International Economics, Globalization, and Policy

A READER

FIFTH EDITION

The McGraw-Hill Series
Economics

ESSENTIALS OF
ECONOMICS

Brue, McConnell, and Flynn
Essentials of Economics
Second Edition

Mandel
Economics: The Basics
First Edition

Schiller
Essentials of Economics
Seventh Edition

PRINCIPLES OF ECONOMICS

Colander
**Economics,
Microeconomics, and
Macroeconomics**
Seventh Edition

Frank and Bernanke
**Principles of Economics,
Principles of
Microeconomics, Principles
of Macroeconomics**
Fourth Edition

Frank and Bernanke
**Brief Editions: Principles of
Economics, Principles of
Microeconomics, Principles
of Macroeconomics**
First Edition

McConnell, Brue, and Flynn
**Economics,
Microeconomics, and
Macroeconomics**
Eighteenth Edition

McConnell, Brue, and Flynn
**Brief Editions: Economics,
Microeconomics,
Macroeconomics**
First Edition

Miller
**Principles of
Microeconomics**
First Edition

Samuelson and Nordhaus
**Economics,
Microeconomics, and
Macroeconomics**
Eighteenth Edition

Schiller
**The Economy Today, The
Micro Economy Today,
and The Macro Economy
Today**
Eleventh Edition

Slavin
**Economics,
Microeconomics, and
Macroeconomics**
Ninth Edition

ECONOMICS OF SOCIAL
ISSUES

Guell
Issues in Economics Today
Fourth Edition

Sharp, Register, and Grimes
Economics of Social Issues
Eighteenth Edition

ECONOMETRICS

Gujarati and Porter
Basic Econometrics
Fifth Edition

Gujarati and Porter
Essentials of Econometrics
Fourth Edition

MANAGERIAL ECONOMICS

Baye
**Managerial Economics
and Business Strategy**
Sixth Edition

Brickley, Smith, and
Zimmerman
**Managerial Economics and
Organizational Architecture**
Fifth Edition

Thomas and Maurice
Managerial Economics
Ninth Edition

INTERMEDIATE ECONOMICS

Bernheim and Whinston
Microeconomics
First Edition

Dornbusch, Fischer, and
Startz
Macroeconomics
Tenth Edition

Frank
**Microeconomics and
Behavior**
Seventh Edition

ADVANCED ECONOMICS

Romer
Advanced Macroeconomics
Third Edition

MONEY AND BANKING

Cecchetti
**Money, Banking, and
Financial Markets**
Second Edition

URBAN ECONOMICS

O'Sullivan
Urban Economics
Seventh Edition

LABOR ECONOMICS

Borjas
Labor Economics
Fourth Edition

McConnell, Brue, and
Macpherson
**Contemporary Labor
Economics**
Eighth Edition

PUBLIC FINANCE

Rosen and Gayer
Public Finance
Eighth Edition

Seidman
Public Finance
First Edition

ENVIRONMENTAL
ECONOMICS

Field and Field
**Environmental Economics:
An Introduction**
Fifth Edition

INTERNATIONAL
ECONOMICS

Appleyard, Field, and Cobb
International Economics
Sixth Edition

King and King
**International Economics,
Globalization, and Policy:
A Reader**
Fifth Edition

Pugel
International Economics
Fourteenth Edition

International Economics, Globalization, and Policy

A READER

FIFTH EDITION

Philip King
San Francisco State University

Sharmila King
University of the Pacific

Boston   Burr Ridge, IL   Dubuque, IA   New York
San Francisco   St. Louis   Bangkok   Bogotá   Caracas   Kuala Lumpur
Lisbon   London   Madrid   Mexico City   Milan   Montreal   New Delhi
Santiago   Seoul   Singapore   Sydney   Taipei   Toronto

McGraw-Hill
Irwin

INTERNATIONAL ECONOMICS, GLOBALIZATION, AND POLICY: A READER
Published by McGraw-Hill/Irwin, a business unit of The McGraw-Hill Companies,
Inc., 1221 Avenue of the Americas, New York, NY, 10020. Copyright © 2009, 2005,
2000, 1995, 1990 by The McGraw-Hill Companies, Inc. All rights reserved. No part
of this publication may be reproduced or distributed in any form or by any means, or
stored in a database or retrieval system, without the prior written consent of The
McGraw-Hill Companies, Inc., including, but not limited to, in any network or other
electronic storage or transmission, or broadcast for distance learning.

Some ancillaries, including electronic and print components, may not be available to
customers outside the United States.

This book is printed on acid-free paper.

1 2 3 4 5 6 7 8 9 0 DOC/DOC 0 9 8

ISBN   978-0-07-337581-6
MHID   0-07-337581-0

Publisher: *Douglas Reiner*
Developmental Editor: *Anne E. Hilbert*
Marketing manager: *Dean Karampelas*
Project manager: *Kathryn D. Mikulic*
Full service project manager: *Deborah L. Darr, Aptara®, Inc.*
Production supervisor: *Gina Hangos*
Design coordinator: *Joanne Mennemeier*
Cover design: *JoAnne Schopler*
Typeface: *9/11 Sabon*
Compositor: *Aptara®, Inc.*
Printer: *R. R. Donnelley*

Library of Congress Cataloging-in-Publication Data

International economics, globalization, and policy : a reader/[edited by] Philip King,
Sharmila King.—5th ed.
      p. cm.
   Revised ed. of: International economics and international economic policy.
   Includes bibliographical references.
   ISBN-13: 978-0-07-337581-6 (alk. paper)
   ISBN-10: 0-07-337581-0 (alk. paper)
   1. International trade. 2. International finance. 3. International economic
relations. I. King, Philip, 1956- II. King, Sharmila. III. International economics and
international economic policy.
   HF1379.I57 2009
   337—dc22

                                                                    2008020241

www.mhhe.com

Table of Contents

Preface ix

International Trade

Section I   *Issues in Trade and Protectionism*

Chapter **1** How Costly Is Protectionism?
              ROBERT C. FEENSTRA 2

         2 Grain Drain: The Hidden Cost of U.S. Rice Subsidies
              DANIEL GRISWOLD 19

         3 International Trade: Why We Don't Have More of It
              EDITH OSTAPIK AND KEI-MU YI 33

Section II   *Outsourcing, the WTO, and the Environment*

         4 Bridging the Trade-Environment Divide
              DANIEL C. ESTY 44

         5 Labor Standards: Where Do They Belong on the International Trade
              Agenda?
              DRUSILLA K. BROWN 60

         6 Beyond the Outsourcing Angst: Making America More Productive
              THOMAS F. SIEMS 80

         7 Offshoring: The Next Industrial Revolution?
              ALAN S. BLINDER 88

         8 Trade in Health Care: Changing Paradigms in a Global Economy
              ANOSHUA CHAUDHURI 98

Section III   *NAFTA, FDI, and Other Trade Issues*

         9 Trade in the Americas From NAFTA to Bilateralism
              JOANNA MOSS 111

        10 Does Foreign Direct Investment Help Emerging Economies?
              ANIL KUMAR 123

        11 Have U.S. Import Prices Become Less Responsive to Changes in the
              Dollar?
              REBECCA HELLERSTEIN, DEIRDRE DALY, AND CHRISTINA MARSH . .133

Section IV   *Immigration*

12 Global Migration: Two Centuries of Mass Migration Offers Insights into the Future of Global Movements of People
    JEFFREY G. WILLIAMSON 145

13 America's Stake in Immigration: Why Almost Everybody Wins
    GIOVANNI PERI 153

Section V   *Globalization*

14 The Global Governance of Trade as if Development Really Mattered
    DANI RODRIK 162

15 Are We Underestimating the Gains from Globalization for the United States?
    CHRISTIAN BRODA AND DAVID WEINSTEIN 188

16 What's So Special About China's Exports?
    DANI RODRIK 198

International Finance

Section VI   *Trade Deficit Disorder*

17 Twin Deficits, Twenty Years Later
    LEONARDO BARTOLINI AND AMARTYA LAHIRI 217

18 Why a Dollar Depreciation May Not Close the U.S. Trade Deficit
    LINDA GOLDBERG AND ELEANOR WISKE DILLON 226

19 Trade Deficits Aren't as Bad as You Think
    GEORGE ALESSANDRIA 236

Section VII   *Exchange Rate Regimes and Macroeconomic Stabilization Policies*

20 Does the Exchange Rate Regime Matter for Inflation and Growth?
    ATISH R. GHOSH, JONATHAN D. OSTRY, ANNE-MARIE GULDE AND HOLGER C. WOLF 251

21 China's Controversial Exchange Rate Policy
    SHARMILA KING 259

22 To Float or Not to Float? Exchange Rate Regimes and Shocks
    MICHELE CAVALLO 264

23 Moving to a Flexible Exchange Rate: How, When, and How Fast?
    RUPA DUTTAGUPTA, GILDA FERNANDEZ AND CEM KARACADAG . .268

24 Official Dollarization and the Banking System in Ecuador and El Salvador
    MYRIAM QUISPE-AGNOLI AND ELENA WHISLER 279

Section VIII   *Europe and the Euro Zone*

25 The Euro: Ever More Global
    AXEL BERTUCH-SAMUELS AND PARMESHWAR RAMLOGAN 298

26 Integration and Globalization: The European Bellwether
    JASON L. SAVING 305

Section IX   *Financial Crises and Capital Flows*

27   Asia Ten Years After
   DAVID BURTON AND ALESSANDRO ZANELLO 316

28   Financial Crises of the Future
   PAOLO MAURO AND YISHAY YAFEH 324

29   Financial-Sector Foreign Direct Investment and Host Countries: New
   and Old Lessons
   LINDA GOLDBERG 331

30   Appraising the IMF's Performance: A Review of the First Three Studies
   by the New Independent Evaluation Office
   PETER B. KENEN 347

31   Sovereign Wealth Funds
   PHILIP KING 354

Section X   *Foreign Aid*

32   Aid and Growth
   STEVEN RADELET, MICHAEL CLEMENS, AND RIKHIL BHAVNANI . .362

33   Microfinance: Banking for the Poor
   INA KOTA 369

   Sources 374

Preface

The title of the fifth edition in this reader has been changed to *International Economics, Globalization, and Policy* for a couple of reasons. First, the original title, *International Economics and International Economic Policy: A Reader,* was always too long and clunky. Phil proposed it to McGraw-Hill over twenty years ago and it stuck, despite some misgivings. The new title is briefer and yet more descriptive, since the term "globalization" has been added to reflect the content of the book, which is also used in courses devoted to globalization, particularly the economic aspects of globalization.

As with previous editions, this one is basically all new, with 80 percent of the articles different from the previous edition. In the last edition the Doha round loomed large, trade agreements were considered extremely important, and the Asian financial crisis was receding. As this edition goes to print, the housing crisis and the U.S. dollar are key headline issues. If one had to capture the theme we have looked for in the fifth edition, we would say that debt, particularly U.S. debt, is the salient issue of the day. The U.S. savings rate is negative (as of the spring of 2008), the U.S. budget deficit is growing, and the U.S. current account has been negative (and growing) for decades. In our opinion, this debt level is unsustainable. It is also odd that China, a poor country, has become a net lender to the U.S. This confounds what one would expect from economic theory. It also makes us wonder if and when other countries will consider the U.S. a bad risk, particularly as the U.S. financial system fits Hyman Minsky's theory of Ponzi finance all too well.

Our section on financial crises focuses on issues that we believe will be critical over the next few years. It has often been remarked that every financial crisis is different, though there are certainly lessons to be learned. For example, the Asian financial crisis involved huge current account imbalances as well as borrowing short (subject to fluctuations in short-term interest rates) and lending long, and also currency movements. Many of these elements will undoubtedly play a role in future crises.

China is also clearly an increasingly important topic. China's importance in the world continues to grow and it has recently taken on the role of creditor to the U.S. as well as becoming a major manufacturing power (producing, for example, 80 percent of the world's toys; as new parents we notice these things).

As with previous editions, this reader focuses on real debates within the discipline of economics and political economy, not on phony "pro-con" debates which often obscure the real issues. In some cases, such as agricultural subsidies in rich countries, there really is very little debate among economists, on the left or the right—agricultural subsidies in rich countries hurt the world's poor and do little to benefit anyone other than rich farmers and agribusiness. This statement, though quite strong, would find almost universal support among economists who have studied the issue seriously. On the other hand, though most economists see globalization as a positive, there are serious dissenters, such as Dani Rodrik of Harvard, and these views are presented.

All of the articles were chosen for an advanced undergraduate or masters level course in international trade or finance, or a course on globalization. We have tried to present a wider array of perspective than is available in a text as well as discussion with a wealth of case specific information.

McGraw-Hill graciously offered to do the formatting of this text as well as the publishing, which has made our life much easier. Anne Hilbert, the Economics Editor at McGraw-Hill, has always made herself available to us and has been extremely responsive to our needs. She has paid careful attention to detail, which is unusual for someone in her role, typically more managerial than editorial. Phil Dunn helped with the permissions while he trained for the Beijing Olympics. Kathryn Mikulic and Deb Darr helped with production.

International Economics, Globalization, and Policy

A READER

FIFTH EDITION

Issues in Trade and Protectionism

I

The vast majority of economists favor free trade. The first section of this reader comprises articles to help make this case. Later sections will look at both the pros and the cons. The first article, "How Costly Is Protectionism," by Robert Feenstra, one of the leading economists in the field of international trade, carries over from the last two editions. Feenstra presents estimates of the familiar welfare triangles that virtually every student of international trade learns. Feenstra's article also contains estimates of these welfare losses for particular industries in the United States. These losses generally range from several billions of dollars to tens of billions. Feenstra examines not only the small domestic (triangle) loss, but also the potential loss from quota rents and losses to other countries as well. While these losses are large in absolute terms, they are small in relationship to U.S. GDP, generally much less than 1 percent. Feenstra points out that these estimates of losses should be taken as a lower bound, since they do not include a number of other losses, such as the costs of lobbying for protectionism by domestic industries (i.e., Posner-Tullock losses).

In "Grain Drain: The Hidden Cost of U.S. Rice Subsidies," Daniel Griswold argues that the current U.S. policies which subsidize rice farmers in the U.S. do far more harm than good. In particular, Griswold points out that Americans pay for these subsidies "three times over" as taxpayers (the subsidies are paid for by government programs), as consumers (the subsidies effectively raise the price of rice to consumers as much as fourfold), and as workers (by distorting decision-making

these programs lower overall economic efficiency and output). These policies also have the net effect of driving down the global price of rice, which is largely produced by poor farmers in developing countries. As with most agricultural subsidies, rice subsidies disproportionately benefit large farmers and agribusiness, not smaller farmers. Overall, Griswold concludes, these programs do not serve the national interest, but rather the special interests of the farm lobby.

In the final article of this section, "International Trade: Why We Don't Have More of It," Ostapik and Yi examine so-called non-tariff barriers, as well as other impediments to trade, in an attempt to explain why international trade does not represent an even larger share of GDP. According to the authors, trade barriers increase the costs of foreign goods by an average of 74 percent. 21 percent of this 74 percent is accounted for by transportation costs including the time costs of shipping these goods, which is almost as significant as the actual shipping costs. 44 percent of the 74 percent increase is due to "border-related" costs. According to the authors, only 8 percent of this 44 percent is accounted for by tariff and non-tariff barriers. Consequently, if the authors are correct, tariff and non-tariff barriers actually comprise a very small portion of the total costs of exporting foreign goods. One interesting policy outcome of this analysis is that to increase trade, lowering other barriers, such as currency costs and language costs, would have a far more significant impact than lowering tariff and non-tariff barriers.

How Costly Is Protectionism?

ROBERT C. **FEENSTRA**

When economists attempt to measure the gains from trade and costs of protection for industrial countries, the resulting estimates often look small. As Krugman (1990, p. 104) recently wrote:

> Just how expensive is protectionism? The answer is a little embarrassing, because standard estimates of the cost of protection are actually very low. America is a case in point. While much US trade takes place with few obstacles, we have several major protectionist measures, restricting imports of autos, steel, and textiles in particular. The combined costs of these major restrictions to the US economy, however, are usually estimated at less than three-quarters of 1 percent of US national income. Most of this loss, furthermore, comes from the fact that the import restrictions, in effect, form foreign producers into cartels that charge higher prices to US consumers. So most of the US losses are matched by higher foreign profits. From the point of view of the world as a whole, the negative effects of US import restrictions on efficiency are therefore much smaller—around one-quarter of 1 percent of US GNP.

Are the efficiency costs of protection really so small? While the estimate cited by Krugman for the US costs of its own protectionism is a plausible lower bound, I will argue that the rents arising from import quotas should not be thought of as simple, nondistortionary transfers to trading partners. On the contrary, the evidence is that US quotas impose a loss on our trading partners, and that in some cases this loss is comparable in magnitude to the transfer of rents. This means that even when foreign firms earn quota rents through higher selling prices in the US, the foreign countries gain by less due to the efficiency losses, and in some cases do not gain at all. It follows that the world efficiency losses from US protection are as large as the US costs.

It is quite common to ignore the efficiency costs imposed on foreign countries through US protection. This approach does not reflect the reality that US protection, like that of other industrial countries, occurs at quite restrictive levels in a small number of industries, and also discriminates against particular supplying countries. The US is not a "small" country in the large world market, and its highly selective pattern of protection generates substantial deadweight losses both at home and abroad.

This paper begins from a US perspective, examining the costs to both the US and other countries from US protectionism. It then moves to a more global policy perspective. The emerging free trade areas in Europe, North America and Asia raise the prospect of gains from trade within each

The Effect of an Import Quota on the U.S. Market
Figure 1

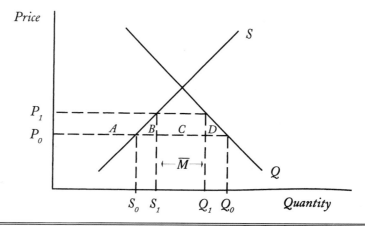

region, but also the possibility of global costs from protectionist actions across the regions. To quantify this, Krugman (1990) considers a world split into three trading regions, where under a hypothetical trade war each region restricts trade with the other regions by one-half. Using a simple triangle calculation, he suggests that the global efficiency losses from this dramatic reduction in trade may be only 2.5 percent of world GNP.

This calculation does not reflect the highly selective pattern of current protection, however, where trade barriers are maintained against specific goods rather than uniformly. Under this form of protection, reducing trade across regions can mean eliminating trade in the varieties of certain goods imported from outside the region, while other internal varieties are still available. This approach is particularly relevant to differentiated manufactured goods such as cars, consumer electronics, footwear, textiles and apparel, and so on. When the range of product varieties is reduced in this manner, the global losses can easily be several times larger than Krugman's estimate.

From a policy perspective, our discussion emphasizes the importance of limiting the use of selective and discriminatory trade protection whenever possible. Of course, the General Agreement on Tariffs and Trade aims at this goal, but GATT may be undercut by the movement towards regional free trade areas. The most important determinant of trade protection in the years ahead is likely to be a choice between the GATT approach of multilateral negotiations to lower all trade barriers, and the more recent shift toward agreements which offer free trade within a region, but also risk discriminatory trade barriers against those outside the region.

Costs of U.S. Import Protection

Figure 1 illustrates the effect of an import quota on the US market. Let S be the US supply curve for a particular good, and let Q be the US demand curve. Suppose that imports are initially available at the free trade price of P_0, so that the quantity imported is $M_0 = Q_0 - S_0$. Then if the US limits the amount imported to M using a quota, the equilibrium price in the US would rise to P_1. Domestic producers would benefit, of course, and their rise in producer surplus is measured by the area A. In contrast, US consumers would suffer from the increase in the price, and their drop in consumer surplus is measured by the entire area A + B + C + D.

When U.S. Protectionism Affects World Prices
Figure 2

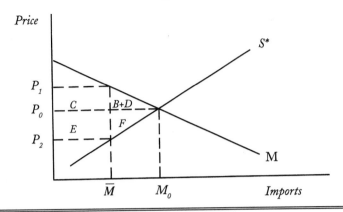

If the US were a "small" country, so that its purchases had no effect on the international price P_0, then the area C would be the "rents" associated with the quota $\overline{M}$. In nearly all the cases of US import quotas we shall consider, the quotas are allocated to foreign exporters by their own governments. Under this system, it is the foreign firms that earn area C in Figure 1, so that the net US loss from the quota is areas B + C + D. In contrast, the global efficiency loss is only B + D, since the quota rents C are a redistribution from the United States to the foreign firms.

However, if protectionist actions by the US have some effect on the world prices, then the measurement of global losses is quite different. This is illustrated in Figure 2, where we incorporate the exporting countries. Let M be the US excess demand curve for imports of the good in question (which is the horizontal difference between domestic demand Q and supply S), and let S* be the excess supply curve from all foreign countries. Under free trade the equilibrium price and quantity of imports are again at P_0 and M_0. With the quota limit of $\overline{M}$, the US price rises to P_1, as before. Foreign firms would have been willing to supply this amount at the reduced price P_2, so that $(P_1 - P_2)$ is the "quota premium" they earn on each

unit sold. Then the quota rents they earn are measured by $(P_1 - P_2)\overline{M}$ = area C + E in Figure 2.

However, not all of the quota rent is a welfare improvement abroad. The drop in foreign producer surplus due to the reduced US sales would be calculated as the area E + F, which represents the losses of those pushed out of the US market as a result of the quota. These losses must be counted against the rents that the foreign firms earn. The net change in the welfare of the supplying countries is therefore (C + E) − (E + F) = C − F. The area F represents the deadweight loss to the foreign countries. These countries are worse off due to the import restriction if this deadweight loss exceeds C, which will certainly occur if the quota $\overline{M}$ is set at a very restrictive level. The efficiency losses to the world as a whole are measured by the areas B + D + F.

In summary, the costs of US import protection in the United States can be measured as the sum of deadweight losses (B + D) and that part of the quota rents which represent the increase in US prices (area C). The measurement of the global losses due to US protectionism would need to subtract the quota rents from US losses, and add the efficiency losses created in the countries supplying to the US (area F).

Annual Cost of U.S. Import Protection (billion dollars, years around 1985)
Table 1

	U.S. Deadweight Loss (B+D)	Quota Rents (C or C+E)	Foreign Deadweight Loss (F)
Automobiles	0.2 − 1.2 [a,b]	2.2 − 7.9 [a,c]	0 − 3 [d]
Dairy*	1.4 [b]	0.25 [c]	0.02 [e]
Steel	0.1 − 0.3 [a,b]	0.7 − 2.0 [a,c]	0.1 [f]
Sugar	0.1 [b]	0.4 − 1.3 [c,g]	0.2 [g]
Textiles & Apparel	4.9 − 5.9 [a,b]	4.0 − 6.1 [a,c]	4 − 15.5 [h]
Average Tariffs	1.2 − 3.4 [i]	0	n.a.
Total	7.9 − 12.3	7.3 − 17.3	4.3 − 18.8

*In dairy the quota rents are earned by U.S. importers, and so are not included in the total.
n.a.— not available

Source:
a. de Melo and Tarr (1990)
b. Hufbauer, Berliner and Elliot (1986)
c. Bergsten et al (1987,. Table 3.3)
d. Feenstra (1988)
e. Anderson (1985)

f. Boorstein (1987)
g. Leu, Schmitz and Knutson (1987)
h. Trela and Whalley (1988, 1990, 1991)
i. Rousslang and Tokarick (1991)

Table 1 offers estimates of these three categories: US deadweight loss (B + D), quota rents (C or C + E), and foreign deadweight losses (F).

U.S. Deadweight Loss

The first column of Table 1 displays estimates of the deadweight loss to the US economy from the major instances of import protection. Other cases of import protection include machine tools and meat, though the losses involved are much less than those in Table 1, and would not substantially affect the totals. The estimates shown are annual costs for years ranging between 1983 and 1987, and are centered around 1985. For each industry, imports are primarily restricted by quotas, though small tariff rates also apply.

The estimates in column one are obtained from two sources: partial equilibrium models estimating the deadweight loss triangles for US consumers and producers (Hufbauer, Berliner and Elliott, 1986); and computable general equilibrium models (de Melo and Tarr, 1990). Both of these methods rely on a wide range of literature for estimates of the demand elasticities, supply elasticities, and the value of the import quota. In some cases the value of the import quotas, or quota premium, is directly observed, while in other cases it is inferred from the reduction in trade and the supply and demand elasticities; some examples will be provided below. The range of estimates in Table 1 is intended to emphasize that the losses are subject to error from both the parameters used and the assumptions imposed.

A few details on each industry should be mentioned. The "voluntary" export restraint on Japanese auto imports was negotiated in 1981, and limited the US sales of each Japanese company. These quotas were increased in 1987, and are still in place today. However, they are not currently binding for most companies, partly because many Japanese firms have established plants in the United States, and sales from these plants are not limited by the agreement. The estimate of the deadweight loss in column one does not reflect this foreign investment, though we shall discuss later the effect of including it.

Dairy products subject to import restrictions include cheese, butter and powdered milk. These restrictions are used in conjunction with domestic support prices, and are intended to preserve income for US farmers, as is the case with sugar. The deadweight loss of $1.4 billion in dairy is primarily due to the restrictive quotas on cheese imports.

The US steel industry has lobbied for various forms of protection during the past two decades, and since 1985 a "voluntary" export restraint has been in place with nearly every trading partner. The complexity of this arrangement is surpassed only by the Multi-Fiber Arrangement, governing world trade in textiles and apparel. Initiated in 1974, this arrangement imposes extremely detailed quotas on every country and product imported to the United States. The distortionary cost of these restrictions to the US is estimated at $4–6 billion, the largest of the industry deadweight losses shown in Table 1.

While tariffs are low in many industries, there are important exceptions. For example, since 1980 there has been a tariff of 25 percent on compact trucks imported from Japan. Estimates of the cost of the tariffs are not available for most industries, so the last row of column one includes a range of estimates for the deadweight loss due to the average tariff rate (3.7 percent) in the US economy.

Summing the estimates in column one, we obtain $8–12 billion. This estimate should be treated as a lower bound to the actual loss, however, since we have ignored many factors that could lead to additional costs for the US For example, the increase in producer surplus as a result of US protection (area A in Figure 1) is many times greater than the deadweight losses, and we might expect some waste of resources as firms attempt to secure this increase in surplus. This waste could occur through lobbying and other "rent-seeking" activities, or more subtly, as firms neglect to modernize their capital equipment to demonstrate the need for continued protection (Matsuyama, 1990).

In addition, it is quite likely that the quotas applied in industries such as autos and steel have allowed US firms to exercise greater market power in setting prices, with associated deadweight losses for US consumers. A simulation model incorporating this idea has been applied to the European car market by Smith and Venables (1991), who find significant costs due to the change in market conduct. Dinopoulos and Kreinin (1988) found that European firms selling cars in the United States increased their prices simultaneously with the US quota on Japanese car imports. This effect is quite plausibly the result of a change in market conduct.

Other areas of US trade legislation can also create deadweight losses. For example, a number of US dumping investigations are settled out of court, thereby allowing the US and foreign firms to raise their prices jointly (Prusa, 1991; Staiger and Wolak, 1991). This outcome should have some added cost to the United States though its magnitude is not known. Finally, the recent literature on trade and growth suggests that protection can have adverse affects on a country's growth rate, leading to welfare losses. While these effects are no doubt important, reliable estimates for the US are not yet available.

Quota Rents

The second column of Table 1 shows estimates of the quota rents. For all the industries shown except dairy products, these rents are earned by foreign firms who are allocated the quotas by an agency of their government. For example, in autos the total number of cars intended for export from Japan to the US is determined by the Japanese government, and then the Ministry of International Trade and Industry allocates the quotas to Japanese firms. For textiles, the quotas for each country are determined under the Multi-Fiber Arrangement (MFA), which are then allocated to firms by their governments. In Hong Kong, the firms are permitted to trade these quotas on a secondary market (Hamilton, 1986). In contrast, for dairy products the quotas are allocated by the Department of Agriculture to US importers, who then earn the rents.

In some cases, the studies we draw on measure only the quota rents leading to US losses (that is, only area C in Figures 1 and 2). For example, Hufbauer, Berliner and Elliott (1986) assume that the US is a "small" country facing a horizontal foreign supply curve at the price P_0, though they recognize that this assumption may not be realistic. For a number of industries, the quota premiums they use are inferred from the reduction in trade and domestic supply and demand elasticities under this "small" country assumption, so that only area C is measured. In contrast, de Melo and Tarr (1990) allow for upward sloping foreign supply curves in some industries, and appear to measure the area C + E by using quota premiums that reflect the full difference between the US price and foreign marginal cost. This is certainly the case for textiles, where their estimate of the quota premium is taken from the observed market price for the quotas (in Hong Kong), and arguably also the case for autos. These authors obtain higher estimates of the quota rents in column two, which is explained partly by the quota premium that they use.

Summing the quota rents in column two, we obtain a range of $7–17 billion. Adding the deadweight losses from the column of Table 1, we obtain an estimate of $15–30 billion as the cost to the US of its own protection, which can be compared to 1985 US GNP of $4 trillion. Thus, the costs we have identified do not exceed three-quarters of one percent of GNP. Despite the fact that the quota rents we have used may overstate the US costs in some cases, we would still treat three-quarters of one percent as a lower bound to the actual losses from protection in the US, for the reasons discussed above: rent-seeking, market power, effects on growth, and so on. To this list, we can add one other factor often resulting from the application of quotas,

with potential costs to the US: the upgrading of imports.

Since US import quotas apply to the quantity sold by foreign firms, a common reaction of the firms is to increase the value of the goods which they send. There are two different arguments for why this phenomena might occur. Under the first (Falvey, 1979), a foreign firm selling multiple types of a product—say, steel—will face a limit on the total tonnage sold in the United States. To maximize profits, the firm will ensure that it earns the same quota premium on the marginal ton of each product sold, regardless of whether that ton is steel bars or specialty steel. This means that each ton will have the same dollar premium due to the quota, which corresponds to a lower percentage price increase on the highly-processed units. Under reasonable assumptions about the elasticity of demand for various products, relative sales will shift towards the more highly-processed units after the quota.

In principle, the US welfare costs of the quota could be measured by applying Figure 1 to each type of steel imported, and no special adjustment for the upgrading would be needed. In practice, however, the US costs are always measured at a more aggregate level (that is, for total steel imported from each country), and this approach misses entirely the shift in the composition of demand across imports types. Boorstein and Feenstra (1991) have argued that an additional welfare cost can be attributed to this upgrading, and that for US import restrictions on steel from 1969–74, the losses due to upgrading are comparable in magnitude to the conventional deadweight loss. Since changes in the composition of imports due to US quotas have been observed in a number of other industries, including footwear and textiles and apparel, we would expect losses in these cases as well.

A second argument for why upgrading might occur focuses on the quality choice for each particular product, rather than the composition across products. For example, US imports of autos from Japan experienced very dramatic increases in their size, horsepower, and luxury equipment as a result of the "voluntary" export restraint. Feenstra (1988) finds that these additional features added about $1,500 to the average value of Japanese cars over the period 1981–1985. Note that this quality upgrading has been omitted from the quota premium used in column two of Table 2, and also from the losses in column one. Winston and Associates (1987) find that the deadweight loss to the United States due to the import restriction was about $2 billion, where this amount includes the loss caused by both the price and quality changes. Unfortunately, an estimate of the loss due to quality upgrading alone is not reported.

When imports are upgraded through the addition of quality characteristics, it is difficult to make a sharp distinction between the efficiency costs to US consumers and to foreign firms: the upgrading can also be viewed as a form of rent-seeking activity by foreign firms. We shall return to a discussion of the auto case below, after considering the foreign deadweight losses in other industries.

Foreign Deadweight Losses

While foreigners earn the rents from nearly all US quotas, it does not necessarily follow that these firms prefer to have the restrictions in place. When the quota limits are very tight, the premium that foreign firms earn on sales to the US may not compensate for the sales they have lost, as was explained earlier in Figure 2.

The textile and apparel industry is one case where countries supplying to the United States do suffer from US import restrictions, despite collecting the quota rents. Trela and Whalley (1990) calculate that all developing countries lose $8 billion from the quotas and tariffs applied to textiles by the industrial countries. The reason for this very large loss is the restrictiveness of the MFA quota and tariffs. In earlier work, Trela and Whalley (1988) report that the losses to developing countries from just the

US import restrictions are about one-half as large, or $4 billion. This amount represents the area F – C in Figure 2, and therefore underestimates the deadweight loss F.

Moreover, the loss to the developing countries grows if the calculation includes the internal costs of allocating the quotas among suppliers. Trela and Whalley (1991) describe how the allocation schemes within the developing countries create losses by not granting export licenses to the most efficient producers, and by requiring that exporters with licenses send some of their product to non-quota countries. Including these efficiency costs, the total losses to the developing countries of the Multi-Fiber Arrangement are estimated as $31 billion. The costs from US restrictions alone might be half this amount (as in Trela and Whalley, 1988), which is the basis for the estimate in the third column of Table 1.

The US quotas on sugar may also be so restrictive that foreign countries do not gain, despite receiving the quota rents. Leu, Schmitz, and Knutson (1987) calculate that the foreign deadweight loss is about $200 million. Again, the drop in foreign producer surplus roughly equals the quota rents, so that supplying countries are not gaining from existing quotas. As the authors note (p. 597): "Interestingly, while countries holding sugar quotas once favored a restrictive US sugar policy which generated high quota rents, in lobbying activities related to the 1985 farm bill, they joined with sugar users and consumers groups in support of lower sugar prices as a means of maintaining a market for sugar in the United States."

For both sugar and textiles and apparel, foreign countries do not benefit from US import quotas; in fact, the losses from greater inefficiency may even exceed the quota rents they receive. For other industries listed in Table 1, there is evidence of costs to foreigners through the upgrading of imports, or through the allocation of quotas which attempts to control this upgrading. Rodriguez (1979) argues that the upgrading of imports has an efficiency cost on foreign firms, for the following reasons.

Consider a firm that is choosing the level of some quality characteristic (such as horsepower) to include in its product. In a competitive market with free trade, it can be argued that the firm will choose the level of quality that can be produced with minimum average cost. If the sales of the firm are restricted by an import quota, however, it will have an incentive to raise the quality level, since this will allow it to increase the sales value and quota rents earned on each unit. This means that the quality level is no longer chosen to minimize average costs, and so the firm has some technological inefficiency. This inefficiency is caused by the attempt to increase rents, and in this sense, is analogous to other forms of rent-seeking activity.

To quantify this efficiency cost for Japanese auto imports, we would need to have evidence on the cost function of Japanese producers, and the extent to which the quality upgrading raised the average costs of producing each characteristic. In the absence of this information, we simply use the total amount of upgrading—$1,500 per car (Feenstra, 1988) times 2 million imports—as an upper bound on the waste of resources associated with adding the extra equipment. Thus, the range $0–3 billion is included as a foreign efficiency cost in the third column. As discussed above, it is difficult to separate the foreign and US losses due to upgrading in this case. The important point is that some additional cost from column three should be added to the US deadweight loss in column one to obtain the global efficiency cost.

Costs of upgrading have also been estimated for the quotas on US cheese imports by Anderson (1985). He finds that the US deadweight loss due to the quota-induced shift in the composition of demand across products (the first reason for upgrading discussed above) is very small at $0.4 million. However, he also finds that the allocation of the quotas across countries promotes supplies from less efficient producers, which results in an excess cost of $22 million, as reported in Table 1. This amount should be treated as a foreign efficiency cost, and would need to be added to the US deadweight loss to obtain the global cost.

In the steel industry, Boorstein (1987) finds that the very detailed, country-by-country allocation of these quotas by the US has led to an increase in the share of supplies from less efficient producers. She argues that this allocation can be seen as an attempt to prevent the upgrading of steel imports which had occurred earlier, particularly in product lines competing closely with US production. Over the 1983–85 period an index of supplier prices rose by 2.3 percent due to this (mis)allocation of quotas. These price increases correspond to a foreign efficiency cost of $110 million, as shown in Table 1, which is also a global loss.

Summing the foreign losses in column three we obtain $4–19 billion, which is comparable to the range of the total quota rents. The implication is that total global losses (columns 1 + 3) are no smaller than the total US losses (columns 1 + 2). Of course, the foreign losses are dominated by the estimates in textiles and apparel, and need to be treated as more tentative than other losses in Table 1. Nevertheless, from the evidence we have presented it is apparent that foreign losses due to US protection are pervasive, and cannot be ignored in any estimate of the global losses.

Foreign Investment

No discussion of the costs of protection would be complete without mentioning the increasing levels of investment by foreign firms within the US economy. The annual value of US businesses acquired or established by foreign investors reached $72.7 billion in 1988, while declining slightly to $64.4 billion in 1990. Japan has now replaced the United Kingdom as the largest source country of new direct investment, with 1990 outlays of $20.5 billion (Fahim-Nader, 1991). A rise in foreign investment is intertwined with the costs of protectionism for several reasons.

Most obviously, foreign investment can be motivated by anticipated or actual trade restrictions, as a means of "defusing" the protectionist sentiment. From a global point of view, of course, this sort of "quid pro quo" foreign investment (Bhagwati, 1986, 1988) would not reflect the most efficient choice of location, and so would have some deadweight loss for this reason. The evidence that investment with this motive has occurred in a number of US industries during the 1980s is anecdotal at present, but plausible.

On the positive side, however, investment attracted into industries protected by quotas will increase supplies within the United States, reduce import demand, and thus lower the quota premium earned by firms exporting to the United States. In the auto industry, for example, de Melo and Tarr (1991) reduce their estimated cost of protection by $0.5 billion due to Japanese investment up to 1984. In addition, foreign investment would have additional benefits if it raises local wages or employment, regardless of protection in the domestic industry.

Increasing foreign investment in the US also raises the issue of special regulations applying to these firms. Beyond rules for the reporting of acquisitions, it may seem obvious that foreign-owned firms would be subject to essentially the same regulations as their US counterparts. However, in one surprising and little known case, an import tariff was applied to a foreign-owned firm producing within the United States. This case illustrates the potential for manipulation of US trade laws to suit the goals of domestic firms and regulators.

The case involves the temporary tariff on heavyweight motorcycle imports to the United States that was in effect from 1983–87. This tariff was put in place to protect the only US producer—Harley Davidson—on the grounds that several Japanese producers had large US inventories, and this was judged to be a "threat of serious injury" to the domestic industry (US International Trade Commission,

1983). Since several countries other than Japan supplied heavyweight motorcycles to the United States, the tariff was applied to all of them, but only for imports in excess of a quota limit specified for each country. However, only for Japan was the quota set low enough to result in any tariff duties being collected.

Moreover, even production by Japanese firms within the United States came under the tariff. During this time, Honda and Kawasaki operated plants in the Midwest to produce motorcycles, both for the United States and abroad. Like much other foreign investment in the United States, these plants were in Foreign Trade Zones, which is a tax status allowing producers to import parts duty-free when the final goods are intended for export. If instead the final goods are sold in the United States, the firms are normally allowed to pay either the tariff on the imported parts, or the tariff on the final good, whichever is less. However, for the US sales of heavyweight motorcycles from the Honda and Kawasaki plants, the US Trade Representative directed that these firms pay the full tariff on the sales of every motorcycle (US International Trade Commission, 1987, Appendix E).

While this is only one case, it does illustrate the potential for discriminatory policy against foreign producers in the United States. Other examples of how US regulations can be manipulated around the issue of foreign investment include: the differential treatment of cars as either domestic or imported, to satisfy US fuel-economy standards and the import quota with Japan; and the recent squabble over whether cars imported from Canada have 50 percent "North American content," and are therefore entitled to duty-free access. The usual view of protection as applying to imports needs to be broadened to incorporate foreign investment. The magnitude and growth of foreign investment has led some to suggest that it will be a more important focus of trade policy than import competition in the years ahead.

Trading Regions

A founding principle of the General Agreement on Tariffs and Trade (GATT) was that all signatories should have "most-favored-nation" status, which means that they should be treated equally when a member country applies any trade restriction. However, exceptions to this principle are becoming more frequent. GATT includes exceptions for agriculture and textiles and apparel, and the quotas in these areas discriminate across supplying countries. The use of "voluntary" export restraints in autos and steel by the US and European countries also discriminates against particular suppliers, with Japan and other Asian exporters frequently being singled out. These export restraints are outside of the GATT framework, but even for actions which follow the GATT guidelines discrimination against particular importers is sometimes achieved, as illustrated by the discussion of US motorcycle imports.

Against the backdrop of these protectionist actions in specific industries, certain groups of countries have been moving toward freer trade within regional areas: Canada and the United States agreed to a free trade area in 1988 and negotiations are now underway to extend this agreement to Mexico, creating a North America Free Trade Area; barriers to trade within Europe are being dismantled by 1992; and Japan may be creating an economic sphere of influence among its Asian neighbors. While reduced trade barriers in each of the regional areas hold the prospect of gain for the member countries, significant costs may also result if the regional trading areas take steps to reduce or eliminate trade with outside countries.

There are two reasons why the formation of trade regions may lead to efficiency losses. First, as described some years ago by Viner (1950), if two countries form a free trade area but maintain tariffs against the rest of the world, their combined income can fall rather than rise. This is because the additional trade from a partner country can occur at higher costs than the goods were formerly produced at abroad: Viner called this "trade diversion," and it would also imply a loss for the outside country that has reduced demand. In contrast, if the free trade area leads to increased trade from a partner country when the goods were formerly produced at higher costs domestically, then "trade creation" has occurred, and it is likely that both countries gain.

A second reason that the formation of trading regions can be harmful is that each region will have greater influence over world prices than did the individual countries, and may be tempted to apply an external tariff to exploit this monopoly power in trade. Krugman (1991a, b) finds that the potential for protectionist action is greatest when the number of trading regions falls in an intermediate range, and for the simulations he presents, the number that minimizes world welfare is three regions! Despite this negative result, he argues that the costs from protectionist actions across the regions may not be that large.

As an example, Krugman (1990) considers a hypothetical trade war between three trading regions, one centered on the United States, one on Europe, and one on Japan. If each region applied a 100 percent tariff on imports from the other, and this restricted trade by one-half, he then suggests the following calculation of global deadweight losses (p. 105):

"With a 100% tariff, some goods would be produced domestically even though they could have been imported at half the price. For these goods, there is thus a waste of resources equal to the value of the original imports . . . Our three hypothetical trading blocs would, however, import only about 10 percent of the goods and services they use from abroad even under free trade. A trade war that cut international trade in half, and which caused an average cost of wasted resources for the displaced production of, say, 50 percent, would therefore cost the world economy only 2.5 percent of its income (50 percent $\times$ 5 percent = 2.5 percent)."

Trade Shares and Costs of Trade War
(percent of income in each region)
Table 2

	Trade with Other Regions	Elasticity of Substitution		
		1.5	2	3
North and South America	7.2	7.2	3.6	1.8
Europe & Asia	6.4	6.4	3.2	1.8
Asia & Oceania	11.7	11.7	5.8	2.9
World Average	8.0	8.0	4.0	2.0

Source: Trade shares calculated from Summers and Heston (1991), and General Agreement on Tariffs and Trade (1990).

However, this calculation contains an implicit assumption: that the tariff applies to all goods imported from the other trading regions. In view of the selective pattern of current protection against particular industries and supplying countries, it is more relevant to consider a case where trade in one-half of the products from other trading regions is eliminated, while the other half of trade is unaffected. Under this scenario, what would the costs of the trade war be?

To tackle this question, we can use a model of trade with monopolistic competition, as in Krugman (1980). We suppose that each good is produced in many different varieties, which can be either imported or purchased from domestic firms. Consumers do not treat these product varieties as identical, but the expenditure on each variety does fall as its price increases. A decrease in the number of varieties imported from outside the region, as could occur through a trade war, lowers the welfare of each consumer. Our approach is to compare the initial equilibrium with a situation where the import varieties for one-half of the traded goods are not available, but the prices and availability of all other goods are unchanged.

In this framework, the size of the welfare loss will depend on what proportion

of income is spent on the varieties that are eliminated, and on the degree of substitution between the imported and domestic varieties. One can derive a simple expression in which the change in the cost of living due to the elimination of import varieties is proportional to the share of income originally spent on those varieties, and inversely proportional to the elasticity of substitution minus one. The elasticity of substitution measures the degree to which consumers are willing to substitute between varieties of traded goods as their prices change, and various estimates are available. For US and imported varieties of autos, Levinsohn (1988) finds elasticities from 1.3 to 2.3. Using data for disaggregated steel and textiles products, elasticities from 1.2 to 4.5 are obtained (Grossman, 1982; Feenstra, 1991), where each country importing to the US is treated as a distinct variety.

Measuring the elasticity of substitution for every variety of every good and calculating the amount of variety eliminated by various trade barriers is obviously an enormous task. The simple calculations presented in this section use two shortcuts. First, I use a single elasticity of substitution for the product varieties of every import, although presenting a range of estimates. Second, I suppose that imports from various countries represent different product varieties, which ignores the possibility that some countries produce more similar product varieties than others.

Using only the member countries of GATT, the world was divided into three trading regions: North and South America; Europe and Africa; Asia and Oceania.[18] The share of regional income spent on trade with the other regions for 1988 was calculated using the system of Real National Accounts from Summers and Heston (1991) and the "direction of trade" statistics in GATT (1990). With the world divided in this way, more than half of international trade is internal to the three regions: total trade is 20 percent of world income, while trade with other regions comprises 8 percent of world income. The extent of trade between regions, as a share of each region's income, is shown in column one of Table 2.

The rest of Table 2 presents estimates based on eliminating one-half of the trade between regions, and considering values of 1.5, 2 and 3 for the elasticity of substitution. These calculations give a range 2 to 8 percent for the decline in world welfare caused by the reduction in product varieties available.[19] Thus, estimates at the lower end of this range are close to Krugman's (1990) 2.5 percent loss, but at the upper end of the range the costs are several times larger. Of course, the exact magnitude is quite sensitive to the elasticity of substitution that is used, with lower costs corresponding to the case where consumers gain little from additional product variety.

The estimates presented in Table 2 probably understate the costs of a trade war, however, since they include only the impact on consumers of reduced product variety. There would also be efficiency losses on the production side, and these losses could be substantial if there were economies of scale in production. Computable models incorporating economies of scale were developed to assess the gains from the Canada-US Free Trade Agreement, and the results from

these can give us some idea of the order of magnitude of the production efficiency effects.

The initial work of Harris (1984) gave dramatic estimates of the effect on Canadian welfare; national income rose by 6.2 to 8.6 percent due to the expansion of outputs and resulting fall in average costs due to economies of scale: the so-called rationalization of production. These gains were obtained by avoiding the duplication of fixed costs across firms, as would occur in a protected market, but did not rely on the presence of product differentiation. Instead, the model used a "focal point" pricing rule, under which Canadian firms set their prices equal to the US price plus any tariff.

Later work has relied on the more familiar monopolistically competitive pricing behavior (or segmented markets across the countries), which lowers the estimates of the Canadian efficiency gains. The Canadian Department of Finance (1988) obtained 2.5 percent of Canadian real income as the calculated gains, while subsequent researchers have obtained estimates of 0.6 percent or less (Brown and Stern, 1989). The message from these studies is that the potential gains due to the expansion of firm outputs in larger markets are substantial, though the exact magnitude of this effect is quite sensitive to the assumptions of the model.

Bilateralism or Multilateralism?

This paper has emphasized the substantial costs imposed on foreign countries by US protectionism. These costs result from the highly selective nature of protection in particular industries and against particular exporting countries. Despite rules to the contrary in the General Agreement on Tariffs and Trade, the use of these discriminatory trade restrictions has been increasing in recent years. Perhaps as a result of the perceived failure of GATT to regulate these actions, the US and other countries have been moving towards the establishment of regional free trade areas, negotiated bilaterally with chosen countries. While holding the promise of significant gains to the countries included in each agreement, this path holds the risk of greater discrimination and losses for the countries excluded.

Economists differ strongly as to whether bilateral negotiations should, or will, be followed. For example, Krugman (1990, p. 131) foresees "the prospect of a fragmentation of the world into mutually protectionist trading blocs—a costly outcome though not a tragic one. Is there a middle way? Perhaps not. It seems likely that the bashers will more or less have their way, and that this decade will be one of growing economic nationalism." In contrast, Bhagwati (1991) argues for incorporating regional agreements more fully into GATT, which would provide some check on the adverse impact on other countries. On the prospects for the current round of multilateral negotiations, he concludes optimistically (p. 96): "The promise of the Uruguay Round is so considerable, and the downside from its failure would be so unfortunate, that it is hard to see an agreement not finally emerging."

A pragmatic path is one that continues to pursue multilateral agreements as a primary strategy, while adding bilateral agreements whenever needed. Richardson (1991) calls this approach "minilateralism," and describes how it has influenced US trade policy in the 1980s. The bilateral agreements should not be seen as an end in themselves, however, since they are not necessarily better from a global point of view than the current system. Indeed, Bergsten (1991) argues that "trade diversion" is actually a goal of recent proposals for trading areas rather than an unintended consequence, and that the costs from reduced world efficiency are substantial. The incentives for regional trading areas to restrict trade from outside countries would very likely lead other nations to pursue free trade areas themselves (as the Asian nations are now being led to consider). The challenge for economists is to ensure

that the movement towards regional trading areas also creates the dynamics for a multilateral agreement

Robert C. Feenstra is Professor of Economics, University of California, Davis, California. The author thanks Jagdish Bhagwati, Severin Borenstein, Jim Levinsohn, Peter Lindert, Andy Rose, Robert Staiger, and the editors for very helpful comments, and Wen Hai for research assistance.

Notes

[1] Note that the foreign excess supply curve S^* is the difference between the supply curve of foreign firms and the demand curve of foreign consumers. Strictly speaking, then the area $E + F$ represents the difference between the gain to foreign consumers as their prices are reduced from P_0 to P_2 and the loss to foreign producers.

[2] This unusually high tariff originally applied to truck imports from West Germany, and was a form of US retaliation against the tariff on poulty sales there, in what became known as the "Chicken War" of 1962–63.

[3] The impact of quotas on market conduct is examined in a monopoly model by Bhagwati (1965), and in oligopoly models by Harris (1985) and Krishna (1989). It is noteworthy that these models of imperfect competition lead to additional costs of protectionist actions, in contrast to the idea of "strategic trade policy" that tariffs or export subsidies might be in the national interest. At least for the industries listed in Table 1, there is no evidence that US trade policies have provided them with any strategic advantage.

[4] As they state (p.33): "In real life, foreign supply curves may not be perfectly elastic . . . Since the measurement of gains or losses to foreign supplies is not our main focus, we will adhere to assumption of perfectly elastic foreign supply curves."

[5] Feenstra (1988) estimates the quota premium in autos by pooling data on car and truck from Japan, where the latter were subject to a 25 percent tariff. He finds that annual changes in the truck prices, net of the tariff, provide an acceptable estimate of the quota-free changes in car prices. In addition, the evidence from Feenstra (1989) is that Japanese firms absorbed about one-third of the tariff in trucks, meaning that the net of tariff price (P_2 in Figure 2) was lower than that of the free trade price (P_0).

[6] In addition, de Melo and Tarr (1990) include "rents" earned by foreign suppliers of autos

who were not covered by the quota agreements, but who nevertheless increased their prices to the United States. Such price increases by "uncovered" suppliers can be explained by a rise in their costs as they expand production for sale to the US or as an exercise of their market power in the quota-restricted market. In either case, the price increase should be counted as a cost to the US economy.

[7] The figure reported in Trela and Whalley (1988) for the losses to developing countries from the US MFA restrictions is actually $6.9 billion, while the losses due to the MFA restrictions in all developed countries was $11.3 billion. The latter estimate was revised downward to $8 billion in subsequent work, but the effect of the US restrictions alone was not calculated again.

[8] This scheme creates an efficiency cost through encouraging firms to sell to non-quota countries at less than marginal cost. See Bark and de Melo (1988), who also cite evidence that this type of scheme applies to Korean exports of footwear and steel to the United States.

[9] Of course, the competitive case may not be the most appropriate for autos, and the monopoly has been analyzed by Krishna (1987).

[10] The foreign supplier prices used by Boorstein (1987) actually include the quota rents, so for steel there is some double-counting between the losses in column three and the quota rents in column two.

[11] The following sort of press report is common and suggestive: "Fearful of trade friction, the Communications Industry Associations of Japan, a trade group, has cautioned its members to avoid explosive increases in exports and to build factories in the United States, according to Ozawa, its president. 'We have learned lessons in the experience with automobile exports to United States and semiconductor exports to the United States,' he said in an interview" (*The New York Times*, June 2, 1984).

[12] Note that this reasoning would not apply if the domestic industry was protected with a tariff, since foreign investment may then lower welfare of the host country; see Brecher and Diaz-Alejandro (1977).

[13] *The Wall Street Journal*, November 11, 1991, p. A1; and February 19, 1992, p A18.

[14] In terms of Figure 2, suppose that the foreign supply curve S* is horizontal. Then if the value of imports P_0M_0 under free trade is 10 percent of world GNP, and the price P_1 is twice P_0 while M_1 is one-half of M_0, it follows that the global deadweight loss B+D equals 2.5 percent of world GDP.

[15] This second situation may not be an equilibrium, but can still be used to isolate the drop in welfare due to the elimination of the import varieties. In this second situation, there would be an incentive for domestic firms to expand the range of product varieties to sell in the protected regional market, but an offsetting incentive to contract the range of varieties due to lost export sales. We are ignoring both of these influences.

[16] At a more formal level, the calculation proceeds like this. A reduction in the number of varieties would raise the cost of living—or true price index—for consumers. Let P denote the price index conrresponding to the preferences with a constant elasticity of substitution between varieties, denoted by ∂. Assume that $\partial > 1$. Suppose that the share of total expenditure going to the varieties which will no longer be available is S_m. Then the increase in the cost of living due to the reduction in product varieties is given by $P = (1 - S_m)^{-1/(\partial-1)}$ (Feenstra, 1991). Thus, the increase in the price index facing consumers is higher if the share of imports that are eliminated (S_m) is larger, or if the elasticity of substitution ∂ is smaller. Conversely, as the varieties become perfect substitutes so that s is very large, then the price index P approaches one: the consumer is not affected by the elimination of imports when they are perfect substitutes with domestic varieties. A slightly simpler form of the equation is obtained by taking logarithms of both sides, and using an approximation which holds when s_m is small: $\ln P = S_m/(S - 1)$. This approximation is the one referred to in the text.

[17] Note that these estimates are higher than those compiled by Shiells, Stern and Deardorff (1986), which include many elasticities which are less than unity, and are therefore inconsistent with pricing under monopolistic competition. These low estimates may arise because many studies first aggregate import countries into groups, and then estimate the elasticity of substitution between the groups of countries. This procedure will lead to a downward bias if, in the language of Chamberlin, the elasticity of the DD curve rather than the dd curve is being estimated. I thank Avinash Dixit for this suggestion.

[18] Oceania includes Australia, New Zealand, and the Pacific Islands. Contrary to the way we divided up the regions, in preliminary proposals for an Asian free trade area, Australia and New Zealand have been excluded (Kreinin and Plummer, 1992).

[19] This calculation uses the formula in note 16, where the share of trade eliminated (s_m) equals one-half of the amounts in column one of Table 2.

References

Anderson, James E., "The Relative Inefficiency of Quotas," *American Economic Review,* March 1985, 75: 1, 178–90.

Bark, Taeho, and Jaime de Melo, "Export Quota Allocations, Export Earnings, and Market Diversification," *The World Bank Economic Review,* September 1988, 2:3, 341–48.

Bergsten, C. Fred, "Commentary: The Move Towards Free Trade Zones." In *Policy Implications of Trade and Currency Zones,* Federal Reserve Bank of Kansas City, 1991, 43–57.

Bergsten, C. Fred, et al., eds., *Auction Quotas and United States Trade Policy.* Washington D.C.: Institute for International Economics, Policy Analyses in International Economics 19, September 1987.

Bhagwati, Jagdish, "On the Equivalence of Tariffs and Quotas." In Baldwin, R.E., et al., eds., *Trade, Growth and the Balance of Payments–Essays in Honor of Gottfried Haberler.* Chicago: Rand McNally, 1965, 52–67.

Bhagwati, Jagdish, "Investing Abroad." Esmee Fairbairn Lecture, University of Lancaster, 1986.

Bhagwati, Jagdish, *Protectionism.* Cambridge: MIT Press, 1988.

Bhagwati, Jagdish, *The World Trading at Risk.* Princeton: Princeton University Press, 1991.

Boorstein, Randi, "The Effect of Trade Restrictions on the Quality and Composition of Imported Products: An Empirical Analysis of the Steel Industry." Ph.D. dissertation. Columbia University, 1987.

Boorstein, Randi, and Robert C. Feenstra, "Quality Upgrading and Its Welfare Cost in US Steel Imports, 1969–74." In Helpman, Elhanan, and Assaf Razin, eds., *International Trade and Trade Policy.* Cambridge: The MIT Press, 1991, 167–86.

Brecher, Richard A., and Carlos F. Diaz-Alejandro, "Tariffs, Foreign Capital, and Immiserizing Growth," *Journal of International,* November 1977, 7:4, 317–22.

Brown, Drusilla K., and Robert M. Stern, "Computable General Equilibrium Estimates of the Gains from U.S.-Canadian Trade Liberalisation." In Greenaway, David, Thomas Hyclak, and Robert J. Thorton, eds., *Economic Aspects of Regional Trading Arrangements.* London: Harvester Wheatsheaf, 1989, 69–108.

de Melo, Jaime, and David Tarr, "Welfare Costs of U.S. Quotas in Textiles, Steel and Autos," *The Review of Economics and Statistics,* August 1990, 72:3, 489–97.

de Melo, Jaime, and David Tarr, "VERs under Imperfect Competition and Foreign Direct Investment: A Case Study of the U.S.-Japan Auto VER." Washington, D.C.: The World Bank, January 1991, mimeo.

Dinopoulos, Elias, and Mordechai E. Kreinin, "Effects of the U.S.-Japan Auto VER on European Prices and on U.S. Welfare," *The Review of Economics and Statistics,* August 1988, 70:3, 484–91.

Fahim-Nader, Mahnaz, "U.S. Business Enterprises Acquired or Established by Foreign Direct Investors in 1990," *Survey of Current Survey of Current Business,* U.S. Department of Commerce, May 1991, 30–39.

Falvey, Rodney E., "The Comparison of Trade within Import-Restricted Product Categories," *Journal of Political Economy,* Part I, October 1979, 87:5, 1105–14.

Feenstra, Robert C., "Quality Change Under Trade Restraints in Japanese Autos," *Quarterly Journal of Economics,* February 1988, 103:1, 131–46.

Feenstra, Robert C., "Symmetric Pass-through of Tariffs and Exchange Rates Under Imperfect Competition: An Empirical Test," *Journal of International Economics,* August 1989, 27: 25–46.

Feenstra, Robert C., "New Goods and Index Numbers: U.S. Import Prices," National Bureau of Economic Research Working Paper No. 3610, February 1991.

General Agreement on Tariffs and Trade, *International Trade International Trade 1989/90.* Geneva, 1990.

Government of Canada, Department of Finance, *The Canada-U.S. Free Trade Agreement: An Economic Assessment.* Ottawa, 1988.

Grossman, Gene M., "Import Competition from Developed and Developing Countries,"

Review of Economics and Statistics, May 1982, 64:2, 271–81.

Hamilton, Carl, "An Assessment of Voluntary Restraints on Hong Kong Exports to Europe and the U.S.," *Economica,* August 1986, 53:2 11, 339–50.

Harris, Richard G., "Why Voluntary Export Restrains are 'Voluntary'," *Canadian Journal of Economics,* November 1985, 18:4, 799–809.

Harris, Richard G., "Applied General Equilibrium Analysis of Small Open Economies with Scale Economies and Imperfect Competition," *American Economic Review,* December 1984, 74:5, 1016–32.

Hufbauer, Gary Clyde, Diane T. Berliner, and Kimberly Ann Elliott, *Trade Protection in the United States: 31 Case Studies.* Washington, D.C.: Institute for International Economics, 1986.

Kreinen, Mordechai E. and Michael G. Plummer, "Economic Effects of the North American Free-Trade Area on Australia and New Zealand," East-West Center, Institute for Economic Development and Policy, Honolulu, 1992.

Krishna, Kala, "Tariffs vs. Quotas with Endogenous Quality," *Journal of International Economics,* August 1987, 23:1/2, 97–112.

Krishna, Kala, "Trade Restrictions as Facilitating Practices," *Journal of International Economics,* May 1989, 26:3/4, 251–70.

Krugman, Paul, "Scale Economies, Product Differentiation, and the Pattern of Trade," *American Economic Review,* December 1980, 70:5, 950–59.

Krugman, Paul, *The Age of Diminished Expectations—U.S. Economic Policy in the 1990s.* Cambridge: The MIT Press, 1990.

Krugman, Paul, "Is Bilateralism Bad?" In Helpman, Elhanan and Assaf Razin, eds., *International Trade and Trade Policy.* Cambridge: MIT Press, 1991a, 9–23.

Krugman, Paul, "The Move Toward Free Trade Zones." *In Policy Implications of Trade and Currency Zones,* Federal Reserve Bank of Kansas City, 1991b, 43–57.

Leu, Gwo-Jiun M., Andrew Schmitz and Ronald D. Knutson, "Gains and Losses of Sugar Program Policy Options," *American Journal of Agricultural Economics,* August 1987, 69:3, 591–602.

Levinsohn, James A., "Empirics of Taxes on Differentiated Products: The Case of Tariffs in the U.S. Automobile Industry." In Baldwin, Robert E., ed., *Trade Policy Issues and Empirical Analysis.* Chicago: The University of Chicago Press, 1988, 11–40.

Matsuyama, Kiminori, " Perfect Equilibria in a Trade Liberalization Game," *American Economic Review,* June 1990, 80:3, 480–92.

Prussa, Thomas, "Why Are So Many Anti-dumping Petitions Withdrawn," State University of New York at Stony Brook, working paper, 1991, *Journal of International Economics,* forthcoming 1992.

Richardson, J. David, "U.S. Trade Policy in the 1980s: Turns and Roads not Taken," National Bureau of Economic Research Working Paper No. 3725, June 1991.

Rodriguez, Carlos A., "The Quality of Imports and the Differential Welfare Effects of Tariffs, Quotas, and Quality Controls as Protective Devices," *Canadian Journal of Economics,* August 1979, 12:3, 439–49.

Rousslang, Donald J., and Stephen P. Tokarick, "Estimating the Welfare Cost of U.S. Tariffs: The Role of the Work-Leisure Choice," Working Paper 91-O l-G, Office of Economics, U.S. International Trade Commission, January 1991.

Shiells, Clinton R., Robert M. Stern, and Alan V. V. Deardorff, "Estimates of the Elasticies of Substitution between Imports and Home Goods for the United States," *Weltwirtschafliches* Archiv, 1986, 122:3, 497–519.

Smith, Alasdair, and Anthony J. Venables, "Counting the Cost of Voluntary Restrains in the European Car Market." In Helpman, Elhanan and Assaf Razin, eds., *International Trade and Trade Policy.* Cambridge: The MIT Press, 1991, 187–220.

Staiger, Robert W., and Frank A. Wolak, "The Determinants and Impacts of Antidumping

Suit Petitions in the United States: An Industry Level Analysis," working paper, Stanford University, 1991.

Summers, Robert, and Alan Heston, "The Penn World Trade (Mark 5): An Expanded Set of International Comparisons, 1950–1988," *Quarterly Journal of Economics*, May 1991, 106:2, 327–68.

Trela, Irene, and John Whalley, "Do Developing Countries Lose from the MFA?" National Bureau of Economic Research Working Paper No. 2618, June 1988.

Trela, Irene, and John Whalley, "Global Effects of Developed Country Restrictions on Textiles and Apparel," *The Economic Journal*, December 1990, 100, 1190–1205.

Trela, Irene, and John Whalley, "Internal Quota Allocation Schemes and the Costs of the MFA," National Bureau of Economic Research Working Paper No. 3627, February 1991.

United States International Trade Commission, *Heavyweight Motorcycles, and Engines and Power Train Subassemblies Therefor,* USITC Publication 1342, Washington D.C., February 1983.

United States International Trade Commission, *Heavyweight Motorcycles,* USITC Publication 1988, Washington D.C., June 1987.

Viner, Jacob, *The Customs Union Issue.* New York: Carnegie Endowment for International Peace, 1950.

Winston, Clifford, and Associates, *Blind Intersection? Policy and the Automobile Industry.* Washington DC.: The Brookings Institution, 1987.

Grain Drain

The Hidden Cost of U.S. Rice Subsidies

D ANIEL **G RISWOLD**

Introduction

No commodity dominates the diets of so many people in the world as rice. Rice constitutes the principal source of caloric intake for about half the world's population, especially among the world's poor, and accounts for one in five calories consumed worldwide.[1] The word for rice in many languages translates literally as "food."

At the same time, no commodity is more distorted by government intervention in its production and trade than rice. Governments around the world maintain tariffs, tariff-rate quotas, escalating barriers to processed rice, production and export subsidies, and state monopoly trading enterprises. According to the World Bank, the weighted average tariff on rice imports as recently as 2000 was 43.3 percent.[2] The Organization for Economic Cooperation and Development estimates that government subsidies and trade barriers provide more than three-quarters of the income of rice farmers in the relatively wealthy OECD member countries.[3]

Hundreds of millions of people pay a price every day for intervention in the rice market. Consumers in countries with protected markets pay as much as four times the world price for rice, which reduces their standard of living. Taxpayers in wealthier countries pay billions of dollars more to support rice farmers and further distort global markets with subsidized exports. And tens of millions of rice farmers in poor countries find it harder to lift their families out of poverty because of the lower, more volatile prices caused by the interventionist policies of other countries.

One opportunity to reduce those costly distortions may be slipping away. The Doha Round of negotiations among members of the World Trade Organization has reached a stalemate with no likely prospect of a breakthrough anytime soon. Launched in 2001, the round was supposed to emphasize expanding market access for agricultural products and other issues of special importance to developing countries. At meetings in June and July 2006, major participants were unable to bridge differences over limits on domestic subsidies, reductions in tariffs, and exclusion of "sensitive" or "special" products. With presidential trade promotion authority due to expire in mid-2007, there is no immediate prospect of an ambitious multilateral agreement that would reduce global distortions in the production and trade of rice.

Another opportunity remains, however, as the U.S. Congress prepares to rewrite the farm bill sometime in the first half of 2007. Like the European Union, Japan, and South Korea, the United States extends significant support to its rice farmers through tariff protection as well as direct payments decoupled from production and through countercyclical and loan-deficiency payments triggered when global prices fall below certain minimums. Those programs have cost American taxpayers an average of more than $1 billion a year since 1998, account for half of all income for U.S. rice farmers, and exert a depressing effect on global rice markets by spurring farmers to overproduce. Subsidies for rice and other U.S. agricultural commodities undermine the U.S. governments bargaining position in global trade talks. They are also liable to challenge from other WTO members for violating our existing commitments to restrict domestic subsidies that injure other members, just as Brazil successfully challenged certain U.S. subsidies for cotton in 2005.

As Congress and the Bush administration begin to reexamine and reshape U.S. farm policy, they should consider the full cost of the U.S. rice program, not only the cost to rice producers in other countries but the cost to American taxpayers and consumers and to the U.S. agenda of promoting a more open and undistorted global market through trade negotiations.

In this study I will examine the peculiar nature of global rice production and trade and describe the significant distortions in global rice markets caused by widespread intervention, with special attention to the U.S. rice program. I will then analyze the many costs that those distortions impose at home in the United States and abroad and suggest reforms to the U.S. rice program that would serve our broader national interests.

The Global Rice Market(s)

The global rice market is not one homogeneous market but many, with four major categories of rice and as many as 50 distinct varieties selling at different prices. Because of global trade barriers, rice markets are "thin," with rice trade relatively small compared to production. And while imports of rice are diffused among nations, rice exports tend to be concentrated among relatively few. All those features have consequences for rice policy.

Although there are a numerous varieties, rice grains fall into four broad categories:

- *Long-grain* (also referred to as Indica) rice is grown in tropical and subtropical climates. Long-grain rice

grains remain separate and relatively dry when cooked. Most long-grain rice is grown in southern and Southeast Asia and in the lower Mississippi River Valley of the United States. It accounts for 75 percent of rice traded in global markets.

- *Medium-grain* (also referred to as Japonica) rice is grown in temperate climates and becomes moist and sticky when cooked. Medium-grain rice is the variety grown primarily in Japan, Korea, northeastern China, and California's Sacramento Valley. It accounts for about 12 percent of global rice trade.

- *Aromatic* rice represents subgroups of long-grain varieties such as jasmine rice from Thailand and basmati rice from India. Aromatic rice varieties sell for premium prices and account for about 12 percent of rice trade.

- *Glutinous* rice is a variety of sweet rice grown in Southeast Asia. It accounts for only about 1 percent of the global rice market.[4]

Rice markets are also differentiated by degree of processing. The least processed form is *rough* or *paddy rice*, in which the husk remains on the grains. Once the husk is removed, it becomes known as *brown rice*, and once the bran coating and its nutrients are removed, it becomes known as *milled or white rice*. Putting the nutrients back into the white rice produces *enriched rice*. Another way of retaining the nutrients involves boiling the rice in the husk, which drives the nutrients into the grain, resulting in *parboiled rice*.

Considered as a single commodity, rice is one of the most important in global agriculture. The grain is grown and eaten on every continent except Antarctica. In 2005 rice farmers worldwide produced a record 628 million metric tons of paddy rice, which equates to 409 million tons of milled rice.[5] The production and exporting of rice tend to be concentrated, while

Top Producers, Exporters, Importers, and Consumers of Rice, 2003–05
Table 1

Production	Exports	Imports	Annual per Capita Consumption
1. China (29.7%)	Thailand (31.9%)	Nigeria (5.2%)	Vietnam (232 kg)
2. India (21.2%)	Vietnam (16.4%)	Indonesia (5.2%)	Bangladesh (196 kg)
3. Indonesia (8.2%)	India (13.6%)	Philippines (4.8%)	Thailand (165 kg)
4. Bangladesh (6.4%)	**United States (13.1%)**	EU (3.7%)	Indonesia (162 kg)
5. Vietnam (5.7%)	Pakistan (8.8%)	Brazil (3.3%)	Philippines (134 kg)
6. Thailand (4.7%)	Egypt (3.3%)	Bangladesh (3.2%)	China (105 kg)
7. Philippines (2.3%)	China (2.8%)	Saudi Arabia (3.1%)	Korea (100 kg)
8. Brazil (2.0%)	Uruguay (2.4%)	Iran (3.0%)	Malaysia (83 kg)
9. Japan (1.9%)	Korea (1.1%)	South Africa (3.0%)	India (78 kg)
10. **United States (1.7%)**	Australia (0.9%)	Japan (2.7%)	Japan (66 kg)

Source: Organization for Economic Cooperation and Development, *OECD-FAO Agricultural Outlook 2006–2015* (Paris: OECD, 2006), Table A.8, pp. 130–33.
Note: Percentages are the share of world production, exports, or imports.

consumption and imports are diffused. Asia accounts for more than 90 percent of global rice production and consumption, with China, India, Indonesia, Bangladesh, Vietnam, and Thailand the world's top producers. Among non-Asian countries, Brazil, the United States, and Egypt are the largest producers. Five countries dominate the export market, Thailand, Vietnam, India, the United States, and Pakistan account for 84 percent of global exports. Imports are much more diffused, with no country accounting for more than about 5 percent of global imports (Table 1).

Those peculiar features of rice mean there is not one homogenous global rice market but several. Most exports of long-grain rice grown in the southern United States go to Latin America, while exports of medium-grain rice grown in the Sacramento Valley in California go to Japan and South Korea. Exports of Asian-grown long-grain rice go to Africa, the Middle East, and Europe, while Thailand and India export aromatic rice to the United States.

Although trade flows of rice have been growing in the past decade, those flows remain constrained and distorted by the high trade barriers and the domestic production and export subsides maintained by a large number of nations.

Global Markets, Global Distortions

For decades, rice trade has been distorted and suppressed by a patchwork of government policies. In the name of "food security" and protecting rice-sector jobs, importing nations have limited imports through tariffs, tariff-rate quotas, and outright bans. Rice-producing countries have sought to stimulate domestic production and stabilize prices through production subsidies, to compete in global markets through export subsidies, and to reduce stocks of oversupply through food aid programs. Exporters and importers alike have sought to exercise market power through state trading monopolies.

Global trade barriers against rice vary widely but on average are extraordinarily high. The World Bank calculates that the global tradeweighted average tariff on all varieties and grades of rice was 43.3 percent in 2000.[6] India imposes a 70 percent tariff on imported milled rice and an 80 percent tariff on paddy rice.[7] Indonesia maintains an official 30 percent tariff supported by nontariff barriers that add up to an effective tariff of 100 percent.[8] Eighteen countries wield "special safeguards" that allow them to enact steep tariffs when rice imports grow beyond certain levels.[9]

The highest barriers to rice trade are found in Northeast Asia against medium-grain rice. Before the Uruguay Round's Agreement on Agriculture came into effect in 1995, Japan and South Korea enforced total bans on imported rice. Today both countries limit rice imports to a fraction of domestic consumption (7.2 percent in Japan) through tariff-rate quotas, which allow a certain amount of rice to be imported at a low or no tariff rate but then impose prohibitive rates on imports above the quota. Steep barriers to rice imports drive a wedge between domestic and global prices, forcing consumers in the more protected countries to pay as much as four times the world price for rice.[10]

Tariffs vary not only by country and type of rice but also by its stage of processing. Many countries practice "tariff escalation," imposing steeper tariffs on imports of more processed forms of rice to protect employment in rice mills and other processing sectors. Other countries discourage or forbid the exportation of paddy (i.e., unprocessed) rice to encourage domestic milling at the expense of the milling sector in other countries. Tariff escalation also adds to the cost of shipping because rice weighs about 43 percent more before the husk is removed than it does after milling, further depressing levels of global trade. Countries in Central America are among the most aggressive practitioners of tariff escalation. The "tariff wedge," or difference between rates imposed on paddy and more processed forms of rice, varies from 10 to 40 percent in Mexico, Guatemala, Honduras, El Salvador, and Nicaragua.[11] Tariff escalation in Latin America is one of the main reasons that U.S. exports have shifted over the past decade from milled to paddy rice.[12]

Distortions at the border are compounded by widespread subsidies for production and export, including the U.S. rice program described in the next section. The United States and the European Union are among the largest dispensers of production subsidies for rice, but developing countries such as China and India also provide subsidies.[13] Progress has been made in the past decade in "decoupling" a growing share of subsidies from production requirements, but significant trade-distorting subsidies still remain. According to the OECD, border protection, domestic subsidies, and other government support accounted for an incredible 77 percent of gross receipts for rice farmers in OECD countries in 2002–04, an incremental improvement from the 81 percent provided in 1986–88.[14]

A number of countries also engage in the direct and indirect subsidy of exports. As a high-cost producer, the European Union relies on direct subsidies for most of its commercial exports.[15] The U.S. government promotes exports through export credit guarantees described below. When they are not subsidizing exports of rice, the United States and the European Union give away large quantities as food aid. According to the UN Food and Agricultural Organization, the two entities combined give away about 1.4 million tons of milled rice a year under various programs, accounting for 5 percent of global trade in rice.[16] Several developing countries, including Indonesia, the Philippines, Malaysia, Sri Lanka, Myanmar, and Kenya, try to influence global prices through monopolistic state trading enterprises.[17]

High trade barriers against rice mean that global markets for the commodity are thin and volatile. Only about 6 percent of global rice production in 2005 was traded on international markets, compared to 11 percent of feed grains (corn, oats, barely, and sorghum) and 17 percent of wheat production.[18] A major negative consequence of a thin global rice market is that production or consumption in a major trading country can have amplified effects on global prices, causing artificial and unnecessarily large disruptions in smaller rice markets.

Distortions in the global rice market were even worse two decades ago. Since the early 1990s, global trade barriers have trended downward and production subsidies have been shifting from the trade-distorting "amber box" to the less distorting "green box" and "blue box" categories, which are used in WTO jargon to designate less distorting subsidies decoupled from production. The Uruguay Round Agreement on Agriculture cracked opened the previously dosed Japanese and Korean markets and required quotas to be converted to more transparent tariffs and tariff rate quotas. Brazil, Bangladesh, Sri Lanka, Indonesia, Nigeria, and other African nations have lowered barriers to imported rice. The European Union under the Blair House Agreement of 1995 has allowed more imported rice, especially through expanded preference programs for low-income countries, and has cut subsidized procurement prices in half. China and Taiwan opened their markets further for rice imports as part of agreements to enter the WTO. Meanwhile, India, Pakistan, and Vietnam have loosened controls on rice exports.[19] The average global tariff wedge against more processed forms of rice has been reduced in the past decade from 23 percent to 17 percent.[20]

Even after piecemeal liberalization, the global rice market remains suppressed and distorted by an array of remaining government subsidies and trade barriers. As one rice trade expert concluded: "In several high-income countries, the rice sector has been isolated from external competition through high border protection, in the form of outright import prohibitions, state trading monopolies, minimum import quotas, high tariffs or variable duties. Rice in those countries is also subject to export subsidies, credit guarantees and food aid."[21]

The U.S. rice program is part of the problem.

The Protected and Subsidized U.S. Rice Industry

The U.S. government supports domestic rice production through tariffs on imported rice and direct taxpayer subsidies based on production, prices, and historical acreage. Those programs make rice one of the most heavily supported commodities in the United States, with ramifications for U.S. taxpayers and consumers and rice producers abroad.

Federal rice programs are aimed at helping about 9,000 rice farmers concentrated almost exclusively in six states. Arkansas farmers alone account for 45 percent of the nation's rice production, producing mostly long-grain rice but also some medium-grain. California farmers account for 18 percent of production, almost all of it medium-grain. Missouri, Mississippi, Louisiana, and Texas account for the rest, almost all of it long-grain.[22]

Collectively, American rice farmers produced an average of 6.9 million metric tons of rice (milled basis) in 2003–05, making the United States the world's 10th-largest producer of rice.[23] U.S. producers export about 40 percent of their crop, with long-grain rice typically exported from the South to Latin America and medium-grain exported from California to East Asia. Imports account for about 13 percent of domestic consumption; imports are predominantly aromatic varieties such as basmati rice from India and Pakistan and jasmine rice from Thailand (varieties not typically grown in the United States).[24]

Supporting the American rice industry are tariff barriers and an array of taxpayer subsidies. According to the Harmonized Tariff Schedule of the United States, the most commonly applied (i.e., the most favored nation) tariffs range from 0.44 cents per kilogram on lower quality, broken rice to 2.1 cents per kilogram on husked brown rice. Imported white and parboiled rice face an ad valorem rate of 11.2 percent. Those per kilogram tariffs translate into ad valorem rates of 3 to 24 percent, depending on the type of rice and fluctuations in global prices. (Because those tariffs are fixed at per kilogram rates, higher global prices per kilogram will mean lower effective ad valorem rates, while lower prices will mean higher rates.)[25]

Triple Subsidies with a Tariff on Top

On top of protection at the border, the U.S. government favors domestic rice producers through three major domestic subsidy programs. The Farm Security and Rural Investment Act of 2002, the most recent farm bill, contains three major provisions extending subsidies to rice farmers through direct payments, countercyclical payments, and marketing assistance loans.[26]

The direct payment program rewards farmers and other landowners on the basis of past acreage planted and average yields. Specifically, the program pays owners of the land $2.35 per hundredweight (100 pounds) times 85 percent of the farm's base acreage times the yield-per-acre level set by the program. Base acreage is not the number of acres currently under cultivation but the area farmed during a previous base year; the per acre yield is based on an industrywide average.

Countercyclical payments kick in when the "effective price" of rice falls below the government-set "target price." The effective price is the sum of the direct payment rate of $2.35 per hundredweight and the higher of the national average farm price of rice for the current marketing year or the national loan rate for rice (set by law at $6.50 per hundredweight). Rice farmers receive such payments whenever the effective price falls below the government-set target price of $10.50 per hundredweight. That means the minimum

effective price is $8.85 (the loan rate plus the direct payment rate) and the maximum countercyclical payment is $1.65 (the target price minus the effective price). As with direct payments, the total payment amount equals the countercyclical payment rate times payment acres times the payment yield per acre. In effect, the lower the domestic market price of rice, the higher the payments to domestic rice farmers, up to $1.65 per hundredweight.

Marketing assistance loans allow farmers to use their actual production as collateral for federal loans. If the adjusted world price, as defined by the USDA, falls below the national average loan rate of $6.50 per hundredweight, the farmer can forfeit the rice pledged as collateral to the Commodity Credit Corporation in full settlement of the loan. If prices are higher than the loan rate, the farmer can sell the rice at market prices and repay the loan at a favorable rate of interest. As an alternative, farmers can receive direct "loan deficiency payments" without needing to first take out a loan. Such payments are also based on the difference between market prices and the loan rate.

Together, those federal programs have delivered between $473 million and $1,774 million in taxpayer subsidies to the rice sector each year since 1998 through the Commodity Credit Corporation (Figure 1). Year-to-year variations in spending are driven by changing global prices, with lower global prices quickly translating into higher taxpayer subsidies.[27] According to the OECD, government protection and subsidies account for fully half of the income of U.S. rice farmers, making rice the single most subsidized commodity in the United States.[28]

Along with income subsidies and tariff protection, the federal government also supports the rice industry with various programs to promote exports. Through the Export Credit Guarantee Program, it guarantees payment to U.S. exporters on private loans to foreign customers, while the Supplier Credit Guarantee Program provides short-term financing. Other programs

Federal Expenditures for Rice Subsidies, 1998–2015 (millions of dollars, fiscal years)
Figure 1

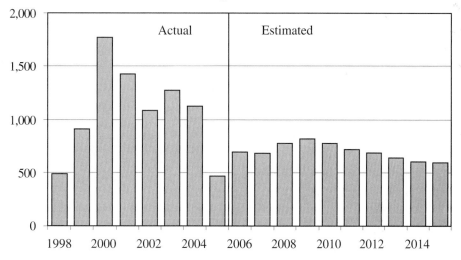

Sources: Commodity Credit Corporation, 1998–2005; Food and Agricultural Policy Research Institute, 2006–2015.

give rice away to poor countries free of charge or under concessionary terms. Through Public Law 480, the USDA channels rice to developing countries by acquiring rice in the open market and selling it through low-interest loans. Through Tide II of the Food for Progress Program, the U.S. Agency for International Development donates rice to poor countries.[29] U.S. food aid accounted for 5.8 percent of U.S. rice exports in fiscal year 2004 and 3.5 percent in FY05.[30]

Concentrated Benefits

Contrary to popular perception, payments do not necessarily go to individual rice farmers. Because direct payments and countercyclical payments are decoupled from actual production, payments can be received by owners of land that has been removed from rice farming altogether. According to a recent nine-month investigation by the *Washington Post*, "[T]he federal government has paid at least $1.3 billion in subsidies for rice and other crops since 2000 to individuals who

do no farming at all." The report cited an 87-year-old homeowner who had collected $191,000 during the past decade and a Houston surgeon who had collected $490,709—all because they owned land in southeast Texas, near Houston, that had once been used to grow rice.[31]

Other nonfarmers collecting payments are the landlords of active rice farmers. Part owners and tenants work almost 80 percent of farms producing rice, compared to 40 percent for farming in general. That causes the "leakage" of intended benefits away from households actually growing the rice to upstream and downstream interests, namely landowners and processors.[32] In the public's mind, farm payments are seen as a way to help small, struggling farmers, when in reality, a significant share of government support payments goes to large, nonfarming interests such as major landowners and agribusinesses. As the U.S. Department of Agriculture's chief rice expert, Nathan Childs, notes, "The rice sector tends to be dominated by a relatively few large producers.[33]

Congress has tried to reduce the relative concentration of payments by setting limits on how much can be received per farm. Rice producers, however, have managed to work around the limits through joint ownership. The "three entity rule," for example, allows rice farmers to claim subsidies for one farm and for a 50 percent stake in two other farms, effectively doubling the limit.

Obviously, federal rice programs benefit certain rice producers through direct taxpayer subsidies for production and exports and tariff restrictions against foreign-grown rice. It should be equally clear that those programs do not benefit most Americans or promote our broader national interests.

Impact on U.S. Taxpayers and Consumers

Americans pay for the rice program three times over—as taxpayers, as consumers, and as producers.

The most obvious cost of the rice program is found in the federal budget. Depending on the market price of rice, the federal government spent from $473 million to $1,774 million a year on direct, countercyclical, and loan payments to the rice sector between fiscal years 1998 and 2005, an average of slightly more than $1 billion per year. Without reforms, those payments are expected to continue to average $700 million a year through FY15—amounting to total outlays on the program during the next decade of $7 billion (see Figure 1). That is $7 billion that will not be available for deficit reduction, tax relief, or national defense.

Consumers also pay a price for the rice program through higher prices because of tariffs. Granted, U.S. tariffs are significantly lower than tariffs imposed by some other OECD member countries, such as Japan and Korea, but existing U.S. tariffs of 3 to 24 percent still keep domestic rice prices higher than they would be if Americans could buy rice freely from producers abroad.

The rice program imposes a drag on the U.S. economy generally through a misallocation of resources. Domestic subsidies and trade barriers artificially divert resources in the market economy—land, capital, production inputs, and labor—to maintaining a level of rice production greater than what the market would call for if the program did not exist. The program drives up the price of land, energy, fresh water, and other inputs to production, making those resources more expensive or unavailable for other sectors where Americans would enjoy a greater comparative advantage. Thus an artificially protected and stimulated rice industry crowds out other, more economical activities, slowing, even if incrementally, the growth rate of the U.S. economy.

The rice program has hurt the U.S. economy generally by compromising the U.S. governments ability to negotiate more effectively for more open markets abroad. U.S. farm subsidies were one of the major obstacles to forging a comprehensive agreement in the Doha Round of negotiations in the WTO. A comprehensive agreement could have delivered significant market access abroad for U.S. manufacturing, service providers, and farm producers. Although other U.S. programs and foreign governments shared the blame, the rice program was part of the problem that prevented a breakthrough in Doha.

There is no evidence that the costs imposed on the rest of American society have bought self-sustaining prosperity for the U.S. rice sector. In fact, subsidies and trade protection have probably contributed to the sector's declining competitiveness in global markets. America's share of the global rice export market has been in steady decline since the 1970s, when the United States was the world's leading exporter. From more than a quarter of global exports in 1975, the U.S. share has dropped steadily to a low of 10.4 percent in 2001 and has recovered only modestly since then.[34] Meanwhile, total rice imports have more than doubled since 1993–94 and now account for 12–14 percent of domestic use.[35]

What about "Food Security"?

One argument made for the rice program and other commodity subsidies and trade barriers is "food security." Although not a precise term, food security typically means pursuing policies that ensure reliable access to food in the face of external shocks such as war, embargoes, and natural disasters abroad. It emphasizes national self-sufficiency over reliance on imports.

Sen. Ken Salazar (D-CO) employed the food security argument in a recent speech to the Rocky Mountain Farmers Union. Salazar told the group that food security needs to be an important element in the next farm bill. "We're talking about a very fundamental issue to the United States of America, and that is our national security," he said. "I would hate to think of a day where the United States of America becomes hostage to other countries [that export food to the United States], in a way that we are held hostage over our energy needs."[36]

True food security does not depend on closed or subsidized markets; it depends on the ability to buy food from a variety of sources. Open global markets with expanding levels of trade are actually less volatile in terms of price changes and supply disruptions than are thin and protected markets. Americans would be less likely to face shortages and price hikes on food commodities if our markets were open to imports rather than closed to global suppliers. Like diversifying when investing, diversifying our food portfolio actually decreases risk and volatility. If food supplies are disrupted in the domestic market because of weather, pests, disease, or other shocks, producers abroad can provide additional supplies through imports. It is more economical to import extra supplies of food than to maintain an expensive domestic storage system vulnerable to pests and rot.

Advocates of protection in the name of food security propose a costly form of insurance against a set of circumstances that is only remotely possible. It is highly unlikely that a significant share of Americas food imports would be cut off by some kind of military blockade against the United Stats, or that major food exporters to the United States would decide to restrict supplies through an embargo. And even if some suppliers decided to reduce exports to the United States, for whatever reason, other global competitors would be eager to fill the gap. Against that negligible risk, food security advocates would have Americans pay a premium of billions of dollars a year in higher food prices and federal outlays. Out of an exaggerated fear that foreign supplies of food might be cut off, we would perversely enact policies that cut off foreign supplies of food.

For U.S. agriculture, the food security argument would be a double-edged sword. Last year, American farmers exported $62.5 billion worth of agricultural commodities, representing 27 percent of U.S. farm receipts.[37] Our major farm exports include soybeans, corn, wheat, meat and poultry, rice, fruits, vegetables, and nuts. U.S. farmers would potentially lose billions in sales abroad if other nations embraced the flawed food security argument.

In the end, the food security argument is no more valid than other arguments put forward to restrict imports and subsidize domestic production of rice. By any objective cost/benefit analysis for the United States as a whole, the rice program has failed to deliver benefits to a significant number of Americans outside the small rice sector.

Impact on Poor Rice Farmers Abroad

America's rice program causes collateral damage beyond our borders. By subsidizing production and exports and restricting imports, U.S. policy drives down global prices for rice. Those lower prices, in turn, perpetuate poverty and hardship for millions of rice farmers in developing countries, undermining our broader interests and our standing in the world.

U.S. Rice Production and Prices, 1990–2005
Figure 2

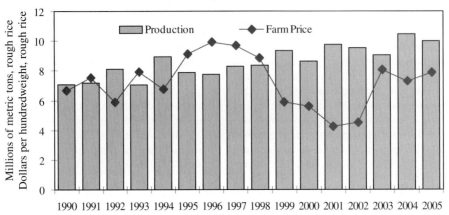

Source: U.S. Department of Agriculture.

The very purpose of the U.S. rice program, as of other commodity support programs, is to insulate domestic production levels from changes in global price signals. In this way the program promotes overproduction during times of lower global prices by promoting exports above the level that a free and open market would determine. Because of those distortions, U.S. rice producers are slow to respond to market signals. The marketing loan benefits and countercyclical payments, in particular, dull incentives to cut back production during periods of falling prices. High fixed costs and a lack of easy alternative crops further inhibit a supply response when rice prices change.

As a result, rice production in the United States has been remarkably unresponsive to changes in market prices. When global prices for rice collapsed in the late 1990s in the aftermath of the East Asian financial crisis, U.S. rice production continued to grow steadily. As Figure 2 shows, from 1997 to 2001, the average farm price for rough rice, as reported by the USDA, plunged by more then half, from $9.70 per hundredweight to $4.25;

U.S. rice farmers ramped up their annual production during that same period from 8.30 million to 9.76 million metric tons of rough rice, an 18 percent increase from 1997 to 2001.[38] Thanks to price-sensitive subsidy programs, federal support payments to rice farmers in the meantime exploded from less than half a billion a year before the price drop to $1.77 billion in 2000 and $1.42 billion in 2001.[39]

In the face of falling prices through 2001, American rice farmers switched from growing for the market to growing for the government. That was undoubtedly welcome relief for U.S. producers, but subsidies merely deflected the cost of adjustment from U.S. farmers to poor farmers in Vietnam, India, and Thailand. As Oxfam International concluded in a 2005 study, "[T]he USA deflected the shock of low prices back to the world market, and forced the adjustment onto other exporting countries."[40]

Rice market intervention by the United States and other countries "thins" the global rice market, reducing trade relative to production and leaving global markets and prices vulnerable to supply shocks in major trading countries. In a thin market, changes in production or consumption in a major market are amplified in global markets, forcing other countries to make disproportionate adjustments in production and supply.

Despite efforts to "decouple" U.S. rice subsidies from production, those subsidies continue to promote overproduction. Even supposedly decoupled subsidies insulate risk-averse farmers from the full impact of changes in prices. By making farmers more financially secure, direct payments make them less risk averse, encouraging them to plant more acreage than they would otherwise. Greater wealth also allows farmers to more easily finance operations and to ride out fluctuations in prices, effectively reducing their costs. Farmers have also been allowed to periodically update their "base acreage," sending the signal that payments are not entirely decoupled and therefore indirectly encouraging higher production in order to qualify for larger payments in the future. A study by agricultural economists Jayson Beckman and Eric J. Wailes found that countercyclical payments, although technically decoupled, still prompted an increase in supply.[41]

"Serious Prejudice" against Foreign Producers

By stimulating overproduction, U.S. rice subsidies increase the global supply of rice and thus put downward pressure on global prices. In a study for the Cato Institute in 2005, agricultural economist Daniel Sumner estimated that U.S. rice subsidies depress global prices by 4 to 6 percent.[42] Most distorting is the marketing loan program followed by countercyclical payments. U.S. subsidies are especially prejudicial against rice exports from Uruguay and Thailand. "The data on com, wheat, and rice programs indicate that there are plausible claims that those subsidies cause serious prejudice to competitors in the U.S. domestic market or international markets," Sumner concluded. "The remedy for those adverse effects is to eliminate the programs,

reduce the subsidy amounts, or reduce the degree of linkage to productions."[43]

Without reform, the U.S. government can expect that its rice program will be successfully challenged in the WTO just as the U.S. cotton program was successfully challenged by Brazil in 2005. Countries as diverse as Costa Rica, Ghana, Guyana, Haiti, India, Mexico, Pakistan, Peru, Suriname, Thailand, Uruguay, Venezuela, and Zambia could all plausibly claim that the U.S. rice program has driven down global prices to the detriment of their citizens.

WTO legality aside, artificially depressed global rice prices can have terrible consequences for poor farmers and their families. A 2002 study for the National Bureau of Economic Research found that higher rice prices in Vietnam were associated with significant declines in child labor rates. Specifically, a 30 percent increase in rice prices accounted for a decrease of children in the workforce of one million, or 9 percent. The drop was most pronounced among girls aged 14 and 15. As the incomes of rice-growing families rose, they chose to use their additional resources to remove their children from work in the field and send them to school.[44] If U.S. rice subsidies are indeed depressing global rice prices, then those same programs are plausibly responsible for keeping tens of thousands of young girls in Vietnam and other poor countries in the labor force rather than in school.[45]

The United States is certainly not alone among OECD countries in maintaining rice policies that are detrimental to farmers in developing countries. Total government support for rice production in OECD countries averaged $25 billion a year in 2000-02, through a combination of direct domestic subsidies and trade barriers, with trade barriers causing the most distortions in global markets. In fact, a number of developing countries, including Nigeria, the Philippines, Mexico, India, and Bangladesh, also maintain high tariffs on rice imports, further distorting global markets.[46]

If the United States were to join with other countries to scrap all subsidies and border protection for rice, global trade in rice would expand, export prices would rise, and import prices would fall. According to a recent World Bank study: "Complete liberalization in 2000 would have resulted in a significant expansion in global rice trade of nearly 3.5 million metric tons, a 15 percent increase in trade. Tradeweighted average export prices would be 32.8 percent higher and trade-weighted import prices would be 13.5 percent lower."[47]

Even if the rest of the world did not join in eliminating subsidies and protection for rice producers, the United States and its citizens would still be better off if we eliminated our program unilaterally.

The 2007 Farm Bill: An Opportunity for Reform

The cost that the U.S. rice program imposes on poor farmers abroad is significant, but the cost it imposes on Americans alone more than justifies radical reform. For our own national interest, the U.S. Congress and the Bush administration should work together to adopt a more market-oriented rice program in the upcoming farm bill. As the evidence presented above indicates, eliminating trade barriers and further reducing and decoupling subsidies would save taxpayers billions of dollars during the next decade, lower domestic rice prices, and spread goodwill toward the United States abroad.

In the new farm bill, expected to be addressed in the first half of 2007, Congress should do the following:

- Repeal all trade barriers against imported rice. Tariffs act as a regressive tax on food while delivering support to a small group of rice farmers through a nontransparent and market-distorting mechanism.
- Eliminate the market loan program, which is the most production- and trade-distorting of the three main support programs. The program is vulnerable to a challenge in the WTO.

- Phase out or buy out the other two subsidy programs, direct payments and counter cyclical payments, which, although less market distorting, amount to an unjust transfer of wealth from tens of millions of American households to a few thousand rice farmers. The payments could be phased out over a period of three to five years, or they could be ended immediately with the payment of a lump sum equal to something less than the net present value of the phased-out payments.

Congress should avoid merely tinkering with the program but instead should end current programs outright or within a limited time period. The chief failure of the 1996 farm bill was that it left much of the agricultural support infrastructure in place. When global agricultural prices fell in the late 1990s, followed by rising demands from certain farm sectors for government relief, it was too easy for Congress to ramp up emergency spending through still-existing programs. If the programs were eliminated entirely, a future Congress would face the additional hurdle of having to re-create the programs from scratch if it were to renew price supports.

A major obstacle to scaling back the rice program is interest-group politics. The rice program exists not because it serves the national interest but because the special interests that benefit from it are more organized, concentrated, and motivated than the general public that pays for the program. In the 2003–04 election cycle, political action committees connected to the rice sector contributed $289,300 to influence elections for the U.S. House and Senate, and those same PACs had contributed $250,076 in the current election cycle through June 30,2006. The three largest contributors were the Farmers' Rice Cooperative, the USA Rice Federation, and Riceland Foods. Not surprisingly, a significant share of contributions went to members of the agricultural subcommittees that oversee the rice program.[48]

The answer is not to restrict campaign donations but to expose the true costs to the public of the federal rice program. In the wake of various lobbying scandals in Washington, reforming the rice program and other farm programs offers members of Congress an opportunity to show that they can serve the broader public interest by asserting their independence from special-interest lobbying.

Congress should also reject any hyperbole about the very survival of the rice sector depending on the rice program. Elimination of the rice program would obviously and intentionally reduce production from uneconomic farms that cannot survive in a free and unsubsidized market. But a reformed and more competitive, if somewhat smaller, U.S. rice sector could be expected to survive and thrive without federal support.

The United States has certain inherent advantages as a rice producer, including plentiful land, human and physical capital, a reputation as a reliable supplier, and proximity to major markets such as Latin America. If other countries respond with lower tariffs and reduced subsidies, American rice producers could even increase their production in a global free market for rice.[49] The recent experience of New Zealand demonstrates that an advanced agricultural nation can sharply reduce its agricultural payments and still retain its competitiveness as a global agricultural producer.[50]

Ending the U.S. rice program would be, not "unilateral disarmament," but an exercise in asserting our own national interest regardless of what other countries may choose to do. The rice program is not an asset to be jealously guarded; it is a national liability to be jettisoned as soon as possible. By reforming the rice program unilaterally, the U.S. government would bolster our national economic well-being, create goodwill among less developed countries, and enhance our nation's role as a leader in the world economy.

Notes

1. United Nations Food and Agricultural Organization, "Rice Liberalization: Predicting Trade and Price Impacts," Policy Brief no. 12, p. 1, ftp://ftp.fao.org/docrep/fao/008/j5931e/j5931e01.pdf, accessed July 27, 2006.

2. Eric J. Wailes, "Rice: Global Trade, Protectionist Policies, and the Impact of Trade Liberalization," in *Global Agricultural Trade and Developing Countries*, ed. M. Ataman Aksoy and John C. Begbin (Washington: World Bank, 2005), p. 185.

3. Organization for Economic Cooperation and Development, *Agricultural Policy and Trade Reform: Potential Effects at Global, National and Household Levels* (Paris: OECD, 2006), p. 21.

4. Concepcion Calpe, "International Trade in Rice, Recent Developments and Prospects," UN Food and Agricultural Organization, Paper presented at the World Rice Research Conference, November 5–7, 2004, p. 6.

5. UN Food and Agricultural Organization, *Rice Market Monitor* 9, no. 1 (March 2006): 1.

6. Wailes, p. 185.

7. Ibid., p. 181.

8. Ibid., p. 182.

9. UN, *Rice Market Monitor*, p. 2.

10. OECD, *Agricultural Policy and Trade Reform*, p. 22.

11. E. Wailes, A Durand-Morat, L. Hoffman, and N. Childs, "Tariff Escalation: Impact on U.S. and Global Rice Trade," Paper prepared for the American Agricultural Economics Association Annual Meeting, August 1–4, 2004, p. 4, agecon.lib.umn.edu.

12. Ibid., p. 21.

13. Nathan Childs, "Rice Situation and Outlook Yearbook," U.S. Department of Agriculture, Economic Research Service, November 2005, p. 5.

14. OECD, *Agricultural Policy and Trade Reform*, p. 21.

15. Childs, "Rice Situation and Outlook Yearbook," p. 57.

16. UN, *Rice Market Monitor*, p. 3.

17. Ibid., p. 2.

18. Organization for Economic Cooperation and Development, *OECD-FAO Agricultural Outlook 2006–2015* (Paris: OECD, 2006), Figure 2.9, p. 46.

19. Calpe, pp. 2–3.

20. Wailes, Durand-Morat, Hoffman, and Childs, p. 4.

21. Calpe, p. 1.

22 Jayson Beckman and Eric J. Wailes, "The Supply Response of U.S. Rice: How Decoupled Are Income Payments?" Paper prepared for the American Agricultural Economics Association Annual Meeting, July 24–27, 2005, p. 3, agecon.lib.umn.edu.

23 OECD, *Agricultural Outlook*, Table A-8, p. 130.

24 Childs, "Rice Situation and Outlook Yearbook," p. 73.

25 U.S. Harmonized Tariff Code, Chapter 10.

26 The description of the major subsidy programs that follows is based on U.S. Department of Agriculture, "Rice: Policy," Economic Research Service Briefing Rooms, www.ers. usda.gov/Briefing/Rice/Policy.htm, accessed June 20, 2006.

27 U.S. Department of Agriculture, "CCC FY 2007 Budget Estimates, Table 35, CCC Net Outlays by Commodity and Function," Farm Service Agency, www.fsa.usda.gov/Internet/ FSA_File/07msr web35.pdf.

28 Cited in Wailes, p. 184.

29 For a description of export subsidy programs, see USDA, "Rice: Policy."

30 Childs, "Rice Situation and Outlook Yearbook," p. 34.

31 Dan Morgan, Gilbert M Gaul, and Sarah Cohen, "Farm Program Pays $1.3 Billion to People Who Don't Farm," *Washington Post,* July 2, 2006, p. Al.

32 Nathan W. Childs, "Rice: Background and Issues for Farm Legislation," Economic Research Service, USDA, RCS-0601-01 July 2001, p. 3, www.ers.usda.gov.

33 Ibid., p. 3.

34 Childs, "Rice Situation and Outlook Yearbook," p. 53.

35 Ibid., p. 15.

36 Steven K. Paulson, "Salazar: Farm Bill Should Aim at National Security," Associated Press, August 21, 2006, cbs4denver.com/politics/ local_story_233201402.html.

37 See Michael Johanns, U.S. secretary of agriculture, Speech to the Bretton Woods Committee Annual Meeting on Agricultural Trade and Farm Policy, Washington, D.C., May 23, 2006, www.usda.gov.

38 U.S. Department of Agriculture, Economic Research Service, *2005 Rice Yearbook*, Appendix Table 11, "U.S. Rice Acreage, Yield, and Production," and Table 16, "Ending Stocks, Prices, and Payment Rates for Rice."

39 U.S. Department of Agriculture, "CCC FY 2007 Budget Estimates, Table 35."

40 Oxfam International, "Kicking Down the Door: How Upcoming WTO Talks Threaten Farmers in Poor Countries," Oxfam Briefing Paper 72, April 11, 2005, p. 38.

41 Beckman and Wailes, p. 3.

42 Daniel A. Sumner, "Boxed In: Conflicts between U.S. Farm Policies and WTO Obligations," Cato Institute Trade Policy Analysis no. 32, December 5, 2005, p. 21.

43 Ibid., p. 25.

44 Eric Edmonds and Nina Pavcnik, "Does Globalization Increase Child Labor? Evidence from Vietnam," NBER Working Paper no. 8760, July 2002.

45 Even in low-income countries that import rice, distorted global markets can have harmful long-term effects. To the extent that artificially low prices depress global trade and production, they add to market volatility and the potential for supply disruptions.

46 Wailes, p. 185.

47 Ibid., p. 186.

48 Figures compiled by the Center for Responsive Politics, www.opensecrets.org/pacs/index.asp.

49 Wailes, p. 189.

50 See Thomas Lambie, "Miracle Down Under: How New Zealand Farmers Prosper without Subsidies or Protection," Cato Institute Free Trade Bulletin no. 16, February 7, 2005.

3

International Trade:
Why We Don't Have More of It

EDITH **OSTAPIK** AND
KEI-MU **YI**

lobalization has many facets. One of the most important is the enormous increase in international trade. Over the past 40 years, world exports as a share of output have doubled to almost 25 percent of world output.[1] However, despite globalization and the increasing share of output that is exported and imported internationally, economic evidence suggests that significant barriers to international trade still exist.[2] We will summarize the latest developments in the measurement of international trade barriers, drawing mainly from a recent comprehensive survey on the subject by James Anderson and Eric van Wincoop. In their survey, these authors report estimates of the magnitudes of different categories of international trade costs. They find that, on average, international trade costs almost double the price of goods in developed countries.[3]

The primary policy implication of the existing research is that globalization still has a long way to go, so that there is still plenty of room for trade to grow. Growth in trade will likely occur primarily through technological changes that reduce transportation or communication costs or from long-run policy choices, such as a national currency or language. Reduction in policy-related barriers, such as tariffs, will also play a role.

Why and How Trade Costs Reduce Trade

The core idea underlying the benefits of international trade goes back to Adam Smith and his famous pin factory parable. According to Smith, when each worker specializes in doing only those tasks he is best suited to do, a factory achieves its maximum economic efficiency. Smith and later economists extended this argument from firms to countries. Economic efficiency occurs when each country specializes in making and exporting only those goods it is relatively efficient at producing. In turn, each country imports those goods other countries produce relatively efficiently.[4]

In other words, international trade enhances a society's economic well-being because it facilitates specialization in production. With trade, prices consumers pay for goods are lower than those they would pay without trade. According to Smith and later economists, when trade is free and unfettered, a society maximizes its economic well-being.

Barriers to international trade prevent the efficient outcome described above from occurring. For example, because these barriers raise the costs of purchasing imported goods, U.S. consumers would buy fewer foreign goods, and foreign consumers would buy fewer U.S. goods. To satisfy the demand for products that previously had been imported under free trade, each country would now be making more goods it is not relatively efficient at producing. In the presence of international trade barriers, there would be less specialization, prices would be higher, and, overall, consumers in all countries would be worse off.

The Two Main Types of Trade Costs

In 19th-century England, economist David Ricardo used these core ideas of the benefits to international trade to argue against a pressing political barrier to trade: the Corn Laws, which protected British agriculture and kept domestic food prices high. Since then, economists have studied many other barriers to trade. We will describe these barriers in terms of costs, following the convention used by Anderson and van Wincoop.[5]

Broadly, trade costs are all costs incurred from the time a good leaves the factory or its place of production to the time it is purchased by the end-user. Such costs can be incurred internationally (for example, at the border) or domestically (that is, within a country). In the case of consumer goods such as automobiles, televisions, clothing, and food, trade costs are the difference between the price at the "factory gate" and the retail price.[6]

International trade costs can be broadly divided into two main categories: border-related costs and international transportation costs. Border-related costs encompass the broad range of trade barriers encountered between nations, excluding international transportation. These barriers include costs that occur specifically at the border, such as tariffs, quotas, and paperwork due to customs and other regulations, as well as those differences between countries that could affect trade, such as different currencies, languages, or laws (contract enforcement).[7] Together with international transport costs, these items make up the costs incurred internationally.

Border-related costs can be classified based on whether they are attributable to (national) government policies. This allows

economists to assess the importance of border costs imposed by government policy relative to other border costs. Border-related costs imposed by government policy are further separated by economists into two categories: tariffs and nontariff barriers.

Tariffs are additional charges added to the price of a good imported from another country. The charge is usually levied as a proportion of the price, similar to a sales tax. Nontariff barriers[8] are loosely defined as all other trade barriers imposed by national governments. The most familiar of these are quotas, which are restrictions on the quantity of a good that can be imported from a country. They also include voluntary export restraints, which occur when the exporting country "voluntarily" agrees to limit its exports to the importing country; anti-dumping actions, which are taken when foreign firms are suspected of selling their goods at a price below that in their home market;[9] paperwork and regulatory procedures encountered specifically at the national border; and "softer" measures, such as product labeling and product quality standards.

Border barriers not due to government policy include information costs (costs incurred by potential importers in finding out more about the goods they are buying); costs due to exchange rate uncertainty, linguistic barriers, or other cultural differences; and contract enforcement costs. International transportation costs are freight charges and transport time associated with moving goods from the exporting to the importing country. These costs include all freight and time costs associated with moving a good from the factory in the exporting country to the first port of entry in the importing country. Freight charges include trucking, shipping, and air charges.

Measuring Trade Costs

We can measure trade costs two ways. The first is to simply measure them directly from concrete data. The second involves an indirect approach whereby the costs are inferred using an economic model of bilateral trade flows known as the gravity model.

Border-Related Costs

Tariffs are the easiest to measure because they are directly collected by U.S. Customs officials. Detailed data are collected on tariff rates for thousands of goods. There are two approaches to combining the detailed tariff data into an overall average tariff measure for the country. One approach is to compute an average across all tariff rates. While this way is simple to implement, it is problematic because it weighs all goods equally, regardless of whether imports of the good are $10,000 or $10 billion.

A second approach is to weigh the tariff rates according to the volume of imports. In the above example, the tariff on the heavily imported good would have a weight 1 million times larger than the weight on the other good. However, this approach is problematic, as well. Suppose that tariff rates on Canadian apples were so high that U.S. consumers did not import them at all. Clearly, the tariffs on apples are negatively affecting imports.[10] But precisely because their impact is so negative that imports fall to zero, they would have a zero weight. In other words, this approach tends to underestimate the true impact of tariffs. Despite this shortcoming, most calculations of overall average tariff rates employ this second approach.

Calculating other border-related trade costs, especially nontariff trade barriers, is considerably more difficult. In his study, Patrick Messerlin converts the nontariff barriers into a tariff equivalent.[11] For quotas, Messerlin uses direct information from case studies to do the conversion. For the antidumping measures, he either directly converts them to tariff-equivalents[12] or uses the ratio of the "dumping" price to the standard world price to convert the measures to tax equivalents. These different measures are summed to an overall tariff equivalent and then combined with the average tariff rate to yield an estimate of border-related trade costs imposed by government policy.

For border-related trade costs not related to government policy, economists generally rely on a combination of direct and indirect measurement based on the gravity model. For example, the costs of not sharing a common currency or a common language, as well as security costs and information costs, are calculated using the gravity model.

In its simplest form, the gravity model is a statistical relationship that seeks to explain trade between two countries (bilateral trade) by three forces: the economic sizes of the two countries and the distance between them. Economists perform a statistical analysis called a regression in order to obtain an estimate, for example, of the effect of an increase in distance on trade flows.

More sophisticated versions of the gravity model include additional variables to further explain bilateral trade flows. In our context, the additional variables capture whether the two countries share a common currency, language, border, trade agreement, or legal system. While the lack of a common currency, for example, will not show up as a direct add-on to the price of the imported good as does a tariff, it will still reduce trade. The gravity regression provides a statistical means for measuring the tariff-equivalent of this reduction in trade.[13]

International Transport Costs

The four primary modes of transport are boat, rail, truck, and airplane. The two key transport costs are direct freight, or shipping, costs and travel time. Exporters must decide on the most efficient mode (or combination of modes) of transport for their goods, balancing per unit shipping costs and travel time. In general, transport by air is more expensive in terms of freight costs but cheaper in terms of time. In addition, countries with poorly developed infrastructure (for example, roads, airports, and ports) will generally have higher freight costs compared with countries that have large stocks of infrastructure.

A Breakdown of Trade Costs*
Table 1

Description	Percent Markup over the Price of the Good
time costs	9
+ shipping costs	11
Total Transport Costs	21
tariffs and NTBs	8
language costs	7
currency costs	14
information costs	6
+ security costs	3
Total Border-Related Barriers	**44%**
TOTAL	**74%**

*The table presents the various trade costs described in this paper, along with categorical sub-totals and the final total. In totaling these components of the overall trade cost, recall the multiplicative accounting procedure employed by Anderson and van Wincoop. . . .

Anderson and van Wincoop explore research on measuring freight costs, where shippers and handlers are interviewed, industry trade journals are examined, and customs data are analyzed. Customs data provide both total imports including freight charges and total imports excluding freight charges. These customs data facilitate the calculation of total freight charges associated with importing.[14]

Anderson and van Wincoop ultimately draw from an article by David Hummels for a measure of international transport costs because he incorporates time into transportation costs.[15] In his article, Hummels develops methodologies to translate time costs into dollars, from which the costs can then be expressed as a percentage of the value of the good transported. Then, the freight costs and the time costs can be totaled to yield an overall measure of international transport costs.

Estimates of Trade Costs

Before beginning the discussion of estimating trade costs, we advise the reader to review Table 1 and Figure 1. Table 1 contains a breakdown of the two main international trade costs and their components. Figure 1 illustrates the importance of tariffs and other border-related costs, on the one hand, and international transport costs, on the other hand, via a hypothetical example of a pair of shoes produced in a foreign country and shipped to the U.S.

Tariffs

To arrive at a single overall tariff measure for a country, economists typically calculate average tariffs according to the trade-weighted method discussed above. Average tariffs can differ across countries for a number of reasons, but the most

Figure 1

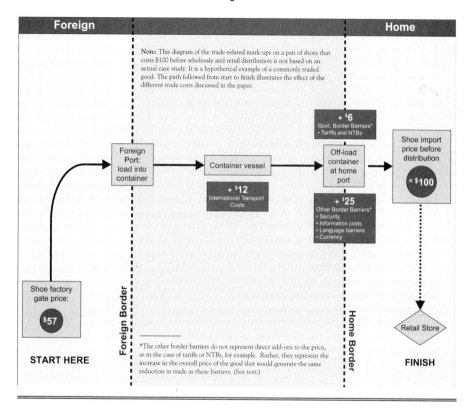

obvious and basic reason is that tariff rates on individual goods are higher in one country than in another.[16] Anderson and van Wincoop report that in 1999, this trade-weighted average tariff rate ranged from 0 to 30 percent across different countries. They find that developed countries' tariffs tended to be considerably lower than tariffs in developing countries: Developing countries tend to have tariffs of more than 10 percent, while developed countries' tariffs are in the range of 0 to 5 percent.

While average tariffs in developed countries are low, there is some variation between countries, as the following numbers from Anderson and van Wincoop indicate. At the low end in 1999, Switzerland, Hong Kong, and Singapore had 0 percent tariffs. At the high end, Australia and Canada had average tariffs of about

4.5 percent. In between were New Zealand and the major advanced economies, including Japan, the United States, and the European Union (EU), which had average tariffs of about 2 to 3 percent.

Nontariff Barriers

Traditionally, the tendency has been to apply nontariff barriers broadly to goods in a few sectors, as Anderson and van Wincoop show using United Nations data.[17] For example, nontariff barriers in 1999 were applied, respectively, to 74 percent, 71 percent, and 39 percent of the categories of goods in the food, textiles, and wood-related sectors.[18] This contrasts with the overall picture of nontariff barrier coverage in 1999, where only 1.5 percent of all goods were protected by such barriers. Additionally, there has been a rise in other types of nontariff barriers, most notably anti-dumping actions. If these anti-dumping actions were included in the nontariff barriers, the share of all goods protected increases to 27.2 percent in 1999.[19]

Incorporating all of these types of trade policy barriers into models, researchers have found that for the EU in 1999, tariffs and nontariff barriers can be translated into a 7.7 percent "tax" on industrial goods. In light of the tariff numbers presented above, this estimate indicates that for the EU, at least, nontariff barriers exert more of a tax than do tariffs.

Other Border-Related Barriers

Using the gravity model described above, a number of researchers have been able to estimate, for developed countries, the indirect trade costs at national borders. Anderson and van Wincoop summarize the main findings as follows: (1) The costs of not sharing the same language are roughly 7 percent of the value of the goods traded. (2) The cost of employing different currencies is about 14 percent. (3) Information costs are 6 percent. (4) Security costs are 3 percent.

Overall, these nonpolicy border-related costs equal 33 percent. Note that the combined effect is not obtained by simply adding up each border cost. Rather, because each border cost is applied to the total value of trade inclusive of all other border costs, a multiplicative formula must be used: $(1.07)*(1.14)*(1.06)*(1.03)-1 = 0.33$ (or 33 percent).[20] Adding government policy barriers to these barriers yields a total border-related trade cost of $(1.33)*(1.077)-1 = 0.44$ (or 44 percent).

International Transport Costs

Anderson and van Wincoop report results on transport costs from another article by David Hummels.[21] Using U.S. national customs data to get detailed data on transport costs and then calculating a simple average across all of the costs, Hummels obtains a freight transport cost estimate of 10.7 percent.

Anderson and van Wincoop also report results from Hummels on-time costs.[22] As of 1998, about half the value of U.S. exports are shipped by air. Hummels imputes a willingness to pay for saved time and translates that into a percentage of the value of the goods shipped. His estimate of U.S. time costs is 9 percent.[23] Combining the freight costs and the time cost estimates yields a total transport cost of $(1.107*1.09-1) = 0.21$, or 21 percent of the price of the good at the factory gate.

To summarize, Anderson and van Wincoop list two main sources of trade costs: border barriers and international transport costs. They then draw on the existing empirical research to obtain a rough approximation of each of these costs for the United States, as well as an approximation of the overall costs. All border barriers, including tariffs, nontariff barriers, and nonpolicy barriers, add up to a 44 percent "tax" on imports. Transportation costs are an additional 21 percent. Combining these costs—again using the multiplicative formula—yields the final overall tax-equivalent international trade cost of 74 percent of the factory gate price.

Conclusion

Barriers to international trade impede the free flow of goods and services, leading to increased production by relatively inefficient firms, thereby reducing the overall economic well-being of societies. While the globalization of the world's economies has seized the attention of policymakers, the media, and economists, researchers have recently collected a great deal of evidence that indicates that barriers to trade remain quite high. The types and magnitudes of these barriers in developed countries are highlighted in an important recent article by James Anderson and Eric van Wincoop.

Combining the results from current research on trade costs, Anderson and van Wincoop find that border barriers and international transport costs are equivalent to a 74 percent tax on the factory gate price—74 percent seems like a high number; imagine a sales tax that high! How is it that in a rapidly globalizing world the costs of international trade are still so high? For evidence of these high trade costs, it is useful to look at the United States data in relation to the predictions of theories of international trade.

The United States is the world's largest economy, yet its output is still less than one-third of the world total. If there were no costs to international trade—if it were as costless to ship goods to Europe and China as it is to send an e-mail—most existing trade theories would predict that the United States would export about two-thirds of its output. In fact, exports are only about 10 percent of U.S. GDP. From the sharp divergence of the theory's prediction and the actual data, we can infer that costs to international trade are quite high.

Anderson and van Wincoop's article shows that nonpolicy barriers account for the vast majority of total trade costs. Policy barriers, such as tariffs and quotas, play a smaller role. Will these nonpolicy and policy barriers ever be completely eliminated? The answer certainly is no. It is not possible that the economists' idealized world of frictionless trade in which trade costs and barriers are zero will ever be realized.

For the world's developed economies, however, significant reductions in trade costs and increases in trade can come from technological improvements that reduce international transportation costs, or from long-run policy changes, such as policies to reduce currency and information costs (or language and cultural barriers). One example is the recent adoption of a single currency, the euro, by 12 nations within Europe in 1999.[24] In addition, Anderson and van Wincoop show that for certain categories of goods, policy barriers have been strongly persistent over time. If these barriers were to be reduced significantly or eliminated, this would further increase international trade. Regardless of which barriers fall, firms and consumers, on the whole, would be better off.

Endnotes

[1] Source: The World Bank's World Development Indicators (we use the world export share of world GDP). Since world exports = world imports, imports have risen by the same amount.

[2] Previous *Business Review* articles have questioned the extent to which globalization has taken place. The article by Janet Ceglowski reviews research on barriers to international trade. Examining another dimension of globalization, Sylvain Leduc explores the lack of international diversification of investment portfolios.

[3] They estimate an overall average increase of 74 percent in the prices of goods in these countries.

[4] David Ricardo formalized the notion of relative efficiency in his theory of comparative advantage. One of the most powerful ideas in economics, comparative advantage shows that countries can gain from trading with each other, even if one country is more productive at producing every single good than another country. Textbooks on international economics (for example, the one by Richard Caves, Jeffrey Frankel, and Ronald Jones or the one by Paul Krugman and Maurice Obstfeld) provide a more detailed description of comparative advantage.

[5] Anderson and van Wincoop divide trade costs into three broad categories: border-related costs, international transportation costs, and distribution costs. We focus only on those costs associated with international trade: border related costs and international transport costs.

[6] In the case of intermediate goods such as automobile engines, semiconductors, textiles, and wheat, trade costs are the difference between the "factory gate" price and the purchase price by the next firm in the production sequence.

[7] Economists have studied the importance of international networks in reducing the negative effect of these country-level differences on trade. For example, James Rauch and Vitor Trindade find that trade flows are greater between countries with larger shares of Chinese population. They hypothesize that this linguistic and cultural network facilitates trade by reducing information and contract enforcement costs otherwise present between pairs of countries.

[8] The main data source for tariffs and nontariff barriers is the United Nations' Conference on Trade and Development TRAINS database. This database lists eight broad categories of trade control measures, which can be further broken down into 150 sub-categories.

[9] Dumping occurs when exports are sold in foreign markets at a price below their domestic price or production costs (according to U.S. policy). An anti-dumping action is the filing, by a domestic firm or industry, of an accusation that a foreign firm or industry has dumped goods in the domestic market. If the foreign firms are found guilty of dumping, the domestic government levies a duty on the goods in question for a fixed period of time.

[10] The following historical example illustrates the effect of a tariff on the volume of imports. In

April 1984, the U.S. government increased the tariff rate on heavyweight motorcycles from 4.4 to 45 percent. From 1983 to 1984, the total customs value (the value at the "entry gate" of a country) of heavyweight motorcycle imports (700–790 cubic centimeters of engine displacement) fell from $5.7 million to $55,000.

[11] In their survey, Anderson and van Wincoop cite Messerlin's article.

[12] Ad valorem duties, which are taxes levied as a percentage of the value of the imported goods, are converted directly.

[13] The tariff-equivalent of the effect of not having a common currency could be calculated if the gravity regression includes both tariff rates and a variable for whether or not the two countries share a common currency. Then, the regression would indicate how much a one-percentage-point change in tariffs reduces trade, and it would also indicate how much not sharing a common currency would reduce trade. From these two pieces of information, the tariff equivalent of not sharing a common currency can be calculated.

[14] From these two measures it is possible to calculate the average free on board (f.o.b.) price (the price on the mode of transport before any trade costs) as well as the average cost, insurance, and freight (c.i.f.) price. The difference between these two numbers is one way of measuring transport costs.

[15] See the 2001a article by Hummels.

[16] Another reason would be if a country happens to heavily import those goods that face high tariff rates. This would be unusual, however, because high tariff rates presumably discourage imports.

[17] United Nations Conference on Trade and Development's Trade Analysis & Information System: TRAINS, and general insight from the work of Jon Haveman available at: www.macalester.edu/research/economics/PAGE/HAVEMAN/Trade.Resources/TradeConcordances.html.

[18] In 2005 the World Trade Organization's textile quota system known as the Multi-Fiber Agreement (MFA) was phased out. However, subsequent dramatic changes in trade flows have caused countries to invoke other methods to control the amount of textiles traded.

[19] All percentages reported are simple averages of the nontariff barrier coverage ratios over the appropriate categories of goods (that is, the share of total goods in a category that are subjected to nontariff barriers).

[20] When border costs are small, the multiplicative formula yields numbers very similar to what would be obtained by adding up the costs. However, when border costs are large, the formula yields numbers quite different from those obtained by simple addition.

[21] See Hummels' 2001b article.

[22] See Hummels' 2001a article.

[23] This is a sharp decrease from 32 percent in 1950.

[24] Between 2000 and 2005, euro-area trade increased by 10.3 percent, which was larger than the increase between 1993 and 1998 (8.3 percent). This is consistent with (but not proof of) the notion that the adoption of the euro reduced trade costs, thus increasing trade.

References

Anderson, James E., and Eric van Wincoop. "Trade Costs," *Journal of Economic Literature,* 42 (September 2004), pp. 692–751.

Caves, Richard E., Jeffrey A. Frankel, and Ronald W. Jones. *World Trade and Payments: An Introduction,* 10th edition. Addison Wesley: New York, 2006.

Ceglowski, Janet. "Has Globalization Created a Borderless World?" Federal Reserve Bank of Philadelphia *Business Review* (March/April 1998), pp. 17–27.

Harrigan, James. "OECD Imports and Trade Barriers in 1983," *Journal of International Economics,* 34:1-2 (1993), pp. 91–111.

Hummels, David. "Time as a Trade Barrier," manuscript, Purdue University (2001a).

Hummels, David. "Toward a Geography of Trade Costs," manuscript, Purdue University (2001b).

Krugman, Paul, and Maurice Obstfeld. *International Economics: Theory and Policy,* 6th edition. Addison Wesley: New York, 2002.

Leduc, Sylvain. "International Risk Sharing: Globalization Is Weaker Than You Think," Federal Reserve Bank of Philadelphia *Business Review* (Second Quarter 2005), pp. 18–25.

Messerlin, Patrick. *Measuring the Cost of Protection in Europe.* Institute of International Economics: Washington, D.C. (2001).

Rauch, James E., and Vitor Trindade. "Ethnic Chinese Networks in International Trade," *Review of Economics and Statistics,* 84:1 (2002), pp. 116–29.

Discussion Questions

I

1. In the estimates of the total welfare loss due to protectionism, why are the losses estimated for the U.S. different than the estimates of global welfare loss?

2. Do you think the losses that Feenstra presents are significant? What losses are left out of the analysis? Do you think that these other losses might be larger or smaller?

3. Besides the U.S., what countries are hurt most by U.S. rice subsidies? What particular individuals in these countries do you believe would be hurt the most?

4. If U.S. rice subsidies are bad policies, why have they, and other agricultural subsidies, persisted?

5. What are the total costs to the U.S. of rice subsidies? (Hint: Include costs to government, industry and consumers.)

6. If one follows the analysis by Ostapik and Yi, how significant would a currency union such as the Euro area be in increasing free trade, compared to tariff and non-tariff barriers?

7. Do you think that developments in communications technology would lower the costs of trade? If so, what particular costs of trade are likely to be reduced?

8. Given what you have learned in the first three articles, what policies would you recommend to encourage more trade?

Outsourcing, the WTO, and the Environment

II

Section 2 looks at the nuts and bolts of critical trade issues and how these could potentially be addressed under the World Trade Organization (WTO). In "Bridging the Trade-Environment Divide," Daniel Esty gives an overview of the key environmental issues being debated in the Doha round. One key issue is the environmental "Kuznets curve," an empirical generalization that poor countries pollute more when they first start to grow, and only reduce pollution when they become high income countries. To the extent that trade encourages economic growth, increased trade could increase pollution in the short run. Esty also discusses "transboundary" externalities, which encompass such concerns as fishing rights, global warming, and CFC pollution, which impact more than one country. Finally, Esty discusses the "race to the bottom" argument, which is a major concern of environmentalists—that poor countries will compete to host polluting industries by lowering their standards. While Esty rejects this hypothesis, he does believe that countries may act in a strategic fashion and create environmental policies which are not in the best interest of the planet.

Labor standards are also a key issue in Doha and in other trade negotiations. Labor unions and activists opposed to the WTO and to globalization have long opposed the use of low wage labor in developing country "sweat shops," which they claim exploits workers in developing countries and leads to unemployment in developed countries as jobs are shipped overseas. Most economists argue that these jobs, generally in manufacturing, pay more than a worker could make elsewhere and thus increase welfare. In "Labor Standards: Where Do They Belong on the International Trade Agenda," Drusilla Brown examines the debate from both sides. While she recognizes that developing countries cannot provide the same wages and benefits as developed countries do, she does believe that some labor standards are necessary. In particular, she favors restrictions on child labor, since children who work will have less time to pursue education. She also notes that restrictions on labor supply can benefit workers by raising wages.

The third article in this section, "Beyond the Outsourcing Angst: Making America More Productive," by Thomas F. Siems, examines one of the most widely reported side-effects of globalization—outsourcing. Siems believes that outsourcing is necessary to keep U.S. companies competitive with other companies in the world and that any attempt to limit outsourcing would backfire. He further argues that although outsourcing does lead to some lost jobs, the increase in jobs created by globalization more than compensates for the temporary loss in jobs due to outsourcing. He sees outsourcing as part of the process of "creative destruction" inherent in a free market.

Alan Blinder, a highly respected economist from Princeton, also examines the outsourcing perspective. Like Siems in the previous article, Blinder favors outsourcing and sees it as inevitable. Blinder focuses on how outsourcing changes the nature of trade and comparative advantage and, in particular, how it will impact the U.S. economy. He believes that we are in a third industrial revolution governed by information technology, and that outsourcing and comparative advantage will be largely governed by jobs that "are easily deliverable through a wire" as opposed to those that are not. Thus, according to Blinder, in the field of medicine, American interns, who must examine patients directly, will thrive, whereas radiologists, who examine x-rays remotely, will face stiff competition from abroad. In the end, Blinder believes that those with computer skills may not do as well as most think. Instead, those with interpersonal skills and creativity may thrive.

The final article by Anoshua Chaudhuri, "Trade in Health Care: Changing Paradigms in a Global Economy," examines one particular industry, health care, and how it has been impacted by trade and globalization. The article begins by examining the pharmaceutical industry, where trade is governed by intellectual property rights and the World Trade Organization's Agreement on Trade-Related Aspects of Intellectual Property Rights (TRIPS) negotiated in the Uruguay round. Since most drugs are patented, at least initially, drug companies have monopoly power. Economic theory would suggest that these companies would charge higher prices in rich countries than in poor countries. (They do.) However, the threat of reimportation—the ability of individuals to buy drugs overseas, sometimes on the internet, limits the price differential and forces drug prices higher in poor countries. A great deal of pressure has been placed on drug companies to keep prices on critical drugs, such as those designed to treat HIV, low enough for the poor to afford them. Dr. Chaudhuri points out that in some cases the WTO allows a developing country drug manufacturer to produce needed pharmaceuticals even if the company holding the patent/license disagrees. The final part of the article addresses medical outsourcing and points out that many procedures are far cheaper outside the U.S., which accounts for the increasing popularity of "medical tourism."

4

Bridging the Trade-Environment Divide

DANIEL C. ESTY

Protection. For free traders, this word represents the consummate evil. For environmentalists, it is the ultimate good. Of course, for the trade community, "protection" conjures up dark images of Smoot and Hawley, while the environmental camp sees clear mountain streams, lush green forests, and piercing blue skies. One cannot blame all of the tensions at the trade environment interface on linguistic differences, but these competing perspectives are emblematic of a deep clash of cultures, theories, and assumptions.

Trade officials often seek to limit efforts to link trade and environmental policymaking, and sometimes to prohibit such efforts altogether. In this regard, the narrow focus and modest efforts of the World Trade Organization's Committee on Trade and Environment are illustrative.[1] The launch of negotiations for a Free Trade Area of the Americas with an express decision to exclude environmental issues from the agenda provides an even starker example of the trade community's hostility toward serious environmental engagement. Economists have been prominent among those arguing that pollution control and natural resource management issues are best kept out of the trade policy-making process (Cooper, 1994; Bhagwati, 1999). Other economists, however, have tried to set trade policymaking in a broader context and to build environmental sensitivity into the international trading system (Runge, 1994; Rodrik, 1997; Summers, 2000).

In fact, there is no real choice about whether to address the trade and environment linkage; this linkage is a matter of fact. The only choice is whether the policies put in place to respond will be designed openly, explicitly, and thoughtfully, with an eye to economic and political logic—or implicitly and without systematic attention to the demands of good policymaking. This article seeks to explain why trade liberalization and environmental protection appear to be in such tension and to push economists to explore more aggressively what economic theory and practice might do to address the concerns being raised.

Trade and Environmental Linkages

Potential Conflicts Between Domestic Regulations and Trade

In recent years, the focus of trade liberalization has shifted from lowering tariffs, which have come down considerably around the world, to the elimination of non-tariff barriers to trade (Jackson, 1992). Since many kinds of domestic regulations can potentially be construed as non-tariff barriers, the extent and impact of the market access commitment and other regulatory disciplines negotiated in the trade domain have expanded.

A number of the most prominent international trade disputes in the last decade have concerned the clash between domestic regulations and trade rules. In the well-known tuna-dolphin case, the United States banned Mexican tuna imports because the fishing methods resulted in incidental dolphin deaths. In 1991, Mexico obtained a GATT panel decision declaring the United States to be in violation of its GATT obligations for imposing such a ban. In the ongoing beef hormone dispute, the European Union has refused to adjust its "no added hormones in beef" food safety standards despite a series of WTO rulings that its regulations had no scientific foundation and were in contravention of the rules of international trade. The U.S. sanctions against Thai shrimp caught using methods that killed endangered sea turtles were recently deemed to be GATT-illegal. Trade and environment friction can be found outside the WTO, as well. Witness the enormous effort that the European Union has put into harmonizing environmental standards over the past several decades (Vogel, 1994).

There is no end in sight to "trade and environment" cases. If anything, the number of disputes seems to be rising (Sampson, 2000). As global economic integration intensifies, so does the potential for conflict (Lawrence et al., 1996; Dua and Esty, 1997). Public health standards, food safety requirements, emissions limits, waste management and disposal rules, packaging and recycling regulations, and labeling policies all may shape trade flows. Trade disciplines may also affect national-scale environmental efforts, especially to the extent that WTO dispute settlement procedures are used to challenge pollution control or natural resource management programs.

Thus, while fearmongering about lost "sovereignty" (Perot, 1993; Wallach and Sforza, 1999) can be dismissed, the suggestion that trade liberalization constrains regulatory flexibility rings true. With new issues like biotechnology and climate change emerging, the potential for significant and divisive battles between trade policy and regulatory choices—including environmental rules—looms large.

Increasing Trade, Economic Growth, and Environmental Risks

The literature on the interaction between economic growth and pollution points to what has been called an environmental "Kuznets curve." The Kuznets curve is a inverted-U relationship which shows that environmental conditions tend to deteriorate in the early stages of industrialization and then improve as nations hit middle-income levels, at a per capita GDP of about $5000 to $8000 (Grossman and Krueger, 1993, 1995; Shafik and Bandyopadhyay, 1992; Seldon and Song, 1994). Since the primary purpose of liberalizing trade is to increase economic growth, trade unavoidably affects the level of environmental protection through its impact on the Kuznets curve.

A first concern stemming from the Kuznets curve is that air and water pollution problems tend to worsen in the early stages of development. Many developing countries are living through the part of the Kuznets curve in which environmental conditions deteriorate. In addition, some problems, especially those that are spread spatially or temporally (such as greenhouse gas emissions), do not yet appear to have reached the downward-sloping part of the Kuznets curve in any country. This empirically derived pattern of ongoing deterioration perhaps reflects the fact that, absent reciprocity, the benefit-cost ratio for policy interventions in response to diffuse problems is always negative from a national perspective.

A second concern is that even if expanded trade and economic growth need not hurt the environment, there is no guarantee that it will not (Harbaugh, Levinson and Wilson, 2000; Hauer and Runge, 2000). The effects of economic growth on trade can be broken down into three effects. "Technique" effects arise from the tendency toward cleaner production processes as wealth increases and trade expands access to better technologies and environmental "best practices." "Composition" effects involve a shift in preferences toward cleaner goods. "Scale" effects refer to increased pollution due to expanded economic activity and greater consumption made possible by more wealth (Grossman and Krueger 1993; Lopez, 1994). Thus, the claim that growth improves the quality of environment can be rephrased as a claim that, above a certain level of per capita income, technique and composition effects will outweigh scale effects. Empirical evidence on the relative sizes of these effects is limited. But at least some of the time, it appears that expanded trade may worsen environmental conditions (Antweiler, Copeland and Taylor, 1998).

Finally, the odds that increased trade will have net negative environmental impacts rise if resources are mispriced (Anderson, 1998; Panayotou, 1993). Around the world, many critical resources like water, timber, oil, coal, fish, and open space are underpriced (or overpriced) (World Bank, 1997; Earth Council, 1997). Even the WTO acknowledges in its most recent "Trade and Environment Special Report" that expanded trade can exacerbate pollution harms and natural resource management mistakes in the absence of appropriate environmental policies (Nordstrom and Vaughan, 1999).

Transboundary Externalities

Transboundary pollution spillovers make attention to trade-environment linkages a matter of normative necessity as well as descriptive reality. Perhaps the most discussed issues involve emissions of ozone-layer-depleting chlorofluorocarbons and greenhouse gases, which threaten global climate change. But recent advances in tracing the movement of pollutants have also demonstrated long-distance impacts from particulates (Grad, 1997), sulfur dioxide and other precursors of acid rain (Howells, 1995), DDT and other pesticides (Lawler, 1995; Rappaport et al., 1985), mercury and other heavy metals (Fitzgerald, 1993), and bioaccumulative toxics (Francis, 1994). Other transboundary issues involve rules governing shared resources such as fisheries in the open ocean and biodiversity.

The need to control transboundary externalities makes trade-environment linkages essential from the point of view of good economic policy-making. After all, uninternalized externalities not only lead to environmental degradation, but also threaten market failures that will diminish the efficiency of international economic exchanges, reduce gains from trade, and lower social welfare. National governments, no matter how well intended, cannot address inherently international problems such as climate change or fisheries depletion unilaterally. A functioning Global Environmental Organization, operating in parallel with the trading system, might be a "first-best" policy option in response to these challenges (Esty, 2000a). But no such regime exists. Thus, the World Trade Organization along with regional trade agreements cannot avoid some shared responsibility for managing ecological interdependence.

The Political Economy of Trade Liberalization

Taking environmental issues seriously must also be understood as a political necessity for free traders. Forward momentum in the trade realm is difficult to sustain (Bergsten, 1992). In this regard, the trade community cannot risk diminishing further the already narrow coalition in favor of freer trade, especially in the United States. Dismissing environmental concerns, which results in broad environmental community opposition to trade agreements, generates unnecessary and avoidable political resistance to liberalized trade (Esty, 1998a).

Certain environmentalists will always be opposed to trade liberalization because they adhere to a "limits to growth" philosophy. But the environmental community is neither monolithic nor uniformly protectionist. Many mainstream environmentalists believe in "sustainable development" and will support freer trade if they feel that pollution and natural resource management concerns are being taken seriously. For example, the congressional vote in favor of the NAFTA depended critically on the fact that a number of environmental groups came out in favor of the agreement, which translated into support from politicians who define themselves as both pro–free trade and environmentally oriented (Audley, 1997). Concomitantly, the several recent failures to obtain a majority for new fast track negotiating authority can be attributed to this swing group voting against the legislation because the proposals lacked environmental credibility (Destler and Balint, 1999).

In practice, moreover, there is no empirical support for the suggestion that environmental linkages detract from trade agreements or trade liberalization. The North American Free Trade Agreement, often considered the "greenest" trade pact ever, contains a number of environmental elements and was adopted with an Environmental Side Agreement. There is no evidence that these provisions have in any way diminished the post-NAFTA U.S.-Canada-Mexico trade flows (Araya, 2002; Hufbauer et al., 2000).

One might argue that this political analysis has little to do with economists' role in the trade and environment debate. To the contrary, if the arguments of economists become disconnected from the reality of political pressures and policy imperfections, then economic logic is unlikely to prevail in trade policy-making.

The Arguments for Separating Trade and Environmental Policy

While many "no linkage" economists and trade officials understand the arguments for taking up environmental issues in the trade context, they fear a scenario in which protectionist wolves find their way into the trading system in environmental sheep's clothing (Bhagwati, 1988; Subramanian, 1992).[2] The sight at the 1999 WTO Ministerial Meeting in Seattle of green activists marching arm-in-arm with avowed protectionists confirmed for many, especially in the developing world, the suspect motives of those advancing the environmental agenda. A related argument for keeping the environment out of the WTO turns on the fear that trade liberalization will grind to a halt under the weight of environmental burdens. Why, ask trade economists, must trade measures be used to enforce international environmental agreements? Shouldn't environmental policy problems be solved with environmental policy tools? Those who wish to separate trade and environmental policy-making also fear that high-income countries will impose lofty environmental standards on low-income countries, depriving them of one aspect of their natural comparative advantage and subjecting them to trade barriers if they fail to perform up to developed country standards (Bhagwati, 1999; 2000).

But while these worries have some basis in reality, they do not provide a justification for complete separation of trade and environmental policies. Certainly, environmentalism should not be used as a cover to disguise trade barriers. Certainly, the tactical partnerships of some environmental groups have been misguided. Certainly, better environmental regulation at both the national and global levels could markedly reduce trade environment tensions.[3] Certainly, global scale environmental efforts should not mean a reduction in the standard of living for people in low-income countries.

But these are not arguments for ignoring the inescapable linkages between trade and the environment. They are arguments for trying to integrate trade and environmental policies in sensible ways. The following sections discuss key areas for research and policy analysis that could help to narrow the divide between trade and environmental policy goals and practices. The next section focuses on strengthening the foundations of environmental policy, while the next two sections focus on issues of economic theory and trade policy.

Strengthening Environmental Policy Foundations

A battle rages among environmentalists over how best to address (and even understand) environmental challenges. Many environmentalists support the concept of "sustainable development" (World Commission on Environment and Development, 1987) and believe that economic growth can, if managed properly, support environmental improvements. A significant number of environmental advocates remain committed, however, to a "limits to growth" paradigm in which trade liberalization contributes to more economic activity and therefore more pollution and unsustainable consumption of natural resources (Meadows et al., 1972; Daly, 1993). But even those who find the promise of sustainable development attractive worry that, in practice, environmental policy tools are not up to the pressures of globalization.

Economists are likely to have little in common with the advocates of lower consumption levels, especially when the burdens of such a policy choice would fall most heavily on those in the poorest countries of the world. But economists can play a role in answering certain persistent environmental research and policy questions which could, in turn, help to expand the common ground between free traders and environmentalists.

Clarifying Concerns about Sustainable Development

Sustainable development has proven hard to define and even harder to put into practice. It is clear that poverty can force people to make short-term choices that degrade the environment, like cutting down nearby trees for firewood despite the likelihood of future soil erosion. But the hope that trade liberalization will lead to economic growth that will alleviate poverty and generate resources for environmental investments sometimes seems to rely on a tenuous chain of events which may well unravel under real-world conditions.

It is useful to examine these issues in terms of the inverted-U environmental Kuznets curve discussed earlier, which shows a general pattern of increasing environmental degradation up to a certain level of per capita GDP and environmental improvements beyond that point. Environmentalists will always be worried about societies which are living through the portion of the Kuznets curve where growth is accompanied by environmental degradation, even if it can be shown that people are receiving other welfare gains. Economists could, however, significantly bridge the gap with green groups if they were to find ways to reduce the duration and intensity of environmental deterioration as low-income countries grow to middle income. Economists might also confirm that ignoring pollution altogether until middle-income levels are reached is a serious policy mistake. Some environmental investments, like protecting drinking water or siting polluting factories downwind of urban areas, have such high benefit-cost ratios that even the poorest countries should undertake them.

As regards the portion of the environmental Kuznets curve in which growth and environmental quality are both improving, many mainstream environmentalists express concerns that either rising wealth or increased population will drive up consumption in ways that undermine prospects for sustainable development. Both economic theory and recent empirical evidence could help to assuage these apprehensions. Development economists have demonstrated that population growth diminishes with wealth. Economists might do more to demonstrate that poverty alleviation is critical for population control, which in turn offers significant potential environmental benefits. More generally, the economics field has had little to say about how to minimize scale effects and maximize the chances that growth will improve environmental quality.

Finally, as noted earlier, certain environmental harms do not appear to diminish with increases in income. Carbon dioxide emissions, for instance, continue to rise, albeit at a decreasing rate, as GDP per capita goes up. It may be that, even for carbon dioxide emissions, the downward portion of the environmental Kuznets curve would be reached at some income level, but no society has achieved the exalted wealth required. If or until that occurs, economists could gain credibility by agreeing that wealth is not an environmental cure all.

The common theme in this discussion is that the environmental Kuznets curve need not be destiny. The present shape of the curve, as estimated from historical experience, reflects a political economy interaction among trade, growth, and the environment. Trade has a positive effect on the environment (and perhaps a net welfare benefit more broadly) only if environmental policy advances alongside trade liberalization (Anderson, 1992, 1998; Esty, 1994). However, institutional failures in the environmental realm often mean that the requisite strengthening of environmental performance in parallel with trade liberalization may not occur (Chichilnisky, 1994; Zhao, 2000). In this regard, economists should take more seriously the need to find policy strategies that lead to a shorter and flatter Kuznets curve.

Disciplining Free Riders

Economists and environmental policymakers generally agree on the wisdom of enforcing the "polluter pays" principle, which holds that those who cause environmental degradation should bear the costs. But as a matter of policy, this goal remains elusive. While economists have demonstrated the value of market-based environmental strategies, they have by and large not managed to convince the environmental and political worlds that pollution fees, emissions allowances, or other economic incentives will work in practice. Environmental policy remains underdeveloped in terms of economic sophistication and largely mired in "command and control" approaches. The collapse of the international negotiations over climate change, in part because

of disputes over how far to go in using market mechanisms, demonstrates the persistence within the environmental policy community of anti-economics sentiment.

Figuring out how to enact policies that embody the polluter pays principle becomes even more difficult when the scope of the environmental harm is broader than the vista of the regulators. Dua and Esty (1997) argue that "super-externalities," which spill beyond the defined jurisdiction of regulatory authorities in either space or time, aggravate the collective action problem.[4] A small number of scholars have looked at the spatial distribution of issues in the trade domain (Krugman, 1991; Bloom and Sachs, 1998) and at the geographic dimensions of the trade and environment problem (Hauer and Runge, 2000; Esty, 1994), but more work needs to be done in the realm of economic geography.

Transboundary environmental spillovers create a risk of allocative inefficiency and market failure in the international economy. Some mechanism for promoting collective action and for disciplining free riders is therefore required (Baumol and Oates, 1988). Whether free traders like it or not, trade measures are one potential candidate for this function. Admittedly, trade sanctions are imperfect, costly to those who impose them, and may backfire. But at least in some cases, trade penalties have worked (Brack, 1996; Barrett, 1997). Moreover, better tools to discipline free riders in the international environmental domain do not seem readily available. As environmentalists point out, the weakness of the extant global environmental regime cannot be wished away nor dismissed as irrelevant to the question of how environmental goals get squared with the trade liberalization agenda.

There are a number of issues to be investigated which could shed light on the use of trade policy as a tool for enforcement of environmental standards. First, refined theory on the use of trade measures to support environmental cost internalization in the international realm is needed, advancing the preliminary analyses of

Charnovitz (1993), Chang (1995), and Barrett (1997). Second, more work to find ways to strengthen the international environmental regime, which could relieve the pressure on the World Trade Organization to play a major environmental role, would be useful (Esty, 1994, 2000a). Such work might build on efforts to investigate the political economy of environmental protection (for example, Keohane, Revesz and Stavins, 1998). Third, the advantages and disadvantages of policy linkages need to be more fully explored. Concerns are sometimes expressed that if trade policy becomes entangled with environmental policy, either or both sets of policies may be unable to advance. Yet the potential benefits of cross-issue policies and trade-offs have been repeatedly demonstrated (Haas, 1958; Carrero and Siniscalco, 1994). Finally, those who wish to limit the trade system's role in enforcing international environmental agreements would find their case greatly strengthened if they could point to workable alternative enforcement mechanisms.[5]

Refining Trade Theory

Environmental perspectives on trade often clash with the settled views of economists. Frequently, the problem reflects a degree of economic misunderstanding by those in the environmental community. But often, there is a kernel (or more) of truth in the environmental position with which the economic community has failed to grapple. In these areas, there are intriguing research opportunities for economists.

Level Playing Fields

Environmentalists often worry that expanded trade will lead to competitive pressures which will push down environmental standards. They fear a regulatory "race toward the bottom" as jurisdictions with high environmental standards relax their rules so as to avoid burdening their industries with pollution control costs higher than competitors operating in low-standard jurisdictions. Thus, they call for harmonization of pollution control regulations at stringent levels, the imposition of "eco-duties" on those with subpar rules, or other policy interventions to "level the playing field."

Economists point out that the existence of divergent circumstances, including variations in societal preferences about the optimal level of environmental protection, is what makes gains from trade possible. If environmental rules vary because of differences in climate, weather, geography, existing pollution levels, population density, risk preferences, level of development, or other "natural" factors, the variation in standards should be considered welfare enhancing and appropriate. Clearly, a sweeping presumption in favor of uniform standards fails to grasp the insight of comparative advantage and makes no sense (Burtless et al., 1998). More generally, economists tend to find arguments in favor of regulatory harmonization in a context of economic integration unpersuasive (Bhagwati, 1996, 2000).

Diversity in circumstances generally makes uniformity less attractive than standards tailored to the heterogenous conditions that exist (Mendelsohn, 1986; Anderson, 1998). But not always. Divergent standards across jurisdictions may impose transaction costs on traded goods that exceed any benefits obtained by allowing each jurisdiction to maintain its own requirements. Sykes (1995, 1999) has demonstrated that market forces will tend, over time, to eliminate such problems. Vogel (1994) argues, in fact, that upward harmonization (a "race to the top") often occurs. But this logic only applies to product standards, and standards that relate to production processes or methods are not subject to the same market pressures.

Some theoretical work has been done to try to understand the different harmonization dynamics (Bhagwati and Hudec, 1996; Esty and Geradin, 1998, 2001), but more would be useful, as would empirical evidence on what happens to environmental standards in the process of trade liberalization.

For example, how often do free trade agreements include commitments to lower environmental standards and how often to higher standards?

Environmentalists also fear that the rules of international trade are biased against their interests. They believe that within the trading system—both WTO and regional trade agreements—free trade principles always trump other policy goals such as environmental protection. Some recent analyses suggest that such a tilt in GATT jurisprudence might once have existed, but is now less pronounced (Charnovitz, 2000; Wofford, 2000). Efforts to illuminate the facts might diminish fears that trade liberalization runs roughshod over environmental issues. Some efforts have been made in this regard (Trachtman, 2000; Burtless et al., 1998), but more would be welcome.

Psychological Spillovers and Ethical Preferences

Most economists acknowledge, at least in theory, that transboundary pollution externalities need to be addressed, but economists tend to be skeptical about claims of psychological spillovers (Blackhurst and Subramanian, 1992; Cooper, 1994). What are we to make of complaints about environmental degradation in China or campaigns to save the rain forest? As long as the harms are localized, shouldn't environmental policy choices (even "mistakes") in other jurisdictions be accepted? Maybe so from a perspective of economic theory, but most people do not see the world this way. The fact that Chinese workers produce goods under adverse environmental conditions is not celebrated, even if the low standards in China translate into cheaper products in export markets. Why not?

Perhaps economists assume a utilitarianism that is oversimplified. Sen (1977) and others have noted the narrow behavioral assumptions on which most of economics builds, ignoring human realities such as the existence of interdependent welfare functions. In fact, many people consider themselves, at least to some

extent, to be part of a global community. In addition, economists may too readily accept as a given that the policy choices in places like China are locally optimal and do not stop to ask whether Chinese environmental standards truly reflect the will of the people.[6] By gliding past "choice of public" questions (Esty, 1996), economists simplify their models but diminish the policy traction of their arguments.

Environmentalist concerns about extraterritorial policy choices frequently seem to be paternalistic or even imperialistic. Green groups often think that they know better than the people or governments of other countries, especially developing nations, what constitutes the "right" environmental standard or policy program. Economists have been quick to condemn those who "are keen to impose their own ethical preferences on others, using trade sanctions to induce or coerce acceptance of such preferences" (Bhagwati, 1993).

But trade, like any realm of human endeavor, cannot exist without baseline rules, defined by community standards and values. One such set of rules concerns what constitutes a fair and legitimate basis for comparative advantage. From nineteenth century British hesitation about trading with the slave holding American south to Article XX(e) of the GATT, which permits trade restrictions on products made by prison labor, the international trading system has always circumscribed the bounds of acceptable commercial behavior.

The issue becomes one of line drawing. When is a divergent policy in another jurisdiction just a "choice," worthy of respect and acceptance in a world of diversity? When does it become a violation of moral minimum standards that should not be abided?

A conservative answer here would be that when environmental harms are purely local in scope, then preservationist demands from abroad are overreaching. In such a case, trade policy should not be the primary tool for international environmental policy, and instead environmental advocates should find a way to pay for their preferences in other countries. But if localized environmental harms are vast and there is reason to doubt whether the will of the people is being fairly represented, it makes sense to leave open the possibility that international pressure for a cleaner environment may be justified.

Is There a Race Toward the Bottom?

Economists have strongly rejected suggestions that country-versus-country competitiveness pressures degrade environmental standards.[7] They argue that the idea that jurisdictions with low environmental standards will become pollution havens, luring industries from high-standard jurisdictions and triggering a back-and-forth downward spiral in environmental standards finds little basis in theory (Revesz, 1992; Drezner, 2000) and lacks empirical support (Kalt, 1988; Low and Yeats, 1992; Repetto, 1995). For example, it does not appear that U.S. pollution control standards have dropped in the aftermath of NAFTA nor following the various rounds of GATT and WTO negotiations over time.

But the real concern is not about a race literally to the bottom. Rather, the concern arises from the possibility that economic integration will create a regulatory dynamic in which standards are set strategically with an eye on the pollution control burdens in competing jurisdictions. The result may be a "political drag" that translates into suboptimal environmental standards in some places.[8] These effects might involve not only weakened environmental laws, but perhaps more importantly, environmental standards not strengthened as much as they would otherwise have been or environmental enforcement cases not brought.

The evidence here is by no means as one-sided as many economists have come to believe. Some recent empirical studies find races to the bottom (Mani and Wheeler, 1999; van Beers and van den Bergh, 1997). Moreover, a growing theoretical literature, largely published in law

journals, suggests that if the market in "locational rights" is flawed, regulatory races toward the bottom may occur (Klevorick, 1996; Engel and Rose-Ackerman, 2001; Esty and Geradin, 2001). A mismatch between the scope of pollution harms and the jurisdiction of regulators, as well as information gaps or technical deficiencies in the regulatory process, or public choice distortions (such as the fact that politicians may be more influenced by highly visible job effects and may overlook more subtle environmental impacts) may lead jurisdictions to set their environmental standards too low (or too high) (Esty, 1996). Moreover, once a trade competitor has deviated from optimal regulatory levels, a welfare maximizing government may benefit by strategically adjusting its own environmental standards.

Within economics, the welfare effects of inter-jurisdictional regulatory competition have been carefully analyzed (Fischel, 1975; Oates and Schwab, 1988). However, the application of the theory to the race-toward-the-bottom question in the international trade and environment context has only recently begun to get attention (Levinson, 1997; Fredriksson and Millimet, 2000). New work is beginning to specify those settings in which regulatory competition will improve outcomes and when some degree of harmonization (not necessarily uniform standards) will improve results.[9]

The Development and Evolution of Trade Policy-Making

Advances in both the procedures and substantive rules of the international trading system could help to alleviate some trade environment tensions. A good bit of the environmentalist animosity toward freer trade arises from the closed process by which trade liberalization has historically proceeded and the sense that any expression of environmental concerns, no matter how valid, would not be taken seriously. The World Trade Organization, like

GATT before it, has usually done its business through negotiations between governments. Mechanisms for participation by nongovernmental organizations including environmental groups and other elements of civil society have been limited. But the obscure nature of the process and the attempt to channel all political debate to the national level has created an image of the WTO as a star chamber or "black box" where insiders take advantage of their access to the levers of power.

The closed nature of the system had a logic; it shielded the trade regime from special interest manipulation and "capture" (Bhagwati, 1988; Subramanian, 1992). But the organization's future now depends on it becoming more transparent. Beyond building public understanding and acceptance, a more open WTO policy-making process has other virtues. Notably, nongovernmental organizations provide critical "intellectual competition" for both national and intergovernmental decision makers (Esty, 1998b). In presenting alternative perspectives, data, policy analyses, and options, these non-government organizations force officials to explain and justify their policy choices. There remains, however, work to be done to find ways to maximize the benefits of the interchange while limiting the risk that access will give special interests undue power to manipulate or block outcomes. In this quest, the learning from public choice theory may be helpful.

Economists could also help the trade community to modernize the WTO's substantive rules on a basis of greater analytic rigor. In this regard, several issues stand out at the trade-environment interface.

First, the reliance on a distinction between product standards imposed on imports (generally acceptable) and production process or methods restrictions (generally unacceptable) makes little sense in a world of ecological interdependence.[10] How things are produced matters. Production related externalities cannot be overlooked. For example, semiconductors manufactured using chlorofluorocarbons destroy everyone's ozone layer. Where international environmental agreements are in place, such as the 1987 Montreal Protocol phasing out chlorofluorocarbons, trade rules should be interpreted to reinforce the agreed upon standards. Indeed, such a principle can be found in Article 104 of the North American Free Trade Agreement.

A recrafted trade principle that accepts the legitimacy of environmental rules aimed at transboundary externalities would eliminate the risk of the trade regime providing cover for those shirking their share of global responsibilities. A number of economists, including some who have been skeptical about trade-environment linkages, have now come around to view that trade rules must not permit free riding on global environmental commitments (Cooper, 2000; Bhagwati, 2000). But how this agreement in principle should be translated into actual trade policies has not been clarified. Economists are in a good position to think through the efficiency and equity implications of the issues and options.

Another opportunity for updating of the trade system centers on the traditional rule that, when trade and environment principles clash, only the "least GATT inconsistent" environmental policies are acceptable. Such an approach lacks balance, because clever policymakers can always come up with a possible policy alternative that is less restrictive to trade. A more neutral decision rule would focus on whether the environmental standards are arbitrary, unjustifiable, or a disguised restriction on trade. Such a principle seems to be emerging in recent WTO dispute settlement cases, notably the 1998 shrimp turtle Appellate Body decision (Wofford, 2000).

Final Thoughts

A traditional piece of received wisdom about trade policy-making is that more can be accomplished by operating in a closed "club system" beneath the radar of public scrutiny rather than through open debate (Keohane and Nye, 2001). Whether this hypothesis was ever correct is now moot. The World Trade Organization has gained a very high profile, and it will never again be able to operate in the policy shadows (Esty, 2000b). When the trade agenda was perceived to be narrow and technical, the trade regime's performance was of interest only to the trade cognoscenti. But today the WTO's work has much broader impacts, and the trade agenda encompasses nontariff barriers and other issues which impinge on commercial and governmental activities beyond the trade domain. Where once the WTO's legitimacy turned on its capacity to produce good results from a trade perspective, the organization is now subject to much wider scrutiny. If the WTO is to play its designated role as one of the key international organizations managing economic interdependence, it must find a new center of gravity (Schott, 2000).

Going forward, the WTO's authority and public acceptance will have to be founded on a more democratic basis and on a refined ability to reflect the political will of the global community. Such a transformation entails a commitment to transparency and an open trade policy-making process that provides access to nongovernment organizations across the spectrum of civil society. The WTO's future legitimacy requires a more robust trade and environment dialogue, not artificial separation of these policy-making realms. Special interest lobbies will have to be disciplined by exposure and argument, not exclusion (Esty, 1998b).

Environmental rules cannot be seen as simple pollution control or natural resource management standards; they also provide the ground rules for international commerce and serve as an essential bulwark against market failure in the international economic system. Building environmental sensitivity into the trade regime in a thoughtful and systematic fashion should therefore be of interest to the trade community as well as environmental advocates. In working toward a world of effective environmental protection that is simultaneously free of trade protectionism, economists could play a substantial role.

Thanks to Monica Araya and Brian Fletcher for research assistance and to the Global Environment and Trade Study (GETS) and its funders, especially the Ford Foundation. Thanks also to INSEAD, Stephan Schmidheiny, and Alqueria for support.

Daniel C. Esty is Associate Dean and Professor of Environmental Law and Policy, Yale School of Forestry and Environmental Studies, New Haven, Connecticut. He has a joint appointment at the Yale Law School and serves as Director of the Yale Center for Environmental Law and Policy. His e-mail address is (daniel.esty@yale.edu)

Endnotes

[1] For a full review of the work of the WTO Committee on Trade and Environment, see (http://www.wto.org/WT/CTE).

[2] Some trade officials, however, seem not to have learned their economics very well. Many of the comments of the trade leaders who spoke at the WTO's 1999 "Trade and Environment Symposium" reflected serious deficiencies in the understanding of core principles, such as the implications of externalities or the Olsonian logic of collective action. See, for example, the speech of de la Calle (WTO, 1999).

[3] Momentum for a revitalized international environmental regime, perhaps including a new Global Environmental Organization to serve as a counterpart and counterbalance to the WTO, seems to be building (Esty, 1994; Ruggiero, 1999; Barrett, 2000; Jospin, 2000).

[4] Issues that cross jurisdictional boundaries create a risk of "structural" failure in the regulatory cost-benefit calculus (Esty, 1996). Related problems arise with long-term environmental issues in which there is a risk of market failure because future citizens are not present to cast their "market votes." Some thinking has gone into how to manage problems with long time horizons (Cline, 1993; Revesz, 1999). But if economic theories are to be persuasive to environmentalists, they will have to deal explicitly with the broader set of issues such as threshold effects, nonlinear cost curves, and irreversibility (for example, species destruction).

[5] The suggestion that there be more use of carrots (financial rewards for compliance) and less of sticks (trade measures) may be useful in some circumstances. But in other cases,

transboundary pollution spillovers represent a serious infringement on property rights, making a "victim pays" strategy inappropriate (Esty, 1996).

[6] A number of economists (Sachs, 1998; Sen, 1999) and others (Esty and Porter, 2000) have begun to argue that a society's underlying legal, political, and economic structure critically affects economic growth trajectories, environmental performance, and other variables. The extent to which economic and trade theory even applies in a nation may therefore depend on these structural conditions.

[7] Economists see any such pressures that emerge as mere market clearing or "pecuniary" effects, not real externalities that distort allocative efficiency (Baumol and Oates, 1988). Interestingly, the legal literature leans in a different direction on this point. Elliott, Ackerman and Millian (1985), for example, explain that real economic externalities will arise if the scope of the cost-bearers and beneficiaries of regulation are not coterminous.

[8] In many instances, the result will be lower standards (Esty, 1994, 1996). But note that, where NIMBYism (that is, not in my backyard–ism) is pervasive, strategic behavior may create pressures for suboptimally high standards as a way of discouraging local development (Levinson, 1999).

[9] For a recent study, drawing on the work of economists, lawyers, political scientists, and business professors, and looking at this issue across regulatory domains (environment, labor, tax, banking) and economic integration experiences (United States versus European Union versus WTO), see Esty and Geradin (2001).

[10] A potentially groundbreaking WTO decision in the asbestos case has shown more sensitivity regarding restrictions based on process and production methods (World Trade Organization, 2001).

References

Anderson, Kym. 1992. "The Standard Welfare Economics of Policies Affecting Trade and the Environment," in *The Greening of World Trade Issues*. Kym Anderson and Richard Blackhurst, eds. Ann Arbor: University of Michigan Press, pp. 25–48.

Anderson, Kym. 1998. "Environmental and Labor Standards: What Role for the WTO?" in *The WTO as an International Organization*. Anne O. Krueger, ed. Chicago: University of Chicago Press, pp. 231–55.

Anderson, Kym and Richard Blackhurst. 1992. "Trade, the Environment and Public Policy," in *The Greening of World Trade Issues*. Kym Anderson and Richard Blackhurst, eds. Ann Arbor: University of Michigan Press, pp. 3–18.

Antweiler, Werner, Brian R. Copeland and M. Scott Taylor. 1998. "Is Free Trade Good for the Environment?" National Bureau of Economic Research Working Paper No. W6707. August.

Araya, Monica. 2002. "Trade and Environment Lessons from NAFTA for the FTAA," in *Trade and Sustainability in the Americas: Lessons from NAFTA*. Carolyn Deere and Daniel C. Esty, eds. Cambridge: MIT Press, forthcoming.

Audley, John. 1997. *Green Politics and Global Trade: NAFTA and the Future of Environmental Politics*. Washington: Georgetown University Press.

Barrett, Scott. 1997. "The Strategy of Trade Sanctions in International Environmental Agreements." *Resource and Energy Economics*. 19:4, pp. 345–61.

Barrett, Scott. 2000. "Trade and Environment: Local Versus Multilateral Reforms." *Environment and Development Economics*. 5, pp. 349–59.

Baumol, William J. and Wallace E. Oates. 1988. *The Theory of Environmental Policy*. Cambridge: Cambridge University Press.

Beckerman, Wilfred. 1992. "Economic Growth and the Environment: Whose Growth? Whose Environment?" *World Development*. 20, pp. 481–96.

Bergsten, C. Fred. 1992. "The Primacy of Economics." *Foreign Policy*. Summer, 87, 3–24.

Bhagwati, Jagdish. 1988. *Protectionism*. Cambridge: MIT Press.

Bhagwati, Jagdish. 1993. "The Case for Free Trade." *Scientific American*. November, pp. 42–49.

Bhagwati, Jagdish. 1996. "Trade and the Environment: Does Environmental Diversity Detract from the Case for Free Trade?" in *Fair Trade and Harmonization: Prerequisites for Free Trade?* Jagdish Bhagwati and Robert Hudec, eds. Cambridge: MIT Press, pp. 159–223.

Bhagwati, Jagdish. 1999. "Third World Intellectuals and NGOs Statement Against Linkage." Letter drafted by Bhagwati and signed by several dozen academics, circulated on the Internet; copy on file with author.

Bhagwati, Jagdish. 2000. "On Thinking Clearly About the Linkage Between Trade and the Environment." *Environment and Development Economics.* 5:4, pp. 485–96.

Bhagwati, Jagdish and Robert E. Hudec. 1996. *Fair Trade and Harmonization: Prerequisites for Free Trade?* Cambridge: MIT Press.

Blackhurst, Richard L. and Arvind Subramanian. 1992. "Promoting Multilateral Cooperation on the Environment," in *The Greening of World Trade Issues.* Kym Anderson and Richard L. Blackhurst, eds. Ann Arbor: University of Michigan Press, pp. 247–68.

Bloom, Dave E. and Jeffrey Sachs. 1998. "Geography, Demography, and Economic Growth in Africa." (Revised) CID/HIID Working Paper. October. Available online at <http//www2.cid.harvard.edu/cidpapers/bro okafr.pdf>

Brack, Duncan. 1996. *International Trade and the Montreal Protocol.* London: Chatham House.

Burtless, Gary et al. 1998. *Globaphobia: Confronting Fears About Open Trade.* Washington: Brookings Institution.

Carrero, C. and D. Siniscalco. 1994. "Policy Coordination for Sustainability," in *The Economics of Sustainable Development.* Goldin and Winters, eds. Cambridge: Cambridge University Press, pp. 264–82.

Chang, Howard F. 1995. "An Economic Analysis of Trade Measures to Protect the Global Environment." *Georgetown Law Journal.* 83, pp. 2131–213.

Charnovitz, Steve. 1993. "Environmentalism Confronts GATT Rules." Journal of World Trade. April, 27:2, pp. 37–52.

Charnovitz, Steve. 2000. "World Trade and the Environment: A Review of the New WTO Report." *Georgetown International Environmental Law Review.* 12:1, pp. 523–41.

Chichilnisky, Graciela. 1994. "North-South Trade and the Global Environment." *American Economic Review.* September, 84:5, pp. 851–75.

Cline, William R. 1993. *The Economics of Global Warming.* Washington: Institute for International Economics.

Cooper, Richard N. 1994. *Environment and Resource Policies for the World Economy.* Washington: Brookings Institution.

Cooper, Richard N. 2000. "Trade and the Environment." *Environment and Development Economics.* 5:4, pp. 501–4.

Daly, Herman E. 1993. "The Perils of Free Trade." *Scientific American.* November, pp. 51–55.

Destler, I.M. and Peter J. Balint. 1999. *The New Politics of American Trade: Trade, Labor and the Environment.* Washington: Institute for International Economics.

Drezner, Daniel W. 2000. "Bottom Feeders." *Foreign Policy.* November/December, 29:6, pp. 64–70.

Dua, André and Daniel C. Esty. 1997. *Sustaining the Asia Pacific Miracle: Environmental Protection and Economic Integration.* Washington: Institute for International Economics.

Earth Council. 1997. *Subsidizing Unsustainable Development.* Vancouver: Earth Council.

Elliott, E. Donald, Bruce A. Ackerman and John C. Millian. 1985. "Toward a Theory of Statutory Evolution: The Federalization of Environmental Law." *Journal of Law Economics and Organization.* Fall, 1:2, pp. 313–40.

Engel, Kirsten and Susan Rose-Ackerman. 2001. "Environmental Federalism in the United States: The Risks of Devolution," in *Regulatory Competition and Economic Integration: Comparative Perspectives.* Daniel C. Esty and Damien Geradin, eds. Oxford: Oxford University Press.

Esty, Daniel C. 1994. *Greening the GATT: Trade, Environment and the Future.* Washington: Institute for International Economics.

Esty, Daniel C. 1996. "Revitalizing Environmental Federalism." *Michigan Law Review.* 95:3, pp. 570–653.

Esty, Daniel C. 1998a. "Environmentalists and Trade Policy-making," in *Constituent Interests and U.S. Trade Policies.* Alan W. Deardorff and Robert M. Stern, eds. Ann Arbor: University of Michigan Press.

Esty, Daniel C. 1998b. "NGOs at the World Trade Organization: Cooperation, Competition or Exclusion." *Journal of International Economic Law*. 1:1, pp. 123–48.

Esty, Daniel C. 2000a. "Global Environment Agency Will Take Pressure off WTO." *Financial Times*. July 13, p. 12.

Esty, Daniel C. 2000b. "Environment and the Trading System: Picking up the Post-Seattle Pieces," in *The WTO After Seattle*. Jeffrey J. Schott, ed. Washington: Institute for International Economics.

Esty, Daniel C. and Damien Geradin. 1998. "Environmental Protection and International Competitiveness: A Conceptual Framework." *Journal of World Trade*. 32:3, p. 5.

Esty, Daniel C. and Damien Geradin. 2001. "Regulatory Co-opetition," in *Regulatory Competition and Economic Integration: Comparative Perspectives*. Daniel C. Esty and Damien Geradin, eds. Oxford: Oxford University Press.

Esty, Daniel C. and Michael E. Porter. 2000. "Measuring National Economic Performance and its Determinants," in *The Global Competitiveness* Report 2000. Michael E. Porter, Jeffrey D. Sachs, et al., eds. New York: Oxford University Press.

Fischel, William A. 1975. "Fiscal and Environmental Considerations in the Location of Firms in Suburban Communities," in *Fiscal Zoning and Land Use Controls*. Edwin S. Mills and Wallace E. Oates, eds. Lexington, Mass.: Lexington Books, pp. 119–74.

Fitzgerald, William F. 1993. "Mercury as a Global Pollutant." *The World and I*. October, 8, pp. 192–223.

Francis, B. Magnus. 1994. *Toxic Substances in the Environment*. New York: John Wiley.

Fredriksson, Per, ed. 2000. *Trade, Global Policy, and the Environment*. World Bank Discussion Paper no. 402. Washington: World Bank.

Fredriksson, Per G. and Daniel L. Millimet. 2000. "Strategic Interaction and the Determination of Environmental Policy and Quality Across the US States: Is There a Race to the Bottom?" Unpublished working paper.

Grad, Franklin P. 1997. *Treatise on Environmental Law*. New York: M. Bender.

Grossman, Gene M. and Alan B. Krueger. 1993. "Environmental Impacts of a North American Free Trade Agreement," in *The Mexico-US Free Trade Agreement*. Peter M. Garber, ed. Cambridge: MIT Press, pp. 13–56.

Grossman, Gene M. and Alan B. Krueger. 1995. "Economic Growth and the Environment." *Quarterly Journal of Economics*. CX:2, pp. 353–77.

Haas, Ernst B. 1958 *The Uniting of Europe: Political, Social and Economic Forces*. Stanford: Stanford University Press.

Harbaugh, William, Arik Levinson and David Wilson. 2000. "Re-examining the Empirical Evidence for an Environmental Kuznets Curve." NBER Working Paper No. 7711, May.

Hauer, Grant and C. Ford Runge. 2000. "Transboundary Pollution and the Kuznet's Curve in the Global Commons." Unpublished manuscript.

Howells, Gwyneth P. 1995. *Acid Rain and Acid Waters*. New York: E. Horwood.

Hufbauer, Gary C. et al. 2000. *NAFTA and the Environment: Seven Years Later*. Washington: Institute for International Economics.

Jackson, John. 1992. *The World Trading System: Law and Policy of International Economic Relations*. Cambridge: MIT Press.

Jospin, Lionel. 2000. "Development Thinking at the Millennium." Speech to the Annual Bank Conference on Development Economics (World Bank), Paris. June 26.

Kalt, Joseph. 1988. "The Impacts of Domestic Environmental Regulatory Policies on US International Competitiveness," in *International Competitiveness*. A. Michael Spence and Heather A. Hazard, eds. Cambridge: Ballinger, pp. 221–62.

Keohane, Robert O. and Joseph S. Nye. 2001. "The Club Model of Multilateral Cooperation and the World Trade Organization: Problems of Democratic Legitimacy," in *Efficiency, Equity and Legitimacy: The Multilateral Trading System at the Millennium*. Robert O. Keohane and Joseph S. Nye, eds.

Cambridge: Harvard University Press, pp. 313–67.

Keohane, Nathaniel, Richard L. Revesz, and Robert N. Stavins. 1998. "The Choice of Regulatory Instruments in Environmental Policy." *Harvard Environmental Law Review.* 22, pp. 313–67.

Klevorick, Alvin K. 1996. "The Race to the Bottom in a Federal System: Lessons from the World of Trade Policy." *Yale Law and Policy Review* and *Yale Journal on Regulation.* Symposium Issue, 14, pp. 177–86.

Krugman, Paul R. 1991. *Geography and Trade.* Cambridge: MIT Press.

Lawler, Andrew. 1995. NASA Mission Gets Down to Earth. *Science.* September, 1, pp. 1208–10.

Lawrence, Robert et al. 1996. *A Vision for the World Economy.* Washington: Brookings Institution.

Levinson, Arik. 1997. "A Note on Environmental Federalism: Interpreting some Contradictory Results." *Journal of Environmental Economics and Management.* 33, pp. 359–66.

Levinson, Arik. 1999. "NIMBY Taxes Matter: The Case of State Hazardous Waste Disposal Taxes." *Journal of Public Economics.* 74, pp. 31–51.

Lopez, Ramon. 1994. "The Environment as a Factor of Production: The Effects of Economic Growth and Trade Liberalization." *Journal of Environmental Economics and Management.* 27, pp. 163–84.

Low, Patrick and Alexander Yeats. 1992. "Do 'Dirty' Industries Migrate?" in *International Trade and the Environment.* Patrick Low, ed. World Bank Discussion Paper 159. Washington: World Bank, pp. 89–103.

Mani, Muthukumara and David Wheeler. 1999. "In Search of Pollution Havens? Dirty Industry in the World Economy 1960–1995," in *Trade, Global Policy and the Environment.* Per G. Fredriksson, ed. Washington: World Bank, pp. 115–27.

Meadows, Donella H. et al. 1972. *The Limits to Growth.* New York: Universe Books.

Mendelsohn, Robert. 1986. "Regulating Heterogeneous Emissions." *Journal of Environmental Economics and Management.* December, 13:4, pp. 301–13.

Nordstrom, Hakan and Scott Vaughan. 1999. *Special Studies: Trade and Environment.* Geneva: World Trade Organization.

Oates, Wallace E. and Robert M. Schwab. 1988. "Economic Competition Among Jurisdictions: Efficiency Enhancing or Distortion Inducing?" *Journal of Public Economics.* 35:1, pp 333–62.

Panayotou, Theodore. 1993. *Green Markets: The Economics of Sustainable Development.* San Francisco: ICS Press.

Perot, Ross. 1993. *Save Your Job, Save Our Country: Why NAFTA Must Be Stopped Now!* New York: Hyperion.

Rappaport, R.A. et al. 1985. "'New' DDT In-puts to North America Atmospheric Deposition." *Chemosphere.* 14, pp. 1167–73.

Repetto, Robert. 1995. *Jobs, Competitiveness and Environmental Regulation: What Are the Real Issues?* Washington: World Resources Institute.

Revesz, Richard L. 1992. "Rehabilitating Interstate Competition: Rethinking the 'Race-to-the-Bottom' Rationale for Federal Environmental Regulation." *New York University Law Review.* December, 67, pp. 1210–54.

Revesz, Richard L. 1999. "Environmental Regulation, Cost-Benefit Analysis and the Discounting of Human Lives." *Columbia Law Review.* May, 99, pp. 941–1017.

Rodrik, Dani. 1997. *Has Globalization Gone Too Far?* Washington: Institute for International Economics.

Ruggiero, Renato. 1999. "Opening Remarks to the High Level Symposium on Trade and the Environment." Speech at the WTO High Level Symposium on Trade and the Environment. Geneva Switzerland. March 15.

Runge, C. Ford. 1994. *Freer Trade, ProtectedEnvironment: Balancing Trade Liberalization and Environmental Interests.* New York: Council on Foreign Relations.

Sachs, Jeffrey. 1998. "Globalization and the Rule of Law." Yale Law School Occasional Papers, 2d ser., no. 4.

Sampson, Gary P. 2000. *Trade, Environment and the WTO: The Post-Seattle Agenda.* Washington: Johns Hopkins University Press.

Schott, Jeffrey. 2000. "The WTO After Seattle, in *The WTO After Seattle.* Jeffrey Schott, ed. Washington: Institute for International Economics, pp. 3–40.

Seldon, Thomas M. and Daqing Song. 1994. "Environmental Quality and Development: Is There a Kuznets Curve for Air Pollution Emissions." *Journal of Environmental Economics and Management.* September, 27:2, pp. 147–52.

Sen, Amartya K. 1977. "Rational Fools." *Philosophy and Public Affairs.* 6:4, pp. 317–44.

Sen, Amartya K. 1999. *Development as Freedom* New York: Knopf.

Shafik, Nemat and Sushenjit Bandyopadhyay. 1992. "Economic Growth and Environmental Quality: Time Series and Cross-Country Evidence." Background Paper prepared for WorldBank, *World Development Report 1992: Development and the Environment.* New York: Oxford University Press.

Subramanian, Arvind. 1992. "Trade Measures for Environment: A Nearly Empty Box?" *World Economy.* 15:1, pp. 135–52.

Summers, Lawrence. 2000. Speech to the Confederation of Indian Industry, Bombay. January 18.

Sykes, Alan O. 1995. *Product Standards for Internationally Integrated Goods Markets.* Washington: Brookings Institution.

Sykes, Alan O. 1999. "Regulatory Protectionism and the Law of International Trade." *University of Chicago Law Review.* 66, pp. 1.

Trachtman, Joel. 2000. "Assessing the Effects of Trade Liberalization on Domestic Environ-mental Regulation: Towards Trade-Environment Policy Integration," in *Assessing the Environmental Effects of Trade Liberalization Agreements: Methodologies.* Paris: OECD.

van Beers, Cees and Jeroen C.J.M. van den Bergh. 1997. "An Empirical Multi-Country Analysis of the Impact of Environmental Regulations on Foreign Trade Flows." *Kyklos.* 50:1, pp. 29–46.

Vogel, David. 1994. *Trading Up: Consumer and Environmental Regulation in a Global Economy.* Cambridge: Harvard University Press.

Wallach, Lori and Michelle Sforza. 1999. *Whose Trade Organization: Corporate Globalization and the Erosion of Democracy.* Washington: Public Citizen.

Wofford, Carrie. 2000. "A Greener Future at the WTO: The Refinement of WTO Jurisprudence on Environmental Exceptions to the GATT." *Harvard Environmental Law Review.* 24:2, pp. 563–92.

World Bank. 1997. *Expanding the Measure of Wealth: Indicators of Environmentally Sustainable Development.* Washington: World Bank.

World Commission on Environment and Development (WCED). 1987. *Our Common Future.* Oxford: Oxford University Press. Commonly known as the "Brundtland Report."

World Trade Organization (WTO). 1999. High Level Symposium on Trade and Environment. Proceedings available online (visited 12/10/00) at www.wto.org/english/ tratop_e/envir_e/ hlspeech.htm.

World Trade Organization (WTO). 2001. Report of the Appellate Body on Measures affecting asbestos and asbestos-containing products. AB-2000-11. WTO/DS/135/AB/ R/. March 12, 2001.

Zhao, Jinhua. 2000. "Trade and Environmental Distortions: Coordinated Intervention." *Environmental and Development Economics.* October, 5:4, pp. 361–76.

5

Labor Standards: Where Do They Belong on the International Trade Agenda?

D R U S I L L A **K . B R O W N**

During the past decade, universal labor standards have become the focus of intense debate among policymakers, international agencies, nongovernmental organizations, college campus activists and the general public. Tension over labor standards has sometimes erupted into violent conflict between police and demonstrators, as it recently did during the spring 2001 Conference of the Americas in Quebec.

Labor rights activists argue that the nations of the world ought to be able to agree on some set of universally accepted human rights regarding working conditions that would apply in all nations. In addition, trade with countries in which labor is protected poorly may create an incentive to lower wages in industrialized countries and weaken existing labor law in order to maintain competitiveness in international trade. As a remedy, some proponents seek to protect the interests of labor by incorporating labor rights into international trade law.

Opponents of internationally established labor standards respond that the regulation of labor markets, as a matter of national sovereignty, should remain primarily in the domain of domestic policy and should not be a topic in international trade negotiations. The promulgation of standards internationally ought to be delegated to the International Labour Organization (ILO) and advanced exclusively through dialogue, monitoring and technical advice.

Our purpose here is to analyze the arguments concerning the value of coordinating labor standards internationally, the arena in which international labor standards ought to be established, and the instruments that can be used constructively to bring about compliance. We will examine the analytical underpinnings of universal rules for labor rights; the evidence on whether labor practices in developing countries have adverse consequences for workers in industrialized countries; and the question of whether labor standards should be introduced formally into the negotiations of the World Trade Organization (WTO) or remain primarily in the purview of the ILO.

Labor Standards Defined: Rights, Outcomes, Efficiency

The regulation of labor markets originally emerged before the fourteenth century in Europe with laws generally written to serve the interests of the elite rather than to protect labor.[1] However, with the onset of the industrial revolution, social activists began advocating labor protections that might mitigate the more brutal aspects of industrialization. Engerman (2001) marks the beginning of the modern labor rights movement with the English Factory Act of 1802. This act regulated the working conditions of pauper apprentices by establishing a twelve-hour day, prohibiting night work and providing for basic academic and religious training.

From its inception, the debate over labor rights addressed the legitimate right of the government to intrude upon market outcomes and the free choices of workers. Thus, most of the labor legislation in Europe and North America throughout the nineteenth century focused only on regulating the working conditions of women and children, with the intention of offsetting their weak bargaining power with employers. Legislation typically controlled the length of the workday and night work, and prohibited the employment of women in hazardous conditions such as underground mines.

There is also a long tradition of concern over the international coordination of labor law to mitigate the effects of labor protections on trade competitiveness.[2] The drive to coordinate labor practices internationally began during the second half of the nineteenth century. However, success was limited largely to the prohibition of production and importation of white phosphorous matches and night work by women.

The international labor rights agenda broadened dramatically at the end of World War I with the creation of the International Labour Organization. The ILO was established in 1919 as an offshoot of the League of Nations and originally had 44 member countries from Europe, Asia, Africa and Latin America.[3] Initially, discussions in the ILO focused on the eradication of slavery and all forms of forced labor. However, a broader labor rights agenda also included the rights to freedom of association and collective bargaining, nondiscrimination in employment, and the elimination of child labor (ILO, 1999).

As part of building an international consensus on labor standards, the ILO promulgates certain "Conventions" and "Recommendations" that member nations may choose to ratify. The early Conventions adopted between 1919 and 1939 included a long list of labor market practices targeted for international standards. For example, Convention 1 establishes the 8-hour day/48-hour workweek, and Convention 5 establishes a minimum work age of 14 years (although children working with family members are excluded). Additional Conventions and Recommendations pertained to wages, occupational health and safety, retirement compensation, severance pay, survivor's benefits and other topics.

The Critique of International Labor Standards

In the face of the lengthy list of labor standards contemplated by the ILO, critics of international labor standards point out the unfairness of attempting to establish standards in all of these areas without regard for the level of economic development and cultural norms. While most countries may be willing to embrace the broad caveat-filled language typical of ILO Conventions, that does not imply that the same countries will be able to agree on specific language pertaining to labor standards that would then be subject to trade disciplines in the World Trade Organization.

For example, there is strong empirical evidence that the optimal length of the workweek is negatively correlated with a nation's level of income; that is, high-income countries have a shorter workweek than many low-income countries. For example, Table 1 reports on typical workweeks, wages and labor costs for a select group of countries for manufacturing, agriculture and wearing apparel. In Costa Rica, a typical worker in manufacturing earned $1.54/hour and worked 49.1 hours a week in 1999. Some textile and wearing apparel workers earning less than $1/hour worked 50 or more hours per week. By contrast, a typical manufacturing worker in the United States earned $13.91/hour and worked 41.7 hours a week in 1999. Similarly, a suitable minimum wage cannot be set uniformly since its effects will depend critically on how high it is relative to the productivity of less-skilled labor.

Child labor practices, which receive the most intensive scrutiny in the public discussions, clearly depend on the level of economic development, and for many families the income earned by their children is a matter of the family's survival. Krueger

Labor Market Characteristics for Select Countries: Hours Worked, Wages and Labor Costs, 1999
Table 1

Country	Manufacturing			Agriculture[a]			Wearing Apparel[a]		
	Hrs. Worked (week)	Wages (US$/hr)	Labor Cost (US$/hr)	Hours/Week Worked	Normal	Wages (US$/hr)	Hours/Week Worked	Normal	Wages (US$/hr)
Africa				41.0		1.57	43.0		0.70
Mauritius									
Latin America									
Costa Rica	49.1	1.54							
El Salvador							44.0		0.81
Mexico	45.4	1.27	3.94						
Peru				49.0	48.0	0.96	50.0	48.0	0.94
Europe									
Cyprus	41.0	6.23							
Estonia	33.8	1.92							
Hungary	34.5	2.02	3.27						
Slovenia	40.5	4.17							
Spain	36.3		18.45						
Middle East									
Israel	41.7	10.11							
Asia									
Hong Kong							45.0		4.69
New Zealand	41.0	8.80							
United States	41.7	13.91	19.20						

Sources: ILO (2000a, b), IMF (2000).

[a]Data for typical production workers in each sector

(1997) finds a very strong negative correlation between child labor force participation and per capita GDP. Children 14 years and younger are not completely withdrawn from the labor force until GDP approaches $5000 per capita.

Virtually every country in the world attempts to regulate child labor by setting minimum educational requirements and minimum age of employment, though with limited success. National regulations on minimum ages for work and compulsory education, along with child labor force participation rates for a select group of countries, are reported in Table 2. For countries in the poorest parts of the world, more than 40 percent of children aged 5–14 work. This is the case even though the legal minimum age of work is typically 14 years old or higher, and in no case is the minimum work age less than 12 years.

Child Labor and Education Labor Force Participation Rates, Minimum Age of Work and Compulsory Education
Table 2

Region	Child Labor Force Participation		Minimum Age for Work		Compulsory Education Ages
	Age Range	Rate	Basic	Hazardous	
Africa	5–14	41.0			
Egypt	6–14	12.0	14	15–17	6–13
Kenya	10–14	41.3	16	16–18	
South Africa	10–14	4.3	15	18	7–13
Tanzania	10–14	39.5	12–18	18	7–13
Asia	5–14	21.0			
Bangladesh	5–14	19.1	12–15	18	6–10
India	5–14	5.4	14	14–18	
Nepal	5–14	41.7	14	16	
Pakistan	5–14	8.0	14	14–21	
Philippines	5–14	10.6	15	18	6–11
Thailand	10–14	16.2	15	18	6–11
Latin America	5–14	17.0			
Brazil	5–14	12.8	14	18–21	7–14
Guatemala	7–14	4.1	14	16	6–15
Mexico	12–14	17.3	14	16–18	6–15
Nicaragua	10–14	9.9	14	18	7–12
Peru	6–14	4.1	12–16	18	6–16
Europe	5–14				
Turkey	6–14	12.6	15	18	6–13

Source: Adapted from U.S. Department of Labor (1998).

Core Labor Standards as Basic Human Rights

Several responses have been offered to the concerns raised by the critics of labor standards. First, even if a global minimum wage applying across all countries seems nonsensical, there are still certain "core standards" that should be imposed universally because they are arguably independent of national income and reflect natural rights or broadly held values. A second line of argument holds that certain basic labor standards will have positive economic effects and can be justified on these grounds.

Cast in these terms, the discussion of core labor standards is closely related to the ongoing debate in political science and philosophy over the notion of natural rights. Some prefer to avoid the language of "rights," but instead argue that something of a consensus has emerged on a broader set of values that are derived from the notion of individual freedom (Maskus, 1997).

Such rights-based or value-based language appears in the charters and declarations of several international organizations that include nearly all countries in the world in their membership. For example,

ILO Core Conventions
Table 3

Convention	Number	Year	Ratification Status	
			Total Members Ratifying	
			Convention[a]	United States
Suppression of Forced Labor	29	1930	153	no
The Abolition of Forced Labor	105	1957	145	yes
Freedom of Association and Protection of the Right to Organize	87	1948	130	no
The Application of the Principles of the Right to Organize	98	1949	146	no
Equal Remuneration for Men and Women Workers for Work of Equal Value	100	1951	147	no
Discrimination in Respect of Employment and Occupation	111	1958	143	no
Minimum Age for Admission to Employment	138	1973	93	no
The Prohibition and Immediate Action for the Elimination of the Worst Forms of Child Labor	182	1999	72	yes

Source: (http://www.ilo.org/public/english/standards/norm/whatare/fundam/index.htm).
[a]As of 2001.

the ILO Conventions pertaining to core labor standards, listed in Table 3, have been ratified by well over 100 countries. Furthermore, the 1998 ILO Declaration on Fundamental Principles at Work binds all 175 ILO members and states that

"...all Members, even if they have not ratified the Conventions in question, have an obligation arising from the very fact of membership in the Organization, to respect, to promote and to realize, in good faith and in accordance with the Constitution, the Principles concerning the fundamental rights which are the subject of those Conventions, namely:

1. freedom of association and the effective recognition of the right to collective bargaining,
2. the elimination of all forms of forced or compulsory labor,
3. the effective abolition of child labor, and
4. the elimination of discrimination in respect of employment and occupation."

Thus, proponents argue that the ILO and UN language can be viewed as a near universally accepted set of humanitarian principles concerning the treatment of labor (Eddy, 1997).

Of course, the fact that an ILO document refers to "fundamental rights" does not end the discussion. Bhagwati (1995) has been a prominent voice among those arguing that in the area of labor standards, there is little universal agreement. We have a near-universal consensus only in favor of prohibiting forced labor.[4] On other issues, like the appropriate rules to regulate collective bargaining or child labor or discrimination, we have a mixture of good intentions, some blood-curdling stories about undoubted abuses in extreme cases, and great uncertainty over what the appropriate labor standard should be.

Some statements about labor standards may be attractive general goals, but they vary too much across countries to be defined as rights. Even the United States, which has been a driving force behind the recent international labor standards initiative, has not ratified any of the ILO Conventions pertaining to nondiscrimination, forced labor, or the right to free association and collective bargaining, as can be seen from Table 3. Similarly, the debate over what constitutes "the elimination of discrimination" has proceeded for decades inconclusively. At this point there appears little closure on the issue.

Labor Process Standards

To avoid the intellectual quagmire of natural rights, other organizing principles have been proposed. For example, Aggarwal (1995) distinguishes labor market standards that are focused on outcomes from those that are focused on processes. Outcome-related standards, like a minimum wage, will always depend on levels of productivity and economic development and, thus, are poor candidates for international standards. By contrast, the core labor standards listed in the 1998 ILO Declaration are largely process-related; that is, they concern the organization of the labor market without specifying any particular market outcome. If we adopt the "process" approach, the question becomes what labor standards should be regulated and how?

An OECD (1996) report isolates labor standards that either reflect (near) universally held values and/or play a role in supporting the efficient function of labor markets. According to this view, standards such as freedom of association, the right to collective bargaining, prohibition of forced labor, the principle of nondiscrimination and prohibition of "exploitative" child labor can be imposed without regard to the degree of development and can actually promote economic growth.

While it would be convenient if efficiency-enhancing labor standards could be linked to humanitarian values, these connections are often ambiguous and controversial. Consider first the prohibition against forced labor. The consensus against slavery or labor contracts that lead to slave-like conditions is one point on which there is virtually no debate. Although it is possible to make an efficiency argument supporting the prohibition of forced labor—for an example, see Swinnerton (1997)—humanitarian concerns typically dwarf any discussion of efficiency.

The grey area concerns bonded labor contracts prohibited under ILO Convention 105. The act of choosing to be bonded may be voluntary, but once bonded, the worker is no longer free (Singh, 2001). Genicot (2000) emphasizes the role of capital market failure in bonded labor contracts. Extremely poor workers frequently have no access to formal capital markets and so are forced to offer their own labor as collateral to obtain a loan. Such arrangements may be mutually agreed upon by the worker and the employer, at least before the bonding contract is signed. Nevertheless, banning such contracts may be justified if they result from limited information or rationality on the part of the worker.

Genicot (2000) further argues that the legality of bonded labor contracts may actually inhibit the development of formal capital markets. He points out that a bank may be unwilling to extend a loan if the worker has the option of obtaining a second loan by bonding his labor. Presumably, the bondholder has greater power to enforce the loan agreement than the bank, thereby raising the default risk for the bank. In such cases, outlawing bonded labor contracts can actually improve the options for the worker by lowering the default risk for formal credit institutions.

Standard efficiency arguments are also weakened when we are constrained by political feasibility. Take, for example, discrimination in employment. Discrimination discourages workers from entering the job to which they are best-suited, thereby lowering the value of output. However, Rodrik (1999) offers a striking example in which discrimination was Pareto-improving for political economy reasons.

Mauritius set out on a development strategy that depended on operating an export-processing zone. To generate a consensus in support of the export-oriented development strategy, the interests of those benefiting from long-standing protection had to be preserved. This was accomplished by following a two-part development strategy: protection for existing industries that hired males was continued, while the export-processing zones employed females. Rodrik (1999) argues that the segmentation of the labor force along gender lines was critical to the policy's success. Male workers and import-competing producers continued to produce under the same conditions as before the introduction of the export-promotion plan, while women and capital owners in the export-processing zones had new opportunities opened to them. In Rodrik's words (p. 21): "New profit opportunities were created at the margin, while leaving old opportunities undisturbed." Thus, the Pareto-improving step was rendered politically feasible by segmenting the labor market along gender lines. Dealing with entrenched cultural patterns that have favored one group over another may sometimes lead to advocacy of policies—either preserving some of the benefits to the favored group or assuring benefits to the disfavored group—that would not pass a strict nondiscrimination test.

The expected outcome of collective bargaining is similarly uncertain. As argued by Freeman (1994), unionism has two faces. In many cases, a union can improve dispute resolution, provide a channel of information from worker to employer, and coordinate the differing views among workers concerning the trade-off between working conditions and wages (for views of unions along these lines, see Stiglitz, 2000; Piore, 1994; and Marshall, 1994). However, if a union behaves like a

monopoly in an otherwise competitive market, favoring the interests of a small elite at the expense of a large group of excluded workers, then the efficiency effects are negative (Bhagwati, 1995; Srinivasan, 1997).

Finally, the OECD (1996) report seeks to include the prohibition of "exploitative" child labor as a core standard. Indeed, the specter of small children working long hours in appalling conditions motivates most analysts to find some analytical basis on which to circumscribe, at the very least, labor practices concerning children.

Bonded child labor is frequently put forward as the most egregious and offensive form of exploitative child labor. Not only do families depend on the income earned by their children for survival, but in some traditional households, children are bonded to finance a dowry or funeral ceremony. Children delivered into bonded servitude are sometimes clothed, housed and fed by their employer, and they may receive only a very small wage. The excess product generated by the child's work that is not devoted to the child's support is paid to the parent, who receives a lump sum at the time the child is delivered into servitude. That is, the child must be subsidizing the standard of living of the rest of the family and thus is exploited in this sense (Brown, Deardorff and Stern, 2001).

Although the OECD (1996) report focuses on "exploitative" child labor, it is possible to make an argument for banning child labor more broadly defined on both equity and efficiency grounds.[5] Basu and Van (1998) analyze the case of families who put their children to work only when the adult wage is below some critical level at which the family's survival is threatened. When child labor decisions depend on the adult wage in this manner, two labor market equilibria may emerge.

In the low-wage child-labor equilibrium, both children and their parents work because the adult wage is below the critical level at which children are withdrawn from the labor market. A ban on child labor that requires parents to withdraw their children from the labor force contracts the supply of labor and may give rise to a second equilibrium with an adult wage above the critical level at which children no longer work. The ban on child labor is effective when it redistributes income from capital to labor in such a way as to alter the family's child-labor decisions.

Although much attention is focused on poverty as the root cause of child labor, Baland and Robinson (2000) refocus on the role of capital market failure. Presumably, poor families analyze the trade-off between work and schooling in part by comparing the present discounted value of an education relative to the income from current work. It is arguably the case that the relative return to education is as high or higher for a poor child than for children generally. However, poor parents may still choose to put their child to work if they cannot borrow against their educated child's future income.[6] In this situation, a ban on child labor may be part of a strategy for improving the efficiency of the labor market when combined with a program that provides poor families access to capital markets or otherwise repairs the capital market failure. Brown (2001) offers a review of policies that combine education and capital market reform.

Taking steps to reduce forced labor, child labor, and discriminatory behavior, or to support free association and collective bargaining will often have a mixture of effects. Realizing the potential efficiency, equity and humanitarian benefits of core standards may depend on first correcting ancillary market or political failures. Further, we cannot make a general statement that universal labor standards derived from commonly held moral values will always produce positive economic outcomes. The effect on economic performance and the lives of workers and their families of legally imposed labor market constraints of the sort contemplated by labor rights activists cannot be presumed to be positive, but instead must be empirically investigated on a country-by-country basis.

Divergent Labor Standards, Trade and Wages of Unskilled Workers in High-Income Countries

While humanitarian concerns have played a prominent role in the debate over international labor standards, a complementary motivation rests on the view that trade with low-wage countries has increased unemployment and slowed the growth in wages of unskilled workers in high-income countries over the past three decades. To the extent that low labor cost in developing countries is the result of poorly protected core labor rights, trade based on low wages is sometimes seen as unfair or illegitimate.

As a matter of theory, poorly protected worker rights in one country can assuredly lower the wages in its trade partner. According to the Stolper-Samuelson (1941) theorem, international trade between a high-wage and a low-wage country will lower the return to unskilled labor in the high-wage country. But to what extent is the decline in the return to unskilled labor in the United States in the last few decades the result of international trade with low-wage countries? Further, to what extent is such trade the consequence of low labor standards?

Has Trade Lowered the Return to Unskilled Labor in the United States over the Past Two Decades?

There appear to be two primary candidates driving the rise in inequality between skilled and unskilled labor in the United States in recent decades. Skill-biased technical change, presumably associated with the new information and communications technologies, would shift up the demand for skilled workers. However, labor rights activists focus on the expansion of international trade with low-wage economies, which they argue has tended to reduce the demand for low-skilled labor in the United States.

A number of pieces of evidence suggest that an important shift toward skill-biased technological change has indeed occurred. For example, the relative supply of skilled labor did expand throughout the 1980s even as the relative wage of skilled labor increased, which suggests that firms were moving up along the skilled-labor supply curve, paying higher wages and adopting a more skill-intensive technique of production (Bound and Johnson, 1992). Similarly, throughout the 1980s, U.S. manufacturing consistently substituted toward skilled labor in spite of its rising costs (Lawrence and Slaughter, 1993). Such a pattern of behavior is cost-minimizing only if there has been a technological change rendering skilled labor relatively more productive. The greater demand for skilled labor seems to have occurred more as a broad-based shift within many sectors of the economy rather than arising only in certain labor-intensive sectors. Such evidence is consistent with skill-biased technological change that drives up the demand for skill in all sectors (Berman, Bound and Griliches, 1994). Finally, there is little evidence that the relative price of labor-intensive goods fell during the 1980s, as one would expect if imports from low-income countries were undercutting less-skilled U.S. labor (Leamer, 1996).

Nevertheless, a number of economists continue to believe that international trade is responsible, at least in part, for the recent decline in the relative wages of unskilled workers in the United States. As one example, Borjas, Freeman and Katz (1992) calculate the factor supplies embodied in U.S. international trade and immigration. They find that for 1985–1986, trade and immigration implicitly increased the supply of workers with a skill level equivalent to a high school dropout in the United States by 27 percent, whereas the comparable number for college graduates was 9 percent. They use a wage equation to relate the implicit change in relative factor supplies to a change in relative wages and conclude that trade and immigration gave rise to a 2 percent increase in the college graduate wage premium, which was 20 percent of the total change in the college premium during the period.[7]

Choosing between skill-biased technology and trade as explanations for the rise in income inequality is further complicated by the reality that these factors may be intertwined; that is, technological improvements may both increase the demand for skilled labor and also increase imports from low-wage countries by making it easier to manage far-flung supply chains.

The controversy over trade and the distribution of income continues.[8] However, at this point, the bulk of the evidence supports the argument that skill-biased technological change is more important than trade as an explanation of wage inequality in the United States, although rising levels of trade with low-income countries may have played a secondary role.

Do National Labor Standards Alter Exports, Competitiveness or Comparative Advantage?

With regard to the issue of international labor standards, the question is whether poorly protected labor rights have played a role in determining comparative advantage and increasing exports from developing countries.

Several studies have examined a simple correlation between the existence and/or observance of core labor standards and various measures of trade performance. For example, Mah (1997) analyzes the trade performance of 45 developing countries and finds that each country's export share of GDP is strongly negatively correlated with rights to nondiscrimination, negatively correlated with freedom-of-association rights, and weakly negatively correlated with the right to organize and collective bargaining.

However, to gauge the marginal contribution of core labor standards, one must compare each country's trade performance against a baseline expectation as to what such a country should be trading given its factor endowments and other determinants of trade. Rodrik (1996) provides an excellent example of how such analysis can be undertaken. He first considers the impact of core labor standards on labor costs per worker in manufacturing. He does this by calculating a regression using labor cost as the dependent variable and per capita income and various measures of labor standards as the independent variables. In this framework, per capita income is being used as a proxy for productivity in the economy. Labor standards are measured in a variety of ways: total number of ILO Conventions ratified; number of ILO Conventions ratified pertaining to labor standards; Freedom House indicators of civil liberties and political rights; statutory hours worked; days of paid annual leave; the unionization rate; and an indicator of child labor.

Rodrik (1996) finds that for the period 1985–88, labor costs are overwhelmingly determined by labor productivity. However, the number of ILO Conventions ratified, Freedom House indicators of democracy, and the index of child labor are large and statistically significant, with laws regulating child labor playing a particularly important role in determining labor costs.

Rodrik (1996) then turns to the determinants of comparative advantage in labor-intensive goods. He uses the fraction of textiles and clothing exports in total exports as a proxy for measuring comparative advantage in labor-intensive goods.

As a theoretical matter, comparative advantage is primarily determined by factor endowments. Therefore, the comparative advantage variable is regressed on the independent variables of population-to-land ratio (a measure of the labor endowment), average years of schooling in the population over 25 (a measure of the stock of human capital) and the labor standards variables. The population and human capital variables have the expected signs and are statistically significant. However, generally the labor standards variables, while having the expected sign, are not statistically significant. The lone exception is statutory hours worked. The longer the workweek, the

stronger is the comparative advantage in textiles and clothing.

Overall, the link from low labor standards in low-income countries to the wage of unskilled workers in industrialized countries is not especially strong. Increased global trade is at most a secondary cause of income inequality in high-income countries, and labor standards are at most a secondary determinant of wages in low-income countries. Moreover, this evidence begs the question as to whether externally imposed labor standards will actually affect labor market practices in developing countries (Brown, 2000). Some evidence on this question is discussed below.

Competition between Labor Standards and the Risk of a Race to the Bottom

Proponents of international coordination of core labor standards argue that, in the absence of coordination, each country might lower its own standards in an attempt to be more attractive to foreign investment or to gain a competitive advantage over foreign exporters. The possibility of a prisoner's dilemma outcome arises, in which each country has an individual incentive to adopt low labor standards, but all nations could benefit from a coordinated choice of higher labor standards.

This scenario raises several questions. How powerful is this incentive to diminish labor standards? Must core labor standards be harmonized according to a universal guideline or will some more limited coordination be more effective? Should the responsibility of promulgating standards and monitoring labor practices remain with the ILO or should the trade disciplines of the WTO be brought to bear on countries with low labor standards?

The Race to the Bottom

Those most concerned with a prisoner's dilemma in labor protections couch their arguments in terms of a "race to the bottom" in which governments may be pressured to loosen labor protections so as not to hamper domestic firms that are competing in the international arena. This line of argument implies that international trade and labor standards are inextricably linked and, therefore, should be negotiated simultaneously within the WTO.

To understand the political economy of this race to the bottom, consider in the spirit of Brown, Deardorff and Stern (1996) the situation of a country that wishes to impose new labor standards on an import-competing sector of the economy. For a small country, the price of the good is fixed on world markets. Consequently, the cost of the labor standard must be borne solely by domestic producers, who have no power to pass the cost of the regulation on to consumers. However, if all countries impose the new labor standard, global supply for the product declines, allowing firms in this sector worldwide to raise their price. In this case, consumers end up bearing some of the cost. Thus, with coordination, the political objection to the labor standards legislation by domestic producers will be less intense, enhancing the chances of passage.

It is important to note for the purposes of the following discussion that this country pays a price for relying on international coordination to discipline the domestic political process. Harmonization is effective in transferring some of the cost of the labor standard from the producer to the consumer precisely because it raises the international price of the imported good. In other words, this country suffers a deterioration in its terms of trade with harmonization—specifically, higher prices for its imports and lower prices for its exports.

International Trade and Some Surprising Incentives for Higher Labor Standards

At first blush, the forces driving a race to the bottom in international standards may seem obvious. However, all countries have an incentive at least to consider the efficiency properties of their labor market policies. We need to consider, then, how international trade alters the political and economic incentives to pursue efficiency-enhancing domestic policies, such as labor standards (Srinivasan, 1998). As it turns out, trade provides at least some incentives for both high- and low-income countries to choose higher labor standards.

Consider first standards-setting in a high-income country. Bagwell and Staiger (2000) analyze a situation in which a government's rationale for establishing labor standards is, at least in part, driven by the true social benefits and costs of such standards. For example, the decision to raise the minimum age of employment by one year reflects an attempt to balance the social benefits of greater educational attainment and the social cost of the forgone production of young workers.

In this situation, when a high-income economy opens to trade, goods formerly produced by inexperienced and low-skilled young workers can now be replaced with low-priced imports. Thus, opening to trade creates an incentive, because of the reduced opportunity cost, to tighten rather than relax labor standards in the high-income country.

Next, consider the effect that international trade has on the incentives to set labor standards in developing countries. Brown, Deardorff and Stern (1996) point out that low-income countries are, typically, labor abundant. They make the plausible assumption that higher labor standards are "labor using," which means that a tightening of world labor standards will contract the world supply of labor. Wages worldwide rise, pushing up the price of labor-intensive goods exported by developing countries. The change in the terms of trade serves the interests of the labor-abundant developing countries at the expense of industrialized countries that are physical and human capital abundant. Therefore, developing countries, as a group, have an incentive to overprotect labor.

This analysis does not suggest that labor standards in developing countries will be higher than in industrialized countries, but only that developing countries with market power in international trade might have higher-than-expected labor standards given their level of economic development. More importantly, when labor standards are used in this way to gain a strategic advantage over the terms of trade, the policy is welfare reducing from a world point of view. A low-income country that uses labor standards for strategic purposes is surrendering efficiency to bring about higher export prices. However, from a world point of view, the terms-of-trade effects are zero-sum. The terms-of-trade gain for the labor-abundant country comes at the expense of their labor-scarce trade partners. Thus, on balance, the efficiency effect is negative.

The Race to the Bottom Revisited

Given the conflicting incentives, where can we find a race to the bottom that is broadly consistent with optimizing behavior on the part of governments? Bagwell and Staiger (1999) point out that lower labor standards may be used to gain a strategic advantage in international trade or to accomplish domestic political objectives when tariffs are also being used to restrict trade. Labor standards, like tariffs, have implications for the international terms of trade and for the well-being of import-competing firms and, thus, are policy substitutes.

For example, an import tariff provides relief to import-competing producers from the pressure of foreign imports by raising the price of imports. A reduction in labor standards similarly provides relief by lowering labor cost for import-competing producers. Both policies expand production by import-competing firms, which has the additional effect of lowering the demand for imports. If the country has international market power, the contraction in the demand for imports will also reduce the world price of imports, giving rise to a terms-of-trade improvement.

When countries remove tariffs and other barriers to trade in the context of international trade negotiations, they give up the policy tools normally used to turn the terms of trade to their advantage and to protect their import-competing producers. These protectionist urges are thus deflected onto domestic policies such as labor standards. Consequently, some mechanism for controlling subsequent competition in domestic policies is necessary if WTO members are to realize the full benefits of trade liberalization.

Labor Standards in International Negotiations

The strategic interaction between tariffs and labor standards raises the question of whether or how labor standards might be included in the negotiations of the WTO. A recent review of trade law by the OECD (1996) considered various ways of trying to link labor standards to existing WTO rules.[9] However, the OECD report found that in each case, either low labor standards do not meet the technical requirements of the article and/or the WTO does not provide for an enforcement mechanism. As a consequence, some revision to the WTO charter will be required if low labor standards are to be addressed directly.

Opponents of a "social clause" in the WTO warn of a morass that will emerge if governments attempt to negotiate trade and domestic policy simultaneously. Concerns for domestic autonomy, to say nothing of complexity, could bring the WTO process to its knees. However, because of the strategic interaction between tariffs and labor standards discussed in the previous section, the "benign neglect" of labor standards in the WTO is also a potential source of inefficient bargaining over trade policy (Bagwell and Staiger, 2000).

Remarkably, Bagwell and Staiger (2000) find a clever device for implicitly drawing domestic policies into the WTO framework without having to negotiate over domestic policies directly. As they argue in this symposium, when governments negotiate over tariffs in the WTO, they are implicitly making a commitment to a particular level of market access. This is the case because, under GATT Article XXIII, any country in the WTO is entitled to "right of redress" for changes in domestic policy that systematically erode market access commitments even if no explicit GATT rule has been violated. Such a "nonviolation" complaint entitles the aggrieved party either to compensation in the form of other tariff concessions to "rebalance" market access commitments or the complaining partner may withdraw equivalent concessions of its own.

In the context of labor standards, any country that attempts to undo its market access commitments made in a round of WTO negotiations may be required to provide additional trade concessions to restore the originally agreed-upon market access commitments. As a consequence, no government has the ability to pass the cost or benefit of their labor standards onto the rest of the world or to achieve a strategic advantage by altering its labor standards.

Of course, a change in labor standards policy may expand, as well as contract, market access. Thus, to achieve symmetry, GATT Article XXIII would have to be amended to allow countries that expand market access as a consequence of changes in domestic policy to retract subsequently some tariff concessions that restore the original market access commitments.

We can gain an intuitive feel for the Bagwell-Staiger mechanism by returning to the race to the bottom presented above. Recall that some governments have a political economy incentive to seek stricter labor standards internationally to offset the cost of domestic labor standards for their import-competing producers. An internationally coordinated labor standard could provide relief to domestic producers, since it reduces worldwide production of the labor-intensive good, thereby raising its price on the world market. However, under the tariff negotiating scenario envisioned by Bagwell and Staiger, a country that raises its labor standards, thereby increasing import demand, would be entitled to a tariff increase that returns market access to the originally agreed-upon level.

Note that a high-income country will prefer the Bagwell-Staiger mechanism to the strategy of harmonizing labor standards internationally. Both provide relief to domestic producers by raising the landed price of imports. However, harmonization entails a deterioration in the terms of trade and requires all countries to agree upon a single standard. By contrast, the Bagwell-Staiger mechanism does not alter the terms of trade and leaves all countries with the option of setting their labor standards in the manner that serves their own economic and domestic political interests.

The essential feature of the Bagwell-Staiger mechanism is that it requires each country to neutralize the international economic repercussions of its domestic policy decisions. As a consequence, countries are not tempted to sacrifice socially desirable labor market policies in order to achieve zero-sum terms-of-trade gains. Perhaps more importantly, each government is also given the ability to offset some of the distributional effects of efficiency-enhancing domestic policies. By internalizing to each country all of the external effects of domestic policy, legislators are free to choose optimizing domestic policies without regard for their strategic consequences for international trade.

Labor Protections and Humanitarian Concerns

The analysis to this point has probably not been particularly satisfying for those motivated by humanitarian concerns. It is morally meaningless to prohibit the domestic production of goods by our own children if the end result is simply to import goods produced by illiterate children in a neighboring country. A similar argument can also be made, albeit in a lower tone, about goods produced by workers who receive low wages or work long hours.

While it is undoubtedly the case that consumers in high-income countries are genuinely concerned with the welfare of foreign workers, it is not at all clear that these concerns can be constructively addressed in the WTO by applying trade disciplines. To understand the role that the WTO might play in mediating humanitarian concerns with the process of production, it is important to distinguish between two different forms in which these moral concerns might manifest themselves.

First, moral distaste may be a private good. For example, a consumer might prefer not to consume goods produced by children or under poor working conditions. In this case, consumers ought to have an opportunity to avoid goods produced in this manner, provided that they are willing to pay the additional cost of production. In some cases, this might be accomplished by attaching a product label detailing the conditions under which the good was produced (Freeman, 1994). But one can also make a case that countries that wish to do so should be allowed to include a broad definition of immoral working conditions and, acting as a country, refuse to import such goods.

However, this particular moral stance focuses only on alleviating the bad feeling consumers have in knowing they have consumed a good produced under unpleasant circumstances. The welfare of the foreign workers themselves is not necessarily at issue. But if consumers in high-income countries can exhaust their moral commitments simply by avoiding consumption of goods produced in ways that they dislike contemplating, without regard for the welfare of the workers involved, then the humanitarian argument begins to lose some of its moral gravity. If, by contrast, humanitarian and moral concerns focus on the welfare of the workers themselves, rather than on the discomfort of the consumer, then the ability of trade sanctions imposed through the WTO to address these concerns is highly limited.

In fact, trade sanctions in the face of low labor standards are as likely or even more likely to harm workers as they are to improve working conditions. Maskus

(1997) provides a detailed discussion of this point, which I draw upon throughout this section.

Consider the problem of child labor in the case of a small open economy in which the export sector is adult labor-intensive, the import sector is capital-intensive, and a nontraded intermediate input to the export sector is produced using child labor. The child's labor supply is increasing in the child's wage and decreasing in the adult wage. The marginal child worker is the youngest, since the opportunity cost in terms of forgone education falls as the child ages.

In this setting, a foreign tax imposed on goods produced by children can lead to the social optimum in the sense of internalizing the external effect of child work on the well-being of western consumers. Those children no longer working who receive an education are also better off. However, if, as a consequence of the tax, the newly unemployed children live in a household with lower income, less nutrition, and otherwise diminished life alternatives, the trade sanction has probably been counterproductive. Children who continue to work after the imposition of the tax are definitely worse off, since the firms who employ children have to pay a tax. In a small open economy, a tax must lower the after-tax wage of the working child.

A similar type of analysis can be applied to discrimination in employment. Suppose, for example, that the supply of female workers is upward-sloping but there is a legally mandated ceiling on the wages paid to female workers in the export sector. A foreign tariff imposed as a sanction against the offending practice will lower the demand for the offending country's exports. By implication, the demand for female labor in the export sector also declines. Since the equilibrium wage for female workers is now lower than before the sanctions were imposed, firms will find it less costly than before to engage in discrimination, thus making discrimination more likely. Women, of course, are made worse off in the process relative to male workers since both their employment and wages have declined.

The foreign tariff will only be successful if the government responds to the threat of sanctions by eliminating the discriminatory practice. However, the threat itself lacks credibility in view of the fact that the tariff harms precisely the group of workers who are already victimized.

A threat with such adverse consequences could hardly be credible. The threat of sanctions will be particularly ineffective if the targeted country simply lacks the resources to respond to the threat. For example, Rogers and Swinnerton (1999) estimate that if GDP per worker falls below $5020, families are so poor that they cannot survive without contributions to family income from children. Thus, no matter how intense the demand for a reduction in child labor, child labor practices will continue.

Furthermore, trade sanctions do little to address the underlying market failure that gives rise to offending labor practices. For example, capital market failure arguably lies at the heart of the most egregious forms of child labor exploitation. If parents had access to capital markets, they would school their children while transferring wealth from the future to the present by borrowing against their own future income or the future income of their children (Baland and Robinson, 2000). However, lacking collateral and facing other capital market pathologies, the only device parents have available to them is to put their children to work. The end result, of course, is inadequate human capital formation.

Nor does it appear that legislating labor practices is likely to be particularly effective when standards are not sensitive to local community conditions. For example, Krueger (1996) examines the relationship between mandatory education and the actual age at which children leave school. In 1947, the United Kingdom raised the age at which children could leave school from 14 to 15 years. In 1973 the age was raised again from 15 to 16 years. In both cases, the modal age at which students left school adjusted with the law. By contrast, in Brazil, 80 percent of students leave school before the age of 13, even though school attendance is mandatory through age 14. In Mexico and Portugal, 25 percent of students leave school before the legal age. More generally, none of the developing countries studied showed a spike in leaving school at the compulsory age for doing so.

The decline in child labor in the United States between 1880 and 1910 suggests a similar pattern (Moehling, 1999). In 1900, twelve states had a minimum age law prohibiting work by children under the age of 14 years. By 1910, 32 states had enacted similar legislation. However, a review of the censuses taken in 1880, 1900 and 1910 suggests that the legislation had little effect on the incidence of child labor.

More broadly, the difficulty in enforcing agreed-upon labor standards has plagued the ILO since its inception. Many countries have ratified ILO Conventions pertaining to both core and other labor practices, but have ultimately lacked the intention or the resources to change their labor market conditions.

For example, many countries that have ratified ILO Conventions pertaining to the right to organize and collective bargaining maintain tight political control over union activity (OECD, 1996). The main union federations in Jordan, Kenya, Singapore and Taiwan are closely linked with the ruling parties. More extremely, China, Egypt, Iran, Kuwait, Syria and Tanzania effectively permit only a single union structure, and the right to strike is severely circumscribed in many countries.

Thus, while international pressure can lead to the passage of stricter labor law, it is unclear to what extent the newly enacted legislation will change the realities of the labor market in low-income countries. If trade sanctions are actually employed in pursuit of higher labor standards, the effect will often be to hurt precisely those who are the focus of humanitarian concerns. Of course there are some cases in which sanctions by the international community can be brought to bear against some more egregious violations of broadly held humanitarian values. However, the routine use of trade sanctions or the threat of sanctions imposed through the WTO does not seem an especially promising mechanism for helping workers in low-income countries.

International Enforcement of Labor Standards

The weight of the argumentation above militates against direct negotiation over labor standards in the WTO, leaving the ILO as the main forum for discussion. Labor rights activists nevertheless argue in favor of some link between the ILO and the WTO on labor issues in order to provide the ILO with enforcement power beyond its current practice of monitoring and providing members with advice and technical support.

Countries who have ratified ILO Conventions are obligated to report regularly on their compliance activities. In addition, ILO Article 24 allows employers' and workers' organizations to report to the ILO on a state's compliance, and under ILO Article 26, another member of the ILO can bring evidence of a state's failure to comply with ratified Conventions. Moreover, freedom-of-association complaints can be brought even against countries that have not ratified the specific Conventions 87 and 98. In cases where problems exist with compliance, the ILO begins a consultative process with the member government, providing technical support and drawing press attention to the matter.

While the ILO may be effective in promoting discussion between workers and member governments, it has none of the remedies available to members of the WTO. For this reason, linkage between the ILO and the WTO has been suggested as a way of transferring some enforcement power on trade policy to labor standards.

It is possible to link two separate issues in a single agreement and, through that linkage, improve enforcement of both issues. Spagnolo (1999) considers the case in which two governments are attempting to cooperate over two separate policy issues.

For our purposes, these two policy issues can be viewed as tariffs and labor standards. Both policy issues are characterized by a prisoner's dilemma; that is, both countries would gain if they could find a sustainable mechanism to cooperate on lower tariffs and higher labor standards, but an inferior outcome emerges in the absence of cooperation.

In a repeated prisoner's dilemma game, cooperation can be self-enforcing if the benefit of defecting in any round of the game is smaller than the cost of the punishment in all succeeding rounds. Thus, one strategy for sustaining cooperation in a repeated prisoner's dilemma game is a "trigger" strategy: cooperate as long as the other party cooperates, but make clear that if the other party ever defects, then there will be no future cooperative behavior. When policy issues become linked in an international agreement, defection on either tariff or labor standards commitments will cause the entire agreement to collapse. Employing linkage to raise the cost of defecting from either tariff or labor standards commitments should help to sustain compliance on both dimensions.

However, it is important to realize that linking trade and labor standards could slow the process of trade liberalization. Limao (2000) considers a case in which the international community has found it relatively easy to achieve a nearly optimal agreement on tariffs but has had greater difficulty finding a self-enforcing agreement on labor standards. If tariffs and labor standards are linked together, the likely agreement would consist of less trade liberalization but tighter labor standards than would have occurred in a partitioned agreement. Nevertheless, in this example world welfare is higher than in the absence of linkage because the gains from improving the relatively inadequate labor standards are larger than the losses from raising the already close-to-optimal tariff levels.

As with most conclusions in economics, the outcome depends on the underlying assumptions. Limao (2000) points out that linkage can become counterproductive in the face of a powerful lobby, which advocates in favor of producers in the import-competing sector. In this scenario, defection on the tariff agreement by raising tariffs makes the import-competing sector larger. The larger is the import-competing sector, the greater the gain in producer surplus from subsequently relaxing labor standards. That is, when it comes to cheating, cheating in labor standards and cheating in tariffs are complements when producer surplus in the import-competing sector plays an important role in the political process. The consequent increase in the returns to cheating makes defection on a linked agreement more attractive when compared to two separate agreements. In this case, the enforcement power of two separate agreements can be destroyed by linkage.

Conclusion

There is clearly a trend in global trade talks to extend coverage beyond traditional tariffs, quotas and subsidies. During the Uruguay round of multilateral trade negotiations, the purview of the GATT process extended well past debate over tariffs to include issues previously relegated to the domestic agenda, such as intellectual property rights, competition policy, and investment regulations. In each case, the argument is that trade policies and domestic policies need to be negotiated simultaneously if all policy tools are to be set optimally.

Labor standards have proved to be one of the most contentious of the domestic policies considered for introduction into the WTO. In spite of the "trade-relatedness" of labor market practices, the case for international labor standards mediated by the WTO is ultimately problematic.

For those whose goal is to protect the wages of low-skilled workers in high-income countries from import competition, it seems unlikely that trade is the primary factor that has caused the stagnant wages of low-skilled workers in recent decades. Nor does it appear that harmonizing labor standards is a powerful tool for improving the distribution of income in industrialized countries.

For those concerned with a race to the bottom in labor standards, there is a strong case that efficiency can be achieved without negotiating over labor standards directly. As long as countries are required to adhere to market access commitments made in a round of tariff negotiations, any subsequent change in domestic policy that erodes that commitment must be offset with additional tariff concessions. If GATT Article XXIII is interpreted and enforced in this way, it can be used to short-circuit any motivation for setting labor standards strategically.

For those motivated by humanitarian concern over the plight of workers in low-income countries, it is an uncomfortable reality that trade sanctions leveled against countries with poor labor practices may well hurt the very workers who are the intended beneficiaries. Moreover, it is by no means clear that attempts to use trade sanctions to enforce labor standards will strengthen either trade or labor standards, at least not in a world of strong political lobbies.

Heterogeneous labor standards across the world are a legitimate source of policy concern. But it seems unlikely that the appropriate policy response is to seek a single set of universal labor rules.

Drusilla K. Brown is Associate Professor of Economics, Tufts University, Medford, Massachusetts. Her e-mail address is <Drusilla.Brown@tufts.edu>.

Endnotes

[1] See Engerman (2001) for a discussion of the history of international labor standards

[2] See in particular the 1818 writings of Robert Owen (Engerman, 2001).

[3] Specifics concerning the ILO and ILO Conventions can be found at http://www.ILO.org.

[4] Portes (1994) offers a four-part taxonomy of labor standards: basic rights, which include the rights against the use of child labor, involuntary servitude, physical coercion and discrimination; civic rights, including free association, collective representation and expression of grievances; survival rights, including a living wage, accident compensation and a limited workweek; and security rights, which protect against arbitrary dismissal and provide for retirement compensation and survivors' compensation.

[5] See Basu (1999) for a review of the literature concerning child labor.

[6] In fact, there is considerable evidence that the presence of household assets lowers the probability of child labor above and beyond their impact on family income. See Psacharopoulos (1994) for a discussion.

[7] The factor content approach relies on certain underlying assumptions that are controversial. For critiques, see Panagariya (2000), Bhagwati and Dehejia (1994) and Leamer (2000). For a defense of the approach, see Krugman (2000).

[8] For discussions of the state of the literature on trade and wages, readers are referred to the "Symposium on Income Inequality and Trade" in the Summer 1995 issue of this journal, with articles by Richard B. Freeman, J. David Richardson, and Adrian Wood. More recently, see Cline (1997), Slaughter and Swagel (1997), and Panagariya (2000).

[9] Specifically, some possible sources of linkage from labor standards to trade in the WTO, based on the articles of the original GATT, include: the prohibition on dumping products at less than normal value (GATT Article VI); the prohibition on export subsidies (GATT Article XVI); the prohibition on goods produced by prison labor (GATT Article XX(e)); the Nullification and Impairment Provision (GATT Article XXIII); the Opt-Out Provision (GATT Article XXXV); and the Trade Policy Review Mechanism. See OECD (1996) for a detailed discussion.

References

Aggarwal, Mita. 1995. "International Trade, Labor Standards, and Labor Market Conditions: An Evaluation of Linkages." USITC, Office of Economics Working Paper No. 95-06-C (June).

Bagwell, Kyle and Robert W. Staiger. 1999. "Domestic Policies, National Sovereignty and International Economic Institutions." NBER Working Paper 7293.

Bagwell, Kyle and Robert W. Staiger. 2000. "The Simple Economics of Labor Standards and the GATT," in *Social Dimensions of U.S. Trade Policy*. A. V. Deardorff and R.M. Stern, eds. Ann Arbor, MI: University Press, pp. 195–231.

Baland, Jean-Marie and James Robinson. 2000. "A Model of Child Labor." *Journal of Political Economy*. 108:4, pp. 663–79.

Basu, Kaushik. 1999. "Child Labor: Cause, Consequence, and Cure, with Remarks on International Labor Standards." *Journal of Economic Literature*. September, 37, pp. 1083–1119.

Basu, Kaushik and Pham Hoang Van. 1998. "The Economics of Child Labor." *American Economic Review*. 88:3, pp. 412–27.

Berman, Eli, John Bound and Eli Griliches. 1994. "Changes in the Demand for Skilled Labor within U.S. Manufacturing: Evidence from Annual Survey of Manufacturers." *Quarterly Journal of Economics*. 109:2, pp. 367–97.

Bhagwati, Jagdish. 1995. "Trade Liberalisation and 'Fair Trade' Demands: Addressing the Environmental and Labour Standards Issues." *World Economy*. 18:6, pp. 745–59.

Bhagwati, Jagdish and V. Dehejia. 1994. "Freer Trade and Wages of the Unskilled? Is Marx Striking Again?" in *Trade and Wages: Leveling Wages Down?* J. Bhagwati and M. Kosters, eds. Washington, D.C.: AEI, pp. 36–75.

Borjas, George J., Richard B. Freeman and Lawrence F. Katz. 1992. *Immigration and the Work Force: Economic Consequences for the United States and Source Areas*. Chicago: University of Chicago Press.

Bound, John and George Johnson. 1992. "Changes in the Structure of Wages in the 1980s: An Evaluation of Alternative Explanations." *American Economic Review*. 82:3, pp. 371–92.

Brown, Drusilla K. 2000. "International Trade and Core Labour Standards: A Survey of the Recent Literature." Labour Market and Social Policy Occasional Papers No. 43, Organization for Cooperation and Development, Paris.

Brown, Drusilla K. 2001. "Child Labor in Latin America: Policy and Evidence." *World Economy*, forthcoming.

Brown, Drusilla K., Alan V. Deardorff and Robert M. Stern. 1996. "International Labor Standards and Trade: A Theoretical Analysis," in *Fair Trade and Harmonization: Prerequisites for Free Trade? Economic Analysis, Vol. 1.* Jagdish Bhagwati and Robert Hudec, eds. Cambridge and London: MIT Press, pp. 227–80.

Brown, Drusilla K., Alan V. Deardorff and Robert M. Stern. 2001. "U.S. Trade and Other Policy Options and Programs to Deter Foreign Exploitation of Child Labor," in *Topics in Empirical International Economics.* Bagnus Blomstrom and Linda S. Goldberg, eds. Chicago and London: The University of Chicago Press.

Cline, William R. 1997. *Trade and Income Distribution.* Washington, D.C.: Institute for International Economics.

Eddy, Lee. 1997. "Globalization and Labour Standards: A Review of Issues." *International Labour Review.* 136:2, pp. 173–89.

Engerman, Stanley L. 2001. "The History and Political Economy of International Labor Standards," mimeo.

Freeman, Richard. 1994. "A Hard-Headed Look at Labour Standards," in *International Labour Standards and Economic Interdependence.* Werner Sengenberger and Duncan Campbell, eds. Geneva: International Institute for Labour Studies, pp. 79–92.

Genicot, Garance. 2000. "Bonded Labor and Serfdom: A Paradox of Choice." Working Paper, University of California, Irvine.

International Labour Organization. 1999. *Promoting Social Justice.* Geneva: International Labour Office.

International Labour Organization. 2000a. *Statistics on Occupational Wages and Hours of Work and on Food Prices.* Geneva: International Labour Office.

International Labour Organization. 2000b. *LABOURST.* Geneva: Bureau of Labour Statistics.

International Monetary Fund. 2000. International Financial Statistics Yearbook. Washington, D.C.: International Monetary Fund.

Katz, Lawrence F. and Kevin M. Murphy. 1992. "Changes in Relative Wages, 1963–1987: Supply and Demand Factors." *Quarterly Journal of Economics.* 107:428, pp. 35–78.

Krueger, Alan. 1997. "International Labor Standards and Trade," in *Annual World Bank Conference on Development Economics.* Michael Bruno and Boris Pleskovic, eds. Washington, D.C.: The World Bank, pp. 281–302.

Krugman, Paul R. 2000. "Technology, Trade and Factor Prices." *Journal of International Economics.* 50, pp. 51–71.

Lawrence, Robert Z. and Matthew Slaughter. 1993. "Trade and U.S. Wages in the 1980s: Giant Sucking Sound or Small Hiccup?" *Brookings Papers on Economic Activity: Microeconomics,* pp. 161–210.

Leamer, Edward E. 1996. "A Trial Economist's View of U.S. Wages and Globalization," in *Imports, Exports, and the American Worker.* Susan Collins, ed. Washington, D.C.: Brookings Institution.

Leamer, Edward E. 2000. "What's the Use of Factor Contents?" *Journal of International Economics.* 50, pp. 17–49.

Limao, Nuno. 2000. "Trade Policy, Cross-Border Externalities and Lobbies: Do Linked Agreements Enforce More Cooperative Outcomes?" Mimeo.

Mah, J.S. 1997. "Core Labor Standards and Export Performance in Developing Countries." *World Economy.* September, 20:6, pp. 773–85.

Marshall, Ray. 1994. "The Importance of International Labour Standards in a More Competitive Global Economy," in *International Labour Standards and Economic Interdependence.* Werner Sengenberger and Duncan Campbell, eds. Geneva: International Institute for Labour Studies, pp. 65–78.

Maskus, Keith. 1997. "Should Core Labor Standards Be Imposed through International Trade Policy?" World Bank Policy Research Working Paper No. 1817, August.

Moehling, Carolyn M. 1999. "State Child Labor Laws and the Decline of Child Labor." *Explorations in Economic History.* January, 36, pp. 72–106.

Organization for Economic Cooperation and Development. 1996. *Trade, Employment and Labour Standards: A Study of Core Workers' Rights and International Trade.* Paris: OECD.

Panagariya, Arvind. 2000. "Evaluating the Factor-Content Approach to Measuring the Effect of Trade on Wage Inequality." *Journal of International Economics.* 50, pp. 91–116.

Piore, Michael. 1994. "International Labor Standards and Business Strategies," in *International Labor Standards and Global Economic Integration: Proceedings of a Symposium.* Washington, D.C.: U.S. Department of Labor, Bureau of International Labor Affairs.

Portes, Alejandro. 1994. "By-Passing the Rules: The Dialectics of Labour Standards and Informalization in Less-Developed Countries," in *International Labour Standards and Economic Interdependence.* Werner Sengenberger and Duncan Campbell, eds. Geneva: International Institute for Labour Studies, pp. 159–76.

Psacharopoulos, George. 1994. "Returns to Investment in Education: A Global Update." *World Development.* 22:9, pp. 1325–43.

Rodrik, Dani. 1996. "Labor Standards in International Trade: Do They Matter and What Do We Do About Them," in *Emerging Agenda For Global Trade: High Stakes for Developing Countries.* Robert Z. Lawrence, Dani Rodrik and John Walley, eds. Overseas Development Council Essay No. 20, Washington, D.C.: Johns Hopkins University Press.

Rodrik, Dani. 1999. "Institutions for High-Quality Growth: What They Are and How to Acquire Them," manuscript.

Rogers, Carol Ann and Kenneth A. Swinnerton. 1999. "Inequality, Productivity, and Child Labor: Theory and Evidence," mimeo, Georgetown University.

Singh, Nirvikar. 2001. "The Impact of International Labor Standards: A Survey of Economic Theory," mimeo, University of California, Santa Cruz.

Slaughter, Matthew J. and Philip Swagel. 1997. "The Effect of Globalization on Wages in the Advanced Economies." IMF Working Paper WP/97/43.

Spagnolo, Giancarlo. 1999. "Issue Linkage, Delegation, and International Policy Cooperation." Cambridge, DEA Working Paper no. 9913.

Srinivasan, T.N. 1997. "Trade and Human Rights," in *Representation of Constituent Interests in Design and Implementation of U.S. Trade Policies.* Alan V. Deardorff and Robert M. Stern, eds. Ann Arbor: University of Michigan Press.

Srinivasan, T.N. 1998. *Developing Countries and the Multilateral Trading System: From the GATT to the Uruguay Round and the Future.* Boulder and Oxford: Harper Collins, Westview Press.

Stiglitz, Joseph. 2000. "Democratic Development as the Fruits of Labor." Keynote Address of the Annual Meetings of the Industrial Relations Research Association, Boston, MA, January.

Stolper, Wolfgang F. and Paul A. Samuelson. 1941. "Protection and Real Wages." *Review of Economic Studies.* 9, pp. 58–73.

Swinnerton, Kenneth A. 1997. "An Essay on Economic Efficiency and Core Labour Standards." *World Economy.* 20:1, pp. 73–86.

U.S. Department of Labor. 1998. *By the Sweat and Toil of Children, Efforts to Eliminate Child Labor, Vol. V.* Washington, D.C.: Bureau of International Labor Affairs.

6

Beyond the Outsourcing Angst:
Making America More Productive

THOMAS F. SIEMS

Outsourcing is not new. For years, American companies have focused on core competencies and contracted out activities that could be accomplished better, faster and cheaper by outside, specialized providers. These vendors may be across town, elsewhere in the country or on the far side of the world.

The motive has always been to remain competitive. In today's business environment, profit and even survival depend on making constant improvements throughout supply chains by lowering costs and improving quality, designs, cycle times and processes. Through specialization and trade, businesses develop important competitive advantages that help them become more flexible and innovative in rapidly changing markets.

Indeed, the best companies keep costs low and boost productivity by doing what they do best and outsourcing the rest.[1]

Even when it involves foreign workers, outsourcing benefits individual companies. Many Americans, however, express a deep unease over reports of firms' "exporting jobs" and displacing domestic workers by moving jobs to India, China or other up-and-coming nations.

The concern is understandable. Job losses are painful, especially when they are related to global economic forces beyond individual workers' control. As reports of outsourcing grow, many Americans are advocating policies designed to preserve existing jobs and industries. But many economists—including such notables as Milton Friedman and Jagdish Bhagwati—discourage these efforts as harmful to the overall economy.[2] They argue that outsourcing increases efficiency and productivity and leads to competitiveness, innovation and ever-larger market opportunities.

Knowledge Workers at Risk

One reason today's overseas outsourcing generates heat is the wider swath of occupations being performed offshore. Computers, software, the Internet and fiber-optic cables form an infrastructure that allows businesses to break apart activities and redistribute them elsewhere—increasingly to knowledge workers all over the world. Digital technologies and inexpensive telecommunications have created an efficient and effective information superhighway: Strings of zeroes and ones can be moved to Bangalore, Beijing or just about anyplace in seconds.

White-collar activities such as processing accounting data, performing standard financial analyses, writing routine software and maintaining call centers are no longer exempt from international competition. With an Internet connection and specialized skills, individuals and companies in the remotest ends of the earth are able to compete and collaborate in today's global economy.

How many knowledge jobs are affected by offshore outsourcing? Data on outsourcing's effect on employment are limited, but one estimate puts the total

Offshoring of U.S. Jobs to Low-Wage Countries
Table 1

Profession	Estimated 2003	Projected By 2005	By 2010	By 2015
Art, design	2,500	8,000	15,000	30,000
Architecture	14,000	46,000	93,000	191,000
Business	30,000	91,000	176,000	356,000
Computer	102,000	181,000	322,000	542,000
Legal	6,000	20,000	39,000	79,000
Life sciences	300	4,000	16,000	39,000
Management	3,500	34,000	106,000	259,000
Office	146,000	410,000	815,000	1,600,000
Sales	11,000	38,000	97,000	218,000
Total	315,300	832,000	1,679,000	3,314,000

Note: Numbers are cumulative and have been rounded.
Source: "Near-Term Growth of Offshoring Accelerating," by John C. McCarthy, Forrester Research Inc., May 14, 2004.

number of U.S. white-collar jobs moving overseas at 832,000 through 2005, nearly triple the figure through 2003 *(Table 1).* In another five years, the total could rise to 1.7 million; in a decade, to 3.3 million. We should keep in mind, however, that the U.S. has added 18 million jobs in the past 10 years. Total employment rose to nearly 135 million workers in early 2006, so the offshore outsourcing estimates represent a relatively small part of a growing economy.

The recent increase in offshore relocation of knowledge work has been followed by a surge in anti-outsourcing legislation by U.S. state governments *(Chart 1).* According to the National Foundation for American Policy, more than 300 bills have been introduced over the past two years to protect American workers against outsourcing to other countries.[3] The Constitution's commerce clause constrains the states' power to interfere with business, so many of these proposals are limited, often covering only companies doing government work.

Outsourcing is fundamentally a trade phenomenon, and empirical evidence suggests protectionist policies entail significant economic costs. They result in higher prices for consumers and declining domestic and global competitiveness. The economy also loses the productivity gains that would have come from shifting resources to their best uses. Trade barriers do long-term harm by short-circuiting healthy economic evolution.[4]

Protectionist measures rarely save jobs. A generation ago, American angst focused on foreign competition's impact on manufacturing employment, particularly in automobiles, steel and textiles. We passed laws to restrict imports. Despite trade restraints and domestic-content laws, manufacturing jobs continued to decline even as overall employment rose. Most significant, some of the biggest job losses have come in autos, steel and textiles.

Saving existing jobs exacts a price. Countries that impose laws aimed at easing the burdens of job loss tend to have lower per capita incomes *(Chart 2).* World Bank data indicate that many countries impose huge burdens on employers who lay off workers—the equivalent of 165 weeks of pay in Brazil, 112 in

Anti-Outsourcing Legislation, 2005
Chart 1

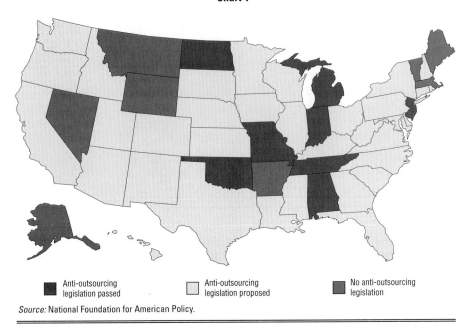

| Anti-outsourcing legislation passed | Anti-outsourcing legislation proposed | No anti-outsourcing legislation |

Source: National Foundation for American Policy.

Turkey, 90 in China, 79 in India. All are poor countries. High firing costs rob economies of their vitality by discouraging companies from hiring new employees in the first place. While generous severance is helpful to the displaced workers, it makes societies poorer by slowing job creation and dragging down labor productivity.

By contrast, countries with lower burdens on firing are usually richer. The United States, for example, mandates no severance at all, allowing companies to determine their own policies. Giving companies a freer hand in staffing decisions allows firms to pare payrolls quickly in response to changing market conditions, and it reduces the risk of hiring and forming new businesses. This labor market flexibility encourages efficiency, productivity and economic growth—all of which contribute to higher incomes.

Outsourcing often creates employment uncertainties because it's not always immediately apparent where the new jobs

will materialize. History tells us, however, that job creation outpaces job destruction in the long run. If the U.S. had tried to hang onto the jobs of its past, we would be far poorer today. Living standards would have stagnated, and American consumers would be paying higher prices.[5]

Economists Milton and Rose Friedman put it this way, "If all we want are jobs, we can create any number—for example, have people dig holes and then fill them up again or perform other useless tasks." The Friedmans conclude that the real objective is not just jobs, but productive jobs—those that will result in more goods and services for consumers around the globe.[6]

Toward Greater Productivity

The most successful economies tend to resist calls for protectionism and keep their markets open. This sometimes means short-term economic dislocations, but in

Job Security and Income per Capita
Chart 2

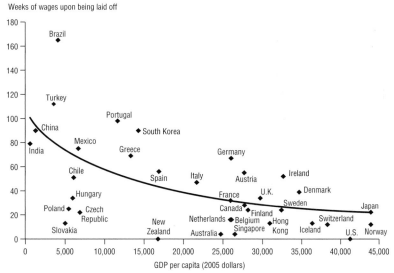

Weeks of wages upon being laid off

GDP per capita (2005 dollars)

Note: A similar relationship is obtained using purchasing power parity adjustments for GDP per capita. James J. Heckman and Carmen Pages, in "The Cost of Job Security Regulation: Evidence from Latin American Labor Markets," NBER Working Paper 7773, June 2000, obtain parallel findings using 1995 GDP data for Latin America.

Source: World Bank, World Development Indicators Database; World Bank Group, Doing Business 2006.

the long run competition spurs economic progress. The challenge for U.S. companies and workers involves reinventing themselves and creating the next generation of jobs, products and services.

Recent history proves that lost jobs, while they often mean hardship for the affected workers and their families, aren't an impediment to growth in one of the world's most resilient, dynamic and flexible economies. From 1980 to 2005, U.S. workers filed 118 million claims for unemployment insurance *(Table 2)*. Many others lost their jobs, of course, but either didn't qualify for benefits, weren't unemployed long enough to file claims, or quickly transitioned to new jobs. It's hard to find the total number of displaced workers, but it surely would be more than 150 million.

Despite all the job losses, the economy performed quite well. Total employment over the same 26-year period rose by 44 million. At annual rates, unemployment fell from 7.2 percent to less than 5 percent today. Productivity increased by 72 percent. Per capita real gross domestic product shot from $25,309 to $41,257. The average workweek fell by nearly two hours to 33.7, and average household real net worth more than doubled to $431,000. All this was accomplished, by the way, with relatively little economic downtime. Since the beginning of 1983, the United States has had just 16 months of recession, fewer than any other major country *(Table 3)*.

Increasing productivity—getting more for less—is key to business success and the ultimate source of higher living standards. Sometimes greater productivity means automating processes and replacing workers with improved technologies. Sometimes it entails adding resources to work on high value-added activities. Sometimes it involves moving noncritical work to lower-cost providers.

The Churn: Recycling America's Labor
Table 2

Year	Initial claims*	Dec.-to-Dec. net job gains*	End-of-year employment*	End-of-year unemployment rate (percent)	Productivity (index, 1980 = 100)
1980	5,850	267	90,936	7.2	100
1981	5,419	(52)	90,884	8.5	102
1982	7,033	(2,128)	88,756	10.8	101
1983	5,294	3,454	92,210	8.3	105
1984	4,484	3,877	96,087	7.3	108
1985	4,702	2,500	98,587	7.0	110
1986	4,529	1,897	100,484	6.6	113
1987	3,897	3,150	103,634	5.7	114
1988	3,704	3,237	106,871	5.3	116
1989	3,950	1,938	108,809	5.4	117
1990	4,616	309	109,118	6.3	119
1991	5,363	(857)	108,261	7.3	121
1992	4,905	1,157	109,418	7.4	126
1993	4,117	2,785	112,203	6.5	127
1994	4,076	3,853	116,056	5.5	128
1995	4,298	2,154	118,210	5.6	128
1996	4,223	2,793	121,003	5.4	132
1997	3,858	3,358	124,361	4.7	135
1998	3,810	3,003	127,364	4.4	139
1999	3,563	3,172	130,536	4.0	143
2000	3,590	1,948	132,484	3.9	147
2001	4,869	(1,763)	130,721	5.7	150
2002	4,852	(535)	130,186	6.0	156
2003	4,823	112	130,298	5.7	163
2004	4,114	2,097	132,395	5.4	168
2005	3,985	1,976	134,371	4.9	172
Total	117,924	43,702			
Avg./month	378	140			

*Establishment survey, data in thousands. Claims are for unemployment insurance.

Sources: Bureau of Labor Statistics; Federal Reserve Board

Economic Downtime, 1983–2005
Table 3

	Recession	
	Months	**Percent of time**
U.S.	16	5.8
U.K.	22	8.0
Australia	23	8.3
Canada	24	8.7
Italy	25	9.1
Austria	36	13.0
Spain	42	15.2
France	42	15.2
Sweden	43	15.6
Germany	70	25.4
Japan	82	29.7
New Zealand	85	30.8
Switzerland	87	31.5

Sources: National Bureau of Economic Research; Economic Cycle Research Institute.

Today, global firms increasingly use outsourcing to redeploy and redirect staff to higher value-added activities. Farming out some tasks frees up talent to work on new products and new ideas. It creates greater worker flexibility and allows firms to put the right resources in the right places at the right times.

Competition gives companies the incentive to move production to lower-cost locations. Large segments of the textile industry left New England for the Southeast; more recently, textile plants in the Carolinas have closed as companies shift production to other parts of the world. Automobile manufacturers sent a lot of their parts and assembly work to Mexico in an effort to compete with Asian rivals. The electronics industry has developed a global supply chain, and it takes components from a hodgepodge of nations to build computers and other gadgets.

Laptops, for example, are assembled in Mexico with memory chips and display screens from South Korea; cases, keyboards and hard drives from Thailand; graphics chips from Taiwan; and batteries from any number of Asian countries. The microprocessor, the machine's highest valued and most complex part, is still made in the United States. This is the future of business— a global integration of production, where countries do what they do best, dictated by David Ricardo's principle of comparative advantage.

As a technological powerhouse, with skilled workers and adept managers, the U.S. should strive for the most complex and rewarding tasks, while other countries will specialize in the routine, labor-intensive tasks. Globalization doesn't just mean increased competition; it opens opportunities for cooperation.

Outsourcing creates partners, not rivals. For example, India has historically been viewed as an attractive place to do knowledge work because of its low production and labor costs, talented and skilled workforce, and English-language proficiency. A.T. Kearney Inc. ranks India as the most attractive offshore location for doing business *(Chart 3)*, particularly for call centers and data-processing operations. Among the U.S. companies expanding their presence in India are Dell, Sun Microsystems, Ford, General Electric and Oracle.

The key differences between India two decades ago and now are twofold: (1) the role that technology has played in quickly and inexpensively subdividing and moving work, and (2) the nation's willingness to remove regulatory burdens and attract foreign firms to establish operations there. The availability, affordability and speed of today's technologies allow Indian workers to instantaneously provide highly competitive services to organizations around the globe. And since the new era of fewer regulatory burdens began in 1991, foreign direct investment into India has increased dramatically *(Chart 4)*.

History has proven the power of letting global competition run its course: Many better, higher-paying jobs have been created as new ideas and technologies

Offshore Location Attractiveness
Chart 3

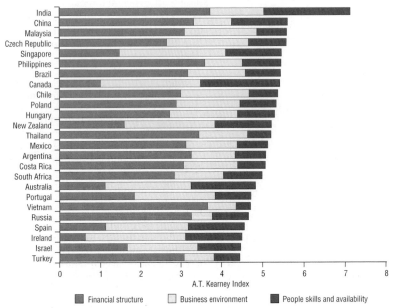

| | Financial structure | | Business environment | | People skills and availability |

A.T. Kearney Index

Note: Financial structure is rated on a scale of 1 to 4; business environment and people skills and availability are on a scale of 1 to 3.

Sourse: A.T. Kearney Inc.

Foreign Direct Investment into India
Chart 4

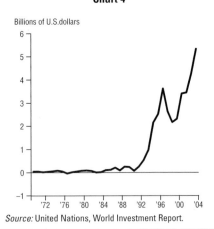

Billions of U.S.dollars

Source: United Nations, World Investment Report.

replace older ones. The key to the U.S. economy's future lies in maintaining a flexible labor market, where resources can flow from declining sectors to emerging ones. Innovation and entrepreneurship depend on it. Job losses and other unsettling aspects of the process can't be ignored, and society can consider policies to make economic change less burdensome. Preparing workers for new opportunities through retraining and education is often mentioned as an alternative to protecting existing jobs.

Outsourcing's Future

Offshore outsourcing presents complex and often divisive issues, but it is unlikely to wither away. The market pressures that create incentives for outsourcing will not abate. Our economy, however, is resilient and flexible. The long-run evidence on employment-turnover patterns demonstrates that offshore outsourcing results in overall economic gains, such as lower consumer prices, better products and higher productivity growth.

Like other trade, offshore outsourcing can have negative impacts on some jobs and wages while affecting others in a positive way. These structural changes influence where jobs are located and what tasks workers perform. While policy can address ways to help displaced workers gain the necessary skills to compete in the global economy, it also can encourage Americans to embrace change and adapt to globalization's effects on the changing nature of work.

We have a choice. Saving specific jobs and industries inhibits innovation and short-circuits the next round of new jobs and services, raising prices for everyone.

Accepting the challenge of competition, however, takes a longer-run view. It leads to innovation and ever-larger market opportunities and, in the end, true productive job creation and a lower cost of living. Indeed, the secret to faster growth and greater prosperity lies in allowing individuals and businesses to do what they do best—and outsource the rest.

Siems is a senior economist and policy advisor in the Research Department of the Federal Reserve Bank of Dallas.

Notes

The author thanks Julia Carter and Timothy J. Schaaf for assistance in research.

[1] A prelude to this article is "Do What You Do Best, Outsource the Rest?" by Thomas F. Siems and Adam S. Ratner, Federal Reserve Bank of Dallas *Southwest Economy,* November/December 2003, pp. 13–14.

[2] The debate over outsourcing is clearly framed in "The Muddles over Outsourcing," by Jagdish Bhagwati, Arvind Panagariya and T.N. Srinivasan, *Journal of Economic Perspectives,* vol. 18, no. 4, Fall 2004, pp. 93–114.

[3] "Outsourcing Saves Money," by Stuart Anderson, *State Legislatures Magazine,* June 2005, and "Outsourcing Attacks Not Over," by Stuart Anderson, *National Review,* February 11, 2005.

[4] Interested readers are directed to *In Defense of Globalization,* by Jagdish Bhagwati, New York: Oxford University Press, 2004.

[5] Job anxieties brought on by offshore outsourcing highlight the tension between efficiency and distributional concerns. See "A Specific-Factors View on Outsourcing," by Wilhelm Kohler, *North American Journal of Economics and Finance,* vol.12, issue 1, 2001, pp. 31–53, and "What Does Evidence Tell Us About Fragmentation and Outsourcing?" by Ronald Jones, Henryk Kierzkowski and Chen Lurong, *International Review of Economics and Finance,* vol. 14, 2005, pp. 305–16.

[6] "The Case for Free Trade," by Milton Friedman and Rose Friedman, *Hoover Digest,* no. 4, 1997.

7

Offshoring: The Next Industrial Revolution?

Alan S. Blinder

A Controversy Reconsidered

In February 2004, when N. Gregory Mankiw, a Harvard professor then serving as chairman of the White House Council of Economic Advisers, caused a national uproar with a "textbook" statement about trade, economists rushed to his defense. Mankiw was commenting on the phenomenon that has been clumsily dubbed "offshoring" (or "offshore outsourcing")—the migration of jobs, but not the people who perform them, from rich countries to poor ones. Offshoring, Mankiw said, is only "the latest manifestation of the gains from trade that economists have talked about at least since Adam Smith. . . . More things are tradable than were tradable in the past, and that's a good thing." Although Democratic and Republican politicians alike excoriated Mankiw for his callous attitude toward American jobs, economists lined up to support his claim that offshoring is simply international business as usual.

Their economics were basically sound: the well-known principle of comparative advantage implies that trade in new kinds of products will bring overall improvements in productivity and well-being. But Mankiw and his defenders underestimated both the importance of offshoring and its disruptive effect on wealthy countries. Sometimes a quantitative change is so large that it brings about qualitative changes, as offshoring likely will. We have so far barely seen the tip of the offshoring iceberg, the eventual dimensions of which may be staggering.

To be sure, the furor over Mankiw's remark was grotesquely out of proportion to the current importance of offshoring, which is still largely a prospective phenomenon. Although there are no reliable national data, fragmentary studies indicate that well under a million service-sector jobs in the United States have been lost to offshoring to date. (A million seems impressive, but in the gigantic and rapidly churning U.S. labor market, a million jobs is less than two weeks' worth of normal gross job losses.) However, constant improvements in technology and global communications virtually guarantee that the future will bring much more offshoring of "impersonal services"—that is, services that can be delivered electronically over long distances with little or no degradation in quality.

That said, we should not view the coming wave of offshoring as an impending catastrophe. Nor should we try to stop it. The normal gains from trade mean that the world as a whole cannot lose from increases in productivity, and the United States and other industrial countries have not only weathered but also benefited from comparable changes in the past. But in order to do so again, the governments and societies of the developed world must face up to the massive, complex, and multifaceted challenges that offshoring will bring. National data systems, trade policies, educational systems, social welfare programs, and politics all must adapt to new realities. Unfortunately, none of this is happening now.

Modernizing Comparative Advantage

COUNTRIES TRADE with one another for the same reasons that individuals, businesses, and regions do: to exploit their comparative advantages. Some advantages are "natural": Texas and Saudi Arabia sit atop massive deposits of oil that are entirely lacking in New York and Japan, and nature has conspired to make Hawaii a more attractive tourist destination than Greenland. There is not much anyone can do about such natural advantages.

But in modern economies, nature's whimsy is far less important than it was in the past. Today, much comparative advantage derives from human effort rather than natural conditions. The concentration of computer companies around Silicon Valley, for example, has nothing to do with bountiful natural deposits of silicon; it has to do with Xerox's fabled Palo Alto Research Center, the proximity of Stanford University, and the arrival of two young men named Hewlett and Packard. Silicon Valley could have sprouted up elsewhere.

One important aspect of this modern reality is that patterns of man-made comparative advantage can and do change over time. The economist Jagdish Bhagwati has labeled this phenomenon "kaleidoscopic comparative advantage," and it is critical to understanding offshoring. Once upon a time, the United Kingdom had a comparative advantage in textile manufacturing. Then that advantage shifted to New England, and so jobs were moved from the United Kingdom to the United States. Then the comparative advantage shifted once again—this time to the Carolinas—and jobs migrated south within the United States. Now the comparative advantage in textile manufacturing resides in China and other low-wage countries, and what many

are wont to call "American jobs" have been moved there as a result.

Of course, not everything can be traded across long distances. At any point in time, the available technology—especially in transportation and communications—largely determines what can be traded internationally and what cannot. Economic theorists accordingly divide the world's goods and services into two bins: tradable and nontradable. Traditionally, any item that could be put in a box and shipped (roughly, manufactured goods) was considered tradable, and anything that could not be put in a box (such as services) or was too heavy to ship (such as houses) was thought of as nontradable. But because technology is always improving and transportation is becoming cheaper and easier, the boundary between what is tradable and what is not is constantly shifting. And unlike comparative advantage, this change is not kaleidoscopic; it moves in only one direction, with more and more items becoming tradable.

The old assumption that if you cannot put it in a box, you cannot trade it is thus hopelessly obsolete. Because packets of digitized information play the role that boxes used to play, many more services are now tradable and many more will surely become so. In the future, and to a great extent already, the key distinction will no longer be between things that can be put in a box and things that cannot. Rather, it will be between services that can be delivered electronically and those that cannot.

The Three Industrial Revolutions

ADAM SMITH wrote *The Wealth of Nations* in 1776, at the beginning of the first Industrial Revolution. Although Smith's vision was extraordinary, even he did not imagine what was to come. As workers in the industrializing countries migrated from farm to factory, societies were transformed beyond recognition. The shift was massive. It has been estimated that in 1810, 84 percent of the U.S. work force was engaged in agriculture, compared to a paltry 3 percent in manufacturing. By 1960, manufacturing's share had risen to almost 25 percent and agriculture's had dwindled to just 8 percent. (Today, agriculture's share is under 2 percent.) How and where people lived, how they educated their children, the organization of businesses, the forms and practices of government—all changed dramatically in order to accommodate this new reality.

Then came the second Industrial Revolution, and jobs shifted once again—this time away from manufacturing and toward services. The shift to services is still viewed with alarm in the United States and many other rich countries, where people bemoan rather than welcome the resulting loss of manufacturing jobs. But in reality, new service-sector jobs have been created far more rapidly than old manufacturing jobs have disappeared. In 1960, about 35 percent of nonagricultural workers in the United States produced goods and 65 percent produced services. By 2004, only about one-sixth of the United States' nonagricultural jobs were in goods-producing industries, while five-sixths produced services. This trend is worldwide and continuing. Between 1967 and 2003, according to the Organization for Economic Cooperation and Development, the service sector's share of total jobs increased by about 19 percentage points in the United States, 21 points in Japan, and roughly 25 points in France, Italy, and the United Kingdom.

We are now in the early stages of a third Industrial Revolution—the information age. The cheap and easy flow of information around the globe has vastly expanded the scope of tradable services, and there is much more to come. Industrial revolutions are big deals. And just like the previous two, the third Industrial Revolution will require vast and unsettling adjustments in the way Americans and residents of other developed countries work, live, and educate their children.

But a bit of historical perspective should help temper fears of offshoring.

The first Industrial Revolution did not spell the end of agriculture, or even the end of food production, in the United States. It just meant that a much smaller percentage of Americans had to work on farms to feed the population. (By charming historical coincidence, the actual number of Americans working on farms today—around 2 million—is about what it was in 1810.) The main reason for this shift was not foreign trade, but soaring farm productivity. And most important, the massive movement of labor off the farms did not result in mass unemployment. Rather, it led to a large-scale reallocation of labor to factories.

Similarly, the second Industrial Revolution has not meant the end of manufacturing, even in the United States, which is running ahead of the rest of the world in the shift toward services. The share of the U.S. work force engaged in manufacturing has fallen dramatically since 1960, but the number of manufacturing workers has declined only modestly. Three main forces have driven this change. First, rising productivity in the manufacturing sector has enabled the production of more and more goods with less and less labor. Second, as people around the world have gotten richer, consumer tastes have changed, with consumers choosing to spend a greater share of their incomes on services (such as restaurant meals and vacations) and a smaller share on goods (such as clothing and refrigerators). Third, the United States now imports a much larger share of the manufactured goods it consumes than it did 50 years ago. All told, the share of manufacturing in U.S. GDP declined from a peak near 30 percent in 1953 to under 13 percent in 2004. That may be the simplest quantitative indicator of the massive extent of the second Industrial Revolution to date. But as with the first Industrial Revolution, the shift has not caused widespread unemployment.

The third Industrial Revolution will play out similarly over the next several decades. The kinds of jobs that can be moved offshore will not disappear entirely from the United States or other rich countries, but their shares of the work force will shrink dramatically. And this reduction will transform societies in many ways, most of them hard to foresee, as workers in rich countries find other things to do. But just as with the first two industrial revolutions, massive offshoring will not lead to massive unemployment. In fact, the world gained enormously from the first two industrial revolutions, and it is likely to do so from the third—so long as it makes the necessary economic and social adjustments.

This Time it's Personal

WHAT SORTS of jobs are at risk of being offshored? In the old days, when tradable goods were things that could be put in a box, the key distinction was between manufacturing and nonmanufacturing jobs. Consistent with that, manufacturing workers in the rich countries have grown accustomed to the idea that they compete with foreign labor. But as the domain of tradable services expands, many service workers will also have to accept the new, and not very pleasant, reality that they too must compete with workers in other countries. And there are many more service than manufacturing workers.

Many people blithely assume that the critical labor-market distinction is, and will remain, between highly educated (or highly skilled) people and less-educated (or less-skilled) people—doctors versus call-center operators, for example. The supposed remedy for the rich countries, accordingly, is more education and a general "upskilling" of the work force. But this view may be mistaken. Other things being equal, education and skills are, of course, good things; education yields higher returns in advanced societies, and more schooling probably makes workers more flexible and more adaptable to change. But the problem with relying on education as the remedy for potential job losses is that

"other things" are not remotely close to equal. The critical divide in the future may instead be between those types of work that are easily deliverable through a wire (or via wireless connections) with little or no diminution in quality and those that are not. And this unconventional divide does not correspond well to traditional distinctions between jobs that require high levels of education and jobs that do not.

A few disparate examples will illustrate just how complex—or, rather, how untraditional—the new divide is. It is unlikely that the services of either taxi drivers or airline pilots will ever be delivered electronically over long distances. The first is a "bad job" with negligible educational requirements; the second is quite the reverse. On the other hand, typing services (a low-skill job) and security analysis (a high-skill job) are already being delivered electronically from India—albeit on a small scale so far. Most physicians need not fear that their jobs will be moved offshore, but radiologists are beginning to see this happening already. Police officers will not be replaced by electronic monitoring, but some security guards will be. Janitors and crane operators are probably immune to foreign competition; accountants and computer programmers are not. In short, the dividing line between the jobs that produce services that are suitable for electronic delivery (and are thus threatened by offshoring) and those that do not does not correspond to traditional distinctions between high-end and low-end work.

The fraction of service jobs in the United States and other rich countries that can potentially be moved offshore is certain to rise as technology improves and as countries such as China and India continue to modernize, prosper, and educate their work forces. Eventually, the number of service-sector jobs that will be vulnerable to competition from abroad will likely exceed the total number of manufacturing jobs. Thus, coping with foreign competition, currently a concern for only a minority of workers in rich countries, will become a major concern for many more.

There is currently not even a vocabulary, much less any systematic data, to help society come to grips with the coming labor-market reality. So here is some suggested nomenclature. Services that cannot be delivered electronically, or that are notably inferior when so delivered, have one essential characteristic: personal, face-to-face contact is either imperative or highly desirable. Think of the waiter who serves you dinner, the doctor who gives you your annual physical, or the cop on the beat. Now think of any of those tasks being performed by robots controlled from India—not quite the same. But such face-to-face human contact is not necessary in the relationship you have with the telephone operator who arranges your conference call or the clerk who takes your airline reservation over the phone. He or she may be in India already.

The first group of tasks can be called personally delivered services, or simply personal services, and the second group impersonally delivered services, or impersonal services. In the brave new world of globalized electronic commerce, impersonal services have more in common with manufactured goods that can be put in boxes than they do with personal services. Thus, many impersonal services are destined to become tradable and therefore vulnerable to offshoring. By contrast, most personal services have attributes that cannot be transmitted through a wire. Some require face-to-face contact (child care), some are inherently "high-touch" (nursing), some involve high levels of personal trust (psychotherapy), and some depend on location-specific attributes (lobbying).

However, the dividing line between personal and impersonal services will move over time. As information technology improves, more and more personal services will become impersonal services. No one knows how far this process will go. Forrester Research caused a media stir a few years ago by estimating that 3.3 million U.S. service-sector jobs will move offshore by 2015, a rate of about 300,000 jobs per year. That figure sounds like a lot until you realize that average gross job losses in the U.S. labor market are more than 500,000 in the average week. In fact, given the ample possibilities for technological change in the next decade, 3.3 million seems low. So do the results of a 2003 Berkeley study and a recent McKinsey study, both of which estimated that 11 percent of U.S. jobs are at risk of being offshored. The Berkeley estimate came from tallying up workers in "occupations where at least some [offshoring] has already taken place or is being planned," which means the researchers considered only the currently visible tip of the offshoring iceberg. The future will reveal much more.

To obtain a ballpark figure of the number of U.S. jobs threatened by offshoring, consider the composition of the U.S. labor market at the end of 2004. There were 14.3 million manufacturing jobs. The vast majority of those workers produced items that could be put in a box, and so virtually all of their jobs were potentially movable offshore. About 7.6 million Americans worked in construction and mining. Even though these people produced goods, not services, their jobs were not in danger of moving offshore. (You can't hammer a nail over the Internet.) Next, there were 22 million local, state, and federal government jobs. Even though many of these jobs provide impersonal services that need not be delivered face to face, hardly any are candidates for offshoring—for obvious political reasons. Retail trade employed 15.6 million Americans. Most of these jobs require physical presence, although online retailing is increasing its share of the market, making a growing share of retail jobs vulnerable to offshoring as well.

Those are the easy cases. But the classification so far leaves out the majority of private-service jobs—some 73.6 million at the end of 2004. This extremely heterogeneous group breaks down into educational and health services (17.3 million), professional and business services (16.7 million), leisure and hospitality services (12.3 million), financial services (8.1 million), wholesale trade (5.7 million), transportation (4.3 million), information services (3.2 million), utilities (0.6 million), and "other services" (5.4 million). It is hard to divide such broad job categories into personal and impersonal services, and it is even more difficult to know what possibilities for long-distance electronic delivery the future will bring. Still, it is possible to get a rough sense of which of these jobs may be vulnerable to offshoring.

The health sector is currently about five times as large as the educational sector, and the vast majority of services in the health sector seem destined to be delivered in person for a very long time (if not forever). But there are exceptions, such as radiology. More generally, laboratory tests are already outsourced by most physicians. Why not out of the country rather than just out of town? And with a little imagination, one can envision other medical procedures being performed by doctors who are thousands of miles away. Indeed, some surgery has already been performed by robots controlled by doctors via fiberoptic links.

Educational services are also best delivered face to face, but they are becoming increasingly expensive. Electronic delivery will probably never replace personal contact in K-12 education, which is where the vast majority of the educational jobs are. But college teaching is more vulnerable. As college tuition grows ever more expensive, cheap electronic delivery will start looking more and more sensible, if not imperative.

The range of professional- and business-service jobs includes everything from CEOS and architects to typists and janitors—a heterogeneous lot. That said, in scanning the list of detailed subcategories, it appears that many of these jobs are at least potentially offshorable. For example, future technological developments may dictate how much accounting stays onshore and how much comes to be delivered electronically from countries with much lower wages.

The leisure and hospitality industries seem much safer. If you vacation in Florida, you do not want the beachboy or the maid to be in China. Reservation clerks can be (and are) located anywhere. But on balance, only a few of these jobs can be moved offshore.

Financial services, a sector that includes many highly paid jobs, is another area where the future may look very different from the present. Today, the United States "onshores" more financial jobs (by selling financial services to foreigners) than it offshores. Perhaps that will remain true for years. But improvements in telecommunications and rising educational levels in countries such as China and, especially, India (where many people speak English) may change the status quo dramatically.

Wholesale trade is much like retail trade, but with a bit less personal contact and thus somewhat greater potential for offshoring. The same holds true for transportation and utilities. Information-service jobs, however, are the quintessential types of jobs that can be delivered electronically with ease. The majority of these jobs are at risk. Finally, the phrase "other services" is not very informative, but detailed scrutiny of the list (repair and laundry workers appear, for example) reveals that most of these services require personal delivery.

The overall picture defies generalization, but a rough estimate, based on the preceding numbers, is that the total number of current U.S. service-sector jobs that will be susceptible to offshoring in the electronic future is two to three times the total number of current manufacturing jobs (which is about 14 million). That said, large swaths of the U.S. labor market look to be immune. But, of course, no one knows exactly what technological changes the future will bring.

A Disease Without a Cure

ONE ADDITIONAL piece of economic analysis will complete the story, and in a somewhat worrisome way. Economists refer to the "cost disease" of the personal services as Baumol's disease, after the economist who discovered it, William Baumol. The problem stems from the fact that in many personal services, productivity improvements are either impossible or highly undesirable. In the "impossible" category, think of how many musician hours it took to play one of Mozart's string quartets in 1790 versus in 1990, or how many bus drivers it takes to get children to school today versus a generation ago. In the "undesirable" category, think of school teachers. Their productivity can be increased rather easily: by raising class size, which squeezes more student output from the same teacher input. But most people view such "productivity improvements" as deteriorations in educational quality, a view that is well supported by research findings. With little room for genuine productivity improvements, and with the general level of real wages rising all the time, personal services are condemned to grow ever more expensive (relative to other items) over time. That is the essence of Baumol's disease.

No such problem besets manufacturing. Over the years, automakers, to take one example, have drastically reduced the number of labor hours it takes to build a car—a gain in productivity that has not come at the expense of quality. Here once again, impersonal services are more like manufactured goods than personal services. Thanks to stunning advances in telecommunications technology, for example, your telephone company now handles vastly more calls with many fewer human operators than it needed a generation ago. And the quality of telephony has improved, not declined, as its relative price has plummeted.

The prediction of Baumol's disease—that the prices of personal services (such as education and entertainment) will rise relative to the prices of manufactured goods and impersonal services (such as cars and telephone calls)—is borne out by history. For example, the theory goes a long way toward explaining why the prices of health care and college tuition have risen faster than the consumer price index for decades.

Constantly rising relative prices have predictable consequences. Demand curves slope downward—meaning that the demand for an item declines as its relative price rises. Applied in this context, this should mean decreasing relative demand for many personal services and increasing relative demand for many goods and impersonal services over time. The main exceptions are personal services that are strong "luxury goods" (as people get richer, they want relatively more of them) and those few goods and impersonal services that economists call "inferior" (as people get richer, they want fewer of them).

Baumol's disease connects to the offshoring problem in a rather disconcerting way. Changing trade patterns will keep most personal-service jobs at home while many jobs producing goods and impersonal services migrate to the developing world. When you add to that the likelihood that the demand for many of the increasingly costly personal services is destined to shrink relative to the demand for ever-cheaper impersonal services and manufactured goods, rich countries are likely to have some major readjustments to make. One of the adjustments will involve reallocating labor from one industry to another. But another will show up in real wages. As more and more rich-country workers seek employment in personal services, real wages for those jobs are likely to decline, unless the offset from rising demand is strong enough. Thus, the wage prognosis is brighter for luxury personal-service jobs (such as plastic surgery and chauffeuring) than for ordinary personal-service jobs (such as cutting hair and teaching elementary school).

Is Forewarned Forearmed?

WHAT IS to be done about all of this? It is easier to describe the broad contours of a solution than to prescribe specific remedies. Indeed, this essay is intended to get as many smart people as possible thinking creatively about the problem.

Most obvious is what to avoid: protectionist barriers against offshoring. Building walls against conventional trade in physical goods is hard enough. Humankind's natural propensity to truck and barter, plus the power of comparative advantage, tends to undermine such efforts—which not only end in failure but also cause wide-ranging collateral damage. But it is vastly harder (read "impossible") to stop electronic trade. There are just too many "ports" to monitor. The Coast Guard cannot interdict "shipments" of electronic services delivered via the Internet. Governments could probably do a great deal of harm by trying to block such trade, but in the end they would not succeed in repealing the laws of economics, nor in holding back the forces of history. What, then, are some more constructive—and promising—approaches to limiting the disruption?

In the first place, rich countries such as the United States will have to reorganize the nature of work to exploit their big advantage in nontradable services: that they are close to where the money is. That will mean, in part, specializing more in the delivery of services where personal presence is either imperative or highly beneficial. Thus, the U.S. work force of the future will likely have more divorce lawyers and fewer attorneys who write routine contracts, more internists and fewer radiologists, more salespeople and fewer typists. The market system is very good at making adjustments like these, even massive ones. It has done so before and will do so again. But it takes time and can move in unpredictable ways. Furthermore, massive transformations in the nature of work tend to bring wrenching social changes in their wake.

In the second place, the United States and other rich nations will have to transform their educational systems so as to prepare workers for the jobs that will actually exist in their societies. Basically, that requires training more workers for personal services and fewer for many impersonal services and manufacturing. But what does that mean, concretely, for how children should be educated? Simply providing more education is probably a good thing on balance, especially if a more educated labor force is a more flexible labor force, one that can cope more readily with nonroutine tasks and occupational change. However, education is far from a panacea, and the examples given earlier show that the rich countries will retain many jobs that require little education. In the future, how children are educated may prove to be more important than how much. But educational specialists have not even begun to think about this problem. They should start right now.

Contrary to what many have come to believe in recent years, people skills may become more valuable than computer skills. The geeks may not inherit the earth after all—at least not the highly paid geeks in the rich countries. Creativity will be prized. Thomas Friedman has rightly emphasized that it is necessary to steer youth away from tasks that are routine or prone to routinization into work that requires real imagination. Unfortunately, creativity and imagination are notoriously difficult to teach in schools—although, in this respect, the United States does seem to have a leg up on countries such as Germany and Japan. Moreover, it is hard to imagine that truly creative positions will ever constitute anything close to the majority of jobs. What will everyone else do?

One other important step for rich countries is to rethink the currently inadequate programs for trade adjustment assistance. Up to now, the performance of trade adjustment assistance has been disappointing. As more and more Americans—and Britons, and Germans, and Japanese—are faced with the necessity of adjusting to the dislocations caused by offshoring, these programs must become both bigger and better.

Thinking about adjustment assistance more broadly, the United States may have to repair and thicken the tattered safety net that supports workers who fall off the labor-market trapeze—improving programs ranging from unemployment insurance to job retraining, health insurance, pensions, and right down to public assistance. At present, the United States has one of the thinnest social safety nets in the industrialized world, and there seems to be little if any political force seeking to improve it. But this may change if a larger fraction of the population starts falling into the safety net more often. The corresponding problem for western Europe is different. By U.S. standards, the social safety nets there are broad and deep. The question is, are they affordable, even now? And if so, will they remain affordable if they come to be utilized more heavily?

To repeat, none of this is to suggest that there will be massive unemployment; rather, there will be a massive transition. An effective safety net would ease the pain and, by so doing, speed up the adjustment.

Imperfect Vision

DESPITE ALL the political sound and fury, little service-sector offshoring has happened to date. But it may eventually amount to a third Industrial Revolution, and industrial revolutions have a way of transforming societies.

That said, the "threat" from offshoring should not be exaggerated. Just as the first Industrial Revolution did not banish agriculture from the rich countries, and the second Industrial Revolution has not banished manufacturing, so the third Industrial Revolution will not drive all impersonal services offshore. Nor will it lead to mass unemployment. But the necessary adjustments will put strains on the societies of the rich countries, which seem completely unprepared for the coming industrial transformation.

Perhaps the most acute need, given the long lead-times, is to figure out how to educate children now for the jobs that will actually be available to them 10 and 20 years from now. Unfortunately, since the distinction between personal services (likely to remain in rich countries) and impersonal services (likely to go) does not correspond to the traditional distinction between high-skilled and low-skilled work, simply providing more education cannot be the whole answer.

As the transition unfolds, the number of people in the rich countries who will feel threatened by foreign job competition will grow enormously. It is predictable that they will become a potent political force in each of their countries. In the United States, job-market stress up to now has been particularly acute for the uneducated and the unskilled, who are less inclined to exercise their political voice and less adept at doing so. But the new cadres of displaced workers, especially those who are drawn from the upper educational reaches, will be neither as passive nor as quiet. They will also be numerous. Open trade may therefore be under great strain.

Large-scale offshoring of impersonal-service jobs from rich countries to poor countries may also bear on the relative economic positions of the United States and Europe. The more flexible, fluid American labor market will probably adapt more quickly and more successfully to dramatic workplace and educational changes than the more rigid European labor markets will.

Contrary to current thinking, Americans, and residents of other English-speaking countries, should be less concerned about the challenge from China, which comes largely in manufacturing, and more concerned about the challenge from India, which comes in services. India is learning to exploit its already strong comparative advantage in English, and that process will continue. The economists Jagdish Bhagwati, Arvind Panagariya, and T. N. Srinivasan meant to reassure Americans when they wrote, "Adding 300 million to the pool of skilled workers in India and China will take some decades." They were probably right. But decades is precisely the time frame that people should be thinking about—and 300 million people is roughly twice the size of the U.S. work force.

Many other effects of the coming industrial transformation are difficult to predict, or even to imagine. Take one possibility: for decades, it has seemed that modern economic life is characterized by the ever more dehumanized workplace parodied by Charlie Chaplin in *Modern Times*. The shift to personal services could well reverse that trend for rich countries—bringing less alienation and greater overall job satisfaction. Alas, the future retains its mystery. But in any case, offshoring will likely prove to be much more than just business as usual.

8

Trade in Health Care: Changing Paradigms in a Global Economy

Anoshua Chaudhuri

I. Introduction

With information being accessible more easily through the World Wide Web, choices in terms of medical care, health products, and health services are expanding for the global consumer. As a result, provision of health care goods and services is no longer confined to a country's border. However, every country has different standards, rules and regulations that have restrained a wider use of cross-border delivery and seeking of medical care. The World Trade Organization (WTO) has played a pivotal role in mediating internationally agreed upon rules and settling disputes amongst countries as far as trade in health goods is concerned. Section II discusses the role that WTO has played in the arena of public health to make pharmaceutical products more accessible to low and middle income countries. As with any policy-making, there are intense debates about the intended and unintended consequences of a policy. Section III provides a description of possible consequences of one such policy that was meant to provide flexibility for trade in drugs. Although prohibitively high drug prices is the primary barrier to affordable medicines for developing nations, even the developed nations have started facing their own problems with respect to access to affordable care, more in the form of services. United States has seen rising numbers of individuals who either do not have health insurance or despite having insurance are routinely denied catastrophically expensive care. Rising costs of medical care has fostered cross-border outsourcing of health services and international medical tourism has become a viable alternative for health providers and patients alike. Section IV contains a discussion on outsourcing of medical services and its economic implications.

II. TRIPS and Public Health: Role of WTO

The majority of the world's pharmaceutical companies are based in developed countries. They incur huge fixed costs to invent, test and introduce new drugs in the market. Typically, the entire process from discovery to sale takes almost a decade. Granting these companies intellectual property rights over their product helps maintain the incentive for these companies to continue to invest in research and development. As a result, for many years, these new drugs are sold under brand names at monopoly prices in the market.

Intellectual property rights (IPR) are the rights given to creators of new and innovative products so that they can use these creations exclusively for their use for a certain period of time. IPRs are usually granted in two areas: artistic and literary creations, and industrial property.

1. Literary and artistic creations are protected by copyright with the main purpose of encouraging and rewarding creative works. Copyright period is usually a minimum of fifty years after the death of the author.
2. Industrial Property can be of two kinds. Distinctive signs such as trademarks and geographical indications (e.g., champagne from France) are protected to ensure fair competition and to protect consumers so that they can make informed choices about goods and services. Other industrial products are protected by patents to stimulate innovation and invention of design, technology, new products and trade secrets. Patents usually last for twenty years.

The social purpose of IPR is to provide protection so that there is incentive to create original works, invest in the development of new technology and finance research and development so that society as a whole is benefitted. However, these exclusive rights have limitations and exceptions to create a balance between the interests of right holders and of users.

As ideas and knowledge started increasingly being exchanged globally, the need for new internationally-agreed upon rules for IPRs became necessary to introduce order, predictability and settle disputes. This was because the extent of protection and enforcement of these rights vary across the world, and these differences can strain international economic relations. The World Trade Organization's Agreement on Trade-Related Aspects of Intellectual Property Rights (TRIPS), negotiated through several rounds in the late 1980s and decided upon at the 1994 Uruguay Round, introduced intellectual property rules into the multilateral trading system for the first time. The WTO's TRIPS Agreement[1] "is an attempt to narrow the gaps in the way these rights are protected around the world, and to bring them under common international rules. It establishes minimum levels of protection that each government has to give to the intellectual property of fellow WTO members. In doing so, it strikes a balance between the long term benefits and possible short term costs to society. Society benefits in the long term when intellectual property protection encourages creation and invention, especially when the period of protection expires and the creations and inventions enter the public domain." Governments are allowed to reduce any short term costs through various exceptions, for example to tackle public health problems. In addition, when there are trade disputes over intellectual property rights, the WTO's dispute settlement system works as the mediator.

According to the Agreement, copyrights, patents, trademarks, industrial designs, etc are all different types of creations or inventions and are treated differently. Patent protection must be available for a minimum of twenty years for both products and processes in almost all fields of technology. There are also several exceptions where governments can refuse to issue patents to protect social order, morality, and public health as well as can exclude certain methods, processes, plants and animals.[2]

One recent issue that has emerged in the health care industry is how to ensure patent protection to maintain incentives for expensive research and development while at the same time allowing poor countries access to expensive medicines. This issue came to the forefront when the spread of HIV/AIDS acquired epidemic proportions, especially in sub-Saharan Africa. By the end of year 2000, a staggering 36.1 million individuals were living with HIV/AIDS worldwide of which more than 70 percent were in sub-Saharan African countries alone. Research had determined that anti-retroviral (ARV) treatments were cost-effective in prolonging life, reducing the spread of the disease and preventing hospitalization as a result of HIV/AIDS or related illnesses. However, the most important reason for ARV treatments not being widely accessible was the price. Anti-retroviral therapy (ART) was very expensive because of the high cost of developing and testing these treatments, monopoly pricing as a result of patent protection and high marketing expenditures by the patent-holders. Price of ART was in excess of $10,000 per year per individual in 2000 whereas per capita GDP in 1999 was $360 in Kenya and $3160 in South Africa.[3] Clearly, ART was out of reach for all but the most affluent. In comparison, ART was expensive but accessible for most in the developed world. Some European nations even made ART free for its citizens. While pharmaceutical companies practiced differential pricing ("price discrimination"), they were reluctant to offer ART at cheap prices for fear of 'parallel importing' (discussed later) and neither did they want to publish prices for fear of having to negotiate with rich countries as well. International concern over the AIDS crisis and threat from nations to allow 'compulsory licensing' led to substantial price discounts given by the pharmaceutical companies to poor nations. However, this was not enough.

The WTO ministers issued a special declaration at the Doha Ministerial Conference in November 2001 where they concluded that the TRIPS Agreement should not prevent members from taking measures to protect public health. They underscored a country's ability to use the flexibilities that are built into the TRIPS Agreement. This allowed countries to use 'compulsory licensing' to meet domestic needs. The WTO also agreed to extend exemptions on pharmaceutical patent protection for least-developed countries until 2016 whereby countries like India and South Africa could produce generic versions of some patented medicines without requiring permission from the patent-holder.

What is Compulsory Licensing?

Compulsory licensing means that a government allows someone else to produce the patented product or process without the consent of the patent owner. Use of a patent without the owner's authorization can only be done under a limited number of conditions which are aimed at protecting the legitimate interests of the patent holder. Normally, the person or company must have attempted unsuccessfully to obtain a voluntary license from the patent holder on reasonable commercial terms (Article 31b of TRIPS Agreement). If a compulsory license is issued, the company must still pay an adequate remuneration to the patent holder (Article 31h). However, for "national emergencies," "other circumstances of extreme urgency" or "public non-commercial use" (or "government use") or anti-competitive practices, there is no requirement to try to get a voluntary license (Article 31b). Compulsory licensing should also meet other requirements. In particular, compulsory license cannot be exclusively given to the licensees because the patent holder can continue to produce for its own existing market. Usually, compulsory licensing is granted to mainly supply the domestic market (Article 31f). This is done to limit the amount the licensee can export when the drug is made under compulsory license. Because this restriction affected countries that were unable to make the medicines themselves and unable to import generics, compulsory licensing did nothing to help such countries.

To alleviate this problem, the WTO members agreed in August 2003 to let countries import cheaper generics made under compulsory licensing if they are unable to manufacture the medicines themselves.

This new decision contains three waivers:

- "Exporting countries' obligations under Article 31(f) are waived—any member country can export generic pharmaceutical products made under compulsory licences to meet the needs of importing countries.
- Importing countries' obligations on remuneration to the patent holder under compulsory licensing are

waived to avoid double payment. Remuneration is only required on the export side.

- Exporting constraints are waived for developing and least-developed countries so that they can export within a regional trade agreement, when at least half of the members were categorized as least-developed countries at the time of the decision. That way, developing countries can make use of economies of scale."

These carefully negotiated conditions applying to pharmaceutical products were aimed to ensure that countries can import generics without undermining patent systems in rich countries. Also included are measures to prevent medicines from being diverted to unintended markets. The conditions also require governments using the system to keep all members informed each time they use the system, although WTO approval is not required. All WTO member countries are eligible to import under this decision, but 23 developed countries (Australia, Austria, Belgium, Canada, Denmark, Finland, France, Germany, Greece, Iceland, Ireland, Italy, Japan, Luxembourg, Netherlands, New Zealand, Norway, Portugal, Spain, Sweden, Switzerland, United Kingdom and the USA) have announced voluntarily that they will not use the system to import. After joining the EU in 2004, 10 countries have been added to this list. They are Czech Republic, Cyprus, Estonia, Hungary, Latvia, Lithuania, Malta, Poland, Slovak Republic and Slovenia. 11 countries that said that they would only use the system to import in national emergencies or other circumstances of extreme urgency are Hong Kong-China, Israel, Korea, Kuwait, Macao-China, Mexico, Qatar, Singapore, Chinese Taipei, Turkey, and United Arab Emirates. Several potential exporting countries like Norway, Canada, India and the EU, changed their laws and regulations in order to implement the waivers and to allow production exclusively for export under compulsory license. This recent

waiver has helped African nations, particularly Rwanda. Despite the need, Rwanda was unable to manufacture a triple combination AIDS therapy drug itself, and informed the WTO that it intended to import 260,000 packs of generic version of patented TriAvir—a fixed-dose combination product of Zidovudine, Lamivudine and Nevirapine. In October of 2007, the WTO received from Canada, the first notification from any government that a Canadian company, Apotex, Inc. has been authorized to make the generic version of TriAvir for export to Rwanda with the generic name ApoTriavir.

According to Global Price Reporting Mechanism for Antiretroviral Drugs at WHO,[4] depending on the regimen, prices of the first line ARV drugs decreased by 37%–53% between 2003 and 2006. In 2006, these first line drugs ranged from $123–$493 in low income countries and $145–$623 in middle income countries. This increased the availability of these drugs to most low to middle income countries but average prices paid for second-line regimens remain too high for most low-middle incomes countries. Second line drugs ranged from $1698 in low income countries to $4735 in middle income countries. Some countries like Brazil, Senegal and more recently Ethiopia, Kenya, Tanzania and Zambia have introduced universal provision of free antiretroviral drugs through public sector health care delivery.

In addition to compulsory licensing, the 2001 Doha declaration on TRIPS and Public health also underscored countries' ability to use 'parallel importing' as one of the flexibilities built into the TRIPS Agreement.[5]

What is Parallel Importing?

When products produced under patent in one country are imported to another country without approval, it is generally referred to as "parallel importing." Parallel importing, also called grey market importing, does not involve counterfeit or illegal goods. For example, suppose Pfizer sells Lipitor (cholesterol reducing medicine) in Canada and the U.S. but at a lower price in Canada. If a person in the United States goes across the border and buys the drug in Canada and brings it back to the U.S. for own use or for sale at a price lower than U.S. retail, it will be parallel or grey import. TRIPS Agreement uses the legal principle of 'exhaustion' (once Pfizer has sold a batch of Lipitor in Canada, it has exhausted its patent rights on that batch and has no more rights over that batch) and allows member countries to choose how to deal with exhaustion in a way that best fits the domestic policy.

III. Critique of Parallel Importing and One-Price Policy

The issue of parallel importing was the subject of considerable debate during the 2004 U.S. presidential election. Although discussion of this subject has waned in the recent years, it is an important debate that will persist, particularly as the nation faces an increase in drug use as a result of an aging population and increased obesity leading to higher incidences of diabetes and heart disease amongst all age groups. Further, a growing number of uninsured individuals will be looking to save on out-of-pocket costs on prescription medication. It is no secret that there is considerable amount of re-importation of drugs across the border with Canada.[6] In fact, there are internet pharmacies based in Canada that routinely fill prescriptions for U.S.-based individuals at a cheaper price and ship them across the border. The main opponents to drug re-importation are the pharmaceutical companies and the Food and Drug Administration (FDA). The primary reason for this opposition is that re-importation of prescription drugs pose a health risk for U.S. consumers. The FDA purports that these drugs could be counterfeit, contaminated, or expired products and that these prescriptions are also subject to incorrect dosage, labeling errors and inadequate instructions. However, several

studies, including ones done by the General Accounting Office (GAO) find that Canadian pharmacies are safe sources of prescription medications.[7]

While most Canadian re-imports may be safe, other parallel imports, transshipments and internet sales from Europe, Asia and even across the border from Mexico, routinely fail to meet U.S. standards. Pharmaceutical counterfeiting is also a threat, and one that is less understood and less visible. The World Health Organization estimates that 10% of the global market for pharmaceuticals consists of counterfeit drugs[8] with almost 50–70% of the entire pharmaceutical markets in some countries comprising of counterfeits. While counterfeit drugs are attractive to consumers in poor nations because they are cheap, they pose a big threat to public health and reduce profitability for drug companies. Counterfeiting reduces incentives to invest in research and development for drugs specifically intended for diseases prominent in developing countries, both for domestic and foreign firms. Counterfeit drugs also damage a drug firm's reputation and increase the cost of legitimate drugs because it induces the firm to invest in anti-counterfeiting technology and packaging.

Since patents allow a firm monopoly status, drug firms charge monopoly prices. Economic theory also suggests that monopoly firms practice price discrimination (differential pricing) to maximize profits. This differential pricing occurs due to differences in income and because healthcare systems differ across different countries. Some countries in Europe provide universal coverage of prescription drugs administered through their public programs. Other countries, such as Switzerland and the United States, cover prescription drugs through private insurance. For individuals who do not have to pay high out-of-pocket costs for prescription drugs, the price elasticity of demand is relatively low resulting in increased use of drugs and less sensitivity to drug price. Hence, pharmaceutical companies have no incentive to keep drug prices low. However, the countries that provide drugs directly through national health services typically negotiate discounted prices further leading to price differentials. For example, Canadian government negotiates lower drug prices with pharmaceutical companies for its citizens as a result of which drug prices are much lower in Canada compared to the United States. Although most prescription drugs are not covered under basic insurance, Canadians buy supplementary insurance to cover drug purchases. At a discounted price, both the citizens and the government pay much lower amounts for prescription drugs in Canada.

Critics have questioned the fairness of national pricing regimes that leave high-income countries with high drug prices while middle to low income countries with lower prices.[9] These critics have also claimed that low income countries are subsidized by high income countries. On the other hand, the high drug prices in wealthy countries help provide a profit for pharmaceutical companies and maintain the incentive for research and development that benefits all. Eliminating price discrimination implies that either drug prices would rise to rich country levels or would fall to poor country levels. Since drug companies make most of their profit in rich countries, eliminating price discrimination would almost certainly make many drugs unavailable to poor and even middle class people in developing countries.

In the short term, a one price policy will result in prices settling between the high and low end of the price spectrum but closer to the higher end.[10] Consumers in the developed countries will be better off and slightly lower prices may even spur higher demand. However, revenue for firms will most definitely go down because developed country consumers are less price-sensitive. The demand in poor-countries will diminish as a result of higher prices leading to a further loss of revenue for the pharmaceutical firms. This will have a longer term effect on R&D and perhaps on investment on the most innovative products. Less R&D will result in lower number of drugs developed

in rich countries which will lead to a loss for all as everybody loses due to less availability of new drugs. However this should not necessarily be viewed negatively as it may free up resources for alternative uses.[11] To improve access to drugs in low-income countries, lower price is not the only mechanism. Investment in infrastructure and delivery mechanisms as well as investment in 'Drugs for Neglected Diseases'[12] might lead to an improvement of global social welfare.

IV. Medical Outsourcing and Gains from Trade

A common refrain of the day is that the medical care system in the United States needs a serious overhaul and there are widespread concerns over rising costs, decreased access, and wide variation in quality. Increasing costs are driving more and more Americans to opt out of buying insurance. Even for those who are insured, increasing co-payments, deductibles and medical costs routinely denied by insurance companies could potentially result in total bankruptcy. A health care model that is emerging and holds promise to substantially reduce costs and provide quality care for those who cannot afford domestic health care is medical outsourcing or medical tourism.

What is Medical Outsourcing?

Medical outsourcing can be broadly defined as off-shoring of health-related needs to a different country for the purpose of obtaining cost-effective services. Medical outsourcing encompasses off-shoring of medical services as well as medical tourism.

Medical services such as diagnostic imaging, intensive care unit monitoring, claims management, medical transcription,[13 14] design, testing and maintenance of medical ERP[15] systems, and HIPAA[16] compliance administration are increasingly being moved off-shore. This is being done by medical providers to ensure quality and efficiency in the face of increasing volume of demand and rising administrative costs.

Surgical Options Overseas
Table 1

Procedure	US Insurer's Cost	U.S. Retail Price	India	Thailand	Singapore
Angioplasty	$25704 to $37128	$57262 to $82711	$11,000	$13,000	$13,000
Heart bypass	$27717 to $40035	$47988 to $69316	$11,000	$12,000	$20,000
Hip replacement	$18281 to $26407	$43780 to $63238	$9,000	$12,000	$12,000
Knee replacement	$17627 to $25462	$40640 to $58702	$8,500	$10,000	$13,000
Mastectomy	$9774 to $14118	$23709 to $34246	$7,500	$9,000	$12,400

Source: Tracey Walker, (2006) "Consumers go abroad in pursuit of cost-effective healthcare," *Managed Healthcare Executive*, 16:7.

By off-shoring these services, medical providers are able to tap into skilled workers, less expensive labor and delivery of services across time zones ensuring lower costs and lower turnaround time for these services. Health care industry's spending on outsourcing was $6.2 billion in 2005 which is projected to increase to $7.7 billion in 2008.[17]

How is Medical Tourism Different?

Medical tourism can be defined as a planned foreign travel to primarily obtain high quality, cost effective, non-emergency medical treatment that includes a vacation element. The outsourcing of medical care has occurred in the United States for many years where patients have travelled considerable distances to get specialized medical care. Even medical products and medicines have been outsourced from abroad. However, there has been a distinctive change in the nature of medical tourism where patients are willing to travel greater distances, often to international locations to not only get low-cost aesthetic enhancements but increasingly to get more affordable heart surgery, knee replacements, dental work and organ transplants. Moreover,

developing countries have started offering top quality, sophisticated procedures in low-cost medical facilities. Medical tourism was initiated in developed countries such as Belgium, Israel and Germany almost a decade ago but even developing countries such as Argentina, Hungary, India, Mexico, South Africa and Thailand have become popular destinations.[18] The global medical tourism market was estimated at $20 billion in 2005 which is projected to double by 2010. In 2005 alone, almost 500,000 Americans traveled to foreign countries for medical treatment ranging from cosmetic procedures to life-saving surgery.[19]

Arguments For and Against Medical Outsourcing

There is little doubt that medical outsourcing lowers costs for providers and patients alike as well as improves access for those who cannot afford domestic care. Cost savings depend on the nature of medical treatment and treatment location. Even with travel costs, treatments could cost between 50 percent to 95 percent less than average costs in the US. Table 1 demonstrates a comparison of costs for typical surgical procedures.[20]

Estimated Gains from Trade in Health Services in the United States
Table 2

Procedure	US Inpatient Price ($)	US Inpatient Volume	US Outpatient Price ($)	Estimated US Outpatient Volume	Foreign Price Including Travel Cost ($)	Savings if 10% of US Patients Undergo Surgery Abroad Instead ($)
Knee Surgery	10, 335	399,139	4,142	60,000	1,321	376,698,470
Hernia Repair	4,753	40,553	3,450	759,447	1,651	149,254,906
Tubal Ligation	5,663	78,771	3,442	621,229	1,280	168,834,441
Cataract Extraction	3,595	2,215	2,325	1,430,785	1,247	154,681,706
Varicose Vein Surgery	7,065	1,957	2,373	148,043	1,411	15,350,137

Source: Adapted from Exhibit 1 in "How health insurance inhibits trade in health care" by Aaditya Matoo and Randeep Rathindran, Health Affairs, Volume 25, Number 2, 2006.

However, medical outsourcing, like any other outsourcing, is not without its fair share of controversy around issues of quality, loss of domestic employment and privacy concerns. Further, there is currently no international legal regulation of medical tourism; hence patients have no legal recourse to combat medical malpractice or unsatisfactory treatment received abroad.[21] Issues around quality have been addressed by accreditation of over 100 hospitals around the world by leading accreditation organizations such as International Organization for Standardization (ISO) and the Joint Commission International Accreditation (JCIA). Further, many foreign outsourcing hospitals have affiliations with reputed hospitals and clinics in the United States. Standardized education and training of physicians and nurses,[22] quality pre and postoperative care, use of state of the art technology and sophisticated services have dispelled the concerns about quality at some of the premier foreign hospitals.

A study done by two economists have estimated that if one in ten patients undergoing fifteen selected procedures in the United States were to go abroad for these procedures, the estimated annual savings would be approximately 1.4 billion dollars based on 2004 prices. This is an underestimate of the actual savings since the study assumed only 15 treatments (out of a large universe), used Medicare payment rates to calculate U.S. prices (which are lower bounds of average prices in the U.S.) and was limited by the lack of availability of patient volume data for all procedure categories. Table 2 shows the estimated gains from trade in health services for the United States for a few selected procedures.

Despite such large gains from trade, there is considerable tardiness in support for medical tourism amongst third party payers. Reasons could be concerns over quality, absence of international malpractice law, moral hazard behavior due to low prices abroad,[23] oligopolistic nature of providers and insurers, and increasing costs for covering U.S. nationals living abroad voluntarily. There may also be internationalal concerns that trade in health services would crowd out poorer local patients. Increased foreign demand could also raise domestic prices and accentuate inequalities in access to care. However, increased demand also creates opportunities in the developing countries and expands health care capacity. With the correct signaling of quality, developing countries could attract foreign patients and cross-subsidize the poor by taxing export revenues.

V. Conclusion

Globalization has broken down traditional ways of seeking medical goods and services. Cross-border trade in goods and services continue to permeate all aspects of the health care industry. It is no longer confined to pharmaceutical products such as drugs but is also increasingly getting extended to services such as medical transcription and medical tourism. There are clear overall gains from trade in medical goods and services, albeit with winners and losers. The pharmaceutical industry is increasingly under pressure to pay attention to humanitarian relief for countries afflicted with devastating diseases such as HIV/AIDS. Waivers negotiated and enforced at the WTO have allowed for certain flexibilities for countries around patent rules. This may have positive consequences of greater accessibility to drugs for the global poor but at the same time may reduce incentives for pharmaceutical innovation. It may also result in the invention of more blockbuster drugs that are aimed towards diseases of the affluent and less innovation in diseases that are more common in poor countries. Outsourcing of medical services to countries where labor is cheaper may bode very well for the consumers in terms of faster and cheaper service, greater profits for the medical industry but at the expense of domestic job losses in the developed countries.

Further, lack of uniform laws and quality control still make such cross-border transactions risky. This field continues to develop and has created the need for global health diplomacy that organizations such as World Trade Organization and World Health Organization have taken up to help member nations attain the highest possible levels of health.

Anoshua Chaudhuri, Ph.D. is a Health Economist and Assistant Professor of Economics at San Francisco State University. The author would like to thank Philip King and Chiradeep Sengupta for very helpful comments.

Notes

[1] http://www.wto.org/english/docs_e/legal_e/27-trips.pdf, accessed March 5, 2008.

[2] There is a considerable amount of controversy around exemption of plants and animals.

[3] Diduch, "Aids, Patents and Prices in Africa: A case Study," 2003.

[4] This is a web-based price monitoring tool launched by Aids Medicine and Diagnostic Service (AMDS) at the World Health Organization. See http://www.who.int/hiv/amds/gprm/en/index.html for more information.

[5] For TRIPS Material on the WTO website, see http://www.wto.org/english/tratop_e/trips_e/trips_e.htm, accessed on March 3, 2008.

[6] Pecorino (2004)

[7] Serio and Shaw (2005)

[8] World Health Organization Action Programme on Essential Drugs, 1997

[9] Greider (2003)

[10] Berndt (2007)

[11] Wagner and McCarthy (2004)

[12] This is a recently announced initiative that will fund investment in R&D for such drugs. For information on Drugs for Neglected Diseases, see http://www.msf.org.

[13] Smith (2006)

[14] Bikman and Whiting (2007)

[15] Enterprise Resource Planning systems (ERPs) integrate (or attempt to integrate) all data and processes of an organization into a unified system.

[16] Health Insurance Portability and Accountability Act of 1996, see http://www.hhs.gov/ocr/hipaa/ for more details.

[17] McDougall (2006)

[18] McCallum and Jacoby (2007)

[19] Crawford (2006)

[20] Walker (2006)

[21] Mirrer-Singer (2007)

[22] International medical graduates account for a quarter of 853,187 U.S. physicians according to American Medical Association, Physician characteristics and Distribution in the U.S. (Chicago, AMA, 2004).

[23] Gaynor et al (2000)

References

Berndt, Ernst A Primer on the Economics of Re-Importation of Prescription Drugs, *Managerial and Decision Economics,* 28 (2007): 415–437.

Bikman, Jeremy and Stacilee Whiting, Medical transcription outsourcing greased lightning?, *Healthcare Financial Management,* June 2007.

Crawford, K., An Rx for Clever Start-ups: Taking Operations Overseas, *Business 2.0,* 7 (August 2006): 25.

Diduch, Amy "Aids, Patents and Prices in Africa: A Case Study," *Microeconomics and Behavior,* 5th edition, Robert Frank, McGraw Hill, 2003.

Gaynor, Martin, D. Haas-Wilson and W.B. Vogt, Are invisible Hands Good Hands? Moral Hazard, Competition, and Second-Best in Health Care Markets, *Journal of Political Economy* 108, no 5 (2000): 992–1005.

Greider, Katherine, *The Big Fix: How the Pharmaceutical Industry Rips off American Consumers,* New York: Public Affairs, 2003.

Matoo, Aaditya and Randeep Rathindran, How health insurance inhibits trade in health care, *Health Affairs,* 25, no 2 (2006): 358–368.

McCallum, Brent T. and Philip F. Jacoby, Medical Outsourcing: Reducing Client's Health Care Risks, *Journal of Financial Planning,* October 2007.

McDougall, Paul, U.S. Health Care Firms Look Overseas for Cheap IT, *Information Week,* July 17, 2006.

Mirrer-Singer, P. Medical Malpractice Overseas: The Legal Uncertainty Surrounding Medical Tourism, *Law and Contemporary Problems* 70 (2007): 211–232.

Pecorino, Paul, The Peculiar Economics of Importing Drugs from Canada, *The Milken Institute Review,* 6(First Quarter 2004):35–41.

Serio, John and Paul Shaw, Studies Suggest Canadian Drug Reimportation Is Not Bad Medicine for United States, *Benefits and Compensation Digest,* May 2005.

Smith, Bryan F, The "write" choice: a primer on outsourcing transcription services, *Healthcare Financial Management,* February 2006.

Wagner, Judith and Elizabeth McCarthy, International Differences in Drug Prices, *Annual Review of Public Health,* 25 (2004): 475–95.

Walker, Tracey (2006) "Consumers go abroad in pursuit of cost-effective Healthcare", *Managed Healthcare Executive,* 16 (July 2006):7.

World Health Organization Action Programme on Essential Drugs, *Health Economics and Drug Financing,* World Health Organization: Geneva, Switzerland, 1997.

World Health Organization, Aids Medicine and Diagnostic Service (AMDS), http://www.who.int/hiv/amds/gprm/en/index.html, accessed March 5, 2008.

World Trade Organization, TRIPS Material on the WTO website, http://www.wto.org/english/tratop_e/trips_e/trips_e.htm, accessed March 3, 2008.

World Trade Organization, Agreement on Trade-Related Aspects of Intellectual Property Rights, http://www.wto.org/english/docs_e/legal_e/27-trips.pdf, accessed March 5, 2008.

Discussion Questions:

1. Esty argues that "transboundary externalities" are a key issue in upcoming trade talks. What are transboundary externalities? Give three examples not mentioned in the article. Why do they matter? What institutions do you believe are necessary to deal with transboundary externalities?

2. Most environmentalists argue that absent restrictions, free trade will lead to a "race to the bottom." What do they mean? Give an example. Does Esty agree with this assessment? How could the WTO or other trade organization deal with this issue? Should they?

3. What is the environmental Kuznet's curve? What are its implications for trade and development? Do you think the relationship holds for greenhouse gases? Why or why not?

4. What labor issues must be addressed in trade talks? Which ones does Brown think are important?

5. How could child labor laws (restricting child labor) encourage economic growth in developing countries?

6. Devise a set of labor standards for the WTO. Which ones are key?

7. Some manufacturers, like Nike, have committed themselves to limit labor abuse and "sweatshop" activity. Do you think this is an effective policy?

8. Why does Siems favor outsourcing? What specific arguments does he use? If you were debating Siems (even if you agree with him) what counterarguments would you use?

9. How does Blinder's view of outsourcing differ from Siems'?

10. What do you believe Blinder sees as the U.S.'s "comparative advantage" in the future? Where will the most job growth be? Be specific.

11. What is "Baumol's law," and how is it relevant to outsourcing?

12. The WTO allows developing countries to produce drugs locally even if the patent holder does not allow it under certain conditions. What are these conditions? Do you agree with this policy? If not, how would you change it?

13. What is price discrimination, and how is it relevant for the drug industry? Does the threat of reimportation impact price discrimination?

14. After reading Blinder's and Chaudhuri's articles, can you predict which professions in the health care industry will expand and which will contract? Why?

NAFTA, FDI, and Other Trade Issues

III

This section examines a number of specific trade issues, including the North American Free Trade Agreement (NAFTA), Foreign Direct Investment (FDI), and the impact of a weaker dollar on import prices. In "Trade in the Americas: From NAFTA to Bilateralism," Joanna Moss examines the development of NAFTA and its impact on the U.S. economy. On balance, most economists agree that NAFTA has benefited the U.S. economy, as well as those of Mexico and Canada. However, as with most trade agreements, the losers are far more visible and vocal than the winners, and the general perception among many Americans is that NAFTA was a mistake. President G. W. Bush pursued a different policy during his administration, focusing on bilateral agreements with a number of Latin American countries, such as Chile.

In "Does Foreign Direct Investment Help Emerging Economies?" Anil Kumar discusses the benefits of FDI for developing countries and compares FDI to other activities that contribute to a country's capital account. Kumar presents empirical evidence as well as an anecdotal discussion to bolster the case for FDI. Kumar believes that FDI is very beneficial to developing countries, encouraging stable flows of capital as well as flows of technology, know-how, and other benefits.

With the decline of the dollar, one important question for economists is the issue of "exchange rate pass through"—that is, if the dollar falls by 10 percent do import prices reflect this 10 percent fall, or do the companies or importers absorb some of the loss—implying that prices will not rise as much as the fall of the dollar would predict? In a perfectly competitive market, all prices would reflect the change in the dollar's value (e.g., most commodity prices directly reflect the fall of the dollar). However, many markets are far from perfectly competitive. For example, if the Euro rises 20 percent against the dollar, that does not imply that a BMW (made in Germany) will increase in price by 20 percent. Indeed, that is precisely what one generally observes. In "Have U.S. Import Prices Become Less Responsive to Changes in the Dollar?" Rebecca Hellerstein, Deirdre Daly, and Christina Marsh find that U.S. import prices are more responsive to exchange rate changes than other studies have suggested. They do find that competitive sectors are more sensitive to exchange rates, as economic theory would suggest.

9

Trade in the Americas
From NAFTA to Bilateralism

J O A N N A **M O S S**

Introduction

Over the past decade US international trade policy has taken a fork in the road away from the World Trade Organization's (WTO) multilateralism and towards bilateral and regional free trade agreements. While the US has never formally abandoned multilateralism, its pursuit of bilateral and regional freer trade and commercial relations is ongoing, worldwide and it includes developed and developing countries.[1] However, the momentum driving "competitive liberalization," the trend towards countries forming free trade agreements is not a US led phenomenon. The European Union has been spearheading these agreements for several decades.[2] Nevertheless, the US has been pursuing bilateral and regional free trade agreements with vigor for the past decade. Not surprisingly, the Western Hemisphere has received its due attention in this regard. This article will examine recent developments in US—Latin American trade arrangements and discuss some of the results of already existing agreements, such as NAFTA.

Types of Agreements Undertaken

US trade liberalization agreements generally encompass more than straight import-export goods and services trade. Most agreements also have trade related provisions such as treatment of foreign investment, customs procedures, and greater transparency in government and commercial regulations. Some agreements focus on investment alone. In fact the US has established bilateral investment treaties with over 40 countries since 1989.[3]

The US has developed several prototype trade arrangements whose provisions serve as frameworks repeated with each additional country. Some arrangements commit the participants to binding actions while others "promote" the establishment of freer trade and business friendly environments. The following are types of treaties and agreements that are negotiated by U.S. Trade Representative and approved by the United States Congress:

A Free Trade Agreement (FTA) lowers or eliminates tariffs and quotas on goods and services traded amongst signatory nations.

A Trade Promotion Agreement (TPA) is a free trade agreement which lowers or eliminates trade tariffs and quotas amongst signatory nations.[4]

A Bilateral Investment Treaty (BIT) obligates signatory governments to treat foreign investors fairly and offer legal protection equal to domestic investors. A BIT also encourages the adoption of market-oriented domestic policies that treat private investment in an open, transparent, and non-discriminatory way; and supports the development of international law standards consistent with these objectives.[5]

United States Free Trade Agreements
North & South America
Table 1

Free Trade Agreements in Force:	Country/Countries	Entered in Force On:
NAFTA: North American Free Trade Agreement	Canada, U.S., Mexico	1/1/1994
DR-CAFTA: Central America-Dominican Republic Free Trade Agreement	Costa Rica, the Dominican Republic, El Salvador, Guatemala, Honduras, Nicaragua and the U.S.	3/1/2007
Chile Free Trade Agreement	Chile	1/1/2004
Free Trade Agreements Awaiting Implementation:	**Country/Countries**	**Signed into law on:**
Peru Trade Promotion Agreement	Peru and the U.S.	12/14/2007
Free Trade Agreements Pending Congressional Approval:	**Country/Countries**	**Signed on:**
Colombia Free Trade Agreement	Colombia and the U.S.	11/22/2006
Panama Trade Promotion Agreement	Panama and the U.S.	6/28/2007

Source: Office of the United States Trade Representative
Source: http://www.ustr.gov/Trade_Agreements/Bilateral/Section_Index.html

A Trade and Investment Framework Agreement (**TIFA**) promotes the establishment of legal protections for investors, improves intellectual property protection, provides for more transparent and efficient customs procedures, and institutes greater transparency in government and commercial regulations. A TIFA may be bilateral or regional.

Regional versus Bilateral Trade Agreements. Regional Trade Agreements (**RTA**) are United States trade and investment agreements that include more than two signatory countries (e.g., the DR-CAFTA includes Costa Rica, the Dominican Republic, El Salvador, Guatemala, Honduras and Nicaragua as signatories with the United States). Bilateral agreements are United States trade and investment agreements between one nation and the United States (e.g., the Colombia FTA). Bilateral Free Trade Agreements (**BTA**) are between the US and one other signatory government.

US—Latin American Agreements

The US has forged two regional trade areas and four bilateral free trade agreements with Latin American countries since 1994. Table 1 below lists all of the agreements in force and those signed but not yet made into law.

The NAFTA Agreement

The North American Free Trade Agreement (NAFTA) went into force in 1994. It was closely modeled on the US-Canadian Free Trade Agreement (1989). However, NAFTA is by-far the most encompassing of the US sponsored agreements. It creates a free trade area for goods and services between the US, Mexico and Canada by the elimination of tariffs and non-tariff barriers, including the phase-out tariffs on textiles and apparel. Free trade in agricultural products will be phased-in by 2009. Automobile trade has been liberalized through the elimination of tariffs on autos and auto parts. A regional content requirement of 62.5% was established for autos to qualify for duty-free status.

Under NAFTA cross-boarder investment flows have been liberalized and there are no longer export performance requirements or local (national) content rules. Rules of Origin have been established for the NAFTA region. Products manufactured with materials or labor from outside North America qualify for NAFTA treatment only if they undergo substantial transformation within Canada, the US or Mexico. A case in point is the above mentioned automobile sector wherein 62.5% of the car's value must be added in the NAFTA region for the car to be exempt from duties. In addition, under NAFTA, there are clauses that call for the respect of intellectual property rights. NAFTA also has protocols on the environment and labor treatment. It contributes to regional trade and economic stability by locking in market reforms in Mexico. Finally, regional trade and investment rules are explicit in a single document, signed and ratified by all three participants.

The Central American Free Trade Agreement—Dominican Republic (CAFTA-DR)

The CAFTA-DR was passed by Congress in the summer of 2005. The CAFTA is the second RTA successfully negotiated by the US. It is closely modeled on the NAFTA agreement. The agreement breaks down most trade barriers between the United States and five nations of Central America (Costa Rica, El Salvador, Guatemala, Honduras and Nicaragua) plus the Caribbean country of the Dominican Republic. Over a period of 15–20 years, CAFTA will also reduce barriers to investment, open state-owned monopolies to foreign competition, eliminate most agricultural tariffs and deepen economic harmonization in the region. (Erikson, 2004–2005) Like NAFTA, the new agreement includes services in the free

trade arrangement and establishes strict rules of origin. Central American exports of sugar to the US are also severely restricted.

Bilateral Free Trade Agreements

The US-Chilean free trade agreement went into force in 2004. It bears a strong resemblance to the NAFTA agreement in including free trade in most goods and services. For example, upon entry into the agreement tariffs on 90% of U.S. exports to Chile and 95% of Chilean exports to the United States were eliminated. The agreement also has NAFTA-like provisions regarding cross-border investment flows, transparency in transactions, intellectual property rights, etc. The agreement also has a labor rights portion which upholds the 1998 ILO Declaration on Fundamental Principles and Rights at Work and an environmental section which sets out general environmental oversight guidelines and a regular review of environmental conditions.

The other bilateral trade agreements with Columbia (2006), Peru (2007), and Panama (2007) are all nearly the same as the US-Chilean agreement. Each seeks to foster free trade in goods and services, safety for investors, transparency in transactions for business, intellectual property rights, etc.

Free Trade Area of the Americas

The Free Trade Area of the Americas (FTAA) was launched by the Western Hemisphere countries at the Summit of the Americas in Miami in December 1994. The FTAA negotiations formally began in April of 1998 with a target date of completion of January 2005. (Schott, 2006). The commitment was renewed at the Quebec City Summit of the Americans in 2001. Although initially a U.S. initiative, the FTAA initially also had the support of Brazil. As the two economically most powerful countries in the hemisphere, their agreement was necessary for any hemisphere-wide trade arrangement. However, ensuing events stalled any progress. An economic downturn in the hemisphere cooled interest in further economic integration. Differences in the inclusion of agricultural reforms in the FTAA talks fueled by disputes in the WTO Doha round of negotiations created a deep divide between Brazil and the United States. The talks came to a halt in November 2003 and have been essentially moribund since that time. Agricultural market access to the US remains at the center of the problem as well as Brazil's hesitation to open its economy to US technology exports, fearing for its own nascent high tech sector. An US invitation to resume talks at the Summit of the Americas in November 2005 was rejected by the Mercosur members (Brazil, Argentina, Paraguay and Uraguay) and then-autonomous Venezuela rejected the agreement over concerns it would lead to increased inequality in the region (Guardian).

The aforementioned difficulties in completing the FTAA negotiations has shifted US policy initiatives towards bilateral and regional free trade agreements patterned on the NAFTA Agreement and the US-Chile FTA. This approach, called the "hub and spokes" model (Carranza, 2004), of dealing with single countries or smaller groupings gives the US an advantage in obtaining concessions due to its enormity compared to the smaller Latin American states. In such talks, the US is in a superior bargaining position and its smaller partners "have no chance to make common cause against it in areas of mutual, small-country interest" (Lipsey, 1992).

The Mercosur Common Market

The Mercosur group is South America's leading trading bloc made up of Argentina, Brazil, Paraguay, Uruguay and Venezuela. Known as the Common Market of the South, it aims to bring about the free movement of goods, capital, services and people among its member states. It has been likened to the European Union, but with a land mass four times as big as Europe's. The bloc's combined market encompasses more than 250m people and accounts for more than three-quarters of the economic activity on the continent (Carranza, 2004).

Mercosur was set up in March 1991 by Argentina, Brazil, Paraguay and Uruguay under the Treaty of Asuncion. The 1994 Treaty of Ouro Preto gave the body a wider international status and formalized a customs union. Its customs union provisions cause its members to maintain a common external tariff towards imports from the rest of the world, while having free trade within the union. In this aspect, Mercosur is different from a free trade agreement which takes away trade barriers between members, but does not have a common external barrier around the member countries.

Brazil and Argentina are Mercosur's economic giants, while Paraguay and Uruguay are the smaller countries. Venezuela, a leading oil and gas producer, became the fifth full member in July of 2006. Several countries have had associate member status such as Bolivia, Chile, Colombia, Ecuador and Peru meaning that they can join free-trade agreements but remain outside the bloc's customs union. Moves to include Chile as a full member were suspended after Santiago signed a free-trade deal with the US in 2002. Mercosur's charter does not allow its member nations to have FTAs with non-member nations. Thus Colombia and Peru are unlikely to be associate members as long as they have both signed free trade area agreements with the US. (http://news.bbc.co.uk/1/hi/world/americas/5195834.stm)

As noted above, Mercosur played a role in the failure of the FTAA. Mercosur's blockage of the FTAA signals its general disinterest in trade with the United States. Mercosur's interest in trade with the European Union is quite another story. The EU is Mercosur's most important trading partner, responsible for buying 23% of their exports. There is even evidence that the European business cycle has a slightly stronger influence upon most

Latin American economies than the influence of the US business cycle (Bezmen and Slover, 2005).

Since 2004 the EU and the Mercosur group have engaged in two rounds of negotiations aimed at creating a greater economic arrangement, such as a joined common market. However, the EU has refused to alter its protectionist agricultural policies and allow farm imports from Mercosur countries. The courtship has been further complicated by Venezuela's entry into Mercosur, whereby the threat of nationalizations of private firms has cooled the EU's interest. Currently, Mercosur—EU talks are on hold. (http://www.coha.org/2004/07/06/eu-mercosur-free-trade-us-a-third-wheel/)

Recent Developments in US Latin American Trade

This section looks at some of the major developments and issues surrounding the US regional and bilateral agreements with Latin America.

NAFTA

There is no doubt that the NAFTA agreement has expanded economic interchange between the US and Mexico over the past fourteen years. Some of the highlights of this expansion are in the trade and investment areas. During the entire tenure of the NAFTA agreement Mexican exports to the US have grown rapidly, increasing 8.5% annually in the last five years alone as shown in Tables 2 and 3. The US purchases about 85% of Mexican exports. Mexican imports from the US, on the other hand have increased at a lackluster 2.8% over the same period. The US has consistently run a trade deficit with Mexico and in 2006 provided about 51% of Mexican imports whereas 5 years earlier the US provided 66% of Mexican imports. The performance of the past 5 years has particular significance as the US has been inundated with labor-intensive cheap imports of all kinds from China; yet despite this competition,

Mexico has managed to significantly expand its exports to the US.

While the overall performance of US exports to Mexico has been disappointing, certain regions and individual regions such as the SouthEast as well as Alabama and Mississippi have benefited considerably from NAFTA exports in the form not only of increased export earnings, but also increased employment (Merkel and Lovik, 2006, Coughlin, 2004).

Encouraged by NAFTA's market access provisions, direct foreign investment in Mexico by US firms has continued, unabated since NAFTA's inception. Thirty-three of the 50 largest firms operating in Mexico are American (Shahabuddin, 2003). While it is possible that the US could renege on the agreement, the market access provisions of the NAFTA agreement appear not only to expand trade, but to serve as a sort of "insurance policy" for investors. As Schott points out, "lenders/investors usually require it as collateral for their placements." In this context, the insurance policy provides greater confidence in the "lock in" effect of the FTA on domestic policies, which can propel investment if the overall policy mix is right" (Schott, 2006, p.128).

Critics of NAFTA point out that Mexican trade with the US was expanding rapidly before NAFTA's inception. Further, they cite Mexico's thirst for imports as export earnings rise, its expanding marginal propensity, as being problematic by siphoning off monies for consumption that could be going into domestic savings, capital formation and foster[ing] growth (Pacheco-Lopez, 2005)

US-Latin American Bilateral Trade Agreements

Currently, Chile, Colombia, Panama and Peru have Free Trade (or Trade Promotion) agreements with the US. Chile's agreement has been operational since 2004, whereas the others all began in 2006 or 2007. Hence, Chile is the only Latin American country with some information to report.

In its short life the US-Chilean free trade agreement is off to a good start. According to the US Trade Representative, bilateral trade between the United States and Chile has more than doubled since the agreement went into force in 2004. Chilean exports to the US have increased 158% between 2003 and 2006. US exports to Chile have also increased markedly and the US is now Chile's largest export market and its largest supplier of imports. This rosy report needs to be tempered by the fact that no account has been taken of the current high prices of Chilean copper or U.S. oil.

Inflation notwithstanding, continued expanded trade and commerce is expected. Chile's rule of law, relative lack of corruption and likely adherence to the trade deal all work in its favor. Federal Reserve economists note the fact that "intellectual property and other legal accords that are part of the new trade agreement will clearly have positive effects on some aspects not only of foreign direct investment but also of portfolio investment"(Gruben and Kiser January/February 2003).

Central American Free Trade Area–Dominican Republic

The negotiation process creating CAFTA lasted only one year. All parties agreed to eliminate most tariffs and nontariff barriers immediately, while quotas would be phased out (Federal Reserve Bank of Atlanta, *EconSouth*, 2004). Over a period of 15–20 years, CAFTA will reduce barriers to investment, open state-owned monopolies to foreign competition, eliminate most agricultural tariffs, and deepen harmonization between the nations in the region (Erikson, 2004/05).

The Central American Free Trade Area was passed in Congress by a razor-thin majority in 2005 and it went into force in 2007. The agreement includes Costa Rica, El Salvador, Guatemala, Honduras, and Nicaragua as well as one Caribbean nation, the Dominican Republic. Congressional approval of the CAFTA-DR pact was a highly contentious issue.

US labor groups vehemently opposed the agreement arguing that it would cost US jobs and that workers' rights in Central America would be trod upon. The textile industry was split between those who see continued cheap imports from Central America as a threat, and those who stood to benefit from further formalization of rules which allow American textiles to be assembled in Central America and sent back duty-free. Currently, yarns and fabrics manufactured in the United States are assembled into garments, many at offshore US firms, and brought back into the US duty-free. This process has been going on, allowing the clothes to be imported duty free since the Caribbean Basin Initiative (giving duty-free access) was renewed in 2000. With passage of CAFTA these rules are broadened and made permanent, hopefully stimulating new American investment in the region (Nash, 2005).

The agreement means some serious compromises for CAFTA countries. On the one hand permanent market access to the US market, especially in textiles, has a special importance for them, especially given the onslaught of cheap Chinese textiles due to the lifting of the Multifiber Agreement in 2005. On the other hand, the lifting of duties and quotas on agricultural imports will mean waves of cheap US foodstuffs which are likely to undersell local farmers and force them off their farms, a potential repeat of the plight of corn producers in Mexico. Critics charge that without more effective social safety nets, an unfair hardship is forced on the agricultural sector, while supporters say that this process is inevitable (Erikson, 2004/05).

The Central American decision to enter CAFTA is no doubt in large part due to the economic importance of the US economy to the region. Central American exports to the US trade have grown over the past five years as a percent of their total exports, increasing from 35.6% to 43.1% of their total world exports. Central American imports from the US have remained steady at about 35% over the past five years. For some countries the US is a virtual life line of export earnings. In 2006 the US bought 70% of Honduran exports and 65% of Nicaraguan exports.

US Trade with South America

The US has been losing ground in South American trade. Expanding trade relations with the EC and with China have hurt the US trade presence in the area. . . . [T]he US has been buying about a quarter of the southern continent's exports for the past five years but in terms of the region's imports the US share has been falling. The US provided 23% of South America's imported goods in 2001 and the share fell every year to 18.2% in 2006.

Conclusion

The US drive to form regional trade entities can be seen as a way to continue the process of market opening where the multilateral effort stalled. This policy focus by the US is likely to continue, absent a reversal of fortune of the Doha Round.

The author wishes to acknowledge Anne R. Wenzel and Ellen Starkman for their valuable research contributions.

Endnotes

1 US efforts to establish bilateral trade agreements have been most active in Latin America, the Asia-Pacific region and the Middle East and North Africa; see USTR.gov.

2 Almost all WTO members participate in one or more of the nearly 300 separate free trade agreements in effect or under negotiation. European countries are involved in one quarter of all agreements while the US has signed on to only 4% of the total (Schott 2004).

3 Source: http://tcc.export.gov/Trade_Agreements/ Bilateral_Investment_Treaties/index.asp.

4 Gretchen Hamel, Deputy Assistant USTR for Public and Media Affairs, phone: 202 395 3230, confirmed on 3/25/2008 that there is no difference between a trade promotion agreement (TPA) and a free trade agreement (FTA).

5 See, "Summary of U.S. Bilateral Investment Treaty (BIT) Program," 2/24/2006, http://www. ustr.gov/Trade_Agreements/BIT/Su-mmary_of_ US_Bilateral_Investment_Treaty_(BIT)_Program. html.

References

Ahrens, Edgar, and Hurtado, Mauricio. 2004. "NAFTA's implications for transfer pricing in Mexico." *International Tax Review.* North America, Jul 2004, pp. 9–13.

Anderson, Sarah. 2003. "The Equity Factor and Free Trade." *World Policy Journal;* Vol. 20, Issue 3, Fall 2003, pp. 45–51.

Anderson, Greg. 2006. "Can Someone Please Settle This Dispute? Canadian Softwood Lumber and the Dispute Settlement Mechanisms of the NAFTA and the WTO." *World Economy,* Vol. 29, Issue 5, May 2006, pp. 585–610.

Baier, Scott L., and Bergstrand, Jeffrey H. 2005. "Do Free Trade Agreements Actually Increase Member's International Trade." Federal Reserve Bank of Atlanta, *Working Paper Series,* Working Paper 2005-3, Feb 2005. www.frbatlanta.org.

Bezmen, Trisha L, and Selover, David D. 2005. "Patterns of Economic Interdependence in Latin America." *International Trade Journal,* Vol. 19, Issue 3, Fall 2005, pp. 217–267.

Bianchi, Eduardo, and Sanguinetti, Pablo. 2006 "Trade Liberalization, Macroeconomic Fluctuations, and Contingent Protection in Latin America." *Economia,* Vol. 6, Issue 2, Spring 2006, pp. 147–183.

Brown, Drusilla K., Kiyota, Kozo, and Stern, Robert M. 2005. "Computational Analysis of the US FTAs with Central America, Australia and Morocco." *World Economy,* Vol. 28, Issue 10, Oct. 2005, pp. 1441–1490.

Carranza, Mario E. *kfinec02@tamuk.edu* 2004. "Mercosur and the End Game of the FTAA Negotiations: Challenges and Prospects After the Argentine Crisis." *Third World Quarterly,* Vol. 25 Issue 2, Mar. 2004, pp. 319–337.

Casal, Elena. "Understanding CAFTA: Perspectives From All Sides." Federal Reserve Bank of Atlanta. *EconSouth.* v. 6, no. 2. Q2, 2004. www.frbatlanta.org.

Chase, Kerry A. 2003. "Economic Interests and Regional Trading Arrangements: The Case of NAFTA." *International Organization.,* Vol. 57, Issue 1, Winter2003, pp. 137–174.

Chozick, Amy and Nick Timiraos. 2008. "Democratic Rivals Hear Ohio's Ills, Set Out Plans for Mortgages, Jobs; Clinton Focuses on Housing, Obama on Nafta in a State Hit Hard in Recent Years." Wall Street Journal. (Eastern Edition). New York, N.Y.:Feb 25, 2008. p. A3. www.proquest.com, San Francisco Public Library, Mar 11, 2008.

Cornejo, Rafael, Granados, Jaime. 2006. "Convergence in the Americas: Some Lessons from the DR-CAFTA Process." World Economy; Vol. 29, Issue 7, Jul. 2006, pp. 857–891.

Coughlin, Cletus C. 2004. "The Increasing Importance of Proximity for Exports from U.S. States." Federal Reserve Bank of St Louis Review, 86(6), Nov/Dec 2004, pp. 1–18. www.stlouisfed.org.

Coughlin, Cletus C. coughlin@stls.frb.org, and Wall, Howard J. wall@stls.frb.org. 2003. "NAFTA and the changing pattern of state exports." Papers in Regional Science, Vol. 82, Issue 4, 2003, pp. 427–450.

Council on Hemispheric Affairs. 2007. "Mercosur: South America's Fractious Trade Bloc." October 25, 2007. http://www.coha.org/2007/10/25/mercosur-south-america%e2%80%99s-fractious-trade-bloc/.

Dickerson, Marla. 2008. "The Nation; NAFTA has had its trade-offs for the U.S.; Consumers and global companies benefited, but critics see pitfalls." Los Angeles Times. Los Angeles, Calif.:Mar 3, 2008. p. A1. www. proquest.com, San Francisco Public Library, Mar 11, 2008.

Duina, Francesco fduina@bates.edu. 2004. "Regional market building as a social process: an analysis of cognitive strategies in NAFTA, the European Union and Mercosur." Economy & Society, Vol. 33, Issue 3, Aug 2004, pp. 359–389.

Durán, Clemente Ruiz. 2003. "NAFTA." International Journal of Political Economy, Vol. 33, Issue 3, Fall 2003, pp. 50–71.

Erikson, Daniel P. 2004/2005. "Central America's Free Trade Gamble." World Policy Journal, Vol. 21, Issue 4, Winter 2004/2005, pp. 19–28.

"Ethanol and Sugar: Consumers Get Squeezed." 2008. Wall Street Journal. (Eastern Edition). New York, N.Y. Feb 2, 2008. p. A9. www. proquest.com, San Francisco Public Library, Mar 11, 2008.

Farrell, Diana, and Puron, Antonio, and Remes, Jaana K. 2005. "Beyond cheap labor: Lessons for developing economies." McKinsey Quarterly. Issue 1, 2005, pp. 98–109.

Funk, Mark, Erick Elder, Vincent Yao, and Ashvin Vibhakar. 2006. "Intra-NAFTA Trade and Surface Traffic: A Very Disaggregated View." Federal Reserve Bank of St Louis, Regional Economic Development, 2(2), 2006, pp. 87–99. www.stlouisfed.org.

Gamper–Rabindran, Shanti. 2006. "NAFTA and the Environment: What Can the Data Tell Us?" Economic Development & Cultural Change, Vol. 54, Issue 3, Apr. 2006, pp. 605–633.

Grayson, Michael M. Michael.M.Grayson@jsums.edu, and Nica, Mihai Mihai.P.Nica@jsums.edu, and Swaidan, Ziad Swaidanz@uhv.edu. 2006. "The Impact of NAFTA on the Mexican-American Trade." International Journal of Commerce & Management, Vol. 16, Issue 3/4, 2006, pp. 222–233.

Gruben, William C. 2005. "Domestic Policy No Match For Trade Stance of Central American Countries." Federal Reserve Bank of Dallas, Southwest Economy, March/April 2005, www.dallasfed.org.

Gruben, William C. and Sherry L. Kiser. 2003. "Beyond the Border Chilean Accord Extends U.S. Free Trade Universe by One, Federal Reserve Bank of Dallas, Southwest Economy, Issue 1, January/February 2003. www.dallasfed.org.

Kehoe, Timothy J. 2003. "An Evaluation of Performance of Applied General Equilibrium Models of the Impact of NAFTA," Federal Reserve Bank of Minneapolis, Research Department Staff Report 320, Aug 2003. www.minneapolisfed.org.

Kovach, Gretel C. 2007. "For Mexican Trucks, a Road Into the U.S." New York Times. (Late Edition (east Coast)). New York, N.Y., Sep 9, 2007. p. 1.32.

www. proquest.com, San Francisco Public Library, Mar 11, 2008.

Lehmann, Christian. 2007. *"COHA Report: The EU and Mercosur—Can the EU Get its Foot in the Door of Mercosur, Latin America's Most Dominant Market? Council on Hemispheric Affairs April 27, 2007. http://www.coha.org/2007/04/27/coha-report-the-eu-and-mercosur-can-the-eu-get-its-foot-in-the-door-of-mercosur-latin-america%e2%80%99s-most-dominant-market/.*

Leonhardt, David. 2008. "The Politics Of Trade In Ohio." *New York Times.* (Late Edition (east Coast)). New York, N.Y., Feb 27, 2008. p. C1. www. proquest.com, San Francisco Public Library, Mar 11, 2008.

Lipsey, R.G. 1992. "Getting there: the path to a western hemisphere free trade area and its structure," S. Saborio (ed.), *The Premise and the Promise: Free Trade in the Americas,* pp 95–116 (New Brunswick, NY: Transaction Publishers).

López-Córdova, Ernesto. 2005. "Globalization, Migration, and Development: The Role of Mexican Migrant Remittances." *Economia.,* Vol. 6, Issue 1, Fall 2005, pp. 217–256.

Lovik, Lawrence W. and Merkel, Edward T. 2006. "The Economic Impact of NAFTA: A Case Study of Alabama." *International Advances in Economic Research,* Vol. 12, Issue 3, Aug 2006, pp. 422–422.

Lozada, Carlos. 2003. "Latin America.." *Foreign Policy,* Issue 135, Mar/Apr2003, pp. 18–22.

Monaghan, Henry Paul. 2007. "Article III and Supranational Judicial Review." Columbia Law Review, Vol. 107, Issue 4, May 2007, pp. 833–882.

Mooney, Kevin. "Trade More with South America to Counter Chavez, Experts Say." http://www.crosswalk.com/news/11556592/.

Moreno-Brid, Juan Carlos *juancarlos.moreno@cepal.org,* Rivas Valdivia, Juan Carlos *juancarlos.rivas@cepal.org,* and Santamaría, Jesús *jsantama99@yahoo.com.* 2005. "Industrialization and Economic Growth in Mexico after NAFTA:

The Road Travelled." *Development & Change,* Vol. 36, Issue 6, Nov 2005, pp. 1095–1119.

Nash, Betty Joyce. 2007. "CAFTA to Have Mixed Effects on Region's Firms," Federal Reserve Bank of Richmond, *Region Focus,* Policy Update, Fall 2007. ww.richmondfed.org.

"Obama's Border Incident." *Wall Street Journal.* (Eastern Edition). New York, N.Y., Mar 4, 2008. p. A16. www. proquest.com, San Francisco Public Library, Mar 11, 2008.

Ocampo, Jose Antonio. 2004. "Latin America's Growth and Equity Frustrations During Structural Reforms." *Journal of Economic Perspectives;* Vol. 18, Issue 2, Spring 2004, p 67–88.

O'Grady, Mary Anastasia. 2007. "Americas: Mexican Truck Stop." *Wall Street Journal.* (Eastern Edition). New York, N.Y., Nov 26, 2007. p. A20. www. proquest.com, San Francisco Public Library, Mar 11, 2008.

Pacheco-López, Penelope. 2005. "The effect of trade liberalization on exports, imports, the balance of trade, and growth: the case of Mexico." *Journal of Post Keynesian Economics,* Vol. 27, Issue 4, Summer 2005, pp. 595–619.

Paus, Eva *epaus@mtholyoke.edu,* Reinhardt, Nola, Robinson, Michael. 2003. "Trade Liberalization and Productivity Growth in Latin American Manufacturing, 1970–98." *Journal of Policy Reform;* 2003, Vol. 6, Issue 1, 2003, pp 1–15.

Philippidis, George *gphilippidis@aragob.es.* 2004. "Membership of NAFTA: A Viable Alternative for UK Agro-Food Producers?" *Economic Issues.* Vol. 9, Issue 2, Sep 2004, pp. 21–41.

Phillips, Nicola. 2005. "U.S. Power and the Politics of Economic Governance in the Americas." *Latin American Politics & Society,* Vol. 47, Issue 4, Winter 2005, pp. 1–25.

Poole, William. 2005. "Despite Flaws, CAFTA is Step in Right Direction," President's Message, Federal Reserve Bank of St Louis, *The Regional Economist,* October 2005. www.stlouisfed.org.

"Profile: Mercosur-Common Market of the South." 2008. BBC News. Jan 27, 2008. http://news.bbc.co.uk/1/hi/world/americas/5195834.stm

Puyana, Alicia. 2006. "Mexican Oil Policy and Energy Security Within NAFTA." *International Journal of Political Economy,* Vol. 35, Issue 2, Summer 2006, pp. 72–97.

Quartner, David. 2006. "Public Choice Theory, Protectionism and the case of NAFTA." *Economic Affairs,* Vol. 26, Issue 1, Mar 2006, pp. 59–60.

Reis, Anabela. 2007. "Mercosur, EU to Restart Free-Trade Talks in May, Estado Reports." Bloomberg, 18, Dec 18, 2007.

Reubens, Edwin. 2003. "Free Trade, or Countervailing Power for the Americas." *Challenge.,* Vol. 46, Issue 4, Jul/Aug 2003, pp. 54.

Schott, Jeffrey. 2006. "Free Trade Agreements and US Trade Policy: A Comparative Analysis of US Initiatives in Latin America, the Asia-Pacific Region, and the Middle East and North Africa." *International Trade Journal,* Vol. 20, Issue 2, Summer 2006, pp. 95–138.

Schott, Jeffry, 2004. *Free Trade Agreements, US Strategies and Priorities,* Institute for International Economics, Washington, D.C.

Shahabuddin, Syed. 2003. "NAFTA: Does it have any Effect on the U.S.A. Economy?" *International Journal of Management;* Vol. 20, Issue 3, Sep 2003, pp. 306–15.

Singer, Matt. 2004. "EU-Mercosur Free Trade: U.S., a Third Wheel?" Council on Hemispheric Affairs. July 6, 2004. http://www.coha.org/2004/07/06/eu-mercosur-free-trade-us-a-third-wheel/

Solomon, Deborah and Greg Hitt. 2007. "A Globalization Winner Joins in Trade Backlash; Exports Boost Iowa, But Workers Still Fret; Campaigns Take Note." *Wall Street Journal.* (Eastern Edition). New York, N.Y., Nov 21, 2007. p. A1.

www. proquest.com, San Francisco Public Library, Mar 11, 2008.

"Sweet and Sour." 2008. *Wall Street Journal.* (Eastern Edition). New York, N.Y. Jan 22, 2008. p. A.18. www. proquest.com, San Francisco Public Library, Mar 11, 2008.

"Texas v. Ohio." 2008. *Wall Street Journal.* (Eastern Edition). New York, N.Y.: Mar 3, 2008. p. A.16. www. proquest.com, San Francisco Public Library, Mar 11, 2008.

Thomson, Adam. 2008. "Mexicans riled by 'ridiculous' threats to ditch trade accord." *Financial Times.* London (UK). USA 2ND EDITION. Mar 4, 2008. p. 4. www. proquest.com, San Francisco Public Library, Mar 11, 2008.

Tobar, Hector. "THE WORLD; Mexican farmers protest NAFTA; The last tariffs on U.S. produce end, raising fears of a glut of cheap corn and beans wiping out local agriculture." *Los Angeles Times.* Los Angeles, Calif., Jan 3, 2008. p. A3. www. proquest.com, San Francisco Public Library, Mar 11, 2008.

Toledo, Hugo. 2004. "Free Trade and Income Redistribution in Columbia." *International Trade Journal,* Vol. 18, Issue 2, Summer 2004, pp. 127–146

Trujillo, Manuel. 2007. "Peru, Yes; Colombia? Free Trade Agreements: Lessons from Latin America's Recent Past." Council on Hemispheric Affairs. December 6th, 2007. http://www.coha.org/2007/12/06/peru-yes-colombia-free-trade-agreements-lessons-from-latin-america%e2%80% 99s-recent-past/

Uchitelle, Louis. 2007. "Nafta Should Have Stopped Illegal Immigration, Right? *New York Times.* (Late Edition (east Coast)). New York, N.Y., Feb 18, 2007. p. 4.4. www. proquest.com, San Francisco Public Library, Mar 11, 2008.

Wall, Howard J. "NAFTA and the Geography of North American Trade" Federal Reserve Bank of St Louis, *Review,* March/April 2003. www.stlouisfed.org.

Latin American Exports to the United States, by Country
(millions of dollars)
Table 2

Exports from:	2001	Percent of World Total	2002	Percent of World Total	2003	Percent of World Total	2004	Percent of World Total	2005	Percent of World Total	2006	Percent of World Total
Mexico	$140,564	88.5%	$141,898	88.0%	$144,293	87.5%	$164,522	87.6%	$183,563	85.7%	$211,871	84.7%
Central America												
Belize	$ 93	37.4%	$ 76	38.7%	$ 97	34.6%	$ 103	34.5%	$ 95	31.3%	$ 142	33.9%
Costa Rica	814	16.3%	807	15.3%	3,013	49.4%	2,957	46.9%	2,991	42.6%	3,713	27.5%
El Salvador	1,878	65.6%	2,010	67.1%	2,117	67.7%	2,169	65.7%	2,067	61.0%	1,745	49.5%
Guatemala	645	26.7%	2,225	53.5%	2,392	53.7%	2,669	53.0%	2,694	50.1%	3,024	44.6%
Honduras	617	54.8%	587	49.9%	657	49.6%	927	54.4%	3,563	73.3%	3,539	70.6%
Nicaragua	202	34.3%	221	39.4%	217	35.9%	283	37.4%	292	34.1%	1,437	65.2%
Panama	402	48.6%	361	47.5%	414	52.1%	445	49.9%	433	44.9%	407	39.8%
Total	$ 4,652	35.6%	$ 6,288	41.6%	$ 8,908	53.4%	$ 9,552	52.2%	$ 12,136	53.3%	$ 14,006	43.1%
South America												
Argentina	$ 2,884	10.9%	$ 2,957	11.5%	$ 3,134	10.6%	$ 3,818	11.0%	$ 4,572	11.3%	$ 4,116	8.9%
Bolivia	188	13.9%	192	14.0%	237	14.1%	359	15.9%	280	12.5%	343	10.8%
Brazil	14,379	24.4%	15,535	25.7%	16,901	22.9%	20,342	20.8%	22,742	19.2%	24,680	17.8%
Chile	3,428	18.5%	3,484	19.1%	3,468	16.2%	4,568	14.0%	6,248	15.8%	8,940	15.6%
Colombia	5,345	43.4%	5,343	44.2%	6,143	46.8%	7,056	42.0%	8,852	41.8%	8,933	35.8%
Ecuador	1,790	38.2%	2,087	41.4%	2,531	40.7%	3,298	42.5%	5,050	50.0%	6,825	53.6%
Guyana	146	25.4%	122	22.4%	124	21.4%	126	19.4%	121	18.9%	128	18.8%
Paraguay	29	3.0%	38	4.0%	45	3.6%	55	3.4%	55	3.3%	67	3.5%
Peru	1,773	25.5%	2,005	26.2%	2,397	27.1%	3,682	29.5%	5,393	31.2%	5,722	24.1%
Suriname	135	27.1%	127	26.7%	134	23.0%	134	15.2%	156	16.4%	156	12.6%
Uruguay	177	8.6%	185	8.5%	251	11.4%	601	20.5%	789	23.2%	498	12.1%
Venezuela	12,849	47.7%	12,024	45.1%	11,635	42.8%	16,946	42.7%	26,975	48.6%	34,897	46.2%
Total	$ 43,123	26.9%	$ 44,099	27.3%	$ 46,998	25.2%	$ 60,985	24.4%	$ 81,232	26.1%	$ 95,304	24.4%

Source: Direction of Trade Statistics, International Monetary Fund.

Latin American Import from the United States, by Country
(millions of dollars)
Table 3

Imported by:	2001	Percent of World Total	2002	Percent of World Total	2003	Percent of World Total	2004	Percent of World Total	2005	Percent of World Total	2006	Percent of World Total
Mexico	$ 125,143	66.1%	$ 117,212	61.3%	$ 115,897	60.6%	$ 121,909	55.1%	$130,402	53.4%	$ 143,421	50.9%
Central America												
Belize	$ 190	39.3%	$ 151	31.6%	$ 219	39.9%	$ 167	30.3%	$ 238	31.1%	$ 263	35.7%
Costa Rica	1,506	22.9%	1,595	22.2%	3,917	51.1%	3,813	46.1%	4,051	41.3%	4,546	41.2%
El Salvador	2,485	49.4%	2,591	50.0%	2,873	49.9%	2,971	46.9%	2,934	43.4%	2,372	32.2%
Guatemala	1,970	35.1%	3,274	42.8%	3,376	41.5%	3,219	34.0%	4,001	38.1%	3,870	33.2%
Honduras	1,337	45.2%	1,199	40.7%	1,331	40.1%	1,494	37.5%	3,568	53.6%	4,063	53.0%
Nicaragua	494	27.8%	476	27.2%	464	24.7%	490	22.4%	522	20.1%	831	20.1%
Panama	986	29.5%	1,043	34.3%	1,096	40.1%	1,049	29.2%	1,142	27.5%	1,306	27.0%
Total	$ 8,967	34.8%	$ 10,330	36.6%	$ 13,277	44.2%	$ 13,202	38.4%	$ 16,458	39.9%	$ 17,250	36.4%
South America												
Argentina	$ 3,781	18.6%	$ 1,804	20.1%	$ 2,264	16.4%	$ 3,432	15.3%	$ 4,046	14.1%	$ 4,294	12.6%
Bolivia	314	18.4%	310	16.9%	310	18.3%	261	13.8%	324	13.8%	237	9.1%
Brazil	14,342	23.3%	11,482	22.1%	10,699	20.1%	12,671	18.3%	14,138	17.5%	16,342	16.2%
Chile	2,867	16.1%	2,528	14.9%	2,525	13.0%	3,402	13.7%	4,722	14.6%	5,593	15.6%
Colombia	4,443	34.7%	4,032	31.8%	4,261	30.1%	5,113	30.0%	6,033	28.5%	7,379	26.8%
Ecuador	1,229	24.9%	1,376	23.1%	1,324	21.7%	1,527	21.0%	1,922	20.1%	2,597	23.1%
Guyana	155	21.9%	141	25.1%	129	22.1%	149	24.5%	193	26.7%	197	21.3%
Paraguay	130	6.0%	85	5.1%	79	3.8%	119	4.1%	190	5.3%	372	6.4%
Peru	1,886	23.8%	2,198	27.0%	2,585	28.6%	3,252	30.3%	2,370	17.9%	2,690	16.5%
Suriname	174	26.2%	137	23.1%	212	31.1%	196	26.1%	268	29.2%	284	29.4%
Uruguay	274	9.0%	230	8.8%	167	7.6%	224	7.2%	261	6.7%	531	8.2%
Venezuela	5,689	28.8%	3,909	29.2%	2,767	25.9%	4,986	28.8%	6,894	31.5%	9,351	30.6%
Total	$ 35,284	23.0%	$ 28,233	22.5%	$ 27,323	20.4%	$ 35,333	19.8%	$41,362	18.9%	$ 49,867	18.2%

Source: Direction of Trade Statistics, International Monetary Fund.

Does Foreign Direct Investment Help Emerging Economies?

ANIL KUMAR

The gap between the world's rich and poor countries largely comes down to the financial and physical assets that create wealth. Developed economies possess more of this capital than developing ones, and what they have usually incorporates more advanced technologies. The implication is clear: A key aspect of economic advancement lies in poorer nations' capacity to acquire more capital and scale the technological ladder. Emerging economies undertake some capital formation on their own, but in this era of globalization, they increasingly rely on foreign capital.

Indeed, total capital flows to developing economies have skyrocketed from $104 billion in 1980 to $472 billion in 2005.[1] The foreign capital has the potential to deliver enormous benefits to developing nations. Besides helping bridge the gap between savings and investment in capital-scarce economies, capital often brings with it modern technology and encourages development of more mature financial sectors. Capital flows have proven effective in promoting growth and productivity in countries that have enough skilled workers and infrastructure. Some economists believe capital flows also help discipline governments' macroeconomic policies (see box titled *"Does Financial Globalization Shape Fiscal Policy?"*).

Capital flows come in three primary forms:

• Portfolio equity investment, which involves buying company shares, usually through stock markets, without gaining effective control.

• Portfolio debt investment, which typically covers bonds and short- and long-term borrowing from banks and multilateral institutions, such as the World Bank.

• Foreign direct investment (FDI), which involves forging long-term relationships with enterprises in foreign countries.

FDI can be made in several ways. First, and most likely, it may involve parent enterprises injecting equity capital by purchasing shares in foreign affiliates. Second, it may take the form of reinvesting the affiliate's earnings. Third, it may entail short- or long-term lending between parents and affiliates. To be categorized as a multinational enterprise for inclusion in FDI data, the parent must hold a minimum equity stake of 10 percent in the affiliate.

Establishing foreign affiliates usually entails starting new production facilities—so-called greenfield investments—or acquiring control of existing entities through cross-border mergers and acquisitions. Recent years have seen a marked shift toward international mergers and acquisitions.

In developing nations, equity investments as a percentage of gross national income have been flat in recent years. Debt flows, however, have picked up since 2002 after plunging to zero in the previous two years. Meanwhile, FDI as a share of GDP has grown rapidly, becoming the largest source of capital moving from developed nations to developing ones *(Chart 1)*.

From 1990 to 2005, developing economies' share of total FDI inflows rose from 18 percent to 36 percent. In addition, the geographical composition of FDI flows has changed dramatically over the past four decades. Within developing economies, Latin America's share of FDI has fallen from 52 percent in the 1970s to 33 percent since the 1990s. Asia's share of inflows has risen from 25 percent to 60 percent during the same period.

Within Asia, China and India have gained FDI share relative to Southeast Asia. Today, these two emerging economic giants are the most attractive markets for FDI. China's FDI shot up from $3.5 billion in 1990 to $60 billion in 2004, while India's rose from a paltry $236 million to $5.3 billion. The shift reflects the two nations' more open economic policies, as well as their sheer size and dynamic growth.

The rush to invest in places like China and India suggests that FDI will continue to be an increasingly important source of development finance. To better understand these capital inflows and their ripples, we need to examine their effect on key aspects of the receiving countries' economic performance—stability, trade, savings, investment and growth.

Does Financial Globalization Shape Fiscal Policy?

Reckless macroeconomic policies that include large fiscal deficits and excessive borrowing can trigger a vicious cycle of speculative capital outflows and higher interest rates, with dire consequences for a developing economy.[1] Facing a crisis of confidence, governments may raise interest rates to keep foreign investors from leaving, and higher borrowing costs may tip the economy into recession.

Because policymakers would want to avoid that outcome, fear of large-scale reversals of international capital flows could have a disciplining effect. Governments may, for example, seek to lessen the risk of capital flight by curbing fiscal deficits.[2]

If we look at financial globalization, as measured by the ratio of foreign assets and liabilities to GDP, we see that it seems to coincide with rising fiscal deficits in 19 emerging economies over 15 years from 1990 to 2004 *(Chart A)*.

The correlation, however, could be misleading if it doesn't account for country-specific factors that may be associated with both capital inflows and budget deficits—for example, inflation and economic growth. Moreover, the relationship would look exactly the same if budget deficits were driving financial globalization.

If we account for these factors, we find a negative correlation between financial globalization and the fiscal deficit *(Chart B)*. Although the list of other factors isn't exhaustive, the data suggest that financial globalization through larger capital flows helps discipline fiscal policies in host countries.

Notes

[1] For more on financial globalization and fiscal policy, see "The Global Capital Market: Benefactor or Menace?" by Maurice *Obsfeld, Journal of Economic Perspectives,* vol. 12, Fall 1998, pp. 9–30, and "Does Financial Globalization Induce Better Macroeconomic Policies?" by Irina Tytell and Shang-Jin Wei, International Monetary Fund, Working Paper no. 04/84, May 2004.

[2] Globalization may also help shape monetary policy with consequences for inflation. For a discussion, see "Openness and Inflation," by Mark A. Wynne and Erasmus K. Kersting, Federal Reserve Bank of *Dallas Staff Papers,* forthcoming.

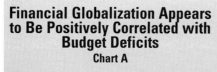

Financial Globalization Appears to Be Positively Correlated with Budget Deficits
Chart A

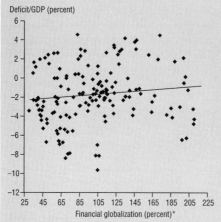

Deficit/GDP (percent)

Financial globalization (percent)*

*Total foreign assets and liabilities as a percentage of GDP.

Sources: Lane and Milesi-Ferretti (2006); World Bank WDI Online database; author's calculations.

After Netting Out Other Factors, Financial Globalization Lowers Deficit
Chart B

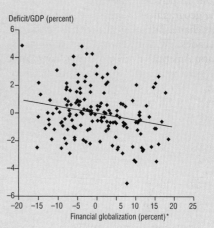

Deficit/GDP (percent)

Financial globalization (percent)*

*Total foreign assets and liabilities as a percentage of GDP, after eliminating other factors for both variables. The result is significant at the 1 percent level.

Sources: Lane and Milesi-Ferretti (2006); World Bank WDI Online database; author's calculations.

FDI Dominates Developing Economies' Capital Flows
Chart 1

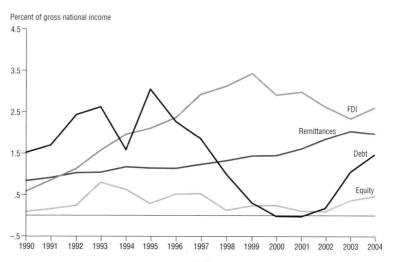

Percent of gross national income

FDI
Remittances
Debt
Equity

Sources: World Bank GDF Online database; author's calculations.

FDI More Stable than Equity and Short-Term Debt
Chart 2

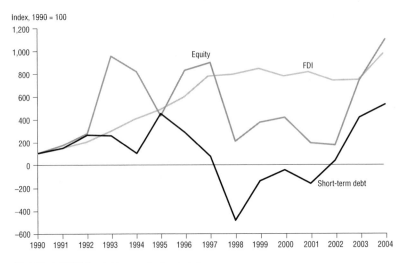

Source: World Bank GDF Online database; author's calculations.

FDI's Stability

For emerging economies, FDI has significant advantages over equity and debt capital flows. Foreign firms' participation in domestic business encourages the transfer of advanced technologies to the host country, and it fosters human capital development by providing employee training. It also strengthens corporate institutions by exposing host countries to developed economies' best business practices and corporate governance.

From a macroeconomic perspective, FDI is more stable than other types of capital flows *(Chart 2)*. Equity and short-term debt in particular tend to be highly volatile and speculative, and their role in igniting and deepening financial crises in the 1990s has been closely scrutinized.[2] FDI's relative stability and long-term character make it the preferred source of foreign capital for many emerging economies. In fact, FDI has been so stable in tumultuous times that some economists have called it "good cholesterol" for emerging economies.[3]

The declining volatility of foreign capital flows has paid off in higher economic growth. With FDI's share of developing nations' foreign investment rising, host countries have experienced less overall volatility in investment flows, as measured by their deviation from average rates of incoming capital. Comparing total capital flows with mean real GDP growth rates for emerging economies, we find that higher volatility coincided with lower economic performance from 1970 to 2004 *(Chart 3)*.

FDI and Trade

Many developing countries pursue FDI as a tool for export promotion, rather than production for the domestic economy. Typically, foreign investors build plants in nations where they can produce goods for export at lower costs. Another way FDI helps boost exports is through preferential access to markets in the parent enterprise's home country.

Multinational enterprises, the creatures of FDI, play a dominant role in world trade, accounting for two-thirds of

Higher Capital Flow Volatility Means Slower GDP Growth
Chart 3

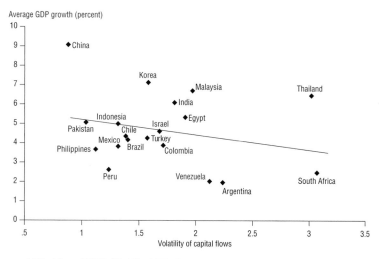

Sources: Lane and Milesi-Ferretti (2006); World Bank WDI Online database; author's calculations.

all cross-border sales.[4] Foreign affiliates were responsible for more than half [of] China's exports in 2001 and 21 percent of Brazil's. They accounted for just 3 percent of India's. At the country's current rate of economic liberalization, however, foreign companies are likely to increase their share of India's exports.

FDI can also provide a path for emerging economies to export the products developed economies usually sell—in effect, increasing their export sophistication.[5] A new study by Dani Rodrik puts the export sophistication of China, a leading FDI recipient, at least three times higher than that of countries with similar per capita GDP. India, another FDI hot spot, also did well on this score.[6] Some emerging economies are fast becoming attractive destinations for multinationals' research and development centers, suggesting further gains for developing nations.

FDI is an important channel for delivery of services across borders—for emerging economies as well as developed ones. Services aren't as widely traded as goods, making up only a fifth of world exports.

That figure is expected to rise rapidly, however, as the Internet and other communications make more services tradable and facilitate the spread of outsourcing. In fact, FDI has grown faster in services than in goods in recent years.[7]

In most developing nations, service industries have been closed to foreign investment. As countries further open their economies, services can be expected to continue outpacing goods. The pattern of services FDI has also been changing. In 1990, finance cornered 57 percent of services FDI in developing economies. By 2002, its share had fallen to 22 percent as business services' share rose from 5 percent to 40 percent.

As services become increasingly tradable, FDI in these industries can forge a strong link with exports of emerging economies. Multinationals operating in such services as banking, telecommunications and trade enhance the efficiency of homegrown providers in myriad ways, contributing to the export competitiveness of these economies' service sectors. With both FDI and trade rising rapidly in services, FDI

Domestic Investment Responds Positively to FDI
Chart 4

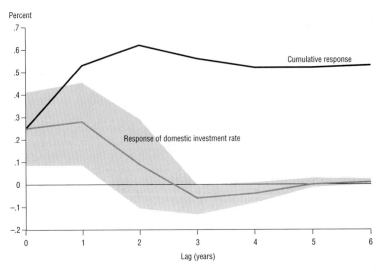

Note: Shaded area represents 95 percent confidence band.
Sources: Lane and Milesi-Ferretti (2006); World Bank WDI Online database; author's calculations.

has an important role in promoting the sector's globalization in other emerging economies.

FDI, Savings and Investment

Foreign investment can ripple through receiving economies in many ways. It can finance current account deficits through its effect on investment or offset other financial transactions, such as increases in reserves or capital outflows. The imported capital may simply result in additional consumption rather than investment. In principle, it needn't always boost the country's productive capital stock. If foreign and homegrown companies vie for the same investment pie in the host country, FDI may simply offset, or crowd out, domestic investment.

Of course, FDI may represent a net capital gain or even "crowd in" domestic investment through a number of channels, such as transfers of technology and key expertise that doesn't exist in host countries. India, for example, has opened up parts of its retail sector to foreign investment, although it limits outsiders to a maximum 49 percent stake. FDI is likely to spur domestic investment in India's retail sector as existing players partner with such foreign giants as Wal-Mart to open stores.

We can test for crowding out by determining how a percentage point increase in the ratio of FDI inflows to GDP impacts domestic investment as a share of GDP. Using data from the World Bank, International Monetary Fund and other sources for 19 emerging economies, our model indicates the domestic investment rate rises in the first year following the FDI increase, with positive effects continuing beyond the second year *(Chart 4).*[8] The 95 percent confidence bands, with upper and lower bounds, suggest the positive response could be as short as a year

FDI Has Positive Effect on Both Savings and Investment
Chart 5

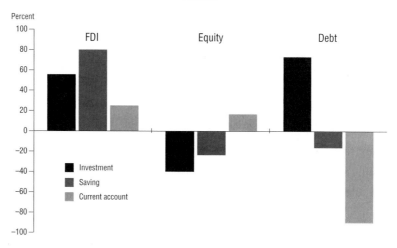

Sources: Lane and Milesi-Ferretti (2006); World Bank WDI Online database; author's calculations.

but may continue as long as two. The cumulative effect of an increase in FDI on domestic investment is positive in the long run.[9]

Of course, this doesn't account for the full range of capital inflows. Equity and debt investments may differ from FDI in the direction and magnitude of their impacts on investment. Because it's more stable, FDI is likely to have a larger impact on domestic investment than equity flows do. Some forms of debt, particularly long-term borrowing from multilateral institutions like the World Bank, may be highly beneficial for domestic investment if used to fund extremely productive infrastructure projects in emerging economies. To compare the impact of FDI and other capital flows, we need to account for all three types of incoming foreign investment.

Our model indicates that FDI has a significant effect on both investment and savings *(Chart 5)*. A percentage point rise in the ratio of FDI to GDP leads to an increase of a half percentage point in domestic investment and three-fourths percentage point in domestic savings. The results suggest that FDI actually crowds

in domestic investment and delivers a positive impact on savings. While FDI has strong positive effects on savings and investment, it has a small positive effect on the current account—the difference between domestic savings and investment.[10]

In our model, FDI performs better than other types of foreign investment. Equity inflows show no discernible effect on investment or savings, possibly because they're considerably more volatile than FDI and may represent largely speculative investment in financial markets. Debt, on the other hand, has a strong positive effect on investment, an indeterminate effect on savings and a significant negative impact on the current account.

The data support the notion that FDI should be the preferred form of foreign investment. It makes a net addition to developing nations' productive resources, without causing deterioration to the current account. This suggests FDI will bolster the receiving country's overall economic performance. The question is whether FDI's desirable effects on savings and investment produce tangible effects on developing nations' growth.

FDI Spurs Economic Growth
Chart 6

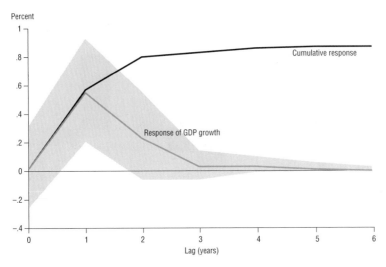

Note: Shaded area represents 95 percent confidence band.
Source: Lane and Milesi-Ferretti (2006); World Bank WDI Online database; author's calculations.

FDI and Growth

Despite FDI's potential to boost technology, productivity, investment and savings, economists have—somewhat surprisingly—struggled to find a strong causal link to economic growth. Some studies have detected a positive impact, but only if the country has a threshold level of human capital.[11] This seems to confirm FDI's important role in propelling growth in China and India, which have vast, untapped technical workforces. China graduates 600,000 engineers every year; India produces 215,000.[12]

A stumbling block to identifying FDI's impact on growth lies in the fact that these investments can be the cause as well as the result of economic vitality because foreign capital beats a path to the world's hottest developing-market economies.

Other problems make it difficult to disentangle FDI's effect on GDP growth. For countries with high tariff and nontariff barriers, FDI may simply be the result of multinational corporations trying to access domestic markets because the export route has been closed. In this case, FDI may contribute to economic growth, but the impact will be reduced to the extent high tariffs stunt growth.

Countries also woo foreign investors with tax breaks and subsidies. Fiscal incentives are doubtlessly a good way to promote FDI. After all, tax havens are prominent FDI recipients. However, researchers have found that such policies aren't effective ways to reap FDI's economic benefits. Indeed, the policies may create distortions that significantly blunt FDF's efficiency and productivity gains. Tax incentives may prove wasteful because FDI responds more to such factors as labor market flexibility, the cost of doing business and the quality of the infrastructure.

As we did with domestic investment, we can examine how a percentage point increase in the FDI-to-GDP ratio affects emerging economies' performance *(Chart 6)*. Although FDI doesn't boost growth immediately, it delivers positive

Riskier Countries Tend to Attract Higher FDI
Chart 7

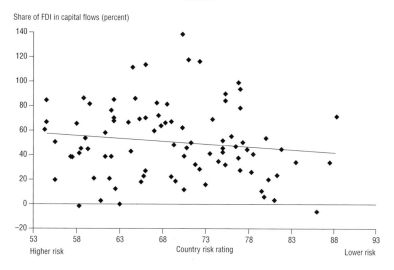

Sources: Lane and Milesi-Ferretti (2006); VNCTAD FDI Inward Potential Index database; author's calculations.

effects in the year after FDI increases. This suggests a significant link between FDI and GDP growth, one that develops over time because investment spending increases the nation's productive capacity. Although the growth effect dies down, the cumulative effect on output is still positive in the long run. The confidence bands indicate that the positive growth effect in the year following FDI inflow is statistically significant.

In addition to spurring growth, FDI may have wage and productivity spillovers in the host country. If multinationals pay more than domestic firms, it may force the latter to raise wages. If foreign investors transfer technology to domestic firms, FDI would also help make workers more efficient.

Is FDI Always Good?

FDI offers attractive benefits that include technology, investments, savings and growth. But emerging economies should exercise caution.

Counter to economic intuition, FDI may flow to riskier destinations. We can see that by plotting FDI's share of a country's total capital inflows against that nation's composite risk rating for developing and emerging countries in December 2003 *(Chart 7)*. The risk measure is obtained from the UNCTAD FDI Inward Potential Index database, which uses higher numbers to indicate lower risk.

The downward-sloping line indicates that FDI tends to make up a greater share of capital inflow in places investors might otherwise avoid. Most likely, such countries pay a premium for FDI through tax breaks and other incentives.

The relative advantages of FDI during crises are well documented. However, capital flight can't be ruled out. In times of extreme financial crisis, FDI may be accompanied by distress sales of domestic assets, which could be harmful.[13] Even in normal times, FDI can be reversed or diminished through domestic borrowing by affiliates of multinational corporations and repatriation of funds.

Too much FDI may not be beneficial. Through ownership and control of domestic companies, foreign firms learn more about the host country's productivity, and they could overinvest, at the expense of domestic producers.[14] There is a possibility that the most solid firms will be financed through FDI, leaving domestic investors stuck with low-productivity firms. Such "adverse selection" isn't the best economic outcome.

Despite these pitfalls, FDI appears to help emerging economies develop. It complements the host country's institutions and human capital. In many countries, however, barriers to FDI remain. These barriers may range from limits on foreign ownership and control to outright bans on FDI in select sectors, such as services. Reducing them may well be a way to speed up economic development. FDI benefits investors, to be sure, but it also pays dividends to the countries that attract it.

Notes

[1] These numbers are calculated using data from the World Bank's Global Development Finance Online database and are not adjusted for inflation.

[2] For more on this, see the following publications: "International Financial Crises: Causes, Prevention, and Cures," by Lawrence H. Summers, American Economic Review Papers and Proceedings, vol. 90, May 2000, pp. 1–16; "Aspects of Global Economic Integration: Outlook for the Future," by Martin Feldstein, National Bureau of Economic Research, Working Paper no. 7899, September 2000; and "The Capital Myth: The Difference Between Trade in Widgets and Dollars," by Jagdish N. Bhagwati, Foreign Affairs, vol. 77, May/June 1998, pp. 7–12.

[3] "Foreign Direct Investment: Good Cholesterol?" by Ricardo Hausmann and Eduardo Fernandez-Arias, Inter-American Development Bank, Research Department Working Paper no. 417, March 2000.

[4] World Investment Report 2002, United Nations Conference on Trade and Development (UNCTAD).

[5] "What You Export Matters," by Ricardo Hausmann, Jason Hwang and Dani Rodrik,

National Bureau of Economic Research, Working Paper no. 11905, December 2005.

[6] "What's So Special About China's Exports?" by Dani Rodrik, National Bureau of Economic Research, Working Paper no. 11947, January 2006.

[7] World Investment Report 2004, UNCTAD.

[8] Unless noted otherwise, this article uses data from the International Monetary Fund's International Finance Statistics; "The External Wealth of Nations Mark II: Revised and Extended Estimates of Foreign Assets and Liabilities, 1970–2004," by P. Lane and G. M. Milesi-Ferretti, International Monetary Fund, Working Paper no. 06/69, March 2006; and World Development Indicators Online database, 1970–2004. The sample of emerging economies consists of Argentina, Brazil, Chile, China, Colombia, Egypt, India, Indonesia, Israel, Korea, Malaysia, Mexico, Pakistan, Peru, Philippines, South Africa, Thailand, Turkey and Venezuela.

[9] Estimation was carried out using panel VAR techniques. See "Financial Development and Dynamic Investment Behavior: Evidence from Panel Vector Autoregression," by Inessa Love and Lea Zicchino, The World Bank, Policy Research Working Paper Series no. 2913, 2002.

[10] These results confirm the findings in "Capital Flows to Developing Economies: Implications for Saving and Investment," by Barry P. Bosworth and Susan M. Collins, Brookings Papers on Economic Activity, no. 1,1999, pp. 143–69.

[11] "How Does Foreign Direct Investment Affect Economic Growth?" by E. Borensztein, J. De Gregorio and J-W. Lee, Journal of International Economics, vol. 45, June 1998, pp. 115–35.

[12] The number of engineers is based on a 2005 study by Duke University researchers Gary Gereffi, Vivek Wadhwa and others. Note that these numbers include engineers with associate degrees and diplomas and are not adjusted for quality, thus not directly comparable with figures for the U.S.

[13] For a discussion of the implications of such distress sales, see "Fire-Sale FDI," by Paul Krugman, Massachusetts Institute of Technology, February 20–21,1998, http://web.mit.edu/krug-man/www/FI RESALE.htm.

[14] "Excessive FDI Flows Under Asymmetric Information," by Assaf Razin, Efraim Sadka and Chi-Wa Yuen, National Bureau of Economic Research, Working Paper no. 7400, October 1999.

Have U.S. Import Prices Become Less Responsive to Changes in the Dollar?

Rebecca **Hellerstein**,
Deirdre **Daly**, and
Christina **Marsh**

Over the past few years, the dollar has depreciated against a number of currencies. In principle, the dollar's fall should help to correct the U.S. trade deficit by altering the relative prices of U.S. and foreign goods. Specifically, the depreciation should prompt foreign producers to protect their profits by raising the dollar price of their exports to the United States. As the cost of foreign goods rises, U.S. demand should weaken, leading to a decrease in the quantity of goods that the United States imports.[1] Although this scenario is quite plausible, the dollar's recent slide has produced neither a substantial fall in imports nor a sizable shrinking of the trade imbalance.

One possible explanation for the U.S. experience of the past few years is that the rate of exchange rate "pass-through"—the degree to which a change in the value of a country's currency induces a change in the price of the country's imports and exports—has fallen relative to historical values. Indeed, while pass-through is almost always "incomplete" (for example, a 10 percent depreciation of a country's currency will lead to an increase of *less than* 10 percent in the price of the country's imports), some recent research suggests that import prices in a number of industrial nations may have become progressively less responsive to changes in exchange rates over the past decade or so.

A potential decline in exchange rate pass-through has important implications for the U.S. economy. First, it has significant bearing on U.S. efforts to correct the country's trade imbalance. If import prices have become much less responsive to changes in currency values, a larger devaluation of the dollar will be needed to narrow the imbalance. Second, pass-through has implications for the stability of domestic prices. Low import prices are believed to contribute to low rates of inflation—in part by constraining domestic producers to keep their prices competitive. By boosting import prices, a dollar depreciation could create inflationary pressures in the U.S. economy, holding all else equal. However, if pass-through has in fact declined, import prices would not rise as much as expected, and the inflationary impact of the dollar's fall would be more muted.

In this edition of *Current Issues*, we take a fresh look at the relationship between exchange rates and U.S. import prices to determine whether a decline in pass-through has indeed occurred. We present new estimates of pass-through for U.S. imported goods both for the 1985–2005:2 period as a whole and for two subperiods, 1985–94 and 1995–2005:2. We also raise two methodological issues that may help explain the recent findings of low pass-through rates.

Overall, we find no conclusive evidence that pass-through has declined significantly from historical levels. Our analysis

The Response of U.S. Import Prices to the Exchange Rate
Chart 1

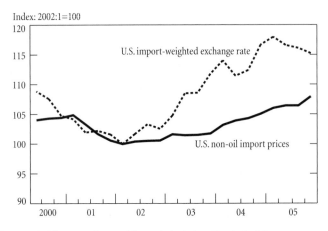

Index: 2002:1=100

Sources: U.S. Department of Commerce, Bureau of Economic Analysis; authors' calculations.

yields an estimate of a 10 percentage point decrease in pass-through—a considerably smaller decrease than that found by other researchers. Moreover, even this small decline may be more apparent than real. Our estimate is not what economists consider to be statistically significant—that is, it may reflect mere chance rather than evidence of a genuine decline that could be expected to persist over time. In addition, we find that changes in the sampling methods used by the Bureau of Labor Statistics (BLS) to produce import price data may create a downward bias in estimates of pass-through for the post-1998 period—including our own estimate. Finally, we show that the inclusion of commodity prices in some estimates may be contributing to findings of a substantial decline in pass-through.

The Dollar's Decline and Exchange Rate Pass-Through

From 2002 to 2005, the dollar depreciated by about 15 percent against an import-weighted index of currencies while U.S. import prices, measured in dollars, rose by approximately 8 percent (Chart 1). Absent any other change in global conditions,

these patterns suggest that about 50 percent of the cumulative change in the dollar has been transmitted to U.S. import prices in recent years.

This figure, based on a casual impression from the chart, accords well with traditional estimates of a one-year pass-through rate of roughly 50 percent.[2] However, it contrasts with recent estimates that put pass-through to U.S. import prices at only 10 or 20 percent.[3] According to these estimates, import prices in the United States and other industrial countries have become significantly less responsive to exchange rate changes since the 1990s. The pass-through rate for the United States is estimated to have fallen 30 percentage points, largely in the past decade.[4] Estimates of the drop in pass-through for other countries range as high as 40 percentage points, for Japan, and more than 80 percentage points, for France.[5]

To explore whether pass-through to U.S. import prices has in fact fallen in recent years, we employ an empirical model that estimates firms' exchange rate pass-through over the period extending from 1985 to the second quarter of 2005 (Box 1

Box 1
Exchange Rate Pass-Through Model

For aggregate import price data, our pricing equation is:

$$p_t = \alpha + \sum_{i=0}^{4} a_i e_{t-i} + \sum_{j=0}^{4} b_j w_{t-j} + c_t(Y_t) + \varepsilon_t,$$

where p_t is an index of U.S. import prices at time t, α is constant, e_{t-i} is the import-weighted nominal exchange rate at time t minus i, w_{t-j} is a control for supply shocks that may affect import prices independently of the exchange rate at time t minus j, Y_t is a control for demand shifts that may affect import prices independently of the exchange rate at time t, and ε_t is an econometric error term. Each of the variables is in percentage-change terms.

Exchange rate pass-through is the sum of the a_i coefficients on the nominal import-weighted exchange rate e at time t plus four lagged periods. U.S. domestic demand, defined as GDP minus exports plus imports, serves as a proxy for domestic demand shifts. Foreign production costs proxy for supply shocks that may affect import prices independently of the exchange rate. An import-weighted foreign consumer price index (CPI) proxies for foreign production costs w. Those specifications that have commodity prices as controls use four lags plus the contemporaneous term. Regressions are also run at the industry level with industry-specific import price, nominal import-weighted exchange rate, and import-weighted CPI indexes.[a]

[a]All regressions use ordinary least squares. The nominal import-weighted exchange rates are constructed from the bilateral exchange rates of thirty-four currencies with the dollar, each weighted by its annual share in U.S. (or for the industry-level regressions, the industry's) imports. The import price indexes exclude petroleum imports and are from the U.S. National Income and Product Accounts; the import volume data are from the U.S. International Trade Commission; the domestic demand data are from the U.S. Commerce Department's Bureau of Economic Analysis.

describes our model). In addition, to test the notion that pass-through to U.S. prices has fallen most dramatically in the past decade, we estimate pass-through rates separately for two subperiods, 1985–94 and 1995–2005:2. We use both aggregate- and industry-level data.

We note at the outset that estimating exchange rate pass-through is not a straightforward exercise. The sensitivity of import prices to changes in the dollar's value may differ from a simple correlation between prices and dollar movements because of independent activity in the production or demand sectors. Thus, models used to estimate pass-through must control for other forces that affect firms' choices of import prices, such as demand conditions in the importing country and cost changes in the exporting country that

should not be attributed to exchange rate movements. Most pass-through models also recognize that import price responses to exchange rate movements can be delayed, with adjustments often taking up to a year or longer.

Our pass-through model controls for foreign cost shocks other than exchange rate fluctuations by using an import-weighted foreign consumer price index. Although foreign producer prices are a better measure of foreign cost shocks, consumer prices usually track changes in producer price indexes—and they are available for more countries and over more years. In addition, our model controls for changes in the demand for imports that reflect variation in consumer tastes or income, rather than in the dollar's value, by including U.S. domestic demand. U.S.

Aggregate-Level Exchange Rate Pass-Through to U.S. Import Prices
Table 1

Percent

	1985–94	1995–2005:2	1985–2005:2
Standard regression	56*	46*	51*
	(.090)	(.098)	(.056)
Standard regression plus commodities	53*	13	36*
	(.093)	(.134)	(.057)

Source: Authors' calculations.

Notes: Figures are long-run estimates. Standard errors are in parentheses.

*Statistically significant at the 5 percent level.

domestic demand is defined as total U.S. GDP minus exports (demand from outside the United States) plus imports (U.S. demand not satisfied by domestic output). Import prices are measured by an index of goods prices upon entry into the United States.[6]

At the aggregate level, we find that over the course of one year, firms pass through 51 percent of an exchange rate change to import prices for the 1985–2005:2 period (Table 1). That is, import prices generally rise by about ½ percentage point following a 1 percent dollar depreciation. Firms pass through less than 10 percent of an exchange rate change to overall consumer prices in the United States over the same period. Dividing the sample into two ten-year subperiods, we find pass-through to be 56 percent for 1985–94 and 46 percent for 1995–2005:2.

Thus, our estimates suggest that pass-through may have declined by 10 percentage points from the first subperiod to the second. Note, however, that in our estimates, the difference in the coefficients between the two subperiods is not statistically significant. That is, the estimated drop in pass-through may be a product of random noise in the data rather than evidence of a genuine decline that could be expected to persist over time.

A more detailed picture of exchange rate pass-through patterns emerges at the industry level (Box 2). Three industries with significant shares of U.S. manufacturing imports—road vehicles, computers and telecommunications equipment, and chemicals—have each exhibited a substantial decrease in pass-through (Table 2). By contrast, other industries—such as primary metals, other metal manufactures, food manufacturing, leather, and rubber and plastic—have each shown a marked rise in pass-through. The average trade-weighted change in pass-through over all industries is −9 percentage points, a figure that is basically identical to the results obtained in our aggregate regressions.

Overall, changes in exchange rate pass-through at the industry level point to the same conclusion as our aggregate results: though some decline in pass-through may have occurred, our estimated decrease of 9 to 10 percentage points is considerably lower than the 30 percentage point decline identified in other studies. Moreover, as we argue in the next section, even the small decline in pass-through that we find may stem from a methodological change: Recent revisions to the import data used in pass-through calculations may contribute to estimates that are biased toward zero.

Box 2
Exchange Rate Pass-Through and Market Power

Pass-through can vary across industries because foreign firms may have different levels of market power relative to domestic firms. If a foreign firm exports goods in an industry in which domestic firms have considerable market power, the foreign firm may be more reluctant to raise prices than it otherwise would when the domestic currency depreciates. As a result, the foreign firm will adjust its markup downward to maintain market share, and exchange rate pass-through will be lower. By contrast, if a foreign firm exports goods in an industry in which domestic firms have less market power than their foreign counterparts, it may have less incentive to keep prices low; in that case, pass-through rates may well be higher.

To test these relationships, we compare pass-through rates across industries using a measure of foreign market power relative to domestic market power, calculated as the ratio of the value of imported goods to the value of domestic production. To provide a more complete picture of the competitive pressures in each industry, we weight domestic production by a measure of market concentration known as a Herfindahl-Hirschman Index (HHI). Market concentration is often positively associated with market power. A foreign firm may have more difficulty competing in an industry with a highly concentrated domestic market dominated by a few firms, which in turn may affect its pass-through patterns. The HHI is calculated by squaring the market share of a number of firms within an industry and summing the resulting shares. We use HHIs calculated by the U.S. Census Bureau employing data on the fifty largest firms in each industry in 1997.

The chart shows that industries with high foreign market power relative to domestic market power do indeed exhibit high pass-through rates. We qualify this finding, however, by noting that pass-through may differ across industries for other reasons. The degree to which imported goods are substitutable for domestic goods may vary by industry. In addition, industries may face diverse trade restrictions, such as import quotas and tariffs.

Exchange Rate Pass-Through and Market Power

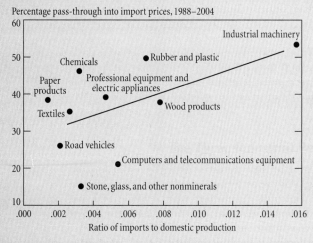

Percentage pass-through into import prices, 1988–2004

Sources: U.S. Department of Commerce, Bureau of Economic Analysis and Bureau of the Census; authors' calculations.
Notes: The industries shown in the chart account for roughly 70 percent of U.S. manufacturing. Those industries for which import and domestic data groupings were not similar (food manufacturing, beverages and tobacco, leather, and apparel) have been dropped. Primary metals, metal manufactures, and miscellaneous products have also been dropped because these industries are outliers.

Industry-Level Exchange Rate Pass-Through to U.S. Import Prices
Table 2

Percent

Industry	1985–94	1995–2005:2
Road vehicles (23.2)	48*	14*
Computers and telecommunications equipment (19.5)	83*	51
Industrial machinery (12.4)	52*	53*
Chemicals (6.5)	47*	31
Toys and miscellaneous manufactures (5.3)	42*	38*
Clothing (4.9)	56*	7
Primary metals (4.6)	80*	186*
Professional equipment and electric appliances (4.3)	68*	64*
Metal manufactures (2.9)	41*	54*
Food manufacturing (2.7)	19*	49*
Leather (2.5)	−5	13*
Paper products (2.4)	18	67
Rubber and plastic (2.3)	15	76*
Wood products (1.8)	20	42
Stone, glass, other nonminerals (1.5)	80*	36*
Furniture (1.4)	51*	35*
Textiles (1.4)	53*	50*
Beverages and tobacco (0.4)	32	5

Source: Authors' calculations.

Notes: Figures are long-run estimates. Import shares, in parentheses, are the average from 1985 to 2005.

*Statistically significant at the 5 percent level.

Changes in BLS Sampling Methods and Estimates of Exchange Rate Pass-Through

One factor that may have contributed to lower estimates of pass-through in recent years is a change in the sampling methodology used by the Bureau of Labor Statistics to collect import price data. In 1998, the BLS altered its methods in order to obtain more information on intrafirm transactions—that is, transactions between domestic and foreign subsidiaries of the same multinational firm. Approximately 40 percent of U.S. imports involve a U.S. subsidiary of a multinational firm importing from a foreign subsidiary. Recognizing that such transactions were underrepresented in the data, the BLS roughly doubled the number of intrafirm prices in its sample, raising the overall number of prices by about 25 percent.

This change in methodology could affect the calculation of exchange rate pass-through because intrafirm prices, set through administrative procedures rather than actual market transactions, may be less sensitive to exchange rate changes than non-intrafirm prices.[7] Clausing (2001, p. 20), for example, finds that "intrafirm imports are less likely to experience a monthly price change in response to changes in the exchange rate than non-intrafirm imports."[8] Moreover, roughly

The Relationship between Higher Intrafirm Trade and Industry-Level Pass-Through
Chart 2

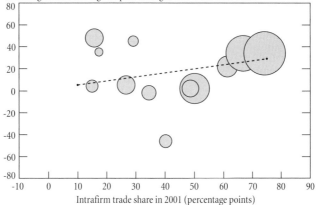

Percentage decline in long-run pass-through, 1985–94 to 1995–2004

x-axis: Intrafirm trade share in 2001 (percentage points)

Sources: U.S. Department of Labor, Bureau of Labor Statistics; authors' calculations.
Notes: Each bubble represents an industry, with more than 80 percent of U.S. manufacturing trade accounted for. The size of each bubble corresponds to the industry's share of total U.S. manufacturing imports. The dashed line is a trend line.

half of the intrafirm prices included in the BLS's expanded sample are cost-based rather than market-based: that is, they are not set with reference to market trends but instead are constructed as a markup over the exporting subsidiary's observable costs. A study by Alterman (1997a) finds that, for particular industries, cost-based prices change less frequently than market-based prices and, in particular, fluctuate less than market-based prices following macroeconomic shocks such as exchange rate changes.

If intrafirm prices are indeed less responsive to exchange rate shifts, then the increased representation of these prices in the BLS import data after 1998 could have introduced a downward bias in measurements of exchange rate pass-through to import prices.[9] This interpretation finds support in Chart 2, which depicts a positive relationship between the share of intrafirm transactions in an industry's total imports and the decrease in annual pass-through elasticities over the past two decades.

Thus, the change in BLS methodology could well have contributed to the perceived decline in exchange rate pass-through in recent years. Estimates of pass-through that use BLS data compiled after the 1998 revision would logically exhibit a lower rate of pass-through than those using pre-1998 data—even though firms' pass-through behavior was unchanged and the underlying relationship between exchange rates and import prices remained the same.

The Inclusion of Commodity Prices in Pass-Through Estimates

A second factor that may have contributed to findings of a pass-through decline is the inclusion of commodity prices (such as those for metals or agricultural raw materials) in economic models of pass-through. Most pass-through models do not control separately for changes in commodity prices, largely because such changes are viewed as a subset of other production cost shocks borne by exporting firms. However, because commodity prices have historically been set in U.S. dollars and may be expected to rise in response to

Ten-Year Rolling Correlations between Commodity Prices and the Dollar Exchange Rate
Chart 3

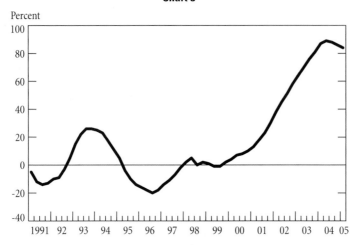

Sources: International Monetary Fund, International Financial Statistics; authors' calculations.

dollar declines, it has been argued that including commodity prices in pass-through models may control for an indirect channel through which exchange rates affect U.S. import prices (Marazzi et al. 2005; Mann 1986).

Significantly, the inclusion of commodity prices in pass-through models produces lower pass-through estimates. When we reestimate exchange rate pass-through to control for commodity prices, we find a 36 percent pass-through rate for the 1985–2005:2 period—a significant departure from the 51 percent found without commodity prices. The inclusion of commodity prices in our model has little effect on our pass-through estimate for 1985–94—which, at 53 percent, is just 3 percentage points below our original estimate of 56 percent. However, the inclusion produces a much lower 13 percent estimate for 1995–2005:2—a 33 percentage point fall from our original estimate of 46 percent.

Our results indicate that the pass-through rate declines dramatically precisely when commodity prices and exchange rates are highly correlated. Over the past five years, commodity prices have been much more strongly correlated with exchange rate movements than in the past (Chart 3). Until about 1998, the correlation fluctuated between plus and minus 20 percent. Since 1999, however, it has risen significantly, reaching 80 percent by the end of our sample period.

What accounts for the high correlation between commodity prices and dollar changes after 1995? One interpretation is that a fundamental change has occurred in the nature of the relationship between the dollar and commodity prices, as argued by Marazzi et al. (2005). If exchange rate changes continue to affect U.S. import prices through commodity prices as much as the recent data suggest, this channel may have to be recognized explicitly and, in a manner of speaking, cumulated to the estimated direct effect of exchange rate changes on import prices. If the post-1998 change in the commodity price–dollar relationship is permanent, the impact of dollar changes on import prices through commodity prices may have risen in importance as a pass-through channel since the 1980s and 1990s, as Marazzi et al. suggest. The lower pass-through estimates that include commodity prices may be more descriptive of conditions going forward given the existence of a new structural pattern in the data.

Even if such a structural change has occurred, however, both the direct (exchange rate) and indirect (commodity price) impact of dollar changes on U.S. import prices should be considered when assessing overall pass-through. That is, having isolated the independent effect of dollar changes operating through a commodity price channel, one must add it to the direct exchange rate effect in order to arrive at an accurate estimate of pass-through. If this is done, then one does not see a sharp drop in pass-through in the past decade.

A second interpretation is that the recent high correlation between dollar changes and commodity price changes is purely coincidental. One could argue that developments in fast-growing economies such as China and India over the past few years are having a sizable influence on commodity prices independent of dollar moves and the U.S. economy. That is, increased demand from these countries may be driving up commodity prices at the same time that developments in the U.S. current account are putting downward pressure on the dollar. If so, the reduction in estimated pass-through may reflect a spurious correlation rather than a structural change in the joint behavior of import prices and exchange rates. Accordingly, it may be more appropriate to exclude commodity prices from exchange rate pass-through models.

Although the first interpretation merits careful consideration, our view is that there is yet no firm evidence of a new and different structural relationship between the dollar and commodity prices. If so, the recent high correlation between the dollar and commodity prices may be coincidental—reflecting the confluence of high demand by China and India and the depreciation of the dollar.

Clearly, the relationship between the value of the dollar and the price of commodities is a complex one, deserving of continued research. Still, whatever position one takes on the importance of commodity prices as a channel for the dollar's impact on the U.S. economy, our analysis suggests that estimates of overall pass-through should focus on the direct and indirect effects of dollar changes on U.S. import prices. There is only weak evidence that this overall rate of pass-through has fallen over the past two decades.

Conclusion

The responsiveness of U.S. import prices, and by extension consumer prices, to exchange rate changes has important implications for the U.S. economy. Although a number of recent studies point to a substantial decline in exchange rate pass-through over the past decade, we find no conclusive evidence of such a trend. While we calculate a drop in pass-through of 10 percentage points from 1985–94 to 1995–2005:2, this estimate is markedly lower than those advanced in other studies and is, based on our empirical model, not significant statistically. We also find that methodological changes—a revision in the BLS procedures for collecting import price data and the inclusion of commodity prices in some pass-through models—may be skewing pass-through estimates in a way that gives the appearance of a decline over the past decade.

These findings lead us to conclude that it is not yet appropriate to treat U.S. import prices as substantially less sensitive to exchange rates. Future studies may show that foreign producers have changed their pricing behavior with regard to U.S. sales, but evidence that such a change has already occurred remains weak.

References

Alterman, William. 1997a. "A Comparison of the Export and Producer Price Indexes for Semiconductors." Paper presented at the National Bureau of Economic Research's Summer Institute, July.

_____. 1997b. "Are Producer Prices Good Proxies for Export Prices?" *Monthly Labor Review* 120, no. 10 (October): 18–32.

Campa, José M., and Linda S. Goldberg. 2005. "Exchange Rate Pass-Through into Import Prices." *Review of Economics and Statistics* 87, no. 4 (November): 679–90.

Clausing, Kimberly A. 2001. "The Behavior of Intrafirm Trade Prices in U.S. International Price Data." Bureau of Labor Statistics Working Paper no. 333, January.

Eden, Lorraine. 2001. "Transfer Pricing, Intrafirm Trade, and the BLS International Price Program." Bureau of Labor Statistics Working Paper no. 334, January.

Feenstra, Robert C. 1989. "Symmetric Pass-Through of Tariffs and Exchange Rates under Imperfect Competition: An Empirical Test." *Journal of International Economics* 27, no. 1–2 (August): 25–45.

Goldberg, Pinelopi K., and Michael M. Knetter. 1997. "Goods Prices and Exchange Rates: What Have We Learned?" *Journal of Economic Literature* 35, no. 3 (September): 1243–72.

Ihrig, Jane E., Mario Marazzi, and Alexander D. Rothenberg. 2006. "Exchange-Rate Pass-Through in the G-7 Countries." Board of Governors of the Federal Reserve System International Finance Discussion Papers, no. 2006–851, January.

Mann, Catherine L. 1986. "Prices, Profit Margins, and Exchange Rates." *Federal Reserve Bulletin* 72, no. 6 (June): 366–79.

Marazzi, Mario, Nathan Sheets, Robert J. Vigfusson, Jon Faust, Joseph E. Gagnon, Jaime R. Marquez, Robert F. Martin, Trevor Reeve, and John H. Rogers. 2005. "Exchange Rate Pass-Through to U.S. Import Prices: Some New Evidence." Board of Governors of the Federal Reserve System International Finance Discussion Papers, no. 833, April.

Rangan, Subramanian, and Robert Z. Lawrence. 1999. *A Prism on Globalization: Corporate Responses to the Dollar*. Washington, D.C.: Brookings Institution Press.

Sekine, Toshitaka. 2006. "Time-Varying Exchange Rate Pass-Through: Experiences of Some Industrial Countries." Bank for International Settlements Working Paper no. 202, March.

Endnotes

[1] By the same logic, the dollar's depreciation should strengthen U.S. export flows, because overseas demand for U.S. goods will increase as those goods become less costly abroad.

[2] See Goldberg and Knetter (1997) and Campa and Goldberg (2005).

[3] See, for instance, Marazzi et al. (2005) and Sekine (2006).

[4] According to Marazzi et al. (2005), pass-through to U.S. import prices declined from more than 0.5 during the 1980s to roughly 0.2 in the past decade; Sekine (2006) sees a decrease from 0.4 in the 1970s to 0.1 in recent periods, with the sharpest fall occurring in the 1990s. Ihrig, Marazzi, and Rothenberg (2006) examine whether pass-through has declined for the Group of Seven countries since the late 1970s and 1980s.

[5] See Sekine (2006).

[6] This index excludes the prices of petroleum products.

[7] Rangan and Lawrence (1999) argue that intrafirm trade may respond differently to exchange rate changes than does trade between firms.

[8] Commenting on Japanese imports to the United States, Clausing notes that "for imports, intrafirm prices clearly respond to a lesser degree to exchange rate changes than do non-intrafirm prices" (p. 21). The study's overall findings on intrafirm import prices are mixed, however. Clausing finds in regressions that intrafirm import prices respond somewhat more to exchange rate changes than do non-intrafirm import prices. Nevertheless, these regressions omit most of the control variables used in pass-through studies, such as foreign cost and domestic demand variables, so the coefficient on the exchange rate variable is difficult to interpret.

[9] Ideally, one could correct estimates of exchange rate pass-through or quantify the impact of the methodological change on pass-through estimates. However, this process would require access to a substantial amount of microeconomic data on the pricing methods of firms in the BLS sample.

Discussion Questions

1. Has NAFTA been a success for the U.S. ? For Canada? For Mexico? What country do you believe has benefited the most?

2. What segments of the U.S. economy have been hurt by NAFTA? Can you think of a reason why people involved in these sectors would be more vocal in expressing their concerns than people in industries who benefit? What are the political implications of this difference in response?

3. How did George Bush's trade policy with Latin America differ from the previous (Bill Clinton) administration?

4. What is foreign direct investment, and how does it differ from other capital flows into a country? Why does Kumar argue that FDI is superior?

5. Give me three potential advantages of FDI. Can you think of reasons why developing countries would oppose FDI?

6. What is exchange rate pass-through?

7. What (import) industries are most likely to be less sensitive to changes in foreign goods due to exchange rate changes? What industries would be most sensitive?

8. If U.S. prices are less sensitive to changes in exchange rates, what are the implications for the U.S. trade deficit?

Immigration

IV

Immigration has become a huge political issue in the United States recently, particularly illegal immigration from Mexico and other Latin American countries. Opponents of immigration argue that illegal immigrants take jobs away from Americans, lower wages, particularly in unskilled jobs, and contribute to our budget deficit by using up resources such as education and medical care. Proponents generally argue that immigrants increase U.S. productivity, perform jobs that others are not willing to do, and reduce outsourcing that would otherwise occur in some of these jobs.

The two articles here discuss immigration. The first article, "Global Migration: Two Centuries of Mass Migration Offers Insights into the Future of Global Movements of People," by noted economist Jeffrey G. Williamson, looks at migration in historical perspective, examining two earlier waves of immigration which brought large numbers of people (mostly European) to the U.S. and other countries. According to Williamson, political opposition to the current wave of immigration is much higher than in the past, mostly due to the objections of people who must compete for lower wages. Williamson believes that the current wave will pass, as others have.

The second article, "America's Stake in Immigration: Why Almost Everybody Wins," by Giovanni Peri, argues that immigration has generated jobs and productivity in complementary industries, creating new jobs for Americans. On balance, Peri believes immigration is good for the U.S.

Global Migration

Two Centuries of Mass Migration Offers Insights Into the Future of Global Movements of People

JEFFREY G. WILLIAMSON

World migration has been going on for centuries, and free mass migration—of those not coerced, like slaves and indentured servants—has been going on for the past two. The reasons people move are no big mystery: they do it today, as they did two centuries ago, to improve their lives. What has changed is who is migrating and where they come from.

Both the demand for long-distance moves from poor to rich countries and the ability of the potential migrants to finance those moves have soared over the past two centuries. As the gap in living standards between the third world and the first world widened in the 20th century, the incentive to move increased. At the same time, improved educational levels and living standards in poor parts of the world—and falling transport costs globally, thanks to new technologies—have made it increasingly possible for potential emigrants to finance the move.

Thus, over time, poorer and poorer potential migrants, those who live the farthest from high-wage labor markets, have escaped the poverty trap. This emigration fact implies an immigration corollary that has important political backlash implications: relative to native-born host country populations, world immigrants have declined in "quality" over time—at least as judged by the way host country markets value their labor.

Adding to the rising demand for emigration, the population pool of the most mobile young adults increased as poor countries started the long process of economic modernization. Every country passes through a demographic transition as modern development unfolds: improved nutrition and health conditions cause child mortality rates to fall, thereby raising the share of surviving children in the population. After a couple of decades, this glut of children becomes a glut of young adults, exactly those who are most responsive to emigration incentives.

These demographic events were important in pushing poor Europeans overseas in swelling numbers in the late 19th century and even more important in pushing poor third-world workers to the first world in the late 20th century. At the other end of this demographic transition are the rich industrial countries, where population aging contributes to a scarcity of working adults and thus to a first-world immigration pull that reinforces the third-world emigration push.

Thus, the dramatic rise in world mass migration after the 1960s should have come as no surprise to any observer who has paid attention to history. But to truly understand world mass migration—and what might lie ahead—it is not enough to look at only the past few decades. We must assess the present relative to a past that stretches back over two centuries.

The First Wave

The discovery of the Americas stimulated a steady stream of voluntary migration from Europe. High transport costs and big risks ensured that only the richest and most fearless made the move. Furthermore, distance mattered: the longer the move, the bigger the cost, and the greater the positive selection. These voluntary migrants, however, were dwarfed by those who came under contract and coercion. About 11.3 million journeyed to the New World before 1820, of whom 8.7 million were African slaves. Another large European emigrant group consisted of indentured servants and convicts, whose migration costs were financed by others. Thus, coercion and contracts were the chief means by which the labor-scarce New World recruited workers before the 19th century.

However, once started, the transition to free migration—which marks a decisive shift in the history of intercontinental migration—was spectacular: the share of free migrants in the total jumped from 20 percent in the 1820s to 80 percent by the 1840s. The combination of incentives, constraints, and policies that underlie the transition speak directly to the global migrations of today.

In the first three decades after 1846, the numbers of emigrants averaged about 300,000 a year; they more than doubled in the next two decades; and, after the turn of the century, they rose to over a million a year (see chart). Their countries of origin also changed dramatically. In the first half of the century, emigrants came predominantly from the richer parts of Europe— the British Isles, followed by Germany. By mid-century, they were joined by a rising tide of Scandinavian and other northwestern European emigrants and, in the 1880s, by southern and eastern Europeans.

The overwhelming majority of these emigrants headed for the Americas, the United States in particular. U.S. immigration from 1846 until the imposition of quotas in the 1920s follows closely the total European emigration pattern. After the mid-1880s, significant numbers of emigrants also went to South America, primarily Argentina and Brazil, and to Canada after the turn of the century. Another stream linked the United Kingdom to Australia, New Zealand, and South Africa. Still, between 1906 and 1910, the United States absorbed 64 percent of all emigration to the Americas (the main competitor being Argentina, which took in 17 percent).

On the go

The number of European emigrants rose from 300,000 a year in 1846 to over a million a year by the end of the century, before plummeting with the U.S. imposition of quotas.

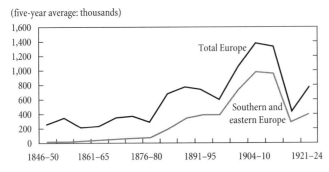

Source: I. Ferencizi and W.F. Willcox, 1929, *International Migrations.* Vol. 1 (New York: National Bureau of Economic Research).

Important migrations also took place within Europe. Spurred by the first industrial revolution, the Irish migration into Britain yielded an Irish-born share of almost 9 percent in British cities by 1851. In the 1890s, more than half of all Italian emigrants went to European destinations, chiefly to France and Germany. A third example is offered by the movement from eastern Europe to Germany, and from east Germany to west, patterns repeated even today. As the cost of migration from rural Europe to the gateway cities of the U.S. east coast fell, return migration soared. The U.S. authorities estimated that, between 1890 and 1914, return migration amounted to 30 percent of the gross inflow.

How large were these mass migrations for the sending and receiving countries? Rates exceeding 50 per 1,000 each decade were common for Britain, Ireland, and Norway throughout the late 19th century, and for Italy, Portugal, and Spain by the end of the century. The lower rates achieved by other countries are still high by modern standards. New World immigration rates were even larger than the European emigration rates, an inevitable arithmetic consequence of the fact that the sending populations were bigger than the receiving populations. In every New World country except Brazil, immigration rates far exceeded 50 per 1,000 in the decade of the 1900s.

Migration rates of this size imply significant economic effects on sending and receiving labor markets. This is especially so when we recognize that migrations tended to self-select those who had most to gain from the move, namely young adult males. Thus, the migrants had far higher labor participation rates than did either the populations they left or the ones they joined. It follows that the *labor migration rates* were even higher than the already-high population migration rates.

What was the resulting foreign-born share of Europe's and the New World's population in the late 19th century? Just before World War I, the highest foreign-born shares were for Argentina and New Zealand, about 30 percent, while the share was 14.7 percent for the biggest immigrant economy, the United States (see Table 1). These proportions are considerably higher than today, with migrant stocks now much more evenly spread around the greater Atlantic economy (Europe, the Americas, Australia, New Zealand, and South Africa). And Western Europe and Latin America are changing roles.

The Mass Emigration Life Cycle

Most of the 60 million Europeans who emigrated to the New World in the century after 1820 did so to escape poverty, and they did it without government assistance or guest worker status. Famine and revolution may have helped push the first great mass migration in the 1840s, but it was the underlying economic and demographic fundamentals that made each subsequent surge bigger than the previous one. If our only purpose were to explain why so many Europeans emigrated in the first global century, this essay would be very short indeed: after all, living standards were a lot higher in labor-scarce host countries.

But why did emigrating countries typically trace out a life cycle pattern? That is, emigration rates typically *rose steeply* from low levels as economic development took place in poor sending countries, after which the rise began to slow, and emigration rates peaked and subsequently fell off. This stylized fact—an emigration life cycle—has been documented in the first global century again and again. What accounts for it?

In preindustrial episodes, low emigration rates and low home wages coexisted: those who had the most to gain from migrating were trapped in poverty. Thus, enormous wage gaps between industrializing, resource-rich, high-wage countries and agrarian, resource-poor, low-wage countries were quite consistent with low emigration rates. As industrialization took place in the poor sending countries, real

Mixing Bowl
Table 1

Western Europe's desirability as an immigrant destination is rising while Latin America's draw is declining.

(share of foreign-born population in percent)

	1870–71	1890–91	1910–11	2000–01
Europe				
Germany	0.5	0.9	1.9	8.9
France	2.0	3.0	3.0	10.0
United Kingdom	0.5	0.7	0.9	4.3
Denmark	3.0	3.3	3.1	5.8
Norway	1.6	2.4	2.3	6.3
Sweden	0.3	0.5	0.9	11.3
New world				
Australia	46.5	31.8	17.1	23.6
New Zealand	63.5	41.5	30.3	19.5
Canada	16.5	13.3	22.0	17.4
United States	14.4	14.7	14.7	11.1
Argentina	12.1	25.5	29.9	5.0
Brazil	3.9	2.5	7.3[1]	

Source: Williamson and Hatton, 2005.

[1] Number of foreign nationals in 1900.

wages rose and the supply constraints on emigration were gradually released: more and more potential emigrants could finance the move. As this trend continued, the backlog of potential migrants was slowly exhausted.

The demographic transition also played a role. The fall in infant mortality rates tended, after a 15- or 20-year lag, to create a fatter cohort of mobile young adults, thus contributing even more to the emigration boom. In addition, remittances from previous emigrants helped finance the move of family members left behind. When the demographic transition reached a crescendo, when remittances leveled off, and when industrialization at home had raised wages and unlocked the migration poverty trap, further increases in the real wage at home caused the emigration rate to decline from the peak.

The first global century thus shows us that country emigration histories typically pass through two regimes—the first constrained by the supply of emigrants, and the second constrained by the demand for emigrants. The first regime was consistent with rising emigration and rising home wages. But, at some point, home wages were high enough that financial constraints became less binding: further increases in the home wage relative to the foreign wage then reduced the incentive to emigrate, the emigration rate fell, and the demand-constrained regime prevailed.

The emigrant life cycle implies that the source and quality of immigrants change over time. The spread of the transport and industrial revolutions, which reduced the cost of long-distance moves and the ratio of migration cost to annual income at home, extended the reach of global migration.

More potential emigrants from the hinterland of western Europe and from distant parts of eastern and southern Europe could make the move. Thus, migrant origins shifted toward the countries that came late to modern economic growth. In addition, as each of these countries went through its own emigration life cycle, the share coming from the poor countries soared.

The powerful positive self-selection that had characterized the global migrations early in the century disappeared, and *negative selection* began to emerge. This dramatic shift obeyed economic and demographic laws of motion and implied a decline in the quality of immigrants—that is, the value of their skills in host country labor markets—and an even bigger decline in the quality of immigrants *relative to the native born,* who were accumulating human capital at a fast pace. There has never been any unambiguous evidence to suggest that immigrants face discrimination in U.S. labor markets, but they earned less than the native born before 1913 and, again, since 1970 have earned less. Why? On average, immigrants have less formal schooling and on-the-job training and poorer English-language skills and knowledge about jobs than do the host country native born. The number of immigrants increased markedly in the decades up to 1913 and has increased even more markedly since 1950.

This deterioration in relative and sometimes absolute immigrant quality had a great deal to do with rising negative attitudes toward immigration in the United States. Rising immigration also helped reinforce anti-immigrant feelings, with the native born feeling crowded out by the newcomers, and anti-immigrant sentiment intensified in the 1890s. Responding to constituent complaints, the House of Representatives proposed the Literacy Act to filter out immigrants from poor source countries; the Literacy Act finally became law in 1917. After the Great War ended, it was an easy matter for Congress to add the more restrictive Quota Acts of 1921, 1924, and 1927, as well as the ban on Asians. Other high-wage immigrant countries followed the U.S. lead, and the first global migration century came to an end.

The Second Wave

Annual immigration to North America and Oceania rose gradually after World War II until the mid-1970s before surging to a million a year in the 1990s. The absolute numbers were, by then, similar to those of a century earlier but were smaller relative to the population and labor force that had to absorb them. Thus, the annual U.S. immigration rate fell from 11.6 per 1,000 in the 1900s to 0.4 per 1,000 in the 1940s, before rising again to 4 immigrants per 1,000 in the 1990s. The proportion of the foreign-born U.S. population fell from a 1910 peak of 15 percent to an all-century low of 4.7 percent in 1970. The postwar immigration boom increased the foreign-born share to more than 8 percent in 1990 and more than 10 percent in 2000. After a half-century retreat, the United States has reclaimed the title "a nation of immigrants."

What happened to the United States after World War II also happened worldwide. The foreign-born share increased by about a third in Oceania between 1965 and 2000 (from 14.4 to 19.1 percent), more than doubled in North America (from 6 to 13 percent), and more than tripled in Europe (from 2.2 to 7.7 percent). Of course, the addition of undocumented immigrants would raise these foreign-born shares and would probably even raise their measured increase over time.

What is amazing about this modern boom in world mass migration is that it has taken place in such a hostile policy environment. Before World War I, most mass migrations took place without visas, quotas, asylum status, smuggled illegals, or security barriers. Since World War II, *all* mass migrations have taken place under those circumstances. Imagine how much bigger world mass migration would be today were we still living in the age of

Where U.S. Immigrants Came From
Table 2

Almost half of U.S. immigrants now come from Latin America, up sharply from about one-fifth in the 1950s.

(percent of total)

Region of origin	1951–60	1961–70	1971–80	1981–90	1991–2000
Europe	52.7	33.8	17.8	10.3	14.9
West	47.1	30.2	14.5	7.2	5.6
East	5.6	3.6	3.3	3.1	9.4
Asia	6.1	12.9	35.3	37.3	30.7
Americas	39.6	51.7	44.1	49.3	49.3
Canada	15.0	12.4	3.8	2.1	2.1
Mexico	11.9	13.7	14.2	22.6	24.7
Caribbean	4.9	14.2	16.5	11.9	10.8
Central America	1.8	3.1	3.0	6.4	5.8
South America	3.6	7.8	6.6	6.3	5.9
Africa	0.6	0.9	1.8	2.4	3.9
Oceania	0.5	0.8	0.9	0.6	0.6
Total (millions)	2.5	3.3	4.5	7.3	9.1

Source: U.S. Citizenship and Immigration Services, 2003.

Notes: National origin based on country of last residence. Totals include 2.7 million former illegal aliens receiving permanent resident status under the U.S. Immigration Reform and Control Act, 1986. Of these, 1.3 million fall in the decade 1981–90 and 1.4 million in the decade 1991–2000.

unrestricted migration that characterized the first global century before 1913. Twice as big? Three times? Five times?

While world migration has surged, the labor market quality of these immigrants has declined. For example, U.S. immigrant males earned 4.1 percent *more* than native-born males in 1960 but 16.3 percent *less* in 1990. Immigrants always suffer an earnings disadvantage before they assimilate, but their initial wage (relative to that of the native born) deteriorated by 24 percentage points between 1960 and 1990. Although the average educational attainment of immigrants improved, it did not increase as rapidly as that of the native born. The percentage of newly arrived immigrants with only a high school education or even less schooling was 5.6 percentage points higher than the better-educated native born in 1970, but 20.4 percentage points higher in 1990, an almost *fourfold* increase.

Most of this decline in immigrant quality was due to changes in the source country composition (Table 2), and it reflects four massive shifts in world migration patterns over the half century since World War II. The first shift involved the decline of European emigrants, part of which can be explained by the resurgence of migration *within* Europe (including Turkey): foreign European nationals increased from 1.3 percent of the western European population in 1950 to 10.3 percent in 2000. The rise would be even higher if it included the foreign born who had become naturalized.

More recently, western and southern Europe have become destinations for immigrants from Asia, the Middle East, and Africa. And, since the collapse of the Soviet Union in the 1990s, western Europe has also absorbed immigrants from the east, including from the former Soviet republics. As a result, annual net immigration into the European Union has soared since the 1980s: it now surpasses that of the United States and would exceed it by even more if illegal immigrants were included.

The second shift involved emigration from eastern Europe. This traditional east-west European flow has a long history but was stopped cold by postwar emigration policy in the centrally planned economies. Things changed dramatically in the 1980s when Poland and Romania opened up and even more dramatically when the Berlin Wall fell in 1989. Emigration from these transition economies increased fivefold between 1985 and 1989 and exceeded a million a year until 1993, when it eased a bit. In any case, Europe seems to have reestablished its old east-west migration tradition.

The third shift involved the transformation of Latin America from a major emigrant destination to a major immigrant source. The first global century leads us to expect that poor, low-wage, agrarian countries should send out more emigrants as they industrialize, but at some point they should start to retain their own and receive immigrants as they continue to industrialize and wages rise. Latin America is an exception to the rule: in 1960, it hosted 1.8 million (net) immigrants; in 1980, it sent abroad 1.8 million (net) of its own. The explanation for this unique regime switch appears to be Latin America's much richer and faster-growing northern neighbor.

The fourth and biggest postwar shift—which repeats the migration life-cycle experience of the first global century—involved Asian, African, and Middle Eastern immigrants, whose numbers rose from a trickle to a flood. Early industrializations and demographic transitions unlock the migration poverty trap and unleash a surge of emigration. Thus, the East Asian "miracle" first fostered an emigration surge, which then slowed, peaked, and subsequently declined as modern development ensued. The Middle Eastern life cycle has been delayed, as has the region's development. In Africa, where per capita income growth over the past half century has been so disappointing, the life cycle has been delayed even more.

In the first global century, demographic booms and early industrial revolutions generated an emigration surge from poor countries, and demographic busts and mature industrial revolutions generated a fall in emigration from now-richer countries. Falling transport costs and the effect of remittances amplified these forces, which slowly reduced positive selection: the really poor could finance the move only late in the first global century, as their incomes at home rose and as the cost of passage fell. Exactly the same forces have also been at work in the modern era although they have been strengthened by policies. In the United States, policies included the 1965 abolition of the country-of-origin quotas (and Asian bans), the shift to a worldwide quota, and the emphasis on family reunification as a key criterion for admission. Australia, Canada, and other industrial countries also leveled the source country playing field, but the effects on immigrant composition were not quite as dramatic as in the United States.

What Can We Expect?

Do the two global centuries of migration—before 1913 and since 1950—offer any insights into the future of global migration? It seems to me that they do.

While the poorest have never been part of any mass migration, it is clear that the European emigration of the 19th century diminished poverty there. Indeed, the living standards of host and sending countries converged during those decades, and the mass migrations did most of the convergence work. That is, world mass migration was *much* more important in contributing to convergence than were booming world trade and booming world capital markets in the first global century. If the same cannot be said of modern Asia, Africa, the Middle East, and Latin America, it is not because the impact of world capital markets and world trade are any more powerful, but rather because the emigrations are so much smaller relative to the huge populations that send their citizens to high-wage host countries. That is, compared with host countries, third-world sending countries have vastly bigger populations than did sending European countries before 1913. Thus, the same host country immigration rates today imply much smaller sending country emigration rates than they did a century ago.

In the first global century, emigration raised living standards in poor sending countries a lot. In the second global century, emigration *could* raise living standards in poor sending countries, but typically it does not. Why? First, successful development in poor countries today depends far more on rapid productivity growth and catch-up at home; second, today's rich countries no longer have open borders.

If more can be gained from world mass migration today than in the first global century, why are so many potential migrants kept out of industrial countries? In large part, the answer has to do with economic adjustment in the host countries and who is doing the adjusting. Thus, it has to do with the economic damage done to low-skilled native-born workers and their political clout. These factors played a central role when the United States, Australia, Argentina, and other overseas high-wage countries retreated from unrestricted immigration before World War I. They play the same role today. Modern immigration restriction also has to do with immigrants' net fiscal impact, who pays for it, and the political clout of those taxed. This issue did not arise during the immigration debates of the first global century because the welfare state did not yet exist.

Still, migrant demand for entrance into high-wage economies will not grow unabated. Indeed, it is unlikely to grow as fast over the next quarter century as it did in the previous quarter century. As the underlying *transitional* forces that have driven the surge in third-world emigration—their demographic and industrial revolutions—die out, so will the pressure to emigrate. That stage has already been reached in most of East Asia and much of Southeast Asia, regions that have completed their growth miracles. And spectacular growth in China and India ensures that it will soon be reached in Asia's two most populous countries. I believe that this stage will soon be reached even in slower-growing Latin America and the Middle East. Africa has yet to release a mass emigration on world markets and remains a wild card. Population aging in the postindustrial part of the world may increase the demand for immigrant labor, but a growth slowdown in host countries is likely to offset it.

My guess is that the next major shift in global migration will be a pronounced relative rise in migration *within* the third world (south-south migration) and a pronounced relative fall in migration *between* the third world and the west (south-north migration).

America's Stake in Immigration

Why Almost Everybody Wins

Giovanni **Peri**

Apart from the Iraq war, no issue seems to polarize American politics as much as immigration policy. And certainly no other issue has revealed as many fissures within both the conservative and liberal camps—a reality that has made it almost impossible to fashion legislative compromises.

The irony here is that while competition from new immigrants does reduce wages in some segments of the labor market, the evidence suggests that a great majority of American workers benefit from the influx. Indeed, foreign workers could greatly contribute to the future prosperity of America if immigration laws evolved toward freer international mobility of labor. While this may surprise those who depend on populist commentators for their analysis of immigration, it follows directly from widely accepted economic principles.

Immigration and Globalization

International migration has increased substantially in recent decades. In 2005, some 190 million people (2.9 percent of the world's population) lived outside their countries of origin—up from 82 million in 1970. But the economic impact has remained modest compared with that of the cross-border movement of goods, services and capital: as of 2004, trade equaled 27 percent of global GDP, while roughly 20 percent of total savings was

invested outside its country of origin. This explains why economists generally agree that by preventing labor from working where it is most productive, immigration restrictions sharply reduce the potential output of the world economy.

This has not always been the case. In the 1870–1920 period (often called the first era of globalization), most destination economies, including the United States, Canada, Latin America and Australia, allowed virtually unrestricted entry for immigrants from Europe. From 1901 to 1913, an average of one million people emigrated annually to the United States, a figure corresponding to about 2.5 percent of the domestic population each and every year.

Only in the last decade has legal U.S. immigration again reached the one million figure. Since the U.S. population is four times larger than a century ago, however, annual immigration represents at most 0.5 percent of the population, even if one allows for generous numbers of undocumented entrants.

The economic pressure to migrate, determined in large part by differences in wages, is much stronger now than during the first globalization era. In 1870, the wage of the average U.S. worker was only 2.5 times that of a worker in Ireland, one of the largest sources of immigrants.

In 1990, by contrast, the average U.S. wage was almost seven times the wage in Mexico. Note, too, that transportation costs are a small fraction of what they were a century ago—and an even smaller fraction of average incomes. Hence, there is no doubt that the current modest migration rates are the product of restrictive immigration laws in place in all developed countries.

Why is it so much more acceptable to stop labor from moving across political borders than to stop goods or capital? Certainly, culture and ideology play a part here: immigration can change everything from the languages spoken in schools, to attitudes toward social welfare programs, to the seasonings included in fast food. But economists believe that much of the explanation lies in the distribution of gains and losses associated with immigration—or, at least, the perception of who wins and who loses.

Not surprisingly, those with the most to gain from freer migration are the migrants themselves. But they do not vote in the receiving country (at least for a while). Incumbent workers can gain or lose, depending on their productive roles and skills. If they are business owners, they benefit from the increased return on investments linked to the availability of cheaper labor. If they are workers, they gain or not, depending on whether their jobs complement or compete with those taken by the immigrants.

Our research looks systematically at these differences—and, in particular, at the effect of the immigration of less educated workers, whose international mobility is most restricted, who are more likely to be undocumented, and who have triggered the current backlash against immigration.

Immigration and Complementarities

In the long run, average wages are determined by average labor productivity, which, in turn, is largely determined by technology and a host of societal institutions affecting the efficiency, competitiveness and openness of markets and governments. Anyone looking for a negative relationship between increases in the supply of labor and the average wage will not find it anywhere. In the last half century, for example, real wages in the United States have risen even as the labor force has doubled in size.

Note one qualification: since it takes some time to adjust productive capital (firms, structures, machines) to increases in the labor force, a large unexpected increase in employment in a short period may temporarily depress wages. But an influx of workers that is smaller than 0.5 percent of current employment and quite regular over the years hardly fits the bill. Each year for the last three decades, new investments have added 2 to 3 percent to the existing stock of capital in the United States, so the adjustment process has been more than adequate to keep pace with employment and keep the average wage on an upward long-run trajectory.

Then consider the effect of immigration on different types of workers. Assume for simplicity that there are two sorts of workers—less-educated (say with a high school degree or less) and highly educated (with at least some college education)—and that they perform different sorts of tasks. The former do jobs requiring mainly manual skills (cooking, cleaning, gardening, construction), while the latter do jobs requiring interactive/analytic skills (managing, coordinating, organizing, computing). The inflow of less-educated workers generates competition for workers already in that group, but also increases the demand for highly educated workers. In the long run, then, the wage of one group relative to the other is critically affected by relative changes in the number in each group.

So what is the contribution of foreign-born workers to the overall size of each group of workers in the United States? While 23 percent of workers with no degree were foreign-born in 2004, the comparable figure for high school and college graduates was just 8 to 10 percent. Then, at the very high end of the education

Brain Gain

The very large inflow of scientific talent to the United States, which by all accounts has been a key to sustaining high rates of technological innovation, has largely been powered by the pull of America's best research institutions—not by its immigration laws. Except for a few ad hoc programs (like the H1B visa program), Washington has shown little inclination to favor the entry of elite scientists. Moreover, since Sept. 11, 2001, indifference has been replaced by vague hostility, with the country adopting a better-safe-than-sorry policy to issuing visas.

Yet, as the figure shows, America is becoming increasingly dependent on foreign-born science workers. The number of new PhDs in science and engineering working here between 1973 and 2003 increased only because of the influx of foreigners. The pool of very talented, well-educated natives is not shrinking, but a larger portion of them are choosing careers in nonscientific professions like management and law. And as other countries begin to understand the importance of attracting talented scientists and engineers and to act on that understanding, the hurdles imposed by the United States immigration laws will almost certainly begin to pinch.

Ph.D. Degrees Awarded By U.S. Universities and National Origin, 1958–2003

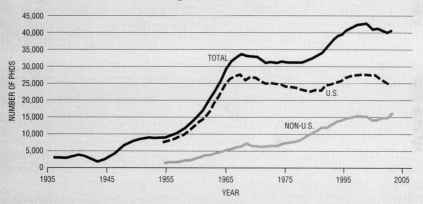

Sources: NSF, *Survey of Earned Doctorates* microdata and, before 1958, National Academy of Sciences (1958). National origin is defined by the country in which an individual went to high school.

spectrum, a whopping 30 percent of those with doctorates in science, engineering and technology were foreign-born.

Leaving aside the PhDs (who represent about 0.5 percent of the labor force), it is clear that immigrants have increased the supply of workers lacking diplomas far more than the supply of high school and college graduates. Accordingly, immigrant labor has depressed the wages of the least-educated workers, but increased the wages of workers with high school diplomas or more.

As of 2004, 89 percent of native workers had a high school degree or more, and only 11 percent lacked any degree. Therefore, roughly 9 in 10 working Americans gain from immigration. Moreover, the number of native workers with no degree has been shrinking fast. In 1960, 50 percent of native workers were in the no-degree group; two decades later, the figure was down to 20 percent, and, as noted above, it is now close to 10 percent.

U.S.-born workers are climbing the educational ladder, acquiring interactive/analytic skills and progressively leaving the manual jobs that would put them in competition with immigrants. If the trend continues as expected, the day is not far off when virtually all manual labor will be performed by foreign-born labor. This implies large wage gains for native workers, since they will be able to specialize in language-intensive and interactive tasks that are typically far better paid.

While some people shudder at the prospect of a more stratified society with immigrants at the bottom, keep in mind that the biggest gainers by far in this situation are the immigrants themselves. They can expect to earn six to seven times what they can now make in similar jobs in their countries of origin.

Let me also emphasize that this trend is not specific to the United States. As citizens of Europe and Japan become both more educated and older (and quickly so), they are becoming increasingly complementary in production to potential immigrants, who are less educated and younger.

Obviously, the gains from complementing one type of labor with another, for both the immigrants and receiving countries, will be realized only to the degree that immigration restrictions are relaxed.

Of course, as John Maynard Keynes pointed out, in the long run we are all dead. In the meantime, how much do less educated American workers stand to lose from more immigration? And how much can the highly educated expect to gain? For that matter, what about past immigrants to the United States? Are they more subject to competition from the new immigrants and thus likely to lose more than their native counterparts?

My colleagues and I found no evidence that immigrants caused unemployment among native workers with similar education and working experience during the 1960–2004 period. This is consistent with the idea that an inflow of workers creates opportunities for more investments and jobs, and thus should not raise unemployment rates in a labor market as competitive and flexible as that of the United States.

The fact that immigration didn't displace native workers doesn't imply that it didn't affect their wages, however. And here, we did find some impact—though most of the shock was felt by previous immigrants rather than by the native-born. This implies that native and foreign-born workers are not perfect substitutes in the labor market—that is, they compete only tangentially for the same jobs and occupations.

Specifically, the big influx of immigrants between 1990 and 2004 reduced the real wages of natives lacking a high school degree by less than 1.5 percent, but hammered the wages of earlier immigrants by 10 to 15 percent. Keep in mind that, because of the complementarities between less- and more-educated, the inflow of immigrants between 1990 and 2004 also *increased* the wages of United States-born workers with at least a high school degree by an average of 2 percent. Aggregating the gains of the more educated (representing 89 percent of United States-born workers) and the losses of the less educated (representing 11 percent) the net impact of immigration was to increase average wages of native workers by about 1.8 percent.

We studied the mechanism through which less educated native workers took advantage of new job opportunities opened by immigrants. Using data from the Department of Labor on skill content, we assayed the "manual" task content and the "language-interactive" task content of all (more than 500) occupational categories. The former measures the use of manual skills in performing such operations as driving, painting, cooking and cultivating. The latter measures the use of managerial and interactive skills in planning, directing, controlling and coordinating people and things.

Table 1

Percentage of Workers Foreign-Born and Manual/Interactive Intensity of Occupations

Occupation	% Of Workers, Foreign-Born, 2000	Manual Intensity	Interactive Intensity
AGRICULTURAL SECTOR			
Agricultural laborer	63%	0.82	0.32
Farm coordinator	4%	0.43	0.99
CONSTRUCTION SECTOR			
Construction helper	66%	0.86	0.02
Construction supervisor	8%	0.43	0.96
FOOD PREPARATION			
Food preparation laborer	33%	0.67	0.41
Supervisor of food preparation	14%	0.39	0.67
TRANSPORTATION SERVICES			
Taxi driver	40%	0.96	0.02
Supervisor/dispatcher of motor vehicles	10%	0.44	0.97

Source: Author, Department of Labor

We found that over the period 1970–2000 in states with large inflows of less-educated immigrants (think California), less-educated natives left manual-intensive jobs to immigrants and took up interactive-intensive job at a much faster pace than in states with small inflows of immigrants. Immigrants have manual skills that are as good as those of natives, but worse interactive skills because they require more knowledge of English and local culture. They thus compete for manual jobs, but in the process create demand for jobs managing and supervising the growing labor force.

Take the case of the construction industry. Workers with college degrees in that industry are likely to be employed as structural engineers, accountants, managers and the like. Workers with less than a high school diploma (but with applied skills like bricklaying and plumbing) might be construction workers or construction supervisors. Immigrants increase the supply of workers with less than a high school degree. But because they are generally young and lack fluency in English,

they largely compete for jobs turning on manual skills.

This added competition at the bottom of the scale tends to decrease the wages of manual construction workers, including many immigrants who have been in the country for some years. At the same time, as more construction companies start up and existing ones expand thanks to the larger availability of immigrant workers, the demand for supervisors and site coordinators increases. And here, less-educated workers (who are, on average, older than the immigrants) have the edge.

Table 1 shows examples of four pairs of occupations that are complementary in the sense that the first of each pair performs mostly manual tasks and the second performs mostly interactive tasks. All four sectors hire lots of immigrants, and none of the occupations requires more than a high school education. The manual and interactive intensity of each occupation is measured as an index between 0 and 1. Occupations that get a 1 in manual intensity (as reported by the Department of Labor) require sophisticated manual tasks (for example, jet pilots, athletes); those with a 1 in interactive intensity require sophisticated organizational-interactive tasks (for example, senior managers, ship captains).

Note that in each sector the occupation with relatively high manual content is disproportionately filled by foreign-born workers (the average in 2000 was 14 percent). By contrast, the occupations with higher interactive content employ smaller-than-average percentages of foreign-born.

The Big Picture

By definition, averages obscure the outliers: older native workers in manual-intensive jobs who haven't managed to take advantage of opportunities to upgrade to supervisory roles have probably suffered significantly from competition with immigrants in recent decades. But our research suggests far larger numbers of workers have gained from immigration.

Indeed, the only identifiable group of incumbent workers to sustain a significant loss from ongoing immigration consists of earlier immigrants.

This is an old story: each successive wave of immigrants has had economic reasons to try to close the door behind it.

But it is not an adequate reason for restricting entry this time around; opinion polls show that immigrants who have arrived in recent decades (those who stand to lose from continuing immigration) generally favor more liberal access, presumably because of the non-economic benefits of being reunited with family and friends. The biggest irony here is that most of the opposition to immigration comes from natives with little to lose and much to gain in economic terms—and that the opposition is largely focused on the least educated immigrants who are the ones most likely to create job opportunities for native workers and to raise their wages.

Discussion Questions

IV

1. What were the two great previous waves of immigration that Williamson discusses? What caused these waves? How do they differ from the current wave?

2. Williamson argues that political opposition to the current wave of U.S. immigration is higher than in the past. Why? Do you think opponents have legitimate reasons for their opposition?

3. Why does Peri believe that immigration is good for the U.S.? What evidence does he cite? Do you agree with him? Can you counter his arguments?

4. Immigration in the U.S. today involves both highly skilled workers and workers with little skill. Peri argues that both have contributed. Do you think that there are differences in terms of impacts to the U.S. economy for these two groups of immigrants?

Globalization

V

lobalization has increasingly become a critical issue for virtually every country in the world today. Economists generally see globalization as an extension of free trade and view globalization positively. However, globalization has a number of critics, including many Americans who see trade as a zero-sum game in which some people gain and some people lose. According to globalization's critics, the U.S. is losing out as China and other countries gain at our expense, exporting goods to the U.S. which lead to a loss in U.S. jobs, particularly in manufacturing.

The first article, "The Global Governance of Trade as if Development Really Mattered," by Dani Rodrik, a professor at Harvard's Kennedy School of Government, argues that most of the multilateral institutions set up to protect the international order, in particular the WTO, have fostered policies than benefit the developed, industrialized world, as opposed to developing countries. He believes that every country has different development needs and must tailor a trade policy to encourage growth and development. Rodrik does not believe that a one-size-fits-all free trade regime is best for everyone. He pre-

sents a detailed overview of trade and development policies over the past 30 years, and argues that the development of stable institutions to reduce conflict within a country is of paramount importance compared to the relatively small gains that economists estimate for free trade versus protectionism. Rodrik also argues that a careful examination of the evidence does not show a strong correlation between free trade policies and growth. In short, a reevaluation of the policies that governed the last 50 years of trade negotiations is in order.

In contrast to Rodrik (above) Christian Broda and David Weinstein, argue in "Are We Underestimating the Gains from Globalization for the United States?" that the U.S. gains enormously from globalization. Further, they believe that standard measures of welfare seriously underestimate the gains from globalization. Their estimates indicate that globalization leads to a gain of $260 billion for the U.S. from 1972 to 2001.

The final article, "What's So Special About China's Exports?" again by Dani Rodrik, focuses on China, a key player in the debate over globalization. Rodrik argues that China's success and its pattern of exports cannot be explained simply by the theory of comparative advantage, which would predict that China would only export goods based on low wages. In addition to cheaper goods, Rodrik argues, China also exports much more sophisticated goods. Rodrik believes that the Chinese government has, in fact followed their own version of an industrial policy, supporting key industries even when market forces might now support them.

The Global Governance of Trade as if Development Really Mattered

Dani **Rodrik**

Introduction

What objectives does (or should) the World Trade Organization (WTO) serve? The first substantive paragraph of the Agreement establishing the WTO lists the following aspirations:

raising standards of living, ensuring full employment and a large and steadily growing volume of real income and effective demand, and expanding the production of and trade in goods and services, while allowing for the optimal use of the world's resources in accordance with the objective of sustainable development, seeking both to protect and preserve the environment and to enhance the means for doing so in a manner consistent with their respective needs and concerns at different levels of economic development. (WTO 1995:9)

A subsequent paragraph cites 'mutually advantageous arrangements directed to the substantial reduction of tariffs and other barriers to trade and to the elimination of discriminatory treatment in international trade relations' as a means of 'contributing to these objectives' (ibid.). It is clear from this preamble that the WTO's framers placed priority on raising standards of living and on sustainable development. Expanding trade was viewed as a means towards that end, rather than an

end in itself. Recently, promoting economic development has acquired an even higher standing in the official rhetoric of the WTO, partly in response to its critics.[1]

That the purpose of the world trade regime is to raise living standards all around the world—rather than to maximize trade per se—has never been controversial. In practice, however, these two goals—promoting development and maximizing trade—have increasingly come to be viewed as synonymous by the WTO and multilateral lending agencies, to the point where the latter easily substitutes for the former. As the WTO's Mike Moore (2000) puts it, 'the surest way to do more to help the poor is to continue to open markets.' This view has the apparent merit that it is backed by a voluminous empirical literature that identifies trade as a key determinant of economic growth. It also fits nicely with traditional modus operandi of the WTO, which is to focus predominantly on reciprocal market access (instead of development-friendly trade rules). However, the net result is a confounding of ends and means. Trade becomes the lens through which development is perceived, rather than the other way around.

Imagine a trading regime that is true to the WTO preamble, one in which trade rules are determined so as to maximize development potential, particularly of the world's poorest nations. Instead of asking, 'How do we maximize trade and market access?' negotiators would ask, 'How do we enable countries to grow out of poverty?' Would such a regime look different from the one that exists currently?

The answer depends on how one interprets recent economic history and the role that trade openness plays in the course of economic development. The prevailing view in G7 capitals and multilateral lending agencies is that integration into the global economy is an essential determinant of economic growth. Successful integration in turn requires both enhanced market access in the advanced industrial countries and a range of institutional reforms at home (ranging from legal and administrative reform to safety nets) to render economic openness viable and growth promoting. This can be regarded as the 'enlightened standard view'—enlightened because of its recognition that there is more to integration than simply lowering tariff and non-tariff barriers to trade, and standard because it represents the prevailing conventional wisdom (see World Bank/IMF 2000). In this conception, today's WTO represents what the doctor ordered: the focus on expanding market access and deepening integration through the harmonization of a wide range of 'trade related' practices is precisely what development requires.

This paper presents an alternative account of economic development, one that questions the centrality of trade and trade policy and emphasizes instead the critical role of domestic institutional innovations that often depart from prevailing orthodoxy. In this view, transitions to high economic growth are rarely sparked by blueprints imported from abroad. Opening up the economy is hardly ever a key factor at the outset. The initiating reforms instead tend to be a combination of unconventional institutional innovations with some of the elements drawn from the orthodox recipe. These combinations tend to be country-specific, requiring local knowledge and experimentation for successful implementation. They are targeted on domestic investors and tailored to domestic institutional realities.

In this alternative view, a development-friendly international trading regime is one that does much more than enhance poor countries' access to markets in the advanced industrial countries. It is one that enables poor countries to experiment with institutional arrangements and leaves room for them to devise their own, possibly divergent solutions to the developmental bottlenecks that they face. It is one that evaluates the demands of institutional reform not from the perspective of integration ('What do countries need to do to integrate?') but from the perspective of development ('What do countries need to do achieve broad-based, equitable economic growth?'). In this vision, the WTO would no longer serve as an instrument for the harmonization of economic policies and practices across countries, but become an organization that manages the interface between different national practices and institutions.

This paper argues that a renewed focus on development and poverty reduction, along with an empirically-based understanding of the development process, would have far-reaching implications for the way in which the international trading regime and the WTO function. It focuses on broad principles, rather than specific recommendations, because it is only through a change in the overall perspective of trade negotiations that significant change can be accomplished.

One of the key propositions is that developing countries are shortchanging themselves when they focus their complaints on specific asymmetries in market access (tariff peaks against developing country exports, industrial country protection in agriculture and textiles, etc.). This approach reflects acceptance of a market–access perspective that does developing countries limited good. They would be far better served by pressing for changes that enshrine development at the top of the WTO agenda, and correspondingly provide them with a better mix of enhanced market access and manoeuvring room to pursue appropriate development strategies.

Since this paper is as much about the approach to development that should inform views about the international trade regime as it is about the WTO itself, much of the discussion is devoted to the empirical content of these ideas. The paper begins with an assertion that the distinction between development strategies that focus on growth versus those that focus on poverty reduction is a false one, since in practice, the two ends are inseparable. The main strike against existing trade rules is not that they over-emphasize trade and growth at the expense of poverty reduction, but that they over-emphasize the expense of poverty reduction and growth. It then argues that the enlightened standard development model encompasses an impossibly broad and unfocused development agenda, and one that is biased towards a particular set of institutional arrangements. It emphasizes instead the centrality of domestic institutional innovations (comprising a mix of orthodoxy with 'local heresies') and of investment strategies that are tailored to the circumstances of each country.

Much of the paper focuses on the link between trade policy and economic performance. The voluminous literature in this area, which forms the basis for the oft-heard claims to the benefits of trade openness, is, upon examination, less unequivocal. A close look reveals that there is no convincing evidence that trade liberalization is predictably associated with subsequent economic growth. This raises serious questions about the priority that the integrationist policy agenda typically receives in orthodox reform programmes. The problem is not trade liberalization per se, but the diversion of financial resources and political capital from more urgent and deserving developmental priorities.

Finally, the paper offers some general principles for a world trade regime that puts development first. First, the trade regime must accept, rather than seek to eliminate, institutional diversity along with the right of countries to 'protect' their institutional arrangements. However, the right to protect one's own social arrangements is distinct from, and does not extend to,

the right to impose it on others. Once these simple principles are accepted and internalized in trade rules, developmental priorities of poor nations and the needs of the industrial countries can be rendered compatible and mutually supportive.

Growth versus Poverty Reduction: A Meaningless Debate

Should governments pursue economic growth first and foremost, or should they focus on poverty reduction? Recent debate on this question has become embroiled in broader political controversies on globalization and its impact on developing economies. Critics of the WTO often take it to task for being overly concerned about the level of economic activity (and its growth) at the expense of poverty reduction. Supporters argue that expanded trade and higher economic growth are the best ways to reduce poverty. This largely sterile debate merely diverts attention from the real issues. In practice, economic growth and poverty reduction do tend to correlate very closely. However, the real question is (or ought to be) whether open trade policies are a reliable mechanism for generating self-sustaining growth and poverty reduction, the evidence for which is far less convincing.

Regarding the relationship between growth and poverty reduction, let's take some of the easier questions. Does growth benefit the poor? Yes, in general. The absolute number of people living in poverty has dropped in all of the developing countries that have sustained rapid growth over the past few decades. In theory, a country could enjoy a high average growth rate without any benefit to its poorest households if income disparities grew significantly—that is, if the rich got richer while the incomes of the poor stagnated or declined. This is unlikely, however; income distribution tends to be stable over time, and rarely changes so much that the poor would experience an absolute decline in incomes while average incomes grow in a sustained fashion.

Moreover, to the extent that income distribution changes, its relationship to economic growth varies from country to country. Growth has been accompanied by greater equality of income in the Taiwan Province of China, Bangladesh and Egypt, for example, but by greater inequality in Chile, China and Poland. This suggests that the magnitude of the poverty reduction payoff from growth depends, in part, on a country's specific circumstances and policies.

Is poverty reduction good for growth? Again, yes, in general. It is hard to think of countries where a large decrease in the absolute number of people living in poverty has not been accompanied by faster growth. Just as we can imagine growth occurring without any reduction of poverty, we can also imagine a strategy of poverty reduction that relies exclusively on redistributing wealth from the rich and the middle classes to the poor. In principle, a country pursuing redistributive policies could reduce poverty even if its total income did not grow. But we would be hard-pressed to find real-world examples. Policies that increase the incomes of the poor, such as investments in primary education, rural infrastructure, health and nutrition, tend to enhance the productive capacity of the whole economy, boosting the incomes of all groups.

What does a high correlation between growth and the incomes of the poor tell us? Practically nothing, for the reasons outlined above. All it shows is that income distribution tends to be stable and fairly unresponsive to policy changes. Moreover, a strong correlation between economic growth and poverty reduction is compatible with both of the following arguments: (1) only policies that target growth can reduce poverty; and (2) only policies that reduce poverty can boost overall economic growth. Therefore, the observed correlation between growth and poverty reduction is of little interest as far as policy choices and priorities are concerned.

A somewhat different question is whether the well-being of the poor should enter as an independent determinant of policy choices, in addition to the usual focus on macroeconomic stability, macroeconomic efficiency, and institutional qual-ity. In other words, should economic reform strategies have a poverty focus? Yes, for at least three reasons. First, in considering social welfare, most people in general, and most democratically elected governments in particular, would give more weight to the well-being of the poor than to that of the rich. An economy's growth rate is not a sufficient statistic for evaluating welfare because it ignores the distribution of the rewards of growth. A policy that increases the income of the poor by one rupee can be worthwhile at the margin even if it costs the rest of society more than a rupee. From this perspective, it may be entirely rational and proper for a government considering two competing growth strategies to choose the one that has greater potential payoff for the poor even if its impact on overall growth is less assured.

Second, even if the welfare of the poor does not receive extra weight, interventions aimed at helping the poor may still be the most effective way to raise average incomes. Poverty is naturally associated with market imperfections and incompleteness. The poor remain poor because they cannot borrow against future earnings to invest in education, skills, new crops and entrepreneurial activities. They are cut off from economic activity because they are deprived of many collective goods (e.g., property rights, public safety, infrastructure) and lack information about market opportunities. It is a standard tenet of economic theory that raising real average incomes requires interventions targeted at closing gaps between private and social costs. There will be a preponderance of such opportunities where there is a preponderance of poverty.

Third, focusing on poverty is also warranted from the perspective of an approach to development that goes beyond an exclusive focus on consumption or income to embrace human capabilities. As Amartya Sen (1999) has emphasized, the overarching goal of development is to maximize people's capabilities—that is, their ability to lead the kind of life they value. The poor face the greatest hurdles in this area and are therefore the most deserving of urgent policy attention.

Policy-makers make choices and determine priorities all the time. The lens through which they perceive development profoundly affects their choices. Keeping poverty in sight ensures that their priorities are not distorted. Consider some illustrative trade-offs.

- *Fiscal policy.* How should a government resolve the trade-off between higher spending on poverty-related projects (rural infrastructure, say) and the need for tight fiscal policies? Should it risk incurring the disapproval of financial markets as the price of better irrigation? How should it allocate its educational budget? Should more be spent on building primary schools in rural areas or on training bank auditors and accountants?
- *Market liberalization.* Should the government maintain price controls on food crops, even if such controls distort resource allocation in the economy? Should it remove capital controls on the balance of payments, even if that means fiscal resources will be tied up in holding additional foreign reserves—resources that could otherwise have been used to finance a social fund?
- *Institutional reform.* How should the government design its anti-corruption strategy? Should it target the large-scale corruption that foreign investors complain about or the petty corruption in the police and judicial systems that affect ordinary citizens? Should legal reform focus on trade and foreign investment or domestic problems? Whose property rights should receive priority, peasants or foreign patent holders? Should the government pursue land reform, even if it threatens politically powerful groups?

As these examples illustrate, in practice, even the standard, growth-oriented desiderata of macroeconomic stability, microeconomic efficiency and institutional reform leave considerable room for manoeuvre. Governments can use this room to better or worse effect. A poverty focus helps ensure that the relevant trade-offs are considered explicitly.

Since growth and poverty reduction go largely hand in hand, the real questions are: What are the policies that yield these rewards? How much do we know about policy impacts? The honest answer is that we do not know nearly enough. We have evidence that land reforms, appropriately targeted price reforms and certain types of health and education expenditures benefit the poor, but we are uncertain about many things. It is one thing to say that development strategies should have a poverty focus, another to identify the relevant policies.

But this is not a strike against poverty-oriented programmes, since we are equally uncertain about growth-oriented programmes. The uncomfortable reality is that our knowledge about the kinds of policies that stimulate growth remains limited. We know that large fiscal and macroeconomic imbalances are bad for growth. We know that 'good' institutions are important, even though we have very little idea about how countries can acquire them. And, despite a voluminous literature on the subject, we know next to nothing about the kinds of trade policies that are most conducive to growth (see below).

For all of these reasons, it is not productive to make a sharp distinction between policies that promote growth and those that target the poor directly. These policies are likely to vary considerably depending on institutional context, making it difficult to generalize with any degree of precision. Our real focus should be on what works, how, and under what circumstances.

Achieving Economic Growth: What Really Matters?

The enlightened standard view of development policy grew out of dissatisfaction with the limited results yielded by the Washington Consensus policies of the 1980s and 1990s. The disappointing

Table 1

The Original Washington Consensus	The Augmented Washington Consensus
Fiscal discipline	*The original list plus:*
Reorientation of public expenditures	Legal/political reform
Tax reform	Regulatory institutions
Financial liberalization	Anti-corruption
Unified and competitive exchange rates	Labour market flexibility
Unified and competitive exchange rates	WTO agreements
Trade liberalization	Financial codes and standards
Openness to DFI	'Prudent' capital-account opening
Privatization	Non-intermediate exchange rate regimes
Deregulations	Social safety nets
Secure property rights	Poverty reduction

growth performance and increasing economic insecurity in Latin America—the region that went furthest with policies of privatization, liberalization and openness—the failures in the former Soviet Union, and the Asian financial crisis of 1997–98 all contributed to a refashioning, resulting in the 'augmented Washington Consensus' (shown in Table 1). This goes beyond liberalization and privatization to emphasize the need to create the institutional underpinnings of market economies. Reforms now include financial regulation and prudential supervision governance and anti-corruption, legal and administrative reform, labour-market 'flexibility' and social safety nets.

Operationally, these institutional reforms are heavily influenced by an Anglo-American conception of what constitutes desirable institutions (as in the preference for arms-length finance over 'development banking' and flexible labour markets over institutionalized labour markets). In addition, they are driven largely by the requirements of integration into the world economy: hence the emphasis on the international harmonization of regulatory practices, as in the case of financial codes and standards and of the WTO agreements.

Market economies rely on a wide array of non-market institutions that perform regulatory stabilization and legitimizing functions (see Rodrik 2001a). Cross-national econometric work shows that the quality of a country's public institutions is a critical and perhaps the most important, determinant of a country's long-term development (Acemoglu et al. 2000). While the recent emphasis on institutions is thus highly welcome, it needs to be borne in mind that the institutional basis for a market economy is not uniquely determined. There is no single mapping between a well-functioning market and the form of non-market institutions required to sustain it, as is clear from the wide variety of regulatory, stabilizing and legitimizing institutions in today's advanced industrial societies. The American style of capitalism is very different from the Japanese style of capitalism. Both differ from the European style. And even within Europe, there are large differences between the institutional arrangements in, say, Sweden and Germany. Over the long term, each of these have performed equally well.[2]

The point about institutional diversity has in fact a more fundamental implication. As Roberto Unger (1998) argues, the institutional arrangements in operation today, varied as they are, themselves constitute a subset of the full range of potential institutional possibilities. There is no reason to suppose that modern societies have exhausted all useful institutional variations that could underpin healthy and vibrant economies. We must avoid thinking that a specific type of institution—mode of corporate governance, social security system or labour market legislation, for example—is the only one compatible with a well-functioning market economy.

Leaving aside the question of long-term choice over institutional forms, the enlightened standard view, insofar as it is presented as a recipe for stimulating economic growth, also suffers from a fatal flaw: it provides no sense of priorities among a long and highly demanding list of institutional prerequisites. This kitchen-sink approach to development strategy flies in the face of practical reality and is at odds with the historical experience of today's advanced industrial economies. What are today regarded as key institutional reforms in areas such as corporate governance, financial supervision, trade law and social safety nets did not take place in Europe or Northern America until quite late in the economic development process (Chang 2000). Indeed, many of the items on the augmented Washington Consensus agenda (Table 1) should be properly viewed as outcomes of successful economic development rather than its prerequisites.

The reality of growth transformations is that they are instigated by an initially narrow set of policy and institutional initiatives, which might be called 'investment strategies' (Rodrik 1999). Adequate human resources, public infrastructure, social peace and stability are all key enabling elements of an investment strategy. But often the critical factor is a set of targeted policy interventions that kindle the animal spirits of domestic investors. These investment strategies set off a period of economic growth, which in turn facilitates a cycle of institutional development and further growth. The initiating reforms are rarely replicas of each other, and they bear only partial resemblance to the requirements highlighted by the enlightened standard

view. Typically, they entail a mix of orthodoxy with unconventional domestic innovations. An analysis of three sets of investment strategies will elucidate this central point and highlight the different paths taken to greater prosperity: import-substitution, East Asian-style outward orientation and two-track reform strategies. The list is not meant to be exhaustive, and in the future successful strategies are likely to differ from all three.

Import-Substituting Industrialization (ISI)

Import-substituting industrialization is based on the idea that domestic investment and technological capabilities can be spurred by providing home producers with (temporary) protection against imports. Although this approach has fallen into disgrace since the 1980s, it actually did quite well for a substantial period of time in scores of developing nations. Until the first oil shock hit in 1973, no fewer than 42 developing countries grew at rates exceeding 2.5 per cent per capita per annum (see Rodrik 1999: ch. 4). At this rate, incomes would double every 28 years or less.

The list of countries which followed ISI policies include 12 countries in South America, six in the Middle East and North Africa, and 15 in Sub-Saharan Africa. In fact, there were no less than six Sub-Saharan African countries among the 20 fastest-growing developing countries in the world prior to 1973: Swaziland, Botswana, Côte d' Ivoire, Lesotho, Gabon and Togo, with Kenya ranking 21st. There can be little doubt that economic growth led to substantial improvements in the living conditions of the vast majority of the house-holds in these countries. Between 1967 and 1977, life expectancy at birth increased by four years in Brazil (from 58 to 62), by five years in Cote d' Ivoire (from 43 to 48), by five years in Mexico (from 60 to 65), and by five years in Pakistan (from 48 to 53). In Kenya, infant mortality fell from 112 (per 1,000 live births) in 1965 to 72 in 1980.

ISI policies spurred growth by creating protected and therefore profitable home markets for domestic entrepreneurs to invest in. Contrary to received wisdom, ISI-driven growth did not produce technological lags and inefficiency on an economy-wide scale. In fact, the productivity performance of many Latin American and Middle Eastern countries was, in comparative perspective, exemplary. According to estimates produced by Collins and Bosworth (1996), not only was average total factor productivity (TFP) growth during the period preceding the first oil shock quite high in the Middle East and Latin America (at 2.3 and 1.8%, respectively), it was actually significantly higher than in East Asia (1.3%)! Countries such as Brazil, the Dominican Republic and Ecuador in Latin America; Iran, Morocco and Tunisia in the Middle East; and Côte d' Ivoire and Kenya in Africa all experienced more rapid TFP growth than any of the East Asian countries in this early period (with the possible exception of Hong Kong, for which comparable data are not available). Mexico, Bolivia, Panama, Egypt, Algeria, Tanzania and Zaire experienced higher TFP growth than all but Taiwan. Of course, not all countries following ISI policies did well: Argentina is a striking counter-example, with an average TFP growth of only 0.2% from 1960 to 1973.

The dismal reputation of ISI is due partly to the subsequent economic collapse experienced by many of the countries pursuing it in the 1980s, and partly to the extremely influential studies of Little, Scott and Scitovsky (1970) and Bela Balassa (1971). What these two studies did was to document in detail some of the static economic inefficiencies generated by high and extremely dispersed effective rates of protection (ERP) in the manufacturing sectors of the countries under study. The discovery of cases of negative value-added at world prices—that is, cases where countries would have been better off by throwing away the inputs than by processing them as they did in highly

protected plants—was particularly shocking. However, neither study claimed to show that countries which had followed 'outward oriented' strategies had been systematically immune from the same kind of inefficiencies. In fact, their evidence can be read as suggesting that there was no such clear dividing line.[3] In addition, the evidence on TFP growth reviewed above shows that the idea that ISI produced more dynamic inefficiency than did 'outward orientation' is simply incorrect.

Hence, as an industrialization strategy intended to raise domestic investment and enhance productivity, import substitution apparently worked pretty well in a very broad range of countries until at least the mid-1970s. However, starting in the second half of the 1970s, a disaster befell the vast majority of the economies that had been doing well. Of the 42 countries with growth rates above 2.5% prior to 1973, less than a third (12) managed the same record over the next decade. The Middle East and Latin America, which had led the developing world in TFP growth prior to 1973, not only fell behind, but actually began to experience negative TFP growth on average. Only East Asia held its own, while South Asia actually improved its performance (see Collins and Bosworth 1996).

Was this a result of the 'exhaustion' of import-substitution policies? As I have argued elsewhere (Rodrik 1999), the common timing implicates the turbulence experienced in the world economy following 1973—the abandonment of the Bretton Woods system of fixed exchange rates, two major oil shocks, various other commodity boom-and-bust cycles, plus the U.S. Federal Reserve interest-rate shock of the early 1980s. The fact that some of the most ardent followers of ISI policies in South Asia—especially India and Pakistan—managed to either hold on to their growth rates after 1973 (Pakistan) or increase them (India) also suggests that more than just ISI was involved.[4]

The actual story implicates macroeconomic policies rather than the trade regime. The proximate reason for the economic collapse was the inability to adjust macro-economic policies appropriately in the wake of these external shocks. Macroeconomic mal-adjustment gave rise to a range of syndromes associated with macroeconomic instability—high or repressed inflation, scarcity of foreign exchange and large black-market premiums, external payments imbalances and debt crises—which greatly magnified the real costs of the shocks. Countries that suffered the most were those with the largest increases in inflation and black-market premiums for foreign currency. The culprits were poor monetary and fiscal policies and inadequate adjustments in exchange-rate policy, sometimes aggravated by shortsighted policies of creditors and the Bretton Woods institutions. The bottom line is that in those countries that experienced a debt crisis, the crisis was the product of monetary and fiscal policies that were incompatible with sustainable external balances: there was too little expenditure reducing and expenditure switching. Trade and industrial policies had very little to do with bringing on the crisis.

Why were some countries quicker to adjust their macroeconomic policies than others? The real determinants of growth performance after the 1970s are rooted in the ability of domestic institutions to manage the distributional conflicts triggered by the external shocks of the period. Social conflicts and their management—whether successful or not—played a key role in transmitting the effects of external shocks on to economic performance. Societies with deep social cleavages and poor institutions of conflict management proved worse at handling shocks (see Rodrik 1999).

'Outward-Oriented' Industrialization

The experience of the East Asian tigers is often presented as one of export-led growth, in which opening up to the world economy unleashed powerful forces of industrial diversification and technological catch-up. However, the conventional account overlooks the active role taken by the governments of Taiwan Province of China and the Republic of Korea (and Japan before them) in shaping the allocation resources. In neither of these countries was there significant import liberalization early in the process of growth. Most of their trade liberalization took place in the 1980s, when high growth was already firmly established.

The key to these and other East Asian countries' success was a coherent strategy of raising the return to private investment, through a range of policies that included credit subsidies and tax incentives, educational policies, establishment of public enterprises, export inducements, duty-free access to inputs and capital goods and actual government coordination of investment plans. In the Republic of Korea, the chief form of investment subsidy was the extension of credit to large business groups at negative real interest rates. Korean banks were nationalized after the military coup of 1961, and consequently the government obtained exclusive control over the allocation of investible funds in the economy. Another important manner in which investment was subsidized in Korea was through the socialization of investment risk in selected sectors. This emerged because the government—most notably President Park—provided an implicit guarantee that the state would bail out entrepreneurs investing in 'desirable' activities if circumstances later threatened the profitability of those investments. In Taiwan, investment subsidies took the form of tax incentives. In both the Republic of Korea and Taiwan, public enterprises played a very important role in enhancing the profitability of private investment by ensuring that key inputs were available locally for private producers downstream. Not only did public enterprises account for a large share of manufacturing output and investment in each country, their importance actually increased during the critical take-off years of the 1960s. Singapore also heavily subsidized investment, but this country differs from the

Republic of Korea and Taiwan in that its investment incentives centred heavily on foreign investors.

While trade policies that spurred exports were part of this complex arsenal of incentives, investment and its promotion was the key goal in all countries. To that end, governments in the Republic of Korea and Taiwan freely resorted to unorthodox strategies: they protected the home markets to raise profits, implemented generous export subsidies, encouraged their firms to reverse-engineer foreign patented products, and imposed performance requirements such as export-import balance requirements and domestic content requirements on foreign investors (when foreign companies were allowed in). All of these strategies are now severely restricted under the WTO agreements.

The Two-Track Strategy

A relatively minimal set of reforms in China in the late 1970s set the stage for the phenomenal economic performance that has been the envy of any poor country since. Initial reforms were relatively simple: they loosened the communal farming system and allowed farmers to sell their crops in free markets once they had fulfilled their quota obligations to the state. Subsequent reforms allowed the creation of township and village enterprises and the extension of the 'market track' into the urban and industrial sectors. Special economic zones were created to attract foreign investments. What stands out about these reforms is that they are based on dual tracks (state and market), on gradualism and on experimentation.

One can interpret Chinese-style gradualism in two ways. One perspective, represented forcefully in work by Sachs and Woo (2000) underplays the relevance of Chinese particularism by arguing that the successes of the economy are not due to any special aspects of the Chinese transition to a market economy, but instead are largely due to a convergence of Chinese institutions with those in non-socialist economies. In this view, the faster the convergence, the better

the outcomes: 'favorable outcomes have emerged not because of gradualism, but despite gradualism' (ibid: 3). The policy message that follows is that countries that look to China for lessons should focus not on institutional experimentation but on harmonizing their institutions with those abroad.

The alternative perspective, perhaps best developed in work by Qian and Roland, is that the peculiarities of the Chinese model represent solutions to particular political or informational problems for which no blueprint-style solution exists. Hence Lau, Qian and Roland (1997) interpret the dual-track approach to liberalization as a way of implementing Pareto-efficient reforms: an alteration in the planned economy that improves incentives at the margin, enhances efficiency in resource allocation, and yet leaves none of the plan beneficiaries worse off. Qian, Roland and Xu (1999) interpret Chinese-style decentralization as all owing to the development of superior institutions of coordination: when economic activity requires products with matched attributes, local experimentation is a more effective way of processing and using local knowledge. These analysts find much to praise in the Chinese model because they think the system generates the right incentives for developing the tacit knowledge required to build and sustain a market economy, and therefore, they are not overly bothered by some of the economic inefficiencies that may be generated along the way.

A less well-known instance of a successful two-track strategy is that of Mauritius, where superior economic performance has been built on a peculiar combination of orthodox and heterodox strategies. An export processing zone (EPZ), operating under free-trade principles, enabled an export boom in garments to European markets and an accompanying investment boom at home. Yet the island's economy has combined the EPZ with a domestic sector that was highly protected until the mid-1980s: the IMF gave the Mauritian economy the highest (i.e., worst) score on its 'policy restrictiveness' index for the early 1990s, reckoning it was one of the world most protected economies even by the late 1990s (see Subramanian 2001). Mauritius is essentially an example of an economy that has followed a two-track strategy not too dissimilar to that followed by China, but which was underpinned by social and political arrangements that encouraged participation, representation and coalition building.

The circumstances under which the Mauritian EPZ was set up in 1970 are instructive, and highlight the manner in which participatory political systems help design creative strategies for building locally adapted institutions. Given the small size of the home market, it was evident that Mauritius would benefit from an outward-oriented strategy. But as in other developing countries, policy-makers had to contend with the import substituting industrialists who had been propped up by the restrictive commercial policies of the early 1960s prior to independence, and who were naturally opposed to relaxing the trade regime.

A Washington economist would have advocated across-the-board liberalization without regard to what that might do the precarious ethnic and political balance of the island. The EPZ scheme provided a neat way around the political difficulties. The creation of the EPZ generated new opportunities of trade and of employment, without taking protection away from the import-substituting groups and from the male workers who dominated the established industries. The segmentation of labour markets early on between male and female workers—with the latter predominantly employed in the EPZ—was particularly crucial as it prevented the expansion of the EPZ from driving wages up in the rest of the economy, thereby disadvantaging import-substituting industries. New employment and profit opportunities were created at the margin, while leaving old opportunities undisturbed. This in turn paved the way for the more substantial liberalizations that took place in the mid-1980s and

in the 1990s. By the 1990s, the female-male earning ratio was higher in the EPZ than in the rest of the economy (ILO 2001, table 28). Mauritius found its own way to economic development because it was able to devise a strategy that was unorthodox, yet effective.

The Bottom Line

These examples suggest that while market incentives, macroeconomic stability and sound institutions are critical to economic development, they can be generated in a number of different ways—by making the best use of existing capabilities in light of resource and other constraints. There is no single model of a successful transition to a high-growth path. Each country has to figure out its own investment strategy. Once the appropriate strategy is identified (or stumbled upon), the institutional reforms needed may not be extensive. Most of the institutional development occurs alongside economic development, not as a prerequisite to it.

Trade Liberalization, Growth and Poverty Reduction: What Do the Facts Really Show?

Consider two countries, A and B. Country A engages in state trading, maintains import monopolies, retains quantitative restrictions and high tariffs (in the range of 30-50 per-cent) on imports of agricultural and industrial products and is not a member of the WTO. Country B, a WTO member, has slashed import tariffs to a maximum of 15 percent and removed all quantitative restrictions, earning a rare recommendation from the U. S. State Department that 'there are few significant barriers to US exports' (US State Department 1999). One of the two economies has experienced GDP growth rates in excess of 8 percent per annum, has sharply reduced poverty, has expanded trade at double-digit rates, and has attracted large amounts of foreign investment. The other economy has stagnated and suffered deteriorating social indicators, and has made little progress in integrating with the world economy as judged by trade and foreign investment flows.

Country A is Viet Nam, which since the mid-1980s has followed Chinese-style gradualism and a two-track reform programme. Country B is Haiti. Viet Nam has been phenomenally successful, achieving not only high growth and poverty reduction but also a rapid pace of integration into the world economy despite high barriers to trade. Haiti's economy has gone nowhere, even though the country undertook a comprehensive trade liberalization in 1994–95.

The contrasting experiences of these two countries highlight two important points. First, a leadership committed to development and standing behind a coherent growth strategy counts for a lot more than trade liberalization, even when the strategy departs sharply from the enlightened standard view on reform. Second, integration with the world economy is an outcome, not a prerequisite of a successful growth strategy. Protected Viet Nam is integrating with the world economy significantly more rapidly than is open Haiti, because Viet Nam is growing and Haiti is not.

This comparison illustrates a common misdiagnosis. A typical World Bank exercise consists of classifying developing countries into 'globalizers' and 'non-globalizers' based on their rates of growth of trade volumes. The analyst asks whether globalizers (i.e., those with the highest rates of trade growth) have experienced faster income growth, greater poverty reduction and worsened income distribution (see Dollar and Kraay 2000). The answers tends to be yes, yes, and no. As the Viet Nam and Haiti cases show, however, this is a highly misleading exercise. Trade volumes are the outcome of many different things, including most importantly an economy's overall performance. They are not something that governments control directly. What governments control are trade policies: the level of tariff and no-tariff

barriers, membership in the WTO, compliance with its agreements and so on. The relevant question is: Do open trade policies reliably produce higher economic growth and greater poverty reduction?

Cross-national comparison of the literature reveals no systematic relationship between a country's average level of tariff and non-tariff restrictions and its subsequent economic growth rate. If anything, the evidence for the 1990s indicates a positive (but statistically insignificant) relationship between tariffs and economic growth (see Figure 1). The only systematic relationship is that countries dismantle trade restrictions as they get richer. That accounts for the fact that today's rich countries, with few exceptions, embarked on modern economic growth behind protective barriers, but now have low trade barriers.

The absence of a robust positive hip between open trade policies and economic growth may come as a surprise in view of the ubiquitous claim that trade liberalization promotes higher growth. Indeed, the literature is replete with cross-national studies concluding that growth and economic dynamism are strongly linked to more liberal trade policies. For example, an influential study by Sachs and Warner (1995) found that economies that are open, by their definition, grew 2.4 percentage points faster annually than did those that are not—an enormous difference. Without such studies, organizations such as the World Bank, IMF and the WTO could not have been so vociferous in their promotion of trade concentric development strategies.

Upon closer look, however, these studies turn out to be flawed. The classification of countries as 'open' or 'closed' in the Sachs-Warner study, for example, is not based on actual trade policies but largely on indicators related to exchange rate policy and location in Sub-Saharan Africa. Their classification of countries in effect conflates macroeconomics, geography and institutions with trade policy. It is so correlated with plausible groupings of alternative

Low Import Tariffs Are Good For Growth? Think Again
Figure 1

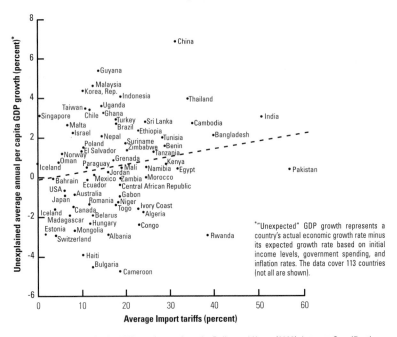

Sources: All data are averages for the 1990s, and come from the Dollar and Kraay (2000) data set. Specifications are based on Dollar and Kraay (2000), replacing trade/GDP with tariff levels and controlling separately for initial income, government consumption/GDP and inflation rate.

explanatory variables—macroeconomic instability, poor institutions, location in Africa—that one cannot draw from the subsequent empirical analysis any strong inferences about the effects of openness on growth (see Rodriguez and Rodrik 2001).

The problem is a general one. In a review of the best-known literature (Dollar 1992; Ben-David 1993; Edwards 1998; Frankel and Romer 1999; Sachs and Warner 1995), Francisco Rodriguez and I found a major gap between the policy clusions that are typically drawn and what the research has actually shown. A common problem has been the misattribution of macroeconomic phenomena (e.g., overvalued currencies or macroeconomic instability) or geographic location (e.g., in the tropical zone) to trade policies. Once these problems are corrected, any meaningful relationship across countries between the level of trade barriers and economic growth evaporates (see also Helleiner 1994).

In practice, the relationship between trade openness and growth is likely to be a contingent one, dependent on a host of internal and external characteristics. The fact that practically all of today's advanced countries embarked on their growth behind tariff barriers, and reduced protection only subsequently, surely offers a clue of sorts. Moreover, the modern theory of endogenous growth yields an ambiguous answer to the question of whether trade liberalization promotes growth, one that depends on whether the forces of comparative advantage push the economy's resources towards activities that generate long-run growth (research and development, expanding product variety, upgrading product quality, etc.) or divert them from such activities.

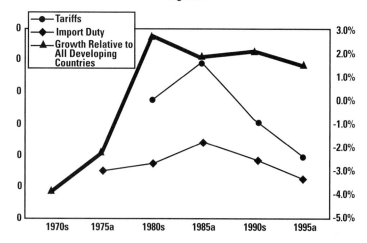

Tariffs and Growth in India
Figure 2

Sources: Author's calculations from data in Dollar and Kraay (2000) and World Bank, *World Development Indicators 2000*, CD-Rom.

No country has developed success-fully by turning its back on international trade and long-term capital flows. Very few countries have grown over long peri-ods of time without experiencing an in-crease in the share of foreign trade in their national product. In practice, the most compelling mechanism that links trade with growth in developing countries is that imported capital goods are likely to be sig-nificantly cheaper than those manufac-tured at home. Policies that restrict imports of capital equipment, raise the price of cap-ital goods at home and thereby reduce real investment levels have to be viewed as un-desirable on the face of it—although this does not rule out the possibility of selective infant industry policies in certain segments of capital-goods industries. Exports, in turn, are important since they permit the purchase of imported capital equipment.

But it is equally true that no country has developed simply by opening itself up to foreign trade and investment. The trick has been to combine the opportunities offered by world markets with a domestic investment and institution-building strategy to stimulate

the animal spirits of domestic entrepreneurs. Almost all of the outstanding cases—East Asia, China, India since the early 1980s—in-volve partial and gradual opening up to im-ports and foreign investment.

The experiences of China and India are particularly noteworthy, as they are two huge countries that have done extremely well recently, and are often cited as exam-ples of what openness can achieve (see Stern 2000: 3). The reality, once again, is more complicated. In both India and China, the main trade reform took place about a decade after the onset of higher growth. Moreover, these countries' trade restrictions remain among the highest in the world. As noted briefly above, the increase in China's growth started in the late 1970s with the introduction of the household responsibil-ity system in agriculture and of two-tier pricing. Trade liberalization did not start in earnest until much later, during the sec-ond half of the 1980s and especially dur-ing the 1990s, once the trend growth rate had already increased substantially.

The case of India is shown in Figure 2. As the figure makes clear, India's trend growth rate increased substantially in the early 1980s (a fact that stands out particularly clearly when it is compared against other developing countries), while serious trade reform did not start until 1991–93. The tariff averages displayed in the chart show that tariffs were actually higher in the rising growth period of the 1980s than in the low-growth 1970s. To be sure, tariffs hardly constitute the most serious trade restrictions in India, but they nonetheless display the trends in Indian trade policy fairly accurately.

Of course, both India and China did 'participate in international trade,' and by that measure they are both globalizers. But the relevant question for policy-makers is not whether trade per se is good or bad—countries that do well also increase their trade/GDP ratios as a by-product—but what the correct sequence of policies is and how much priority deep trade liberalization should receive early in the reform process. With regard to the latter questions, the experiences of India and China are suggestive of the benefits of a gradual, sequenced approach.

To repeat, the appropriate conclusion is not that trade protection is inherently preferable to trade liberalization; certainly, there is scant evidence from the last 50 years that inward looking economies experience systematically faster economic growth than open ones. But the benefits of trade openness are now greatly oversold. Deep trade liberalization cannot be relied on to deliver high rates of economic growth and therefore does not deserve the high priority it typically receives in the development strategies pushed by leading multilateral organizations.[5]

As Helleiner (2000: 3) puts it, there are 'few reputable developing country analysts or governments who question the positive potential roles of international trade or capital inflow in economic growth and overall development. How could they question the inevitable need for participation in, indeed a considerable degree of integration with, the global economy?' The real debate is not over whether integration is good or bad, but over matters of policy and priorities: 'It isn't at all obvious either (1) that further external liberalization ("openness") is now in every country's interest and in all dimensions or (2) that in the overarching sweep of global economic history what the world now most requires is a set of global rules that promote or ease the path to greater freedom for global market actors, and are universal in application' (ibid: 4).

The Integrationist Agenda and the Crowding Out of Development Priorities

Priorities are important because in the enlightened standard view, insertion into the world economy is no longer a matter of simply removing trade and investment barriers. Countries have to satisfy a long list of institutional requirements in order to maximize the gains and minimize the risks of participation in the world economy. Global integration remains the key prerequisite for economic development, but there is now a lot more to it than just throwing the borders open. Reaping the gains from openness requires a full complement of institutional reforms.

So trade liberalization entails not only the lowering of tariff and non-tariff barriers, but also compliance with WTO requirements on subsidies, intellectual property, customs procedures, sanitary standards and policies vis-à-vis foreign investors. Moreover, these legal requirements have to be complemented with additional reforms to ensure favourable economic outcomes: tax reform to make up for lost tariff revenues; social safety nets to compensate displaced workers; credibility enhancing institutional innovations to quell doubts about the permanence of the reforms; labour-market reform to enhance labour mobility across industries; technological assistance to upgrade firms adversely affected by import competition; training programmes to ensure that export-oriented firms and investors have access to skilled workers; and so on. Reading World Bank reports on trade policy, one can be excused for thinking that the list of complementary reforms is virtually endless.

Not withstanding the overly Anglo-American conception of institutional possibilities reflected in the Washington agenda for integrationist reform, many of the proposed institutional reforms are perfectly sensible ones, and in a world without financial, administrative or political constraints, there would be little argument about the need to adopt them. But in the real world, fiscal resources, administrative capabilities and political capital are all scarce, and choices need to be made about how to deploy them. In such a world, viewing institutional priorities from the vantage point of insertion in the global economy has real opportunity costs.

Some trade-offs are illustrative. It has been estimated that it costs a typical developing country $150 million to implement requirements under just three of the WTO agreements: customs valuation, sanitary and phytosanitary measures (SPS) and intellectual property rights (TRIPs). As the World Bank's Michael Finger points out, this is a sum equal to a year's development budget for many of the least-developed countries (Finger and Schuler 1999).

In the area of legal reform, should the government focus its energies on 'importing' legal codes and standards, or on improving existing domestic legal institutions? In Turkey, a weak coalition government spent several months gathering political support for a bill that would provide foreign investors the protection of international arbitration. Wouldn't it have been a better strategy, for the long run, to reform the existing legal regime for the benefit of foreign and domestic investors alike?

In public health, should the government pursue tough policies on compulsory licensing and/or parallel importation of basic medicines, even if that means running afoul of existing WTO rules? The United States has charged that Brazil's highly successful treatment programme for HIV/AIDS violates WTO rules because it

allows the government to seek compulsory licensing when a foreign patent holder does not 'work' the patent locally.

In industrial strategy, should the government simply open up and let the chips drop wherever they might, or should it emulate East Asian experience of industrial policies through export subsidies, directed credit and selective protection?

How should the government focus its anti-corruption strategy? Should it target the 'grand' corruption that foreign investors complain about, or the petty corruption that affects the poor the most? Perhaps, as proponents of permanent normal trade relations with China argued in the recent US Congressional debate, a government that is forced to protect the rights of foreign investors becomes more inclined to protect the human rights of its own citizens too. But isn't this at best a trickle-down strategy of institutional reform? Shouldn't institutional reform be targeted on the desired ends directly—whether those ends are the rule of law, improved observance of human rights or reduced corruption?

The rules for admission into the world economy not only reflect little awareness of development priorities, they are often completely unrelated to sensible economic principles. WTO rules on anti-dumping, subsidies and countervailing measures, agriculture, textiles, trade related investment measures (TRIMs) and trade related intellectual property rights (TRIPs) are utterly devoid of any economic rationale beyond the mercantilist interests of a narrow set of powerful groups in the advanced industrial countries. The developmental pay-off of most of these requirements is hard to see.

Bilateral and regional trade agreements are often far worse, as they impose even tighter prerequisites on developing countries in return for crumbs of enhanced 'market access' in the larger partners. The Africa Growth and Opportunity Act passed by the U. S. Congress in 2000, for example, contains a long list of eligibility criteria, including the requirement that African governments minimize interference in the economy. It provides free access to U.S. markets only under strict rules of origin, thereby ensuring that few economic linkages are generated in the African countries themselves. The U.S.-Jordan Free Trade Agreement imposes more restrictive intellectual property rules on Jordan than exist under the WTO.

In each of these areas, a strategy focused on integration crowds out more development-friendly alternatives. Many of the institutional reforms needed for insertion in the world economy can be independently desirable, or produce broader spillovers. But these priorities do not necessarily coincide with the priorities of a broader development agenda. A strategy that focuses on getting the state out of the way of the market overlooks the important functions that the state must play during the process of economic transformation. What belongs on the agenda of institutional reform is building up state capacity—not diminishing it (Evans 2000).

World markets are a source of technology and capital; it would be silly for the developing world not to exploit these opportunities. But, as I have argued above, successful development strategies have always required a judicious blend of imported practices with domestic institutional innovations. Policy-makers need to forge a domestic growth strategy, relying on domestic investors and domestic institutions. The most costly downside of the integrationist agenda is that it is crowding out serious thinking and efforts along such lines.

An International Trade Regime That Puts Development First: General Principles

Access to the markets of the industrial countries matters for development. But so does the autonomy to experiment with institutional innovations that diverge from orthodoxy. The exchange of reduced policy autonomy in the South for improved market access in the North is a bad bargain where development is concerned.

Consider the old GATT system, under which the international trade regime did not reach much beyond tariff and non-tariff barriers to trade. The developing countries were effectively exempt from prevailing disciplines. The 'most favoured nation' principle ensured that they benefited from the tariff cuts negotiated among the industrial countries, while they themselves 'gave up' little in return. The resulting pattern of liberalization may have been asymmetric (with many products of interest to developing countries either excluded or receiving less beneficial treatment, but the net effect for the developing world was still highly salutary.

It is in such an environment that the most successful 'globalizers' of an earlier era—the East Asian tigers—managed to prosper. These countries were free to do their own thing, and did so, combining trade reliance with unorthodox policies—export subsidies, domestic-content requirements, import-export linkages, patent and copyright infringement restrictions on capital flows (including direct foreign investment), directed credit and so on—that are largely precluded by today's rules.[6] In fact, such policies were part of the arsenal of today's advanced industrial countries until quite recently (see Scherer and Watal 2001). The environment for today's globalizers is significantly more restrictive (see Amsden 2000).

For the word's poorest economies, the so-called least developed countries (LLSDCs), something along the old GATT lines is still achievable, and would constitute a more development-friendly regime than the one that exists currently. LLSDCs are economies that are individually and collectively small enough that 'adjustment' issues in the advanced countries are not a serious obstacle to the provision of one-sided free-market access in the North to the vast majority of products of interest to them. Instead of encumbering these countries with all kinds of institutional requirements that come attached to a 'single undertaking,' it would be far better to leave them the room to follow their own institutional priorities, while providing them with access into northern markets that is both duty free and free of quantitative restrictions. In practice, this can be done either by extending existing 'phase-in' periods until certain income thresholds are reached, or incorporating a general LLSDC exception.

In the case of middle-income and other developing nations, it is unrealistic to expect that advanced industrial countries would be willing to accept a similar arrangement. The amount of political opposition that imports from developing countries generate in the advanced industrial countries is already disproportionate to the volume of trade in question. Some of these objectives have a legitimate core, and it is important that developing nations understand and accept this (see Mayda and Rodrik 2001). Under a sensible set of global trade rules, industrialized countries would have as much right to protect their own social arrangements—in areas such as labour and environmental standards, welfare-state arrangements, rural communities, or industrial organization—as developing nations have to adopt divergent institutional practices. Countries such as India, Brazil, or China, whose exports can have a sizable impact on, say, labour-market institutions and employment relations within the advanced countries, cannot ask importing countries to overlook these effects while demanding at the same time that the constraints on their own developmental agenda be lifted. Middle-income developing countries have to accept a more balanced set of rights and obligations.

Is it possible to preserve developing countries' autonomy while also respecting the legitimate objectives of advanced industrial countries to maintain high labour, social and environmental standards at home? Would such a regime of world trade avoid collapsing into protectionism, bilateralism or regional trade blocs? Would it in fact be development-friendly? The answer to all these questions is yes, provided we accept five simple principles.

Trade is a means to an end, not an end in itself. Step number one is to move away from attaching normative significance to trade itself. The scope of market access generated by the international trade regime and the volume of trade thereby stimulated are poor measures of how well the system functions. As the WTO's preamble emphasizes, trade is useful only insofar as it serves broader developmental and social goals. Developing countries should not be obsessed with market access abroad, at the cost of overlooking more fundamental developmental challenges at home. Industrial countries should balance the interests of their exporters and multinational companies with those of their workers and consumers.

Advocates of globalization lecture the rest of the world incessantly about the adjustments countries have to undertake in their policies and institutions in order to expand their international trade and become more attractive to foreign investors. This is another instance of confusing means for ends. Trade serves at best as an instrument for achieving the goals that societies seek: propriety, stability, freedom and quality of life. Nothing enrages WTO bashers more than the suspicion that, when push comes to shove, the WTO allows trade to trump the environment or human rights. And developing countries are right to resist a system that evaluates their needs from the perspective of expanding world trade instead of poverty reduction.

Reversing our priorities would have a simple but powerful implication. Instead of asking what kind of multilateral trading system maximizes foreign trade and investment opportunities, we would ask what kind of multilateral system best enables nations around the world to pursue their own values and developmental objectives.

Trade rules have to allow for diversity in national institutions and standards. As I have emphasized above, there is no single recipe for economic advancement. This does not mean that anything and everything works: market-based incentives, clear property-control rights, competition and macroeconomic stability are essential everywhere. But even these universal requirements can be and have been embodied in diverse institutional forms. Investment strategies, needed to jump-start economies, can also take different forms.

Moreover, citizens of different countries have varying preferences over the role of government regulations or provision of social welfare, however imperfectly these preferences are articulated or determined. They differ over the nature and extent of regulations to govern new technologies (such things as genetically modified organisms) or protect the environment, of policies to extend social safety nets and, more broadly, about the entire relationship between efficiency and equity. Rich and poor nations have very different needs in the areas of labour standards or patent protection. Poor countries need the space to follow developmental policies that richer countries no longer require. When countries use the trade system to impose their institutional preferences on others, the result is erosion of the system's legitimacy and efficacy. Trade rules should seek peaceful co-existence among national practices, not harmonization.

Non-democratic countries cannot count on the same trade privileges as democratic ones. National standards that deviate from those in trade partners and thereby provide 'trade advantages' are legitimate only to the extent that they are grounded in free choices made by citizens. Think of labour and environmental standards, for example. Poor countries argue that they cannot afford to have the same stringent standards in these areas as the advanced countries. Indeed, tough emission standards or regulations against the use of child labour can easily backfire if they lead to fewer jobs and greater poverty. Democratic countries such as India and Brazil can legitimately argue that their practices are consistent with the wishes of their own citizens, and that therefore it is inappropriate for labour groups or NGOs in advanced countries to tell them what standard they should have. Of course, democracy never works perfectly (in either developing countries or in advanced countries), and one would not want to argue that there are no human rights abuses in the countries just mentioned. The point is simply that the presence of civil liberties and political freedoms provides a presumptive cover against the charge that labour, environmental and other standards in the developing nations are inappropriately low.

But in non-democratic countries, such as China, the assertion that labour rights and the environment are trampled for the benefit of commercial advantage cannot be as easily dismissed. Consequently, exports of non-democratic countries deserve greater scrutiny when they entail costly dislocations or adverse distributional consequences in importing countries. In the absence of the presumptive cover provided by democratic rights such countries need to make a 'developmental' case for policies that generate adjustment difficulties in the importing countries. For example, minimum wages that are significantly lower than in rich countries or health and other benefits that are less generous can be justified by pointing to lower labour productivity and living standards in poor nations. Lax child labour regulations can sometimes be justified by the argument that under conditions of widespread poverty it is not feasible or desirable to withdraw young workers from the labour force. In other cases, the 'affordability' argument carries less weight: non-discrimination, freedom of association, collective bargaining, prohibition of forced labour do not 'cost' anything; compliance with these 'core labour rights' does not harm, and indeed possibly benefits, economic development. The latter are examples that do not pass the 'development test.'

Countries have the right to protect their own institutions and development priorities. Opponents of today's trade regime argue that trade sets off a 'race to the bottom,' with nations converging towards the lowest levels of environmental, labour and consumer protections. Advocates counter that there is little evidence that trade leads to the erosion of national standards. Developing nations complain that current trade laws are too intrusive, and leave little room for development-friendly policies. Advocates of the WTO reply that these rules provide useful discipline to rein in harmful policies that would otherwise end up wasting resources and hampering development.

One way to cut through this impasse is to accept that countries can uphold national standards and policies, by withholding market access or suspending WTO obligations if necessary, when trade demonstrably undermines domestic practices that enjoy broad popular support. For example, poor nations might be allowed to subsidize industrial activities (and indirectly, their exports) when this is part of a broadly supported development strategy aimed at stimulating technological capabilities. Advanced countries might seek temporary protection against imports originating from countries with weak enforcement of labour rights when such imports serve to worsen working conditions at home. The WTO already has a 'safeguards' system in place to protect firms from import surges. An extension of this principle to protect developmental priorities or environmental, labour and consumer-safety standards at home—with appropriate procedural restraints against abuse—might make the world trading system more development-friendly, more resilient and less resistant to ad-hoc protectionism.

Currently, the Agreement on Safeguards allows (temporary) increases in trade restrictions under a very narrow set of conditions (see Rodrik 1997). It requires a determination that increased imports 'cause or threaten to cause serious injury to the domestic industry,' that causality be firmly established and that if there are multiple causes, injury not be attributed to imports. Safeguards cannot be applied to developing country exporters unless their share of imports of the product concerned is above a threshold. A country applying safeguard measures has to compensate the affected exporters by providing 'equivalent concessions,' lacking which the exporter is free to retaliate.

A broader interpretation of safeguards would acknowledge that countries may legitimately seek to restrict trade or suspend existing WTO obligations—to exercise what I call 'opt-outs'—for reasons going beyond competitive threats to their industries. Among such reasons are, as I have discussed, developmental priorities as well as distributional concerns or conflicts with domestic norms or social arrangements in the industrial countries. We could imagine recasting the current agreement into an Agreement on Developmental and Social Safeguards, which would permit the application of opt-outs under a broader range of circumstances. This would require re-casting the 'serious injury' test and replacing it with the need to demonstrate broad domestic support, among all concerned parties, for the proposed measure.

To see how that might work in practice, consider what the current agreement says:

> A Member may apply a safeguard measure only following an investigation by the competent authorities of that Member pursuant to procedures previously established and made public in consonance with Article X of the GATT 1994. This investigation shall include reasonable public notice to all interested parties and public hearings or other appropriate means in which *importers, exporters and other interested parties could present evidence and their views,* including the opportunity to respond to the presentations of other parties and to submit their views, inter alia, as to ***whether or not the application of a safeguard measure would be in the public interest.*** The competent authorities shall publish a report setting forth their findings and reasoned conclusions reached on all

pertinent issues of fact and law. (WTO 1995: 9; emphasis added)

The main shortcoming of this clause is that while it allows all relevant groups, and exporters and importers in particular, to make their views known, it does not actually compel them to do so. Consequently, it results in a strong bias in the domestic investigative process towards the interests of import-competing groups, who are the petitioners for import relief and its obvious beneficiaries. Indeed, this is a key problem with hearings in anti-dumping proceedings, where testimony from other groups besides the import-competing industry is typically not allowed.

The most significant and reliable guarantee against the abuse of opt-outs is informed deliberation, at the national level. A critical reform, then, would be to require the investigative process in each country to: (1) gather testimony and views from all relevant parties, including consumer and public-interest groups, importers and exporters, civil society organizations, and (2) determine whether there exists sufficiently broad support among these groups for the exercise of the opt-out or safeguard in question. The requirements that groups whose incomes might be adversely affected by the opt-out—importers and exporters—be compelled to testify, and that the investigative body trade off the competing interests in a transparent manner would help ensure that protectionist measures that benefit a small segment of industry at a large cost to society would not have much chance of success. When the opt-out in question is part of a broader development strategy that has already been adopted after broad debate and participation, an additional investigative process need not be launched. This last point deserves to be highlighted in view of the emphasis placed on 'local ownership' and 'participatory mechanisms' in strategies of poverty reduction and growth promoted by the international financial institutions.

The main advantage of this procedure is that it would force a public debate on the legitimacy of trade rules and when to suspend them, ensuring that all sides would be heard. This is something that rarely happens even in the industrial countries, let alone in developing nations. This procedure could be complemented with a strengthened monitoring and surveillance role for the WTO, to ensure that domestic opt-out procedures are in compliance with the expanded safeguard clause. An automatic sunset clause could ensure that trade restrictions and opt-outs do not become entrenched long after their perceived need has disappeared.

Allowing opt-outs in this manner would not be without its risks. The possibility that the new procedures would be abused for protectionist ends and open the door to unilateral action on a broad front, despite the high threshold envisaged here, has to be taken into account. But as I have already argued, the current arrangements also have risks. The 'more of the same' approach embodied in the industrialized countries' efforts to launch a comprehensive new round of trade negotiations is unlikely to produce benefits for developing nations. Absent creative thinking and novel institutional designs, the narrowing of the room for institutional divergence harms development prospects. It may also lead to the emergence of a new set of 'grey area' measures entirely outside multilateral discipline. These are consequences that are far worse than the expanded safeguard regime I have just described.

But countries do not have the right to impose their institutional preferences on others. The exercise of opt-outs to uphold a country's own priorities has to be sharply distinguished from using them to impose these priorities on other countries. Trade rules should not force Americans to consume shrimp that are caught in ways that most Americans find unacceptable; but neither should they allow the United States to use trade sanctions to alter the way that foreign nations go about their fishing business. Citizens of rich countries who are genuinely concerned about the state of the environment or of workers in the developing world can be more effective through channels other than trade—via diplomacy or foreign aid, for example. Trade sanctions to promote a country's own preferences are rarely effective, and have no moral legitimacy (except for when they are used against repressive political regimes).

This and the previous principle help us draw a useful distinction between two styles of 'unilateralism'—one that is aimed at protecting differences, and the other aimed at reducing them. When the European Union drags its feet on agricultural trade liberalization, it is out of a desire to 'protect' a set of domestic social arrangements that Europeans, through their democratic procedures, have decided are worth maintaining. When, on the other hand, the United States threatens trade sanctions against Japan because its retailing practices are perceived to harm American exporters or against South Africa because its patent laws are perceived as too lax, it does so out of a desire to bring these countries' practices into line with its own. A well-designed world trade regime would leave room for the former, but prohibit the latter.

Other development-friendly measures. In addition to providing unrestricted access to least developed countries' exports and enabling developing countries to exercise greater autonomy in the use of subsidies, 'trade-related' investment, patent regulations and other measures, a development-friendly trade regime would do the following (see UNCTAD 2000; Raghavan 1996):

- Greatly restrict the use of anti-dumping (AD) measures in advanced industrial countries when exports originate from developing countries. A small, but important step would be to require that the relevant investigating bodies take fully into account the consumer costs of anti-dumping action.
- Allow greater mobility of workers across international boundaries, by

liberalizing for example the movement of natural persons connected to trade in labour-intensive services (such as construction).
- Require that all existing and future WTO agreements be fully costed out (in terms of implementation and other costs). It would condition the phasing in of these agreements in the developing countries on the provision of commensurate financial assistance.
- Require additional compensation when a dispute settlement panel rules in favour of a developing country complainant, or (when compensation is not forthcoming) require that other countries join in the retaliation.
- Provide expanded legal and fact-finding assistance to developing country members of the WTO in prospective dispute settlement cases.

Conclusions: From a Market-Exchange Perspective to a Development Perspective

Economists think of the WTO as an institution designed to expand free trade and thereby enhance consumer welfare, in the South no less than in the North. In reality, it is an institution that enables countries to bargain about market access. 'Free trade' is not the typical outcome of this process; nor is consumer welfare (much less development) what the negotiators have chiefly in mind. Traditionally, the agenda of multilateral trade negotiations has been shaped in response to a tug-of-war between exporters and multinational corporations in the advanced industrial countries (which have had the upper hand), on the one hand, and import-competing interests (typically, but not solely, labour) on the other. The chief textbook beneficiaries of free trade—consumers—do not sit at the table. The WTO can best be understood, in this context, as the product of intense lobbying by specific exporter groups in the United States or Europe or of specific compromises between such groups and other domestic groups. The differential treatment of manufactures and agriculture, or of clothing and other goods within manufacturing, the anti-dumping regime, and the intellectual property rights (IPR) regime, to pick some of the major anomalies, are all results of this political process. Understanding this is essential, as it underscores the fact that there is very little in the structure of multilateral trade negotiations to ensure that their outcomes are consistent with development goals, let alone that they be designed to further development.

Hence there are at least three sources of slippage between what development requires and what the WTO does. First, even if free trade were optimal for development in its broad sense, the WTO does not fundamentally pursue free trade. Second, even if it did, there is no guarantee that free trade is the best trade policy for countries at low levels of development. Third, compliance with WTO rules, even when these rules are not harmful in themselves, crowds outs a more fully developmental agenda—at both the international and national level.

My main argument has been that the world trading regime has to shift from a 'market access' perspective to a 'development' perspective (see Helleiner 2000:19). Essentially, the shift means that we should stop evaluating the trade regime from the perspective of whether it maximizes the flow of trade in goods and services, and ask instead, 'Do the trading arrangements—current and proposed—maximize the possibilities of development at the national level?' I have discussed why these two perspectives are not the same, even though they sometimes overlap, and have outlined some of the operational implications of such a shift. One is that developing nations have to articulate their needs not in terms of market access, but in terms of the policy autonomy that will allow them to exercise institutional innovations that depart from prevailing orthodoxies. A second is that the WTO should be conceived of not as an

institution devoted to harmonization and the reduction of national institutional differences, but as one that manages the interface between different national systems.

This shift to a development perspective would have several important advantages. The first and more obvious is that it would provide for a more development friendly international economic environment. Countries would be able to use trade as a means for development, rather than being forced to view trade as an end in itself (and being forced to sacrifice development goals in the bargain). It would save developing countries precious political capital by obviating the need to bargain for 'special and differential treatment'—a principle that in any case is more form than substance at this point.

Second, viewing the WTO as an institution that manages institutional diversity (rather than imposing uniformity) provides developing countries a way out of a conundrum inherent in their current negotiating stance. The problem arises from the inconsistency between their demands for space to implement their development policies on the one hand, and their complaints about northern protectionism in agriculture, textiles and labour and environmental standards, on the other. As long as the issues are viewed in market-access terms, developing countries will be unable to make a sound and principled defense of their legitimate need for space. And the only way they can gain enhanced market access is by restricting their own policy autonomy in exchange. Once the objective of the trading regime is seen as letting different national economic systems prosper side by side, the debate can become one about each nation's institutional priorities and how they may be rendered compatible in a development friendly way.

The third advantage of this shift in perspective is that it provides a way out of the impasse that the trading system finds itself in post-Seattle. At present, two groups feel particularly excluded from the decision-making machinery of the global trade regime: developing country governments and northern NGOs. The former complain about the asymmetry in trade rules, while the latter charge that the system pays inadequate attention to values such as transparency, accountability, human rights and environmental sustainability. The demands of these two disenfranchised groups are often perceived to be conflicting—over questions such as labour and environmental standards or the transparency of the dispute settlement procedures—allowing the advanced industrial countries and the WTO leadership to seize the 'middle' ground. It is the demands of these two groups, and the apparent tension between them, that has paralyzed the process of multilateral trade negotiations in recent years.

But once the trade regime—and the governance challenges it poses—is seen from a development perspective, it becomes clear that developing country governments and many of the northern NGOs share the same goals: policy autonomy to pursue independent values and priorities, poverty reduction, and human development in an environmentally sustainable manner. The tensions over issues such as labour standards become manageable if the debate is couched in terms of development processes—broadly defined—instead of the requirements of market access. On all counts, then, the shift in perspective provides a better foundation for the multilateral trading regime.

Dani Rodrik is the Rafiq Hariri Professor of International Political Economy at the John F. Kennedy School of Government, Harvard University. He has published widely in the areas of international economics, economic development, and political economy. Rodrik is the research coordinator of the Group of 24 (G-24), and is also affiliated with the National Bureau of Economic Research and the Centre for Economic Policy Research (London). He is the recipient of a Carnegie Scholar award for 2001, and his work has been supported also by the Ford and Rockefeller Foundations. He is the faculty chair of the new MPA in International Development (MPAID) degree programme at Harvard. He holds a Ph.D. in economics and an MPA from Princeton University, and an A.B. from Harvard College.

Endnotes

1. See, for example, Mike Moore (2000) or his speech at the London Ministerial roundtable 19 March 2001 (www.wto.org/english/news).

2. The supposition that one set of institutional arrangements must dominate in terms of overall performance has produced the fads of the decade: Europe, with its low unemployment, high growth and thriving culture, was the continent to emulate throughout much of the 1970s; during the trade-conscious 1980s, Japan became the exemplar of choice; and the 1990s have been the decade of US-style free-wheeling capitalism.

3. For example, although Taiwan and Mexico are commonly regarded as following diametrically opposed development paths, figures provided by Little et al. (1970:174–90) show that long after introducing trade reforms, Taiwan had a higher average ERP in manufacturing and greater variation in ERPs than did Mexico.

4. Although India did gradually liberalize its trade regime after 1991, its relative performance began to improve a full decade before these reforms went into effect (in the early 1980s).

5. The same is true of the promotion and subsidization of inward flows of direct foreign investment (see Hanson 2001).

6. A recent illustration is the dispute between Brazil and Canada over Brazil's subsidization of its aircraft manufacturer, Embraer. Brazil lost this case in the WTO, and will either remove the subsidies or have to put up with retaliation from Canada. The Republic of Korea, the Taiwan province of China and Mauritius subsidized their export industries for years without incurring similar sanctions.

References

Acemoglu, Daron, Simon Johnson and James A. Robinson. 2000 'The Colonial Origins of Comparative Development: An Empirical Investigation,' unpublished paper, Massachusetts Institute of Technology, Cambridge, MA.

Amsden, Alice. 2000. 'Industrialization Under New WTO Law,' paper prepared for the High-Level Round Table on Trade and

Development, UNCTAD X, Bankok, February 12.

Balassa, Bela. 1971. *The Structure of Protection in Developing Countries*. Baltimore: Johns Hopkins University Press.

Ben-David, Dan. 1993. 'Equalizing Exchange: Trade Liberalization and Income Convergence,' *Quarterly Journal of Economics,* 108, no. 3.

Chang, Ha-Joon. 2000. 'Institutional Development in Developing Countries in a Historical Perspective,' unpublished paper, Faculty of Economics and Politics, Cambridge University.

Collins, Susan and Barry Bosworth. 1996. 'Economic Growth in East Asia: Accumulation versus Assimilation.' Brookings Papers on Economic Activity 2: 135–191.

Dollar, David. 1992. 'Outward-Oriented Developing Economies Really Do Grow More Rapidly: Evidence from 95 LDCs, 1976–85.' *Economic Development and Cultural Change,* pp. 523–44.

Dollar, David and Aart Kraay. 2000. 'Trade, Growth, and Poverty,' World Bank, Washington, DC, October.

Edwards, Sebastian. 1998. 'Openness, Productivity and Growth: What Do We Really Know?' *Economic Journal* 108 (March): 383–98.

Evans, Peter. 2000. 'Economic Governance Institutions in a Global Political Economy: Implications for Developing Countries.' Paper prepared for the High-Level Round Table on Trade and Development, 'UNCTAD X, Bankok, February 12.

Finger, Michael J. and Philip Schuler. 1999. 'Implementation of Uruguay Round Commitments: the Development Challenge,' World Bank policy research working paper no. 2215, September.

Frankel, Jeffrey and David Romer. 1999. 'Does Trade Cause Growth?' *American Economic Review* 89, no.3 (June): 379–99

Hanson, Gordon. 2001. 'Should Countries Promote Foreign Direct Investment,' Group of 24 Discussion Paper no. 9, February.

Helleiner, Gerald K. 2000. 'Markets, Politics, and the Global Economy: Can the Global Economy Be Civilized?' Prebisch Lecture, UNCTAD, Geneva.

———. 1994. *Trade Policy and Industrialization in Turbulent Times*. New York: Routledge.

International Labour Office. 2001. Mauritius. Studies on the Social Dimensions of Globalization. Geneva: ILO.

Lau, Lawrence J., Yingyi Quian and Gerard Roland. 1997. 'Reform Without Losers: An Interpretation of China's Dual-Track Approach to Transition,' unpublished paper, November.

Little, Ian, Tibor Scitovsky and Maurice Scott. 1970. *Industry and Trade in Some Developing Countries*. London and New York: Oxford University Press for OECD.

Mayda, Anna Maria and Dani Rodrik. 2001 'Why Are Some People (or Countries) More Protectionist than Others? Harvard University, Cambridge, MA. http://www.harvard.edu/rodrik.

Moore, Mike. 2000. 'The WTO Is a Friend of the Poor,' *Financial Times,* June 19, 2000.

Qian, Yingi, Gerare Roland and Chenggang Xu. 1999. 'Coordinating Changes in M-Form and U-Form Organizations,' paper prepared for the Nobel Symposium, August.

Raghavan, Chakravarthi. 1996. "The New Issues and Developing Countries,' TWN Trade & Development Series, no. 4, Third World Network, Penang, Malaysia.

Rodriguez, Francisco and Dani Rodrik. 2001. "Trade Policy an Economic Growth: A Skeptic's Guide to the Cross-National Literature.' Forthcoming in Ben Bernanke and Kenneth S. Rogoff, eds., NBER Macro Annual 2000. Cambridge, MA:NBER. (http://wwwl.ksg.harvard.edu/rodrik/skepti1299.pdf)

Rodrik, Dani. 2001a. 'Institutions for High-Quality Growth: What They Are and How to Acquire Them,' *Studies in Comparative International Development,* forthcoming.

———. 2001b. "Trading in Illusions,' *Foreign Policy.* March-April.

———. 2000a. 'Five Simple Principles for World Trade," *The American Prospect,* January 17.

———. 2001b 'Trading in Illusions,' *Foreign Policy,* March – April.

———. 2000b. "Growth versus Poverty Reduction: A Hollow Debate,' *Finance & Develoment* 37, no. 4 (December)

———. 1999. 'The New Global Economy and the Developing Countries: Making Openness Work,' Overseas Development Council, Washington, DC, 1999.

———. 1997. 'Has Globalization Gone Too Far?' Institute for International Economics, Washington, DC 1997.

Sachs, Jeffrey D., and Wing Thye Woo. 2000. 'Understanding China's Economic Performance,' *Journal of Policy Reform* 4, no. 1.

Sachs, Jeffrey, and Andrew Warner, 1995. 'Economic Reform and the Process of Global Integration,' Brookings Papers on Economic Activity. No. 1:1–118.

Scherer, F.M. and Jayashree Watal. 2001. 'Post-TRIPs Options for Access to Patented Medicines in Developing Countries,' John F. Kennedy School of Government, Harvard University.

Sen, Amartya. 1999. *Development As Freedom.* New York: Alfred Knopf.

———. 1993. "Capability and Well-being." In Martha Nussbaum and Amartya Sen, eds., *The Quality of Life.* Oxford: Clarendon Press.

Stern, Nicholas. 2000. "Globalization and Poverty." Presented at the Institute of Economic and Social Research, Faculty of Economics, University of Indonesia, December 15.

Subramanian, Arvind. 2001. 'Mauritius' Trade and Development Strategy: What Lessons Does It Offer?' paper presented at the IMF High-Level Seminar on Globalization and Africa, March.

UNCTAD. 2000. Positive Agenda and Future Trade Negotiations. Geneva: UNCTAD.

Unger, Roberto Mangabeira. 1998. *Democracy Realized: The Progressive Alternative.* London and New York: Verso Books.

United States, Department of State. 1999. '1999 Country Report on Economic Policy and Trade Practices: Haiti,' http://www.state.gov/www/issues/economic/trade_reports/1999/haiti.pdf.

World Bank. 2000. World Development Indicators 2000. Washington, DC: World Bank.

World Bank and IMF. 2000. "Trade, Development and Poverty Reduction,' joint paper prepared for the consideration of the Development Committee, March 31.

World Trade Organization (WTO). 1995. 'Agreement Establishing the World Trade Organization.' WTO Information and Media Relations Divisions, Geneva. http://wto.org/english/docs_e/legal_e/04-wto.pdf.

15

Are We Underestimating the Gains from Globalization for the United States?

CHRISTIAN **BRODA** AND
DAVID **WEINSTEIN**

The U.S. economy has advanced considerably since Henry Ford quipped that customers could have cars in "any color as long as it is black." Today's consumers are able to purchase a wide variety of goods that were not available in the past. Not only can they choose their cars from hundreds of makes and models, but they can also purchase a wealth of technologically sophisticated new products. One development that has significantly broadened consumers' choice of goods in recent decades is the growth of international trade. As trade with other nations has expanded, U.S. consumers have been able to acquire varieties of goods not available from domestic producers—Japanese cars, for example, and French wine.

We examine how the availability of new goods and varieties through international trade has affected the welfare of U.S. citizens. While the benefits of free trade have traditionally been associated with declines in the price of existing products, recent trade theory suggests that the introduction of new imported goods constitutes another important gain from trade. Our task in this article is to provide a measure of this gain over the past three decades.

To do so, we first estimate the increase in global varieties from 1972 to 2001. We then estimate how the change in import prices over this period—a standard gauge of consumer welfare—would be affected if this increase in variety were taken into account. Using our results, we determine what consumers would be willing to pay to access the wider range of goods available in 2001 than in 1972.

Significantly, we find that global varieties grew more than threefold over the 1972–2001 period. When we adjust import price growth for the increased variety, we find that import prices in this period fell markedly faster—by about 1.2 percentage points per year—than the conventional, or unadjusted, import price index would suggest.[1] Taking our calculations one step further, we conclude that consumers would be willing to pay $260 billion, or roughly 3 percent of GDP in 2001, to avail themselves of the expanded range of goods on the market. This sizable sum indicates that U.S. consumers see increased choice in goods as an important benefit of international trade.

Why Do Varieties Matter?

Classical international trade theory postulates that the opening of an economy to trade improves welfare by allowing consumers to access cheaper imported goods. In the new models of international trade, however, countries benefit from trade not only because the prices of individual goods change, but also because consumers in open economies have access to a wider range of goods than consumers in closed economies. The new models are typically predicated on an assumption that no one country can produce all of the varieties available in the world. If consumers value new varieties and individual countries cannot supply them, then consumers stand to benefit from the increased choice of goods that comes with trade.

In these new trade models, the gains from trade hinge directly on a number of variables. The first is the "elasticity of substitution" among varieties, or how substitutable consumers believe varieties to be. If varieties of a particular good are so alike that consumers will readily substitute one for another—as in the case of gasoline, for example—then having two varieties of that good will have little impact on welfare. However, if the varieties are quite distinct— consider Irish and American beer, or Italian and American cheese—then U.S. consumers will benefit from the opportunity to obtain both varieties.

The gains from trade also depend on differences in quality across varieties. Consumers will place a higher value on access to varieties regarded as superior. Thus, most Americans would presumably prefer the opportunity to buy French red wine to the opportunity to buy Japanese red wine. The final variable affecting the gains from trade is import quantity: All things being equal, consumers will place a higher value on variety growth in product sectors that command a large share of spending—for example, automobiles— than on variety growth in small sectors.

Calculating the Growth of Variety in U.S. Imports since 1972

To track the growth of variety in goods entering the United States over the past three decades, we examine the most disaggregated, or finely detailed, import data available. For the 1972–88 period, we use the seven-digit import classifications of the Tariff Schedule of the United States Annotated (TSUSA) system; for the 1990–2001 period, we use the ten-digit import classifications of the Harmonized Tariff Schedule (HTS), the system that replaced the TSUSA in 1989.

These classifications break down U.S. imports into approximately 15,000 goods, each characterized by a level of detail on the order of "red wine in bottles of under one liter."

We define a variety to be a good emanating from a particular country—for example, French red wine. This definition suggests both the power and the limitations of working with trade data. On the one hand, our definition is specific enough to enable us to examine the interactions of literally hundreds of thousands of good-country pairs. On the other hand, as the example of French red wine indicates, our definition is still very general, collapsing many kinds of French red wine into a single "variety."[2]

Looking at the composition of U.S. imports over the 1972–2001 period (Table 1), we see two unmistakable trends. The first is a dramatic increase in the number of measured goods. Between 1972 and 1988, the number of goods imported by the United States almost doubled, rising from 7,731 to 12,822. Similarly, between 1990 and 2001, the number of imported goods rose from 14,572 to 16,390. Closer scrutiny reveals that the increases in these two sample periods did not consist simply of new imports being added to the old (Table 1, rows 3 and 4 and rows 9 and 10). Indeed, it appears that only half to two-thirds of the goods in each of the two samples were imported both at the start and at the end of the period. Moreover, approximately one-third of the goods in each sample had disappeared by the end of the sample period. It is possible, of course, that the shifting composition of the imported goods over the sample periods may owe as much to changes in the way the goods are classified as to actual changes in the goods themselves. Nevertheless, the data do suggest that the growth of international trade in recent decades has led to both the creation and the elimination of imports—a fact often overlooked in discussions of globalization.

The second trend that emerges from the import data is a dramatic increase in the

Variety in U.S. Imports, 1972–2001
Table 1

Year (1)	Number of Goods (2)	Median Number of Exporting Countries (3)	Total Number of Varieties (Good-Country Pairs) (4)
U.S. Imports, 1972–88			
All 1972 goods	1972	7,731	6	74,667
All 1988 goods	1988	12,822	9	173,937
Goods common to				
1972 and 1988	1972	4,171	6	36,191
1972 and 1988	1988	4,171	10	56,183
Goods in 1972 not in 1988	1972	3,560	7	38,476
Goods in 1988 not in 1972	1988	8,651	8	117,754
U.S. Imports, 1990–2001			
All 1990 goods	1990	14,572	10	182,375
All 2001 goods	2001	16,390	12	259,215
Goods common to				
1990 and 2001	1990	10,636	10	132,417
1990 and 2001	2001	10,636	13	173,776
Goods in 1990 not in 2001	1990	3,936	10	49,958
Goods in 2001 not in 1990	2001	5,754	11	85,439

Sources: NBER Trade Data on CD-ROM; Center for International Data at UC Davis, <http://data.econ.ucdavis.edu>.

Note: For the 1972–88 period, goods are defined at the seven-digit level of the TSUSA (Tariff Schedule of the United States Annotated); for the 1990–2001 period, they are defined at the ten-digit level of the HTS (Harmonized Tariff Schedule).

number of countries exporting each good to the United States (Table 1, column 3). Over the full 1972–2001 period, the median number of countries supplying each good doubled, rising from six countries at the start of the period to twelve at the end.

Taken together, the data in Table 1 indicate that the number of good-country pairs—that is, the number of varieties (column 4)—rose 133 percent in the first period and 42 percent in the second period, for a total increase of 231 percent. This increase constitutes more than a threefold rise in the number of varieties over the three decades from 1972 to 2001. Roughly half of this increase is attributable to a doubling in the number of goods and half to a doubling in the number of countries supplying each good. While we have not yet explored how consumers value these new varieties, the dramatic growth in the count of new varieties makes a prima facie case that understanding variety growth is important for measuring changes in consumer welfare.

To get a more concrete sense of what is driving the surge in import variety, consider how specific goods have fared. In some cases, variety growth stems primarily from an increase in the number of countries exporting the good. For example, in 1972, the United States imported roasted or ground coffee from twenty-five countries. By 2001, however, the nation was importing roasted coffee from fifty-two countries.[3] Similarly, the number of countries supplying beer and wine to the United States rose by about 195 percent and 50 percent, respectively, over the period. The number of countries supplying eyeglasses rose from nine to forty-seven.

In other cases, variety growth stems from both new goods and new sources for each good. Car audio is a prime example: In 1972, twenty-one countries exported car radios of all types to the United States. By 2001, there were nine different classifications for car audio systems and as many as twenty-eight countries exporting each of the nine. Overall, the number of varieties would appear to have risen from 21 to 174. Clearly some portion of this increase—for example, the splitting of the single 1972 classification of car audio into the 2001 classifications of AM radios and AM/FM radios—does not represent the addition of new goods. However, other 2001 classifications for car audio systems—radios with tape and compact disc players, for example—probably do constitute new goods that have produced a genuine increase in choice.

Countries Exporting to the United States: Changes in the Rankings

The rapid growth of import varieties has been accompanied by changes in the relative importance of various countries as exporters to the United States. In the first column of Table 2, countries are ordered according to the number of goods they exported to the United States in 1972, with the largest exporter placed first; the following columns report the rankings of these same countries in 1988, 1990, and 2001. Although the countries exporting the most goods to the United States have tended, throughout the 1972–2001 period, to be large and high-income economies, the position of individual countries within the ranking has changed. Canada moved from fourth to first place, and Mexico moved from thirteenth to eighth place. The sharp rise in the ranking of these two countries may reflect their adoption of a free trade policy: Canada's jump to first place followed a trade liberalization in the 1970s and 1980s; Mexico rose from tenth to eighth place after it liberalized trade in the 1990s.

In the case of other countries, economic growth, perhaps coupled with liberalization, may help explain the change in rank. Fast-growing economies such as China and Korea have advanced rapidly as import sources for the United States. The increase in the number of U.S. imports from China has been especially stunning. In 1972, China exported only 510 goods to the United States; by 2001, that number had risen to 10,199 (Table 3). In other words, while Chinese firms competed in only 0.6 percent of the import markets in existence in 1972, they participated in 62 percent of the markets in 2001. Thus, although Chinese firms account for only 9 percent of all imports to the United States, there is a Chinese firm selling in almost two-thirds of the U.S. import markets.

The twenty-fold increase in the number of goods exported by China has elevated China from the twenty-eighth position in the 1972 ranking of exporters to the fourth position today. Similarly, India has risen in the rankings—from twenty-third in 1990 to thirteenth in 2001—with the sharp rise in exports that began with the country's liberalization in the last decade. At the other extreme,

Countries Ranked by the Number of Goods Exported
to the United States
Table 2

Country	Ranking in Year			
	1972	**1988**	**1990**	**2001**
Japan	1	1	3	7
United Kingdom	2	4	4	3
Germany	3	3	2	2
Canada	4	2	1	1
France	5	6	5	6
Italy	6	5	6	5
Switzerland	7	11	11	11
Hong Kong	8	9	12	16
Netherlands	9	13	13	14
Taiwan	10	7	7	9
Spain	11	14	15	12
Belgium-Luxembourg	12	15	14	15
Mexico	13	12	10	8
Sweden	14	17	16	19
Denmark	15	22	21	23
Austria	16	18	18	21
India	17	19	23	13
South Korea	18	8	9	10
Brazil	19	16	17	18
Australia	20	20	20	20
Israel	21	21	22	22
Portugal	22	26	28	32
Norway	23	31	31	37
Ireland	24	27	26	28
Finland	25	28	30	31
Colombia	26	33	34	35
Philippines	27	25	25	26
China	28	10	8	4
Argentina	29	29	29	39
Greece	30	38	44	47

Sources: NBER Trade Data on CD-ROM; Center for International Data at UC Davis,
<http://data.econ.ucdavis.edu>.
Notes: The table reports rankings for the thirty countries that exported the highest number of goods to
the United States in 1972. For 1972 and 1988, goods are defined at the seven-digit level of the TSUSA
(Tariff Schedule of the United States Annotated); for 1990 and 2001, they are defined at the ten-digit level
of the HTS (Harmonized Tariff Schedule).

U.S. Imports from China, 1972–2001
Table 3

	Year	Number of Goods	Percentage of Total U.S. Imports in Year
		1972–88	
All 1972 goods	1972	510	0.1
All 1988 goods	1988	4,673	1.9
Goods common to			
1972 and 1988	1972	215	0.0
1972 and 1988	1988	215	0.2
Goods in 1972 not in 1988	1988	295	0.0
Goods in 1988 not in 1972	1988	4,363	1.7
		1989–2001	
All 1989 goods	1989	5,587	2.5
All 2001 goods	2001	10,199	9.0
Goods common to			
1989 and 2001	1989	3,567	1.3
1989 and 2001	2001	3,567	3.9
Goods in 1989 not in 2001	1989	2,002	1.2
Goods in 2001 not in 1989	2001	6,582	5.0

Sources: NBER Trade Data on CD-ROM; Center for International Data at UC Davis, <http://data.econ.ucdavis.edu>.

countries such as Japan and Argentina, whose economies grew slowly at the end of the 1990–2001 sample period, have seen fairly substantial drops in the number of varieties they export.

Calculating the Welfare Gains from New Varieties

Although increased product variety is generally believed to bring welfare gains, standard national measures of welfare and prices do not assess how much better off consumers are when a new variety of an existing good or a new good becomes available. Both the U.S. import price index and the consumer price index (CPI) mea-

sure the current cost of a particular basket of goods and services relative to the cost of those same goods and services in some base period in the past. Thus, both indexes largely fail to capture the introduction of new varieties and the increase in the standard of living that new varieties bring about.[4] Indeed, in this regard, the two indexes fall short of being a true cost-of-living index—one that measures the cost of maintaining a certain level of welfare without restrictions on what is in the basket of goods and services examined.[5]

In this section, we report our efforts to recalculate the U.S. import price index for 1972–2001 taking variety growth into account. Our object—both here and in the

Box: Empirical Methodology

Our empirical calculation of the import price index begins with some assumptions about how consumers think about varieties. Here, we assume that all consumers evaluate varieties using a constant elasticity of substitution (CES) utility function that places equal weights on imports from every country. If the prices of all varieties of an imported good are identical and there are no differences in quality across varieties (an assumption we relax in the longer version of this article), we can write the price index that takes variety growth into account, P_c^V, as

$$P_c^V = P_c \times \prod_g \left(\frac{n_{gc72}}{n_{gc01}} \right)^{\frac{1}{\sigma_g - 1}},$$

where P_c is the conventional price index (that is, the index with no adjustment for variety growth), n_{gc72} is the number of varieties of good g imported by country c in the year 1972, n_{gc01} is this number for 2001, and $\sigma_{gc} > 1$ is the elasticity of substitution among varieties of a different good. As the equation makes clear, the effect of variety growth on the import price index depends on two factors. First, increasing the number of source countries for a given good will lower the ratio of old to new varieties, n_{gc72}/n_{gc01}, hence the price index.[a] This fall in the price index reflects the assumption that consumers value greater choice. Second, the precise amount by which new varieties affect the price index depends on how substitutable varieties of each good are. If varieties are very similar, then, σ_g is large, the exponent in the above equation is small, and increases in the number of varieties will have little effect on the price index. In sum, our methodology assumes that there are two determinants underlying how varieties affect the price index: the magnitude of the increase in varieties and the degree of similarity among varieties.

[a]One drawback of this method of measuring growth in the number of varieties is that it erroneously captures splits or mergers of product classifications as a change in the number of varieties and hence could artificially impact the calculation of the variety-adjusted price index. Fortunately, the methodology we use in our longer technical paper (Broda and Weinstein 2004) is robust to a wide variety of data problems arising from the creation and elimination of product classifications. For example, if goods are randomly split or merged, then the index remains unchanged. Moreover, the methodology is robust to new goods being of higher quality than old goods because superior-quality goods will claim a larger share of total import expenditures at fixed prices.

longer, technical study on which this article is based[6]—is to provide a truer measure of the cost, over this thirty-year period, of maintaining a particular level of satisfaction from the consumption of imports. If new varieties of goods enhance the standard of living, then consumers can spend less to achieve the same level of satisfaction as in the past. By comparing our variety-adjusted estimate of the rate of change in import prices over the sample period with the conventional estimate that does not include variety growth, we obtain a measure of the nation's welfare gains from variety growth.

In the box above, we present an equation for calculating a variety-adjusted price index. Although the equation describes a simple case in which all varieties are uniform in quality and priced identically, it nonetheless captures the most important elements of the more sophisticated calculations performed in our longer study.

The key variables in our adjusted estimate of the price index are (1) the extent of the growth in varieties for each good over the sample period and (2) the degree of similarity, or elasticity of substitution, among the varieties of each good. The simplest way to measure variety growth for a particular good is to compare the number of varieties in that product category at the beginning of the sample period with the number of varieties at the end of the period. For instance, we used this method earlier in the article to calculate the extent of variety growth in coffee, beer, and other products. However, a simple count of varieties ignores the fact that we may import a huge quantity of one variety and a small quantity of another. While we make no allowance for differences in quantity in the simple case we present in the box, we adjust for the share of each variety in total import expenditures in our longer paper (Broda and Weinstein 2004).

The second key variable—the elasticity of substitution—is a measure of the degree to which consumers value new varieties of a particular good. If U.S. consumers see blueberries from Chile and Argentina as equivalent or "perfectly substitutable," then they will not value access to the Chilean berries if they already have access to Argentinean blueberries. In other words, the opportunity to buy both products will do nothing to enhance consumers' standard of living. By contrast, if consumers see Italian and Chinese shirts as essentially different, then they will regard themselves as better off if they are able to purchase shirts from both countries. *How much* better off depends on the degree of substitutability between the two varieties of shirts.

For our recalculation of the import price index, we document the degree of substitutability for varieties of more than 30,000 goods imported by the United States (see Broda and Weinstein [2004]). We find that for the period between 1972 and 1988, the goods sector with the highest substitutability among its varieties was crude petroleum and shale oil. The goods sector in which varieties were the least substitutable was footwear. In general, the degree of substitutability was higher for homogeneous products (petroleum is an apt example) than for highly differentiated products.[7]

The Impact of Increased Import Variety on U.S. Welfare

Our recalculation of the import price index, based on a more sophisticated version of the methodology outlined in the box, suggests that the variety-adjusted index fell 28.0 percent faster than the conventional index between 1972 and 2001, or about 1.2 percentage points per year. The difference in the rate of decline was particularly marked for the earlier sample period: the variety-adjusted price of imports fell 19.7 percent faster than the unadjusted price between 1972 and 1988, or about 1.4 percentage points per year. For the later sample period, the impact of variety growth was much smaller, with the adjusted index falling 8.3 percent faster than the official index between 1990 and 2001, or about 0.8 percentage point per year. The lower rate of decline in the later period may reflect the fact that many of the gains resulting from the rising importance of East Asian trade may have been realized before 1990.

To calculate the impact of variety growth on consumer welfare, we have to make an additional assumption about how the increased availability of foreign varieties affects domestic production. For this exercise, we follow Krugman's (1980) argument that the number of domestic varieties remains the same as the number of import varieties changes. In reality, some imported varieties replace domestic varieties while others just complement them. However, if domestic varieties are replaced, the resources used in their production may be put to work in the production of a new variety of that product or some other good.

With the assumption that the number of domestic varieties is unchanged, we can proceed to estimate the impact of global variety growth on the well-being of U.S. consumers. We found earlier that the official import price index understates the rate of decline in import prices by 28.0 percent over the three decades from 1972 to 2001. If imports account for about 10 percent of U.S. GDP, then the value to consumers of the increase in global varieties is about 3 percent of GDP[8] in 2001, or roughly $260 billion.[9] This sum represents what consumers would be willing to pay to access the expanded set of varieties available in 2001.

Putting Our Findings in Context

Our estimates should be viewed with some caution. As we noted earlier, we treat the interaction of domestic and imported varieties very simply, relying on the assumption that the number of domestic varieties remains the same when the number of imported varieties increases. In addition, we choose one way of modeling variety—the CES model presented in Dixit and Stiglitz (1977)—while recognizing that other researchers might adopt a different approach.[10]

Although our method has certain limitations, our findings are striking indeed. A welfare gain of $260 billion from global variety growth is three to six times larger than traditional estimates of the gains from eliminating protectionism (see, for example, Feenstra [1992] and Romer [1994]). Our finding that the conventional import price index, by failing to correct for the increase in varieties, understates the decline in import prices by 1.2 percentage points per year also underscores the considerable impact of variety growth.

To understand the magnitude of this understatement, or "bias," consider how it compares with other estimates of bias in aggregate prices. In 1996, the Advisory Commission to Study the Consumer Price Index found that the CPI at that time overstated the increase in the cost of living by about 1.1 percentage points per year (Boskin et al. 1996). Improvements in the quality of consumer goods—which were not taken into account in the calculation of the CPI—accounted for about 0.6 percentage point of this bias.[11] These numbers

suggest that the variety-growth bias we find in the import price index is, in fact, quite large: specifically, it is twice as large as the quality-change bias in the overall price index and as large as the total bias from all sources.[12]

Conclusion

This article reports the results from the first attempt to estimate the impact of new varieties on the U.S. import price index.[13] We find that the index overstates import price inflation by 1.2 percentage points per year for the 1972–2001 period. The real cost of imports was almost 30 percent lower at the end of this period than the conventional price index would suggest. This drop in import prices, we contend, has raised U.S. welfare by $260 billion, or about 3 percent of 2001 GDP.

The magnitude of this gain from trade suggests that the effects of variety growth on prices and welfare merit further exploration. Additional research is needed on the interaction between imported and domestic varieties. Our own future work on these issues will consider how the growth and elimination of domestic varieties affect consumer prices and welfare.

Notes

[1] The conventional index used as a benchmark in our analysis mimics the official U.S. import price index in that it makes no adjustment for the impact of variety growth. Although it is derived from a different formula, it is closely related to the official index in practice.

[2] Whether consumers assess goods coming from different countries as different "varieties" is something we will be able to determine by estimating the degree of substitutability between them. For example, high levels of substitutability between Brazilian and Colombian coffees would suggest that consumers do not regard these products as distinct varieties. An alternative definition of a variety that appears in the trade literature is "goods coming from a particular firm." The problem with this definition, however, is that all goods from a given firm are not the same variety. More practically, it is very difficult to get firm- or plant-level data for a large set of countries that export to the United States.

[3] The 2001 classification for roasted coffee contains only caffeinated coffee in packages of under two kilograms. The actual number of suppliers could be higher.

[4] In calculating the CPI, the Bureau of Labor Statistics omits the introduction of new goods until they are eventually discovered as part of the gradual rotation of the sample of goods. Even when the no-longer-new good enters the CPI calculation, no adjustment is made for the consumer gains it provides in relation to the earlier goods. For a good summary of CPI biases, see Lebow and Rudd (2003).

[5] The import price index and the CPI are both fixed-weight indexes; they assign weights to the prices of individual goods and services that are fixed over time. While the assessment of cost-of-living changes is a recognized measurement goal of the fixed-weight index, it is a theoretical construct that cannot readily be translated into a single, straightforward index formula. Therefore, the fixed-weight index cannot easily track all of the factors that affect the cost of living in today's dynamic economy.

[6] This article summarizes the findings of empirical work described in detail in Broda and Weinstein (2004).

[7] Broda and Weinstein (2004) show that the estimates obtained are reasonable under a number of criteria.

[8] Intuitively, if the price of 10 percent of the goods in the CPI falls by 30 percent, then the CPI falls by 3 percent. This implies a rise in real GDP of 3 percent.

[9] About 2 percentage points of the welfare gain accrue to the earlier sample period.

[10] We choose the Dixit and Stiglitz model because of its prominence, tractability, and empirical feasibility.

[11] While we compare the magnitude of the import index and CPI biases, we cannot add the variety-growth bias to the existing CPI bias. This is mainly to avoid a "double counting" of the effect of imported varieties. Many of the imported goods are intermediate goods that already show up as lower prices in final consumption goods.

[12] We note, however, that the average quality-improvement bias in the CPI masks a large variance across different CPI expenditure categories. Both the 1996 Boskin et al. study and a more recent paper by Lebow and Rudd (2003) present estimates of quality bias in many important CPI subindexes—including medical care, personal computers, televisions, toys, and audio equipment—that are larger than our estimate of variety bias. Overall, the weighted sum of the bias found for these categories, which account for 9.7 percent of the CPI, is 2.25 percentage points per year. Another category, "personal computer services (Internet)," accounts for 0.1 percent of the CPI but has an estimated annual bias of 19.0 percentage points.

[13] Although some researchers have studied the price impact of variety growth at the micro level (a single good, or at most a few goods), we know of no other study that considers the effects of variety growth on aggregate prices.

References

Boskin, Michael J., Ellen R. Dulberger, Robert J. Gordon, Zvi Griliches, and Dale Jorgensen. 1996. *Toward a More Accurate Measure of the Cost of Living. Final Report to the Senate Finance Committee from the Advisory Commission to Study the Consumer Price Index.* December 4.

Broda, Christian, and David Weinstein. 2004. "Globalization and the Gains from Variety." NBER Working Paper, no. 10314, February.

Dixit, Avinash K., and Joseph E. Stiglitz. 1977. "Monopolistic Competition and Optimum Product Diversity." *American Economic Review* 67, no. 3 (June): 297–308.

Feenstra, Robert C. 1992. "How Costly Is Protectionism?" *Journal of Economic Perspectives* 6, no. 3 (summer): 159–78.

———. 1994. "New Product Varieties and the Measurement of International Prices." *American Economic Review* 84, no. 1 (March): 157–77.

Krugman, Paul. 1980. "Scale Economies, Product Differentiation, and the Pattern of Trade." *American Economic Review* 70, no. 5 (December): 950–9.

Lebow, David E., and Jeremy B. Rudd. 2003. "Measurement Error in the Consumer Price Index: Where Do We Stand?" *Journal of Economic Literature* 41, no. 1 (March): 159–201.

Romer, Paul M. 1994. "New Goods, Old Theory, and the Welfare Costs of Trade Restrictions." *Journal of Development Economics* 43, no. 1 (February): 5–38.

What's So Special About China's Exports?

16

DANI RODRIK

I. Introduction

The phenomenal performance of China constitutes the great economic miracle of the last quarter century. China's economy has expanded by leaps and bounds, at historically unprecedented rates that few economists would have found plausible or feasible ex ante. More importantly, this growth has lifted hundreds of millions of people from deep poverty and has helped improve health, education, and other social standards. China has accomplished all this using its own brand of experimental gradualism—increasingly relying on markets and on price signals, yet until very recently doing so within the boundaries of a highly unorthodox set of institutions.

That trade has played a significant role in this transformation is beyond dispute. China would likely have grown even if the global economy had been closed. And the very early stages of Chinese growth, based on rural reform, did not in any significant way rely on global markets. But from the mid-1980s on, one must suppose that China's growth was fueled and sustained by the opportunities that the world market offered. We can see the increasing footprint of foreign trade and investment in all the major aggregates. The share of exports in GDP rose from virtually nothing in the 1960s to close to 30 percent in 2003, a rate of increase that is much larger than what has been experienced elsewhere in

the world (see Figure 1). Inward direct foreign investment has risen from close to zero in the early 1980s to around 5 percent of GDP. The flip side of these figures is that China has become one of the world's biggest trading powers, accounting for 6% of global trade flows (Figure 2).

The success with which China has integrated itself into the world economy raises many questions. Drawing the real lessons from this experience is important, not only because China is the stellar example which other developing countries are trying to emulate, but also because the shape of China's own future policies depend (or should depend) on these lessons.

The task is not made easier by the highly unconventional manner in which China has achieved its global integration. The standard list of recommendations for countries pursuing this goal includes: dismantling quantitative restrictions on imports, reducing import tariffs and their dispersion, making the currency convertible for current account transactions, eliminating bureacratic red tape and other impediments to direct foreign investment, improving customs procedures, and establishing the rule of law. Measured by these guidelines, China's policies resemble more those of a country that messed up big time than those of a country that became a formidable competitive threat in world markets to rich and poor countries alike. In brief, China

Exports as a Share of GDP
Figure 1

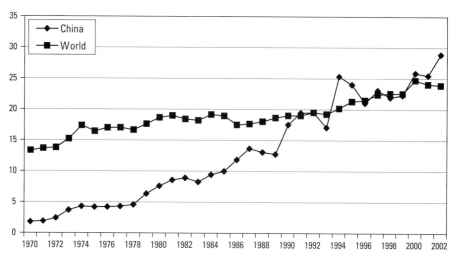

Source: World Development Indicators Database

China's Share of World Merchandise Exports
Figure 2

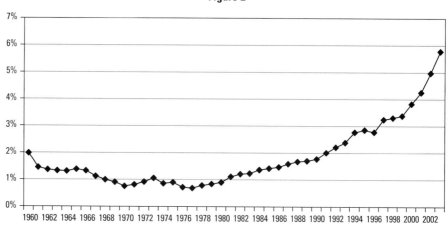

Source: World Development Indicators Database

opened up very gradually, and significant reforms lagged behind growth (in exports and overall incomes) by at least a decade or more. While monopoly state trading was liberalized relatively early (starting in the late 1970s), what took its place was a com-plex and highly restrictive set of tariffs, non-tariff barriers, and licenses. These were not substantially relaxed until the early 1990s.

Table 1 shows the trend for import tariffs: In the early 1990s, tariffs still aver-aged above 40 percent (among the highest

China's Import Tariffs
Table 1

	Unweighted average	Weighted average	Dispersion (st. dev)	Maximum
1982	55.6	—	—	—
1985	43.3	—	—	—
1988	43.7	—	—	—
1991	44.1	—	—	—
1992	42.9	40.6	—	220.0
1993	39.9	38.4	29.9	220.0
1994	36.2	35.5	27.9	—
1995	35.2	26.8	—	220.0
1996	23.6	22.6	17.4	121.6
1997	17.6	16.0	13.0	121.6
1998	17.5	15.7	13.0	121.6
2000	16.4	—	—	—
2001	15.3	9.1	12.1	121.6
2002	12.3	6.4	9.1	70.0

Source: Prasad (2004), p. 10.

in the world at the time), with significant dispersion and a maximum rate above 200%. While the home market was highly protected, the penalizing effect of these tariffs on export production was neutralized through duty drawbacks and other incentives for export oriented investment projects. Currency markets were not unified until 1994. Foreign investors were straddled with requirements to form joint ventures, transfer technology to local partners, and source their inputs locally. And corruption and weak rule of law remain significant problems. So China is not a straightforward story of export growth achieved through trade openness and free market forces.

Neither is China a simple story of specialization according to comparative advantage. While labor intensive exports (toys, garments, simple electronics assembly) have always played an important role in China's export basket, China also exports a wide range of highly sophisticated products. Indeed, a major argument

of this paper is that China is an outlier in terms of the overall sophistication of its exports: its export bundle is that of a country with an income-per-capita level *three times* higher than China's. China has somehow managed to latch on to advanced, high-productivity products that one would not normally expect a poor, labor abundant country like China to produce, let alone export. I will provide some evidence below that suggests this has been an important contributor to China's recent growth. China's experience indicates that it not how much you export, but what you export that matters.

The extent to which China's sophisticated export basket has been a direct consequence of its unorthodox policy regime is not clear. But it is not too much of a stretch to imagine that China's industrial structure has indeed been shaped by policies of promotion and protection, just as in the cases of earlier East Asian tigers. I will return to this theme at the end of the paper, and offer some general remarks that may help frame future policy decisions in the general areas of trade and industrialization.

The outline of this paper is as follows. In section II, I will provide a quantitative evaluation of China's export structure in comparative context and argue that China's trade pattern cannot be explained solely by factor endowments and other "economic fundamentals." In section III, I will provide some evidence that links the types of goods that countries export with their growth performance, and show that China has benefited from having developed export industries that one would not normally associate with a country at that level of income. Section IV briefly reviews the development of the consumer electronics industry in China to put some flesh on the statistical picture developed in previous sections and to highlight the role of government policies. Section V provides concluding remarks and derives some implications for Chinese policymakers.

II. The Indeterminacy of Comparative Advantage

Consider how a country's pattern of specialization and trade is determined. The principle of comparative advantage dictates that trade patterns are determined by how relative costs of production within a country differ from those in the rest of the world. These differences are in turn linked to differences in productivity levels across industries (as in the Ricardian model of trade) or to differences in relative factor endowments across countries (as in the Heckscher-Ohlin model). In these models, entrepreneurs observe costs directly and make their investment decisions accordingly.

But in a poor developing country, investors contemplating entry into new, non-traditional activities face considerable uncertainty about the costs of operation. These costs will likely depend not just on factor endowments, but also on

the investor's success with technology adoption and adaptation, on the policy environment, and (perhaps also) on the number of other investors making similar investment choices. The risks that arise from such uncertainty are borne disproportionately by early entrants into new industries, who therefore provide valuable informational spillovers to the rest of the economy. If they are successful, later entrants can observe the profitability of the incumbents and emulate them. If they fail, they pay the full cost of their failure. This externality implies that market forces on their own generate too little investments in new activities; to use the terminology of Hausmann and Rodrik (2003), they induce too little "self-discovery." The result is that low-income countries produce too few high-productivity goods that they could be producing (and selling in world markets) and incomes are lower than they would otherwise be. Conversely, rapidly growing countries are those that are able to somehow generate the investments in these non-traditional, higher-productivity tradables.

To put some empirical flesh on these conceptual ideas, Ricardo Hausmann and I have recently developed an indicator that measures the productivity level associated with a country's export basket. This indicator, which we call *EXPY* is calculated in two steps. First, for each 6-digit commodity that is traded we compute the weighted average of the incomes of the countries exporting that commodity, where the weights are the revealed comparative advantage of each country in that commodity (normalized so that the weights sum up to 1). This gives us the income level of that commodity, which we call *PRODY*. The 6-digit level of classification yields more than 5,000 products for which *PRODY* can be calculated. Next we calculate *EXPY* as the weighted average of the *PRODY* for each country, where the weights are the share of each commodity in that country's total exports. More details on the construction of these indices are provided in the appendix.

Relationship between *EXPY* and Per-Capita Incomes in 1992
Figure 3

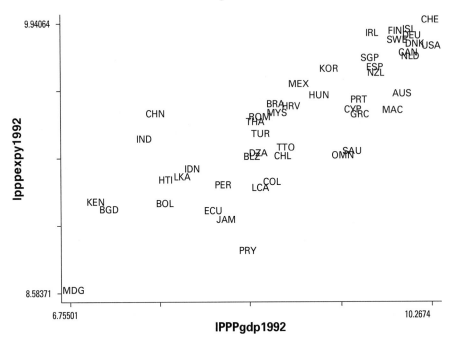

As would be expected, *EXPY* is strongly correlated with per-capita income: rich countries export goods that other rich countries export. Figure 3 shows the scatter plot of *EXPY* against per-capita GDP for 1992. The correlation coefficient is 0.83. But countries do not neatly lie alongside the regression line. Some countries are way below the regression line, while others are way above it. In the latter group, India and China stand out. It is striking that these two high-performing economies have export profiles that are especially skewed towards high productivity goods. In 1992, China's exports were associated with an income level that is more than six times higher than China's per-capita GDP at the time. As we shall see, this gap has diminished somewhat over time, but it still remains high.

Neither is *EXPY* well explained by other economic fundamentals that one can think of. Figures 4 and 5 show the partial correlations between *EXPY* said human

capital and institutional quality, respectively, controlling for per-capita GDP. These scatter plots use more recent trade data from 2002 to maximize the sample of countries. We find a very weak positive partial correlation with the stock of human capital (Figure 4) and virtually no partial correlation with our index of institutional quality, the "rule of law" (Figure 5). Hence the evidence on the fundamentals is mixed. While the productivity of a country's exports is determined in part by its overall productive capacity and its human capital endowment, idiosyncratic characteristics also matter. To take one telling example, a country like Bangladesh with a much similar set of relative factor endowments—abundant in labor, and scarce in human and physical capital—has an *EXPY* that is roughly 50% lower than China's. It is clear that whatever these idiosyncratic features may be (about which I speculate below), they seem to have China with an inordinately high level of

Partial Scatter Plot between *EXPY* and Human Capital
Figure 4

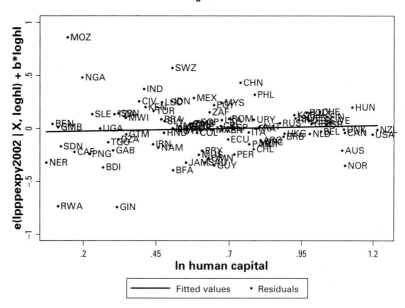

Partial Scatter Plot between *EXPY* and Institutional Quality
Figure 5

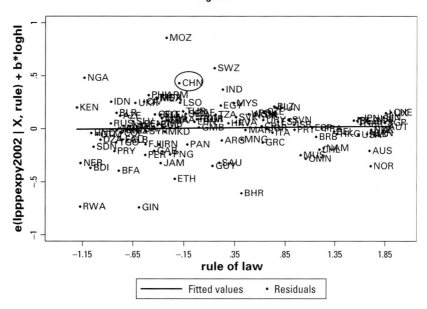

Income Content of Exports
Figure 6

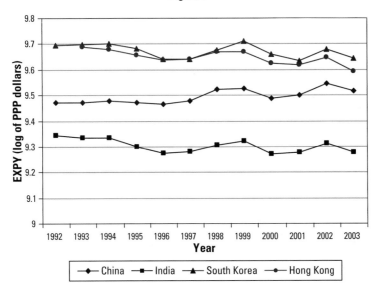

EXPY.[1] In turn, this has apparently been an important driver of its recent economic growth as I will show in the next section.

It is also interesting to compare the progress over time of China's *EXPY with* that of some of its important competitors. This is done in Figure 6, which shows the trends for *EXPY* in China, India, Hong Kong, and South Korea. China has experienced the most rapid rate of growth in the sophistication of its exports since 1992. While China still lags behind South Korea and Hong Kong, the difference in *EXPY* has steadily closed over time. Moreover, the gap between China and India has actually increased over the past decade.[2]

The findings here contrast with those of Wood (2001), who has argued that China's export performance in skill-intensive products is below the level that

would be expected on the basis of the country's factor endowments. Wood's analysis is based on a cross-national benchmark derived from regressing the ratio of skill-intensive to labor-intensive exports on a measure of skill per worker in that country. Wood reports that China's actual share of skill-intensive exports within manufactures in 1990 stood at 33 percent, compared to a predicted ratio of 40 percent (Wood 1991, Table 5). One plausible reason for the difference in the results is that Wood's method relies on a binary classification of goods (skill-intensive or not). Furhermore, the classification is carried out at a much more aggregate level than here. (Remember that we calculate *EXPY* using the information from more than 5,000 distinct products.) In practice, it is common for skill-intensive components of some "goods" to be done in one country and the less

---

[1] Lo and Chan (1998) also emphasize that China's trade structure can not be explained only by comparative advantage, and they emphasize (like do below) the role of production- and technology-oriented policies of the government.

[2] Note that *EXPY* is calculated using commodity exports, so India's software exports are not included in this comparison. Presumably, India's *EXPY* would be significantly higher with software included.

Unit Value Comparisons: Electrical Goods and Equipment Exports (US$ Per Unit, 2003)
Table 2

product name	China	S. Korea	Malaysia	Singapore
Electric transformers, static converters and rectifier	0.855	5.713	0.884	0.229
Electric accumulators	1.317	2.519	17.295	1.248
Electric apparatus for line telephony, telegraphy	14.488	66.581	46.995	36.496
Electronic sound reproducing equipment, non-recording	13.520	50.003	52.966	68.260
Video recording and reproducing apparatus	48.733	39.356	90.926	112.492
Parts, accessories of audio, video recording equipment	9.875	26.222	14.299	n.a.
Radio and TV transmitters, television cameras	62.040	259.014	117.773	92.389
Radio, radio-telephony receivers	7.370	38.552	83.770	68.803
Television receivers, video monitors, projectors	72.903	17.987	144.185	195.939
Parts for radio, tv transmission, receive equipment	31.982	47.988	15.007	n.a.
Electronic printed circuits	1.774	65.973	2.281	49.581
Electronic integrated circuits and microassemblies	1.101	960.988	1.478	2.337

Source: UN Comtrade Database.

skill-intensive components in others, as Wood himself notes (1991, 10). An analysis at the 6-digit level of disaggregation is more likely to capture these distinctions.

It is worth noting however that there are often significant quality differences even *within* 6-digit product categories. Even at this level of aggregation, Chinese exports often concentrate on the more labor-intensive, less sophisticated end of the product spectrum, at least when we compare them to the exports of significantly richer countries. Table 2 shows unit value comparisons for some of China's leading electronics exports. In most cases, China's unit values are lower than those of South Korea, Malaysia, or Singapore. There is therefore some truth to the argument that Chinese exports of electronics products tend to be low-cost, high volume products with not much technological sophistication, and that they therefore pose little threat to U.S. pre-eminence (see Lardy 2004). But here too there are interesting exceptions. For example, Chinese exports of video recorders and TV and video monitors have higher unit values than South

Korean exports in these product lines. And in any case, what is surprising is that a country at China's income level is able to export such electronics products in the first place. That is hardly the norm for other countries with similar factor endowments, as the cross-country comparisons above show.

III. It Is Not How Much but What You Export That Matters

How do we know that the productivity level of a country's exports (measured by *EXPY*) matters to economic performance? It turns out that there is a robust relationship between the initial level of a country's *EXPY* said the subsequent rate of economic growth experienced by that country. Figure 7 is the relevant scatter plot: it shows the relationship between *EXPY* in 1992 and growth over the 1992–2003 period, holding initial levels of income constant. This is a positive and statistically significant relationship (at the 95% confidence level). The estimated coefficient implies that a doubling of the productivity level of a country's exports results in an

Relationship between Initial Level of *EXPY* and Growth, Controlling for Initial Income
Figure 7

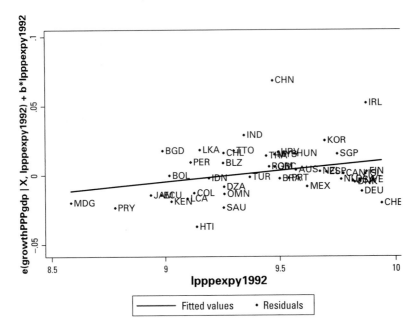

increase in its overall per-capita GDP growth of around 6 percent. Therefore, had China exported only those goods that countries at China's level of income tend to export, its growth rate would have been significantly lower. As the chart shows, a high level of *EXPY* does not fully account for China's growth performance over this period—the other significant outlier is Ireland—but it does help explain it.

Is this a truly causal relationship? Even though the regressor is the level of *EXPY* at the beginning of the period, it is still possible that causality goes from growth to *EXPY* rather than the other way around (if growth and *EXPY* are both persistent over time). To rule this possibility out, we can use an instrumental variable approach, which requires locating an exogenous variable that plausibly influences growth only through the impact it has on *EXPY*. Population (or population density) is in fact one such instrument. The basic economic theory underlying this is simple. Go back to the original story of how

comparative advantage is determined in part by a process of cost discovery by initial entrants in a new industry. High productivity "discoveries" naturally attract more emulation, and the productivity of an economy's tradable sector tends to converge towards the productivity level of the most profitable (most productive) activities discovered to date. Larger economies have more entrepreneurs engaged in discovery, and therefore, everything else being the same, will have maximum levels of productivity in tradables that are higher.[3] And indeed, just as this theory predicts, country size does turn out to have a positive and statistically significant impact on *EXPY*, even when we control for income, human capital, and other plausible regressors. Hence, we can use this theoretical argument as a motivation for using measures of country size as an instrumental variable for *EXPY*. When we do this, we find the

[3] For a formal model of this process, see Hausmann, Hwang, and Rodrik (2006).

Productivity Level of Exports and GDP per Capita (Log of PPP Dollars)
Figure 8

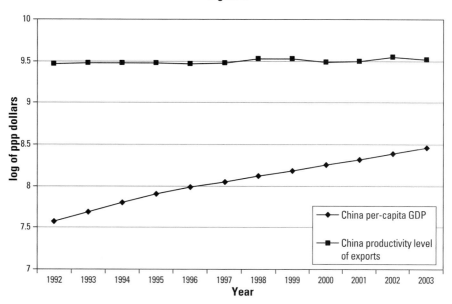

same result that we did with simple OLS regressions. Initial levels of *EXPY* are predictive of subsequent growth.

What is precisely the mechanism that makes *EXPY* a potent force for growth? The theory is that once investors in a country "discover" a number of high productivity exportables, this sets off a powerful demonstration effect. Other investors are drawn in, and as the sector and its suppliers expand, the economy's resources get pulled from lower productivity activities into higher productivity activities. This kind of growth driven by differential productivity across sectors and structural change lies at the root of China's economic performance. A visual indication of this is provided in Figure 8, which shows the progress of per-capita GDP in China alongside *EXPY* since 1992. As we saw previously, the "quality" of China's exports has increased somewhat, especially when compared to competitors. But when we plot *EXPY* alongside per-capita GDP, what really stands out is the stability of *EXPY* relative to per-capita GDP. Per-capita GDP has been rapidly converging to the productivity

level of the country's export basket: it rose from 15% of *EXPY* to 35% in 2003. This picture is strongly indicative of a process of productivity diffusion within the economy: the productivity gains associated with producing a set of sophisticated exportables is spread around the economy as labor moves across industries and across space to the higher productivity exportable activities.

But the pattern shown in Figure 8 also raises a future challenge for China. If much of China's growth today is due to this particular pattern of convergence, will the economy not run out of steam once the process nears completion and the rest of the economy catches up to the productivity level of exportables? As we have seen, the "quality" of China's exportables has been increasing, but not nearly as rapidly as overall income. As a result, China is much less of an outlier today than it was in 1992 in terms of the cross-national relationship between income and *EXPY* (see Figure 9). Using the estimated coefficients from the growth regression presented earlier, this necessarily implies a significant growth slowdown in China. Furthermore,

Relationship between *EXPY* and per-capita Incomes in 2003 (Restricted to Same Sample as in Figure 3)
Figure 9

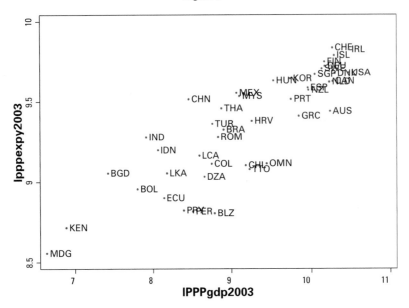

disaggregated analysis shows that the in-crease in China's *EXPY* level over time is ac-counted for exclusively by a compositional shift from goods associated with low productivity to goods associated with high productivity. New goods, that is goods that were not already exported in 1992, have made a negligible contribution to the rise in overall *EXPY.*[4] Sooner or later, therefore, China will have to "discover" new prod-ucts to sell on world markets if growth is to continue at rates resembling recent ones. On the other hand, full GDP conver-gence to the current level of *EXPY* still im-plies a per-capita GDP for China that is much higher than today's level.

IV. The Roots of Success: Consumer Electronics

Among areas where China has been successful, consumer electronics stands out

as one of those that would not have been expected a priori for a country at China's level of income. While low labor costs have helped, this cannot account for the entire story. Indeed, estimates by the McKinsey Global Institute show that labor productiv-ity in China's consumer electronics industry equals that in Mexico, a country where PPP-adjusted per-capita GDP is almost two times larger (McKinsey 2003, 86).[5] Furthermore, China has steadily moved away from being simply an assembler of components. Increasingly, production is integrated backwards and the supply chain is moving to where the assembly is under-taken. So China's success in consumer electronics is based on its ability to make a productivity jump. I will briefly discuss this case as it is emblematic of the broader statistical picture painted above.

Foreign investors have played a key role in the industry's evolution. They are the

[4] Remember that the analysis here is carried out at the 6-digit level, so the absence of many new goods is meaningful.

[5] It is also telling that China's *EXPY* exceeded Mexico's by 2003.

most productive of the producers, they are the source of technology, and they dominate exports. China's openness to foreign investment and its willingness to create special economic zones where foreign producers could operate with good infrastructure and with minimum hassles must therefore receive considerable credit. But if China has welcomed foreign companies, it has always done so with the objective of fostering domestic capabilities. To that end, China has used a number of policies to ensure that technology transfer would take place and strong domestic players would emerge. Early on, reliance was placed predominantly on state-owned national champions. Later, the government used a variety of carrots and sticks. Foreign investors were required to enter into joint ventures with domestic firms (in mobile phones and in computers). Domestic markets were protected to attract market-seeking investors, in addition to those that looked for cost savings. Weak enforcement of intellectual protection laws enabled domestic producers to reverse engineer and imitate foreign technologies with little fear of prosecution. And localities were given substantial freedoms to fashion their own policies of stimulation and support, which led to the creation of industrial clusters in particular areas of the country. Huchet characterizes China's policies as of the mid-1990s thus: "China's technological acquisition strategy is clear: It allows foreign firms access to the domestic market in exchange for technology transfer through joint production or joint ventures" (1997, 270).

The end result of all this can be seen in an industry structure that is very different from the one, say, in Mexico. As Table 3 shows, domestic firms play a significant role in China. In fact, 100% foreign owned firms are a rarity among the leading players in the industry. Most of the significant firms tend to be joint ventures between foreign firms and domestic (mostly state-owned) entities. A strong domestic producer base has been important in diffusing imported technologies and in creating domestic supply chains. In the words of the McKinsey Global Institute, "the international companies' *interaction with domestic companies* has created a genuine global success story" (McKinsey 2003, 79, emphasis added).

It is true that many of the Chinese companies created through government efforts ended up as failures. Accounts of industrial policy in China point to the low productivity and low technology absorption of many SOEs, and to the lack of coordination (across national ministries as well as across different levels of government) that characterizes Chinese policies (see Huchet 1997, Kraemer and Dedrick 2001). But as in other areas of policy, government attitudes have been pragmatic and open to trying new approaches when old ones fail. A well-known case of failure was the early development of the color TV industry, which consisted in the 1980s of more than 100 companies operating at short production runs and high cost. By the early 1990s, the industry had been consolidated thanks to the efforts of local governments and national leadership, which forced mergers and joint ventures with foreign firms. This reversal of policies led to the emergence in quick order of a profitable, export-oriented industry (see Lo and Chan 1998).

Moreover, it is possible that the importance of the weaknesses of the Chinese bureaucratic model is exaggerated. The essence of the self-discovery model of economic development is that you need only a few successes: once a small number of high-productivity activities are identified, they act as the lever for economic convergence by pulling resources in from lower productivity activities. Without state support and publicly funded R&D, a company like Lenovo (previously known as Legend) which became large and profitable enough to purchase IBM's PC business recently would never have come into being.[6] Better to experiment and identify these higher-end activities than not try at all. Lack of

---

[6] Lenovo's majority owner is a state-owned entity.

Major Consumer Electronics Firms in China by Ownership Type
Table 3

Market Segment	Foreign Owned	Joint Venture	Non-FDI
Mobile phone	• Motorola	• Motorola/Eastcom • Nokia/Capitel, Southern • Siemens/MII Subsidiaries • Samsung/Kejian • SAGEM/Bird	• TCL
PCs	• HP • Dell	• IBM/Great Wall • Toshiba/Toshiba Computer (Shanghai) • Epson/Start • Taiwan GVC/TCL	• Lenovo (previously Legend) • Founder • Tongfang
"Brown" goods		• Sony/SVA • Philips/Suzhou CTV • Toshiba/Dalian Daxian • Great Wall Electronics/TCL	• Changhong • Konka • Hisense • Skyworth • Haier • Panda • Xoceco
"White" goods	• Siemens	• Samsung/Suzhou Xiangxuehai • Electrolux/Changsha Zhongyi • LG/Chunlan • Mitsubishi/Haier • Sanyo/Kelon, Rongshida • Sigma/Meiling • Hong Leong (SG)/Xinfei • Toshiba Carrier/Midea	• Changling • Gree

Source: McKinsey (2003), p. 83.

coordination can be an advantage in these circumstances, as it allows different things to be tried and for successes in one region to be copied elsewhere. Somewhat paradoxically, the hesitant, gradual, often conflicting manner in which policies have been formulated and implemented in China may have presented a more suitable environment for entrepreneurial experimentation and cost discovery than one that is centralized, top-down, and overly coordinated.

In sum, China has benefited both from good fundamentals—low labor and materials costs, "outward orientation" in the form of SEZs, large market size—and from a determined government effort to acquire domestic capabilities and build a modern industry. The large size of the economy has allowed policy experimentation. It also has allowed the government to use the carrot of the internal market to force foreign investors into joint ventures with domestic producers. If China is producing an increasingly sophisticated set of consumer electronics product, it would appear that this is due as much to the policy environment as it is to the free play of market forces.

While I have focused on the consumer electronics sector here, the same could be said of other export successes as well. For example, the auto parts industry has been heavily promoted through local content requirements. The Chinese government required foreign car companies investing in the market to achieve a relatively high level of domestic content within a short period of time (typically 70% within three years) (Sutton 2005, 9). This forced these companies to cooperate closely with local suppliers to ensure that their technology and quality were up to par. In his study of the auto supply chain in China, John Sutton found that the domestic first-tier suppliers had achieved quality levels close to international best practice (Sutton 2005). One indicator of success is that China exported $1.7 billion worth of auto components by 2001. Another is that none of the foreign car manufacturers intended to switch to imports, once domestic content requirements were phased out to comply with WTO rules. Sutton reports that "the view expressed in all cases was that the car-maker had developed local sources of supply that were superior, in terms of combination of cost and quality, to imported alternatives" (Sutton 2005, 25). Domestic-content requirements are widely derided as an inefficient tool of industrial policy. The Chinese case stands in stark contrast to this.[7]

V. Implications

I close with three sets of implications for Chinese policymakers. The first has to do with the need to understand better the fundamental underpinnings of China's export performance and its economic success. As I have argued above, much more than comparative advantage and "free markets" have been at play here. China's pattern of production and exports would have looked very different if the traditional forces of comparative advantage, pushing China to specialize in labor-intensive products "appropriate" to low income economies, were the sole determinant. Instead, China has ended up with an export basket that is significantly more sophisticated than what would be normally expected. Government policies have helped nurture domestic capabilities in consumer electronics and other advanced areas that would most likely not have developed in their absence. Whatever static inefficiency costs may have been engendered in the process, this has had favorable implications for China's growth. This is an important point to remember as the inevitable debate between "market fundamentalists" and "planners" plays itself out in the Chinese context.

---

[7] Sutton's portrayal of domestic content requirements in India is not much different; there too, it appears that these requirements helped promote a successful auto parts industry during the 1990s, prior to the coming into effect of WTO rules.

The second implication has to do with the sustainability of China's export-oriented growth. The question here is whether, with exports-to-GDP so high and rising, the Chinese growth model is inevitably running out of steam. The ideas developed in this paper teach us that what matters for China's future growth is not the volume of exports or its relation to GDP, but the "quality" of these exports. Indeed, what is so special about China's exports is not that they are voluminous or that its large pool of labor gives it a huge labor cost advantage. What stands out is that China sells products that are associated with a productivity level that is much higher than a country at China's level of income. This helps account both for why China's trade is viewed as problematic in advanced countries, and for China's rapid economic growth. The economically relevant question for sustainability is not whether trade-GDP can keep on rising, but whether China will manage to latch on to higher- and higher-income products over time, and continue to fuel its growth thereby. As we have seen, there has been a dramatic reduction over the last decade in the gap between *EXPY* and per-capita GDP. Everything else being the same, this is something that is likely to slow down growth.

This brings us to the third point, having to do with the nature of future industrial policies. A clear implication of this paper is that China's industrial policies—however incoherent they may have been—have had a hand in China's past success. Future economic performance may also need to be supported by such policies. This is of course also a lesson from the experience of other East Asian success stories: Japan, Taiwan, South Korea, and Singapore.

The usual criticism of industrial policy is that governments cannot pick winners, and therefore should not try. But this is not the right way to think about industrial policy. In environments that are rife with uncertainty and with technological and informational spillovers, markets under-provide investment in non-traditional products. The appropriate role for industrial policy is to fill in this market incompleteness by subsidizing investments in new products. It is a given that not all of these additional investments will prove to be socially profitable. Good industrial policy consists of withdrawing support from those projects that are revealed to be failures, so that resources do not get bottled up in unproductive activities. Hence the appropriate criterion of success for industrial policy is not that "only winners should be picked" (an impossible task) but that "losers should be let go" (a much less demanding and more doable task). The latter is the relevant yardstick against which industrial policies ought to be measured.

Therefore, a key question for China going forward is whether Chinese policies will maintain their experimental and flexible nature—whether governments will remain willing to support new industries but also willing to turn against ventures that under-perform. Designing the appropriate institutional structure to foster such an experimental, carrot-and-stick approach to industrial policy is an important challenge facing Chinese policy makers.[8] This is an area where institutional transplantation does not work very well. We can identify the higher-order principles involved at a sufficient level of generality, but need to fashion blueprints that are suited to the local context. The challenge for China therefore is to develop institutional models that are based on Chinese realities.

[8] In Rodrik (2004) I discuss some of the issues involved and present some broad guidelines drawing from examples in East Asia and Latin America.

* This is a paper prepared for the project on "China and the Global Economy 2010" of the China Economic Research and Advisory Programme. I am indebted to Edwin Lim for his guidance and comments, and to the Programme for financial support. Comments from Yu Yongding and Adrian Wood have also been very helpful. Oeindrila Dube performed superb research assistance.

Appendix: Construction of *PRODY* and *EXPY*

PRODY is the weighted sum of the per capita GDP of countries exporting a given product, and thus represents the income level associated with each of these goods. Let countries be indexed by j and goods be indexed by l. For any given year, the value of total exports of country j equals:

$$X_j = \sum_l x_{jl}$$

Let the per-capita GDP of country j be denoted by Y_j. Then the *PRODY* index for good k is:

$$PRODY_k = \sum_j \frac{x_{jk}/X_j}{\sum_j (x_{jk}/X_j)} Y_j$$

The numerator of the weight x_{jk}/X_j is the value-share of the commodity in the country's overall export basket. The denominator of the weight, $\sum_j (x_{jk}/X_j)$, aggregates the value-share across all countries exporting the good. By using export share rather than export volume, the weighting scheme tries to ensure that adequate weight is given exports that are important to smaller poorer countries.

EXPY far country i is given in turn by:

$$EXPY_j = \sum_i \frac{x_{jl}}{X_j} PRODY_l$$

This is a weighted index of the representative income associated a country's exports, where the weight is simply the value share of the product in the country's total exports.

Our trade data comes from the United Nations Commodity Trade Statistics Database (COMTRADE). The dataset includes products at the 6-digit level in the Harmonized System for the years 1992 to 2003. The value of exports is measured in current US dollars, which we then convert to 2000 dollars for comparison with real GDP per capita series. The number of countries that report the

trade data vary considerably from year to year. However, we construct the *PRODY* measure for a consistent sample of countries that reported trade data in each of the years 1999, 2000 and 2001. After deleting some missing observations, our data set consists of 5,023 *PRODY* observations. Note that we use the average *PRODY* from 1999–2001 to construct the *EXPY* index, so that the *PRODY* that go into the construction of *EXPY* themselves do not vary over the years.

References

Hausmann, Ricardo, and Dani Rodrik, "Economic Development as Self-Discovery," *Journal of Development Economics,* December 2003.

Hausmann, Ricardo, Jason Hwang, and Dani Rodrik, "What You Export Matters," NBER Working Paper, January 2006.

Huchet, Jean-Francois, "The China Circle and Technological Development in the Chinese Electronics Industry," in B. Naughton, ed., *The China Circle: Economics and Electronics in the PRC. Taiwan, and Hong Kong,* Washington, DC: Brookings Institution Press, 1997.

Kraemer, Kenneth L., and Jason Dedrick, "Creating a Computer Industry Giant: China's Industrial Policies and Outcomes in the 1990s," Center for Research on Information Technology and Organizations, UC Irvine, 2001.

Lardy, Nicholas, "China: The Great New Economic Challenge?" Institute for International Economics, Washington, DC, 2004.

Lo, Die and Thomas M. H. Chan, "Machinery and China's nexus of foreign trade and economic growth." *Journal of International Development,* 10(6), 1998, 733–749.

Mayer, Jorg, and Adrian Wood, "South Asia's Exports in a Comparative Perspective," *Oxford Development Studies,* 29(1), 2001.

McKinsey Global Institute, *New Horizons: Multinational Company Investment in*

Developing Economies, San Francisco, October 2003.

Prasad, Eswar, ed., *China's Growth and Integration into the World Economy: Prospects and Challenges,* IMF Occasional Paper 232, Washington, DC, 2004.

Rodrik, Dani, "Industrial Policy for the Twenty-First Century," unpublished paper, Harvard University, September 2004 *(http://ksghome.harvard.edu/~drodrik/ UNIDOSep.pdf).*

Sutton, John, "The Auto-Component Supply Chain in China and India: A Benchmarking Study," London School of Economics, unpublished paper, 2005.

Discussion Questions

1. Does Rodrik oppose free trade? Why or why not?

2. Why does Rodrik argue that institutions are so important? Why does he believe that the WTO and other institutions can inhibit development?

3. Why do farm subsidies hurt the poor? If these policies are so bad, why do developed countries support them?

4. What benefits of globalization do Christian Broda and David Weinstein believe have been estimated? How important do you believe these gains are?

5. Compare and contrast Rodrik's views on globalization to Christian Broda and David Weinstein's views. Who do you believe is correct?

6. What is an industrial policy? Why does Rodrik believe that China has followed an industrial policy? Has it been successful?

7. Can you think of an alternative explanation to Rodrik's for China's success and for the composition of its exports?

Trade Deficit Disorder

VI

The United States has moved from being the largest creditor nation to becoming (by far) the largest debtor nation as its current account deficit has skyrocketed. Indeed the U.S. current account deficit is one of the most important international economic issues in the last decade, along with the rise of China's trade surplus, which mirrors the U.S. deficit. Any understanding of international finance must begin by recognizing this salient event. One key factor in understanding the rise of the U.S. trade deficit is the relationship between the U.S. budget deficit and the U.S. trade deficit—the so-called "twin deficit hypothesis."

The first article, "Twin Deficits, Twenty Years Later," by Leonardo Bartolini and Amartya Lahiri examines the twin deficits hypothesis and finds mixed evidence of this hypothesis in the U.S. and elsewhere. Overall, they conclude that lowering budget deficits will not necessarily lead to a lowering of trade deficits.

The second article, Why a Dollar Depreciation May Not Close the U.S. Trade Deficit," by Linda Goldberg and Eleanor Wiske Dillon, examines another factor often mentioned as a way to reduce the U.S. trade deficit—dollar depreciation. Similar to the analysis in the first article, the authors here also believe that a fall in the dollar will not be sufficient to reduce demand for imported goods, though a weaker dollar will lead to increased exports.

The final article, "Trade Deficits Aren't as Bad as You Think," by George Alessandria argues, as the title implies, that trade deficits aren't so bad. Alessandria argues that trade deficits simply reflect decisions by rational consumers across the globe to allocate resources, not only geographically, but also over time, as people "consumption-smooth," that is, try to even out consumption patterns over time by alternating saving and spending.

Twin Deficits, Twenty Years Later

17

Leonardo **Bartolini** and
Amartya **Lahiri**

In recent years, the twin-deficit hypothesis—the argument that fiscal deficits fuel current account deficits—has returned to the forefront of the policy debate. The argument first emerged in the 1980s, when a significant deterioration in the U.S. current account balance accompanied a sharp rise in the federal budget deficit. Now, with the U.S. current account and fiscal balances plunging by 3 and 4 percent of GDP, respectively, from 2001 to 2005, the view that the two deficits might be closely linked has attracted new interest.[1] Changes in U.S. fiscal policy have also been viewed as playing a key role in widening the nation's current account deficit since the turn of the millennium and thus in determining whether global current accounts will be rebalanced over the next decade.[2]

According to the twin-deficit hypothesis, when a government increases its fiscal deficit—for instance, by cutting taxes—domestic residents use some of the income windfall to boost consumption, causing total national (private and public) saving to decline. The decline in saving requires the country either to borrow from abroad or reduce its foreign lending, unless domestic investment decreases enough to offset the saving shortfall. Thus, a wider fiscal deficit typically should be accompanied by a wider current account deficit.

Casual observation suggests that the twin-deficit hypothesis accurately captures the U.S. experience in the 1980s and the first years of the new century. However, the hypothesis does not explain the U.S. record of the late 1990s, when a substantial current account deficit coexisted with a federal budget surplus. Nor does it accord with Japan's experience during the 1990s, or the experience of many other countries undergoing sharp swings in fiscal policy over the past two decades. Many empirical studies have also failed to find a strong relationship between fiscal and current account deficits, perhaps because they have used data on a very limited number of countries or have focused on periods that were too short to yield reliable evidence in a variety of environments and over time.[3]

We contribute to the debate on the twin-deficit hypothesis by analyzing the link between fiscal and current account deficits across a larger sample of countries and over a longer period than examined in earlier studies. Reviewing the international record over the past thirty years, we revisit both key components of the twin-deficit hypothesis: the relationship between fiscal policy and private saving, and the response of current account balances to fiscal policy changes. Our findings confirm the broad wisdom that private saving indeed tends to decline when fiscal policy loosens. However, this response may have weakened over time. Saving now tends to fall by about 35 cents in response to each extra dollar of fiscal deficit, down from the decline of 40 to 50 cents that researchers have reported for earlier periods. In addition, much of the decrease in national saving is matched by a drop in the current account, whose deficit rises by 30 cents for each extra dollar of fiscal deficit.

These results offer some support for the twin-deficit view. They suggest, however, that the effects of fiscal policy on saving and the current account balance are too weak for deficit reductions in the United States to play a central role in correcting the nation's current account imbalance with the rest of the world.

Fiscal Policy and Current Account Deficits in Industrial Countries, 1990–2005

Most industrial countries enhanced their fiscal accounts significantly during the 1990s. Fiscal balances started to improve in the Organisation for Economic Co-operation and Development (OECD) area as a whole around 1993 (see Figure 1).[4] By 2000, OECD countries' primary deficits—overall fiscal deficits net of interest payments—had turned to surpluses, increasing by more than 4 percent of GDP

since their 1993 trough. Overall fiscal balances grew by a similar amount.

Since the turn of the millennium, however, much of this fiscal improvement has been reversed, with the largest OECD countries making especially sharp U-turns. As the chart shows, from 2000 to 2004 the primary fiscal balances of the industrial area as a whole deteriorated by nearly 5 percent of GDP. This poor performance was led by a massive decline in fiscal balances in the United States, the United Kingdom, Germany, and Italy.

At first glance, post-1990 data on fiscal and current account deficits for the largest industrial countries offer some support for the twin-deficit hypothesis. Dividing these data over the critical 1990–2000 and 2000–2005 periods, Table 1 reveals that most of the changes in fiscal and current account balances (specifically, those depicted in blue) accord with the predictions of the twin-deficit view. However, there are notable exceptions. For example, improving U.S. fiscal accounts from 1992 to 2000 were associated with a worsening U.S. current account. The stability of Japan's current account surplus during the

Fiscal and Current Account Balances in OECD Countries, 1990–2005
Figure 1

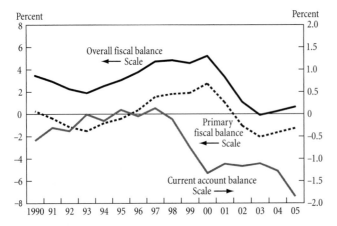

Source: Organisation for Economic Co-operation and Development (OECD).
Note: Primary fiscal balances equal overall fiscal balances net of interest payments.

Fiscal and Current Account Balances in the Largest Industrial Countries
Table 1
Changes over Period (Percentage of GDP)

Country	1990–2000		2000–2005	
	Primary Fiscal Balance	**Current Account Balance**	**Primary Fiscal Balance**	**Current Account Balance**
United States	5.0	−2.9	−6.0	−2.2
Japan	−9.3	1.0	1.2	0.9
Germany	3.8	−4.6	−5.4	5.7
France	0.7	2.1	−1.8	−2.9
United Kingdom	5.0	1.4	−7.3	0.7
Italy	7.2	0.9	−5.4	−0.9
Canada	6.7	6.1	−3.3	−1.0

Source: Organisation for Economic Co-operation and Development.
Notes: Primary fiscal balances equal overall fiscal balances net of interest payments. Pairs in blue accord qualitatively with the predictions of the twin-deficit hypothesis.

1990s, despite the country's sharply declining fiscal condition, is another exception to the twin-deficit hypothesis. Indeed, Japan's experience in the 1990s is frequently cited as evidence that changes in private saving can offset changes in fiscal policy, leaving a country's current account balance largely unaffected.

While the evidence presented in Table 1 is informative, it provides only a weak basis for assessing the validity of the twin-deficit hypothesis. The reason is that such a hypothesis pertains to the response of current account deficits to *isolated* changes in fiscal deficits, keeping factors such as government debt and expenditures and other variables associated with business cycles unchanged. Similarly, Table 1 displays only historical data, without attempting to control for any variable that might have influenced the link between fiscal and current account deficits. It is possible, for instance, that the U.S. current account deficit of the late 1990s might have turned into a surplus had the U.S. economy stagnated in this period instead of booming. It is also possible that Japan's current account surplus might have turned

into a large deficit during the 1990s had Japanese growth not collapsed after 1990.

To assess the twin-deficit hypothesis more formally, we broaden our analysis by using data from a large group of countries over a long period. This approach enables us to account for both the common characteristics of the countries in our sample and the impact of business cycles and other key factors.

Fiscal Policy and National Saving

Two views on the effect of fiscal deficits on private saving and investment behavior have been historically prominent. The first view, sometimes associated with the Keynesian analysis of fiscal policy, is a key ingredient of the twin-deficit hypothesis. According to this view, a tax cut or other fiscal expansion financed by the issuance of public debt lowers national saving by increasing private disposable income and hence private consumption. The implications of this saving shortfall for investment and the current account depend on a country's degree of openness to capital transactions with the rest of the world. In countries that are relatively closed to capital flows, reduced domestic saving must be matched by decreased domestic investment, because residents cannot borrow from abroad to keep investment high. Thus, fiscal expansions "crowd out" domestic investment, usually by lifting domestic interest rates. More open economies, by comparison, may keep domestic investment stable by turning to foreign credit and thus may not see interest rates rise. In these scenarios, a decline in national saving is matched by a rise in the current account deficit, leading to twin fiscal and current account deficits.

The second prominent view on the effect of fiscal deficits on private saving and investment is the so-called Ricardian view. According to this view, tax cuts financed by the issuance of new public debt lead residents to expect the government to raise taxes eventually to repay the new debt.[5] To prepare for future tax increases, residents save all the cash freed by the tax cut; consumption, national saving, and the current account are therefore unchanged.[6]

To date, the most well-known assessment of the relative accuracy of these two views is found in Bernheim (1987). The author reviewed time series U.S. data as well as crosscountry evidence on the effect of fiscal deficits on consumption. For the United States, Bernheim concluded that each dollar of tax cuts raised private consumption by 20 to 30 cents. Similarly, his evidence from thirty-nine countries from 1972 to 1983 revealed that each dollar of tax cuts raised private consumption by 40 to 50 cents. Thus, according to Bernheim, the world accorded somewhat more closely with the pure Ricardian view (according to which private consumption should rise by zero cents for each dollar of tax cuts) than with the pure twin-deficit view (according to which consumption should rise by 100 cents for each dollar of tax cuts). Bernheim's separate analysis of U.S. data suggested that the consumption effects for the United States were even closer to the pure Ricardian view than were those for its foreign partners.[7]

While a number of studies have explored the link between fiscal policy and private saving since Bernheim's classic work,[8] they have focused mostly on data from individual countries and paid little attention to cross-country evidence. We depart from these studies by adopting the cross-country methodology of Bernheim. However, we include a substantial amount of new data in our analysis and, unlike Bernheim, we use data adjusted to eliminate the blurring effects of cyclical relationships.

We begin by essentially replicating Bernheim's analysis of the response of private consumption to fiscal policy for two groups of countries: the same twenty-six countries used by Bernheim and the OECD countries exclusively. By focusing on the latter group, we can estimate our relationships using cyclically adjusted data provided by the OECD. Our estimation strategy, described in the box, involves linking consumption behavior to fiscal balances, both of which are measured as shares of GDP, by controlling for changes in other fiscal variables (government consumption and public debt) and in other variables traditionally associated with consumption behavior (income growth and population growth).

Our estimation results, presented in Table 2, yield three main conclusions.[9] First, each dollar rise in fiscal deficits in our sample countries is associated with an average rise in private consumption of 33 to 37 cents. This finding supports the argument that consumption responds significantly to fiscal policy changes. However, the estimated rise in consumption is smaller than the increase of 40 to 50 cents calculated by Bernheim, suggesting that the effects of fiscal policy changes on consumption and saving may have weakened over time.

Second, our result is essentially unchanged if we restrict our sample to include only OECD countries, for which cyclically adjusted data are available, rather than examine Bernheim's larger group of countries, the estimates for which are not cyclically adjusted. This robustness suggests that the estimated link between fiscal policy and consumption cannot be attributed

---

**Estimating the Link between Fiscal Policy,
Saving, and the Current Account**
Box 1

We estimate the link between fiscal deficits and both private consumption and the current account by using the equations:

$$C/Y = \beta_1 + \beta_2(FISCDEF/Y) + \beta_3(G/Y) + \beta_4(D/Y) + \beta_5 YG + \beta_6 PG$$

and

$$CA/Y = \alpha_1 + \alpha_2(FISCDEF/Y) + \alpha_3(G/Y) + \alpha_4(D/Y) + \alpha_5 YG + \alpha_6 PG,$$

where C is private consumption, Y is GDP, $FISCDEF$ is the fiscal deficit, G is government consumption, D is public debt, YG is GDP growth, PG is population growth, and CA is the current account balance. Our focus is on the coefficients β_2 and α_2. The pure Ricardian view predicts $\beta_2 = \alpha_2 = 0$, that is, neither consumption nor the current account should respond to changes in the fiscal deficit. According to the twin-deficit hypothesis, we

should instead observe $\beta_2 > 0$ and $\alpha_2 < 0$ because consumption should increase and the current account should worsen in response to an increase in the fiscal deficit.

Our model is estimated using a panel regression technique with fixed effects. We first estimate the model for the 1972–98 period for the same twenty-six countries studied by Bernheim (1987), using data from the International Monetary Fund's International Financial Statistics (IFS) and ending our sample in 1998 to avoid consistency problems in the IFS data after that year. We then estimate the model for the 1972–2003 period using Organisation for Economic Co-operation and Development (OECD) data and cyclically adjusted budget deficits for the eighteen OECD countries for which sufficient data are available.

---

to business-cycle relationships that might vanish over longer horizons.

Third, the effect of public debt on private consumption is statistically significant but economically small. That is, historically the fiscal policy changes that have most affected consumption in our group of countries are changes in fiscal deficits, rather than changes in public debt.[10]

We also produced estimates only for the United States, and obtained results similar to those found for other countries. Specifically, a dollar increase in the U.S. budget deficit led to a rise of 23 cents in private consumption. However, this smaller, one-country sample resulted in estimates that were less precise and less stable across different specifications of our empirical model.

Fiscal Policy and the Current Account

Our finding that each dollar increase in fiscal deficit is typically associated with a decline in national saving of 33 to 37 cents helps clarify the link between fiscal policy

changes and consumption. We now consider the implications of this finding for the effect of fiscal policy changes on current account balances.

One approach to linking fiscal policy changes to current account changes involves uncovering the relationship between fiscal policy and domestic investment. This line of inquiry allows one to determine the amount of foreign financing required to close the domestic savings–investment gap. This strategy can be problematic, however, because the empirical behavior of investment is usually hard to characterize. Investment responds to many factors, such as domestic and foreign interest rates and productivity, and the response is often unstable and unpredictable (see, for instance, McCarthy [2001]). Accordingly, we pursue a more direct line of inquiry: we replace consumption with the current account balance as the variable to be explained in our regression equation (see box). This substitution enables us to estimate a direct relationship between fiscal balances and the current account in our sample of countries.

The Impact of Fiscal Policy Changes
Table 2

	Dependent Variable			
	Consumption/GDP		Current Account/GDP	
Sample	**Bernheim 26**	**OECD 18**	**Bernheim 26**	**OECD 18**
Independent variables				
Fiscal deficit	0.33	0.37	0.38	0.30
	(0.04)	(0.05)	(0.05)	(0.05)
Government consumption	−0.33	−0.24	0.33	−0.23
	(0.08)	(0.1)	(0.10)	(0.11)
Income growth	0.00003	−0.001	0.0001	−0.0003
	(0.0001)	(0.0004)	(0.0001)	(0.0003)
Population growth	−0.003	−0.0001	0.03	−0.001
	(0.005)	(0.001)	(0.01)	(0.001)
Public debt	−0.02	0.02	0.004	0.04
	(0.004)	(0.007)	(0.006)	(0.07)
R^2 (within)	0.47	0.28	0.14	0.19
Number of observations	681	444	576	457
Period	1972–98	1972–2003	1972–98	1972–2003

Source: Authors' calculations.

Notes: Public saving, government consumption, and public debt are measured as ratios over GDP. Standard errors are in parentheses. The "Bernheim 26" sample comprises Australia, Austria, Belgium, Canada, Costa Rica, Finland, France, Germany, Guyana, Iceland, India, Indonesia, Italy, Korea, Luxembourg, Mexico, Morocco, Norway, Singapore, South Africa, Spain, Sweden, Switzerland, Thailand, the United Kingdom, and the United States. The "OECD 18" sample comprises the countries of the Organisation for Economic Co-operation and Development: Australia, Austria, Belgium, Canada, Denmark, Finland, France, Germany, Greece, Iceland, Ireland, Italy, Japan, the Netherlands, Norway, Sweden, the United Kingdom, and the United States.

Our estimates reveal that each dollar rise in the fiscal deficit is associated on average with a 30 cent decline in the current account (Table 2). In conjunction with our earlier finding—that each dollar rise in the fiscal deficit leads to a fall in national saving of 33 to 37 cents—this result implies that changes in national saving are reflected almost one-for-one in changes in current accounts in our country group.

The fact that fiscal deficits have a similar impact on private domestic saving and on the current account suggests that investment has exhibited only a tenuous response to fiscal policy changes, failing to decline to offset the drop in national saving. This weak relationship accords with much of the research on the determinants of investment. In the context of our analysis, it suggests that the current account is chiefly responsible for accommodating changes in national saving.

Explaining the Declining Impact of Fiscal Deficits

The earlier comparison of our empirical findings with those of Bernheim suggests that changes in fiscal policy have had a declining impact on consumption and current accounts in our group of mostly industrial and emerging economies. We now consider possible explanations for this phenomenon.

Over the past few decades, at least three factors observed in industrial countries could have led consumers to be more conscious of the need to set aside a larger share of a fiscal windfall in anticipation of future fiscal retrenchments.

The first factor is financial innovation, which has made it easier for households to borrow against future income and thus reduced their need for liquid funds to finance consumption.[11] In these circumstances, tax cuts and other expansionary fiscal initiatives are less likely to spur consumption. Conversely, fiscal retrenchments are less likely to dampen consumption, as households have become more apt to borrow or liquidate some of their financial assets to mitigate the impact of a tax increase or a fall in public spending. Altogether, financial innovation is likely to have weakened the response of consumption to fiscal policy changes in recent decades.

A second factor is the more favorable demographics and associated lengthening of work lifetimes recorded in the industrial and emerging markets over the past few decades. Between 1950 and 2000, life expectancy rose by seven years in the United States, by ten years in Germany, and by sixteen years in Japan (Kinsella and Velkoff 2001; Groshen and Klitgaard 2002). Increases in life expectancy in other industrial countries have been comparable. In other words, adult taxpayers today—unlike their predecessors a few decades ago—are more likely to live long enough to face the eventual bill for a current tax cut. Furthermore, to the extent that the tax obligation weighs disproportionately on the working population, widespread reforms to retirement systems in industrial countries during the past decade may have increased the effective burden of fiscal expansions on today's workers. Customary retirement ages have risen in many industrial countries—most typically, from about sixty to sixty-five—thus increasing workers' stake in the future implications of current fiscal policies.[12]

Finally, the adoption of "fiscal rules" is also likely to have contributed to forward-looking behavior among households in our sample of countries. During the past decade, fiscal rules have taken the form of balanced-budget requirements and/or debt limits for the public sector in many advanced as well as emerging economies.[13] These rules, such as those articulated in Europe's Maastricht Treaty and the Stability and Growth Pact, are generally designed to limit the discretion of fiscal authorities and make them accountable for tax cuts and other expansionary fiscal initiatives. The rules likely have sharpened consumers' perception of the need to plan ahead in response to fiscal expansions.

Conclusion

The twin-deficit hypothesis has resurfaced in the policy debate twenty years after the large U.S. fiscal and current account deficits of the 1980s. The hypothesis suggests that a larger fiscal deficit, through its effect on national saving and consumption, leads to an expanded current account deficit.

Our study offers a mild endorsement of this view. Examining the link between changes in public and private saving in recent decades, we find that lower public saving in advanced economies continues to be associated with higher private consumption and hence reduced national saving. This relationship holds true even as consumers, in anticipation of future fiscal retrenchments, have saved larger shares of the income made available by higher fiscal deficits than they did in earlier decades. We find that, on average, each extra dollar of fiscal deficit is associated with a rise in private consumption—or a fall in national saving—of about 35 cents in the 1972–2003 period, compared with a rise in consumption of 40 to 50 cents in the 1972–83 period.

We also find that changes in national saving have led to very similar changes in current accounts in our sample of countries. Accordingly, we conclude that investment continues to show no systematic response to fiscal policy changes. Much of the saving shortfall observed in our sample of countries—about 30 cents for each extra dollar of fiscal deficit—thus requires an increase in foreign borrowing.

While these findings provide some support for the twin-deficit hypothesis, they do not support the view that future deficit reductions can play a critical role in eliminating the U.S. current account imbalance with the rest of the world. Our estimates suggest that even if the federal fiscal deficit—currently about 2 percent of GDP—were fully erased, the nation's current account deficit would improve by only a fraction of its current 7 percent of GDP. For example, if the U.S. current account continues to respond to fiscal changes as it has, on average, in our sample of OECD countries—by 30 cents on the dollar—a full elimination of the federal fiscal deficit would improve the U.S. current account by only 0.6 percent of GDP, or less than one-tenth of its current level. While these calculations are based on historical correlations that could break down if circumstances change in unexpected ways, they are nonetheless suggestive of the likely magnitude of the effects at work.

Endnotes

[1] A country's fiscal balance measures the difference between government revenues and expenditures, while a country's current account balance measures the difference between the country's current receipts from and payments to the rest of the world.

[2] See, for example, International Monetary Fund (2004), Organisation for Economic Co-operation and Development (2004), and Chinn (2005).

[3] For instance, while studies such as Miller and Russek (1989) and Enders and Lee (1990) have found fiscal deficits to be prime determinants of trade deficits, others (such as Dewald and Ulan [1990], Gruber and Kamin [2005], and Kim and Roubini [2003]) have observed no firm link or even a link in the opposite direction of the one predicted by the twin-deficit hypothesis. Some studies, such as Chinn and Prasad (2003), estimate a response of current accounts to fiscal deficits similar to ours, but they do not explore the direct link from fiscal deficits to private consumption.

[4] All balances plotted in the chart and used in our analysis pertain to the general (national plus local) government sector, including balances of social security systems.

[5] Whether the Ricardian view can actually be traced to the writing of economic theorist David Ricardo (1772–1823) is a controversial issue. In any case, the modern incarnation of the Ricardian view is typically attributed to Robert Barro (see, in particular, Barro [1974]).

[6] Needless to say, this mechanism can operate smoothly only when domestic residents live long enough to care about their own future tax burdens or the tax burdens of future generations, when domestic residents have unfettered access to capital markets to transfer wealth over time, and when taxes have no effect on resource allocation other than through their impact on private saving. Hardly any scholar nowadays holds a pure Ricardian view. However, a key question is how closely the world adheres empirically to this benchmark.

[7] Bernheim also examined the effect of fiscal deficits on interest rates, but found no stable link. More recent studies have found a firmer link (see, for instance, Gale and Orszag [2004] for evidence on the United States and International Monetary Fund [2004] for a survey of international results). Despite these contributions, the link between interest rates and investment is still not clearly understood.

[8] See Seater (1993) and Elmendorf and Mankiw (1999) for reviews of this work.

[9] Note that our empirical approach greatly simplifies the complex link between fiscal deficits on the one side and private consumption and current account deficits on the other. Such a link is likely to depend on factors such as the specific mix of each tax/expenditure package, its persistence, and a variety of initial conditions not captured by our simple empirical model.

[10] Our estimates of the impact of fiscal balances on private consumption and current accounts changed minimally when we excluded public debt from the independent variables, added past values of the independent variables, or defined variables as changes rather than as levels. By contrast, our estimates were more variable across different country groups and specifications of the econometric model.

[11] See, for instance, Dynan, Elmendorf, and Sichel (2006).

[12] Casey et al. (2003) review many such reforms, including measures increasing retirement ages enacted in twelve industrial countries since the early 1990s.

[13] See Kopits (2001) for a review of the fiscal rules adopted in many industrial countries since the mid-1990s.

References

Barro, Robert. 1974. "Are Government Bonds Net Wealth?" *Journal of Political Economy* 82, no. 6 (November-December): 1095–1117.

Bernheim, B. Douglas. 1987. "Ricardian Equivalence: An Evaluation of Theory and Evidence." *NBER Macroeconomics Annual* 1987, 263–304. London and Cambridge, Mass.: MIT Press.

Casey, Bernard, Howard Oxley, Edward Whitehouse, Pablo Antolin, Romain Duval, and Willi Leibfritz. 2003. "Policies for an Aging Society: Recent Measures and Areas for Further Reform." Organisation for Economic Cooperation and Development, Economics Department Working Paper no. 369, November 20.

Chinn, Menzie D. 2005. "Getting Serious about the Twin Deficits." Council on Foreign Relations, Council Special Report no. 10, September.

Chinn, Menzie D., and Eswar S. Prasad. 2003. "Medium-Term Determinants of Current Accounts in Industrial and Developing Countries: An Empirical Exploration" *Journal of International Economics* 59, no. 1 (January): 47–76.

Dewald, William G., and Michael Ulan. 1990. "Twin-Deficit Illusion." *Cato Journal* 9, no. 3 (winter): 689–707.

Dynan, Karen E., Douglas W. Elmendorf, and Daniel E. Sichel. 2006. "Can Financial Innovation Help to Explain the Reduced Volatility of Economic Activity?" *Journal of Monetary Economics* 53, no. 1 (January): 123–50.

Elmendorf, Douglas W., and N. Gregory Mankiw. 1999. "Government Debt." In *Handbook of Macroeconomics* 15: 1615–69. Amsterdam: Elsevier Science and North-Holland.

Enders, Walter, and Bong-Soo Lee. 1990. "Current Account and Budget Deficits: Twins or Distant Cousins?" *Review of Economics and Statistics* 72, no. 3 (August): 373–81.

Gale, William G., and Peter R. Orszag. 2004. "Budget Deficits, National Saving, and Interest Rates." Unpublished paper, Brookings Institution.

Groshen, Erica L., and Thomas Klitgaard. 2002. "Live Long and Prosper: Challenges Ahead for an Aging Population." Federal Reserve Bank of New York *Current Issues in Economics and Finance* 8, no. 2 (February).

Gruber, Joseph W., and Steven B. Kamin. 2005. "Explaining the Global Pattern of Current Account Imbalances." Board of Governors of the Federal Reserve System, International Finance Discussion Papers, no. 846, November.

International Monetary Fund. 2004. "The Global Implications of the U.S. Fiscal Deficit and of China's Growth." In *World Economic Outlook: Advancing Structural Reforms*, 63–102. A Survey by the Staff of the International Monetary Fund. April.

Kim, Soyoung, and Nouriel Roubini. 2003. "Twin Deficit or Twin Divergence? Fiscal Policy, Current Account, and the Real Exchange Rate in the U.S." Unpublished paper, New York University, February. Revised 2004.

Kinsella, Kevin, and Victoria Velkoff. 2001. "An Aging World: 2001." Washington, D.C.: U.S. Census Bureau.

Kopits, George. 2001. "Fiscal Rules: Useful Policy Framework or Unnecessary Ornament?" International Monetary Fund Working Paper no. 01/145, September.

McCarthy, Jonathan. 2001. "Equipment Expenditures since 1995: The Boom and the Bust." Federal Reserve Bank of New York *Current Issues in Economics and Finance* 7, no. 9 (October).

Miller, Stephen M., and Frank S. Russek. 1989. "Are the Twin Deficits Really Related?" *Contemporary Policy Issues* 7, no. 4 (October): 91–115.

Organisation for Economic Co-operation and Development. 2004. "The Challenges of Narrowing the U.S. Current Account Deficit." *OECD Economic Outlook*, no. 75, June: 29–52.

Seater, John J. 1993. "Ricardian Equivalence." *Journal of Economic Literature* 31, no. 1 (March): 142–90.

Why a Dollar Depreciation May Not Close the U.S. Trade Deficit

18

LINDA **GOLDBERG** AND
ELEANOR WISKE **DILLON**

In 2006, the U.S. trade deficit reached $759 billion—equivalent to almost 6 percent of GDP—as U.S. imports of foreign goods continued to outstrip the nation's exports to other countries (see Figure 1). In the view of many analysts and policymakers, a dollar depreciation remains a key mechanism for addressing this export-import imbalance and restoring the international competitiveness of American producers.[1] Indeed, in theory, a weaker dollar should raise the cost of foreign goods for U.S. consumers, thereby reducing U.S. demand for imports, at the same time that it boosts foreign demand for U.S. goods by making the nation's exports more price-competitive abroad.[2]

We take a fresh look at the effectiveness of dollar depreciation as a means of narrowing U.S. trade deficits. We go beyond the standard discussion of relative price and demand to consider three other factors that influence the nation's trade balance adjustment: the special role of the dollar in invoicing international trade transactions, the market share concerns of foreign exporters, and the high U.S. distribution costs (relative to those of the country's trading partners) that form part of the final consumption prices of imported goods.

Our analysis reveals that a dollar depreciation is unlikely to close the trade gap single-handedly. To be sure, foreign demand for U.S. exports should grow, as theory predicts. Because virtually all U.S. exports to

other countries are invoiced in dollars, foreign purchasers will derive an immediate benefit from a dollar depreciation as the cost of their purchases declines in foreign currency terms. However, the price of foreign imports for U.S. consumers will be considerably more resilient to exchange rate changes.

Trade invoicing practices, we argue, contribute significantly to the insensitivity of import prices to exchange rates. Because almost all of the goods that the United States imports, like those it exports, are invoiced in dollars, the prices of imported goods remain fixed for a period when exchange rates change. Moreover, even in the longer term—over, say, the year following a dollar depreciation—the desire of foreign producers to remain competitive in the large U.S. market may lead them to resist increasing the dollar price of their goods. Finally, the unusually high marketing and distribution costs added to imports once they enter the United States—costs denominated in dollars—further insulate the final consumption price of imported goods from exchange rate changes.

Together, these three factors suggest that, all else equal, we may not see the sort of significant escalation in import prices that would prompt U.S. consumers to curtail their demand for foreign goods and switch their purchases to equivalent goods produced at home. Improvement in the trade balance following a dollar depreciation will most likely be achieved instead

Nominal Trade Balance
Figure 1

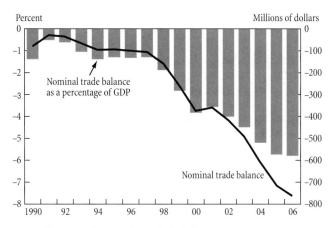

Source: U.S. Department of Commerce, Bureau of Economic Analysis.

through increased foreign purchases of newly affordable U.S. goods. Nevertheless, if the nation's consumption patterns are not "rebalanced" away from imports, then the total adjustment in U.S. trade following the depreciation of the dollar could still fall markedly short of expectations.

Exchange Rates and Traded Goods Prices

To understand how exchange rate changes affect traded goods prices and alter demand, consider what happens to a European good marketed to the United States following a dollar depreciation against the euro. First, the European producer who sells the good to the U.S. market must decide what share of the dollar depreciation, if any, to absorb in his or her profit margins and what share to pass on to U.S. consumers in the form of a higher price for the good in dollar terms. This decision will determine how much of the exchange rate change is transmitted to the import price observed at the U.S. border.

Once at the border, the imported good is stored, shipped to its distributor,

marketed by a retailer, and ultimately sold to the final consumer. The many steps in this distribution stage within the United States add dollar-denominated costs to the final price of the good and thus reduce the share of the final price that is affected by exchange rate movements. Moreover, this stage offers distributors and retailers an opportunity to stabilize some of the fluctuations in the price of the imported good by adjusting their markups. If they do so, the final consumption price of the imported good will increase by a much lower percentage than the price observed at the border.

In the next sections, we present empirical evidence that this pricing process has played out differently in the United States than in many of its trading partners. One key finding is how little exchange rate movements are reflected in import prices at the U.S. border, even before the imported goods are distributed to retailers and then consumers. With transmission rates in the United States much below those observed in other OECD (Organisation for Economic Co-operation and Development) countries, the effect of a dollar depreciation on U.S. demand for any particular type of import could be relatively small.

Estimates of Exchange Rate Pass-Through across Countries

The rate of exchange rate "pass-through" is the degree to which a change in the value of a country's currency induces a change in the price of the country's imports and exports. Table 1 presents estimates of pass-through rates into import prices for the United States, Japan, euro-area countries, other advanced economies, and the OECD countries as a group over the 1975–2003 period.[3] These estimates are calculated as the cumulative percentage change in a country's aggregate import prices at the border over the year following a depreciation of the country's currency against the currencies of its trading partners.[4]

For all OECD countries, a 1 percent change in the exchange rate will, on average, generate a 0.64 percent change in import prices over the course of a year, although there is wide variation around this mean. For the euro area, the average pass-through rate is substantially higher, at 0.81. Estimates of pass-through for Japan differ considerably, but the rate is usually found to be high and close to complete.

By contrast, for the United States over this three-decade period, a 1 percent change in the exchange rate has, on average, yielded only a 0.42 percent change in import prices. Clearly, the pass-through of exchange rate movements into import prices at the border is markedly lower for the United States than for most of the world. This pattern continues to hold, although somewhat less dramatically, in estimates using data only since 1990: the United States exhibits an average rate of exchange rate pass-through into import prices of 0.32, compared with an average across countries of 0.48.[5]

Explaining Low U.S. Pass-Through Rates at the Border

Why is the transmission of exchange rate changes to the import prices observed at the border so much weaker for the United States than for other countries? Two factors—invoicing practices and market share considerations—appear to play an important role.

Invoicing Practices

Producers involved in foreign trade can choose the currency they want to use to express the price of their exports. They can invoice in their own home currency, in the currency of their buyers, or in a third, "vehicle" currency. In selecting an invoicing currency, producers will consider transaction costs across currencies and macroeconomic volatility across countries. They will also consider the competitive structure of the industry in which their goods are being sold: For example, producers in very competitive industries may have strong incentives to keep the price of their goods steady relative to the prices maintained by their rivals in the destination market (Goldberg and Tille 2005).

Cross-country evidence on import and export invoicing in recent years reveals that the dollar is the dominant currency of invoicing across non-European countries (Table 2).[6] While the exports and imports of European countries are increasingly invoiced in euros (even for trade with countries outside the euro area), a high percentage of the traded goods of Asian countries, Latin American countries, and Australia are invoiced in U.S. dollars.

Exchange Rate Pass-Through to Import Prices after One Year
Table 1

OECD average	0.64
United States	0.42
Euro area	0.81
Japan	0.57–1.00
Other advanced economies	0.60

Sources: Campa and Goldberg (2005); Faruquee (2006).

Notes: Estimates are based on data from 1975 to 2003. The pass-through rate for Japan is a range, reflecting differences in study findings.

Use of the U.S. Dollar in Export and Import Invoicing
Table 2

	Date	Dollar Share in Export Invoicing	Dollar Share in Import Invoicing	U.S. Share in Exports
United States	2003	99.8	92.8	
Asia				
Japan	2003	48.0	68.7	24.8
Korea	2004	83.2	79.6	17.0
Malaysia	2000	90.0	90.0	20.5
Thailand	2003	84.4	76.0	17.0
Australia	2004	69.6	50.5	8.1
United Kingdom	2002	26.0	37.0	15.5
Euro area				
Belgium[a]	2004	29.6	35.1	17.9
France[a]	2003	33.6	46.9	13.7
Germany[a]	2004	24.1	35.9	15.6
Greece[a]	2003	17.5	24.9	15.3
Italy	2004	51.2	55.3	8.6
Portugal[a]	2004	27.4	32.6	18.3
Spain[a]	2004	29.1	35.5	9.9
EU accession countries				
Bulgaria	2004	35.2	34.1	5.3
Czech Republic	2004	12.0	18.5	2.3
Estonia	2004	9.4	21.9	2.3
Hungary	2004	9.6	18.8	3.5
Poland	2004	21.4	26.1	2.4

Sources: Goldberg and Tille (2006); Kamps (2006).

[a] Invoicing data refer only to trade outside the euro area.

Moreover, for every country, the share of exports invoiced in dollars exceeds, often by a fairly large margin, the U.S. share in the country's exports—a clear indicator that the dollar is frequently used as a vehicle currency for trade with other countries.

Also notable is the very high percentage of U.S. imports and exports invoiced in dollars in the early 2000s. No other country has had its trade so overwhelmingly invoiced in its own currency. For euro-area countries on average, 54 percent of imports and 59 percent of exports were invoiced in

euros; in the case of Japan, 26 percent of imports and 38 percent of exports were invoiced in yen. By contrast, 93 percent of U.S. imports and 99 percent of U.S. exports were priced in dollars.

Data on invoicing currencies over a longer horizon are available only for some countries. This evidence suggests that since the advent of the euro in the late 1990s, dollar use in import and export invoicing has fallen. Nevertheless, the decline is largely confined to euro-area and European Union (EU) accession countries and, even for these countries, direct trade with the United States remains almost exclusively invoiced in dollars.[7]

The widespread use of dollars in invoicing U.S. trade helps explain the weak pass-through of exchange rate changes to the import prices observed at the U.S. border. When foreign producers invoice their exports to the United States in dollars, the price of these goods remains fixed in the buyer's currency if the dollar depreciates against other currencies.[8] The exchange rate movements affect only the foreign producers' profits and will not increase the dollar price paid by U.S. importers.[9] After a time, of course, foreign producers may choose to adjust their prices in response to the exchange rate change. But evidence suggests that exporters set prices in dollars well in advance of the delivery of their goods and change those prices only periodically.

Market Share Considerations

While the invoicing of U.S. imports in dollars automatically reduces exchange rate pass-through for a period following a dollar depreciation, foreign producers' desire to preserve market share for goods sold in the United States may keep the pass-through rate low over the longer term. That is, exporters to the United States may accept a lower profit margin when their currency appreciates in order to keep their dollar prices constant against competitors.

Moreover, the incentives to forgo a price markup may be stronger for producers exporting goods to the United States than for producers marketing goods to smaller industrialized countries. The U.S. market is very large, and imports command a lower share of consumption than they do in smaller markets. As a result, foreign producers may be reluctant to raise their prices in the event of a dollar depreciation because for many types of goods, U.S. consumers will be able to turn to domestic sources for comparable products. In smaller countries, consumers will be less able to substitute domestic goods for foreign imports; thus, exporters can more readily pass exchange rate movements into prices without losing market share.

In sum, both the use of the dollar in invoicing U.S. imports and the desire of exporters to keep their dollar prices constant against competitors may help to explain the low pass-through rates into U.S. import prices. Support for this view is provided by Gopinath, Itskhoki, and Rigobon (2006), who show that there is lower pass-through for U.S. imports invoiced in dollars, even a year or more after an exchange rate move.

Explaining Low Pass-Through Rates into Final Consumption Prices

Thus far we have considered the transmission of exchange rate changes into the prices of imports arriving at a country's borders, but other forces come into play between the time a good arrives at the border and the time it is sold to the consumer. As we noted earlier, the imported good must be stored, transported, and marketed by a retailer. The share of an exchange rate movement that appears in the final price of an import observed by consumers will be even smaller than the share passed into the price at the border because the final price includes domestic value added—that is, the dollar costs incurred in distributing the good in the United States.

When consumers purchase a good produced abroad, they are really purchasing a bundle of imported and domestic products, with the domestic portion consisting mostly of transportation, storage, and wholesale and retail trade services. Typically, only the portion of the price that comes from imports is directly affected by exchange rates. The share of distribution costs in the final household consumption price of goods for several industry categories generally ranges between 30 and 50 percent across countries (Campa and Goldberg 2006). Significantly, in every industry category, the share of distribution costs in U.S. goods prices is well above the average share and higher than the share of distribution costs in all other countries. The unusually high share of distribution costs in U.S. goods prices thus has the effect of further insulating U.S. import prices from exchange rate movements.

How Pass-Through Affects Trade Balance Adjustment

In theory, currency depreciations play an important role in trade balance adjustment by inducing "expenditure switching." If the U.S. dollar depreciates against the euro, for example, the dollar price of imports from Europe should rise, prompting U.S. consumers to shift their expenditures to domestically produced alternatives or imports from other regions (holding other exchange rates constant). At the same time, the depreciation of the dollar should lower the price, in euros, of U.S. exports to Europe, with the result that European consumers will begin to buy more U.S. exports.

The magnitude of this expenditure switching, relative to the size of the depreciation, will depend in part on how fully exchange rate movements are reflected in the prices faced by consumers. We have seen that invoicing practices, market share considerations, and high distribution costs may weaken the transmission of exchange rate changes to the prices U.S. consumers pay for imported goods. Exchange rate pass-through to U.S. export prices, however, is likely to be stronger. Given that virtually all U.S. exports are invoiced in dollars, a dollar depreciation produces an immediate drop in the price (in foreign currency terms) that foreign consumers will pay for U.S. goods and thereby increases demand for these goods abroad. These differences in pass-through between the United States and its trading partners mean that a dollar depreciation will likely elicit more expenditure switching by foreign consumers than by U.S. consumers. In other words, a weaker dollar is more likely to prompt foreign consumers to increase their purchases of U.S. goods than to induce U.S. consumers to

shift their purchases from imported to domestic goods.

The extent of import and export quantity changes depends on elasticities of demand, the percentage change in the quantity of a traded good demanded for a given percentage change in the price of that good. Researchers have attempted to estimate the elasticity of demand for individual countries' imports and exports with respect to changes in traded goods prices. Hooper, Johnson, and Marquez (2000) compare trade elasticities across the Group of Seven (G7) countries and find a strong asymmetry in export and import elasticities for the United States. Using data from the 1960s to the mid-1990s, they estimate that demand for U.S. exports reacts more than proportionally to changes in export prices, rising 1.5 percent for every 1 percent drop in export prices. U.S. demand for imports, however, reacts less than proportionally to price changes, rising only 0.3 percent for a 1 percent drop in import prices. While this asymmetry is present in the trade elasticities of most other G7 countries, it is most pronounced for the United States.

Researchers have also found that the responsiveness of demand to changes in export and import prices grows over the course of a year and longer. For example, the price elasticity of trade flows is generally considerably higher in the longer run than in the months immediately following a relative price change on goods (Gallaway, McDaniel, and Rivera 2003). Demand may become more responsive in a year's time because in that period, producers are able to reorient their production mix toward goods or varieties that can be profitably produced after the currency depreciation, allowing greater substitution of domestic goods for imports.

The price and quantity adjustments in traded commodities following a dollar depreciation will be reflected in total U.S. export revenues and import expenditures—in other words, the U.S. trade balance. If significant expenditure switching takes place, the real trade balance of the United States, which reflects the relative *quantities* of

Demand Adjustment to a 10 Percent Dollar Depreciation
Table 3

Percentage Change

	United States	Foreign Markets
Change in home currency price of bilateral imports	+4	−7
Change in bilateral demand for imports	−1	+10

Source: Authors' calculations.

exports from and imports to the United States, will improve. The *nominal* trade balance, which measures the total *expenditure* on imports and exports, will also improve, but to a lesser extent.

The reason that the nominal trade balance might lag the real balance is straightforward: while the quantity of goods imported by the United States has fallen, the price in dollars of each unit imported has increased. Similarly, the unit price of exports has decreased as the quantity has increased. This decrease in the ratio of the price of exports to the price of imports, called the terms of trade, partially offsets the improvement in the relative quantities of exports and imports, causing a smaller improvement in the nominal trade balance.

Scenario: The Effects of a 10 Percent Dollar Depreciation

To get a more concrete sense of how exchange rate movements, price adjustments, and demand reactions play out across countries, consider a scenario in which the dollar depreciates 10 percent against a basket of trade partner currencies. For this scenario, we adopt the pass-through rates identified earlier for the 1975–2003 period. That is, we assume that 42 percent of an exchange rate change is passed through to U.S. import prices over the course of a year while the corresponding figure for countries other than the United States is 77 percent—the OECD average excluding the United States. We also assume

the demand elasticities calculated by Hooper, Johnson, and Marquez.

In this scenario, a 10 percent dollar depreciation lowers the foreign currency price of U.S. exports by 7 percent, holding other factors constant (Table 3).[10] The same drop generates at most a 4 percent rise in the prices of imported goods at the U.S. border. Incorporating the demand elasticities from Hooper, Johnson, and Marquez, we estimate that foreign demand for U.S. exports would rise 10 percent while U.S. demand for imports from abroad would decrease only 1 percent in the six quarters after the depreciation. Note that the decline in import demand may be overestimated because we omit the distribution services that further cushion the effects of the depreciation on the prices ultimately paid by consumers.

The price and demand movements calculated here highlight the asymmetric effects of a dollar depreciation on U.S. exports and imports. U.S. consumers see only a very modest increase in the price of imports, and their appetite for imports diminishes only slightly. By contrast, U.S. exports become considerably more affordable abroad, prompting a large increase in demand. It is easy to see from this exercise how a dollar depreciation would lead to significant changes in foreign, but not U.S., consumption patterns.

Who bears the burden of this asymmetric trade balance adjustment? When the dollar depreciation is only partially passed on to import prices, the remainder is reflected in declining profits for foreign exporters. For example, if only 32 percent of the dollar depreciation is passed on to U.S. import prices—the average pass-through rate since 1990— the other 68 percent of the dollar depreciation would be reflected in lower unit revenues for the foreign producers. By contrast, American exporters get a boost in dollar-denominated income, since the dollar price of exports rises slightly while still becoming more price competitive in foreign markets.

Trade Balance Adjustment in a Complex Model

Our simple scenario analysis focuses narrowly on the chain of responses that links an exchange rate change to price adjustment and the subsequent demand reaction. More complex models of trade balance adjustment, by contrast, consider the source of the exchange rate movement, recognizing that the ultimate effects of, say, a dollar depreciation will depend on the developments that triggered it. Here we compare the results of our scenario exercise with those generated by a model developed by Federal Reserve Board economists Christopher Gust and Nathan Sheets (2006).[11] Interestingly, although the adjustment process described by Gust and Sheets is much more complicated, their findings largely parallel our own, providing confirmation for our broad conclusions.

The authors consider a dollar depreciation that stems from a change in the risk premium required by investors to hold U.S. assets. Gust and Sheets track the effects of this depreciation throughout the full economy under various pass-through assumptions, including the assumption that pass-through is low in the United States and high abroad. The adjustment process incorporates inflationary pressures from a depreciation of the dollar and the monetary authority's response to such pressures, as well as the responses of consumption and investment activity.

Under the assumption that exchange rate pass-through is low in the United

States and higher in the nation's trading partners, a change in the risk premium on U.S. assets triggers a 10 percent depreciation of the dollar in the first quarter. Over five quarters—the time horizon we considered in our earlier exercise—the depreciation rises to about 11.5 percent. With weak pass-through in the United States, the effects on U.S. imports are small. Nominal imports (calculated as the price of imports times the quantity of imports) rise modestly as prices adjust faster than demand, and then fall as demand reacts to higher prices, ending up about 1 percent above steady-state levels after five quarters. The dollar price of U.S. exports changes very little with the depreciation, but the price in foreign currency terms drops the full 10 percent of the depreciation, driving up the quantity of U.S. exports demanded. Nominal exports (the price of exports times the quantity of exports) in dollar terms rise 10 percent above steady-state levels after five quarters, exclusively from the change in quantities.

Gust and Sheets go on to compute the improvement in the real and nominal trade balances that would result from these estimated changes in exports and imports. Specifically, they find that a 10 percent depreciation of the dollar would improve the real trade balance by about 12 percent over five quarters and the nominal trade balance by a somewhat smaller margin, about 10 percent after five quarters.[12]

Although Gust and Sheets' analysis yields a much more detailed and complete account of the effects of a dollar depreciation than our simple exercise, the broad consequences described are very similar. In both cases, the dollar depreciation has markedly asymmetric effects on exports and imports, with import prices and quantities responding much more weakly than the price and quantity of exports. Thus, the complex model bears out the results of the scenario analysis: U.S. imports will play only a minor role in easing the U.S. trade deficit; improvement in the trade balance following a dollar depreciation will be driven largely by exports.

Conclusion

In theory, a dollar depreciation should help narrow the U.S. trade deficit by raising the price of imports for U.S. consumers and lowering the price of U.S. exports for consumers overseas. However, three factors that carry particular force for the United States—the near-exclusive use of dollars in invoicing U.S. trade, foreign exporters' market share concerns, and the unusually high distribution costs added to U.S. imports—blunt the pass-through of the currency depreciation to U.S. import prices. With import prices rising only modestly from their pre-depreciation levels, U.S. consumers have little incentive to reduce their demand for imports significantly or to seek out comparable goods produced at home.

The unresponsiveness of U.S. import prices to a dollar depreciation suggests that any substantial trade balance adjustment achieved through exchange rate changes must come instead from a reduction in export prices. Invoicing practices may contribute to the adjustment: Since U.S. exports are invoiced in dollars, foreign consumers will see an immediate reduction in the price of these goods—in home currency terms—when the dollar depreciates.

Quantitative analysis underscores the asymmetric response of import and export prices and confirms that U.S. demand for imports will be little diminished by a weaker dollar. A recent study by Gust and Sheets concludes that both the real and the nominal trade balances are likely to improve following a dollar depreciation, but mainly through a rise in the quantity of U.S. exports, with little change in U.S. imports.

Even a marked rise in exports, however, is by itself unlikely to erase the U.S. trade deficit. In 2006, that deficit stood at $759 billion. If imports and terms of trade remained constant, exports would have to grow 52 percent to single-handedly close this gap. Either import demand will have to become more responsive to exchange rate movements or adjustment will have to take place through other developments that would affect demand. These other developments might include increases in U.S. public or private saving (with related declines in U.S. consumption of all goods) or a rise in global demand driven by economic growth abroad or increased market access for U.S. exporters.

Endnotes

[1] Feldstein (2006). A recent NBER volume (Clarida 2007) provides a useful overview of some alternative positions in the debate over the trade deficit.

[2] Following common practice, we assume that exports and imports are sufficiently responsive to exchange rate changes, a requirement known in the economics literature as the Marshall-Lerner-Robinson condition.

[3] The estimates in Campa and Goldberg (2005) follow a standard approach that uses GDP to control for aggregate demand and a constructed foreign price index to control for changes in the exporting country's production costs.

[4] Different studies have generated varying estimates of pass-through. In the case of Japan, the variation is so great that we report a range of pass-through values; for other countries cited in the table, we present a point estimate that preserves the rank order of country pass-through rates identified in other studies.

[5] Pass-through estimates for the post-1990 period are drawn from Ihrig, Marazzi, and Rothenberg (2006).

[6] Extensive details on currency invoicing of trade are reported in Goldberg and Tille (2006) and Kamps (2006).

[7] Goldberg (2007) explores the evidence on the invoicing practices of the accession countries to the euro area.

[8] For U.S. exports, the situation is reversed. By default, the profit margins for U.S. producers remain fixed in their own currency while the foreign currency price of U.S. exports varies with exchange rates.

[9] Bils and Klenow (2004) provide extensive evidence on the degree of price stickiness in U.S. goods.

[10] This estimate applies to pass-through into the prices of all OECD country imports, not just the imports that are sourced from the United States. Given that U.S. exports are priced almost exclusively in dollars, the true pass-through of a dollar depreciation into the foreign market price of U.S. exports is probably even higher.

[11] See also the careful scenario analyses presented in International Monetary Fund (2005, 2006).

[12] Significantly, Gust and Sheets assume price elasticities of demand near unity in their analysis. If the authors were to use trade elasticities like those estimated by Hooper, Johnson, and Marquez—above unity abroad and well below unity in the United States—the dollar depreciation would induce a smaller improvement of the real trade balance.

References

Bils, Mark, and Peter J. Klenow. 2004. "Some Evidence on the Importance of Sticky Prices." *Journal of Political Economy* 112, no.5 (October): 947–85.

Campa, José, and Linda Goldberg. 2005. "Exchange Rate Pass-Through into Import Prices." *Review of Economics and Statistics* 87, no. 4 (November): 679–90.

———. 2006. "Distribution Margins, Imported Inputs, and the Sensitivity of the CPI to Exchange Rates." NBER Working Paper no. 12121, March.

Clarida, Richard H., ed. 2007. *G7 Current Account Imbalances: Sustainability and Adjustment.* NBER conference volume. Chicago: University of Chicago Press.

Faruquee, Hamid. 2006. "Exchange Rate Pass-Through in the Euro Area." *IMF Staff Papers* 53, no. 1 (April): 63–88.

Feldstein, Martin. 2006. "The Case for a Competitive Dollar." Remarks presented at the Economic Summit of the Stanford Institute for Economic Policy Research, Stanford, Calif, March 3.

Frankel, Jeffrey A., David C. Parsley, and Shang-Jin Wei. 2005. "Slow Passthrough around the World: A New Import for Developing Countries?" NBER Working Paper no. 11199, March.

Gallaway, Michael P., Christine A. McDaniel, and Sandra A. Rivera. 2003. "Short-Run and Long-Run Industry-Level Estimates of U.S. Armington Elasticities." *North American Journal of Economics and Finance* 14, no. 1 (March): 49–68.

Goldberg, Linda. 2007. "Trade Invoicing in the Accession Countries: Are They Suited to the Euro?" In Jeffrey A. Frankel and Christopher A. Pissarides, eds., *NBER International Seminar on Macroeconomics* 2005, 357–93. NBER conference volume. Cambridge, Mass.: MIT Press.

Goldberg, Linda, and Cédric Tille. 2005. "Vehicle Currency Use in International Trade." NBER Working Paper no. 11127, February.

———. 2006. "The International Role of the Dollar and Trade Balance Adjustment." Group of Thirty Occasional Paper no. 71.

Gopinath, Gita, Oleg Itskhoki, and Roberto Rigobon. 2006. "Pass-Through at the Dock: Pricing to Currency and to Market?" Unpublished paper, Harvard University, November.

Gust, Christopher, and Nathan Sheets. 2006. "The Adjustment of Global External Imbalances: Does Partial Exchange Rate Pass-Through to Trade Prices Matter?" Board of Governors of the Federal Reserve System, International Finance Discussion Papers, no. 850.

Hooper, Peter, Karen Johnson, and Jaime Marquez. 2000. "Trade Elasticities for the G-7 Countries." *Princeton Studies in International Economics*, no. 87, August.

Ihrig, Jane E., Mario Marazzi, and Alexander D. Rothenberg. 2006. "Exchange-Rate Pass-Through in the G-7 Countries." Board of Governors of the Federal Reserve System International Finance Discussion Papers, no. 2006–851, January.

International Monetary Fund. 2005. *World Economic Outlook: Building Institutions.* Washington, D.C.: International Monetary Fund, September.

———. 2006. *World Economic Outlook: Financial Systems and Economic Cycles.* Washington, D.C.: International Monetary Fund, September.

Kamps, Annette. 2006. "The Determinants of Currency Invoicing in International Trade." European Central Bank Working Paper no. 665, August.

Trade Deficits Aren't as Bad as You Think

19

GEORGE ALESSANDRIA

We live in a global world. Americans drive automobiles produced in Germany and drink Italian wine. Europeans watch movies of Jedi Knights battling the Dark Side on televisions produced in Mexico. This was not always the case.

For instance, the value of U.S. imports of goods and services has grown from 5.1 percent of gross domestic product (GDP) in 1969 to 15.2 percent of GDP in 2004. Likewise, the value of U.S. exports of goods and services has grown from 5.3 percent of GDP in 1969 to 10.0 percent of GDP in 2004.

The amount of U.S imports and exports has also varied quite a lot over time. At times, the U.S. has run trade surpluses, with exports exceeding imports, and at other times, it has run trade deficits, with imports exceeding exports. Recently, though, the U.S. has imported a lot more goods and services from abroad than it has exported to the rest of the world. In 2004, this resulted in the U.S. running a trade deficit of 5.2 percent of GDP. Through the third quarter of 2005, the trade deficit has averaged 5.7 percent of GDP.

Some people react to the trade deficit with doom and gloom. They argue that the trade deficit is evidence that American firms are unproductive and can't compete with foreign firms. Others point to it as clear evidence that foreign governments are not playing fair in U.S. markets. Still others argue that it demonstrates that we are living beyond our means.

But there is an alternative view. In this view, these unbalanced trade flows have two benefits: They shift worldwide production to its most productive location, and they allow individuals to smooth out their consumption over the business cycle. According to this view, the trade balance declines, or moves into deficit, when a country's firms or government is investing in physical capital to take advantage of productive opportunities. These investments expand the infrastructure, build capacity to access natural resources, and take advantage of new technologies. This increase in investment is financed in part by borrowing in international financial markets. By borrowing internationally, a country can invest more without cutting current consumption. When it repays this borrowing in the future, the trade balance increases or goes into surplus. In this respect, a trade deficit may be a sign of a growing and robust economy. Moreover, by increasing a country's productive capacity, these unbalanced trade flows are vital to sustaining the economy's expansion into the future. This view is consistent with some properties of the trade balance in the U.S. and other countries.

Measuring International Transactions

Before discussing the reasons that a country runs a trade deficit or surplus, it's useful to review the different measures of a country's international transactions. These

U.S. Balance of Payments, 2004*
(Billions of Dollars)
Table 1

Current Account		Capital and Financial Account	
Net Exports	−617.5	Capital Account	−1.6
Net Income Receipts	30.4	Financial Account	584.6
Net Unilateral Transfers	−80.9	Statistical Discrepancy	85.1
Current Account Balance	−668	Capital and Financial Account Balance	668

*Data are from the Bureau of Economic Analysis' Balance of Payments Accounts. Details may not add to totals because of rounding. For more details, see the July issue of the Bureau of Economic Analysis' Survey of Current Business.

are recorded in the balance of payment accounts (Table 1). The two main components of the balance of payments are the current account and the capital and financial account. The current account records the value of currently produced goods and services, both imported and exported, as well as the international payment of interest, dividends, wages, and transfers. The capital and financial account records transactions in real and financial assets.[1]

The easiest way to understand the components of the balance of payments is to think of a monthly credit card statement. One part of the statement reports the difference between new charges and payments. This difference corresponds to the current account. The second part of the statement shows the change in the balance on the account. This measures the amount of new borrowing from the credit card company and corresponds to the capital and financial account.

By definition, any unpaid portion of the bill adds one-for-one to the balance. Similarly, a current account deficit generates a capital and financial account surplus of equal magnitude. When a country is spending more than it earns, it is also selling assets to foreigners.

The left half of Table 1 summarizes the different components of the U.S.'s $668 billion current account deficit in 2004. From this we see that the trade balance, which is the difference between the value

of exports and the value of imports, was the largest determinant of the current account deficit. But there are two additional, smaller components: net unilateral transfers and net income from abroad. Net unilateral transfers measure the value of gifts, foreign aid, and non-military grants. Net foreign income measures the difference of income payments to American capital and workers employed overseas and income payments to foreign capital and workers employed here.[2] For the U.S., net foreign income mostly depends on the difference in capital income—that is, the difference between interest and profit payments to Americans on overseas investments and interest and profit payments to foreigners from investments in the U.S.

To finance its current account deficit, the U.S. ran a capital and financial account surplus of $668 billion. Foreign purchases of U.S. assets exceeded U.S. purchases of foreign assets by $668 billion. These foreign purchases of American assets funneled foreign savings toward the U.S. Thus, a current account deficit represents periods when foreign savings are flowing into a country.

This brings us to another way of measuring the current account: as the difference between a country's savings and investment. Savings is the difference between what a country produces, measured as GDP, and what is consumed privately and by the government.[3] When investment exceeds savings, a country finances this gap by borrowing from abroad.

Since 1929, the current account and the trade balance have been nearly identical. The average difference is 0.02 percent of GDP. There have been some large differences of up to 1 percent of GDP, but these have generally been short-lived. This may not continue to be the case. If the U.S. continues to run large current account deficits and to borrow from the rest of the world, the stock of foreign assets in the U.S. will grow relative to the stock of U.S. assets overseas. The payments on this debt can lead to deficits in the future, just as a high credit card balance today means more interest payments in the future.

For now, though, we will consider the current account and the trade balance interchangeably, partly because, as we have seen, historically they have not differed by much.

Introducing Intertemporal Trade

Just as an increase in the balance on a credit card bill involves new borrowing from the credit card company, when foreigners buy U.S. assets, Americans are borrowing from the rest of the world. This international borrowing and lending is based on the concept of intertemporal trade. The notion of intertemporal trade is based on the idea that people's purchases and income may not always match up over time. When this occurs, people use financial markets to borrow and save to make up the difference between what they buy and what they earn.

Countries are just a collection of individuals:[4] When these individuals collectively spend more than they earn, they finance the difference by either selling assets or borrowing. However, I might go to my neighbor (indirectly through a bank or credit card) to borrow the amount by which my purchases exceed my income. When a country's purchases exceed its income, it pays for the difference by borrowing from its trading partners. Thus, a country can have a trade deficit either because it is borrowing or because it has made some loans in the past for which it is currently being repaid.

A useful way to think about intertemporal trade is to consider the life cycle of a typical doctor. When she is young, she does not have many skills. Rather than work at a low-wage job, she goes to college and then on to medical school, followed by an internship and residency. Before starting to work, she has little to no income, so she must borrow to pay for school and her living expenses. While in school, she is investing in accumulating skills. These skills raise the wage she can command once she is working. In this case, she borrows when she is young and invests in education. Once out of school, she can repay these loans and start accumulating savings for retirement. Through financial markets she lends her savings to finance other people's investments. Once she has retired, her income is low again, and she lives off the income from her savings.

This borrowing and lending over her lifetime reflects intertemporal trade. She has traded part of her income stream when she is working for some payments when she is young and some payments when she is old. This intertemporal trade can involve long periods of borrowing and long periods of saving.[5] This borrowing and lending is efficient, since it allows a person to enter a profession, such as medicine, that makes the best use of her abilities.

International financial markets allow countries to borrow and lend over time through the purchase and sale of financial assets. Just as the doctor benefits from intertemporal trade, international financial markets generate similar benefits. Let's consider two important reasons why countries borrow and lend over time.

International Production Shifting.

The basis of the idea of international production shifting is the notion that you want to make hay while the sun shines. That is, when good productive opportunities present themselves, people can take advantage of them by investing and working more.

Norwegian Investment and Trade Balance
Figure 1

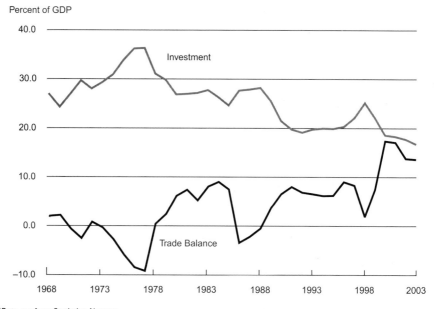

*Data are from Statistics Norway.

Over time, the productive opportunities in a country change. New opportunities present themselves and old ones close. Some industries make technological advances, while others become obsolete. Some of these opportunities are small, and others are large. To take advantage of these opportunities, firms need to hire workers and invest in new equipment, structures, and software.

Norway provides a clear example of one of these productive opportunities. In the 1960s, rich petroleum deposits were discovered in the North Sea. Norway was one of the major beneficiaries of this discovery. Getting to these valuable oil and gas deposits required large and repeated investments in infrastructure, such as offshore oil platforms, transport pipelines, ships, and helicopters. Norway also needed to develop a knowledge of exploration and extraction to precisely locate and exploit these resources. At the time of these discoveries, Norway lacked the equipment and expertise to take advantage of the opportunity. To do so, it borrowed from the rest of the world.

Because of the time involved in building infrastructure, oil production did not start in earnest until the mid 1970s. Although the oil revenue would eventually pay for them, the investments had to be paid for in advance. Norway financed these investments by borrowing from abroad (Figure 1). From the figure, we can see Norwegian investment grew substantially from 1969 to 1977, financed in part by a series of almost continual trade deficits from 1969 to 1977.

Once the oil came online, Norway began running persistent trade surpluses, which were used to repay its original borrowing and to save for the day when the petroleum reserves are exhausted. We can see that, since 1978, Norway has annually run trade surpluses that average 6 percent of GDP. There have been some fluctuations in the size of these trade surpluses because of changes in the price of oil and the Norwegian business cycle. (See *The Terms of Trade* and A *Theory of International Business Cycles,* for a further discussion of these two forms of trade-balance fluctuations.)

The Norway story is an example of a large productive opportunity, but there are also smaller changes in productivity that may be important over the business cycle. For instance, in the 1990s, the information technology and telecommunication sectors in the U.S. developed many new technologies.

These productive opportunities affect both the private and public sectors. For instance, in Norway, the state had sovereignty over the exploration and production of sub-sea natural resources, and much of the development was done within state-owned enterprises. To take advantage of productive opportunities, firms and governments need to invest in machines and infrastructure. This can be done by borrowing capital from the rest of the world. Foreign investors are happy to make these loans, even if it means less investment in the investors' own countries, because the capital is more productive overseas and thus earns a higher return.[6] This increase in investment increases the productive capacity of an economy in subsequent periods and keeps the economy going strong into the future.

Smoothing Consumption.

Another important idea for understanding the dynamics of the current account is consumption smoothing: the notion that people would prefer a relatively stable consumption pattern to a variable one.

A simple example should make this clear. Suppose you could choose between consuming $50,000 this year and $100,000 the following year or consuming $75,000 each year for the next two years. Most people would prefer the second plan, that is, a smooth pattern of consumption.

Now, suppose your income varies, as in the first plan. These types of income variations tend to occur because some workers receive bonuses and others may temporarily lose their jobs. If households can't save or borrow, their consumption will follow their income and will vary over time. Suppose one can borrow at a zero interest rate. Then by borrowing $25,000 in the first year and repaying it in the second year, a household can even out this variation in income to achieve a smooth pattern of consumption.

Now imagine we restrict households to borrowing and lending from households in the same country. To smooth out consumption, we need to find someone from the same country willing to lend $25,000 in the first year and be repaid in the second year. Financial markets do this for us. They channel savings from those households with temporarily high incomes to those households with temporarily low incomes. This lets us smooth out the household-specific fluctuations in individual income.

The Terms of Trade

There is another important determinant of the trade balance: the terms of trade. This is the price of imports relative to the price of exports.

Over time, the terms of trade may vary because the cost of producing imports or exports changes or the demand for these goods changes. Quite often, we see that when the terms of trade worsen, so that imports become more expensive, the trade balance declines. This often occurs because, despite the relatively high price of imports, we do not cut back much on our purchase of these imports. If we hold quantities roughly constant, and the terms of trade increase, the trade balance will decrease. This has been an important source of fluctuations in the trade balance over time.

Oil is one good that the U.S. imports a lot of, and the demand for oil is fairly slow to respond to price changes. This slow response occurs in part because oil is an important input into production in industries such as transportation and energy and there are few substitutes for oil. These industries have made large investments in airplanes, trucks, and power plants whose energy efficiency is largely fixed.

Therefore, just as it is costly for the owner of a gas-guzzling SUV to sell that car and buy a smaller, more energy-efficient car, it is difficult for an industry to change its use of oil in the short run. Thus, an increase in the price of oil tends to raise the value of imports almost one-for-one and lowers the trade balance by the same amount in the short run. In the long run, after firms and individuals invest in new, energy-efficient technologies, the demand for oil declines, so imports decline and the trade balance increases.

The figure bears this out. It shows the trade balance in petroleum and the price of petroleum imports deflated by the price of exports. Notice that these variables tend to move in opposite directions. In particular, notice that the large increases in oil prices in 1973 and 1979 were associated with large decreases in the trade balance. More recently, the rising price of oil has contributed to the worsening trade balance.*

If we return to the case of Norway, which is a large exporter of oil, we see that changes in the price of oil affect its trade balance in the exact opposite way. From Figure 1 in the text, we can see that Norway's trade balance has increased substantially along with the increase in oil prices since 1998. Similarly, the big drop in Norway's trade balance in 1985 coincided with a drop in the price of oil.

More generally, the terms of trade can matter for other goods, such as certain industrial supplies, agricultural products, and capital equipment, for which demand is relatively insensitive to changes in price in the short run.

* David Backus and Mario Crucini have shown that the market for oil can help to explain some of the behavior of the U.S. trade balance in the 1970s and 1980s.

U.S. Oil Trade Balance and Oil Terms of Trade

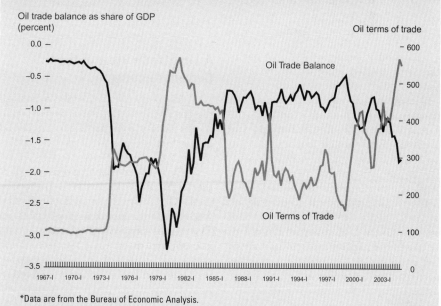

*Data are from the Bureau of Economic Analysis.

A Theory of International Business Cycles

Economists David Backus, Patrick Kehoe, and Nobel Prize recipient Finn Kydland have shown that an international real-business-cycle model can account for the properties of business cycles in the G7 countries.* This is a model that includes both consumption smoothing and production shifting.

In their view, the efficiency with which countries use capital and labor varies over time. These changes in productivity are generally not synchronized across countries, so that productivity may differ internationally. When there are productivity differences across countries, it makes sense to reduce investment in those countries where productivity is relatively low while increasing investment in the country where productivity is relatively high.

Initially, this requires the trade balance of the high productivity country to decline. This effectively shifts production to the more productive location. The larger the differences in international productivity, the greater the incentives to shift production toward the more productive countries and the larger the trade deficit.

Because investment raises a country's stock of capital, these capital flows tend to raise future output and lead to sustained increases in output. Foreign investors are happy to make these loans because they can get a better return by lending to firms in the country with more productive opportunities. Notice that by borrowing from abroad, the more productive country does not have to sacrifice consumption to invest in these opportunities, allowing it to keep its consumption smoother.

Economist Martin Boileau has shown that the effect of production shifting is particularly important, since a large part of trade consists of capital and durable goods, such as industrial machines, aircraft, and automobiles. Thus, periods when investment is high are also periods in which imports will tend to be high. Moreover, if investment is low in the rest of the world, a country will tend to run a trade deficit.

* For a primer on the real-business-cycle view of the macroeconomy, see the article by Satyajit Chatterjee.

But what happens when everyone in the same country experiences the same shock to their income, as in a recession? For instance, suppose average income in a country is $50,000 in year 1 and $100,000 in year 2. If we restrict borrowing and lending with foreign countries, consumption will vary along with income. If we allow international borrowing and lending, consumption smoothing will lead to a $25,000 current account deficit in year 1 and a $25,000 current account surplus in year 2. So countries can use international financial markets to smooth out countrywide fluctuations in income, such as those that occur over the business cycle.[7]

With these ideas in mind, let's take a look at the U.S. current account over time.

A Long-Term View of the U.S. Current Account

It's not possible to describe in detail all the ups and downs of the current account, so let's focus on some particular periods and events that are important in U.S. history (Figure 2).[8]

First, let's consider the second-half of the 19th century. In this period, the U.S. was still a relatively small economy that was poised for major economic expansion. The country experienced substantial immigration, and there was a great migration westward. The American railroad network was built, and municipalities invested in infrastructure such as ports, roads, and municipal sewage.[9] During this period, the U.S. ran current account deficits each year

U.S. Current Account
Figure 2

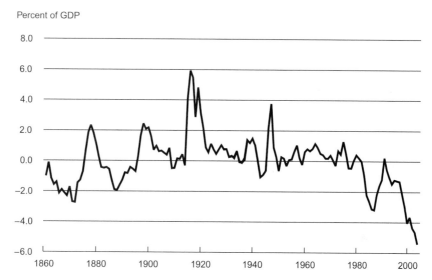

Percent of GDP

*The U.S. current account is constructed from multiple sources. The period from 1929 is based on data from the Bureau of Economic Analysis. The data from 1869 to 1929 are from the study by Maurice Obstfeld and Matthew Jones. The current account data from 1860 to 1869 are also from Obstfeld and Jones. The U.S. data from 1860 to 1869 are only an approximation.

from 1862 to 1876 and 1882 to 1896. Over these two periods, the average annual current account deficit was 1.5 percent of GDP. Investors in London invested heavily in these enterprises, since the returns to these projects exceeded those to be found in England.[10] These trade deficits helped finance the American economic expansion and were followed by a long period of current account surpluses.

Second, let's consider the periods around the two world wars, during which the U.S. ran large and persistent current account surpluses. From 1915 to 1921, the U.S. annually ran current account surpluses, on average, of 4.1 percent of GDP. These loans financed both the war effort of its allies as well as their subsequent postwar reconstruction.

The dynamics of the U.S. current account around World War II are similar to those in the period around World War I. In the buildup to the second world war and before the U.S. entered the war, from 1938 to 1941, the U.S. ran annual current

account surpluses of 1.3 percent of GDP. Much of this lending financed the United Kingdom's war effort. From the U.S. perspective, this was a very good investment. Once the U.S. entered the war, it financed its war effort in part by borrowing from its trading partners. Thus, from 1942 to 1945, the U.S. ran small current account deficits.

Following World War II, the U.S. ran some very large trade surpluses from 1946 to 1949. A large amount of both lending and foreign aid was directed toward Europe and Japan to help them rebuild. Given the lack of productive capital in place in these countries and their relatively highly skilled work forces, the goods from the U.S. were effectively used to build up the productive capacity of these countries. These surpluses were very important for rebuilding the European nations and Japan following WWII.

Finally, a careful eye may notice that the behavior of the current account since 1980 appears to have a lot in common with the period from 1860 to 1914. In both

Business Cycle Statistics*
Table 2

	Standard deviation relative to GDP		Correlation with GDP		
	Consumption	*Investment*	*Consumption*	*Investment*	*Trade Balance*
Canada	0.80	2.84	0.88	0.70	−0.15
France	0.92	3.14	0.74	0.89	−0.43
Germany	0.88	2.32	0.66	0.78	−0.16
Italy	1.32	3.28	0.66	0.76	−0.37
Japan	0.67	2.54	0.64	0.91	−0.48
United Kingdom	1.17	3.34	0.86	0.74	−0.52
United States	0.75	2.75	0.85	0.94	−0.52
Mean—G7	0.93	2.89	0.75	0.82	−0.38

*Consumption, investment, GDP, and trade data are from the OECD's Quarterly National Accounts data set, from 1980:Q1 to 2002:Q2. The Hodrick-Prescott filter was used to remove the long-term trends in each data series.

periods, there are large, sustained swings in the current account. In contrast, in the interwar and postwar periods, fluctuations tended to be small and tended toward balanced trade. These differences across eras are a sign of the uneven progress toward the current world of unrestricted capital flows across borders.

International financial flows were much greater in the period before World War I because there were very few restrictions on them. Following WWI, a number of restrictions were placed on the mobility of international capital, and they were further increased during the Great Depression (1929 to 1939). The postwar financial system maintained these restrictions, which were only gradually loosened in the 1970s. Thus, while today's current account deficits are quite large, the comparison with the postwar period, when capital flows were partially restricted, exaggerates their magnitude.

Common Features of Recent Trade Dynamics Across Countries

Over long periods of American history, we've seen that production shifting and consumption smoothing have mattered for the trade balance. Now, we want to see

if the same is true over the business cycle and for other countries. We can do this by studying how the trade balance and other key measures of economic activity vary over time for a group of industrialized countries.

First, we can look at some properties of the trade balance, output, consumption, and investment for the G7 countries[11] in the period 1980 to 2002 (Table 2).[12] From the table we see that certain features of the business cycle are quite similar across countries.[13] From the first two columns, we see that fluctuations in consumption are generally smaller than fluctuations in output, while fluctuations in investment are much larger than fluctuations in output. The second common feature is that both consumption and investment are highly correlated with output. What this means is that when output is growing fast, as in an economic expansion, both investment and consumption are also growing. Since investment is more volatile than output, investment grows much faster than output. From our earlier accounting, this implies that the trade balance should be declining. In fact, from the fifth column we see that trade balances are negatively correlated with output, so that during economic expansions a country's trade balance tends to decline.

If we put these facts together, a common picture of business cycles emerges. When countries are expanding, they tend to be investing quite a bit. Some of the extra production not consumed is invested, but a lot of the resources for investment come from outside the country, so the country runs a trade deficit. Borrowing abroad to increase investment contributes to future increases in GDP without requiring cuts in current consumption.

A Contrarian View of the Trade Deficit

The view developed here is that the trade balance reflects the optimal response of individuals, firms, investors, and governments to changes in productive opportunities and needs throughout the world. However, an alternative view argues that trade deficits may result from individuals borrowing to spend beyond their means. For instance, individuals may not fully take into account the size of their future expenditures, such as those from government-sponsored old-age and medical benefit programs, and not save enough today. Proponents of this "overspending" view argue that closing the current U.S. trade deficit will require some policy actions to increase savings in the U.S. Absent these policy changes, researchers expect that closing the trade deficit may involve some dramatic events. For instance, economists Maurice Obstfeld and Kenneth Rogoff argue that restoring trade balance will require a large depreciation of the U.S. dollar. Similarly, economists Nouriel Roubini and Brad Setser have argued that financing the international debt incurred following these persistent trade deficits will require an increase in interest rates that will discourage investment and economic growth.

The properties of the trade balance, evident over the last almost century and a half in the U.S. as well as over the business cycle among industrialized countries, provide ample evidence of substantial production shifting and consumption smoothing and cast doubt on this overspending view.

Summary

The current U.S. trade deficit appears unusually large when compared with that in the postwar period. But in the postwar period, the mobility of capital was fairly limited. In comparison to an earlier era of fairly free mobility of international capital, the current U.S. trade deficits don't look so unusual.

Trade deficits tend to be a sign of good things to come. Countries tend to run trade deficits when they are borrowing to finance productive investment opportunities. This is a way to shift world production toward more productive locations. This international borrowing and lending has played a prominent role in some of the most significant events in U.S. history—from the western expansion after the Civil War to the financing of the two world wars. Over the business cycle, we also see that trade deficits are often associated with strong and continued economic growth and are a sign of good things to come.

Endnotes

[1] In the balance of payments accounts, the purchase and sale of assets by central banks, such as the Federal Reserve in the U.S., are often measured separately in the official settlements balance. To simplify the presentation, we have included these transactions in the capital and financial account. In 2004, net purchases by foreign central banks equaled $392 billion, or 59 percent, of the capital and financial account. For more information on the official settlements balance, see the Survey of Current Business, Bureau of Economic Analysis, July 2005.

[2] A growing and serious concern about measuring the current account is how we treat capital gains and losses on cross-border asset holdings. Economists Pierre-Olivier Gourinchas and Helene Rey construct a measure of the current account with this adjustment and show that current account fluctuations are substantially smaller. In fact, recently, those periods in which the U.S. has run large trade deficits also tended to be those periods in which American asset holdings overseas made large capital gains relative to foreign assets in the U.S.

[3] For those familiar with national income and product accounts, this is the familiar relationship: Trade Balance = Savings-Investment, where Savings = GDP-Private Consumption-Government Consumption.

[4] Countries are composed of individuals, firms, and governments. However, individuals own firms and governments are made up of people. So, for simplicity, we view countries as a collection of individuals.

[5] Strictly speaking, when our doctor borrows to finance her education and expenditures, she is selling a financial asset with a claim against her future income. Lenders carry these assets as a credit on their balance sheets.

[6] Some international lending is done by foreign governments. In the case of the U.S., recently these foreign investments have tended to be in relatively low-interest bearing, highly liquid assets. Arguably, the liquidity these investments provide is highly valued by foreign governments and compensates for the relatively low returns.

[7] Similarly, fluctuations in government expenditures can be smoothed out by borrowing internationally. When government expenditures exceed tax revenue, the resulting government fiscal deficit is financed by borrowing. Whether this borrowing results in a current account deficit depends on the private savings response of a country's citizens. It is often claimed that fiscal deficits go hand-in-hand with trade deficits. For the U.S., there are certainly periods with these twin deficits, but there are also periods of government surpluses and trade deficits. See the article by Michele Cavallo for a summary of the links between fiscal and current account deficits.

[8] The U.S. GDP data from 1860 to 1869 are only an approximation, assuming a 2 percent annual growth rate.

[9] From the conclusion of the American Civil War, the American railroad system expanded from 35,021 miles in 1865 to 74,096 miles in 1875 and 128,320 miles in 1885. (*Statistical Abstract of the United States*: Bicentennial edition, 1975)

[10] See the book by Kevin O'Rourke and Jeffrey Williamson, p. 211.

[11] The Group of 7 is a coalition of the major industrial nations: Canada, France, Germany, Italy, Japan, the United Kingdom, and the United States.

[12] Nobel laureate Robert Lucas has argued that business cycles can be thought of as deviations from a trend around which variables tend to move together. Thus, we want to focus on the medium-term fluctuations in economic activity. These are the fluctuations that last from a year and a half to eight years. We don't think of very short-run changes in the economic environment, such as those due to really bad weather, as being part of the business cycle. We also don't think of the really long-term changes in the economy, such as those arising from increased female participation in the labor force, as being part of the business cycle. These are more related to the trend component of the economy. All of the statistics reported in Table 2 are based on these medium-term fluctuations.

[13] Economists David Backus and Patrick Kehoe find similar properties of the data for a broader group of countries over different periods.

References

Backus, David, and Mario Crucini. "Oil Prices and the Terms of Trade," *Journal of International Economics* 50 (2000), pp. 185–213.

Backus, David, and Patrick Kehoe. "International Evidence on the Historical Properties of Business Cycles," *American Economic Review*, 82, 4 (1992), pp. 864–88.

Backus, David, Patrick Kehoe, and Finn Kydland. "International Business Cycles: Theory and Evidence," in T. Cooley (ed.), *Frontiers of Business Cycle Research*. Princeton: Princeton University Press (1995).

Boileau, Martin. "Trade in Capital Goods and the Volatility of Net Exports and the Terms of Trade," *Journal of International Economics* (1999), pp. 347–65.

Cavallo, Michele. "Understanding the Twin Deficits: New Approaches, New Results," Federal Reserve Bank of San Francisco *Economic Letter*, Number 2005–16 (July 22, 2005).

Chatterjee, Satyajit. "Real Business Cycles: A Legacy of Countercyclical Policies?" Federal Reserve Bank of Philadelphia *Business Review* (January/ February 1999).

Gourinchas, Pierre-Olivier, and Helene Rey. "International Financial Adjustment," National Bureau of Economic Research Working Paper 11155 (2005).

Hodrick, Robert J., and Edward C. Prescott. "Postwar U.S. Business Cycles: An Empirical Investigation," *Journal of Money, Credit, and Banking* 29:1 (1997), pp. 1–16.

Leduc, Sylvain. "Globalization Is Weaker Than You Think," Federal Reserve Bank of Philadelphia *Business Review* (Second Quarter 2005).

Obstfeld, Maurice, and Matthew T. Jones. "Saving, Investment, and Gold: A Reassessment of Historical Current Account Data" in G. Calvo, R. Dornbusch, and M. Obstfeld (eds.), *Money, Capital Mobility, and Trade: Essays in Honor of Robert Mundell*. Cambridge, MA: MIT Press (2001).

Obstfeld, Maurice, and Kenneth S. Rogoff. "Global Current Account Imbalances and Exchange Rate Adjustments," Brookings Papers on Economic Activity, 1 (2005), pp. 67–146.

O'Rourke, Kevin H., and Jeffrey G. Williamson. *Globalization and History: The Evolution of a Nineteenth-Century Atlantic Economy.* Cambridge, MA: MIT Press (1999).

Roubini, Nouriel, and Brad Setser. "The U.S. as a Net Debtor: The Sustainability of the U.S. External Balance," mimeo, Stern School of Business, NYU (September 2004).

Sill, Keith. "The Gains from International Risk-Sharing," Federal Reserve Bank of Philadelphia *Business Review* (Third Quarter 2001).

Discussion Questions

VI

1. What is the twin deficits hypothesis? What evidence do Bartolini and Lahiri present to support and refute it?

2. Using the basic accounting identities for current and capital accounts, one can also think of a current account deficit as a lack of domestic savings. Show this algebraically. Further assume that U.S. savings (or dis-savings) can be decomposed into government savings (surplus vs. deficit), household savings and business savings. If the U.S. government deficit falls, but the current account deficit does not fall in accordance, what must be happening to private (household and business) savings?

3. What reason do Goldberg and Dillon give for their argument that a fall in the dollar will not necessarily reduce the trade deficit? Which one of their arguments do you find most compelling? Do you believe that their empirical evidence makes sense?

4. If reducing the budget deficit and reducing the dollar's value do not reduce the current account deficit, what other factors, besides increased exports, could bring about a trade balance? (Hint: What other factor besides the price of imported goods would reduce U.S. demand?)

5. What arguments does Alessandria present to argue that the current account deficit is not so bad? Do you agree? Be specific.

6. One consequence of the U.S. current account deficit is that the U.S. has become a net borrower against the rest of the world while many poor countries, such as China, have become net lenders. Do you think this fact is consistent with Alessandria's argument?

Exchange Rate Regimes and Macroeconomic Stabilization Policies

VII

This section examines exchanges rate regimes. "Does the Exchange Rate Regime Matter for Inflation and Growth" by Ghosh, Ostry, Gulde and Wolf empirically examine the macroeconomic performance of developing and developed economies. They find that there is a statistically significant relationship between low inflation rates and economies with fixed exchange rates resulting from monetary discipline. They also find that productivity growth rates are higher for countries with flexible exchange rates.

Sharmila King's article on "China's Controversial Exchange Rate Policy" provides an overview of the exchange rate controversy between the U.S. and China. China had unofficially fixed its exchange rate to the U.S. dollar; China set an exchange rate which the U.S. deemed undervalued, giving China a competitive advantage in international trade. In response to U.S. complaints, China recently adopted a more "flexible" regime by fixing its currency to a basket of currencies of its major trading partners.

"Float or Not to Float? Exchange Rate Regimes and Shocks" by Michele Cavallo examines whether flexible exchange rates insulate economies from adverse external shocks, as many economists claim. The relative merits of a flexible or fixed exchange rate regime depends on the composition of firm's balance sheets, specifically the degree to which liabilities are denominated in foreign currency. For example, if domestic interest rates fall relative to foreign rates, the domestic currency depreciates causing a decline in a firm's net worth if their liabilities are denominated foreign currency. However, the depreciation increases export revenue raising net worth. Net worth rises if the positive effect dominates the negative effect of the depreciation. Cavallo finds that flexible exchange rates are preferable to manage external shocks when liabilities are minimally exposed to foreign currency liabilities. However since many emerging markets do have foreign currency liabilities, the costs of adopting a flexible rate can be high since a depreciation can reduce a country's ability to access international financial markets as net worth falls.

Duttagupta, Fernandez, and Karacadag from the IMF investigate how, when, and how fast a country should shift from a fixed exchange rate to a flexible rate. The authors argue that countries transitioning from a fixed rate to a flexible rate need to develop and deepen their foreign exchange markets by increasing market information and transparency, reducing foreign exchange interventions, and phasing out regulations that discourage market activity such as taxes on foreign exchange transactions, capital controls, and submitting foreign exchange receipts to the central bank. Further, countries should adopt an alternative nominal anchor to control inflationary expectations and redesign monetary policy around the new anchor to maintain central bank credibility. Also, the government should manage the exposure to exchange rate risk by monitoring, regulating, and supervising sources of exchange rate risk.

The final article examines banking in dollarized Ecuador and El Salvador. Dollarization occurs when a country adopts another country's currency rather than adopting a fixed exchange rate. In 2000 and 2001 respectively, Ecuador and El Salvador adopted the U.S. dollar. Since dollarization, both countries have enjoyed low country risk, low inflation rates, and gains in policy credibility. Banking in both countries has been stable since dollarization. Since stabilization of their macroeconomies, bank asset quality and bank liquidity have improved. To date, dollarization has produced successful results for both countries.

20

Does the Exchange Rate Regime Matter for Inflation and Growth?

ATISH R. **GHOSH**,
JONATHAN D. **OSTRY**,
ANNE-MARIE **GULDE**,
& HOLGER C. **WOLF**

Although the theoretical relationships are ambiguous, evidence suggests a strong link between the choice of the exchange rate regime and macroeconomic performance. Adopting a pegged exchange rate can lead to lower inflation, but also to slower productivity growth.

Few questions in international economics have aroused more debate than the choice of exchange rate regime. Should a country fix the exchange rate or allow it to float? And if pegged, to a single "hard" currency or a basket of currencies? Economic literature pullulates with models, theories, and propositions. Yet little consensus has emerged about how exchange rate regimes affect common macroeconomic targets, such as inflation and growth. At a theoretical level, it is difficult to establish unambiguous relationships because of the many ways in which exchange rates can influence—and be influenced by—other macroeconomic variables. Likewise, empirical studies typically find no clear link between the exchange rate regime and macroeconomic performance.

This paper seeks to identify how various exchange rate regimes influence inflation and growth. It goes beyond previous studies in three important respects. First, it uses more comprehensive data—comprising all IMF members from 1960 to 1990. Second, it classifies exchange rate regimes in more detail than the traditional dichotomy between fixed and floating exchange rates. Third, it distinguishes between the central banks' declared exchange rate regimes and the behavior of the exchange rates in practice.

There is indeed a strong link between fixed exchange rates and low inflation. This results from a discipline effect (the political costs of abandoning the peg induce tighter policies) and a confidence effect (greater confidence leads to a greater willingness to hold domestic currency rather than goods or foreign currencies). In part, low inflation is associated with fixed exchange rates because countries with low inflation are better able to maintain an exchange rate peg. But there is also evidence of causality in the other direction: countries that choose fixed exchange rates achieve lower inflation.

There is also a link, albeit weaker, between the exchange rate regime and the growth of output. To the extent that fixing the exchange rate engenders greater policy confidence, it can foster higher investment. Conversely, a fixed rate, if set at the "wrong" level, can result in a misallocation of resources. In our data, countries that maintained pegged exchange rates did indeed have higher investment. But productivity grew more slowly than in countries with floating exchange rates. Overall, per capita growth was slightly lower in countries with pegged exchange rates.

This paper begins with a brief discussion of difficulties encountered in classifying exchange rate regimes. It then shows how alternative regimes affect inflation and growth. A few observations conclude the essay.

Classifying Regimes

Beyond the traditional fixed-floating dichotomy lies a spectrum of exchange rate regimes. The de facto behavior of an exchange rate, moreover, may diverge from its de jure classification.

While it is customary to speak of fixed and floating exchange rates, regimes actually span a continuum, ranging from pegs to target zones, to floats with heavy, light, or no intervention. The traditional dichotomy can mask important differences among regimes. Accordingly, this analysis uses a three-way classification: pegged, intermediate (i.e., floating rates, but within a predetermined range), and floating.

Regimes can be classified according to either the publicly stated commitment of the central bank (a de jure classification) or the observed behavior of the exchange rate (a de facto classification). Neither method is entirely satisfactory. A country that claims to have a pegged exchange rate might in fact instigate frequent changes in parity. On the other hand, a country might experience very small exchange rate movements, even though the central bank has no obligation to maintain a parity. The approach taken here is to report results according to the stated intention of the central bank, but to supplement these results by categorizing the non-floating regimes according to whether or not changes in parity were frequent. The de jure classification uses the IMF's Annual Report on Exchange Arrangements and Exchange Restrictions, while the de facto classification is based on a survey of IMF desk officers for each country. The data are taken from the World Economic Outlook database. In all, observations of GDP growth and consumer price inflation cover 145 countries and 30 years.

Inflation

Pegging the exchange rate can lower inflation by inducing greater policy discipline and instilling greater confidence in the currency. Empirically, both effects are important.

Policymakers have long maintained that a pegged exchange rate can be an anti-inflationary tool. Two reasons are typically cited. A pegged exchange rate provides a highly visible commitment and thus raises the political costs of loose monetary and fiscal policies. To the extent that the peg is credible, there is a stronger readiness to hold domestic currency, which reduces the inflationary consequences of a given expansion in the money supply.

Inflation Performance

Inflation over our sample averaged 10 percent a year, with pronounced differences in various exchange rate regimes (Chart 1). Countries with pegged exchange rates had an average annual inflation rate of 8 percent, compared with 14 percent for intermediate regimes, and 16 percent for floating regimes.

The differences among regimes are starker for the lower-income countries, where the differential between pegged and floating rates was almost 10 percentage points. As might be expected, countries without capital controls tended to have lower inflation in general. Even for these countries, however, inflation was lower under pegged regimes compared with either intermediate or floating exchange rates.

Although inflation performance is generally better under pegged exchange rates, the last panel in Chart 1 illustrates an important caveat: mere declaration of a pegged exchange rate is insufficient to reap the full anti-inflationary benefits. Countries that changed their parity frequently—though notionally maintaining a pegged exchange rate—on average experienced 13 percent inflation. While this is still better than the performance under non-pegged

Inflation Performance (in percent per year)
Chart 1

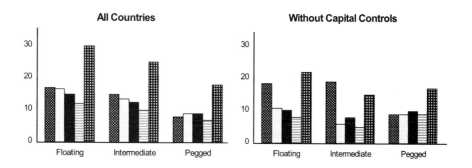

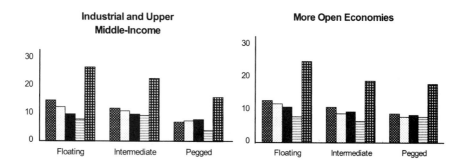

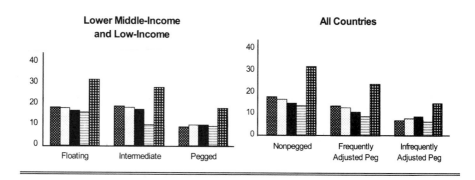

exchange rates (17 percent), it is significantly worse than countries that maintained a stable parity (7 percent).

Since there was a preponderance of pegged exchange rate regimes in the 1960s—when inflation rates were low—the association between low inflation and pegged rates might be more an artifact of the general macroeconomic climate than a property of the regime itself. One way to purge the data of such effects is to measure inflation rates for each regime relative to the average inflation rate (across all regimes) in that year. Doing so, however, leaves the story largely unchanged: as Chart 1 shows, under pegged rates, inflation was 3 percentage points lower than under intermediate and 6 percentage points less than under floating regimes. Again, countries with only occasional changes in parity fared significantly better than those with frequent changes.

Explaining the Differences

What accounts for these results? They derive, in fact, from two separate effects. The first is discipline. Countries with pegged exchange rates have lower rates of growth in money supply, presumably because of the political costs of abandoning a peg. The growth of broad money (currency and deposits) averaged 17 percent a year under pegged exchange rates compared with almost 30 percent under floating regimes. This difference holds regardless of the income level of the country.

In addition, for a given growth rate of the money supply, higher money demand (the desire to hold money rather than spend it) will imply lower inflation. Pegged exchange rates, by enhancing confidence, can engender a greater demand for the domestic currency. This will be reflected in a lower velocity of circulation and a faster decline of domestic interest rates. In the extreme case of perfect credibility, domestic interest rates—even in countries with a history of high inflation—should fall immediately to the world level. Over the sample period, nominal interest rates have tended to rise, but the rate of increase for countries with

floating rates was almost 6 percent, as against 2 percent for countries with pegged rates. It was actually highest for countries with intermediate regimes, where the growth rate of interest rates was almost 9 percent. A change in nominal interest rates is of importance because a fall in these rates will lead to a stronger demand for money. But the level of real interest rates (i.e., the nominal rates adjusted for inflation) also gives a direct measure of confidence. On average, the real interest rates were 0.2 percent a year under pegged regimes, 1.8 percent under intermediate regimes, and 2.3 percent under floating regimes.

For a variety of reasons—including interest rates that are set by the authorities rather than being determined by the market—the greater confidence that pegged exchanges can bring may not be fully reflected in the observed domestic interest rate. Nonetheless, it is possible to identify the "confidence effect" of various regimes by considering the residual inflation once the effects of money expansion, real growth, and domestic interest rates have been removed. A higher residual inflation implies lower confidence.

Do pegged rates lead to greater confidence? They do. Chart 1 shows the residual inflation rates. Countries with pegged exchange rates had inflation 2 percentage points lower than those with intermediate regimes, and 4 percentage points lower than those with floating regimes. This differential in favor of pegged rates is as large as 6 percentage points in the lower-income countries, but only 3 percentage points for countries without capital controls—perhaps because abjuring capital controls itself inspires confidence in the domestic currency.

Not only do countries with pegged exchange rates have lower inflation on average, they are also associated with lower inflation variability.

The Dog or the Tail?

Does pegging the exchange rate cause lower inflation? Or is it merely that countries with low inflation are better able to maintain a pegged exchange rate regime?

Quite obviously, a country with reckless monetary policy will not be able to keep its exchange rate fixed for long. Part of the argument for pegged rates is precisely that they result in greater monetary discipline. But that still leaves the question of whether other variables—such as the degree of central bank independence—determine both a country's disposition toward low inflation and its ability to adopt a pegged exchange rate.

Econometric studies of this simultaneity between the choice of the exchange rate regime and inflation (using the same data) suggest that countries with low inflation do indeed have a greater proclivity toward pegged exchange rates. But they also show that, even allowing for this, pegged exchange rates lead to lower inflation.

Simpler, if less compelling, evidence comes from a comparison of countries that switched to a pegged exchange rate (from a floating regime) or vice versa. Relative to the year preceding the regime change, inflation was 0.6 percentage points lower one year after a switch to a fixed exchange rate regime, 0.5 percentage points lower after two years, and 0.5 percentage points lower after three years. Conversely, inflation was higher by 3 percentage points one year after a switch to a floating regime, 1.8 percentage points higher after two years, and 2.3 percentage points higher after three years.

A second piece of evidence comes from a comparison of countries with similar volatility in nominal effective exchange rates but different exchange rate regimes. Countries with pegged exchanges rates, of course, tend to exhibit lower effective exchange rate variability. But if the exchange rate regime matters for inflation, there should still be a difference between countries with pegged and floating exchange rates even after controlling for nominal exchange rate variability. It turns out that this is indeed the case. Controlling for nominal exchange rate variability, there remain significant differences in inflation in the various regimes. In other words, pegging the nominal exchange rate—which may instill greater confidence—has an effect on inflation beyond simply lowering nominal exchange rate variability.

Finally, it is worth checking that the results are not driven by contamination across regimes. For instance, it is possible for inflationary pressure to build up—but be held in check—during a period of pegged exchange rates and then explode into open inflation when a float is adopted. In such a case, the high inflation would be blamed on the floating regime, though it should more properly be attributed to the fixed exchange rate period. This suggests dropping the first year or two following a regime change from the data. Conversely, if a regime is not sustained, then it is debatable whether the macroeconomic performance under that regime should be attributed to it. The last couple of years prior to a regime change ought also to be omitted. Neither modification alters the results. Dropping the first two years following a regime change lowers the differential in favor of pegged rates from 6.0 percentage points to 5.7 percentage points. Dropping the last two years of each regime lowers it to 5.8 percentage points.

Growth

The exchange rate regime can influence economic growth through investment or increased productivity. Pegged regimes have higher investment; floating regimes have faster productivity growth. On net, per capita GDP growth was slightly faster under floating regimes.

Economic theory has relatively little to say about the effects of the nominal exchange rate regime on the growth of output. Typically, arguments focus on the impact on investment and international trade. Advocates argue that pegged exchange rates foster investment by reducing policy uncertainties and lowering real interest rates. But equally, by eliminating an important adjustment mechanism, fixed exchange rates can increase protectionist pressure, distort price signals in the economy, and prevent the efficient allocation of resources across sectors.

Growth Performance

Annual GDP growth per capita averaged 1.6 percent over our sample. Although differences exist across exchange rate regimes, these are generally less marked than the differences in inflation rates (Chart 2). Different samples, moreover, lead to varied conclusions about growth under fixed and floating exchange rates. Growth was actually fastest under the intermediate regimes, averaging more than 2 percent a year. It was 1.4 percent a year under pegged exchange rates and 1.7 percent under floating rates. This pattern emerges mainly because of the lower middle-income and low-income countries; growth was somewhat higher under pegged rates for the industrial and upper middle-income countries.

Just as inflation was generally lower in the 1960s, growth rates tended to be higher. Controlling for this widens the differential in favor of floating exchange rates to 0.8 percent over all countries, and as much as 1.5 percent for the lower-income countries.

Explaining the Differences

By definition, economic growth can be explained by the use of more capital and labor (the factors of production) or by residual productivity growth. This productivity growth reflects both technological progress and—perhaps more important—changes in the economic efficiency with which capital and labor are used.

Investment rates were highest under pegged exchange rates—by as much as 2 percentage points of GDP—with the largest difference for the industrial and upper middle-income countries and almost none for the lower-income countries. With higher investment rates and lower output growth, productivity increases must have been smaller under fixed exchange rates.

Part of the higher productivity growth under floating rates is reflected in faster growth of external trade. Trade growth (measured as the sum of export growth and import growth) is almost 3 percentage

points higher under floating rates. The lower-income countries—where real exchange rate misalignments under fixed rates have been more common—show an even larger difference in trade growth between pegged and floating exchange rates.

While not overwhelming, the evidence suggests that fixing the nominal exchange rate can prevent relative prices (including, perhaps, real wages) from adjusting. This lowers economic efficiency. Part, though not all, of this lower productivity growth is offset by higher investment under pegged exchange rates. A comparison of countries that switched regimes shows that a move to floating exchange rates results in an increase of GDP growth of 0.3 percentage points one year after the switch and of more than 1 percentage point three years after the switch. One manifestation of the rigidities that pegged exchange rates can engender is the higher volatility of GDP growth and of employment. As the last rows of Chart 2 indicate, GDP growth was more volatile under pegged exchange rates, as was employment.

Conclusions

Does the exchange rate regime matter for macroeconomic performance? The experience of IMF member countries since the 1960s suggests that it does.

The strongest results concern inflation. Pegged exchange rates are associated with significantly better inflation performance (lower inflation and less variability), and there is at least some evidence of a causal relationship. There is, however, an important caveat. Countries that have frequent parity changes—while notionally maintaining a peg—are unlikely to reap the full anti-inflationary benefits of a fixed exchange rate regime.

The choice of exchange rate regime also has implications for economic growth. Pegged rates are associated with higher investment. But they are also correlated with slower productivity growth. On net, output growth is slightly lower under pegged exchange rates. The inability to use

Per Capita GDP Growth (in percent per year)
Chart 2

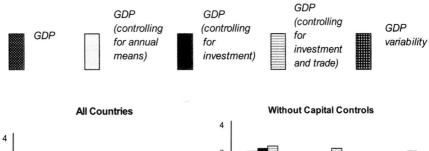

GDP | GDP (controlling for annual means) | GDP (controlling for investment) | GDP (controlling for investment and trade) | GDP variability

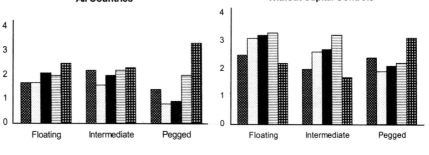

All Countries

Without Capital Controls

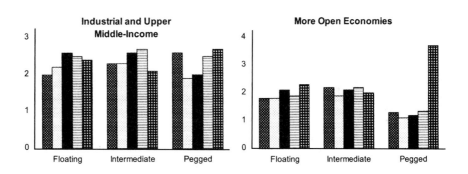

Industrial and Upper Middle-Income

More Open Economies

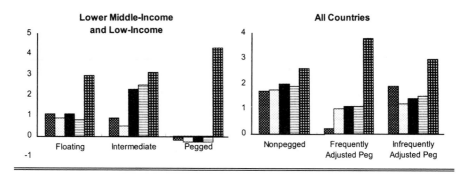

Lower Middle-Income and Low-Income

All Countries

the nominal exchange rate as an adjustment mechanism, moreover, results in greater variability of growth and employment.

Ultimately, the exchange rate regime is but one facet of a country's overall macroeconomic policy. No regime is likely to serve all countries at all times. Countries facing disinflation may find pegging the exchange rate an important tool. But where growth has been sluggish, and real exchange rate misalignments common, a more flexible regime might be called for. The choice, like the trade-off, is the country's own.

Anne-Marie Gulde is an Economist in the IMF's Monetary and Exchange Affairs Department.

Atish R. Ghosh is an Economist in the IMF's European II Department. He holds degrees from Harvard and Oxford Universities.

Jonathan D. Ostry is a Senior Economist in the IMF's Southeast Asia and Pacific Department and holds a doctorate from the University of Chicago.

Holger C. Wolf is a faculty member of the Stern Business School of New York University and holds a doctorate from Massachusetts Institute of Technology.

Bibliography

There is a vast literature on the link between the exchange rate regime and macroeconomic performance. The following provide useful surveys.

Argy, Victor, "The Choice of Exchange Rate Regime for a Smaller Economy: A Survey of Some Key Issues," in *Choosing an Exchange Rate Regime*, ed. by Victor Argy and Paul De Grauwe (Washington: International Monetary Fund, 1990).

Barth, Richard, and Chorng-Huey Wong (eds.), *Approaches to Exchange Rate Policy* (Washington: International Monetary Fund, 1994).

Baxter, Marianne, and Alan C. Stockman, *Business Cycles and the Exchange Rate System: Some Internal Evidence* (Cambridge, Massachusetts: National Bureau of Economic Research, 1988).

Crockett, Andrew, and Morris Goldstein, "Inflation Under Fixed and Flexible Exchange Rates," International Monetary Fund, *Staff Papers*, Vol. 23 (November 1976), pp. 509–44.

Frenkel, Jacob, Morris Goldstein, and Paul Masson, *Characteristics of a Successful Exchange Rate System*, Occasional Paper 82 (Washington: International Monetary Fund, 1991).

Friedman, Milton, "The Case For Flexible Exchange Rates," in *Essays in Positive Economics* (Chicago: University of Chicago Press, 1953).

Ghosh, Atish, Anne-Marie Gulde, Jonathan Ostry, and Holger Wolf, "Does the Nominal Exchange Rate Regime Matter?" IMF Working Paper 95/121 (December 1995).

Guitián, Manuel, "The Choice of an Exchange Rate Regime," in *Approaches to Exchange Rate Policy*, ed. by Richard Barth and Chorng-Huey Wong (Washington: International Monetary Fund, 1994).

Krugman, Paul, *Exchange Rate Instability* (Cambridge, Massachusetts: MIT Press, 1989).

Mussa, Michael, "Nominal Exchange Rate Regimes and the Behavior of Real Exchange Rates, Evidence and Implications," in *Real Business Cycles, Real Exchange Rates, and Actual Policies*, ed. by Karl Brunner and Alan Meltzer (Amsterdam: North-Holland, 1986).

Nurkse, Ragnar, *International Currency Experience* (Geneva: League of Nations, 1944).

Obstfeld, Maurice, "Floating Exchange Rates: Experience and Prospects," *Brookings Papers on Economic Activity*: 2 (1985), pp. 369–450.

Quirk, Peter, "Fixed or Floating Exchange Regimes: Does It Matter for Inflation?" IMF Working Paper 94/134 (December 1994).

Williamson, John, "A Survey of the Literature on the Optimal Peg," *Journal of Development Economics*, Vol. 2 (August 1982), pp. 39–61.

21

China's Controversial Exchange Rate Policy

Sharmila **King**

Introduction

China's exchange rate policy is often the epicenter of trade disputes with China and the US. The US Treasury and Congress have stated publicly and repeatedly that China has artificially held the value of its currency, the Renminbi (RMB)/Yuan, below market value and it is this exchange rate policy that drives China's trade surplus and propels China's rapid economic growth. The Treasury's position is if the Chinese allow the RMB to float, it would appreciate against the US dollar and the US trade deficit with China will shrink. The US has asked the Chinese authorities to revalue their currency against the dollar, while the Chinese have stated emphatically that their currency is not undervalued. This paper provides a brief overview of the controversy surrounding China's exchange rate policy.

China's Exchange Rate Policy: the Dispute between the US and China

Starting in 1997 China has unofficially pegged the value of its currency the RMB or Yuan to the US dollar at 8.28 Yuan to $1 (see figure 1). In 2003, the US pressured China to abandon its currency peg. The US contends that China's undervalued RMB keeps Chinese goods cheap relative to US goods giving Chinese manufacturers a competitive edge against US manufactured goods. Cheap Chinese goods raise the demand for those goods propelling China's trade surplus (US deficit). Figure 2 shows the US-China trade balance in goods. The data shows that the US trade deficit with China has grown steadily since 2001. The US has argued that China's refusal to revalue its currency constitutes currency manipulation and violates IMF rules. The People's Bank of China argue that the poor performance in US manufacturing is not a result of exchange rate manipulation but rather lower labor costs in China and low US savings. The US position is fuelled by poor macroeconomic performance and job losses in the US manufacturing sector. In February 2005, Senators Schumer and Graham sponsored a bi-partisan bill to impose a 27.5% tariff on Chinese exports to the US. The bill passed the senate but its implementation was delayed to allow the Bush Administration to negotiate greater currency flexibility.

Ironically, the political pressure for a revaluation from Washington is spurring speculation for an RMB appreciation. However, pressure for a RMB appreciation is growing not just from political forces but also other endogenous macroeconomic forces. China's economy has been growing at a rapid rate; over the past 5 years China has experienced double digit growth rates. In 2007 China's GDP growth rate was 11.4%.[1] Industrial output grew at a rate of 18.5%. The IMF forecasts that China's

The Value of the Chinese RMB in US Dollars, 1999–2008
Figure 1

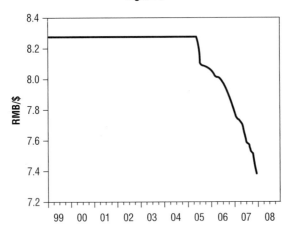

Source: FRED

China-US Trade Balance in Goods, 1998–2007
Figure 2

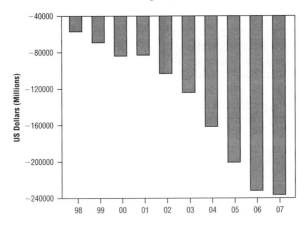

Source: US Census Bureau

growth will slow to 10% in 2008. China is now the fourth largest economy in the world. Fixed asset investment grew at a rate of 24.8%.[2] China is also a net creditor to the US. As of October 2007, Japan held $591.8 billion, Mainland China held $388.1 billion and UK held $296.5 billion making China the second largest holder of US Treasury securities.[3] All these fac-

tors place upward pressure on the RMB. If China does not allow its currency to appreciate, China's economy will overheat and inflation will ensue. Rising prices are already evident in the economy. China's inflation rate rose to 7.1% in 2007. Pork prices rose 59% and cooking oil rose 37% in 2007.[4] Increasing foreign reserves increase China's monetary base which increases prices. China has successfully sterilized capital inflows (see Revaluation by Stealth) but declining interest rates in the US, rising rates in China, and an expected RMB appreciation is a catalyst for more capital inflows further fuelling inflation in China.

Estimates of the degree of the exchange rate misalignment vary. Goldstein (2004) finds that the RMB is undervalued by 15–25%. According to *The Economist*'s Big Mac Index for 2007, China's currency is undervalued by 58%. By contrast Stephen Jen at Morgan Stanley estimates the RMB is undervalued by a meager 1%. According to Spiegel (2005), China's main trading partners in 2005 were the US (20%), the Euro Area (16%), Japan (18%), Korea (10%), Hong Kong (15%), 10% were other Asian countries (India, Philippines, Indonesia, Malaysia and Singapore), and 11% were other non-Asian countries (Brazil, Canada, the UK, Russia, Australia). To examine how China's exchange rate may have moved since 2001 if pegged to a trade weighted basket of currencies Spiegel examines the differences in China's exchange rate if it had followed a trade-weighted peg versus a dollar peg and he finds that the trade weighted peg would show an appreciation of approximately 9–11% partly because the Euro has appreciated against the dollar since 2001.

China's New Currency Regime

Bowing to international pressure, on July 21, 2005 China announced that it would allow the value of its RMB to appreciate against the dollar by cumulative 6% by the end 2007 (see Figure 1 and Frankel and Wei 2007). Further, in July 2005 China announced that the RMB would be pegged to a basket of other currencies (unannounced numerical weights) that would allow the RMB to move within a +/− 0.3% band. The Governor of the People's Bank of China suggested that the currency basket primarily would consist of currencies from countries whose bilateral trade with China exceeds $10 billion. The precise na-

ture of China's new currency peg is unclear. Frankel and Wei (2007) examine China's new exchange rate basket. In particular, the numerical weights placed on other currencies in valuing the RMB from July 21, 2005 to the beginning of 2007. Using Ordinary Least Squares to uncover the currency weights, they find only two currencies that are statistically significant in explaining movements in the RMB, the US dollar (90% weight) and the Malaysian Ringgit (5% weight). The Euro and the Yen received a zero weight in the basket. Frankel and Wei conclude that the Chinese authorities appear to be concerned with maintaining trade competitiveness among major Asian rivals rather than maintaining stability in the RMB on a global level. Further, they conclude that despite the Chinese claims of the abandonment of its dollar peg, the dollar still has a 90% weight in the new basket.

Frankel and Wei (2007) also examine the claims that changes in RMB movements are related to US trade complaints against China. They find evidence that cumulative complaints from Washington are associated with a *reduced dollar weight* in the currency basket *not* the relative appreciation of the RMB to the basket. At the time of the exchange rate regime change in July 2005 the dollar received a weight of 0.98 and based on a non-linear time trend, the weight could fall to 0.87 by 2010. In short, the US dollar still carries significant weight (approximately 90%) in the current RMB trade-weighted basket.

Is a RMB Revaluation in the Interest of the US and China?

It is in China's interest to allow the RMB to appreciate. An undervalued RMB increases the likelihood of an expected RMB revaluation which increases the return on China's financial assets causing capital inflow. Capital inflows encourage excessive credit expansion which must be controlled if inflation is to be kept in check. One lesson we learned from the Asian Financial Crisis of 1997 is that rapid credit expansion by an immature, inexperienced banking sector can destabilize economies. An undervalued RMB increases foreign reserves which increase the monetary base. If inflation is to be controlled, the increase in the monetary base must be sterilized. The cost of sterilization depends on the Chinese interest rate minus the US interest rate since the Chinese hold US dollar assets while selling Chinese bonds to sterilize the rise in the monetary base. Since Chinese rates have been rising while US rate falling, sterilization costs are rising. All these factors results in the rising cost of maintaining an undervalued RMB which means it is in China's interest to allow the RMB appreciate.

Since 2005 the RMB has risen against the dollar by 14%. In 2007 alone, the RMB rose against the dollar by 7% in part because the People's Bank of China increased interest rates 6 times to stem inflationary pressures.[5] As Figure 2 illustrates, during the same time period, the bilateral trade deficit with China grew to an amount in excess of $250 billion by the beginning of 2008. The US dollar would have to depreciate substantially to correct the US trade deficit. Following the RMB appreciation, the bilateral US trade deficit with China failed to improve. McKinnon (2003) argues that China's trade surpluses—and the US trade deficit—is a result of surplus savings in China and low net saving in the US. He argues that changing the exchange rate will not significantly alter the saving propensities and hence the trade imbalances. One step to correct the external imbalance is increase US savings by running a government budget surplus.

McKinnon (2003) further argues that allowing the RMB to float could hurt the US since China is a large US creditor. As mentioned previously, China is the second largest holder of US Treasury securities. If the RMB fluctuates significantly against the US dollar, US dollar assets will become riskier to Chinese investors and could prompt a sell-off. If China ceases to intervene in the currency market and buys Treasury securities, Treasury security

prices would fall causing US interest rates to rise.

In contrast to McKinnon, Bergsten (2006) argues that that China's exchange rate policy of an undervalued RMB perpetuates global imbalances since it deters other Asian countries, such as Japan and India, from allowing their currencies to rise against the dollar in order to remain competitive. Consequently, it is no surprise that many Asian countries are accumulating US dollar reserves. He further states that these global imbalances are unsustainable. On average, the US must attract approximately $7 billion in capital everyday from the rest of the world to finance the current account deficit. Allowing the RMB to appreciate by 20–40% over 2–3 years is a step in the right direction to correct these external imbalances. China's adoption of a flexible exchange rate in the long run will prevent global imbalances forming.

Conclusions

Many economists believe that China should adopt a flexible exchange rate and it is in China's interest to allow its currency to appreciate. However, allowing the RMB to appreciate alone is a necessary but not sufficient condition to cure the US bilateral trade deficit with China.

Endnotes

[1] International Herald Tribune published January 24th, 2008, http://www.iht.com/articles/2008/01/24/business/24yuan.php

[2] http://www.china-embassy.org/eng/gyzg/t402831.htm

[3] http://www.treas.gov/tic/mfh.txt

[4] Bloomberg.com published February 19th, 2008, http://www.bloomberg.com/apps/news?pid=20601087&refer=home&sid=aZmlGxtDTz7c

[5] "Revaluation by Stealth" The Economist, January 10th, 2008

References

Bergsten Fred C., "The US Trade Deficit and China" Petersen Institute for International Economics, Testimony before the Hearing on US-China Economic Relations Revisited, Committee on Finance, United States Senate, March 29, 2006.

Goldstein, Morris "Adjusting China's Exchange Rate Policies" Petersen Institute for International Economics Working Paper 04-1, May 2004.

Frankel J.A. and S. Wei, "Assessing China's Exchange Rate Regime" NBER Working Paper 13100 April 2007.

McKinnon, Ronald, "China's Exchange Rate," *Asian Wall Street Journal*, June 27, 2003.

"Misleading Misalignments" *The Economist*, June 21st, 2007.

"Revaluation by Stealth," *The Economist*, January 10th, 2008

"The Big Mac Index: Sizzling," *The Economist*, July 5th, 2007

Spiegel, Mark, "A Look at China's New Exchange Rate Regime" *FRBSF Economic Letter*, No. 2005-23, September 9th, 2005.

22

To Float or Not to Float?
Exchange Rate Regimes and Shocks

MICHELE CAVALLO

Many economists argue that a flexible exchange rate regime is preferable to a fixed exchange rate regime because it helps to insulate the domestic economy from adverse external shocks. For example, when export demand declines, a depreciation makes domestic goods more competitive abroad, stimulates an offsetting expansion in demand, and dampens the contraction in domestic economic activity.

In reality, however, exchange rate depreciations in many emerging market economies over the past decade typically have been associated with financial distress and output contractions. Consequently, recent research has reconsidered the stabilization properties of a flexible exchange rate regime when exchange rate movements affect financial conditions, and these, in turn, influence economic activity.

We summarize some of the findings of these studies and their policy prescriptions for the choice of the exchange rate regime. Some studies find that, in spite of the adverse impact of changing exchange rates on financial conditions and aggregate economic activity, a flexible exchange rate regime is still preferable. Yet, this is difficult to reconcile with the observation that many emerging market economies prefer to avoid exchange rate adjustments. Other studies explain this behavior by showing how changing exchange rates can produce severe financial distress that, in turn, leads to a net loss of wealth. This mechanism explains why emerging market economies may prefer to keep the exchange rate fixed, at least in the short run, to mitigate the costs arising from exchange rate adjustment.

Balance Sheet Effects

Episodes of large exchange rate adjustments in emerging market economies during the 1990s were characterized by widespread defaults by domestic firms and output contractions. This led many researchers to evaluate how financial conditions affect the impact of exchange rate adjustments on aggregate economic activity.

Financial conditions can influence aggregate demand through balance sheet effects on borrowing and investment expenditure. These effects occur when the interest rate at which firms borrow from financial intermediaries to finance investment depends on the level of net worth, which is essentially a firm's gross value of assets net of liabilities. Firms with a lower net worth tend to finance a greater share of their investment through debt. Since these firms will be more leveraged, they are less likely to meet their loan obligations in the event of some negative shock to their activity. Consequently, to compensate for the greater expected likelihood of default, lenders will charge these firms a higher risk premium. Therefore, a lower net worth, through an increase in the risk premium, leads to a higher cost of borrowing that, in turn, reduces investment.

When external liabilities are denominated in foreign currencies, as is the case for almost all emerging market economies, exchange rate depreciation may have negative balance sheet effects. Since domestic firms typically earn their revenues in their domestic currency, depreciation makes these revenues worth less in terms of foreign currency, thereby reducing their capacity to service foreign currency debt. The associated reduction in net worth generates an increase in the risk premium on borrowing that dampens investment expenditure and aggregate demand. Therefore, the interaction of balance sheet effects and foreign currency denomination of liabilities can lead exchange rate depreciations to be contractionary and render flexible exchange rate regimes less attractive.

The question is: Are these balance sheet effects large enough to make policymakers prefer a fixed exchange rate regime? Céspedes, Chang, and Velasco (2004) and Gertler, Gilchrist, and Natalucci (2003) address this question by analyzing the reaction of an emerging market model economy to an adverse external shock, such as an increase in the foreign interest rate. These studies conclude that, even in the presence of balance sheet effects, flexible exchange rates still provide more output stabilization in response to a negative external shock.

For example, consider the effect of an increase in the foreign interest rate above the domestic interest rate. Under flexible exchange rates, this induces a financial outflow and a depreciation of the domestic currency. With liabilities denominated in foreign currency, this channel produces a decrease in net worth. However, there are also positive consequences from the asset side of firms' balance sheets. Because the depreciation makes domestic goods relatively cheaper, export revenue rises, creating a positive impact on net worth. If this positive effect dominates and net worth rises, the overall effect of depreciation need not be contractionary.

Alternatively, under fixed exchange rates, the central bank must raise the domestic interest rate to match the increase in the foreign interest rate so as to prevent the domestic currency from depreciating. This interest rate rise leads to a decrease

in a firm's net worth because future revenues are worth less in current value terms. As net worth shrinks, the risk premium rises, inducing a contraction in investment spending and output. Therefore, under fixed exchange rates, balance sheet effects exacerbate the contractionary effects of an increase in the foreign interest rate on investment, aggregate demand, and output.

Some Stylized Facts

Despite these theoretical arguments in favor of a floating exchange rate policy, many emerging market economies appear averse to exchange rate adjustments. Calvo and Reinhart (2002), notably, report evidence of widespread fear of large exchange rate adjustment in emerging market economies. In addition, Hausmann, Panizza, and Stein (2001) find that this is particularly so for countries that borrow heavily abroad in foreign currency, as they are exposed to the potential for balance sheet deterioration.

Cavallo et al. (2004) find that balance sheet effects are, in fact, at the root of the output contraction in the aftermath of an exchange rate adjustment. As shown in Figure 1, they detect a positive relation between the severity of output contractions and an index of intensity of balance sheet effects, where the latter is measured by the product of total real exchange rate (REER) depreciation and the ratio of net foreign currency liabilities to output. In addition, they observe that many of the recent exchange rate adjustment episodes in emerging market economies have been characterized by exchange rate overshooting; that is, the degree of exchange rate depreciation in the short run was considerably larger than in the long run. Cavallo et al. (2004) also find that exchange rate overshooting is greater the higher is the ratio of foreign currency debt to GDP, as Figure 2 indicates.

Which Exchange Rate Policy?

Cavallo et al. (2004) formulate a model that relates these stylized facts by recognizing one additional feature of most recent episodes of exchange rate adjustment

Output Contractions and Balance Sheet Effects
Figure 1

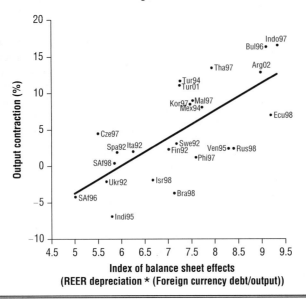

Real Exchange Rate Overshooting and Foreign Currency Debt
Figure 2

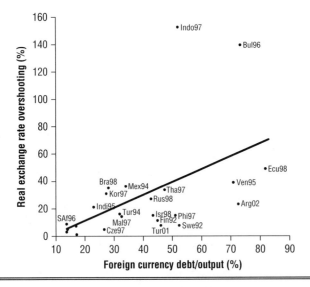

in emerging market economies; specifically, these countries also experienced a decline in the confidence of foreign investors that sharply curbed their ability to borrow from abroad.

In their model, exchange rate depreciation produces negative balance sheet effects that interact with the reduced ability to borrow abroad, which, in turn, generates the need to reduce external indebtedness even further. This can be achieved through two channels: reducing imports of foreign goods and selling equity claims in domestic firms to foreign investors. Each channel of adjustment has further effects. The drop in imports induces a further depreciation of the exchange rate that results in exchange rate overshooting, while the sale of domestic assets prompts a decline in domestic equity prices (see Aguiar and Gopinath 2005 for evidence on East Asian countries during the late 1990s). Both effects are stronger when the exposure to foreign currency liabilities is larger, as any depreciation creates a greater need to reduce external indebtedness. In addition, they magnify the costs of exchange rate depreciation: exchange rate overshooting interacts with sizable foreign currency liabilities and exacerbates the adverse balance sheet effect of depreciation on output, while the sale of domestic assets at a discount implies a net loss of wealth that permanently affects domestic consumption.

Preventing exchange rate depreciation avoids the negative balance sheet effects and lessens the need to sell off domestic equity assets, but at the cost of making domestic goods less competitive. This hampers aggregate demand and depresses domestic output. For this reason, as other studies have concluded, a regime of flexible exchange rates may in fact dominate in the long run. In the short run, however, matters can be quite different: in the face of a sharp reduction in the ability to borrow externally, keeping the exchange rate fixed mitigates the disruption caused by the necessary sales of domestic equity assets and the resulting loss of wealth, so that, in this case fixed exchange rates dominate.

Conclusions

In answer to the question posed in the title, "to float or not to float," the evidence and the models discussed in this paper point to the relevance of foreign currency liabilities in choosing the appropriate exchange rate policies in response to adverse external shocks. Specifically, recent research has found that, even when financial conditions influence aggregate economic activity, flexible exchange rates can be more desirable than fixed exchange rates as a tool to deal with adverse external shocks. However, in emerging market economies these shocks often involve temporarily reduced access to international financial markets. Under such scenarios, a policy of flexible exchange rates can lead to substantial costs. Conversely, a policy of fixed exchange rates dampens these costs, and, at least in the short run, can be preferred to an exchange rate adjustment.

References

[*URL accessed January 2005.*]

Aguiar, Mark, and Gita Gopinath. 2005. "Fire-sale FDI and Liquidity Crises." *Review of Economics and Statistics*, forthcoming.

Calvo, Guillermo A., and Carmen M. Reinhart. 2002. "Fear of Floating." *Quarterly Journal of Economics* 117 (May) pp. 379–408.

Cavallo, Michele, Kate Kisselev, Fabrizio Perri, and Nouriel Roubini. 2004. "Exchange Rate Overshooting and the Costs of Floating." Mimeo. New York University.

Céspedes, Luis Felipe, Roberto Chang, and Andrés Velasco. 2004. "Balance Sheets and Exchange Rate Policy." *American Economic Review* 94 (September) pp. 1183–1193.

Gertler, Mark, Simon Gilchrist, and Fabio M. Natalucci. 2003. "External Constraints on Monetary Policy and the Financial Accelerator." NBER Working Paper no. 10128. http://papers.nber.org/papers/w10128.pdf

Hausmann, Ricardo, Ugo Panizza, and Ernesto Stem. 2001. "Why Do Countries Float the Way They Float?" *Journal of Development Economics* 66 (December) pp. 387–414.

23

Moving to a Flexible Exchange Rate

How, When, and How Fast?

RUPA DUTTAGUPTA,
GILDA FERNANDEZ,
AND CEM KARACADAG

Some countries have made the transition from fixed to flexible exchange rates gradually and smoothly, by adopting intermediate types of exchange rate regimes—soft pegs, horizontal and crawling bands, and managed floats—before allowing the currency to float freely. (See Box 1 for a list of exchange rate regimes.) Other transitions have been disorderly—that is, characterized by a sharp depreciation of the currency. A large share of the exits to flexible exchange rate regimes during 1990–2002 were disorderly (Box 2). But whether an exit from a fixed rate is orderly or not, it is always complicated.

What conditions are necessary—from an operational perspective—for a successful shift from a fixed exchange rate to one that is determined, at least in part, by market forces? How fast should the transition be? And in what sequence should the policies needed for flexibility be put in place?

Country experiences indicate that four ingredients are generally needed for a successful transition to exchange rate flexibility:

- a deep and liquid foreign exchange market;
- a coherent policy governing central bank intervention in the foreign exchange market (the practice of buying or selling the local currency to influence its price, or exchange rate);

- an appropriate alternative nominal anchor to replace the fixed exchange rate; and
- effective systems for reviewing and managing the exposure of both the public and the private sectors to exchange rate risk.

The timing and priority accorded to each of these areas naturally vary from country to country depending on initial conditions and economic structure.

Developing the Foreign Exchange Market

Operating a flexible exchange rate regime requires a foreign exchange market that is liquid and efficient enough to allow the exchange rate to respond to market forces and that limits both the number and the duration of episodes of excessive volatility and deviations from the equilibrium exchange rate (the rate that is in line with a country's economic fundamentals) so that "price discovery" can occur.

In general, the foreign exchange market consists of a wholesale interbank market where authorized dealers (usually banks and other financial institutions) trade with each other and a retail market where authorized dealers transact with final customers like households and firms. A liquid market is one with relatively narrow bid-offer spreads; low transaction costs;

Types of exchange rate regimes
Box 1

Exchange arrangements with no separate legal tender

The currency of another country circulates as the sole legal tender (formal dollarization), or the member belongs to a monetary or currency union in which the same legal tender is shared by the members of the union. Adopting such regimes implies the complete surrender of the monetary authorities' independent control over domestic monetary policy.

Currency boards

A monetary regime based on an explicit legislative commitment to exchange domestic currency for a specified foreign currency at a fixed exchange rate, combined with restrictions on the issuing authority to ensure the fulfillment of its legal obligation. This implies that domestic currency will be issued only against foreign exchange and that it remains fully backed by foreign assets, eliminating traditional central bank functions, such as monetary control and lender of last resort, and leaving little scope for discretionary monetary policy. Some flexibility may still be afforded, depending on how strict the banking rules of the currency board arrangement are.

Other conventional fixed-peg arrangements

The country (formally or de facto) pegs its currency at a fixed rate to another currency or a basket of the currencies of major trading or financial partners, weighted to reflect the geographical distribution of trade, services, or capital flows. The parity is not irrevocable. The exchange rate may fluctuate within narrow margins of less than ± 1 percent around a central rate, or the maximum and minimum values of the exchange rate may remain within a narrow margin of 2 percent for at least three months. The monetary authority stands ready to maintain the fixed parity through direct intervention (sale/purchase of foreign exchange in the market) or indirect intervention (aggressive use of interest rate policy, imposition of foreign exchange regulations, moral suasion,

or intervention by other public institutions). Independence of monetary policy, though limited, is greater than under exchange arrangements with no separate legal tender and currency boards because traditional central banking functions are still possible, and the monetary authority can adjust the level of the exchange rate, although relatively infrequently.

Pegged exchange rates within horizontal bands

The value of the currency is maintained within certain margins of fluctuation of at least ± 1 percent around a fixed central rate, or the margin between the maximum and minimum values of the exchange rate exceeds 2 percent. The exchange rate mechanism (ERM) of the European Monetary System (EMS), which was replaced with ERM II on January 1, 1999, is an example of this type of peg. There is a limited degree of monetary policy discretion, depending on the band's width.

Crawling pegs

The currency is adjusted periodically in small amounts at a fixed rate or in response to changes in selective quantitative indicators, such as past inflation differentials vis-à-vis major trading partners, differentials between the inflation target and expected inflation in major trading partners, and so forth. The rate of crawl can be set to generate inflation-adjusted changes in the exchange rate (backward looking), or it can be set at a preannounced fixed rate and/or below the projected inflation differentials (forward looking). A crawling peg imposes the same kinds of constraints on monetary policy as a fixed peg.

Exchange rates within crawling bands

The currency is maintained within fluctuation margins of at least ± 1 percent around a central rate, or the margin between the maximum and minimum values of the exchange rate exceeds 2 percent, and the central rate or margins are adjusted periodically at a fixed rate or in response to changes in selective

(*continued on next page*)

Types of exchange rate regimes (*concluded*)
Box 1

quantitative indicators. The degree of exchange rate flexibility is a function of the width of the band. Bands are either symmetric around a crawling central parity or widen gradually with an asymmetric choice of the crawl of upper and lower bands (in the latter case, there may be no preannounced central rate). The commitment to maintaining the exchange rate within the band imposes constraints on monetary policy, with the degree of policy independence being a function of the band width.

Managed floating

The monetary authority attempts to influence the exchange rate without having a predetermined path or target for it. Indicators for managing the rate include the balance of payments position, the level of international reserves, and parallel market developments, and adjustments may not be automatic. Intervention may be direct or indirect.

Independent floating

The exchange rate is determined by the markets. Official intervention in the foreign exchange market is infrequent and discretionary and is usually aimed at moderating the rate of change of, and preventing undue fluctuations in, the exchange rate, rather than at establishing a level for it.

---

enough turnover to limit the impact of individual trades on prices; trading, clearing, and settlement systems that facilitate the swift execution of orders; and a wide range of active market participants.

The foreign exchange markets of many developing countries are shallow and inefficient, however, in part because of extensive foreign exchange regulations—such as controls on cross-border capital flows (these controls reduce market turnover), tight prudential limits on net open foreign exchange positions, and requirements to surrender foreign exchange receipts to the central bank. Interbank foreign exchange markets—where they exist—are often small relative to retail markets, limiting the scope for price discovery.

Exchange rate rigidity itself may be a factor in foreign exchange market illiquidity. A central bank operating a fixed exchange rate regime is usually active in the market by necessity, which keeps market participants from gaining experience in price formation and exchange rate risk management and constrains interbank activity. In extreme cases, the central bank may dominate the interbank foreign exchange market and act as the primary foreign exchange intermediary. With a fixed exchange rate, market participants have less incentive to form views on exchange rate trends, take positions, or trade foreign exchange, which limits foreign exchange activity in both the spot and the forward markets. In addition, to reduce the scope for speculation, forward market activity tends to be discouraged under pegged exchange rate regimes. The small size of the forward markets, in turn, limits opportunities for hedging risks.

The following steps can help a country improve the depth and efficiency of its foreign exchange market:

- Allowing some exchange rate flexibility (for example, within a band around a peg) to stimulate foreign exchange activity. Authorities should also foster a sense of *two-way risk* in the exchange rate—the risk that the currency may either appreciate or depreciate—to encourage market participants to take both short and long positions. Between 1995 and 2001, turnover increased in the foreign exchange markets of countries that adopted more flexible exchange rate regimes and declined in countries that adopted less flexible regimes.

Orderly versus disorderly exits to flexible rates
Box 2

Exits to flexible regimes fall into three categories: exits from all hard pegs and fixed and crawling pegs to bands and floats; exits from bands to floats; and exits from managed floats to independent floats. A total of 139 exits to flexible regimes are identified in the figures below. Exits are included only for regimes that lasted at least one year or if the country continued to increase its exchange rate flexibility during the year of the exit.

Number and Type of Exits, 1990–2002
Figure 1

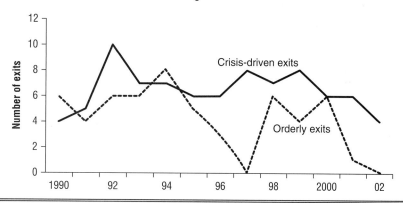

Exits by Exchange Rate Regime, 1990–2002
Figure 2

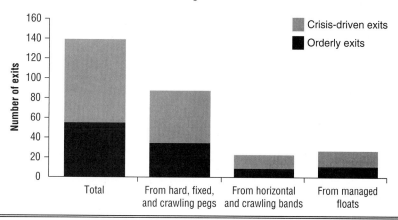

- Reducing the central bank's market-making role by cutting back its trade with banks and its interventions to allow scope for other market makers. The central bank should not trade with nonfinancial customers.
- Increasing market information on the sources and uses of foreign exchange and on balance of payments trends to enable market participants to develop credible views on exchange rate and monetary policy and price foreign exchange efficiently. Authorities should also ensure that information systems and trading platforms provide real-time bid and offer quotations in the interbank market.
- Phasing out or eliminating regulations that stifle market activity. Important measures would include abolishing requirements to surrender foreign exchange receipts to the central bank, taxes and surcharges on foreign exchange transactions, and restrictions on interbank trading; unifying segmented foreign exchange markets; and relaxing current and some capital account restrictions to increase the sources and uses of foreign exchange in the market. Capital controls should be eased gradually, however, and only after certain macroeconomic and institutional preconditions have been met.
- Unifying and simplifying foreign exchange legislation and avoiding frequent, ad hoc changes to the law, so as to increase market transparency and reduce transaction costs.
- Improving the market's microstructure by reducing market segmentation, increasing the effectiveness of market intermediaries, and securing reliable and efficient settlement systems.

Developing and deepening the foreign exchange market is more complicated when a country is forced to abandon a peg under market pressure and has not had time to prepare for an orderly exit. The government is likely to face conflicting objectives. On the one hand, it needs to sell foreign exchange to prevent excessive depreciation. On the other, to maintain market credibility it needs to signal that it will not intervene to defend a particular exchange rate level. Under these circumstances, many countries have gradually renounced the central bank's market-making role, removed barriers to foreign exchange market operations, and tolerated greater exchange rate volatility, while allowing interest rates to rise to counter market pressure and monitoring market transactions to determine the sources and direction of order flows.

Central Bank Intervention

Under currency pegs, official purchases and sales of foreign currency to bridge the gap between foreign currency supply and demand at a given price are often rules-based in that the timing and amount of intervention are predetermined. In contrast, official intervention in the foreign exchange market is optional, or discretionary, under a flexible exchange rate regime, although authorities still can and do intervene, usually to correct misalignments, calm disorderly markets, supply foreign exchange, and accumulate reserves. Thus, a government that is shifting to a flexible regime needs to formulate policies on the objectives, timing, and amounts of intervention.

Like all other markets, foreign exchange markets are imperfect. For example, "herding" (when investors buy or sell en masse) and "feedback trading" (trading driven by price movements rather than fundamentals) may result in the misalignment of a currency with a country's economic fundamentals, with serious repercussions. Among other things, an overvalued currency undermines the competitiveness of the country's exports, while an undervalued exchange rate could stoke inflation. Moreover, when a country's capital account is not fully liberalized, or its capital market is inefficient, temporary shocks may trigger exchange rate volatility in "thin" markets.

Volatility can be politically costly because the exchange rate serves as a symbolic measure of a government's success in macroeconomic management. And long-lasting misalignments and erratic exchange rate movements can subject cost and income projections in the real sector to wide margins of error, making long-term planning and investment difficult.

However, misalignments are difficult to detect, and there is no consensus on a methodology for estimating the equilibrium exchange rate. The indicators used most frequently—the nominal and real effective exchange rates, productivity and other competitiveness measures, the terms of trade, the balance of payments, interest rate differentials, and parallel market exchange rates—usually do not enable policymakers to assess the degree of misalignment accurately enough to help them determine the optimal timing and amount of intervention.

And even when policymakers detect exchange rate misalignment or destabilizing volatility, central bank intervention may not always correct the problem. The empirical evidence on the effectiveness of intervention in influencing the exchange rate is mixed, and the impact of intervention on the exchange rate level appears to be short-lived. Empirical studies have also found that intervention tends to increase, rather than decrease, exchange rate volatility. Thus, short-term exchange rate volatility may not warrant intervention, especially when it occurs in a liquid, or orderly, market. Volatility may reflect the market process of price discovery and provide useful signals to policymakers and market participants.

Central bank intervention is usually justified, however, to calm disorderly markets—that is, markets with unequal numbers of sellers and buyers of foreign exchange, resulting in illiquidity. If market illiquidity persists, it can hurt the real economy. Although volatility that is due to disorderly markets and that is likely to lead to a collapse of liquidity is also difficult to detect, acceleration in exchange rate changes, widening bid-offer spreads,

and a sharp increase in interbank trades relative to customer-bank turnover are signs to watch for.

Central banks may also have to intervene in the foreign exchange market to supply foreign currency or build up their reserves. First, many central banks have a regular supply of foreign currency because of income on foreign reserves and their roles as the bankers of governments that borrow or receive aid in foreign currency. Second, they normally target a certain level of reserves, requiring the regular purchase of foreign currency to maintain core reserve coverage ratios.

A country may need to reevaluate its international-reserve-management policy when it moves to a flexible exchange rate regime. On the one hand, the level of reserves required to maintain a flexible rate may be lower than that required to maintain a fixed one. In addition, improved supervision of private sector foreign currency exposures may reduce reserve requirements. On the other hand, the elimination of capital controls may create a need for higher reserves to maintain or boost market confidence and lower exchange rate volatility, reduce the likelihood of crises, and increase the effectiveness of intervention, while providing funds for the government to invest in longer-term assets with higher returns.

In general, central banks should be selective in their interventions and parsimonious in their use of foreign reserves. The difficulty of detecting exchange rate misalignments and disorderly markets means that decisions on the timing and amount of intervention are subjective and may be off the mark. Moreover, by entering the market infrequently, central banks can convince the markets of their commitment to exchange rate flexibility and improve the potential effectiveness of the occasional intervention. When a country introduces a band as part of a gradual move to exchange rate flexibility, intervention episodes may be more frequent than under more flexible regimes; nonetheless, central banks should minimize the number of interventions and make full use of the exchange rate flexibility allowed by the width of the band. Central banks in many advanced economies (for example, Canada, New Zealand, and the United Kingdom) seldom intervene in the foreign exchange market.

Transparency also helps build confidence in the new exchange rate regime, especially in the aftermath of a forced exit. Many countries, including the Philippines and Turkey, issued statements and policy reports affirming that they were committed to a flexible exchange rate regime and that they would not intervene in the foreign exchange market to target a certain exchange rate level. The published intervention policies of Australia and Sweden are good examples of the policies that need to be developed and communicated to the market to enhance the effectiveness of official foreign exchange operations. Disclosing information on intervention with a time lag can improve market transparency and central bank accountability. The United Kingdom discloses information on intervention in a monthly press release, the European Central Bank in a monthly bulletin; the U.S. Treasury confirms interventions on the day they take place and provides additional details in quarterly reports.

Selected country experiences suggest that rules-based intervention may be useful when the exchange rate is not under a lot of pressure in a one-sided market. Such a policy may help countries supply foreign exchange or accumulate reserves without affecting the exchange rate. Eventually however, central banks will gain enough experience and credibility to intervene on a more discretionary basis. Rules-based intervention policies tend to be transitory, abandoned or modified by most countries (for example, Brazil and Canada).

Adopting an Alternative Nominal Anchor

A country exiting a peg must replace it with another nominal anchor and redesign its monetary policy framework around the new anchor. While some central banks maintain flexible regimes without a formal nominal anchor—for example, in the euro area, Singapore, Switzerland, and the United States—these economies enjoy a high level of credibility, which may be difficult for developing countries to build quickly, especially if they relied on a rigid exchange rate anchor before the exit or had a history of high inflation.

The most important function of a country's monetary policy is control of the money supply (or liquidity). This is especially true when countries have exited a peg under market pressure, since a currency depreciation is likely to spark inflation. As a country moves to a more flexible exchange rate regime, the burden of managing liquidity shifts from intervention in the foreign exchange market to other monetary policy instruments, such as standing facilities, open market operations, and repurchase agreements. While such instruments, along with liquid money markets, are important for managing liquidity under any type of exchange rate regime, their importance rises with exchange rate flexibility.

The difficulty of developing a credible alternative nominal anchor has caused many countries to give up the exchange rate anchor slowly, for example, by adopting a crawling band as an intermediate regime while they shift to another nominal anchor, possibly over a long period. The band is usually set symmetrically around a crawling central parity and gradually widened as the tension between exchange rate and inflation objectives is eventually resolved in favor of the latter. Chile, Hungary, Israel, and Poland successfully made the transition using crawling bands that were widened over time in response to increases in capital inflows. Their experience has yielded some useful lessons:

- The narrow scope for exchange rate flexibility in the early stages of the transition can constrain the independence of monetary policy and put the burden of aggregate-demand management on fiscal and incomes policies.
- Restricting exchange rate movements within a narrower band than the one

that was publicly announced can create the perception of an implicit exchange rate guarantee and reduce the sensitivity of market participants to exchange rate risk. Two-way exchange rate movements are necessary to give participants an incentive to develop hedging instruments and manage exchange rate risk.

- Governments that maintain two nominal anchors—the exchange rate and the inflation target—can bolster public confidence in their commitment to the inflation target by making it clear that price stability will be their first priority in the event of a conflict between the two anchors.

Many countries moving to flexible rate regimes have opted for inflation targeting over monetary targeting. A consensus seems to be emerging that an inflation target is a more reliable and effective nominal anchor. While monetary targeting can serve as an alternative nominal anchor after a country abandons a peg, the weak relationship between monetary aggregates and inflation limits the effectiveness of money targets. Countries that have managed orderly exits from pegs have generally adopted inflation targeting over long time horizons, in part because of the time required to put the necessary institutions and macroeconomic conditions in place, including a central bank mandate to pursue an explicit inflation target as the overriding objective of monetary policy; central bank independence and accountability; transparency that promotes accountability in the conduct and evaluation of monetary policy; a reliable methodology for forecasting inflation; a forward-looking procedure that systematically incorporates forecasts into policy and responds to deviations from targets; a supportive fiscal policy; and a well-regulated, supervised, and managed financial sector.

Until these preconditions are established, many countries have followed various versions of the monetary-targeting approach (targeting base money, broad monetary aggregates, or bank reserves), especially after a disorderly exit. For example, several of the countries hit by the Asian crisis adopted monetary targets immediately after exiting from pegged exchange rate regimes to establish a new nominal anchor and restore policy credibility as quickly as possible. In Korea, the Philippines, and Thailand, the monetary-targeting approach laid the groundwork for a fairly rapid move to inflation targeting. Brazil has followed a similar path. In Indonesia, however, the transition from monetary targeting to inflation targeting was slower because the severity of the crisis hampered the country's efforts to move ahead.

Managing and Supervising Exchange Rate Risk

When a country floats its currency, exchange rate risk shifts from the public sector (the central bank) to the private sector, as the former no longer stands ready to intervene at fixed rates. Indeed, disorderly exits often happen because of unmanageable imbalances in the public sector's balance sheet. Thus, determining the scale and scope of exchange rate risk exposures in the financial and nonfinancial sectors is also key to achieving an orderly exit from pegs. The private sector's exposure to exchange rate risk can have an important bearing on the pace of the exit, the type of flexible exchange rate regime adopted (for example, a band versus a float), and official intervention policies.

The evaluation of exchange rate risk exposures entails detailed balance sheet analysis focusing on the currency composition, maturities, liquidity, and credit quality of assets and liabilities denominated in foreign currencies. The Asian crisis, for example, showed how unhedged foreign exchange borrowing by the corporate sector could turn into massive losses for creditor banks and a surge in demand for foreign currency. Even when banks ensure that foreign currency liabilities and assets are matched, the use of short-term foreign currency funds to finance long-term foreign currency loans to unhedged customers results in sizable credit and liquidity risks. Similarly, the corporate and the banking sectors' exposure to interest rate risk can limit the central bank's ability to use interest rates, instead of interventions in the foreign exchange market, in conducting monetary policy. It can be very difficult for corporations in developing and emerging market countries to off-load interest rate risk, in particular when their assets are not interest bearing and they have difficulty obtaining long-term fixed rates for their liabilities, as is often the case.

The management of exchange rate risk is composed of four elements:

- Information systems to monitor the various sources of exchange rate risk, including the sources and uses of foreign currency funds, and formal reporting requirements. Indirect exchange rate risk should be monitored through regular surveys of the corporate sector or by requiring borrowers to provide information on their foreign currency incomes, foreign debts, and hedging operations.

- Formulas and analytical techniques to measure exchange rate risk. Measures of risk include accounting-based measures of the overall foreign currency position and more forward-looking risk-management techniques such as value-at-risk models and stress testing.

- Internal risk policies and procedures, including, among other things, limits on concentration in foreign currency loans, specific provisions for the additional credit risks associated with foreign currency lending, requirements for foreign earnings or collateral for borrowers of foreign currency, and analysis of the potential impact of exchange rate movements on foreign currency borrowers. Also important are strong internal controls—including a written policy on foreign exchange operations, exposure limits, risk-management

procedures, and a system of monitoring compliance where front and back offices are fully separate—as well as good corporate governance, including regular monitoring, review, and approval of risk policies and procedures by the board of directors to maintain appropriate checks and balances within the institution. Banks should encourage clients to hedge against exchange rate risks.

- Prudential regulation and supervision of foreign exchange risk. Prudential measures may include limits on net open positions (as a percentage of capital), foreign currency lending (as a percentage of foreign currency liabilities), and overseas borrowing and bond issuance (as a percentage of capital); limits on the range of foreign exchange operations banks are allowed to perform through licensing requirements; capital requirements against foreign exchange risk; and the issuance of regulations or guidelines on the design of banks' internal controls. Foreign currency borrowing by sectors that do not generate foreign currency revenues or that are exposed to volatile returns warrants special vigilance.

Facilitating the development of risk-hedging instruments by lifting controls on forward market activity can be a double-edged sword. In addition to improving risk management, it can contribute to the development of the foreign exchange market. However, derivatives can easily be misused—in Thailand, in 1997, for example, investors used them to take highly leveraged bets on unsustainable exchange rates. Corporations and financial institutions—and the authorities that supervise them—need to acquire considerable sophistication to ensure that such instruments are used properly. In addition, their use must be closely monitored, bank trading of derivative products must be standardized and accounting standards for fair valuation and a reliable legal system for contract enforcement must be established, and the central bank should promote market transparency and high reporting standards.

Pace and Sequencing

Countries face certain trade-offs in choosing between a rapid exit from a peg and a more gradual move to a floating exchange rate regime. A rapid approach involves fewer intermediate steps, if any, between fixed and floating regimes than a gradual approach.

For a country with a strong macroeconomy and a prudent monetary policy, a rapid approach can be a more credible signal of commitment to exchange rate flexibility than a gradual approach, while allowing the country to limit its interventions in the foreign exchange market and thereby conserve its foreign exchange reserves. Countries seeking greater monetary policy independence may also be better off moving rapidly, as may those with an open capital account—it may be harder to pursue a gradual exit strategy in the presence of large and volatile capital flows. However, a gradual approach is preferable if a country lacks the appropriate institutional framework, including a deep foreign exchange market and the ability to monitor and manage exchange rate risk; such a country runs a high risk of experiencing excessive exchange rate volatility if it moves too quickly.

The absence of a full-fledged inflation-targeting framework as an alternative nominal anchor need not preclude a rapid exit strategy, if there is a robust commitment to price stability. The building blocks of inflation targeting—such as fiscal discipline, the monetary authorities' operational independence in pursuit of low inflation, credible steps to contain inflation, and transparency and accountability—are fundamental to the success of any monetary policy regime regardless of whether inflation targeting is formally adopted. South Africa exited from a fixed peg to a float in the early 1980s but did not formally adopt inflation targeting until 2000. Other countries forced to float in one step—for example, Mexico and Turkey—used monetary targeting as an interim strategy before adopting inflation targeting.

A gradual approach allows the country to move toward a free float in measured steps—for example, by shifting from a fixed peg against a single currency to a fixed or crawling peg against a basket of currencies, and then to an exchange rate band that is increased in increments. In July 2005, for example, China revalued the yuan and replaced its peg to the dollar with a peg to a basket of currencies. Pegging to a basket of currencies has the advantage of reducing the transmission of external shocks to the domestic economy and tempering the exchange rate's exposure to the potentially erratic movements of a single currency. The basket may be composed of a weighted average of the currencies of a country's main trading partners. A shift to a crawling peg against a basket of currencies can help a country maintain its external competitiveness if its inflation rates are different from those of its trading partners. Moving to a horizontal or crawling exchange rate band can provide greater exchange rate flexibility and monetary policy independence. While these variants of pegged regimes are easier to maintain than wide exchange rate bands and floats, they constrain monetary policy and can be difficult for countries with liberalized capital accounts to sustain. In either case, whether the exit is rapid or gradual, each step forward should ensure two-way risk in exchange rate movements.

Early preparation for the move to a floating exchange rate increases the likelihood that the exit will be successful. A country should begin to lay the groundwork for the exit while it still has a peg, securing central bank independence, improving its ability to forecast inflation, making monetary policy more transparent, developing information systems on foreign exchange risk, and increasing information on balance of payments developments. Once it has laid the groundwork, it can move to a second stage, introducing some exchange rate flexibility to stimulate activity in the foreign exchange market, while it develops the other tools it will need to operate the new regime. Intervention policies can be addressed later in the transition.

Although policymakers have no control over the pace of a disorderly exit, they still need to make decisions about sequencing. Their top priority should be to stabilize the exchange rate; often, this can be done by eliminating the shortage of dollars in the market and maintaining monetary control. Policymakers should also attempt to signal a conservative monetary policy, although the design of an alternative nominal anchor will probably require more time.

Adopting a flexible exchange rate before liberalizing the capital account enables a country to absorb capital account shocks at a lower cost to the real economy than under a fixed exchange rate. By contrast, liberalizing the capital account first can help offset temporary current account shocks, expand the range of instruments available for risk management, and deepen the foreign exchange market. Accordingly, when an exchange rate is floated before the capital account is liberalized, central bank intervention may be needed to offset temporary current account shocks and to limit excessive real exchange rate volatility.

The experiences of emerging market economies over the past decade highlight the risks of opening the capital account before adopting a flexible exchange rate. Many countries were forced off pegs after sudden reversals of capital flows under open capital accounts (for example, Mexico at the end of 1994, Thailand in July 1997, and Brazil in early 1999). Others faced heavy inflows and upward pressure on pegged rates and had to allow exchange rate flexibility to avoid overheating the economy (for example, Chile and Poland during the 1990s). Thus, even under favorable economic conditions, opening the capital account before introducing exchange rate flexibility can threaten domestic liquidity, create macroeconomic imbalances, and precipitate speculative attacks. Uganda did not liberalize its capital account until after it had completed its move to a float; New Zealand successfully moved to a float and liberalized its capital account simultaneously; and Chile's capital account liberalization moved in parallel with its transition to a floating exchange rate, but very gradually.

To Float or not to Float

It is no doubt better to plan an exit in a calm economic environment. But even planned exits do not necessarily last. Many countries have reversed course after adopting exchange rate flexibility. Either macroeconomic conditions or a lack of institutions or both may contribute to the reversal from a float to a fixed regime. Fiscal dominance played an important role in the reversals of both Russia (1993–95) and Venezuela (2002–03), while Egypt's reversal occurred amid concerns about excessive depreciation (2003). Other obstacles to floating in many developing countries include the limited number of participants in the foreign exchange market, pervasive exchange controls, a weak technological infrastructure, and underdeveloped money markets.

Both fixed and floating exchange rates have distinct and different advantages. No single exchange rate regime is appropriate for all countries in all circumstances. Countries will have to weigh the costs and benefits of floating in light of both their economic and their institutional readiness.

24

Official Dollarization and the Banking System in Ecuador and El Salvador

MYRIAM QUISPE-AGNOLI
AND ELENA WHISLER

Since Ecuadorian president Jamil Mahuad announced the adoption of the U.S. dollar as legal tender in January 2000, the discussion about the pros and cons of full dollarization has intensified. In 2001 El Salvador engaged in full dollarization to enhance its economic reform process. The two economies adopted the U.S. dollar as their currency for diametrically opposite reasons: In Ecuador full dollarization occurred in the midst of an economic and banking crisis. In contrast, in El Salvador full dollarization was expected to enhance the set of previous structural reforms put in place to support economic stability and thus attract foreign investors. This article studies the evolution of the banking system in these two countries before and after the adoption of full, or official, dollarization.[1]

Under full or official dollarization, a country adopts as legal tender another country's currency, in this case the U.S. dollar. The adopted currency takes over all the functions of domestic currency: a unit of account, medium of exchange, and store of value. The country's policymakers thus give up any possibility of monetary and exchange rate policies. Official dollarization is equivalent to pegging the domestic currency to the U.S. dollar, but it is different from a currency board because it is irreversible. This irreversibility theoretically makes full dollarization a credible economic policy and a way to avoid currency and balance-of-payments crises.

The expected benefits of full dollarization include the elimination of exchange rate risk, contributing to the decline of the country risk premium and interest rates, as well as the reduction of the inflation rate and inflationary expectations. These outcomes are expected to encourage foreign investment and a stable capital flow. One cost of full dollarization is the elimination of the government's ability to generate seigniorage—that is, revenue from issuing domestic money—to finance its fiscal deficit. Without this possibility, the dollarizing country must look for alternative revenue sources or reduce government expenditures. By giving up control of its money supply, a full dollarization regime encourages fiscal discipline (enhancing policy credibility) but also constrains the fiscal response to stabilize the economy in difficult times.

Some initial conditions could be relevant in the decision to implement official dollarization. Minda (2005) and Edwards and Magendzo (2006) observe that small countries with close trade or financial ties to the United States could favor official dollarization, as Panama did in 1904. Ecuador, El Salvador, and Panama, the largest countries that have implemented official dollarization, are still relatively small and are very open to U.S. trade and finance, with an average gross domestic product (GDP) of $11 billion (in 2000 dollars) and an average population of 7 million in 2004.[2]

A relevant factor in policymakers' decision to adopt full dollarization is the depth and type of partial dollarization already present in the economy.[3] A banking system with a large portion of deposits or loans denominated in foreign currency might have a smaller adjustment with the adoption of official dollarization than a system whose share is small or negligible. Banks in a dollarized economy might have internalized the costs of operating in such environment. They could already have foreign currency liquid assets, or the financial system could have adopted other prudential regulations to control or reduce liquidity and solvency risks. In addition, a country that is experiencing a currency or banking crisis might be more likely to implement official dollarization. Edwards (1995) points out that policymakers might be willing to make radical decisions in times of crisis rather than in times of economic stability. The realization and timing of expected benefits from full dollarization might depend on whether a country implemented it after an economic crisis, such as the currency and banking crisis in Ecuador, or as part of its structural reform process.

Official Dollarization and the Banking System

Three effects on the banking system under full dollarization are considered in this article: restrictions on the central bank as lender of last resort, the effect of economic stability on the performance of banks, and the promotion of financial integration with the world economy.

The restriction on the role of the monetary authority as lender of last resort is one of the costs of full dollarization. Central banks provide loans to banks facing liquidity problems. Under official dollarization, printing money is no longer a feasible source of liquidity, and the central bank needs to look for alternative responses to episodes of financial distress. Chang and Velasco (2000) study the case of an economy under a fixed exchange rate regime with a central bank that does not act as a

lender of last resort, concluding that this regime is more prone to bank runs than a currency board. In this case, the liabilities of the banking system as a whole are, implicitly, obligations in international currency. Consequently, a bank run is possible if the banking system's implicit liabilities are greater than its liquid assets (in foreign currency). Under full dollarization, the economy is shielded from a currency or balance-of-payments crisis, but the risk of a banking crisis is real. Financial instability is endemic to this regimen.

The solution includes external lines of credit with banks from abroad and reserve funds from taxes or other revenues (Calvo 2001). In their analysis, Chang and Velasco show that a policy of high bank reserve requirements dominates over a policy of large international reserves. "The intuition is that increasing the international liquidity of the banking system has a social opportunity cost. Under a policy of high reserve requirements, banks internalize this cost; under a policy of large international reserves, they do not" (2000, 3).

Paradoxically, even though full dollarization limits the central bank's role as lender of last resort and therefore monetary authority responses to financial crises, it might make banks runs less likely because consumers and businesses may have greater confidence in the domestic banking system. The reason is that official dollarization reduces the moral hazard present in highly dollarized banking systems. In a partially dollarized economy, the impact of a large depreciation is widespread in the banking system. Banks expect that the monetary authority would come to the rescue of troubled banks or would delay any sharp devaluations. However, under official dollarization and without exchange rate risk, banks would have to manage their own solvency and liquidity risks better, taking the respective precautionary measures.

Gale and Vives (2002) show that dollarization provides a credible commitment not to help banks in trouble even though it would be ex ante optimal to do so. Their study concludes that dollarization is

Dollarization: Some Definitions and Measurements

Official or *full (de jure) dollarization* is a country's adoption of another country's currency as legal tender.

Under *partial (de facto) dollarization,* a country's domestic currency remains the official legal tender, but transactions can also be carried out in foreign currency, effectively giving the country a bicurrency system.

Other types of dollarization can be distinguished:

- *Currency* or *payments dollarization,* sometimes referred to as currency substitution, is a country's use of foreign currency for transaction purposes.
- *Real dollarization* is the indexing, formally or de facto, of prices and wages to the dollar,
- *Financial dollarization,* also called asset substitution, occurs when a country's residents hold financial assets and liabilities in foreign currency. Financial dollarization can be external (using the dollar in claims between residents and nonresidents) or domestic (using the dollar in claims between residents),

Data limitations on cash holdings in foreign currency restrict the measurement of currency or payments dollarization. Financial dollarization can be measured in several different ways. Domestic financial dollarization can be measured as the ratio of foreign currency deposits or loans to GDP or to total deposits or to total loans. External financial dollarization can be measured as the ratio of foreign assets held by banks to foreign currency deposits or cross-border deposits to foreign currency deposits.

Source: Guide et al. (2004) and Minda (2005)

beneficial when the costs of establishing a reputation for the central bank are high, monitoring by the central bank is important in improving returns, and the cost of liquidating projects is moderate.

Under official dollarization, the lack of a lender of last resort encourages changes in the way supervisory and regulatory institutions manage liquidity and solvency risks. Prudential norms to manage liquidity risk include higher reserve requirements, liquidity requirements, and deposit insurance.[4] Guide et al. (2004) point out that these norms reduce banks' profits because banks have to hold more liquid assets, which have a lower return, and required reserves that pay below-market rates and must increase their expenditures to pay for insurance. Official dollarization also eliminates banks' exchange rate services, a good source of revenues, especially in partially dollarized countries.[5]

Banks ultimately benefit from the reduction of inflation, the elimination of inflationary expectations, and price stability, which fosters an environment beneficial to financial intermediation. With the return of confidence in the currency and financial stability, one expects an increase in bank deposits and loans supporting the development of the banking system. In addition, the elimination of currency risk and currency mismatch contributes to a more efficient banking system. As a net result, reserve requirements are expected to be lower given that banks do not have to distinguish between foreign and domestic currency deposits. Moreno-Villalaz (1999) points out that official dollarization in Panama allowed banks to reduce their reserves by an equivalent of 5 percent of GDP.

Official dollarization also lowers transaction and information costs, encouraging trade and financial integration. According to Minda (2005), even if the risk of external shocks cannot be eliminated, full dollarization contributes to diiranishing their impact and lowering contagion risk by eliminating exchange risk, signaling to international markets the country's commitment to currency stability. This commitment could foster foreign investment and stable capital flows, promoting the integration of the domestic financial market with the world.

Official Dollarization in Ecuador and El Salvador

In 2000 and 2001, Ecuador and El Salvador, respectively, implemented official dollarization for diametrically opposite reasons. In this section, we discuss the economic background before and after the adoption of the U.S. dollar as their domestic currency.

Ecuador

During the 1990s, attempts to open the Ecuadorian economy to international trade and capital markets failed, for the most part. Large fiscal deficits and increasing external debt led to imbalances that became unsustainable with the decline of world oil prices and El Nino's devastating impact on production and infrastructure in 1998. These external shocks resulted in low economic growth, inflation, and liquidity problems in an already fragile banking sector. Several developments contributed to Ecuador's economic collapse in 1999: the devaluation of the sucre in February, a freeze on bank deposits in March, a default on external debt payments in September, and the country's overall political uncertainty and lack of policy direction.

In January 2000, in an environment of social unrest and lacking congressional support for the implementation of structural reforms then President Jamil Mahuad called for full dollarization to avoid the collapse of the banking system. Days later, Mahuad was deposed. Congress confirmed Gustavo Noboa, the elected vice president, as the new president. Noboa continued with full dollarization to promote a return to economic stability. In this already partially dollarized economy, the exchange rate was set at 25,000 sucres per U.S. dollar.

Along with full dollarization, the Economic Transformation Law (Ley de Transformatión Económica) introduced reforms that provided incentives to private investment in the energy sector, encouraged privatization of state enterprises, and made labor markets more flexible. Over the course of the year, the central bank repurchased almost all the outstanding stock of sucres, and all bank accounts were converted into dollars. The International Monetary Fund (IMF) signed a standby agreement with the Ecuadorian government to support economic stability and recovery, helping to attract additional funding from other multilateral institutions.

Ecuador started enjoying the expected benefits of full dollarization even before the U.S. dollar was officially adopted on September 9, 2000. As a sign of the enhanced credibility provided by full dollarization, the release of frozen bank deposits in March did not translate into a bank run. Economic recovery in the first quarter of 2000 and lower inflation in July represented the stabilizing effect of full dollarization. Ecuador also restructured its external debt in August 2000, reducing the total external debt ratio from 106 percent of GDP at the end of 1999 to around 98 percent in 2000.

Full dollarization eliminated currency risk in Ecuador although country risk did not decline immediately with the announcement of full dollarization in January 2000.[6] However, country risk became less volatile after dollarization took effect in September and diminished after debt renegotiations with international organizations (see Figure 1).

Initially, dollarization did not help reduce inflation; the adjustment to lower rates has taken some years. The lag in the adjustment of administered prices and the increase in fiscal spending have delayed the convergence of prices to international levels. By 2003 the inflation rate reached 7.9 percent, the first year since 1972 to have only single-digit growth. In 2004 inflation rose only 2.7 percent for the year, thus converging to U.S. inflation rates (see Figure 2).

Country Risk and Full Dollarization
Figure 1

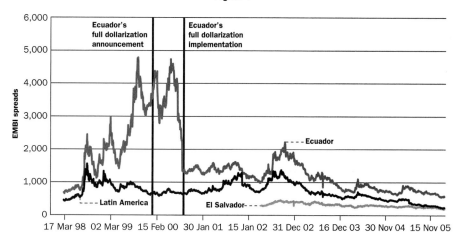

Source: Bloomberg

Inflation in Fully Dollarized Countries
Figure 2

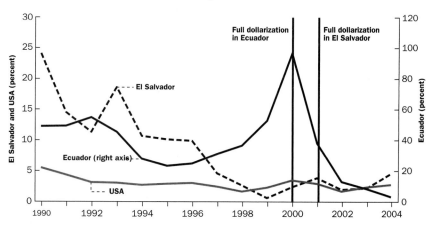

Source: World Development Indicators, World Bank

In addition to a more stable and lower inflation rate, clear signs of economic recovery emerged in 2001, with the country reporting real GDP growth of 5.1 percent in 2001. While economic growth reached only 3.4 percent and 2.7 percent in 2002 and 2003, respectively, the economy bounced back in 2004 with almost 7 percent growth, with the help of an increase in oil output from the new oil pipeline, the Oleoducto de Crudos Pesados. Currently, high global commodity prices continue to support economic growth, but the economy had an estimated growth of 2.9 percent in 2005 and is expecting similar growth of 3.0 percent in 2006, according to Economic Intelligence Unit forecasts.

El Salvador

After reaching a peace agreement in the early 1990s resolving a civil war, El Salvador implemented comprehensive structural reforms in the mid-1990s in an attempt to rebuild and stabilize the economy. These reforms included the simplification of the tax structure, reprivatization of the financial system, and financial and trade liberalization (IMF 1998). In addition, in 1993, the central bank adopted a fixed exchange rate policy with respect to the U.S. dollar to minimize exchange rate risk and to foster price stability.[7]

These structural reforms and overall political and economic stability helped bring El Salvador back into the global economy. Export growth and diversification and the growth of the maquila industries helped the economy become less dependent on coffee production.[8] Additionally, stability and comprehensive reforms have contributed slightly to improvements in per capita income and social conditions. However, even after a decade of steady growth, most measures of poverty and social conditions have not fully recovered from the deterioration of the civil war in the 1980s.

Since 1992, El Salvador's economy has enjoyed stability and a steady decline of inflation rates, from 18.5 percent in 1993 to 2.3 percent in 2000. Interest rates have remained high, however, mainly because of the lack of confidence in the fixed exchange rate regime. Interest rates declined slightly from 19 percent in 1993 to 14 percent in 2000. Remittances from abroad also increased significantly, growing approximately 155 percent from 1992 to 2000. In 2000, total remittances reached $1.75 billion, approximately 13 percent of real GDP. GDP growth averaged 6 percent between 1990 and 1995. In 1998 Hurricane Mitch caused widespread flooding and landslides, affecting agriculture, the transportation

infrastructure (mainly highways), and housing. But the economy continued growing, albeit at a slower pace, averaging 3.7 percent between 1998 and 2000.

Beginning January 1, 2001, the Salvadoran government implemented the Monetary Integration Law (Ley de Integración Monetaria), which established a fixed exchange rate of 8.75 colones per U.S. dollar and made the dollar legal tender and the only unit of account in the financial system. The colón is still considered legal tender and continues to circulate alongside the dollar, but dollars have gradually replaced colones, which are no longer printed. All financial operations are denominated in dollars, and currently the use of the colón is generally limited to some rural areas.

Unlike Ecuador, which adopted the dollar as a policy alternative to bring economic stability, El Salvador had enjoyed economic stability and low inflation rates before official dollarization (see Figures 2 and 3). (Further, El Salvador is currently one of four investment-graded countries in Latin America, a status that demonstrates the confidence of international investors.) The government decided to dollarize in an attempt to lower interest rates, increase foreign investment, improve financial conditions, and decrease transaction costs in international trade, thereby further accelerating economic growth and stability (see Towers and Borzutzky 2004). In addition, the government argued that dollarization would protect wages and savings against devaluations. Dollarization would also benefit Salvadorans living in the United States by making their remittance transfer costs cheaper.[9] Officials also pointed out that full dollarization was the logical next step, considering that historically the colón has been pegged to the dollar, especially since 1993. Moreover, the country's economy is closely linked to the United States: Two-thirds of total exports are sent to U.S. markets, and the United States is the origin of a large portion of remittances.

Right after the adoption of dollarization, El Salvador faced several severe

Real GDP Growth
Figure 3

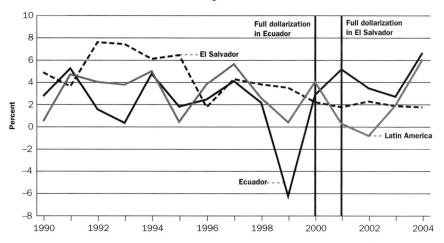

Source: World Development Indicators, World Bank

shocks, including two earthquakes, declining international coffee prices, increasing oil prices, and the slowdown of the U.S. economy. These shocks dampened economic growth and other expected benefits from full dollarization. Real GDP grew by only 1.8 percent in 2004 and has averaged less than 2 percent since 2001. Trade growth has also been sluggish, with export growth averaging only 3 percent and imports averaging 6.7 percent since 2001—a sharp contrast to the 17.5 percent export growth in 2000. Foreign investment growth has also been slow, with gross fixed capital formation increasing slightly more than 1 percent since 2001.

While economic growth has decelerated, interest rates, inflation rates, and remittances have improved since full dollarization was adopted. In 2004, lending interest rates (in foreign currency) averaged 6.3 percent, declining considerably from 11 percent in 2000.[10] Although inflation increased slightly to 4.5 percent in 2004, it has averaged around 3 percent since 2001 compared to 7.8 percent from 1992 to 2000. Remittance inflows have also improved significantly, reaching $2.55 billion

(approximately 16 percent of GDP) in 2004, according to the central bank. Economic growth is expected to increase in the coming years as the implementation of the Dominican Republic–Central American Free Trade Agreement (DR–CAFTA) and reforms to deepen the financial sector, along with prudent fiscal policies, support productivity gains and investment.[11]

Comparing Results

For Ecuador and El Salvador, the implementation of official dollarization has resulted, as expected, in lower inflation rates, lower country risk premiums, and gains in policy credibility. The expected benefits have taken longer to materialize in Ecuador than in El Salvador, however. In Ecuador, even though inflation rates started to decline in 2000, not until 2004 did the rates reach levels similar to the U.S. inflation rate. In addition, the fall in the volatility of monthly inflation in Ecuador also was noticeable only after February 2003. El Salvador, on the other hand, continued to enjoy low inflation rates, and inflation volatility declined smoothly after full dollarization.

The same picture can be drawn for country risk; in Ecuador it took eight months after President Mahuad announced full dollarization in January 2000 for international markets to show lower levels of risk premiums, which declined sharply the day that the debt was renegotiated with international organizations in September 2000. But country risk reached levels of below 1000 basis points only after May 2004.[12] In El Salvador, country risk has been below the average spread for the Latin American region since country risk for the country was introduced in May 2002 (see Figure 1).

Economic growth has been influenced heavily by internal and external conditions. In Ecuador the persistence of high oil prices has helped anchor official dollarization in the last two years, thus compensating for the lack of external financing and increases in fiscal expenditures. Higher oil exports have helped pay down public debt and stimulate the economy during a period of political instability. In El Salvador the slow recovery of the U.S. economy, political uncertainty surrounding the elections, low coffee prices, and high oil prices have decelerated economic activity. Figure 3 shows lower, but less volatile, economic growth for El Salvador in 2000 and 2004 than for Ecuador and Latin America. Under official dollarization, both economies continue to be vulnerable to external and internal shocks. But policy credibility and economic stability brought by full dollarization can encourage reforms to promote competitiveness and productivity to overcome such vulnerabilities.

Banking Systems before Official Dollarization

In Latin America, banks are the most significant institutions in the financial system, representing approximately 70 percent of total financial assets. Latin American banks, however, do not reach levels of financial deepening and development observed in developed economies. Throughout the 1960s and 1970s, banks in Ecuador and El Salvador faced a period of stability, which gave way to disruptions caused by the external debt crisis in the 1980s in Ecuador and by a civil war in El Salvador late in that decade. The economic instability, high inflation, and depreciation of the domestic currency that ensued, along with other political and external shocks, did not foster an environment of financial deepening. In this section, we will analyze the banking systems in Ecuador and El Salvador after this period of instability.

Banking Crisis in Ecuador

In Ecuador, the banking crisis of the late 1990s really began a decade earlier and had "[its] roots in a 'boom and bust' cycle in the middle of financial liberalization, coupled with lax financial surveillance and bad banking practices" (Jacome 2004, 12). De la Torre, Garcia-Saltos, and Mascaró (2001) argue that the banking crisis can be explained in three dimensions: failure to establish an effective regulatory and supervisory environment in the face of financial liberalization, a credit boom and sudden stop phenomenon, and the exacerbation of financial vulnerability during 1997 and 1998 due to lax fiscal policy and failure to introduce financial reform.

In 1994 the General Law of Financial Institutions (Ley General de Instituciones del Sistema Financiero) created the legal basis for financial liberalization, fostering financial intermediation and investment allocation. Banks could then perform dollar-denominated services, and commercial banks were now legally allowed to have offshore operations. The central bank also underwent significant reform, retaining the ability to provide monetary support to banks in liquidity and solvency troubles (see Beckerman and Solimano 2002). In addition, the law established a modern framework for the development of risk-based prudential regulations.

But the implementation of these new prudential regulations did not materialize quickly. Regulations continued to be outdated, and enforcement continued to be extremely lax, deficient, and uneven.

Monitoring difficulties and lack of information from banks, mainly from their offshore branches, limited the ability to produce an accurate assessment of the soundness of the financial system. In addition, the supervisory authority had no proper strategy or power to intervene in a troubled bank, thus restricting the use of preventive measures to avoid bankruptcies and bank failures.

With lax prudential supervision and regulation, banks increasingly performed risky transactions, encouraged by moral hazard stemming from successive bailouts granted over the 1980s. Related-party lending intensified, loan portfolios became heavily concentrated in certain economic sectors, and dollar-denominated operations increased without the proper measures to hedge currency mismatches, mainly with borrowers earning in local currency but acquiring loans in dollars.

Financial liberalization coincided with a period of foreign capital Inflows attracted by higher domestic returns in an environment of domestic macroeconomic stability. The rapid monetization of the economy brought in a sizable credit boom. Credit increased in real terms by 40 percent in 1993 and 50 percent in 1994. The increase in liquidity was encouraged by a decline in reserve requirements from 28 to 10 percent in domestic currency deposits and from 35 to 10 percent for foreign currency deposits (see Jacome 2004).

In 1995, as risky activities intensified in the banking system, Ecuador experienced a sudden stop and reversal of capital Inflows, mainly because of domestic political problems, the short but costly war with Peru, and the Mexican Tequila crisis. In addition, the continued depreciation of the currency under the new exchange rate regime created difficulties for banks with currency and maturity mismatches. In an environment of political and economic instability, residents began to shift their deposits to stronger and more stable banks and to dollar-denominated deposits. Nevertheless, the money was kept in the banking system. But the failure of two banks in 1995 and 1996 increased residents'

fears. Liquidity pressures on the banking system increased as residents began to panic, triggering deposit runs.

In early December 1998, the government passed the "AGO Law," which established a blanket guarantee through the Guarantee of Deposits Agency (Agencia de Garantia de Depósitos)(AGD), in an effort to restore a sense of stability in the banking system (see Jacome 2004). The government also included a 1 percent tax on financial transactions (debits and credits) to substitute for income tax. In an effort to avoid the tax, residents began to store money in foreign currency outside of the banking system, further hurting bank liquidity. Deposits contracted 15 and 60 percent in 1998 and 1999, respectively. However, as shown in Figure 4, bank deposits as a percentage of GDP remained at 23 percent in 1998 and 1999 because of the decline in GDP of 7.3 percent.

Since the AGD Law was not helping the banking system, the government imposed a widespread deposit freeze in March 1999. Time deposits and repurchase agreements were locked for at least one year, and savings deposits in excess of U.S. $500 and half of checking account balances were frozen for six months. Despite the deposit freeze, only three banks became insolvent and had to shut down.

An examination of banking system data shows the effects of the crisis. From 1995 to 1997, loans grew 29 percent but fell 31 percent in 1998 and 1999 (see Figure 5). Total assets also grew 29 percent from 1995 to 1997 but fell 9 and 29 percent, respectively, in 1998 and 1999. Bank assets' share in total financial assets went from 98 percent in 1997 to 77 percent in 1999, a 22 percent decline. In addition, past-due loans' performance also deteriorated quite sharply; past-due loans increased a dramatic 307.6 percent in 1999, reaching $1.1 million.

In summary, prior to official dollarization the banking system in Ecuador underwent a crisis that resulted in a reduction in the system's size (in terms of both assets and number of banks), in a deposit

Bank Deposits as a Percentage of GDP
Figure 4

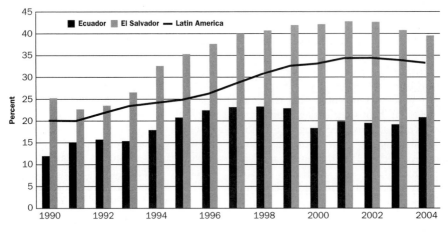

Source: Financial Structure Database, World Bank

Bank Credit to the Private Sector as a Percentage of GDP
Figure 5

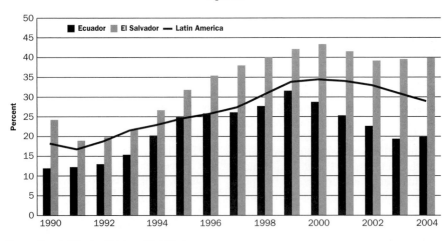

Source: Financial Structure Database, World Bank

freeze to avoid a bank run, and in a decline in banks' lending activities.

Banking Stability in El Salvador

In the first half of the 1990s, the Financial System Reform Program (Programa de Fortalecimiento y Privatización del Sistema Financiero) was initiated as part of the country's structural reform, which established a new role for the central bank; redefined monetary, credit, and exchange rate policies; readjusted the legal and institutional framework; and strengthened and privatized the banking system.[13] In 1990 the Organic Law for the Superintendence of the Financial System (Ley Orgánica de la Superintendencia del Sistema Financiero) was approved, establishing an autonomous institution to oversee banks, *financieras* (formerly known as savings and loans associations), the central bank, and other institutions of the financial system. In addition, commercial banks and *financieras* were privatized through a process that involved several stages, from analyzing each bank's loan portfolio to institutional restructuring. According to the central bank, ownership was returned to the private sector by distributing the largest banks to individual shareholders and bank employees. During the 1990s financial liberalization was consolidated by implementing laws that established the autonomy of the central bank and its limitations on public financing.

The process of financial liberalization promoted growth in the banking system. Assets rose from 27 percent of GDP in 1990 to 51 percent in 2000. In the first half of 1990s, nonperforming loans were small while indicators of liquidity, efficiency, solvency, and profitability were satisfactory. Assets performed well, and total deposits increased dramatically (see SAPRIN 2001).

In the second half of the 1990s, however, adverse economic conditions affected the performance of the banking sector. Two bank failures in 1997 and 1998 brought to light some weaknesses of the banking system and its supervision and regulation. Banco Fincomer and Insepro-Finsepro were linked to illegal transfers of funds from corporate firms to bank branches, highlighting the fact that resources could be transferred outside the surveillance of supervision and regulation.

While deposits and loans continued to grow, their growth rates declined. From rates of 19.6 percent in 1996, deposits' growth rates slowed to 5.4 and 5.1 percent in 1999 and 2000, respectively. Loan activity growth demonstrated a similar pattern, declining from 20.1 percent in 1996 to only 4.3 percent in 1999 and 1.8 percent in 2000. The performance of nonperforming loans also began to deteriorate along with asset quality.

In response, the 1999 Banking Law (Ley de Bancos) was established, bringing greater transparency in financial activities and forcing banks to monitor credit risk. The law, one of the most progressive in Central America, brought the banking system in line with internationally accepted standards.

Banks after Official Dollarization

The previous discussion raises several questions: Did the banking system introduce changes to overcome the restrictions imposed on the central bank in the role of lender of last resort? Given the expected reduction in inflation, interest rates, country risk, and volatility that ensued from dollarization, how did the banking system evolve? Did banks in fact perform better in an environment of expected economic stability? And, finally, did full dollarization help in the financial integration of the banking system with international markets?

Lender of Last Resort

In Ecuador the Economic Transformation Law that supported the implementation of full dollarization in September 2000 included changes in the role of the central bank, the development of a liquidity fund, and the modernization and tightening of banking supervision and regulation. Under the new law, the central bank is able to conduct liquidity operations with banks, including transactions in stabilization bonds with commercial banks and repurchase operations. In addition, a separate Liquidity Support Fund was established to supplement the central bank's capacity during liquidity problems (see Beckerman and Solimano 2002). Banks are required to allocate 1 percent of their deposit base to the fund.[14]

Under full dollarization, banking regulations were restructured and tightened, and regulators were given more power to take preventive measures against banks that showed signs of instability.

More stringent capital adequacy regulations (which are now much closer to Basel standards) and new credit risk centers were established to improve prudent supervision. In addition, the General Law of Financial Institutions was overhauled in 2001, including reforms such as a prohibition against related-party lending, more stringent loan-loss reserves and capital definitions and requirements, and mandatory consolidated financial reporting. These reforms improved transparency and brought the banking system closer to international standards. Deficiencies do remain, however, and while regulations were updated, actual implementation and enforcement continue to be poor (see Fitch Ratings 2003). Bank accounting standards continue to deviate from international norms while some regulations continue to be lenient, including rules for loan write-offs.

Compared to the experience in Ecuador, where full dollarization supported the banking system in its rebuilding process, full dollarization in El Salvador supported the performance of an already well-established banking system. The absence of a lender of last resort has encouraged Salvadoran banks to hold a growing proportion of their assets in highly liquid instruments. Also, banking system deposits are now insured under the Deposit Guarantee Fund (Institute de Garantia de los Depósitos) (IGD) set by the 1999 Banking Law. The IGD guarantees deposits up to U.S. $6,700, or roughly three times GDP per capita.[15] One of the main weaknesses of the fund is that it does not provide adequate coverage for the deposits that it currently insures (U.S. $2.2 billion). In case of need, it would cover only about 2 percent of the insured funds.

The Banking Environment

In Ecuador, after the banking crisis and during the initial stages of full dollarization, the government initiated an evaluation process to assess banks' solvency. External auditors determined that the government should intervene in sixteen banks,

with all but two closing soon afterward. This restructuring process removed the weakest, most problematic banks from the system. But none of the banks was exempt from the devastating impact of the crisis, and those that remained in operation were weakened by asset quality problems, liquidity pressures, and a sharp decline in the level of activity and, thus, sustainable operating profitability.[16] Consequently, immediately after dollarization, the size of the banking system (in terms of financial penetration) shrank. In 2001, total assets fell to 28.6 percent of GDP (from 38.2 percent in 2000). By 2003, total assets declined to 21.4 percent of GDP, levels similar to those in the 1980s. Since then, deposit growth and loan growth reached 86.4 percent and 111.7 percent, respectively, from 2000 to 2004 in response to the rebound in investor confidence and more robust economic growth. Nonperforming loans over total loans have declined, indicating better asset quality and more stability in the banking system.

Although prior to 2001 Salvadoran banks already operated in an environment of free capital flows and low inflation, full dollarization contributed to a reduction in banks' intermediation margins. On the deposit side, local banks compete among themselves within the domestic market. Although large banks have a comparative advantage with their expansive networks, small banks have benefited from full dollarization as their funding costs have converged with those of their larger competitors. Lower lending rates and recent depressed credit have given Salvadoran banks a comparative advantage versus other Central American banks, encouraging larger Salvadoran banks to expand their lending to neighboring countries (Honduras, Guatemala, and Nicaragua). Recent reforms to the banking law in 2003 have limited cross-border lending; however, banks are circumventing restrictions by establishing holding companies in Panama. This practice results in additional risk to the Salvadoran operations of these institutions.

As a response to lower intermediation margins, there has been a process of consolidation to allow banks to compete more effectively. Between 2000 and 2002 four mergers occurred that resulted in a high concentration: Four banks now account for more than 80 percent of the sector's assets and deposits. These banks are among the largest in Central America but are still small by international standards.

Financial Integration

Foreign bank presence in El Salvador remains negligible despite the absence of barriers to entering the market. The country has only two foreign-owned institutions that have operated for some time. It is also estimated that about fifty other foreign banks that do not have a local presence provide financing to El Salvador's private sector, on the order of $1.8 billion as of June 2002, nearly double the amount at the end of 1999 (see Fitch Ratings 2003). Ecuador has twenty-five private banks, of which two are foreign.

Overall, full dollarization helped the stabilization of the banking system in Ecuador by stopping the collapse of the economy. In 2005, despite political uncertainty, financial conditions remained stable, deposits had grown steadily over the previous four years, and banks continued to maintain high levels of liquidity and to improve asset quality. But the long-term sustainability of this policy remains uncertain as institutional weaknesses in the economy and banking system continue. In El Salvador, banks have improved their performance despite the economic deceleration, gaining competitiveness in the Central American region. The regulatory and supervisory institutions have set up regulations comparable to international standards.

Did Official Dollarization Have an Impact on Bank Performance?

To examine how full dollarization and other macroeconomic and institutional factors affected bank performance indicators such as profitability, liquidity, and asset quality, we use panel data including all banks in Ecuador and El Salvador from 1995 to 2004. Following Demirguc-Kunt and Huizinga (1999), we define bank performance Y_{it} for bank i at time t as follows:

$$(1) \quad Y_{it} = f(DOLL, MACRO_t, BANK_{it}) + \text{error}_{it},$$

where Y_{it} is the dependent variable—bank performance—measured by its profitability, loan quality, and loan growth. Profitability or before-tax profits can be decomposed as net interest income plus noninterest income minus overhead costs minus loan-loss provisions, usually as a ratio of total assets. The indicator for loan quality is loan-loss provisions as a ratio of total loans (LLP), and, for liquidity, net loans as a ratio of total deposits.

The explanatory variables are a dollarization dummy indicating when the country implemented official dollarization. We also include macroeconomic variables reflecting the state of the economy, including economic growth rates, inflation rates, interest rates, gross domestic product (GDP) per capita, and trade as a percentage of GDP. As indicators of financial structure, we use credit to the private sector as a percentage of GDP, bank deposits as a percentage of GDP, and banks' asset share in the banking system. Another set of variables is specific to banks' activity. These include loan-to-asset ratios and equity-to-asset ratio indicators of capital strength as well as bank size variables such as individual banks' share of loans and deposits as a portion of loans and deposits in the banking system. Country and year dummies are included to capture idiosyncratic effects. These bank activity variables are lagged one period to prevent simultaneity, in particular because balance-sheet variables refer to year-end balances.

The data set, published by Latin Finance, includes information from all banks from 1995 to 2004 in Ecuador and El Salvador. Macroeconomic variables come from International Financial Statistics published by the IMF, financial structure

Regressions on Bank Performance Indicators for Ecuador and El Salvador, 1995–2004
Table 1

Independent Variables	Loan Quality: Loan-Loss Provisions	Liquidity: Net Loans/Deposits	Profitability: Before-Tax Profits
Dollarization dummy	0.1532**	−2.1611**	−0.168
	(0.0772)	(0.8520)	(0.1727)
Macroeconomic variables			
Economic growth	−0.0106***	−0.4524***	0.017*
	(0.0035)	(0.1704)	(0.0097)
GDP per capita	−0.0003	−0.0047	0.0010
	(0.0003)	(0.0040)	(0.0010)
Inflation	−0.0010**	0.0547***	0.0033
	(0.00068)	(0.0206)	(0.0030)
Trade as a percent of GDP	0.0039**	0.2588***	−0.0096
	(0.0016)	(0.0952)	(0.0066)
Interest rate	−0.0014**	0.0645*	0.0095
	(0.0005)	(0.0355)	(0.0092)
Financial structure variables			
Bank assets/central bank assets			−1.676
			(1.9096)
Private credit by banks as a percent of GDP		−58.8336**	
		(22.6876)	
Bank deposits as a percent of GDP	0.0111		
	(0.6214)		
Bank variables			
Asset share in total banks	0.0006	−0.0213	0.0003
	(0.0016)	(0.0119)	(0.0013)
Equity-to-loan ratio $(t-1)$	−0.00002	0.0004	0.00004***
	(0.000016)	(0.00048)	(0.00002)
Number of observations	391	391	391

Notes: The table does not include country dummies and year dummies. *, **, and *** indicate significance at the 10, 5, and 1 percent levels, respectively.
Source: Authors' regressions using data from Latin Finance, the IMF, Banco Central del Ecuador, Banco Central de Reserva de El Salvador, and the World Bank

variables come from the Financial Structure Database of the World Bank (2004), and data on dollarization ratios come from the Web sites of the central banks of Ecuador and El Salvador.

Table 1 shows the results of the regression for loan-loss provisions (or loan quality), liquidity, and profitability. As expected, the coefficient of the dollarization dummy is positive and significant in the explanation of loan quality. Given the absence of a lender of last resort, banks need to hold adequate reserves to respond to any sudden increase in nonperforming loans. Trade as a percentage of GDP has a direct relationship with loan provisions, indicating that banks may allocate more reserves for loans given an increase in the openness of the economy that could bring more fluctuations as a result of external shocks. The coefficient on the interest rate is negative and significant, suggesting that an increase in the interest rate could reduce the demand for loans. Economic growth is significant with a negative sign, meaning that economic growth is an incentive to decrease loan-loss provisions. Inflation is also significant with a negative sign; a possible explanation is that unexpected inflation will benefit borrowers and reduce the incentive to increase loan-loss provisions. Relatively larger banks will have a greater loan-loss provision ratio.

The second column of the table shows the results for liquidity, which is net loans over deposits. The dollarization dummy has a negative and significant coefficient; as expected, official dollarization will restrict liquidity in the overall economy, and banks need to make reserves to support their liquidity needs. In this regression, macroeconomic variables and financial structure indicators are also significant. Economic growth has a negative and significant coefficient, showing a direct relationship between economic growth and liquidity. Inflation and bank liquidity have an inverse and significant relationship: Higher inflation increases the demand for money (for example, less deposits) competing with banks. In the case of trade as a percentage of GDP, the relationship with bank liquidity is also indirect: The more open an economy is, the higher the demand for cash for international transactions, competing with bank liquidity.

The regression on profitability indicates that neither the official dollarization dummy, macroeconomic variables (except for economic growth), nor financial

structure variables explain bank profitability. Lagged variables that are specific to the bank—such as the ratio of equity to assets and to loans, indicators of bank solvency—are positive and significant in the explanation of bank profitability. This result is similar to that found in the general literature on bank performance. Economic growth has a direct relation with profitability, as expected.

Conclusion

In both Ecuador and El Salvador, the banking system has initially benefited from the implementation of full dollarization. Even though the two countries adopted the U.S. dollar as their country's currency for entirely different reasons, both countries have experienced improvements in banking regulations and in the overall stability of the banking systems. According to our estimations, official dollarization has played a significant role in improving bank liquidity and asset quality. Macroeconomic variables and financial structure indicators have also been relevant in explaining bank liquidity and loan quality, and bank profitability has responded to variables that are bank specific.

While it is still too early to determine whether these initial benefits of dollarization will be sustainable in the long term, both countries have been able to modernize and improve upon the overall safety and soundness of the banking system.

Endnotes

[1] In this article, the terms "official" and "full" dollarization will be used interchangeably.

[2] Minda (2005) points out that full dollarization affects small countries and territories; a majority are insular (such as the Marshall Islands and Micronesia) and are closely connected to another country (Guam, Puerto Rico, San Marino).

[3] See the dollarization box on page 283 for a description of the types and measures of dollarization.

[4] These norms reduce banks' profits, but banks have to face this level of protection voluntarily given that full dollarization has removed currency risk.

[5] Duncan (2003) notes that in Peru, a highly dollarized economy, currency exchange transactions represented 2.1 percent of the banks' revenues.

[6] The indicator for country risk is the interest rate spread in basis points between Ecuador's emerging market bond index and thirty-year U.S. treasury instruments.

[7] Even before 1993, the historical preference was a fixed exchange rate with respect to the U.S. dollar, in which the rate changed only during the period of the civil war from 2.5 colones per U.S. dollar to 8 colones per U.S. dollar. In 1993, the exchange rate became fixed at 8.75 colones per U.S. dollar. See IMF (1998) for more details.

[8] Maquila industries are plants that assemble imported materials and parts and re-export the finished product to the original market.

[9] There would be no foreign exchange transaction cost associated with sending remittances after dollarization.

[10] The interest rate for loans in domestic currency was 14 percent in 2000.

[11] The Central American countries involved in DR-CAFTA are Costa Rica, El Salvador, Guatemala, Honduras, and Nicaragua.

[12] JPMorgan raised Ecuadorian debt from underweight to market weight, despite political uncertainty. In addition, the government was negotiating a new standby agreement with the IMF.

[13] See the historical outline at the central bank of El Salvador's Web site, www.bcr.gob.sv.

[14] This fund is in addition to the reserve requirement of 8 percent.

[15] Offshore deposits are not insured.

[16] Most banks remained in profit thanks to hefty gains on foreign currency positions when the sucre devalued and to inflation adjustments, which were used to boost capital and increase loan-loss reserves (see Fitch Ratings 2003).

References

Beckerman, Paul, and Andres Solimano, eds. 2002. *Crisis and dollarization in Ecuador: Stability, growth and social equity.* Washington, D.C.: World Bank.

Calvo, Guillermo A. 2001. Capital markets and the exchange rate with special reference to the dollarization debate in Latin America. *Journal of Money, Credit, and Banking* 33, no. 2, pt. 2:312–34.

Chang, Roberto, and Andrés Velasco. 2000. Financial fragility and the exchange rate regime. *Journal of Economic Theory* 92, no. 1:1–34.

De la Torre, Augusto, Roberto Garcia-Saltos, and Yira Mascaró. 2001. Banking, currency and debt meltdown: Ecuador crisis in the late 1990s. Washington, D.C.: World Bank manuscript.

Demirguc-Kunt, Asli, and Harry Huizinga. 1999. Determinants of commercial bank interest margins and profitability: Some international evidence. *World Bank Economic Review* 13, no. 2:379–408.

Duncan, Roberto. 2003. Exploring the implications of official dollarization on macroeconomic volatility. Central Bank of Chile Working Paper 200, February.

Edwards, Sebastian. 1995. *Crisis and reform in Latin America: From despair to hope.* Washington, D.C.: World Bank.

Edwards, Sebastian, and I. Igal Magendzo. 2006. Strict dollarization and economic performance: An empirical investigation. *Journal of Money, Credit, and Banking* 38, no. 1:269–82.

Fitch Ratings. 2003. Country Reports, Financial Institutions. *The Ecuadorian prudential regulations* and *The Ecuadorian banking system: An overview,* January 31. <www.fitchratings.com>.

Gale, Douglas, and Xavier Vives. 2002. Dollarization, bailouts, and the stability of the banking system. *Quarterly Journal of Economics* 117, no. 2:467–502.

Guide, Anne-Marie, David Hoelscher, Alan Ize, David Marston, and Gianni De Nicoló. 2004. Financial stability in dollarized economies. International Monetary Fund Occasional Paper 230.

International Monetary Fund. 1998. El Salvador: Recent economic developments. Staff country report 98/32, April.

Jacome, Luis. 2004. The late 1990s financial crisis in Ecuador: Institutional weaknesses, fiscal rigidities, and financial dollarization at work. International Monetary Fund Working Paper WP/04/12, January.

Minda, Alexandre. 2005. Official dollarization: A last resort solution to financial stability in Latin America? Groupment de Recherches Economiques et Sociales Working Paper 2, January.

Moreno-Villalaz, Juan Luis. 1999. Lessons from the monetary experience of Panama:

A dollar economy with financial integration. *Cato Journal* 18, no. 30:421–39.

Structural Adjustment Participatory Review International Network (SAPRIN). 2001. The liberalization of the financial system in El Salvador: Executive summary. <http://www.saprin.org/elsalvador/research/els_sum_financial_sys.pdf> (September 11, 2006).

Towers, Marcia, and Silvia Borzutzky. 2004. The socio-economic implications of dollarization in El Salvador. *Latin American Politics and Society* 46, no. 3:29–54.

World Bank. 2004. Financial structure database. <www.worldbank.org/research/projects/finstructure/index.htm> (September 11, 2006).

Discussion Questions

VII

1. Does the exchange rate regime matter for inflation and growth?

2. Why is credibility important to maintain a fixed exchange rate?

3. What is the primary complaint the U.S. has against China's fixed exchange rate?

4. If China floats its currency, will the U.S. trade deficit fall?

5. Is a floating exchange rate ideal for all countries?

6. Under what conditions are floating exchange rates desirable to absorb adverse external macroeconomic shocks?

7. How should a country with a fixed exchange rate transition to a floating exchange rate?

8. At what speed should the transition from a fixed exchange rate to a floating rate occur?

9. What is the difference between dollarization and a fixed exchange rate regime?

10. Why did Ecuador and El Salvador dollarize?

Europe and the Euro Zone

VIII

On January 1999, the European Union (EU) took the unprecedented step of adopting a new currency, the euro. Euro notes and coins did not circulate until January 2002. The introduction of the euro was a success, however, during the few years the value of the euro steadily declined against the U.S. dollar. For the past five years the euro has gained strength against the dollar, and since February 2008 the euro has traded over $1.50. This section investigates the relative success of the euro since its inception and the economic success of euro-area countries compared to the U.S. Proponents of the European Monetary Union (EMU) have long argued that as countries become more integrated, lower transactions costs and greater competition will boost economic growth. The last article examines this issue.

"The Euro: Ever More Global" by Bertuch-Samuels and Ramlogan compares the international use of the euro compared to the U.S. dollar. While the success of the euro is unprecedented, the euro still is primarily used by countries that have ties to the EU and the CFA franc zone in Africa. The article points out that still two thirds of global foreign reserve holdings are U.S. dollar denominated while one fourth are euro denominated. However, in private international financial transactions such as international bonds and notes, the euro has surpassed the U.S. dollar, and in international banking the euro is catching up to the U.S. dollar. The authors argue that greater use of the euro as an international currency has been influenced by the relative size and openness of the EU, the ECB's credibility in maintaining price stability, and the existence of well-developed and integrated capital markets.

Jason Saving's article "Integration and Globalization: The European Bellwether" focuses on the benefits and costs of EU integration and the relative success of an integrated EU to the U.S. In productivity and unemployment rates, the EU (15 countries) has lagged behind the U.S. For example, the EU post-war average annual productivity rate is 1.4% compared to 2.5% for the U.S. Savings argues that one reason for the relative poor performance of the EU compared to the U.S. is globalization. Inflexible labor markets and government policies (such as high tax rates) hinder the EU's competitiveness at a global level.

The Euro: Ever More Global

25

AXEL BERTUCH-SAMUELS
AND PARMESHWAR RAMLOGAN

More than eight years ago, the euro was launched amid enormous hopes and expectations about its future international role. Some even speculated that it might someday supplant the U.S. dollar as the most important international currency. There is no question its introduction was an unqualified technical success. The euro has quickly and firmly established itself as the world's second most important international currency. Today, its international prominence far surpasses not only that of the legacy European currencies the euro replaced, but also that of the pound sterling and the Japanese yen, the other main international currencies. And even though the European Central Bank (ECB) is not actively seeking to promote the euro's use abroad, its role continues to grow.

An international currency is one that is used by residents both outside and inside the country of issue. In contrast, a domestic currency is used only inside the country of issue. In the case of the euro, international use would mean use by residents outside the countries comprising the euro area. On the plus side, having a strong international currency confers political and economic advantages on the issuing country or group of countries. Politically, the country or group gains international prestige and its global influence expands. Economic benefits include lower transaction costs and interest rates and higher profitability of financial institutions, resulting from increased activity and efficiency in domestic capital markets; the ability to finance current account deficits in the country's own currency, thus avoiding the need to accumulate foreign reserves; and seigniorage revenue from the country's issue of non-interest-bearing claims on itself in exchange for goods and services.

But internationalization of the currency also carries risks and responsibilities. Sound macroeconomic policies to maintain price and exchange rate stability will be crucial. But even with sound policies, the country becomes more exposed to volatile capital flows that could generate financial and macroeconomic instability and constrain policy choices. At the same time, specification of a monetary target becomes more difficult because part of the currency is held abroad, which complicates the conduct of monetary policy.

How the Euro Is Currently Used

The euro's advance as an international currency has not been even. From a functional perspective, it has made the most progress in international financial transactions—particularly as a currency in which international debt securities are denominated—and the least progress in international trade transactions. From a geographical perspective, the euro's role as an international currency is still confined largely to countries that have regional and political ties to the euro area, including

European Union (EU) members that have not adopted the euro, EU accession countries, and the CFA franc zone in Africa. Some may argue that the euro's limited geographical role means it is still not in the same class as the dollar.

So how does current use of the euro as an international currency compare with use of the dollar? In *official* use, roughly one-third of countries that peg their currency in one form or another use the euro as their anchor currency. They comprise mostly non–euro area EU members, EU accession or potential accession countries, and French-speaking African countries. Most of the remaining two-thirds—in Asia, Africa, the Middle East, and Latin America—use the dollar as their anchor currency. Reflecting this, at the end of September 2006, dollar-denominated foreign exchange reserves comprised almost two-thirds of total world holdings of official foreign exchange reserves for which the currency composition is known (see Chart 1). Euro-denominated reserves comprised one-fourth of the total

whereas yen- and sterling-denominated reserves together comprised only 7 percent. The euro's share has risen at the expense of the dollar and the yen. Developing countries hold a larger share of their reserves in euros than do industrial countries, reflecting the dominance of euro reserves in countries neighboring the euro area and in French-speaking Africa.

In *private* use, the euro has surpassed the dollar as the most important currency of issue for international bonds and notes (defined as foreign-currency issues and domestic-currency issues targeted at non-residents). Indeed, net issues in euros have risen faster than issues in other currencies, and by end-September 2006, euro issues comprised nearly half the outstanding global stock of international bonds and notes (see Chart 2). In central Europe and the Baltic states, 83 percent of outstanding international bonds, on average, were denominated in euros at the end of 2005, whereas in Asia and Latin America issues in euros remain very small.

Coming in Second for Reserves
While the use of the euro in foreign exchange reserves has increased everywhere in the world, much of the rise has taken place in countries with ties to the euro area.
(percent of total allocated reserves)
Chart 1

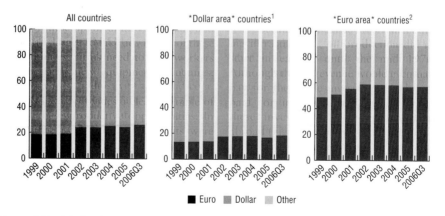

Sources: IMF and Lim (2006).
[1]Asia plus Western Hemisphere plus other countries that largely peg to the dollar.
[2]Countries around the euro area plus several countries in Africa.

Taking the Lead on Bonds
**The euro has experienced phenomenal growth as a
currency of issue for international bonds and notes.
(percent of total amount of international bonds and notes outstanding)**
Chart 2

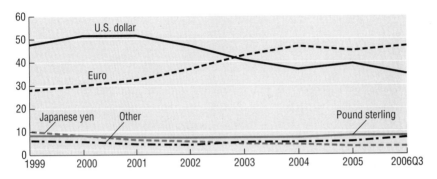

Source: Bank for International Settlements.

In *international banking,* 39 percent of all loans and 28 percent of all deposits were denominated in euros at end-June 2006, compared with 41 percent and 48 percent, respectively, denominated in dollars. Again, most transactions involved the non–euro area countries in Europe; the euro is not used much in international banking outside Europe. In foreign exchange markets, the euro is currently the second most widely traded currency after the dollar, and euro-dollar the most frequently traded currency pair, suggesting that the euro is a significant vehicle currency in foreign exchange transactions. Limited invoicing data available from the ECB indicate that the euro is the most important currency for invoicing trade between euro area and non–euro area countries in Europe, but that it is rarely used in international trade transactions outside the euro area (see Chart 3). This may reflect, in part, the fact that trade in commodities is traditionally invoiced in dollars.

In many countries surrounding the euro area, the euro is also used alongside or in place of the national currency—what is called *euroization.* This growing trend is evident for all the functions of money: as a means of payment (cash and credit), as a store of value (bank deposits), and as a unit of account (loan contracts). It is not surprising that this is happening. Many countries in eastern and southeastern Europe are aiming for EU membership (which entails adopting the euro once certain criteria are fulfilled), and loans in euros often carry lower interest rates. But the largely unhedged borrowing and lending in euros have made these countries more vulnerable to swings in investor sentiment, not least because they expose residents to foreign exchange risks.

Factors Influencing Use of the Euro

The euro's role as an international currency is shaped largely by the following four factors:

Economic Size and Openness

The larger and more dynamic an economy, the greater the potential global economic influence it wields, in part because economic size and openness are highly correlated with capital and trade flows. With a population larger than that

Not Much of a Trade Impact
Use of the euro for trade remains modest outside its zone of influence.
(euro's use as a percent of total trade)
Chart 3

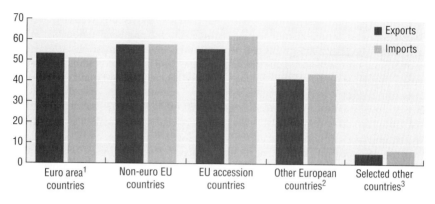

Sources: European Central Bank; and IMF staff calculations.
[1]Selected countries
[2]FYR Macedonia and Ukraine.
[3]Australia, Indonesia, Japan, Korea, Pakistan, and Thailand. Data for these countries refer to 2003.

of the United States, and an aggregate economy that is relatively open and almost as large (or potentially larger when the entire EU is considered), the euro area is well placed to forge a major international role for the euro. However, the euro area's economic growth has lagged that of the rest of the world, averaging only 1.4 percent during 2003–05 compared with 5.7 percent elsewhere. Higher growth would boost the attractiveness of the euro area as an investment destination, as well as confidence in the euro area economies and in the euro, and would likely lead to larger capital inflows of a longer-term nature. Policies that strengthen the foundations for economic growth, including a sustained qualitative improvement of public sector balance sheets and structural reforms to raise productivity and labor use, will also matter.

Price and Exchange Rate Stability

The greater the issuing country's price and exchange rate stability, the lower the cost and risk in financial markets and the higher the confidence in the currency. The Maastricht Treaty has given the ECB

a firm mandate and operational independence to maintain price stability, and the ECB's track record has been strong. Inflation and inflation expectations in the euro area have been low and stable, and exchange rate volatility has also been low. The euro itself has facilitated the conduct of monetary policy and the maintenance of price stability by stimulating money market development.

Financial Market Development and Integration

The existence of well-developed and integrated domestic financial markets is critical. Such markets provide liquidity; lower transaction costs; reduce uncertainty and risk and, hence, hedging costs; and lead to lower interest rates. They also boost productivity and economic growth and strengthen confidence in the euro. All these factors influence the degree to which the euro is used as a global currency for saving, investing, and borrowing.

Traditionally, euro area financial systems have been largely bank-based, with euro area financial markets less developed and less integrated than those of the United States. However, European financial systems have been undergoing a steady transformation over the past two decades—a process that accelerated with the euro's introduction and the adoption of the Financial Services Action Plan (FSAP) in March 2000. The plan's objective is to create a single market for financial services by removing regulatory and market barriers to the cross-border provision of financial services, thereby encouraging the free movement of capital within the EU.

The ongoing development and integration of European financial markets manifests itself in several ways. First, corporate and government bond markets in Europe have expanded significantly and become much more liquid since the euro's introduction. Second, there is evidence of increased integration of stock markets within the euro area. Co-movements of stock prices have increased, the share of Europe-wide funds in the aggregate equity market has risen substantially, and market participants are paying more attention to industry and company factors and less to country-specific factors in valuing stocks. Third, sovereign interest rate differentials across euro area countries have come down. Fourth, financial innovation is progressing rapidly. Market infrastructures are being transformed, the range and complexity of financial instruments have increased, and trading volumes have expanded.

Even so, European financial markets are not yet fully integrated. The markets for debt securities and retail finance remain fragmented, the commercial paper market is underdeveloped, and national stock markets are not sufficiently harmonized. Several obstacles to greater financial market integration persist. First, the legal systems governing securities issuance are not standardized across countries, leading to a heterogeneity of securities that are not readily interchangeable. Second, securities clearing and settlement systems vary from country to country. As a result, accounting and other business conventions are different and cross-border transaction costs are relatively high. Third,

differences in tax structures, consumer protection, and commercial law still discourage cross-border financial investments. Fourth, the segmented supervisory framework hinders cross-border optimization of banks' operations and is not cost-efficient. Over time, the full implementation of the FSAP should help remove these obstacles and contribute to a much more efficient and integrated pan-European financial market.

Habit and Inertia

Economies of scale increase efficiency and lower transaction costs, and the convenience and availability of a wider range of financial market instruments provide strong incentives for economic agents to continue to use the incumbent dominant currency. For example, the pound sterling continued to be the primary world currency in the first half of the 20th century, long after Britain had lost its 19th-century status as the world's leading military and economic power. The dollar gradually replaced sterling as the main international currency, becoming the dominant currency only after the Second World War, when the stability of the pound had been seriously undermined and New York's financial markets had developed sufficiently to rival London's. From this perspective, it will take a long time before the euro becomes a truly viable alternative to the dollar.

What the Future May Hold

If the euro is to become a truly global currency, it will need to extend the frontiers of its international use beyond the immediate vicinity of the euro area. The ability of the euro to rise to this challenge will depend in large part on the extent to which structural and other impediments to economic growth and financial market development in Europe are overcome. The ability of Europe to speak increasingly with one voice in the international arena, including on international financial issues, will also be important.

A promising sign for the euro is that net foreign capital inflows into the euro area have risen since its introduction, reflected in a more than doubling of the stock of net assets held by nonresidents between 1999 and the end of 2006. The increase was particularly rapid during 2002–04, when net inflows to the euro area grew faster than net inflows to the United States. These trends may reflect exchange rate developments (the euro appreciated against the dollar during 2002–06, except for a break in 2005) but may also indicate that the euro area remains a competitive investment destination. The enactment of the U.S. Sarbanes-Oxley Act in 2002—particularly Section 404, which requires certification of internal controls—has probably made it less attractive for foreign companies to list their stocks in U.S. capital markets. Evidence of this is an increase in the number of foreign companies delisting their shares from U.S. stock exchanges, a decline in the number of initial public offerings (IPOs) in the United States by foreign firms, and the fact that London's stock exchange has overtaken New York's as the location of choice for IPOs by foreign firms. There has also been an increase in IPO activity in continental European stock exchanges, especially in the alternative exchanges for smaller companies (this is also the case in the United Kingdom). If the United Kingdom decides to join the euro area and European stock exchanges consolidate, this could further boost liquidity in European capital markets to the detriment of U.S. capital markets.

Two other developments could influence the euro's future role. The first is the extent to which global imbalances will adjust through changes in the dollar exchange rate and a shift in global asset allocation. There is a large body of research on this issue. For example, recent editions of the IMF's *World Economic Outlook* and *Global Financial Stability Report* examine alternative scenarios of gradual and abrupt exchange rate adjustment, and the conditions and policies under which each of these scenarios is likely to materialize (IMF, 2005 and 2006). There is a consensus that adjustment of global imbalances

will involve efforts to rebalance global saving, investment, and consumption and that there are several ways in which this can come about. The question is to what extent and how fast the adjustment will take place. Global asset allocation preferences are crucial in this debate. The gradual adjustment scenario depends partly on the willingness of foreigners to continue to purchase U.S. assets. A sudden shift in portfolio preferences away from U.S. assets could precipitate a sharp deterioration in the dollar, altering relative confidence in the euro and the dollar and boosting the euro's use as an international currency at the expense of the dollar. But a more gradual correction of current account imbalances that avoids a sudden and substantial depreciation of the dollar is unlikely to significantly affect the euro's international role.

According to U.S. treasury data, investors from Asian countries are by far the largest foreign holders of U.S. treasury securities (57 percent at end-October 2006), followed by those from European countries (21 percent). Oil-exporting countries account for a relatively small share (less than 5 percent). But investors from European countries are the biggest foreign holders of U.S. equities (53 percent in June 2005), followed by those from Western Hemisphere countries (26 percent) and Asian countries (18 percent). Investor behavior in Asia and Europe thus appears to be a key factor in the continued strong demand for dollar assets. This demand mirrors the strength of the U.S. economy, the depth and liquidity of U.S. capital markets, and interest rate differentials. The willingness of public and private investors in these two regions to continue to hold dollar assets if the risk of a substantial dollar appreciation intensifies will be crucial for orderly global adjustment and the euro's international role.

The second development is China's and India's continued rapid economic growth and the accumulation of foreign reserves by Asian countries. The rise of these two economies would reduce the relative global importance and influence of the euro area and shift trade and capital transactions to the Chinese and Indian currencies. But it is not certain that international usage of these two currencies will grow over the foreseeable future at a pace commensurate with the growth of the real economy. Thus, the important question is what direction China's and India's increased participation in world trade and financial markets is likely to take. And because Asian countries hold a substantial portion of global official reserves, their reaction to a potential continued depreciation of the dollar will also matter greatly.

References:

Bertuch-Samuels, Axel, 2006, "The Role of the Euro as an International Currency," in Conference on, Experience with, and Preparations for the Euro, ed. by Franz Naushnigg and Paul Schmidt (Vienna, Austria: Oesterreichische Nationalbank).

International Monetary Fund, 2005, "How Will Global Imbalances Adjust?" World Economic Outlook, September, Chapter 1, Appendix 1.2 (Washington).

———, 2006, Global Financial Stability Report, September (Washington).

Lim, Ewe-Ghee, 2006, "The Euro's Challenge to the Dollar: Different Views from Economists and Evidence from COFER (Currency Composition of Foreign Exchange Reserves) and Other Data," IMF Working Paper No. 06/153 (Washington: International Monetary Fund).

U.S. Treasury, 2006, Treasury Bulletin, December (Washington).

26

Integration and Globalization:
The European Bellwether

JASON L. SAVING

The European Union owes its very existence to the economic integration that defines today's increasingly global economy. From the ashes of World War II, six core European nations forged a coal-and-steel community designed to foster industrial competitiveness. Over time, the nations realized that a common market would best promote European growth, and the mission gradually broadened to include the general goal of ever-closer union.

Successive waves of integration raised membership to 15 countries a decade ago, then to 25 today, with Turkey and several other nations eager to join in the near future *(see map)*. Along the way, Europe has seen significant increases in its standard of living as it became economically freer and more integrated.

Creating a common market has brought benefits. At the same time, it has meant exposure to worldwide competition, which creates difficulties for nations with high taxes and inflexible labor markets. EU members maintain less competitive economic policies than the United States, and globalization has exacerbated the consequences of these policies for their economies. Some analysts question whether further economic liberalization offers the best path to future prosperity, advocating instead greater policy coordination to bring taxes, regulations and other measures into even closer alignment.

Should EU members integrate their economies in a way that resists global economic pressures? Or should they embrace globalization through greater economic freedom, with each nation vying to compete effectively in the world economy? As technology and freer trade integrate economies, the EU stands at a policy crossroads. Two conflicting strategies of integration are facing off to see which will guide Europe's future. The stakes are nothing less than the continued advance of globalization and its consequences for national and regional economies.

Integration's Costs and Benefits

Economic integration is the process through which nations lessen the economic significance of their borders. It can take the form of pacts—such as the North American Free Trade Agreement and the World Trade Organization—that reduce tariffs and other barriers, letting goods and services move more freely. It can take the form of investor protections that foster capital mobility or visa programs that help firms find willing workers. When goods, services, capital and labor can move to where they are most efficiently employed, economies can grow at faster rates than they otherwise could.[1]

But increasing mobility for goods, labor and capital entails greater exposure to global economic pressures. When nations in a common market choose different labor policies, for example, those who receive government benefits have an incentive to

The European Union Today

Joined 1973–1995
Joined 2004

Iceland

Sweden
Finland

Norway

Estonia
Russia

Denmark
Latvia

Lithuania

Ireland

United
Kingdom

Belarus

Netherlands

Belgium
Germany
Poland

Luxembourg
Ukraine

Czech
Republic
Slovakia
Moldova

France
Austria

Switzerland
Hungary

Slovenia
Romania

Croatia
Bosnia
and
Herze-
Govina
Serbia
and
Montenegro

Portugal

Spain
Bulgaria

Macedonia

Italy
Albania

Greece
Turkey

Cyprus

Malta

move from less generous nations to more generous ones. When tax policies differ, workers and businesses have an incentive to move from high-tax nations to low-tax ones.[2] High-tax, high-benefit nations find themselves in a squeeze, simultaneously facing increases in the amount they must spend and reductions in the tax revenue available to meet their obligations. The more economically integrated the world, the greater this penalty becomes because firms,

workers and capital can search for greener pastures more readily than ever before.

Does this apply to Europe? Let's look at the competitiveness of Europe's 15-nation core compared with the U.S. (*Chart 1*). The Fraser Institute compiles an annual ranking of economic freedom, based on such factors as size of government, legal structure and security of property rights, access to sound money, freedom to exchange with foreigners, and regulation of credit, labor

EU Economies Trail in Economic Freedom
U.S. and EU-15 economic freedom
Chart 1

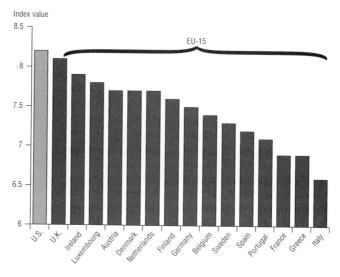

Source: The Fraser Institute.

and business. The latest readings show that the United States eclipses any current EU member. Past years also reflect this pattern. While some economists may question the precise placement of particular countries, few would dispute the overall conclusion that Europe's economy is less free than the United States'.

The consequences are evident in broad measures of economic performance. Over the past decade, for example, the U.S. economy has grown at an annual rate of 3 percent—relatively healthy by postwar standards (*Chart 2*). In contrast, the EU has grown by barely 2 percent a year, a rate disappointing to economists and policymakers alike. The U.S. doesn't grow faster than every European nation in every year, but it does better than most EU members most of the time.

The unemployment rate also shows America's edge in economic performance. In the U.S., it has hovered around 5 percent for most of the decade, a rate many economists consider close to full employment

(*Chart 3*). In contrast, Europe's relatively inflexible labor markets have produced an unemployment rate 3 to 5 percentage points higher. Unemployment rates in France and Germany remain around 10 percent, despite several initiatives over the past few years to deal with the issue.

Perhaps the single most telling statistic is productivity—the amount of output per hour worked. Largely dependent on the extent to which government policies foster a dynamic economy, productivity has grown by roughly 2.5 percent annually in the U.S. over the past decade but only 1.4 percent in Europe (*Chart 4*).

It has not always been so. In the heady days of postwar reconstruction and the formation of the common market, some economists spoke of a permanent productivity advantage for Europe. Now, an emerging consensus holds that labor and tax policies have combined with the relatively sluggish introduction of new technologies to produce a sustained productivity deficit for the European economies.

EU Has Relatively Low Growth
U.S. and EU-15 real output
Chart 2

Source: Organization for Economic Cooperation and Development.

EU Has Relatively High Unemployment
U. S. and EU-15 unemployment
Chart 3

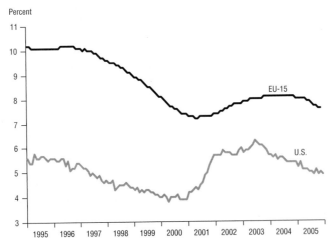

Sources: Bureau of Labor Statistics (U.S.), EuroStat (EU).

Commentators may point to the current economic performance of France and Germany as proof of the "Eurosclerosis" that besets the continent's major economies, but a snapshot in time can't tell the whole story of economic fundamentals or future prospects. It is the sustained differences that suggest something more fundamental—

EU Has Low Productivity Growth
U.S. and EU-15 productivity
Chart 4

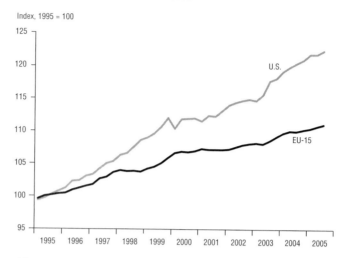

Index, 1995 = 100

Sources: Bureau of Economic Analysis (U.S.); Statistical Office of European Communities (EU); Haver Analytics.

namely, a gap in competitiveness—has been at work here.

Globalization and Growth

Europe once kept pace with the United States. Tracking GDP back to the early 1970s shows that Europe managed to keep up with the U.S. until diverging markedly in the 1980s (*Chart 5*). This raises an interesting question. If more competitive economic policies enabled the U.S. to outperform Europe in the 1980s and 1990s, why didn't they also enable us to outperform Europe before then?

The answer boils down to one word: globalization.

In earlier decades, the world simply wasn't as global as it is today. The consequences of high taxes and inflexible labor markets weren't especially severe in the low-tech, low-mobility 1960s and 1970s. As globalization heated up in the 1980s and 1990s, the cost of these policy decisions—in lost output, slower job creation and forgone productivity—became plain for all to see.

Empirical evidence supports this globalization story. The U.S. leads all 25 EU members in the Harvard Business School rankings of national policies that foster innovation (*Chart 6A*). The entire EU, on the other hand, does worse than the U.S. on the World Bank's measure of labor-market policies that inhibit growth (*Chart 6B*). Business-climate indicators paint a similar picture: For example, an entrepreneur can create a new U.S. firm in five days, but it requires an average of 37 days to start one in the EU. Such data indicate the U.S. should participate more fully in the global economy, and a globalization index devised by A.T. Kearney and *Foreign Policy* magazine does indeed show the U.S. ahead of all but one EU member (*Chart 6C*).

The underlying message is as simple as it is accurate: Nations that offer more competitive economic environments will reap greater benefits from a more open world economy.

Globalization places a premium on economic freedom and gives nations greater incentive to engage in policy competition aimed at liberalizing their economies. But

Europe Didn't Always Lag the U.S.
U.S. and EU-15 real output
Chart 5

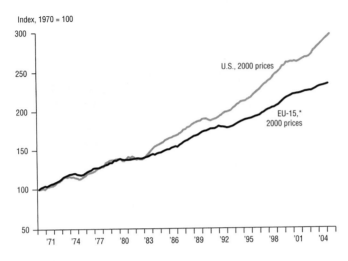

Index, 1970 = 100

U.S., 2000 prices

EU-15,*
2000 prices

'71 '74 '77 '80 '83 '86 '89 '92 '95 '98 '01 '04

* Purchasing power parity.
Source: Organization for Economic Cooperation and Development.

some worry that policy competition has gone too far. A recent report from the Organization for Economic Cooperation and Development, for example, concludes that the developed world should eliminate the "harmful tax competition" that tempts firms to move in search of better business climates. A few months ago, the finance minister of Germany's new coalition government echoed this concern when he urged the 10 newest EU members to raise taxes in the name of fairness.

Can economics contemplate a means to thwart cross-border policy competition? Yes. A federation could impose minimum tax rates and labor standards—or even mandate a single set of tax rates and labor standards—so no nation could "unfairly" undercut another and "poach" workers and businesses.[3] Under this view, Europe would need an integration that discourages rather than encourages further liberalization.

At times, the EU has done exactly that. In the mid-1990s, Sweden had to raise its farm subsidies as a condition for EU entry. In early 2004, the EU forced the Czech Republic to adopt labor-market regulations the country deemed onerous. And in January 2006, Poland fought a pitched battle with European leaders to keep its tax rates below what EU leaders wanted. In each case, countries shared the goal of binding economies together but diverged over the terms.

Some analysts have cast the great continental debate as a contest between Europhiles desperate to bind EU countries together and Euroskeptics determined to maintain national sovereignty. But integration per se need not be the issue. After all, a uniformly low-tax Europe with flexible labor markets would be just as integrated as a Europe with uniformly high tax rates and inflexible labor markets. The key question centers on the kind of integration Europe ought to undertake. Should it pursue an integration that fosters free markets and the economic growth they bring, or should it pursue an integration in which member states band together to resist the economic consequences of high taxes and heavily regulated labor markets in a global era?

U.S. Bests EU in Globalization
Chart 6

A. Innovation Policy Index

Index value (100 = best)

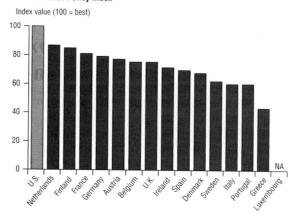

Source: Harvard Business School.

B. Labor Rigidity Index

Index value (100 = best)

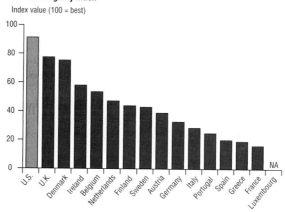

Source: The World Bank.

C. Globalization Index

Index value (100 = best)

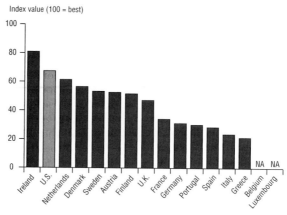

Source: A.T. Kearney.

What Will the Future Hold?

What are the prospects for further liberalization? Last year, the EU considered a proposal for free trade in services. With goods now accounting for a dwindling portion of the EU economy, free trade in services would seem a logical step for a federation dedicated to providing a common market across Europe. Yet, the specter of increased competition from Eastern Europe's cheap labor undermined public support. Bowing to opposition in several countries, the EU adopted only minimal changes in its services trade policies. More recently, a months-long drama featuring massive street protests forced the French government to withdraw a proposal to increase labor market flexibility with a probationary employment period during which young workers would enjoy fewer benefits and less job security.

These incidents are balanced by signs favorable to reform. Current European Commission President José Manuel Barroso has spoken movingly of the need for Europe to further liberalize its economy to better compete in the global marketplace. And to give just one example where this is happening, Germany has renegotiated labor contracts in a few high-cost sectors and has discussed limiting labor's historic influence over corporate strategy. These and other events within the EU suggest Europe's future policy direction is far from decided.

The EU stands at a crossroads as it debates further economic liberalization. Some EU members wish to preserve and even expand Europe's social protections, so that workers can have much-needed security in an era of ever-more-rapid change. Other EU members want Europe's economy to become more flexible, so that economic growth can equal and perhaps even exceed that of the U.S.

Europe can't simultaneously satisfy these competing visions. Either the EU must liberalize its economy to compete in a globalized world, knowing its workers will have to retrain faster—and become more highly educated—than ever before. Or EU nations can band together to resist further liberalization, knowing that unemployment will become more prevalent and economic growth will remain slow.

The European Union has a clear choice, but the challenge of globalization is an issue for every economic entity on every continent, including the United States. U.S. labor markets may be somewhat more flexible than Europe's, and the U.S. economy somewhat more open. But make no mistake: In areas ranging from steel to softwood lumber to clothing to autos, the U.S. faces pressure to ward off globalization rather than embrace it.

With technologies knitting economies closer and policies aligned toward openness, globalization has advanced steadily in the postwar era. Future policy choices in the European Union, United States and other entities will determine whether the world continues its progress toward increasing economic integration.

Saving is a senior economist in the Research Department of the Federal Reserve Bank of Dallas.

Notes

[1] See *International Economics: Theory and Policy,* by Paul R. Krugman and Maurice Obstfeld, 7th ed., Addison-Wesley, 2005, for an overview of this and other economic issues relevant to the global economy.

[2] See "A Pure Theory of Local Expenditures," by Charles M. Tiebout, *Journal of Political Economy,* vol. 64, no. 5, 1956, pp. 416–24, for more on this phenomenon.

[3] "A Single Welfare Benefit Level for Europe? Efficiency Implications of Policy Harmonization in a Federal System," by Jason L. Saving, *Southern Economic Journal,* vol. 70, no. 1, 2003, pp. 184–94, contains a more rigorous examination of the conditions under which economic integration can be harmful rather than helpful.

Discussion Questions

VIII

1. How is the euro used as an international currency?

2. How does the euro compare to the U.S. dollar for use in international transactions?

3. What factors increase the use of the euro for international transactions?

4. Will the euro surpass the U.S. dollar in future international economic transactions?

5. How does the economic performance of the EU-15 compare to the U.S.?

6. What government policies hinder the economic performance of the EU-15 in a global economy?

7. What must the EU governments do to increase economic performance in a globalized world?

8. What are the two conflicting strategies of EU integration that Jason Saving refers to in his article?

Financial Crises and Capital Flows

IX

This section covers key topics in international capital flows from global financial crises to IMF readiness to respond to such crises. Interest in sovereign wealth funds has been rekindled by the rapid growth in these funds. The final article in this section "Asia Ten Years After" by Burton and Zanello discusses the economic outlook of south-east Asia ten years after the Asian financial crisis of 1997. In 1997, doubts over the financial integrity of regional financial institutions prompted investor panic and mass capital outflows from the region causing exchange rate collapse, balance sheet effects and insolvencies, and a collapse in aggregate demand and GDP. However by 2003, GDP in all countries had recovered to precrisis levels. Ten years on, Asia's governments still have to address the problem of increasing income inequality and high, volatile capital inflows to the region. These capital inflows are a concern for policy makers as the flows can cause the real exchange rate to appreciate, asset prices to bubble, and bank lending to become lax, which can jeopardize economic stability.

Two economists at the IMF, Mauro and Yafeh, examine the nature of future financial crises. To examine what future financial crises may look like, the authors examine the country-specific financial crises of the 1890s and the contagion crises of the 1990s. The authors measure risk using interest rate spreads (the difference in yields between emerging market countries' bonds and U.S. Treasury bonds) and they find that bond spreads moved together across emerging market countries during the 1990s. In contrast, in the 1890s spread movements were limited to one country. This suggests that the determinants on asset prices are different between the two periods. In the 1990s, emerging market bonds spreads moved together because economic effects were similar across countries today compared to the 1890s. The authors argue that the extent of future contagion depends on the influence of hedge funds, private equity funds, and sovereign wealth funds.

Linda Goldberg's article on financial sector foreign direct investment (FDI) investigates the economic impact of banks in industrialized countries, such as the U.S. and U.K., establishing branches in developing countries. During the 1990s the largest source of external finance for developing countries was FDI. FDI in manufacturing and natural resources does provide increases in productivity and technology for host countries, and Goldberg argues that financial sector FDI increases the efficiency of foreign-owned and domestically-owned banks. However, the efficiency gains could be attributed to increased competition or technology transfers. If host countries have a sufficient level of human capital, FDI can increase economic growth. Empirical studies show that financial sector FDI can improve economic growth by improving the efficient allocation of funds from savers to investors. Further, at the institutional level host countries improve banking oversight through better regulation and supervision. One potential problem with financial sector FDI is the increased probability of contagion should a crisis ensue.

Peter Kenen assesses the studies performed by the Independent Evaluation Office (IEO) of the International Monetary Fund (IMF). The studies address criticisms of IMF fiscal strategy and implementation, the IMF's response to capital account crises, and the prolonged use of IMF resources. Fiscal and monetary adjustment is a necessary condition for countries requiring IMF resources. In particular, countries must tighten fiscal and monetary policy to reduce their current account deficit and achieve an exchange rate appreciation. The studies evaluate whether the adjustments have been excessive and whether it is a one-size-fits-all policy. The IEO finds that an improvement in the government's budget does improve the current account; however the policy is not a one-size-fits-all policy

since the extent of the adjustments varies according to the initial size of the fiscal deficit and the policy does not reduce economic growth. The empirical evidence of raising interest rates to strengthen a currency is less clear. In terms of prolonged use of IMF resources, the IEO finds that IMF resource use has risen since the 1970s. Kenen argues that the IEO fails to investigate whether the IMF approves additional programs, and thus IMF resources, to avoid the economic or political fallout when additional IMF funds are denied.

The final article examines the nature of sovereign wealth funds, funds controlled by sovereign states. The term "sovereign wealth fund" is only just becoming a household name but these funds have been around for decades. The recent interest in these funds has been rekindled by the size of these funds, estimated at over $3 trillion U.S. dollars. Further, the sheer size of these funds provides some governments with economic, and therefore political, leverage over foreign policy that may not be in the interests of the U.S.

27

Asia Ten Years After

D A V I D **B U R T O N**
A N D A L E S S A N D R O **Z A N E L L O**

Ten years ago, the Asian financial crisis of 1997–98 began to unfold. Few countries in the region were left untouched, and the aftereffects reverberated across the globe. A decade later, Asia shines in the global economic landscape, and its vitality stands out as a remarkable achievement. But what lies behind this success, and what are the new challenges for a region that has become a dynamo for the world economy?

A Look Back

In retrospect, the Asian financial crisis proved to be a temporary setback, despite its enormous economic and social costs. Its hallmark was the sudden reversal of investor sentiment and abrupt withdrawal of international capital. Doubts about the soundness of financial institutions and corporates spread quickly across national borders, creating a vicious circle of capital outflows, plummeting exchange rates, and crippling balance-sheet effects in the crisis-struck countries. Private demand collapsed and output in the most affected economies contracted quickly and sharply. The underdevelopment of social safety nets to protect those most exposed to economic disruptions exacerbated the social and economic impact of the slumps.

The international community stepped in to help as private investors were stampeding for the exits, providing external financing (including IMF assistance), while governments in the region adjusted policies, taking increasingly strong and appropriate action, and steps were taken to coordinate private sector financing. After some adjustments, this combination eventually turned the tide: confidence recovered and capital started returning. As financial and real sector weaknesses were tackled, output in the hardest-hit countries began expanding again. The most determined reformers were the first to claw back the ground lost and, by 2003, GDP in all crisis countries had surpassed its precrisis level (see Chart 1). GDP per capita took a bit longer to do so.

Fast-Forward

Today, Asia is among the star performers in the global economy. The region found strength in no small part by turning crisis into opportunity. The testing times of the late 1990s have rekindled a sense of regional identity and shared economic destiny. Regional policy forums have taken on renewed importance. Policy cooperation is gaining traction, and initiatives like the Chiang Mai network of bilateral swap lines among Asian central banks, which is now being converted into a reserve-pooling arrangement, and the Asian Bond Fund project provide a welcome measure of self-insurance and commonality of purpose. In addition, intraregional trade has grown rapidly, with the development of complex supply chains centered on China.

Temporary Setback
**The Asian crisis resulted in a large initial output contraction,
but a recovery started relatively quickly.**
Chart 1

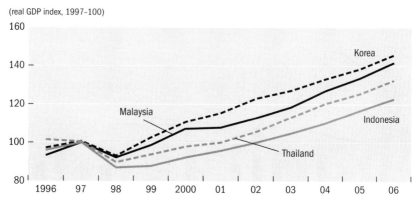

(real GDP index, 1997-100)

Source: IMF, World Economic Outlook database.

At the same time, Asia has not turned its back to the outward-looking orientation that propelled its spectacular rise on the world's economic stage. Intraregional commerce is so far complementing—not substituting for—global trade. With deepening financial and trade connections inside and outside the region, Asia's economic vitality 10 years after the crisis stands out. The countries that were most affected by the crisis have made good progress in laying solid foundations for continued growth and their medium-term prospects are bright.

What lies behind their success? The key to today's dynamism has been nimbler macroeconomic policy frameworks and comprehensive reforms in the financial and corporate sectors. More flexible exchange rate regimes have cushioned external shocks and an impressive war chest of official reserves has been built up; inflation targeting has provided a monetary anchor in many cases; and fiscal policies have taken on a longer-term perspective to safeguard debt sustainability. As for structural reforms, measures to deal with the immediate strains in the financial system have

been complemented by steps to address the underlying weaknesses. Mechanisms to facilitate financial restructuring are now in place, regulatory and prudential frameworks have been upgraded, and corporate governance has been strengthened. More work lies ahead, but financial institutions and corporates in Southeast Asia have, on the whole, regained a solid footing (see Charts 2 and 3).

While the hardest-hit countries were busy cleaning up the legacies of the crisis, the rest of Asia was not standing still (see table). China and India have made further strides as regional powerhouses, the Philippines has weathered bouts of turbulence and gained considerable resilience, Vietnam has burst onto the global economic scene, and Japan has finally extricated itself from its "lost decade" and entrenched deflation.

The IMF has worked closely with economies in the region on their reform programs throughout the past decade. Increasingly, this has been done as part of the Fund's normal surveillance activities, including under new transparency and financial sector initiatives.

Stronger Corporates . . .

In the worst-hit countries, once overgeared companies have reduced their debt.

Chart 2

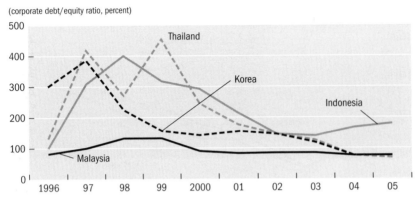

(corporate debt/equity ratio, percent)

Source: IMF, Corporate Vulnerability Utility.

. . . and Stronger Banks

Through vigorous restructuring, nonperforming loans at banks have been brought down to more manageable levels.

Chart 3

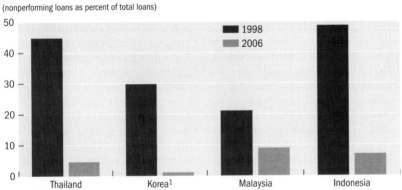

(nonperforming loans as percent of total loans)

Sources: CEIC Data Company Ltd.; and the World Bank.
[1]1998 World Bank estimate.

The Next 10 Years?

So what is ahead for Asia? Much will depend on whether it can tackle a number of issues over the medium term. While priorities differ across countries, a common theme stands out—coping with globalization and harnessing the tremendous upside it could deliver. For instance, the ever-greater participation of China and India in the global economy is opening up new horizons for the rest of the region, but the potential benefits do not come without risks. Nor

High Fliers
Asia includes some of the world's fastest-growing economies.

	2005	2006	2007 Latest projecton	2008 Latest projecton
Industrial Asia	**2.0**	**2.3**	**2.4**	**2.1**
Japan	1.9	2.2	2.3	1.9
Australia	3.1	2.4	2.6	3.3
New Zealand	2.2	1.5	2.5	2.6
Emerging Asia	**8.6**	**9.0**	**8.5**	**8.1**
Hong Kong SAR	7.5	6.8	5.5	5.0
Korea	4.2	5.0	4.4	4.4
Singapore	6.6	7.9	5.5	5.7
Taiwan POC	4.0	4.6	4.2	4.3
China	10.4	10.7	10.0	9.5
India	8.7	9.1	8.4	7.8
Indonesia	5.7	5.5	6.0	6.3
Malaysia	5.2	5.9	5.5	5.8
Philippines	5.0	5.4	5.8	5.8
Thailand	4.5	5.0	4.5	4.8
Vietnam	8.4	8.2	8.0	7.8
NIEs[1]	*4.7*	*5.3*	*4.6*	*4.6*
ASEAN-5[2]	*5.5*	*5.7*	*5.8*	*6.0*
Asia	**7.2**	**7.6**	**7.2**	**6.9**

Source: IMF, World Economic Outlook database; and staff estimates.

[1]NIEs = Newly industrializing economies.

[2]ASEAN-5 = Indonesia, Malaysia, Philippines, Singapore, and Thailand.

does the increased fluidity of global capital movements. More broadly, as the pace of world integration quickens, vulnerabilities and social strains from rapid structural change and external shocks are bound to come to the fore, hand in hand with new opportunities. Governments—in Asia, as elsewhere—need to put in place shock absorbers to mitigate the impact of negative outcomes, as well as adopt policies that help capture the gains from deeper integration.

Although the challenges are many, here we focus on just two of the most important—the need to address worsening income inequality and learning to live with potentially unstable capital flows (for a more comprehensive take on Asia's policy agenda, see "Asia's Winds of Change," F&D, June 2006).

Income Inequality

Over the past decade, inequality has risen steadily across the region. For example, China displays now a more skewed income distribution than the United States or Russia. Even Japan, once the poster child of a fairly equalitarian society, is today more unequal than the average industrial country. In fact, widely used measures of income dispersion, such as the Gini coefficient and indicators of the size of the middle class, all point in the same direction—a more unequal sharing of income (including

Growing Inequality
**Over the past 10 years, measures of income dispersion have
deteriorated in most Asian countries.**
Chart 4

(Gini coefficient, percent change over 10 years)[1]

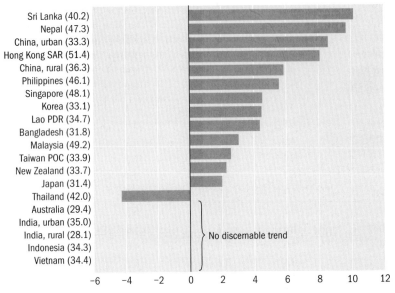

Sources: World Bank, PovCalNet database; WIDER World Income Inequality Database; OECD; Australian and Korean authorities.
[1]The Gini coefficient is a measure of inequality, with the index running from 0 to 100. A low score indicates a more equal income distribution. Values in parentheses give the latest Gini index measure, with the bars showing the change compared with 10 years earlier.

along a rural-urban divide) and more polarization for Asian societies (see Chart 4).

The causes of Asia's growing disparities are complex. Several factors may be at play, but skill-biased technical progress in the more advanced economies and the transition from agriculture to industry in developing ones appear to be the main forces shaping income distribution in the region. Globalization is of course providing the broader context for the changes in technology and patterns of production that are at the root of differential wage and sectoral developments. Besides ethical or social implications, worsening inequality is a concern for economic policymakers. If unattended, growing disparities could strain social cohesion and undermine the support for further engagement in the global economy, in spite

of great potential benefits. More broadly, tears in the social fabric could lead to inferior economic outcomes—namely, lower long-term growth, macroeconomic instability, and dwindling room for maneuver when adverse shocks occur.

Asian policymakers are looking for ways to stem the trend. Specific measures depend on individual country circumstances, but in all cases need to be supported by sound macroeconomic management, which is necessary for sustainable growth. Growth holds out the greatest promise for lifting the poor out of poverty and providing better opportunities to the disadvantaged. Policy options to address inequality more directly include greater and more effective spending on education and infrastructure to build human capital and enhance the allocation of resources; labor market re-forms that facilitate hiring and improve the employment conditions of nonregular work-ers; more equal access to financial markets to empower the poor and improve economic efficiency; and regulatory reforms to bolster the investment climate. Because the old tend to be poorer, steps to better absorb the fiscal impact of rapid population aging will also help redress income and geographical dis-parities in several countries.

Unstable Capital Flows

The other big challenge facing Asia re-lates to the ongoing integration of its capital market, both within the region and globally. The region's large current account surplus continues to be the main reason for its over-all balance of payments surplus. But, whereas net inflows to emerging Asia re-main close to their long-run average relative to aggregate GDP, gross capital inflows and outflows are at record highs (see Chart 5). Capital is pouring in because of ample global liquidity and an expanded interna-tional investor base. It is being attracted by improved fundamentals, favorable interest rate differentials on domestic assets (espe-cially against the yen), and broader and deeper regional financial integration. Savings have also been flowing out of the re-gion as never before. Active official reserve management in some cases, more relaxed restrictions on residents' investment abroad in others, and—throughout the region—better integration of markets and produc-tion structures have provided powerful drivers for gross outflows.

Gross flows have also become more volatile in recent years. The increased im-portance of portfolio and other invest-ments (notably bank lending and derivative transactions) explains the trend and under-scores the possibility of financial swings in either direction. Surges in capital move-ments (at times, in the context of yen carry trades—the practice of borrowing yen to invest in higher-yielding assets denomi-nated in foreign currencies) have become a policy concern (see Chart 6). As the 1997–98 crisis made all too clear, rapid

capital inflows carry the dangers of disrup-tive real appreciations, asset price bubbles, and imprudent domestic lending, on the one hand—and may lead to widespread economic and financial dislocations if they come to a sudden stop or turn into panic outflows, on the other.

No surefire policy tool exists to deal with potentially unstable financial flows, but mutually reinforcing and consistent poli-cies hold the best promise. Greater exchange rate flexibility in the context of sound macroeconomic policies—and, perhaps, in-tervention to smooth exchange rate move-ments without undue "leaning against the wind"—may be the least costly approach to absorb surges in capital inflows, after all.

A complementary strategy for Asia is to push forward with the development of domestic financial markets, including in the context of intraregional financial integra-tion. Regional financial markets outside Hong Kong SAR, Singapore, and Tokyo are small, especially bond markets, and equity markets are less liquid than those in mature economies. Deeper and broader capital markets will provide a first bulwark against disruptions from unpredictable capital movements and perhaps add a measure of stability by retaining Asian savings within the region. Intraregional financial integra-tion can be spurred by further steps to strengthen market infrastructure, corporate governance, and risk management at finan-cial institutions, as well as coordinated ef-forts to harmonize financial regulations and tax treatments. Government-led initiatives in these areas are providing helpful support to a market-driven, bottom-up process in the background. Further liberalization of remaining restrictions on outflows can also support deeper integration and potentially offset swings in capital inflows.

Growing income inequality and po-tentially erratic capital flows are but two ex-amples of the challenges that globalization presents to Asia. The to-do list for Asia's policymakers is longer. Steps are needed in many cases to encourage household con-sumption and private investment to rein-force the domestic underpinnings of growth

Flowing in . . .

Gross capital inflows to emerging Asia, which dipped abruptly during the crisis, are now higher than precrisis levels.

Chart 5

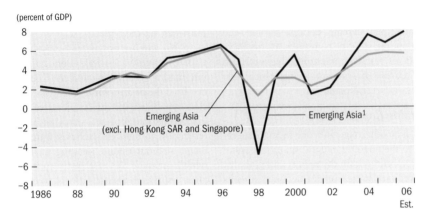

(percent of GDP)

. . . and Flowing Out

Gross outflows are also at record highs, driven by several factors, including active management of reserves and better integration of markets.

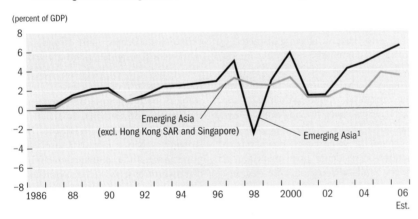

(percent of GDP)

Sources: CEIC Data Company, Ltd.; IMF, *International Financial Statistics;* World Economic Outlook database; and staff estimates.
[1]Excludes Hong Kong SAR until 1997.

and limit the region's reliance on external demand. Stronger domestic demand will go hand in hand with stronger currencies throughout the region, facilitating a global rebalancing of world growth and an orderly resolution of current account imbalances.

At the same time, protectionism must be resisted as external pressures to open up domestic markets build. By the same token, it will be important to avoid distortions to trade that the proliferation of preferential trade agreements in the region threatens to create. Additional product and labor market reforms may also be necessary to facilitate the development of new areas of comparative advantage as patterns of production and trade shift. Finally, many countries need to put in

More Volatile
Surges in capital movements in either direction have become a policy concern.
Chart 6

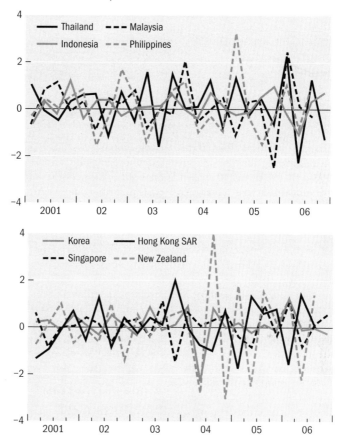

(standardized deviation of quarterly changes in portfolio and other investment inflows)

Sources: CEIC Data Company, Ltd.; IMF, *International Financial Statistics* and staff estimates.

place welfare systems that cushion, but do not obstruct, structural change, while policy space must be found to deal with the environmental impact of rapid growth.

Ten years after a major financial crisis, Asia is looking at the future with renewed confidence and has good reason to do so. Ground has been regained where it had been lost, and Asia is well positioned to be an ever-greater force in the world economy. Encouragingly, policies are increasingly attuned to the quickening pace of globalization, and the foundations for a sustained expansion are being laid. Although the list of policy issues still to address might seem daunting at first, reforms must be a continuous process in today's fast-paced and interconnected economy, and policies that address any one of these issues are likely to help on the other fronts as well. For its part, the IMF will continue to work closely with economies in the region to help them move forward with this reform process.

Financial Crises of the Future

28

PAOLO **MAURO**
AND YISHAY **YAFEH**

THE damaging financial crises of the 1990s—originating in Mexico in 1994, Asia in 1997, and Russia in 1998—spread quickly across emerging markets, prompting calls for reform of the financial architecture. That was a decade ago, however. The only major, full-blown emerging market crisis of this century—in Argentina in 2001—led to little spillover, or "contagion," except in neighboring Uruguay. In recent years, commentary in the financial press and in publications by investment banks and rating agencies has often emphasized an apparent decline in international contagion risk.

That is not to say that investors are not occasionally reminded of the issue of contagion: recent episodes of financial market turbulence include the drop in equity prices in emerging markets in May–June 2006, the global equity sell-off that began with an unwinding of positions on the Chinese stock market in February–March 2007, and the most recent woes that began in mid-2007, triggered by developments in the subprime mortgage markets in the United States.

On the whole, however, over the past few years emerging markets have enjoyed abundant liquidity, low bond spreads, and surges in capital inflows. Moreover, a very long-term perspective suggests that the contagious crises of the 1990s were not the norm but an unusual phenomenon. During the last period of financial globalization—the half century prior to World War I—the world witnessed several crises, but essentially no contagion. Even the most famous financial collapse of the period, the Barings crisis that originated in Argentina in 1890, did not have much impact outside the borders of that nation.

Will future crises look more like those of the 1990s or of the 1890s? Was the Argentine crisis of 2001 a harbinger of a return to self-contained crises? And if international spillovers remain possible, are there implications for global governance in the area of financial markets? To shed light on these questions, it is useful to analyze the historical record.

A Tale of Two Eras

The 1870–1913 period of financial globalization—characterized by free trade, nearly unrestricted migration, large international capital flows, and sophisticated financial markets—resembles, and in some respects surpasses, globalization as we know it today. The London market for bonds issued by the "emerging economies" of the day was large (with an overall capitalization amounting to more than half of Britain's GDP), liquid (with bond spreads fluctuating considerably and reported daily in the newspapers), and supported by timely and reliable information (with political and economic news about emerging economies widely available in the British press). The typical portfolio of a British investor around the turn of the 20th century was probably more internationally diversified, and included a far larger share of emerging market securities, than that of his great-grandchild living at the beginning of the 21st century.

This global integration came to an abrupt end with the outbreak of World War I and the subsequent upheaval of the Great Depression and World War II. International financial flows resumed in the 1970s, but only in the final years of the 20th century did financial globalization achieve a level and a form reminiscent of the pre-1914 period. In particular, reliance on tradable emerging market bonds was jump-started by the Brady deals of the early 1990s, which repackaged the defaulted bank debt of the 1970s and early 1980s into bonds.

Despite these similarities in scale and reliance on bond finance, a striking difference between the 1870–1913 era and the 1990s relates to the extent that asset prices—specifically, sovereign bond spreads—moved together. Sovereign bond spreads are defined, for the historical period, as the yields on emerging market countries' bonds issued in pounds sterling on the London Stock Exchange, minus yields on British consols; and, for the modern period, as the yields on emerging market countries' bonds issued in U.S. dollars, minus yields on long-term U.S. treasury bonds. Whereas bond spreads followed country-specific trajectories during the pre-1914 era (see Chart 1), emerging market bond spreads tended to move in tandem to a much greater extent in the 1990s (see Chart 2). The message is similar when one focuses on comovement in times of crisis: sharp increases in sovereign bond spreads (of, say, more than 200 basis points) often took place simultaneously in several emerging markets in the 1990s, but they were typically restricted to one country in the pre-1914 period.

Changing Influences on Asset Prices

What explains the observed differences in the extent of comovement of asset prices between the two periods? The evidence (based on event studies and econometric analysis of data on asset prices, macroeconomic variables, and contemporary newspaper articles) shows that the determinants of asset prices were different. Bond spreads a century ago were driven primarily by country-specific events such as droughts, rebellions, wars, other changes in the political climate, and economic fundamentals. In particular, episodes of politically motivated violence had the most visible impact on bond spreads. By contrast, in the 1990s, country-specific macroeconomic data and events, while still relevant, had more limited power in explaining individual-country bond spreads, with developments in the overall emerging market indices (and, especially, contagious emerging market crises) playing a greater role.

To some extent, the greater degree of comovement of emerging market bond spreads in modern times than in the past is explained by greater similarity in the economic structures of emerging market economies today. Before World War I, these economies tended to be very specialized (for example, Argentina produced wheat and wool and Brazil produced coffee and rubber). Now, they are better diversified and, as a result, engage in more similar economic activities, so that their economic fundamentals tend to move together to a greater extent than they did a century ago. Nevertheless, the increased similarity in the economies of today's emerging markets cannot fully account for the rise in asset price comovement and shared crises.

Changes in investor behavior and the way in which international investment is organized and undertaken also contribute to greater comovement of asset prices in modern times. During the 1990s, losses incurred at the outset of a crisis in a given country induced large investment funds (including mutual funds and hedge funds) to sell assets in (initially) unaffected countries to maintain certain liquidity and risk profiles. For example, when open-end mutual funds foresaw future redemptions

Moving on Their Own Merits
During the 50 years before World War I, spreads on sovereign debt changed in response to country-specific events.
Chart 1

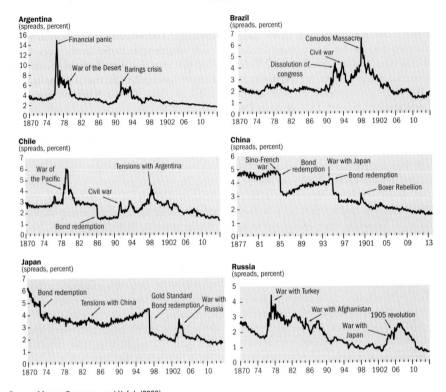

Source: Mauro, Sussman, and Yafeh (2006).
Note: Spreads are the yields on the emerging market country's bonds issued in pounds sterling on the London Stock Exchange minus yields on British consols (British bonds that have no specified maturity date and pay a coupon forever).

after a shock in one country, they raised cash by selling assets they held in other countries. Similarly, leveraged investors, such as banks and especially hedge funds, faced regulatory requirements, internal provisioning practices, or margin calls that led them to rebalance their portfolios by selling their asset holdings in countries that were initially unscathed. By contrast, investors in the past operated primarily as individuals at a time when trading technologies were also slower. In times of impending crisis, investors may have responded to trouble in one emerging market by buying assets in another, thus shifting assets rather than selling them en masse.

The Strange Case of Argentina

Why was there a near absence of contagion in the case of the Argentine crisis of late 2001 (only Uruguay was affected, mainly because of withdrawals by Argentines who had deposits in its banking system)? Here too investor behavior is the key. Whereas the crises of the 1990s took many investors by surprise, the Argentine crisis was widely expected and market players had ample opportunities to adjust their exposure. Data on international mutual funds reveal a major decline in Argentine holdings throughout 2001. By the time the Argentine currency board collapsed in December, such holdings were extremely low. At a more technical level, a timely reduction of Argentina's weight in the Emerging Markets Bond Index tracked by many market participants may have facilitated an orderly shift of investment positions out of Argentina into other emerging markets.

Although there are some who argue that the 2001 Argentine crisis indicates that contagion may have permanently "vanished," the anticipated nature of this crisis casts doubt on that view. On the contrary, the generalized surge of capital inflows into emerging markets observed in recent years is consistent with the view that in some cases investors fail to discriminate sufficiently among emerging markets, based on fundamentals.

Trouble in the Core and on the Periphery

An additional factor determining whether contagion occurs has to do with whether financial market players in the "core" advanced countries are adversely affected by developments in the country in which a crisis originates. Indeed, in many of the best-known contagious emerging market crises, advanced-country financial institutions played a role in transmitting the initial shock to countries on the "periphery." For example, losses incurred by advanced-country banks and other financial institutions were an important transmission channel of contagion during the Asian crisis.

The debacle of Long-Term Capital Management was a key factor in the spread of the Russian crisis of August 1998 to other emerging market economies. And the most recent woes that began with developments in the subprime market in the United States caused concern, though not a full-blown crisis, in a number

of emerging markets. In fact, prompt liquidity provision by the central banks of the main advanced countries—while obviously aimed squarely at restoring confidence domestically—may also have reduced the likelihood of contagion to the emerging markets. The importance of liquidity provision by central banks in the core financial markets has not changed much since the previous era of financial globalization. Prompt action by the Bank of England is often credited with averting international contagion that might otherwise have emanated from the collapse of the investment house of Barings in 1890.

The Future of Contagion

The likelihood of contagious financial crises and high comovement across global financial markets in the future is reinforced by the entry and increased importance of new financial instruments and new players on international financial markets:

Hedge funds have grown tremendously in recent years and manage assets in excess of $1 trillion. As seen in the 1990s and in the recent crisis in subprime mortgages, hedge funds' operations have often added to asset price comovement. Some commentators, however, have suggested that hedge funds may also occasionally mitigate the severity of financial crises by trading "against" the market when prices fall too low for investors with lower risk appetite.

Private equity funds affect comovement and the nature of financial crises, but how they do so is less clear. Private equity funds are typically long-term investors, so their presence might mitigate crises and contribute to stability. But were they to unwind a large position suddenly, the opposite would occur. Moreover, private equity funds occasionally have shorter investment horizons, which lead them to invest in fashionable sectors in several countries at the same time, contributing to comovement across countries.

Moving in Tandem
Since 1990, bond spreads in emerging market countries have moved together, with a handful of exceptions.
Chart 2

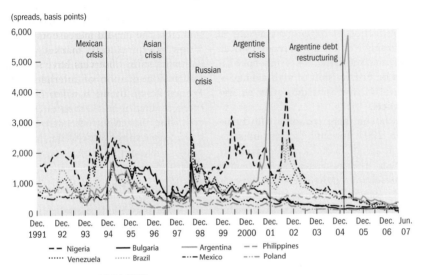

(spreads, basis points)

Mexican crisis

Asian crisis

Russian crisis

Argentine crisis

Argentine debt restructuring

6,000 — 5,000 — 4,000 — 3,000 — 2,000 — 1,000 — 0

Dec. 1991 Dec. 92 Dec. 93 Dec. 94 Dec. 95 Dec. 96 Dec. 97 Dec. 98 Dec. 99 Dec. 2000 Dec. 01 Dec. 02 Dec. 03 Dec. 04 Dec. 05 Dec. 06 Jun. 07

– – Nigeria   —— Bulgaria   —— Argentina   – – Philippines
······ Venezuela   ······ Brazil   –··– Mexico   –··– Poland

Source: Mauro, Sussman, and Yafeh (2006).
Note: Spreads are the yields on the emerging market country's bonds issued in U.S. dollars minus yields on long-term U.S. treasury bonds. A basis point is 1/100th of a percentage point.

Sovereign wealth funds are sparking new interest, although they have been investing sovereign nations' international reserves for years. The sudden interest has been kindled by various factors: these funds have grown rapidly in the past decade, attaining a vast scale; they have acquired large stakes in both emerging market and advanced country corporations and financial institutions, occasionally raising concerns about the perceived strategic importance of the target companies; and several of them do not make their investments public. By some estimates, sovereign funds manage assets well in excess of $1½ trillion, with most of this amount accounted for by a handful of such funds. Although most have used conservative and long-term investment strategies, in principle they could play a destabilizing role if they reversed a position abruptly, particularly one in a small emerging market country.

Beyond the emergence of new players, new investment vehicles for individual investors also have the potential to increase asset price comovement across countries. For example, the rise and growing popularity of index-based investing—through index mutual funds and, more recently, exchange-traded funds—leads to investment in aggregate country or regional indices rather than in individual securities (or countries). Exchange-traded funds are open-end mutual funds that typically seek to replicate a well-established market index. Flows into and out of them may cause all underlying securities to move together, with limited regard for country-specific information. On the other hand, the introduction of new financial instruments, such as exchange-traded funds, may help investors diversify their portfolios and increase market liquidity, contributing to investors' willingness to invest in individual stocks and bonds. The growth in cross-border banking has no doubt also played a role in increasing the potential for international transmission of financial and other shocks.

Prepare for the Future

It is difficult to predict the nature of financial crises in the 21st century, but it is quite likely that they will incorporate features from both the more distant past and the 1990s. Financial crises in the pre–World War I era occurred against the background of macroeconomic difficulties, but were typically triggered by such events as wars or other episodes of politically motivated violence, reflecting institutional deficiencies and political instability. Macroeconomic policies have improved in many emerging markets. But, in some, institutional weaknesses remain, so future crises may well also be triggered by political upheaval. And today's greater financial linkages—including those generated by the activities of new players—may lead to the rapid transmission of crises to other countries, much as happened in the 1990s.

A prudent working assumption, then, would be that contagion is likely to reemerge, suggesting the need to be prepared at both the domestic and the international level. At the domestic level, many countries have taken steps—including improved macroeconomic policies and debt management—aimed at reducing their vulnerability and at softening the blow in the event of a crisis. At the international level, to the extent that market failures and externalities require global governance and coordination, the debate has focused on the possible role of international financial or other supranational institutions, for example, in establishing mechanisms committed to providing liquidity in a crisis. Regional groups of countries have arranged to pool their international reserves to provide a backstop in case of a crisis.

Beyond increased stockpiles of official sector liquidity—whether through self-insurance in the form of international reserves, or international arrangements among countries or with international institutions—are there additional implications for global governance in the area of international financial flows? The debate is likely to concentrate on whether the official sector should increase its scrutiny of private financial market players. Although some observers have suggested forms of regulation of international financial flows, attention will probably be focused on the possible need for additional transparency and data provision, and refinements to existing prudential regulations. This will include a discussion of whether gaps were uncovered by the recent turmoil originating in the subprime market.

The implications of newly important players, such as hedge funds, private equity funds, and sovereign wealth funds, are not yet fully understood, and reasonable arguments can be made for whether—on a net basis—each of these players is likely to foster stability or volatility. Regardless, it is not difficult to imagine scenarios in which these players would be a source of volatility and contagion; a careful discussion of how to avoid such scenarios seems warranted. In particular, the policy debate is likely to concentrate on whether these players should provide additional information about their strategies and investments (that is, greater transparency), and on the possibility that new (voluntary) codes of conduct will be conceived for these new players. Progress in these areas will require identifying exactly what information is needed to permit effective prudential regulation and to facilitate informed decisions by investors without unnecessarily hampering the operation of the financial system.

What seems clear is that both advanced and emerging market countries will pay close attention to this debate. Traditionally, the importance of good governance and transparency has been emphasized with regard to avoiding hidden liabilities, and related vulnerabilities, in crisis-prone emerging markets. The focus on transparency in emerging markets has shifted to the asset side, with frequent calls for greater transparency in the operations of emerging market sovereign wealth funds. However, the financial turmoil that began during the summer of 2007 has shined the spotlight on issues related to transparency of advanced-country financial institutions and the importance of preserving stability in the core financial markets—not only for the well-being of domestic investors, but also to avoid harmful international contagion. The debate on these issues is likely to become more prominent still in the years ahead.

References:

Mauro, Paolo, Nathan Sussman, and Yishay Yafeh, 2006, Emerging Markets and Financial Globalization: Sovereign Bond Spreads in 1870–1913 and Today (London: Oxford University Press).

Didier, Tatiana, Paolo Mauro, and Sergio Schmukler, 2006, "Vanishing Financial Contagion?" IMF Policy Discussion Paper 06/1 (Washington: International Monetary Fund).

29

Financial-Sector Foreign Direct Investment and Host Countries: New and Old Lessons

LINDA GOLDBERG

I. Introduction

In the 1990s, foreign direct investment (FDI) became the largest single source of external finance for many developing countries. For the most part, discussions of the causes and effects of FDI have mainly focussed on manufacturing and real production activity ("general" FDI). Financial-sector FDI also has soared. Yet, research efforts on the general FDI and the financial-sector FDI have been orthogonal, and cross citation has been rare. This orthogonality is surprising: financial FDI shares many of the features of more general FDI in productive services. This paper attempts to bridge this gap and emphasize the parallels and differences between the real and financial-sector FDI.

Conceptually, in each case a foreign producer of goods or services makes a two-fold decision. First, he decides whether to service a particular market; second, he determines whether this market should be served through exports or through setting up local production. While manufacturers use the language of exports or production by multinationals, there is a direct financial services (and in particular banking) analogue to this two-step decision: first, the bank decides whether to provide lending, deposit-taking and other services to a market; second, if so, the bank determines whether to service this market via cross-border activities (arms-length transactions) or foreign direct investment in the form of setting up branches or subsidiaries followed by local lending.

FDI is an activity that occurs as part of a multinational's broader strategic plan. Flows can respond to both microeconomic stimuli, such as tax incentives,[1] and macroeconomic stimuli, such as fluctuations in exchange rates and business cycles. The sometimes lumpy reallocation of capital across borders may occur when governments reduce their protection of inefficient or corrupt local industries.[2] Opportunities to gain local market share and exploit sales or production networks also trigger entry. These features are common to manufacturing industries, extractive resource industries, and financial services.

A well-established literature explores the causes and consequences of FDI in productive services, generally interpreted as manufacturing but sometimes extending to mining and natural resource extractive services. This research often uses data from individual countries or industries within countries, as opposed to taking the form of sweeping multi-country studies. Consequently, the resulting stylized are usually based on theoretical arguments supplemented by selective case studies.[3] Mainly due to data limitations, distinctions are seldom made between FDI conducted in the form of mergers and acquisitions, versus those done as greenfield (*de novo*) investments.

A distinct and more recent literature has been addressing themes related to cross-border flows of products or ownership in the financial services industry. This literature generally focuses on the implications of foreign entry into local banking systems, either from the perspective of risk management by the investing firms and parents, or from the perspective of host markets that sometimes are skeptical about foreign entry.[4] Events of the early 1990s accelerated interest in this financial-sector FDI. Following the breakup of the Soviet Union, foreign bank entry into Central and Eastern European countries led to foreign ownership in local banking system often in excess of 80 percent of local banking system assets. Liberalizations in Latin America also may have been partially prompted by these events, especially where there were concerns about potential competitiveness losses relative to the East. Financial crises of the mid- to late 1990s prompted further openings as countries sought to recapitalize and spur efficiency improvements in their financial systems.

Observers of these changes in financial sector ownership have appropriately begun to analyze the implications of this financial sector FDI on the host countries. In this paper, I argue that many of the lessons from the general FDI research (which has a manufacturing sector and extractive resource industry focus) directly pertain to financial-sector FDI (FSFDI). I review—without attempting to be exhaustive—some of the main findings and policy themes, taking as a primary focus the host country implications of FDI, especially for emerging markets. I emphasize evidence on technology transfers, productivity spillovers, wage effects, macroeconomic growth, institutional development, and fiscal and tax concerns. Throughout the paper, I cite the applicable parallel results that have independently been reached in studies of financial sector FDI. While the language of these orthogonal research areas may have subtle differences, I emphasize that many of the conclusions from such research are similar. In cases where parallel results are not

available, I discuss which host country implications of general FDI are likely to extend to financial services.

I conclude that both types of FDI can induce limited technology transfers and productivity and wage gains in the host country. Both types of FDI can also induce increased integration of the host country into world business cycles. Yet, FDI in banking and finance raises distinct concerns and benefits for the host country, including in the areas of institutional development and crisis avoidance. These differences, more so than the similarities, warrant further study. In particular, the balance of such evidence may provoke an examination of the question of whether emerging market governments should encourage financial-sector FDI even to the extent of providing explicit incentives for inflows.

II. Does FDI Lead to Technology Transfer and Productivity Spillovers?

Development economists argue that multinationals, through FDI, can help to fill an "idea gap" between developed and developing countries and provide enhanced opportunities for developing country growth (Romer 1993). According to this view, foreign direct investors in a country presumably have access to productive knowledge that is not otherwise readily available to producers in the host country. However potent, such productive knowledge may be intangible, taking the form of technological know-how, marketing and managing skills, export contacts, coordinated relationships with suppliers and customers, and reputation (Markusen 1995). Technology transfer from FDI is posited to stimulate developing country growth.

This concept of technology transfer between countries has a long and rich research history.[5] Nonetheless, formal evidence is mixed on the extent that technology transfers and productivity spillovers have occurred as a result of foreign direct investment. Some studies conclude that domestic firms in sectors with more foreign ownership are more productive than firms in sectors with less foreign participation.[6] Other studies dispute the spillover benefits of FDI into local markets[7]. Part of the disagreement among researchers stems from the extent to which the studies properly control for the conditions in a country or sector prior to the advent of FDI. Sometimes foreign investment enters sectors where firms are ex ante more productive. Observations of *ex post* high productivity are not, therefore, proof that foreign entry contributed to enhanced productivity via technology transfer or some other channel.

On balance, FDI researchers conclude that positive productivity and technology spillovers exist, but depend on the structure of host country production activity.[8] Small plants may have the largest productivity gains from foreign entry. Some local plants may lose workers and experience productivity declines. In some cases the gains from foreign investment appeared to be entirely captured by the joint ventures.[9] Overall, while the theoretical point of technology transfer from FDI is compelling, empirically the strength of technology transfer and aggregate productivity effects remains debated in the context of "manufacturing" FDI. Difficulty in quantifying the strength of this channel has complicated the proof of the idea that growth in developing countries is unambiguously spurred by the closing of idea gaps.

Another positive effect from FDI could arise if non-recipient-industries experience positive spillovers from the recipient industry. The view that a new plant will stimulate the local development of services and attract related producers is sometimes offered as a justification for (possibly excessive) incentive packages offered to foreign investors.[10] There is emerging support for a view of positive spillovers. Using data on Lithuanian firms, Smarzynska (2004) finds evidence of productivity spillovers from FDI taking place through contacts between foreign affiliates and their local suppliers in upstream

sectors (i.e. vertical linkages). This careful study finds no support for a claim of spillovers taking place within the same industry (i.e. horizontal linkages).

These technology transfer and productivity themes have close counterparts in the financial-sector FDI literature. Instead of using the language of *productivity,* recent research in this area asks whether foreign bank entry alters the *efficiency* of foreign-owned and domestically-owned banks. Efficiency calculations are done by using data on overhead costs (the ratio of bank overhead costs to bank total assets) and bank net interest margin (bank interest income minus interest expense over bank total assets). Foreign banks operating in developing countries appear to be more efficient than their domestic counterparts, whether privately-owned or government owned. Domestic banks are forced to become more efficient after foreign entry, especially in the business lines in which foreign banks choose to compete. Relevant research studies rely on either cross-country or case study approaches, and also are "within industry." For example, Claessens, Demiriguc-Kunt and Huizinga (2000) use data from a sample of 80 countries to show that foreign entry reduces the profitability of domestic banks and enhances their efficiency. Country studies mainly using bank balance sheet data reach similar types of conclusions for the Philippines (Unite and Sullivan 2001), Colombia (Barajas, Steiner and Salazar 2000), and Argentina (Clarke, Cull, D'Amato and Molinari 2000).

This financial-sector FDI research, to my knowledge, does not directly distinguish between within-sector productivity enhancements due to changes in the market structure of the industries versus those due to technology transfers between foreign banks and domestic banks. Despite anecdotal accounts, direct evidence for technology transfer has not been formalized in relation to financial-sector FDI. Most of the discussion in the area of financial-sector FDI argues that these efficiency gains are induced by changes in industry competitive structure: foreign entry reduces the monopolistic excesses of domestic banks. Bank exit or mergers and acquisitions have changed local competitive structures in ways largely unparalleled in other sectors that have received FDI. The significant amount of bank consolidation during the past decade has been fostered by technological change and foreign entrants into emerging markets. Interestingly, Gelos and Roldos (2002) show convincingly that while this consolidation has been associated with efficiency improvements, as previously noted, consolidation has not reduced competition in local financial markets.

III. Do FDI Inflows Change Host Country Wages?

The productivity and technology transfer arguments lead directly to the question of whether local workers benefit (in terms of wages) from foreign entry. When the foreign firm possesses some intangible productive knowledge, technology transfer and other training after foreign entry should spur expanded human capital by the host-country employees of the foreign firm. This accumulation of human capital should manifest itself in greater worker productivity and be rewarded by higher wages.

Empirical studies of manufacturing industries have tied higher levels of foreign direct investment to higher wages. In Mexico and Venezuela, this wage growth was experienced only for the workers in foreign-owned firms without broader spillovers through the host country labor markets. In the United States, there have been smaller wage effects from foreign investment, but these wage gains have spilled over more into local labor markets (Aitken, Harrison and Lipsey 1996). In Indonesian industries, wages paid in domestically-owned manufacturing plants taken over by foreign firms increased sharply relative to wages paid in those plants that remained in domestic hands. These results persisted even after controlling

for the initial characteristics of the plants that were taken over by foreign investors (Lipsey and Sjoholm 2002). On balance, some workers directly benefit from FDI through higher wages. Whether due to the accumulated capital being firm-specific, or foreign firm efforts to limit out-mobility of productive workers, analogous growth in wages and productivity are not generally observed outside the sector which receives FDI.

The same arguments for wage effects of FDI should apply to workers in emerging market financial services industries. However, the data on this issue has not yet been parsed out. There is evidence from bank balance sheet data that foreign bank operating costs are lower and domestic bank costs are pushed down by foreign entry. In some cases the wage expenditures decline for banks. More analysis is needed to decompose these cost reductions into components of reduced numbers of workers (often a result of acquisitions and consolidations of banks) versus higher wages paid to the remaining workers.

A related theme is the employment effects of FDI. The overall employment implications for the host economy, summing across the jobs of the entrant firms and surrounding economy, most likely depend on whether the FDI takes the form of greenfield investment (referred to as *de novo* in the financial services industry) or occurs via mergers and acquisitions of preexisting plants (or banking networks). Greenfield investments, like the construction of a new production plant, are expected to generate increased host country employment. This job growth might be strongest if the new plant does not directly compete with other local production facilities, especially in serving thin host country markets. The net employment effects also could be strong if there are agglomeration externalities, so that the infrastructural improvements have spillovers on other firms locally and all local producers gain.[11] These points are relevant for studies of general FDI, which do not typically distinguish between types of FDI, and would be expected to also be quite relevant for financial FDI.

The net employment effects of merger and acquisition FDI are less transparent. If the M&As imply that consolidation occurs over an inherited bloated infrastructure, there may be job loss. There may be fewer individuals employed at higher wages in a plant or banking system that ultimately is operating more efficiently. Financial-sector FDI is often done through acquisitions of host country banks. Evidence on branch closures and reduced wage bills post-acquisition are suggestive of within industry job loss with this form of FDI.

IV. Do FDI Inflows Accelerate Macroeconomic Growth?

Studies of the aggregate implications of FDI sometimes using data from larger groups of countries and taking the form of growth regressions[sic]. One level of motivation is drawn from the question of whether an idea gap had held back EME growth, with FDI inducing a catch-up process (Romer 1993). Indeed, the most robust evidence on FDI and aggregate growth is found in studies of developing countries.[12] Some researchers conclude that inward investments to Greece, Taiwan, Indonesia, and Mexico have contributed significantly to their growth. However, research that uses detailed industry-level data also finds that growth spillovers across industries may be driven by the industries into which FDI is targeted. Spillovers are not expected to occur across all industries. The spillovers and growth ramifications are expected to be strongest when foreign affiliates and local firms compete most directly with each other, as may be the case in previously protected industries.[13] Borensztein, DeGregorio, and Lee (1998) find positive threshold effects between FDI and growth, with human capital accumulation needing to be large enough before countries can absorb the beneficial effects of the foreign inflows.

Two strands of research specifically tie into the question of whether financial-sector FDI stimulates emerging market growth.[14] Cross-country growth regressions reach a broader finding that financial development is both positively and causally related to economic growth.[15] Beck, Demirguc-Kunt and Maksimovic (2001), however, find no evidence that distinguishing countries by financial structure (i.e. bank-based versus market-based) explain[s] country differences in economic growth performance. None of the related studies have identified whether foreign bank entry per se is a growth driver.

A second relevant literature is more suggestive of positive growth effects from financial-sector FDI since it provides evidence of more efficient credit allocation within economies that receive financial-sector FDI. Prior to financial sector liberalization and reform, some governments use the local banking system as a tool for providing directed credit to politically favored constituents or favored but loss-making sectors of the economy. The banks implicitly play a role in patronage, "development finance," and subsidize levels of activities that might not be viable on market terms. Suggestive evidence of the costliness of such strategies is found in work by LaPorta, Lopez-de-Silances, Shleifer (2002). Using data from around the world, they argue that higher levels of government ownership of banks is [sic] associated with lower growth of per capita income and productivity. Sapienza (2002), in a fascinating study of state-owned banks in Italy, shows that public bank lending has a pattern of rewarding political supporters.

While serving as a means of fiscal stimulus, this type of directed lending crowds out intermediation to worthy private borrowers. If banks are better regulated and subject to parent bank oversight, foreign banks operating in emerging markets may be better able to resist local suasion. As such, they may better discipline host country fiscal or monetary "irresponsibility" and be less amenable to forced purchases of government bonds or forced lending to favored political constituents.

Galindo and Schiantarelli (2002) document that financial liberalization tends to relax financing constraints on producers in developing countries, and make them less adversely influenced by financial crises. Foreign banks sometimes enter as a component of a larger scale financial liberalization and banking privatization effort, and sometimes enter as local governments seek to recapitalize their financial systems in the wake of crises. Outside of crisis periods, foreign banks might be expected to contribute to growth by providing capital to worthy but previously credit-constrained borrowers, and by not crowding out credit provision to worthy borrowers who are outside the scope of their business model. During crises, if foreign-owned banks are the destinations for local flight capital, instead of this capital leaving the country there are greater opportunities for these funds to continue to be intermediated locally.

Further evidence supportive of financial-sector FDI as a stimulus to growth is from research on lending comparisons across banks differentiated by owner types. U.S. bank credit provision to Latin American countries grew faster and was less sensitive to local cycles than credit provision by domestically-owned banks (Dages, Crystal and Goldberg 2002). The composition of credit provision also is important for long-term growth, raising the concern that small businesses that rely on bank credit might have constrained access with foreign bank entry. In Latin America, foreign-owned banks operating have been providing credit to local constituents in similar patterns as healthy domestically-owned banks (Dages, Goldberg, and Kinney 2000). Other than possible biases in borrower orientation that often are linked to bank size (large banks lend relatively less to small and medium-sized enterprises), detailed evidence for Latin American countries shows that there has not been a systematic bias in orientation specifically associated with foreignness (Clarke, Cull, and Martinez Peria 2002). In Eastern Europe (specifically Hungary),

on aggregate, foreign entry may even have been associated with expanded SME credits when the domestic banks had to more aggressively search for a broader clientele for lending (Bonin and Abel 2000).

Overall, these observations from research on credit provision in country and bank studies are supportive of the more general growth regression results. Namely, financial-sector FDI appears to support more rapid economic growth rates within economies.

V. FDI, Business Cycles, and Institutional Development

FDI can also be important for the multiplier on foreign and domestically generated business cycles, crisis contagion, and institutional development.[16] Recently, researchers engaged in analyses of business cycle comovements across countries have looked for explanations for changes in synchronization. Kose, Prasad, and Terrones (2003) explore the changes in global linkages across different types of developing countries in recent decades. They divide developing countries into two coarse groups—more financially integrated economies (MFI) and less financially integrated countries (LFI). Both groups have low correlations with "world macroeconomic aggregates, with these correlations not statistically higher in recent decades compared, for example, with the 1960s and the 1970s.[17]

The independent role of general FDI, and specifically multinational firms in business cycle integration, is less well explored. While Hanson and Slaughter (2003) posit a role for multinationals that relies on profit sharing between parent and affiliate firms, especially through wages, the strength of this channel has not been tested empirically or assessed relative to other channels.[18] As a general point, the specific contribution of FDI to business cycle linkages, as opposed to financial integration more broadly defined, remains a largely open question. Likewise, the relative importance of general FDI versus financial-sector FDI in changing the nature of local business cycles has not been determined.

Empirical analyses show that financial-sector FDI clearly has consequences for local business cycles. This type of research typically uses bank-level data to relate lending activities to shock transmission within and across national borders. In principle, bank lending activity can either be procyclical or countercyclical with respect to local business cycles and other shocks. On the loan supply side, the availability of loanable funds via the deposit base contributes to procyclicality. To the extent that foreign bank entrants are less reliant on host country funding sources, and more reliant on foreign sources of funds, the procyclicality of their supply of loanable funds may be reduced. Loan demand can either be procyclical or countercyclical. Procyclicality can arise as individuals or businesses borrow more to expand their holdings in good times, or countercyclical as individuals try to intertemporally smooth consumption.

Researchers typically find strong evidence of procyclicality in bank lending. In addition to the aforementioned points, other arguments for procyclicality rely on information asymmetries between borrowers and lenders, as within a financial accelerator view of credit cycles.[19] Or, as Borio, Furfine, and Lowe (2001) contend, procyclicality may be the result of inappropriate responses by financial market participants to changes in risk over time. These inappropriate responses can be caused by under-estimating risk in good times and over-overestimating risk in bad times. Inappropriate credit cycles can also derive from market participants having incentives to react to risk, even if correctly measured, in ways that are socially suboptimal. Related arguments for procyclicality stem from bank provisioning practices and their links to rules on regulatory capital (Cavallo and Majnoni 2001).

These cyclical lending responses could potentially differ between foreign-owned and domestically owned banks.

Goldberg, Dages, and Crystal (2002) find that while foreign banks are procyclical lenders, they do not appear to magnify the boom-bust cycles in emerging markets. Analysis of individual bank data from Chile, Colombia, and Argentina supports broad similarities between the lending patterns of private domestically-owned domestic banks and longer-established foreign banks. The similarities with newer established foreign banks are less systematic. While foreign banks had higher average loan growth, they did not add significant volatility to local financial systems or act as relatively destabilizing lenders.[20]

Financial-sector FDI can reduce the magnitude of host country cycles if foreign bank involvement reduces the incidence of crises. The boom/bust cycles in international capital flows are often derided as wreaking havoc on economies, with lending booms contributing to financial crises. Financial liberalization, by giving banks and other intermediaries more freedom of action and allowing them to take greater risks, is sometimes argued to increase the financial fragility in an emerging market. Studies by Demirguc-Kunt and Detragiache (1998, 2001), as well as work by Rojas-Suarez (2001), find that financial liberalization (defined as interest rate liberalization) has costs in terms of increased financial fragility, especially in developing countries where the institutions needed to support a well-functioning financial system are generally not well-established.

Yet institutions in developing countries can respond positively to FDFDI. Crystal, Dages, and Goldberg (2002) show that foreign owned banks appear to contribute to the overall soundness of local banking systems via more aggressive screening and treatment of problem loans. If foreign entry spurs additional regulatory improvements, financial crisis risk declines. Demiriguc-Kunt, Levine, and Min (1998) relate foreign bank entry per se to the probability that a banking crisis will occur. The foreign bank presence was found to have a negative and statistically significant coefficient, leading the authors to conclude that (controlling for other factors likely to produce banking crises) greater foreign bank participation had a stabilizing effect.

The transmission of shocks across borders is another issue that bears on financial crises. Foreign banks may contribute to contagion through common lender effects, as documented in Van Rijckeghem and Weder (2000). Foreign banks could also be subject to foreign cyclical flows. However, any private bank with access to foreign loanable funds can be similarly effected: foreign cycles have been shown to effect the lending and deposit bases of both domestically and foreign owned private banks in emerging markets (Crystal, Dages, and Goldberg 2002). More evidence is needed on the question of whether foreign banks have access to—and receive—additional capital from their head offices in times of stress. Anecdotal evidence suggests that there is not a systematic relationship, but this warrants more rigorous study.

On the issue of crises it is worth noting that foreign banks may contribute to domestic financial stability by being within a country's borders, rather than abroad. If flight to quality occurs under stress periods, it may be better to have domestic depositors keep their money within the domestic financial system (to be reintermediated locally) rather than leave the country through capital flight. Martinez-Peria and Schmukler (1999) document that depositors recognize differences in health and efficiency of banks, moving their assets to better functioning banks or demanding higher deposit rates. Locally generated claims from foreign-owned banks substitute, in part, for cross border flows, with the latter sometimes more volatile.[21]

Host Country Institutional Development

In theory, general and financial-sector FDI can play a causal role in host country institutional development. The direct role of general FDI in host country institutional reform is not well-documented by researchers. Financial-sector FDI has been more closely linked to institutional reforms, but systematic analysis of this institutional response is warranted. The recent availability of rich institutional databases, such as the World Bank database on Bank Regulation and Supervision, may facilitate this type of testing.[22]

Numerous studies assert the financial-sector FDI spurs improvements in bank supervision, with regulatory spillovers. The entry into emerging markets of foreign banks that are healthier than domestic banks implicitly allows a country to import stronger prudential regulation and increase the soundness of the local banking sector. In the cases of Argentina, Chile, and Colombia, for example, foreign banks have contributed to enhanced domestic financial stability by engaging in more aggressive risk management techniques (Crystal, Dages and Goldberg 2002). Calomiris and Powell (2001) argued that Argentina's bank regulatory system in the late 1990s was one of the most successful among emerging market economies. Reliance on market discipline was viewed as playing an important role in prudential regulation by strengthening risk management among banks.

The transitions to improved local supervision might be bumpy. Major international banks may try to build market share by offering a variety of new financial products, including OTC derivatives, structured notes, and equity swaps. These new derivative products can provide improved opportunities for hedging a variety of risks. Yet, some new products may also be used to evade prudential regulations and take on excess risks, especially in countries with weak financial systems with underprepared supervisors (Garber 2000). One clear implication is that local supervisors in emerging markets may need to make early investments in upgrading their skills in order to better evaluate the use and effects of new products. Other challenges for supervisors arise in the context of relationships with parent banks, and may depend on whether the foreign entry is accomplished through branches or subsidiaries.[23]

Foreign bank entry also raises issues of competition policy within host country banking systems. While the actual experiences of host countries have been extensively elaborated elsewhere (see the collection of articles in BIS 2001, and its overview by Hawkins and Mihaljek), on average consolidation has occurred without deterioration of the competitiveness of the financial services industry within a country (Gelos and Roldos 2002).

Another challenge arises in the case where the financial services industry becomes highly concentrated with monopolistic pricing tendencies exerted by banks (for example). If foreign banks are among the few surviving banks, local regulators may be tempted to conclude that foreign banks bear specific responsibility for adverse outcomes. Yet in many cases, foreign bank entry occurs as part of a process of larger scale restructuring and recapitalization of the EME financial system. More concentrated market power may have occurred regardless of whether owners were foreign or domestic. Even with monopolistic pricing, there may be other benefits through scale economies and improved services that are the by-products of consolidation. These issues challenge regulators to engage in careful cost-benefit analyses and policy reactions.

VI. Fiscal and Tax Questions Raised by FDI

Public finance decisions concerning multinationals[24] and host country governments have received considerable analytical attention, particularly in the area of general FDI. One pertinent and very important issue is that of incentives offered to foreign investors in order to attract them to a country (or locality within a country). Such efforts to attract multinationals and foreign investment capital have been extensive. As reported in UNCTAD (2001:6–7), nearly 95 percent of the almost 1200 changes in national FDI legislation during 1991 through 2000 were favorable to foreign investors—sometimes taking the form of special incentives to foreign enterprises, including lower income taxes, income tax holidays, import duty exemptions, and subsidies for infrastructure.

Researchers and policymakers correctly ask whether (quantitatively) there is reason to believe that the benefits from FDI justify the costs. When governments compete actively against each other for FDI, profits from the investments are shifted from the host country to multinational enterprises (Oman 2000).[25] While debate over this point remains, Blomstrom and Kokko (2003) provide a compelling argument that the types of long-term benefits that are generated by FDI may not justify the short-term costs. These benefits include the positive spillovers between firms and across sectors that researchers continue to try to identify. Governments may make excessive long-term financial commitments for the employment and political gains that are received in the short term.

> "strong promotion efforts show that the government is actively doing something to strengthen employment, productivity, growth, or some other policy objective . . . Another reason is that some of the perceived benefits (in particular, the jobs created by FDI) are easily observable while some of the costs (particularly related to tax breaks and fiscal incentives) are distributed over long periods of time and hard to measure."
>
> Blomstrom and Kokko 2003.

The same questions, to date applied almost exclusively in the area of general FDI, also are pertinent in the area of financial-sector FDI. We have suggested a number of important dimensions along which financial-sector FDI is expected to have distinct implications from the more general forms of FDI. These areas include changes in crisis incidence, business cycle magnitudes, and institutional development. Clearly, given the welfare consequences of business cycles and crises, the calculus of costs and benefits of actively promoting and subsidizing such foreign entry is a topic worthy of further analysis. The quantities that have been implicitly or explicitly put on the table for attracting financial FDI have not been, to my knowledge, systematically studied.

VII. Concluding Remarks.

This paper has argued that multinationals and FDI into emerging markets generally have a number of important effects on host countries, with some of these effects specific to FDI in financial services. Some effects are associated with changes in allocative efficiency, technology transfer and diffusion, wage spillovers, institution building, macroeconomic cycles, and overall economic stability.

In brief, research concludes that FDI is typically associated with improved allocative efficiency. This improvement can occur when foreign investors enter into industries with high entry barriers and then reduce local monopolistic distortions. The presence of foreign producers may also induce higher technical efficiency: the increased competitive pressure or some demonstration effect may spur local firms to more efficient use of existing resources.

FDI also is associated with higher rates of technology transfer and diffusion, and higher wages. While there is evidence of technological improvements from FDI, and a presumption that FDI will consequently stimulate economic growth, the strength of these effects is disputed. Higher wages also are induced by FDI into host countries, although sometimes these wage effects are limited to the foreign-owned production facilities and do not spillover more broadly.

Institutional change is another potential implication of FDI. At least in the context of FDI in financial services, the outcome is in the direction of improved regulation and supervision. Sometimes these improvements occur with a lag, as supervisors in host countries may be initially

unprepared for evaluating the new products and processes introduced by foreign entrants.

FDI can also play a role in non-crisis and crisis macroeconomic conditions. Foreign banks are procyclical lenders in emerging markets. Domestic privately-owned banks also are procyclical lenders, so the presence of foreign banks does not aggravate the boom-bust cycle in lending and international capital flows. Foreign entrants may introduce a more diversified supply of funds, in principle leading loan supply to be less procyclical but also more sensitive to foreign fluctuations. Foreign bank entry into emerging markets reduces the incidence of crises, but enhances the potential for greater contagion through common lender effects. The contagion issue is reduced when foreign banks have a stronger subsidiary presence, as opposed to supporting local markets through cross-border flows.

A debate actively rages on the issue of whether governments should actively pursue FDI through subsidies and other incentive programs. In the literature on FDI (real side) there is some skepticism about whether the real benefits from FDI to the host country justify the sometimes large incentives offered to attract foreign investors. These investment incentives may be off-budget items in developing countries—for example as tax holidays that do not require payment of scare public funds.

The special features of financial FDI add other dimensions to this debate, and warrant further exploration. There are some broad similarities, but also some differences, between the effects of manufacturing FDI and financial FDI. The employment effects of financial FDI are more subtle,[26] depending in part on whether the investment is greenfield or merger and acquisition. In the latter case, the effects also depend on whether the acquired institution was financially sound or needing restructuring, regardless of the nationality of the new owners.

The institutional effects are clearer. Financial FDI from well-regulated and supervised source countries can support emerging market institutional development and governance, improve the mix of financial services and risk management tools of a host country, and potentially reduce the sharp crises associated with financial underdevelopment in emerging markets. This type of financial FDI can initially pose strong regulatory challenges to local supervisors, who need to develop expertise in the practices and products introduced into their local economies. A range of analytical and policy questions arise. The most basic decision point is whether developing countries should open up to foreign financial-sector entrants. Many emerging markets have responded with strong affirmative statements in the past decade. A second question, goes beyond the decision point of whether or not to open to financial foreign investment, and asks whether the benefits of this financial sector FDI are such that a country should actively encourage and support entry. Careful discussion and further rigorous analyses would better inform this important issue.

Endnotes

1. See the edited volume by Feldstein, Hines, and Hubbard (1995) for a range of analyses of tax and FDI questions.

2. Dixit and Kyle (1985) provide an elegant conceptual exposition.

3. The case studies employ distinct "definitions" of FDI—sometimes using a flow definition (for example, covering the foreign investment that took place within a particular period of time) or a stock definition, which is meant to represent the total cumulative value of all foreign investment up until some point in time. Data availability often drives the type of analysis conducted.

4. The insurance industry has also received significant foreign investment flows, but less research attention. For example, see Skipper (2001).

5. See Horstmann and Markusen 1989 for an early discussion and formalization of this concept.

6. For example, Blomstrom 1989 on Mexico.

7. See Germidis 1977 for an early discussion of spillovers in the OECD.

8. Gorg and Greenaway (2003) provide a rich and more exhaustive review of the evidence on this point. They are more skeptical that the balance of evidence is positive, but also emphasize

that methodological issues need to be better addressed.

9. Aitken and Harrison 1993, 1999 provide evidence for Venezuela and preliminary results for Indonesia.

10. Such themes were developed in the elegant theoretical analysis of Markusen and Venables (1999) and in Rodriguez-Clare (1996).

11. Job creation by a single plant is generally not an appropriate welfare metric for employment calculations. The foreign plant employs workers and pays higher wages, drawing some workers from other local plants. In a situation where the foreign investor takes over a local plant, restructuring could lead to job loss, with only the remaining employees getting higher wages. The producer potentially generates larger income and tax revenues for local governments.

12. See Lipsey 2000 for an informative overview.

13. Markusen (1995) was an early advocate of the view that the competitive structure of an industry is a key driver behind FDI implications.

14. A related strand of research looks broader than only financial-sector FDI and considers the growth implications of overall financial liberalization. The issue of financial FDI, as opposed to portfolio investments or other forms of capital inflows, is not explicitly addressed. In this literature, financial liberalization events are usually defined in terms of regulatory changes such as the relaxation of capital controls or lifting of interest rate ceilings. Despite considerable research output, the extent of long term growth benefits of capital account liberalizations is hotly debated and a consensus view has not developed. Sharply contrasting results have been generated by researchers due to differences in country coverage, sample periods, inclusion of crisis controls, and indicators of financial liberalization used in research. For recent examples and surveys, see Edison, Klein, Ricci, and Slok 2002; Eichengreen and Leblang 2002.

15. For example, see Levine, Loayza and Beck (2000) and Rajan and Zingales (1998).

16. I do not delve substantively into the other important range of issues surrounding the alternative modes of entry into a country (*de novo* versus merger and/or acquisitions with local banks) or the alternative organizational forms for bank entrants (branch, subsidiary, or as a representative agent of the parent bank).

17. Prasad, Rogoff, Wei, and Kose (2003) provide an extensive review of this evidence, noting the broad group of papers that look at financial integration and growth. The role of FDI within financial integration is less well documented. Imbs (2003) finds that financial integration raises correlations among a sample of industrialized countries. Kose and Yi (2003) argue that

the increased vertical integration of production in world trade poses a powerful channel for business cycle transmission. Such vertical production linkages are frequently supported by patterns of general FDI, and would be suggestive of FDI in manufacturing and extractive resource industries as stimulating business cycle comovements.

[18] The arguments draw from Budd and Slaughter (2003) on international rent sharing.

[19] The "financial accelerator" argument maintains that information asymmetries between lenders and borrowers contribute to the procyclicality of lending. When economic conditions are subject to an adverse shock, and collateral values decline, even those borrowers with profitable projects have difficulty obtaining funding.

[20] See also Goldberg (2002), Dages, Kinney and Goldberg (2000), and Horvath (2002).

[21] More evidence is needed on the extent to which there is substitutability between cross border flows and locally-generated claims by foreign branches and subsidiaries. There are direct parallels between these types of questions in financial FDI and questions long raised in the area of real-side FDI. In manufacturing industries, there is no clear pattern of substitutability versus complementarity in bilateral flows between Latin American countries and the United States. But, manufacturers in different countries may engage in distinct FDI strategies. Research has shown that for Southeast Asian countries, FDI from Japan enhanced Japanese exports to those countries (consistent with intermediate input trade) while FDI from the United States substituted for exports from the United States to Southeast Asia. FDI from these two sources did not systematically influence exports from the U.S. or Japan to Latin American countries. (Goldberg and Klein 1998, 2001).

[22] See Barth, Caprio, and Levine (2002).

[23] One recent study considers the stability of cross border versus FDI flows in banking for Central and Eastern European countries (Buch, Kleinert, and Zajc 2003). In preliminary work, the authors argue that FDI should have an additional stabilizing feature since it should allow banks in CEECs to draw on the liquidity buffer of their headquarters abroad. Branches and subsidiaries are not distinguished in the conceptual presentation.

[24] See The Effects of Taxation on Multinational Corporations, edited by Martin Feldstein, James Hines, Jr. and R. Glenn Hubbard (NBER and U. Chicago Press, 1995).

[25] Similar arguments apply to states within countries that compete against each other to attract new production facilities.

[26] If manufacturing FDI evidence is a guide to where spillovers are likely, Kokko (1994) shows that the incidence of spillovers is related to a host country's ability to absorb them.

References

Aitken, Brian and Ann Harrison. 1999. "Do Domestic Firms Benefit from Direct Foreign Investment? Evidence from Venezuela" *American Economic Review* vol. 89 no. 3 (June) pp. 606–618.

Aitken, Brian, Ann Harrison, and Robert E. Lipsey. 1996. "Wages and Foreign Ownership: A Comparative Study of Mexico, Venezuela, and the United States," *Journal of International Economics,* Vol. 40, No. 3/4, (May), pp. 345–371.

Bank for International Settlements, 2001. *The banking industry in the emerging market economies: competition, consolidation, and systemic stability.* BIS papers no. 4 Monetary and Economics Department (August).

Barajas, Adolfo, Roberto Steiner, and Natalia Salazar. 2000. "The Impact of Liberalization and Foreign Investment in Colombia's Financial Sector." *Journal of Development Economics* 63 (1): 157–96.

Barth, James, Gerard Caprio, and Ross Levine. 2001. "Banking Systems Around the Globe: Do Regulation and Ownership Affect Performance and Stability?" in Frederic Mishkin, ed., *Prudential Regulation and Supervision: What Works and What Doesn't.* (Boston Ma: National Bureau of Economic Research).

Barth, James, Gerard Caprio, and Ross Levine. 2002. "Bank Regulation and Supervision: What Works Best?" NBER working paper 9323 (November).

Blomstrom, Magnus. 1989. *Foreign Investment and Spillovers.* London: Routledge.

Blomstrom, Magnus, and Ari Kokko. 2003. "The Economics of Foreign Direct Investment Incentives" NBER 9489. http://papers.nber.org/papers/W9489

Bonin, John and I. Abel. 2000. "Retail Banking in Hungary: A Foreign Affair?" William Davidson Institute working paper no. 356.

Borensztein, Eduardo, Jose de Gregorio, and J.W. Lee. 1998. "How does foreign direct investment affect economic growth?"

Journal of International Economics vol. 45, pp. 115–135.

Borio, C., C. Furfine, and P. Lowe. 2001. *Procyclicality of the financial system and financial stability: Issues and Policy options.* BIS working paper.

Buch, Claudia, Jorn Kleinert, and Peter Zajc. January 2003. "Financial Integration and Stability in Transition Economies: Does the Mode of Entry Matter?" manuscript, Kiel Institute for World Economics.

Budd, John, and Matthew Slaughter. forthcoming. "Are Profits Shared Across Borders? Evidence on International Rent Sharing," *Journal of Labor Economics.*

Burdisso, Tamaro, Laura D'Amato, and Andrea Molinari. 1998. "The Bank Privatization Process in Argentina: Toward a More Efficient Banking System?" Unpublished paper, Banco Central de la República Argentina (October).

Calomiris, Charles and Andrew Powell. 2001. "Can Emerging Market Bank Regulators Establish Credible Discipline? The Case of Argentina, 1992–1999." In *Prudential Supervision: What Works and What Doesn't,* edited by Frederic Mishkin (NBER and University of Chicago Press).

Cavallo, Michele and Giovanni Majnoni. 2001. "Do Banks Provision for Bad Loans in Good Times?" World Bank Policy Research working paper no. 2619.

Claessens, Stijn, Asli Demiriguc-Kunt, and Harry Huizinga. 2000. "The Role of Foreign Banks in Domestic Banking Systems." In Stijn Claessens and Marion Jansen, eds. *The Internationalization of Financial Services: Issues and Lessons for Developing Countries.* (Boston MA: Kluwer Academic Press)

Claessens, Stijn, Asli Demiriguc-Kunt, and Harry Huizinga. 2001. "How does foreign entry affect domestic banking markets?" *Journal of Banking and Finance,* 25, pp. 891–911.

Clarke, George, Robert Cull, Laura D'Amato, and Andrea Molinari. 1999. "The Effect of Foreign Entry on Argentina's Banking System." In *The Internationalization of Financial Services: Issues and Lessons for Developing Countries,* edited by Stijn Claessens and Marion Jansen. (Doredrecht, The Netherlands: Kluwer Academic).

Clarke, George, Robert Cull and Maria Soledad Martinez Peria. 2002. Does Foreign Bank Penetration Reduce Access to Credit in Developing Countries? Evidence from Asking Borrowers. Manuscript.

Clarke, George, Robert Cull and Maria Soledad Martinez Peria. 2002. "Foreign Bank Entry: Experience, Implications for Developing Countries, and Agenda for Further Research." Manuscript (June).

Crystal, Jennifer, B. Gerard Dages, and Linda Goldberg. 2001. "Does Foreign Ownership Contribute to Sounder Banks? The Latin American Experience." In *Open Doors: Foreign Participation in Financial Systems in Developing Countries,* edited by Robert Litan, Paul Masson, and Michael Pomerleano (Washington DC: Brookings Institution and the World Bank): 217–266.

Dages, B. Gerard, Daniel Kinney, and Linda Goldberg. 2000. "Foreign and Domestic Bank Participation in Emerging Markets: Lessons from Mexico and Argentina" in Federal Reserve Bank of New York, *Economic Policy Review* 6(3): 17–36.

Demirgic-Kunt, Asli and Enrica Detragiache. 1998. "The Determinants of Banking Crises: Evidence from Industrial and Developing Countries." *IMF Staff Papers* 45(1): 81–109.

Demirgic-Kunt, Asli and Enrica Detragiache. 2001. "Financial Liberalization and Financial Fragility" in *Financial Liberalization: How Far, How Fast?* Edited by Gerard Caprio, Patrick Honohan, and Joseph Stiglitz (New York: Cambridge University Press).

Demirguc-Kunt, Asli, Ross Levine, and Hong-Ghi Min. 1998. "Opening to Foreign Banks: Issues of Stability, Efficiency, and Growth." In Seongtae Lee, ed., *The Implications of Globalization of World Financial Markets.* (Seoul: Bank of Korea).

Detragaiche, Enrica and Poonam Gupta. 2002. "Foreign Bank in Emerging Market Crises: Malaysia, 1996–98" International Monetary Fund, Washington DC.

Dixit, Avinash and A.S. Kyle. 1985. "The Use of Protection and Subsidies for Entry Promotion and Deterrence." *American Economic Review* 75: 139–152.

Edison, Hali, Michael Klein, Luca Ricci, and Torsten Slok. 2002. Capital Account Liberalization and Economic Performance:

Survey and Synthesis. IMF working paper (May).

Eichengreen, Barry and David Leblang. 2002. Capital Account Liberalization and Growth: Was Mr. Mahathir Right? NBER working paper no. 9427 (December).

Feldstein, Martin, James R. Hines, and R. Glenn Hubbard. *The Effects of Taxation on Multinational Corporations.* (Chicago: NBER and University of Chicago Press).

Focarelli, Daio and Alberto Franco Pozzolo. "Where do Banks Expand Abroad? An Empirical Analysis." Manuscript.

Fosfuri, A., M. Motta, and T. Ronde. 2001. "Foreign Direct Investment and Spillovers through Worker's Mobility." *Journal of International Economics* vol. 53, pp. 205–222.

Galindo, Arturo, Alejandro Micco, and Serra, "Better the Devil that You Know: Evidence on Entry Costs Faced by Foreign Banks" IADB September 2002.

Galindo, Arturo, and Fabio Schiantarelli, "Credit Constraints on Firms in Latin America: An Overview of the Micro Evidence" IADB 2002.

Garber, Peter. 2000. "What you see vs. what you get: Derivatives in International Capital Flows" in Managing Financial and Corporate Distress: Lessons from Asia, edited by Charles Adams, Robert E. Litan, Michael Pomerleano (Brookings). http://brookings.nap.edu/books/0815701039/html/362.html#pagetop

Gelos, Gaston and Jorge Roldos. 2002. Consolidation and Market Structure in Emerging Market Banking Systems. Manuscript.

Germidis, Dimitri. Transfers of technology by multinational corporations. Paris. OECD 1977.

Goldberg, Linda. 2002. "When Is Foreign Bank Lending to Emerging Markets Volatile?" in *Preventing Currency Crises in Emerging Markets,* edited by Sebastian Edwards and Jeffrey Frankel (NBER and University of Chicago Press).

Goldberg, Linda, B. Gerard Dages, and Jennifer Crystal. 2002. "The Lending Cycles of Banks in Emerging Markets: Foreign and Domestic

Owners Compared." Manuscript, Federal Reserve Bank of New York.

Goldberg, Linda and Michael Klein. 1998. "Foreign Direct Investment, Trade and Real Exchange Rate Linkages in Developing Countries," 1998, in *Managing Capital Flows and Exchange Rates: Perspectives from the Pacific Basin,* edited by Reuven Glick. (Cambridge University Press).

Goldberg, Linda and Michael Klein. 2001. "International Trade and Factor Mobility: An Empirical Investigation," in *Money, Capital Mobility and Trade: Essays in Honor of Robert Mundell,* edited by G. Calvo, R. Dornbusch, and M. Obstfeld. (M.I.T. Press).

Gorg, Holger and David Greenaway. 2003. "Much Ado About Nothing? Do Domestic Firms Really Benefit from Foreign Direct Investment?" *World Bank Research Observer* (forthcoming).

Hanson, Gordon and Matthew Slaughter. 2003. "The Role of Multinational Corporations in International Business Cycle Transmission." Manuscript.

Hawkins, John and Dubravko Mihaljek. 2001. "The banking industry in the emerging market economies: competition, consolidation and systemic stability: an overview." In *The banking industry in the emerging market economies: competition, consolidation and systemic stability* Bank for International Settlements papers no. 4 (August).

Horstmann, Ignatius and James Markusen. "Firm-specific Assets and the Gains from Direct Foreign Investment." *Economica,* February 1989, 56 (221) pp. 41–48.

Horvath, E. 2002. Lending booms, credit risk and the dynamic provisioning system, in Studies on the Procyclical Behaviour of Banks, National Bank of Hungary Occasional Papers #10. http://www.mnb.hu/english/

Imbs, Jean. 2003. "Trade, Finance, Specialization, and Synchronization" *Review of Economics and Statistics.* August.

Kiraly, Julia, Bea Majer, Lazlo Matyas, Bela Ocsi, Andras Sugar and Eva Varhegyi. 2000. "Experience with Internationalization of Financial Services Providers—Case Study:

Hungary." In Stijn Claessens and Marion Jansen, eds *The Internationalization of Financial Services: Issues and Lessons for Developing Countries*. (Boston, Mass.: Kluwer Academic Press.)

Kokko, Ari, 1994. "Technology, Market Characteristics, and Spillovers," *Journal of Development Economics* vol. 43 pp. 279–293.

Kose, M. Ayhan, Eswar S. Prasad, and Marco E. Terrones. 2003. "Volatility and Comovement in a Globalized World Economy: An Empirical Exploration." International Monetary Fund, working paper wp/03/246.

LaPorta, Rafael, Florencio Lopez-de-Silances, and Andrei Shleifer. 2002. "Government Ownership of Banks" *Journal of Finance*, forthcoming.

Levine, Ross. 1999. "Foreign Bank Entry and Capital Control Liberalization: Effects on Growth and Stability." Manuscript, University of Minnesota.

Levine, Ross, Norman Loayza, and Thorsten Beck. 2000. "Financial Intermediation and Growth: Causality and Causes." *Journal of Monetary Economics,* vol. 46 (1): 31–77.

Lipsey. 2000. "Inward FDI and Economic Growth in Developing Countries," *Transnational Corporations*, Vol. 9, No. 1, (April), Geneva, United Nations Conference on Trade and Development, pp. 67–96.

Lipsey, Robert E. and Frederik Sjoholm. 2002. "Foreign Firms and Indonesian Manufacturing Wages: An Analysis with Panel Data." NBER working paper no. 9417 (December).

Markusen, James R. 1995. "The Boundaries of Multinational Enterprises and the Theory of International Trade." *Journal of Economic Perspectives* vol. 9, pp. 169–189.

Markusen, James R. and Anthony J. Venables. 1999. "Foreign Direct Investment as a Catalyst for Industrial Development." *European Economic Review,* vol. 43, pp. 335–356.

Mathieson, Donald J. and Jorge Roldas, 2001. "Foreign Banks in Emerging Markets." In Robert E. Litan, Paul Masson, and Michael Pomerleano, eds. *Open Doors: Foreign Participation in Financial Systems in Developing Countries*. (Washington DC: Brookings Institute Press.)

Martinez Peria, Maria Soledad, and Sergio Schmukler. 1999. "Do Depositors Punish Banks for 'Bad' Behavior? Market Discipline in Argentina, Chile, and Mexico." World Bank Policy Research Working Paper no. 2058 (February).

Novaes and Sergio Werlang. "Political Risk and Capital Structure Choice of Foreign Subsidiaries: An Empirical Analysis" November 2001 http://www.bis.org/pub/joint04.pdf

Oman, C. 2000. *Policy Competition for Foreign Direct Investment: A Study of Competition Among Governments to Attract FDI.* (Paris OECD).

Peek, Joe, and Eric Rosengren. 1997. "The International Transmission of Financial Shocks: The Case of Japan." *American Economic Review* 87, no. 4 (September): 495–505.

Peek, Joe, and Eric Rosengren. 2000. "The Role of Foreign Banks in Latin America." Manuscript.

Prasad, Eswar, Kenneth Rogoff, Shang-Jin Wei, and M. Ayhan Kose. 2003. "Effects of Financial Globalization on Developing Countries: Some Empirical Evidence." International Monetary Fund Occasional Paper #220 (Washington D.C.).

Rajan, Raghuram G. and Luigi Zingales. "Financial Dependence and Growth." *American Economic Review* vol. 88 (3). June. Pp. 559–586.

Rodriguez-Clare, Andres. 1996. "Multinational Linkages and Economic Development." *American Economic Review* vol. 86 pp. 852–873.

Rojas-Suarez, Liliana. 2001. "Rating banks in emerging markets: What credit rating agencies should learn from financial indicators." Institute for International Economics working paper 01–6.

Romer, Paul. 1993. "Idea gaps and object gaps in economic development" *Journal of Monetary Economics* 32 pp. 543–573.

Sapienza, Paola. "Lending Incentives of State-Owned Banks" Northwestern University working paper. 2002.

Seth, Rama, Daniel E. Nolle, and Sunil K. Mohanty. 1998. "Do Banks Follow Their Customers Abroad?" *Financial Markets, Institutions, and Instruments* 7 (4): 1–25.

Skipper, Harold, Jr.. 2001. "Liberalization of Insurance Markets: Issues and Concerns." In *Open Doors: Foreign Participation in Financial Systems in Developing Countries,* edited by Robert Litan, Paul Masson, and Michael Pomerleano (Washington DC: Brookings Institution and the World Bank): 105–156.

Smarzynska, Beata. 2004. "Does Foreign Direct Investment Increase the Productivity of Domestic Firms? In Search of Spillovers through Backward Linkages." *American Economic Review,* forthcoming.

Stallings, Barbara and Rogerio Studart. 2001. "Financial Regulation and Supervision in Emerging Markets: The Experience of Latin America since the Tequila Crisis." CEPAL.

Ter Wengel. 1995. "International Trade in Banking Services," *Journal of International Money and Finance*, 14, 47–64.

UNCTAD. 2001. *World Investment Report 2001. Promoting Linkages.* (Switzerland: The United Nations)

Unite, Angelo and Michael Sullivan. 2001. "The Impact of Liberalization of Foreign Bank Entry on the Philippine Domestic Banking Market." Philippine Institute PASCN discussion paper 2001–08.

Van Rijckeghem, Caroline and Beatrice Weder. 2000. "Spillovers through Banking Centers: A Panel Data Analysis of Bank Flows" *Journal of International Money and Finance* (forthcoming).

Weller (2001) "The Supply of Credit by Multinational Banks in Developing and Transition Economies: Determinants and Effects." United Nations DESA Discussion Paper no. 16 http://www.un.org/esa/esa01dp16.pdf

Zhang, Kevin Honglin and James Markusen. 1999. "Vertical Multinational and Host-Country Characteristics." *Journal of Development Economics* 59: 233–252.

30

Appraising the IMF's Performance

A Review of the First Three Studies by the New Independent Evaluation Office

PETER B. **KENEN**

DOES THE IMF adopt a one-size-fits-all approach to fiscal policy in countries that seek its assistance, requiring retrenchment in every instance? Were the fiscal provisions of IMF programs responsible for the large output contractions in the countries beset by the Asian crisis of 1997–98? Why were those programs so slow to halt the capital outflows from those countries? Do IMF programs depress growth, and do they hurt the poor? And why have some countries been chronically dependent on IMF financing, which is supposed to be temporary?

Fresh answers to these questions are now available in the first set of studies produced by the Independent Evaluation Office (IEO) of the IMF, and if they are typical of the studies it will produce in the future, the IMF and its member countries will benefit significantly. Its analyses are thorough, combining careful quantitative work, detailed country studies, and discussions with IMF staff, national officials, and others. Its conclusions are eminently sensible, and most of its recommendations should be adopted, although some of them run afoul of an intractable conflict between candor and transparency.

The IEO chose three subjects for its first year's studies: fiscal adjustment in IMF-supported programs, the role of the IMF in three capital account crises (Indonesia, Korea, and Brazil), and the prolonged use of IMF resources.

Assessing Fiscal Strategy

The IEO report on fiscal adjustment poses two main questions: Have IMF programs required excessive fiscal adjustment? Has the fiscal adjustment been adequate in quality—in composition, sustainability, and incidence, especially in its impact on social spending and the vulnerable members of society?

A country obliged to improve its current account balance often has to make more resources available for the production of exports and import-competing goods and must then reduce aggregate domestic demand. For this reason, if no other, it is often necessary to tighten fiscal policy. But the amount of tightening cannot be chosen without first projecting aggregate expenditure, especially domestic investment. In some cases, moreover, a tightening is needed because of constraints on governments' ability to borrow or the need to achieve or maintain debt sustainability.

Yet the IEO finds that the link between the fiscal and current account balances in IMF programs is weaker than might be expected. A cross-sectional analysis covering 143 recent programs does reveal a positive link between the sign of the targeted change in the primary fiscal balance and the sign of the projected change in the current account balance, but the two are quite different in size. When the current account is projected to improve by 1 percent

Varying Approaches
Not all IMF programs called for improvements in both
the fiscal balance and the current account balance.
Table 1

Category	Percent of programs	Initial as percent of GDP	
		Current account	Fiscal balance
Improvement in fiscal balance:			
Improvement in current account	43	−6.6	−5.7
Deterioration in current account	27	−1.9	−4.4
Deterioration in fiscal balance:			
Improvement in current account	15	−8.2	−1.1
Deterioration in current account	15	−3.7	−1.1

Source: IEO, *Evaluation of Fiscal Adjustment,* Table 2.3.

of GDP, the fiscal balance is supposed to improve by only one-fifth as much. A far larger share of the targeted change in the fiscal balance is explained by the initial state of that balance. If a government has a big budget deficit, it is supposed to reduce it.

The same pattern emerges in Table 1, which classifies most of those same programs by the projected changes in the two balances. Although 70 percent of them call for an improvement in the fiscal balance, only two-thirds of that group call for improvement in the current account balance. The main feature of programs that call for an improvement in the fiscal balance is the initial size of the fiscal deficit. Conversely, half of the programs that contemplate a deterioration in the fiscal balance still call for an improvement in the current account balance.

Invoking these and other findings, the IEO concludes convincingly that IMF programs do *not* display a one-size-fits-all strategy. Furthermore, its findings suggest that IMF programs do not depress economic growth. Table 2 presents some of the relevant evidence. Typically, GDP growth in the preprogram year was much slower than trend growth in the prior decade, save in low-income countries. And, in all but one country group, growth in the first program year was faster than in the preprogram

year, and it was typically higher in the second program year. The table also shows that the exceptional case—slower growth in the first program year—was due chiefly to sharp economic contractions in the small number of countries beset by the capital account crises of the past few years, a subject discussed below.

The IEO evaluation also addresses the common criticism of the IMF that it is not sufficiently sensitive to the effect of fiscal adjustment on vital social programs, such as health care and education. To this end, the IEO compares the relevant levels of government spending by individual countries in years when they had IMF programs with levels of spending in other years. In the vast majority of cases, there was no significant difference, no matter how spending was measured. Where there were significant differences, moreover, the number of cases in which spending rose typically exceeded the number in which it fell. The IEO points out, however, that the vulnerable members of society are not always well protected from the effects of fiscal tightening, and it cites a distressing example:

In 1999, Ecuador suffered a macroeconomic crisis. Inflation rose to 60 percent, public sector wages rose by 34 percent, and the currency depreciated sharply. But the health budget rose by only 12 percent.

Is Growth Depressed?

The IEO found that countries grew *faster* with an IMF program in place, (percent)

Table 2

Category	Trend in prior decade	Preprogram year	Program years	
			First	Second
All programs	1.6	1.4	2.2	3.8
Low-income countries[1]	1.7	2.8	4.4	4.3
Transition countries[2]	−2.1	−3.3	0.4	3.0
All other countries[3]	3.6	2.4	0.9	3.7
Capital account crises	4.8	2.9	−5.0	4.7
Other programs	3.4	2.3	2.1	3.5

Source: IEO, *Evaluation of Fiscal Adjustment,* Table 5.1.

[1]Average for 64 programs using the Enhanced Structural Adjustment Facility or the Poverty Reduction and Growth Facility.

[2]Average for 34 programs using a Stand-by Arrangement or the Extended Fund Facility.

[3]Average for 61 programs using a Stand-by Arrangement or the Extended Fund Facility, of which 10 involved the capital account crises for which the outcomes are shown separately.

Therefore, six public hospitals were visited to see how they coped with higher wage costs and the much higher costs of medical inputs caused by the depreciation. As the hospitals had to cut back patient care, outpatient care fell by more than 25 percent, the number of prescriptions dispensed dropped sharply in three hospitals, and patients' food rations were cut in at least one hospital although staff rations stayed relatively constant.

The IEO concludes that the protection of small but critical nonwage budgetary items poses a major challenge for the design and monitoring of fiscal adjustment—and one that the IMF cannot meet by itself. Help from the World Bank is needed to design the requisite expenditure safeguards.

Design and Implementation of Fiscal Adjustment

Although the IEO rejects the most common criticisms of the fiscal measures in IMF programs, it raises three concerns about the design and implementation of those measures.

First, excessive optimism about the recovery of output and, especially, investment tends to impart a contractionary bias to those fiscal measures. As a result, the current account balance adjusts more strongly than projected. Reviewing 52 conventional programs (those that did not involve the transition countries or the low-income countries eligible for concessional financing), the IEO finds that the projected change in the current account during the second program year was typically close to zero, yet the actual improvement was typically larger than 1 percent of GDP. And this result obtained even though the actual improvement in the fiscal balance was typically smaller than the projected improvement. Although the IMF does not require fiscal tightening in every program, it may call for too much tightening in too many programs.

Second, the IEO is dissatisfied with the rationale provided for the fiscal aspects of IMF programs. Having examined the documents pertaining to 15 programs, it finds that they often fail to justify the size and pace of the fiscal measures and do not explain how the fiscal targets mesh with the assumptions about economic recovery or with the rest of the program. These matters, it notes, are covered more thoroughly in subsequent reports on the progress of programs, but not in the initial briefs. It urges the staff to undertake more intensive brainstorming in the initial briefs—to articulate clearly the rationale for the fiscal measures, as well as the risks to programs and the revisions that might be needed if those risks materialize. In its response to the IEO, the staff points out that the key assumptions of IMF programs have to be negotiated with the governments involved and that the excessive optimism mentioned earlier may reflect the governments' desire to achieve a rapid revival of confidence and to generate domestic support for the programs. When that is true, however, the viability of the programs may well be at risk.

These two concerns, taken together, are reinforced by another finding. When programs are reviewed for the first time, most of the revisions in the fiscal measure are minor, and the few major revisions are distributed rather evenly between upward and downward changes in the fiscal targets. But when programs are reviewed for the second time, more fiscal targets have to be relaxed than tightened, suggesting that the initial fiscal targets were too demanding.

Finally, the IEO criticizes the sorts of fiscal measures found in many programs. They stress the revenue side more than the expenditure side, and the revenue measures themselves are too narrowly focused. On the revenue side, the IEO says, the IMF rightly views the value-added tax as the cornerstone of a modern tax system, but it has not paid enough attention to income and property taxes and to the need to combat tax evasion. On the expenditure side, the IEO says, the IMF has focused too heavily on cutting public employment or capping public sector wages, measures that tend to be short lived because they are easily reversed.

The IEO concedes that these defects reflect an unavoidable mismatch of time frames; IMF programs do not last long enough to see deeper reforms to completion.

Therefore, the IEO rightly urges the closer integration of programs and surveillance. Programs should exploit the previous findings of surveillance, and surveillance should monitor the completion of reforms introduced by programs.

The IMF and Recent Capital Account Crises

Concerns about fiscal adjustment in IMF programs also appear in the IEO study of three capital account crises: the Indonesian and Korean crises of 1997–98 and the Brazilian crisis of 1998–99. In the first two crises, it says, the IMF called for too much fiscal tightening because it failed to foresee the collapse of investment and resulting fall in output. In the Brazilian crisis, it says, the IMF called for too little tightening, given the need to achieve debt sustainability. Like IMF staff studies of these crises (the 1999 account of the Asian crisis by Timothy Lane and others, and the 2002 study of capital account crises by Atish Ghosh and others), the IEO blames the collapse of investment in Indonesia and Korea on the balance sheet effects of the currency depreciations, effects that were not foreseen at the time. Like those staff studies, moreover, the IEO notes that the IMF modified its fiscal targets quickly and thus absolves it of blame for the large fall in output. In Brazil, by contrast, the IMF went in the opposite direction. It called for more fiscal tightening after Brazil had to let its currency float and the subsequent depreciation raised the government's debt burden, as much of its debt was dollar denominated or dollar linked.

The IEO is less firmly supportive of the monetary policies prescribed by the IMF, apart from noting that Indonesia and Brazil failed to follow those policies during the early stages of their crises. Recent research, it says, has not dispelled doubts about the net benefit of raising interest rates when a country confronts a currency crisis. Theoretical work has shown that higher interest rates can strengthen or weaken a currency, empirical work has not settled the matter, and the issue is even harder to resolve when a country faces a banking crisis as well as a currency crisis. In light of these considerations, the IEO concludes, it is difficult to pronounce definitively on the appropriateness of monetary conditionality in the three crisis countries.

The IEO is less circumspect when assessing the results of the IMF programs. The initial programs failed in that they did not stabilize the three countries' currencies. In Indonesia, the IEO blames the government for refusing to take ownership of the program and, indeed, subverting it. In Korea, it blames the IMF's major shareholders for attaching vague conditions to the use of the bilateral financing they provided and for taking too long to involve Korea's private sector creditors. In Brazil, it divides blame between the government and the IMF for trying to defend an overvalued currency and failing to address the government's adverse debt dynamics. But it also faults the IMF for failing to detect some of the vulnerabilities that explain the severity of the Korean and Indonesian crises and for failing to flag the vulnerabilities it did, in fact, detect.

The detailed accounts of the crises in the IEO evaluation are well worth reading for the light they shed on relations between the IMF and its major shareholders. It is widely believed that the IMF and the U.S. Treasury worked closely together to resolve the crises under study. There were marked differences of view, however, between the IMF and its major shareholders. In Korea, the IMF quickly concluded that the available financing was insufficient and immediately pressed its major shareholder governments to achieve a rollover of bank credit lines, but to no avail. In Indonesia, a long list of structural reforms was attached to the January 1998 program at the urging of major shareholders in the belief that confidence could be restored only by signaling a clean break with the past. The IEO finds that this strategy deflected attention from vital reforms in the banking sector and reduced the willingness of the Suharto government to take ownership of the program.

The IMF has already addressed some of the issues raised in the IEO evaluation—a fact that the IEO readily acknowledges. The IMF has decided, for example, that programs should not include structural reforms unless they are required to achieve the macroeconomic objectives of the programs. We should not expect to see again long lists of structural reforms like those in the Indonesian and Korean programs. It may be harder, however, to implement some of the IEO's other recommendations, notably those that pertain to IMF surveillance. At times, the IEO suggests that candor and transparency are complementary—that the publication of the IMF's views can stimulate public debate about national policies and bring market pressure to bear on a recalcitrant government. Elsewhere, it concedes that they can conflict. When candor is combined with transparency, markets may react abruptly—faster than governments can react constructively.

In an effort to marry candor and transparency, the IEO suggests that the IMF find ways of engaging in escalated signaling when, in the course of surveillance, the staff has identified key vulnerabilities and they have not been cured after several more rounds of surveillance. This approach, it says, would strike a balance between the role of the IMF as confidential advisor to governments and its role in providing information to markets. But this approach assumes implicitly that markets will respond in a graduated way to the escalating signals from the IMF, and there is little reason to expect that outcome. It may thus be better to rely on confidential warnings that a government will not qualify for large-scale IMF financing if, by failing to cure key vulnerabilities, it succumbs eventually to a capital account crisis.

What should the staff tell the Board, however, when the risk to an IMF program does not derive from unforeseen shocks or perceived vulnerabilities but is instead political—the risk that a government will be unwilling or unable to implement an IMF program? The IEO tackled this question in its report on prolonged use.

Prolonged Use of IMF Resources

The IEO treats a country as being a prolonged user if it has had IMF programs for 7 or more years in any 10-year period. Under this definition, a country is not likely to be a prolonged user unless it has had at least two 3-year programs within a 10-year period. Nevertheless, the IEO finds that prolonged use has risen since the 1970s, whether measured by the number of countries involved or the total financial exposure of the IMF. To a significant extent, prolonged use reflects the adaptation of IMF policies and financial facilities to meet the special needs of low-income countries. Most prolonged users belong to that group. But much of the increase in financial exposure resulting from prolonged use reflects the involvement of middle-income countries, such as Argentina, Mexico, and Turkey. The IEO finds, moreover, that both sorts of prolonged use are due partly to flaws in IMF policies and programs.

Though the findings in this report derive from studying prolonged use, some have wider applicability. The IEO's case studies of prolonged use, for example, yield valuable findings about the design of conditionality:

- The specific structure of conditionality is less important than an underlying domestic political commitment to core policy adjustment.
- Excessively detailed conditionality—whether used because of a weak track record, doubts about ownership, or to support reform-minded groups within a government—does not appear to have been effective.
- Conditionality focused on policy rules or procedures, rather than discretionary onetime actions, was ultimately more effective.

The IEO also discusses the political economy of conditionality and the problem raised above: How and where should political feasibility enter into the IMF's decision-making processes? The IEO finds that judgments about political feasibility influence IMF mission chiefs working with national governments on the design of programs and that staff members often understand the political risks to a program. It also finds, however, that these judgments do not surface in staff reports to the Board. But its conclusion suggests a different solution to this crucial problem. Judgments about political risks should be clearly distinguished from judgments about other risks and should be made in a transparent manner at the level of the Managing Director and the Executive Board, who are accountable for them. But this surely implies that the staff should be strongly encouraged to advise the Managing Director, if not the Board itself, of the concerns that it may have about the political risks to a particular program.

Returning to the narrower problem of prolonged use, the IEO finds that aid donors and others, including the Paris Club of official creditors, often key their own decisions to those of the IMF—that is, an IMF program is seen as a seal of approval. This practice, it says, may lead the IMF to tolerate prolonged use, and it should therefore develop other ways to signal its approval of a country's policies, including more frequent use of enhanced surveillance, shadow programs, and precautionary arrangements.

Unfortunately, the IEO does not explore sufficiently another explanation for prolonged use. The IMF may tolerate prolonged use because it is loath to face the obvious consequence of refusing to approve an additional program—the failure of a large middle-income country to repay what it already owes. When tracing the involvement of the IMF in concessional lending to the low-income countries, IMF historian James Boughton notes that it began when the IMF started to worry about the ability of those countries to repay concessional loans from the trust fund set up in the wake of the first oil crisis. Similar concerns may help to explain the recent growth of prolonged use by some middle-income countries. It is hard to believe that those concerns did not influence the decision to approve a new program for Argentina in 2003.

Looking Ahead

Reflecting on the lEO's work to date, the topics of its next three studies, and the published list of topics on which it may work thereafter, I offer two general observations:

The lEO's initial studies dealt with a large subject, although two of them also contained detailed country studies. As a result, some of its recommendations have been cast too broadly to elicit firm responses from the Executive Board. Almost all of the recommendations made in the study of prolonged use are applicable generally to the work of the IMF and have thus far elicited rather vague responses. The IEO has made operational recommendations, one of which the Board rejected— the proposal that prolonged users be charged higher interest rates. Yet concrete recommendations may stand the best chance of producing focused debate in the Board and, when they find favor, subsequent implementation. The Board, for example, has agreed to adopt an operational definition of prolonged use and to use that definition to assess the effectiveness of IMF programs involving prolonged use.

Broad subjects, moreover, tend to spawn long documents, and the first three from the IEO were rather long indeed. To be sure, they were well organized, with executive summaries at the start and technical annexes at the end. Nevertheless, they may be too long to serve effectively one of the main purposes of the IEO—promoting wider understanding of the IMF. Shorter studies of narrower subjects might be read more widely.

Looking further ahead, the IEO should contemplate follow-up studies to ask whether its recommendations have had the expected effect. It will not run out of new subjects to study but should not wait long to revisit old ones.

Peter B. Kenen is Walker Professor of Economics and International Finance at Princeton University

References

Boughton, James M., 2001, Silent Revolution: The International Monetary Fund, 1979–1989 *(Washington: International Monetary Fund).*

Ghosh, Atish, and others, *2002,* IMF-Supported Programs in Capital Account Crises, *Occasional Paper 210 (Washington: International Monetary Fund).*

Independent Evaluation Office, *2002,* Evaluation of Prolonged Use of IMF Resources *(Washington: International Monetary Fund).*

———, 2003, The IMF and Recent Capital Account Crises:

Indonesia, Korea, Brazil *(Washington, International Monetary Fund).*

———, Fiscal Adjustment in IMF-Supported Programs *(Washington: International Monetary Fund).*

Lane, Timothy, and others, *1999,* IMF-Supported Programs in Indonesia, Korea, and Thailand: A Preliminary Assessment, *Occasional Paper 178 (Washington: International Monetary Fund).*

Sovereign Wealth Funds

PHILIP **KING**

When Citibank faced a capital shortage in late 2007, it turned to an obscure source for funding—the Abu Dhabi's sovereign wealth fund (SWF), which loaned Citibank $7.5 billion in exchange for convertible equity. Since then sovereign wealth funds have become a household word, at least on Wall Street. Overall, these funds control approximately three trillion dollars in capital and have the ability to deploy their funds without the constraints that apply to many other funds, such as pension funds. This article will examine the nature of sovereign wealth funds.

What is a Sovereign Wealth Fund?

Sovereign wealth funds are controlled by sovereign states and are designed to invest a country's savings to earn a high rate of return. In some cases, SWFs have been established to promote macroeconomic stability in addition to managing huge influxes of cash related to commodity exports which might otherwise destabilize a small economy. SWFs may invest in stocks, bond, commodities, real estate, or any other asset. They can buy companies directly or hold equity in a company through the purchase of stock. As such, they are not that different from many other private funds, such as mutual funds, pension funds, or private equity funds. What makes SWFs unique is the fact that they are controlled by foreign countries, generally resulting from foreign reserves created by a large trade surplus. The scale of SWFs and the fact that they can engage in multi-billion dollar trades almost overnight also makes them significant.

History of Sovereign Wealth Funds

Although the term "sovereign wealth fund" is relatively new, the concept has been around for quite some time. It is often acknowledged that the first SWF was the Kiribati Revenue Equalization Fund, established in 1956 when the British placed a levy on phosphate exports used for fertilizer on an island in Micronesia. A number of similar funds were established in the 1970s and 1980s, mostly by oil exporting countries that developed large trade surpluses when oil prices rose. Some countries have also established SWFs when fiscal surpluses arose or when large state owned companies were privatized, creating a windfall for the state. However, the majority of SWFs are related to natural resource exports, in particular oil. It is not a coincidence that the boom in [the price of] resources in the late 1970s, early 1980s and then again in the early 21st century gave rise to SWFs. The huge current account surpluses that China, Singapore, and other countries experienced as a result of massive export booms also contribute to the growth in SWFs.

How Large are SWFs and Which Are the Most Significant?

Table 1 below lists the twelve largest SWFs along with the country of origin and date of inception. Since SWFs are not always required to disclose assets and since investments can fluctuate, these estimates may vary. Of these twelve funds, nine are owned by oil exporting countries. With the exception of Norway, all of these oil exporting countries are in the Middle East. Two other countries with substantial SWFs are Singapore and China; both countries have large trade surpluses. Singapore controls two of the twelve largest funds: Temasek holdings and GIC. A number of other countries, including Russia, Canada, Iran, Botswana, New Zealand, Chile, own much smaller funds.

Most of these funds are also related to oil or other resource based exports.

Including all known funds, the total assets controlled by SWFs are estimated at $3 trillion in 2008, but this amount will grow rapidly. Morgan Stanley estimates that by 2012, SWFs will control $12 trillion. If oil prices continue to rise and the US dollar falls, this may well be an underestimate. While this may sound like a huge amount of money, it is still relatively small compared to the over $20 trillion managed by pension funds or the amount managed by mutual funds, insurance companies, or official reserve assets of sovereign countries. However, the dramatic growth of sovereign wealth funds, along with fact that many have few restrictions, has been cause for concern in some circles.

Largest Sovereign Wealth Funds
League of Nations
Sovereign-wealth funds Latest
Table 1

Country: Name	Assets* $bn	Inception Year
UAE: Abu Dhabi Investment Authority	875.0	1976
Norway: Government Pension Fund—Global	380.0	1996
Singapore: GIC	330.0	1981
Saudi Arabia: various	300.0	*no*
Kuwait: Reserve Fund for Future Generations	250.0	1953
China: China Investment Corporation[1]	200.0	2007
Singapore: Temasek Holdings	159.2	1974
Libya: Oil Reserve Fund	50.0	2005
Qatar: Qatar Inv. Auth.	50.0	2005
Algeria: Fond de Régulation des Recettes	42.6	2000
US: Alaska Permanent Fund Corporation	38.0	1976
Brunei: Brunei Inv. Auth.	30.0	1983
Other	171.4	—
Total	**2,876.3**	—
of which oil- and gas-related	*2,103.4*	—

*Estimated, excluding Norway
[1]Includes Central Huijin Investment Co.
Source: Morgan Stanley

How Large Are SWFs Compared to Other Asset Classes?

A lot, or a little?

Global assets under management

Latest available, trillion

Table 2

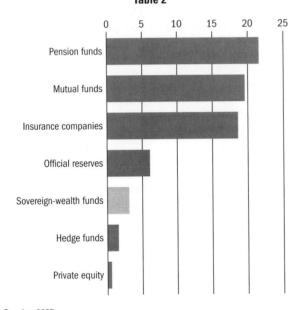

Source: Morgan Stanley 2007

What Are the Criticisms of Sovereign Wealth Funds?

Critics of SWFs point to the fact that SWFs are controlled by foreign governments whose interests may not be the same as the U.S. or other sources of the SWFs investment. The vast majority of SWFs are controlled by countries that are not democratic and that may have interests opposed to the U.S. or other countries where the SWFs investments are located. Indeed, it is possible that a country could use its SWF strategically to influence policy abroad. Even if an initial investment was made for other reasons, it might be hard to ignore a substantial investment in a key company. For example, Citibank is one of the largest banks in the world and a key part of the U.S.'s financial system. As such it is generally considered "too big to fail." What are the implications when a substantial portion of such a company is owned by an entity that is controlled by a foreign government?

The debate over SWFs does not fall neatly into the laissez-faire versus government regulation divide that often surrounds public policy debates. Some supporters of free markets argue that SWFs, since they are controlled by foreign governments, are not really part of a free market and hence violate laissez-faire principles. On the other hand, proponents of government regulations, such as Dani Rodrik, have argued that SWFs do not constitute a threat.

One other issue that frequently arises is the potential lack of transparency with SWFs. Unlike most pension funds, insurance companies or other large asset funds, SWFs are not always required to disclose their transactions or holdings, though large transactions are usually reported widely in the press. SWFs face few regulations as well, unlike banks and other financial intermediaries. Finally, publicly owned companies are also required to disclose a great deal of financial information. No such requirements extend to SWFs, though some are required by their host countries to disclose much information.

As one might expect, SWFs in Norway, the U.S. (Alaska) and Canada generally have a higher degree of transparency, publishing annual reports that disclose a great deal of information. Singapore's two SWFs also score high in terms of transparency, as does Malaysia's SWF.

However, the SWFs controlled by OPEC countries, as well as China, score relatively low in terms of transparency. Table 3 presents a ranking of the largest SWFs in four important categories, according to Edwin Truman of the Peterson Institute for International Economics. The first category, structure, focuses on whether the source of the SWFs funding and the subsequent use of the SWFs proceeds are clearly stated, whether there are guidelines for corporate responsibility and ethical behavior as well as whether the SWF has a clear budget and clear goals. The second category, governance, focuses on how the SWF has been set up, whether the SWF can be directly influenced by the political whims of a country's leaders, and whether a SWF has guidelines for ethical behavior and corporate governance. The third category, transparency and accountability, examines whether the SWF has an annual report as well as quarterly reports, whether investments and holdings are clearly disclosed publicly, as well as whether these reports are audited by independent accounting firms. The final category is behavior, which focuses on the speed of adjustment in a SWFs portfolio.

As can be seen in Table 3, New Zealand and Norway scores the highest, with the U.S. and Canada not far behind in terms of transparency. Most OPEC countries score quite low (though Kuwait is a bit of an exception). The Table also ranks the California Public Employees

Retirement System (PERS) for comparison and it scored relatively high, though below New Zealand and Norway's SWFs.

What Is to Be Done?

First, one should recognize that SWFs are not going to disappear. The low savings rate in the U.S. and corresponding trade deficits over the last decade have given rise to huge current account surpluses in oil exporting countries as well as a number of export oriented countries in Asia, particularly China. Traditionally, these surpluses were held in the form of dollars or US government debt. However, these assets have very low rates of return. Indeed, when the dollar is falling, these assets may yield negative returns in terms of the host country's currency. SWFs allow a country to reinvest their surpluses in a manner that can earn a higher return. SWFs also make sense for a country (like China) that already has a huge amount in reserves and wants to diversify its holdings of foreign assets.

A number of organizations, including the U.S. Treasury and G-7 countries, have publicly endorsed any actions that would increase transparency, governance and accountability by SWFs. Singapore has already taken a step in this direction. Larry Summers of Harvard University has suggested that SWFs take a more conventional approach and hire asset managers in the same way that mutual funds and pension funds do. It has also been suggested that SWFs limit their holdings in one particular company (as most mutual funds are required) or even that they buy non-voting shares of stock. While this restriction may seem tame, it's clear that one role SWFs have played is to "bail-out" companies such as Citibank, which were in need of a large amount of capital in a short period of time. In many aspects, SWFs are playing the same role that Warren Buffet, Carl Icahn, and other wealthy individuals often play: buyer of last resort. Without a large influx of capital, these firms may face severe liquidity problems and potential

Summary Scoreboard for Sovereign Wealth Funds
Table 3

		Structure	Governance	Transparency & Accountability	Behavior	Total
New Zealand	Superannuation Fund	8.00	4.00	12.00	0.00	24.00
Norway	Government Pension Fund—Global	7.50	4.00	10.50	1.00	23.00
Timor-Leste	Petroleum Fund	8.00	2.00	11.75	0.00	21.75
Canada	Alberta Heritage Savings Trust Fund	7.50	3.00	9.00	0.00	19.50
United States	Alaska Permanent Fund	7.50	2.00	8.50	0.00	18.00
Australia	Future Fund	8.00	2.00	7.00	0.00	17.00
Azerbaijan	State Oil Fund of the Republic of Azerbaijan	5.00	2.00	9.50	0.00	16.50
Chile	Economic and Social Stabilization Fund	7.00	2.00	6.50	0.00	15.50
Botswana	Pula Fund	5.50	2.00	7.00	0.00	14.50
Kazakhstan	National Oil Fund	6.00	2.00	6.50	0.00	14.50
Singapore	Temasek Holdings	4.00	1.50	8.00	0.00	13.50
São Tomé and Príncipe	National Oil Account	8.00	2.00	2.25	0.00	12.25
Trinidad and Tobago	Heritage and Stabilization Fund	6.50	2.00	3.75	0.00	12.25
Kuwait	Kuwait Investment Authority	6.00	3.00	3.00	0.00	12.00
Malaysia	Khazanah Nasional	4.00	1.50	4.00	0.00	9.50
Russia	Stabilization Fund of the Russian Federation	4.00	2.00	3.50	0.00	9.50
Korea	Korea Investment Corporation	6.00	2.00	1.00	0.00	9.00
Kiribati	Revenue Equalization Reserve Fund	5.00	2.00	0.50	0.00	7.50
Mexico	Oil Income Stabilization Fund	5.00	0.00	2.00	0.00	7.00
China	Central Huijin Investment Company	5.50	0.00	0.50	0.00	6.00
Venezuela	National Development Fund	1.50	0.50	4.00	0.00	6.00
Iran	Oil Stabilization Fund	4.00	1.00	0.50	0.00	5.50
Venezuela	Macroeconomic Stabilization Fund	3.00	0.50	2.00	0.00	5.50
Oman	State General Reserve Fund	3.00	0.00	2.00	0.00	5.00
Sudan	Oil Revenue Stabilization Account	4.00	0.00	1.00	0.00	5.00
Algeria	Revenue Regulation Fund	3.00	1.00	0.50	0.00	4.50
United Arab Emirates	Istithmar	3.00	0.50	0.25	0.00	3.75
United Arab Emirates	Mubadala Development Company	3.00	0.50	0.00	0.00	3.50
Brunei	Brunei Investment Agency	1.00	0.50	1.00	0.00	2.50
Singapore	Government of Singapore Investment Corporation	1.50	0.00	0.75	0.00	2.25
Qatar	Qatar Investment Authority	2.00	0.00	0.00	0.00	2.00
United Arab Emirates	Abu Dhabi Investment Authority and Corporation	0.50	0.00	0.00	0.00	0.50
Total Possible Points		8.00	4.00	12.00	1.00	25.00
Average Number of Points		4.80	1.42	4.02	0.03	10.27
United States	California Public Employees' Retirement System	8.00	3.00	10.25	0.50	21.75

Source: A Scoreboard for Sovereign Wealth Funds, Edwin Truman, Peterson Institute for International Economics, 2007.

bankruptcy. Further, since corporate governance requires active stockholders to hold management accountable, it is quite possible that restrictions on SWF voting may create unintended consequences if management is not held accountable.

The most likely solution, which has been proposed by the U.S. Treasury, is for the IMF to develop a code of conduct for SWFs with transparency being the first issue on the agenda. The Organization for Economic Cooperation and Development (OECD) may play a similar role to the IMF in proposing guidelines. SWFs which do not meet these guidelines may find it more difficult to access U.S. and European markets, though the U.S. and Europe should not make the restrictions so onerous that foreign capital would simply go elsewhere. Further, SWFs always face a small but powerful possibility that assets could be expropriated.

If SWFs want access to developed capital markets, their best bet is to "be boring." In other words, they will need to use index funds (which buy the entire stock market) and conventional asset management, disclose all assets and all transactions quarterly, as do most conventional fund managers, and follow Norway's example.

References

Will Devlin and Bill Brummitt, "A few sovereigns more: the rise of sovereign wealth funds, unpublished, 2007.

Jen, S, 'How big could Sovereign Wealth Funds be by 2015?', Morgan Stanley, 4 May, 2007

Johnson, S., 'The rise of sovereign wealth funds', IMF *Finance and Development,* September. vol. 44, no. 3, 2007.

Miles, David K. & Jen, Stephen, 'Sovereign wealth funds and bond and equity prices', Morgan Stanley, 31 May, 2007.

The Economist Magazine, various issues.

Federal Reserve Bank of San Francisco, Sovereign Wealth Funds: Stumbling Blocks or Stepping Stones to Financial Globalization? *FRBSF Economic Letter,* 2007-38; December 14, 2007.

Edwin Truman, "A Scoreboard for Sovereign Wealth Funds," Peterson Institute for International Economics, 2007.

Discussion Questions

IX

1. According to Burton and Zenello, what policies did the South-East Asian countries employ to recover from the crisis and to reduce their exposure to future crises?

2. What are the similarities in capital markets during the 1890s versus the 1990s?

3. What are the differences in capital markets during the 1890s versus the 1990s?

4. What are the primary advantages of FDI for a host country and local workers?

5. How do the effects of "real-side" FDI differ from financial sector FDI?

6. What are the criticisms often applied to IMF policies dealing with financial crises?

7. Given Kenen's summary of the IEO study, is the IMF's response to financial crises appropriate?

8. What are sovereign wealth funds, and where do the funds come from?

9. What are some of the criticisms leveled at sovereign wealth funds?

Foreign Aid

This last section focuses on developing country issues in international finance. The first article by Radelet, Clemens and Bhavnani, "Aid and Growth," discusses the effectiveness of foreign aid. Critics of foreign aid argue that aid fosters government bureaucracies, waste, and poor government policies with little or no positive results. Radelet et al. argue that previous assessments on the effectiveness of aid on economic growth are flawed because they do not take into account the type of aid, only the total amount of aid donated. When accounting for the type of aid received, the authors find that there is a strong, positive and causal effect of aid on economic growth. However, they find diminishing returns to aid; that is, larger amounts of aid do have a smaller impact on growth.

The Grameen Bank was one of the first institutions to offer microfinance and earned the 2006 Nobel Peace Prize. Most developing countries have under-developed financial markets and the poorest individuals are often denied basic banking services. Micro-financing offers small loans to those that cannot even verify income, credit history or have no collateral. Microfinance has grown in importance for developing countries. Along with the growth in microfinance, there is growth in microinsurance. Ina Kota's article on "Microfinance: Banking for the Poor" provides an overview of the microfinance model and its development beyond the Grameen Bank.

Aid and Growth

32

S T E V E N **R A D E L E T ,**
M I C H A E L **C L E M E N S ,**
A N D R I K H I L **B H A V N A N I**

Controversies about aid effectiveness go back decades. Critics such as Milton Friedman, Peter Bauer, and William Easterly have leveled stinging critiques, charging that aid has enlarged government bureaucracies, perpetuated bad governments, enriched the elite in poor countries, or just been wasted. They cite widespread poverty in Africa and South Asia despite three decades of aid, and point to countries that have received substantial aid yet have had disastrous records—such as the Democratic Republic of the Congo, Haiti, Papua New Guinea, and Somalia. In their eyes, aid programs should be dramatically reformed, substantially curtailed, or eliminated altogether.

Supporters counter that these arguments, while partially correct, are overstated. Jeffrey Sachs, Joseph Stiglitz, Nicholas Stern, and others have argued that, although aid has sometimes failed, it has supported poverty reduction and growth in some countries and prevented worse performance in others. They believe that many of the weaknesses of aid have more to do with donors than recipients, especially since much aid is given to political allies rather than to support development. They point to a range of successful countries that have received significant aid such as Botswana, Indonesia, Korea, and, more recently, Tanzania and Mozambique, along with successful initiatives such as the Green Revolution, the campaign against river blindness, and the introduction of oral rehydration therapy. In the 40 years since aid became widespread, they say, poverty indicators have fallen in many countries worldwide, and health and education indicators have risen faster than during any other 40-year period in human history.

Throughout this debate, however, most analysts have missed a critical point by treating all aid as if it were alike in its impact on growth. In a recent Center for Global Development study, we try to rectify this gap by exploring the impact on growth of aid flows that actually are aimed at growth.

Three Prevailing Views on Aid

Over the past three decades, three broad views have emerged on the relationship between aid and growth:

Aid has No Effect on Growth, and May Actually Undermine Growth

There are several reasons why aid might not support growth. It can be wasted on frivolous expenses such as limousines or presidential palaces, or it can encourage corruption. It can undermine incentives for private sector production, including by causing the currency to appreciate, which weakens the profitability of tradable goods production (an effect known as "Dutch disease"). Similarly, food aid, if not managed appropriately, can reduce farm prices and hurt farmer income. Aid flows potentially can undermine incentives for both private and government saving. They can also sustain bad governments in power, helping to perpetuate poor economic policies and postpone reform.

This view has been supported by a range of empirical studies, mostly published from the early 1970s through the mid-1990s. While these studies have been influential, many are of questionable quality, especially using today's research standards. For example, most assume only a simple linear relationship between aid and growth in which each new dollar of aid has exactly the same impact on growth as the first (eliminating the possibility of diminishing returns) and ignore possible endogeneity (in which faster growth might attract higher aid, or both might be caused by something else), among other issues. A recent paper by Raghuram Rajan and Arvind Subramanian (2005), which also assumes a simple linear relationship for most of its results, stands in sharp contrast to the bulk of recent research on the issue, as discussed below.

Aid has a Positive Relationship with Growth on Average (Although not in Every Country), but with Diminishing Returns

Aid could support growth by financing investment or by increasing worker productivity (for example, through investments in health or education). It can bring new technology or knowledge, either imbedded in capital goods imports or through technical assistance. Several early studies found a positive relationship between aid and growth, but this strand of the literature took a significant turn in the mid-1990s when researchers began to investigate whether aid might spur growth with diminishing returns—that is, that the impact of additional aid would decline as aid amounts grew. Oddly, since economic theory and research had recognized the importance of diminishing returns on investment since the 1950s, research on aid and growth until the mid-1990s tested only a linear relationship, a specification that (surprisingly) persists in some studies even today.

Although they have received comparatively less popular attention, most of these studies (some published in top peer-reviewed journals) have found a strong aid-growth relationship, including research by Michael Hadjimichael and colleagues at the IMF in the mid–1990s, and the work of Carl-Johan Dalgaard, Henrik Hansen, Finn Tarp, Robert Lensink, Howard White, and others between 1999 and 2005. These studies typically do not conclude that aid has always worked, but rather that, on average, higher aid flows have been associated with more rapid growth.

Aid has a Conditional Relationship with Growth, Helping to Accelerate Growth Only Under Certain Circumstances

The "conditional" view usually argues that aid effectiveness hinges on either recipient characteristics or donor practices.

Recipient country characteristics. World Bank researchers Jonathon Isham, Daniel Kaufmann, and Lant Pritchett opened this line of enquiry in 1995 by finding that World Bank projects had higher rates of returns in countries with stronger civil liberties. Craig Burnside and David Dollar followed with their influential study that concluded that aid stimulated growth in countries with good policies, but not otherwise. Others have proposed different characteristics that might affect the aid-growth relationship, including vulnerability to trade shocks, climate, institutional quality, political conflict, and geography. The statistical results of these studies tend to be fragile, however, and subsequent research has questioned some of the results.

Nevertheless, the view that aid works best (or in a stronger version, aid works only) in countries with good policies and institutions has become the conventional wisdom among donors, partly based on this research and partly due to development practitioners' own experiences. The appeal of this approach is that it can explain why aid seems to have supported growth in some countries but not others. This reasoning has had an enormous impact on donors, especially the multilateral development banks, and is the foundation of the U.S. Millennium Challenge Account (Radelet, 2003).

Donor practices. Multilateral aid might be more effective than bilateral aid, and untied aid is thought to have higher returns than aid tied to purchases in the donor country. Donors with large bureaucracies, heavy reporting requirements, or ineffective monitoring and evaluation systems probably undermine the effectiveness of their own programs. Two influential and overlapping views argue that aid is more effective when donors allow for greater "country ownership" or broader "participation" in setting priorities and designing programs (country ownership allows for the recipient country to have a stronger say in these decisions; broader participation allows civil society and faith-based and nongovernmental organizations to have a voice alongside the government in these choices). These issues have been regularly debated and have begun to change donor practices, but have been subject to little systematic research.

The Type of Aid Matters

New research has taken a different tack by exploring the idea that not all aid is alike in its impact on growth. This view suggests that most research on aid and growth is flawed regarding both substance and timing. On substance, almost all studies look at the relationship between total aid and growth, even though large portions of aid are not primarily directed at growth. For example, food and humanitarian aid are aimed primarily at supporting consumption, not growth, as is the provision of medicines, bed nets, and school books. And aid to support democracy or judicial reform is not primarily aimed at stimulating growth. These important aid-financed activities help improve recipient welfare by supporting basic consumption needs, developing political institutions, and strengthening health and education—but they are likely to affect growth only indirectly, if at all. By contrast, aid to build roads, bridges, or telecommunications facilities or to support agriculture and industry is more directly aimed at production and should be expected to accelerate growth. Given the range of likely impacts of different kinds of aid, it is not surprising that some research on aid and growth has shown a weak relationship.

On timing, most cross-country growth research uses panel data, with each observation (usually) corresponding to four years, but then investigates aid flows that cannot possibly affect growth in that period. Aid to support education and health, for example, may stimulate growth, but the impact is likely to take decades. One option for researchers is to use a longer time period, but there is a trade-off: the longer the time period, the harder it is to isolate the impact of aid (or other variables) on growth from other influences. Only a few studies have explored this idea, and most focus on specific countries. For example, one study found that household welfare in Zimbabwe was increased by "development aid" (such as infrastructure and agricultural extension) far more than by "humanitarian aid" (such as food aid and emergency transfers).

To remedy this weakness, our recent research focuses on the type of aid that is directed primarily at growth (Clemens, Radelet, and Bhavnani, 2004). We examined aid flows to 67 countries between 1974 and 2001 and divided aid into three categories:

1. *Aid for disasters, emergencies, and humanitarian relief efforts, including food aid.* Here we find a negative simple relationship, since disasters simultaneously cause growth to fall and aid to increase. The recent tsunami undermined growth in Sri Lanka, and donors responded with more aid. In a simplistic growth regression, cases like this would show up as high aid with low or negative growth, making it appear that aid had a poor relationship with growth, an obviously misleading result.

Method matters

In conducting our empirical research, we focused on three issues: (1) ensuring the basic model was consistent with theory and evidence; (2) controlling for the possible two-way relationship between aid and growth; and (3) testing the results with a broad yet reasonable set of robustness checks.

At the core of our model is a nonlinear relationship between "early impact" aid and growth that allows for diminishing returns: each additional dollar of aid has a smaller impact on growth than the last. This specification is consistent with both theory and extensive evidence, but it is often overlooked in the literature, giving rise to the weak relationships found in some studies. We then control for a wide variety of other factors that influence growth, including income level, institutional quality, trade policy, inflation, budget deficits, life expectancy, location in the tropics, and the incidence of civil war. Our results show that each of these variables is strongly related to growth, with the exceptions of initial income and budget deficits.

A positive relationship between aid and growth does not prove causality. More aid could cause higher growth, but faster growth could attract more aid, or both could be caused by something else (such as a change in government). To control for potential endogeneity, we estimate the relationship using instrumental variables, using as instruments geopolitical variables and past aid flows that have been used in previous peer-reviewed journal articles. But since no instrumentation strategy is perfect, we also estimate the model using ordinary least squares with aid lagged one four-year period, and find essentially the same results.

We further test the robustness of the results by examining differences rather than levels, eliminating outlier observations, estimating the model using the generalized method of moments procedure, controlling for more or fewer variables, and examining alternative definitions for key variables, among other tests. The results hold firm across this array of tests, giving us confidence in the robustness of the results.

2. *Aid that might affect growth, but indirectly and over a long period of time.* No one would expect aid aimed at environmental conservation or democratic reform to affect economic growth quickly, and certainly not over a four-year period. Similarly, aid to strengthen health and education is likely to affect labor productivity over many years, but not immediately (with some exceptions). In a standard cross-country growth regression, these observations are likely to appear as high aid and zero or very little growth, again weakening the results. As expected, we detect only a weak positive association between this "late-impact" aid and growth.

3. *Aid aimed more directly to support growth relatively quickly.* Aid to build infrastructure—roads, irrigation systems, electricity generators, and ports—should affect growth rates fairly quickly. So should aid to directly support productive sectors, such as agriculture, industry, trade, and services. Aid that comes as cash, such as budget or balance of payments support, could be spent on a wide variety of activities, but to be conservative we assume it is directed at growth (to the extent it is not, our assumption would only weaken our results). For this "early impact" aid (which accounts for about half of all aid), it is perfectly reasonable for policymakers to expect, and

for researchers to test for, a positive relationship with growth over a four-year period.

Early Impact Aid Boosts Growth

Our research shows a strong, positive, and causal effect of early impact aid on economic growth. The results exhibit diminishing returns, with larger amounts of aid having a progressively smaller impact. The estimated impact is nearly triple the magnitude found in other studies. We test the results over a very wide set of specifications and estimation techniques that control for other influences on growth, possible endogeneity, lags, and other factors. Throughout, the results remain strong and robust. We estimate the model over a four-year period, following the standard used in many studies, but we show (using lags) that the impact carries into a subsequent four-year period. We find no evidence that the effect is a short-run phenomenon that is later reversed. The results do not imply that aid has worked everywhere—it most definitely has not—but that, on average, growth-oriented aid has had a positive and significant impact on growth. The results underscore that the impact of early impact aid differs significantly from other types of aid (see Chart 1).

How great is the effect of early impact aid on growth? Consider the mean observation, where early impact aid is 2.7 percent of GDP (roughly equivalent to where total aid is about 5.4 percent of GDP). Using our most conservative results, at the mean, a 1 percentage point of GDP increase in early impact aid produces an additional 0.31 percentage point of annual growth over the four-year period. With plausible assumptions about discount and depreciation rates (summing to 35 percent), we calculate that each $1 in early impact aid yields $1.64 in increased income in the recipient country in net present value terms. This country-level return roughly corresponds to a project-level rate of return of around 13 percent. For sub-Saharan Africa, we find that higher-than-average

early impact aid raised per capita growth rates by about 1 percentage point over the growth that would have been achieved by average aid flows. This suggests that, while growth in sub-Saharan Africa has been disappointing, it would have been worse in the absence of this kind of aid.

What about the claim that aid works best in countries with good policies and institutions? To explore this idea, we looked at one of the most commonly used measures of institutional quality, drawn from the International Country Risk Guide. This index, which has been shown to be strongly correlated with growth, includes measures of the extent of corruption, rule of law, risk of expropriation or repudiation of contracts, and bureaucratic quality. We find some evidence that in countries with better institutions, the relationship between early impact aid and growth is stronger than otherwise. In addition, in countries with higher life expectancy (that is, better health), the aid–growth relationship is stronger than otherwise. But unlike other studies, we do not find that aid works only in countries with strong institutions or better health, and our results do not hinge on this interaction.

Are there limits on how much early impact aid typical recipients can absorb? The answer appears to be yes, but the maximum growth rate occurs on average when early impact aid represents 8–9 percent of GDP, more than three times the typical amount. As a rule of thumb, since early impact aid is slightly more than half of total aid on average, this implies that the maximum growth rate occurs when total aid reaches around 16–18 percent of GDP in the typical country. This does not mean that in any particular country, aid flows greater than this amount are necessarily a bad idea. Instead, this represents the typical pattern over the last 30 years—some countries can absorb more, and others less. Moreover, we find that absorptive capacity depends to some extent on the quality of institutions and general health of the population. In countries with stronger institutions and higher life expectancy, the

Not All Aid is Alike

Some types of aid have a much bigger impact on growth than others—possibly why some studies examining aggregate aid find weak results.

Chart 1

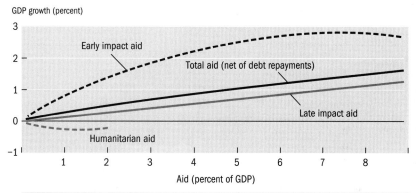

Humanitarian aid	Early Impact aid	Late Impact aid
Disaster relief	Transport and storage	Government and civil society
Emergency aid	Communications	General environmental protection
Humanitarian relief	Energy generation and supply	Women in development
Food aid	Most banking and financial services	Health
	Business and other services	Education
	Agriculture, forestry, and fishing	Populations policies
	Industry, mineral resources, and mining	Water supply and sanitation
	Construction	Policy and administrative management
	Structural adjustment assistance	Support to nongovernmental
	Budget support	organizations
	Debt relief	Other social infrastructure and services

Source: Clemens (2004).

Note: All three curves are estimated using a similar model and include a nonlinear relationship between aid and growth (which is hard to detect visually in the curve for late impact aid). The curve for humanitarian aid is cut off at 2 percent of GDP because there are no data in our sample beyond this point, and to show an upward curve would be misleading. Although only the coefficient an early impact aid is statistically significantly different from zero, the weather relationships for late impact and humanitarian aid do not necessarily mean these flows have no impact on growth, but rather that a different modeling technique is required to explore these relationships (which we leave for future research).

---

impact of early impact aid is stronger throughout, and more aid can be absorbed before reaching the maximum growth rate.

The results also suggest that aid is not fully fungible, at least in the sense that all aid is interchangeable. If this were true, different subcategories would show similar relationships with growth. Instead, we find that aid flows intended for different purposes have significantly different relationships with growth. It is more likely that aid is only partially fungible, not fully so, in accordance with several recent studies.

Going Forward

The intense pessimism on aid effectiveness expressed by some analysts appears to be too strong: we find a positive, causal relationship between growth-oriented aid and growth. At the same time, no one should conclude that aid has always worked or that it cannot work better. There are many countries that have received substantial aid and have stagnated or worse, and much aid has been wasted, stolen, or otherwise used to support countries with poor governance. The evidence suggests, however, that on average aid that has been aimed at growth in fact has boosted growth.

Those who argue that aid works *only* in countries with good institutions overstate their case. It would be more accurate to say that aid works *better* in countries with strong institutions, but at times can be effective in other situations. Aid has helped support growth in Mozambique and Uganda over the past decade, even though policies and institutions were far from ideal, and aid has played an important role in stabilizing Sierra Leone since its cease-fire. Aid helped to support sustained growth and poverty reduction in Indonesia during the Suharto regime—even in the 1970s and 1980s when institutions were weak, corruption was problematic, and policies were less than ideal.

We hasten to add that the weak relationship between late impact and humanitarian aid and growth over a four-year period should not be interpreted to mean that they are ineffective. Different modeling techniques are required to examine those questions, which we are exploring in subsequent research. Although (surprisingly) there is no systematic cross-country research on the relationship between health-oriented aid and health, there is evidence that at least some aid for health has been effective. For example, aid played an important role in supporting several large-scale successful health interventions, such as eradicating smallpox, significantly reducing the prevalence of polio and river blindness, and reducing the incidence of diarrheal diseases (Levine and others, 2004).

Finally, the evidence suggests that absorptive capacity constraints are real, but should not be seen as an immutable barrier to growth. Although the impact of aid on growth diminishes as aid increases, in countries with stronger institutions or better health, more aid can be absorbed effectively. This finding suggests that efforts to strengthen institutions and build human capital can increase returns to aid and help countries effectively absorb larger amounts of aid. Thus, policy discussions should not focus exclusively on determining the limits of aid on growth—but rather on how those limits can be expanded, and how aid can be made even more effective in supporting growth and development.

References

Burnside, Craig, and David Dollar, 2000, "Aid, Policies, and Growth," *American Economic Review*, Vol. 90. (September), pp. 847–68.

Clemens, Michael, Steven Radelet, and Rikhil Bhavnani, 2004, "Counting Chickens When They Hatch: the Short-Term Effect of Aid on Growth," *Center for Global Development Working Paper 44 (Washington: Center for Global Development).*

Isham, Jonathan, Daniel Kaufmann, and Lant Pritchett, 1995, "Governance and Returns on Investment: An Empirical Investigation," *World Bank Policy Research Working Paper 1550 (Washington: World Bank).*

Levine, Ruth, and the "What Works" Working Group (with Molly Kinder), 2004, Millions Saved: Proven Success in Global Health *(Washington: Center for Global Development).*

Steven Radelet, 2003, Challenging Foreign Aid: A Policymaker's Guide to the Millennium Challenge Account *(Washington: Center for Global Development).*

Rajan, Raghuram and Arvind Subramanian, 2005, "Aid and Growth: What Does the Cross-Country Evidence Really Show?" *IMF Working Paper 05/127 (Washington: International Monetary Fund).*

Microfinance: Banking for the Poor

33

I N A **K O T A**

Mufiya Khatoon—a poor, illiterate young woman in rural Bangladesh—used to spend her days begging for a few ounces of rice to feed her children. She desperately wanted a livelihood, but lacked the funds to start a small business, and there was nowhere she could borrow on terms she could afford. That is, until she discovered Grameen Bank, one of the first microfinance institutions (MFIs), which set up shop in rural Bangladesh in the wake of the 1976 famine. In 1979, Grameen made Mufiya a one-year loan of 500 taka (about $22), enough to start a bamboo business. To qualify, she had to form a group with four others in similar circumstances. She paid an interest rate of 20 percent, with repayments of 2 percent of the loan each week. Stiff terms perhaps, but better than the 150 percent interest rate a local money lender would have demanded. Mufiya was able to start her bamboo products business and, one year later, she repaid her loan. She is better off materially and more in control of her own destiny.

Microfinance gave Mufiya—as it did to millions of other poor people with no credit history, collateral, or steady income—access to basic financial services. Half of the world's population, nearly three billion poor people, lack such access. Most mainstream banks have considered the poor high-risk and hard to serve because they often live scattered across remote areas and because the small loans they need are costly to make and maintain. But microfinance, which specializes in providing small loans and other financial services even to the world's most destitute, challenges those traditional assumptions.

In the past three decades, microfinance has mushroomed from Grameen's tiny nonprofit experiment in Bangladesh to a global industry. Grameen Bank and its founder Muhummad Yunus won the 2006 Nobel Peace Prize for pioneering efforts to provide financial services to the poorest of the poor. Many enthusiasts believe microfinance is an important tool in the effort to end world poverty. Whether they are right is still open to question.

The Current Landscape

Today, microfinance players include governments, philanthropists, social investors, and commercial banks, such as Citicorp and ING, that are attracted by the potential for profit and corporate social responsibility. Customers can still go to a Grameen-type bank, but they can also go to microfinance credit unions, public sector and commercial banks, and, relatively recently, Islamic banks (which apply Islamic financial principles, such as risk sharing). Besides tiny business loans, MFIs offer deposit, savings, pension, and insurance products. Microinsurance is growing because borrowers need to insure assets such as farming equipment that they purchase with microcredit. In fact, MFIs are

Big Business
The Microcredit Summit Campaign says microfinance has shot up
globally in just the past six years.
Table 1

Year	Number of Institutions Verified	Number of Poorest Clients Verified
2000	78	9,274,385
2001	138	12,752,645
2002	211	21,771,448
2003	234	35,837,356
2004	286	47,458,191
2005	330	58,450,926
2006	420	64,062,221

Source: State of the Microcredit Summit Campaign Report (2006).

as important in providing savings vehicles and transaction services as they are in lending.

Microfinance customers live in both rural and urban areas—the rural poor borrow for cattle fattening, dairy farming, bamboo making, or weaving, whereas the urban poor borrow to become street vendors, rickshaw drivers, or seamstresses. Moreover, microfinance has moved well beyond its roots in developing countries—some MFIs now serve poor people in industrial countries.

Still, reliable data are hard to come by. The number of MFIs operating today is estimated to range anywhere from 300 to 25,000, depending on the definition. The Microfinance Information eXchange (MIX), known as the "Bloomberg" of microfinance, reports on nearly 1,000 microfinance institutions worldwide, nearly half of which are self-sustainable. The number of borrowers is hard to pin down, with estimates ranging from 30 to 500 million. The Washington D.C.–based advocacy group Microcredit Summit Campaign verified more than 64 million worldwide in 2006, up from more than 9 million borrowers in 2000 (see Table 1). Many more millions of poor people have their savings in MFIs.

How it Works

MFIs assume that their clients are clever enough to handle their own affairs, but do not assume that all the poor will be reliable borrowers. They have adopted two basic approaches:

Group Lending

Grameen Bank is considered the pioneer of the group lending model, which has now been adopted in many countries. Individual borrowers are required to form a group and take responsiblity for each other's loans. Grameen Bank depends primarily on peer pressure to guarantee repayment. Moreover, it limits risk by targeting female borrowers, who are considered more reliable because of family-based community ties. In early 2007, Grameen Bank reported almost 7 million borrowers—96 percent of them poor, illiterate women from remote villages. And since 1976, it says, $6 billion has been lent, with a repayment rate of 98 percent.

Individual Lending

These loans are bigger and are made to individuals without a collective guarantee and on more flexible terms. Typical borrowers are not the very poor seeking to start businesses, but the self-employed poor who are skilled business people. In some cases, the borrower has a small amount of collateral. Accion, a leading MFI that operates in Latin America and the Caribbean, Africa, and Asia, has adopted individual lending in the form of small, short-term loans of $100 to $500 at interest rates that it says reflect the cost of lending. Loan officers look not only at a borrower's financial wherewithal but also at references from customers and neighbors. Incentives such as the possibility of borrowing progressively larger amounts and the opportunity to get business and vocational training encourage repayment. In countries like Bolivia, credit bureaus have been set up to enforce repayment.

The Road Ahead

Although microfinance appears to be a promising way to provide financial services to the poor, there is considerable debate about its future.

Is Microfinance Sustainable?

If microfinance can achieve commercial success, it can move beyond relying on subsidies, which today total hundreds of millions of dollars. MFIs are expected to increase their reach among the urban poor—who, because they are concentrated, are easier to serve. But it will be challenging to achieve sustainability while reaching the remote rural poor, especially those at the bottom of the income ladder, because of the high costs and risks involved.

Should Microfinance be Sustainable?

A microfinance movement that becomes mainly commercial might shift its focus from the poorest borrowers to relatively better off, more conventionally safe customers. Thus, MFIs may evolve into direct competitors with conventional banks, and the special benefit for the poorest may be lost in the search for commercial sustainability. Yet in some locations, heavily subsidized MFIs may be crowding out sustainable MFIs, and the subsidies may therefore be of little additional benefit. One may also ask whether MFIs should concentrate on the poorest borrowers, or are other mechanisms better, given constraints on aid budgets?

Why are Interest Rates So High?

The interest rates on microloans range from 20 percent to 35 percent (even after adjusting for inflation). MFIs are subject to significantly higher costs than commercial banks, because of lending and administrative costs (for example, identifying and screening clients). For some MFIs, interest rates cover the cost of doing business, whereas others add a premium for risk. Some say that despite the high interest rates, the loans still provide positive welfare benefits for borrowers and that costs will fall as the infrastructure of the industry grows. There is a broad consensus that increased competition is the key to driving down interest rates.

What Regulatory and Legal Framework is Necessary?

The regulatory and legal approach used for large-scale commercial financial institutions may not be appropriate for microfinance. Countries such as Morocco and Kenya have developed legal frameworks to regulate MFIs. Key challenges are how best to protect depositors and borrowers while promoting the MFI sector, how to limit the costs of MFI supervision, and how to prevent regulation from restricting innovation and competition. What, for example, is the balance between consumer protection, the regulatory burden, and sustainability and development?

Going Digital

Technology may provide some answers. Today, "branchless banking" is active in the Philippines, South Africa, and Colombia. Commercial players are using point-of-sale devices and mobile phones to connect with the rural poor, licensing local merchants and shop owners to make cash transactions on their behalf. The availability of such transfer services is especially important in areas where families rely on remittances from relatives working in economic centers or abroad. Technology will likely reduce transaction costs, allowing MFIs to grow and reach more customers.

The latest innovation is the digital microfinance marketplace, where Web-based MFIs like Kiva.org team up with local credit providers to match low-income borrowers with higher-income social investors—individual lenders who make electronic loans for amounts as small as $25. One potential borrower, Zemfira Bayramova of Azerbaijan, can advertise her need for $1,000 to buy three calves. Once $1,000 has been received, the funds are sent to a local partner, Komak Credit Union, which disburses the funds to Zemfira. Kiva.org claims to have processed nearly $5 million in loans in April 2007, up from $400,00 in October 2006.

Discussion Questions

X

1. What are the three predominant views on foreign aid? How accurate are these views?

2. Radelet et al. argue that previous assessments of the effectiveness of aid on economic growth are flawed because they do not account for the type of aid. Why is it necessary to control for the type of aid given to countries?

3. What are the other factors that affect the success of early impact growth-oriented aid?

4. What is microfinance, and how does it work?

5. What are some of the problems facing the future of microfinance institutions?

6. Why are the interest rates on micro-loans high, and do you think these high rates exploit the poor?

Sources

INTERNATIONAL TRADE

Section I: *Issues in Trade and Protectionism*

1. Robert Feenstra, "How Costly Is Protectionism?" *Journal of Economic Perspectives,* Summer 1992, pp. 159–178.

2. Daniel Griswold, "Grain Drain: The Hidden Cost of U.S. Rice Subsidies," Cato Institute, November 16, 2006.

3. Edith Ostapik and Kei-Mu Yi, "International Trade: Why We Don't Have More of It," Federal Reserve Bank of Philadelphia *Business Review,* Third Quarter, 2007.

Section II: *Outsourcing, the WTO, and the Environment*

4. Daniel Esty, "Bridging the Trade-Environment Divide," *Journal of Economic Perspectives,* Summer 2001, pp. 113–130.

5. Drusilla Brown, "Labor Standards: Where Do They Belong on the International Trade Agenda?" *Journal of Economic Perspectives,* Summer 2001, pp. 89–112.

6. Thomas F. Siems, "Beyond the Outsourcing Angst: Making America More Productive," Federal Reserve Bank of Dallas *Economic Letter,* February 2006.

7. Alan S. Blinder, "Offshoring: The Next Industrial Revolution?" *Foreign Affairs,* March/April 2006, p. 113–128.

8. Anoshua Chaudhuri, "Trade in Health Care: Changing Paradigms in a Global Economy," 2008.

Section III: *NAFTA, FDI, and Other Trade Issues*

9. Joanna Moss, "Trade in the Americas: From NAFTA to Bilateralism," 2008.

10. Anil Kumar, "Does Foreign Direct Investment Help Emerging Economies?" Federal Reserve Bank of Dallas *Economic Letter,* January 2007.

11. Rebecca Hellerstein, Deirdre Daly, and Christina Marsh, "Have U.S. Import Prices Become Less Responsive to Changes in the Dollar?" FRB New York *Current Issues in Economics and Finance,* September 2006.

Section IV: *Immigration*

12. Jeffrey G. Williamson, "Global Migration: Two Centuries of Mass Migration Offers Insights into the Future of Global Movements of People," *Finance and Development,* September 2006.

13. Giovanni Peri, "America's Stake in Immigration: Why Almost Everybody Wins," The Milken Institute Review, Third Quarter, 2007, p. 40–49.

Section V: *Globalization*

14. Dani Rodrik, "The Global Governance of Trade as if Development Really Mattered," Report to United Nations Development Programme, July 2001.

15. Christian Broda and David Weinstein, "Are We Underestimating the Gains from Globalization for the United States?" Federal Reserve Bank of New York *Current Issues in Economics and Finance,* April 2005.

16. Dani Rodrik, "What's So Special About China's Exports?" China & World Economy, September/October 2006, p. 1–19.

INTERNATIONAL FINANCE

Section VI: *Trade Deficit Disorder*

17. Leonardo Bartolini and Amartya Lahiri, "Twin Deficits, Twenty Years Later," FRBNY *Current Issues in Economics and Finance,* October, 2006.

18. Linda Goldberg and Eleanor Wiske Dillon, "Why a Dollar Depreciation May Not Close the U.S. Trade Deficit," FRBNY *Current Issues in Economics and Finance,* June 2007.

19. George Alessandria, "Trade Deficits Aren't as Bad as You Think," Federal Reserve Bank of Philadelphia *Business Review,* First Quarter, 2007.

Section VII: *Exchange Rate Regimes and Macroeconomic Stabilization Policies*

20. Atish R. Ghosh, Jonathan D. Ostry, Anne-Marie Gulde and Holger C. Wolf, "Does the Exchange Rate Regime Matter for Inflation and Growth?" IMF Economic Issues, September 1996.

21. Sharmila King, "China's Controversial Exchange Rate Policy," 2008.

22. Michele Cavallo, "To Float or Not to Float? Exchange Rate Regimes and Shocks," FRBSF *Economic Letter,* January 7, 2005.

23. Rupa Duttagupta, Gilda Fernandez and Cem Karacadag, "Moving to a Flexible Exchange Rate: How, When, and How Fast?" IMF Economic Issues, December 2005.

24. Myriam Quispe-Agnoli and Elena Whisler, "Official Dollarization and the Banking System in Ecuador and El Salvador," Federal Reserve Bank of Atlanta *Economic Review,* Third Quarter, 2006.

Section VIII: *Europe and the Euro Zone*

25. Axel Bertuch-Samuels and Parmeshwar Ramlogan, "The Euro: Ever More Global," IMF *Finance and Development*, March 2007.

26. Jason L. Saving, "Integration and Globalization: The European Bellwether," Federal Reserve Bank of Dallas *Economic Letter*, May 2006.

Section IX: *Financial Crises and Capital Flows*

27. David Burton and Alessandro Zanello, "Asia Ten Years After," *Finance and Development*, June 2007.

28. Paolo Mauro and Yishay Yafeh, "Financial Crises of the Future," *Finance and Development*, December 2007.

29. Linda Goldberg, "Financial-Sector Foreign Direct Investment and Host Countries: New and Old Lessons," Federal Reserve Bank of New York Staff Reports, April 2004.

30. Peter B. Kenen, "Appraising the IMF's Performance: A Review of the First Three Studies by the New Independent Evaluation Office," *Finance and Development*, March 2004.

31. Philip King, "Sovereign Wealth Funds" 2008.

Section X: *Foreign Aid*

32. Steven Radelet, Michael Clemens, and Rikhil Bhavnani, "Aid and Growth," IMF *Finance and Development*, September 2005.

33. Ina Kota, "Microfinance: Banking for the Poor," *Finance and Development*, June 2007.